To Chris

In u

HUMAN RIGHTS
& Religion

A READER

HUMAN RIGHTS & Religion
A READER

Edited by
LIAM GEARON

sussex
ACADEMIC
PRESS

BRIGHTON • PORTLAND

2 4 6 8 10 9 7 5 3 1

First published in 2002 in Great Britain by
SUSSEX ACADEMIC PRESS
PO Box 2950
Brighton BN2 5SP

and in the United States of America by
SUSSEX ACADEMIC PRESS
5824 N.E. Hassalo St.
Portland, Oregon 97213-3644

British Library Cataloguing in Publication Data
A CIP catalogue record for this book is available from the British Library.

Library of Congress Cataloging-in-Publication Data

Human rights and religion / edited by Liam Gearon.
p. cm.
Includes bibliographical references and index.
ISBN 1–902210–94–8 (alk. paper) — ISBN 1–902210–95–6 (pbk. : alk. paper)
1. Human rights—Relgious aspects. I. Gearon, Liam

BL65.H78 H859 2002
291.1'77—dc21   2002066939

Typeset and designed by G&G Editorial, Brighton
Printed by TJ International, Padstow, Cornwall
This book is printed on acid-free paper.

Contents

Foreword

Sumner B. Twiss

Although religion has been a significant factor in the modern human rights movement from its inception, only within the past decade or so have scholars and advocates of human rights begun to take religion seriously in both its positive and negative effects on the well-being of persons and communities. The present volume introduces the reader to some of the most significant and representative work from that decade. Guided by a vision of the importance of collaboration between academic inquiry and human rights praxis, Dr. Liam Gearon has designed this model anthology for courses and reflection on persistent and emerging human rights issues that foreground tensions between the universality of human rights norms and the particularity of many religious traditions and their respective norms for human behavior. Following a helpful contextualization of religion within the realm of international politics and law, the volume explores the meaning and role of human rights (or their equivalent) in diverse religious, philosophical, and cultural traditions across the world in a way that is sensitive to how the ideals of these traditions can deviate from their real-world expression. The subsequent regional case-studies – many of which are drawn from country and situation reports of professional human rights NGOs – encourage the reader to appreciate the dynamics and complexity of trying to instantiate a human rights ethos in a world rife with ethnic and religious conflict and government violations of norms of religious freedom and tolerance, not to mention the systematic violations of personal dignity and cultural integrity by repressive governments in collusion with transnational corporate interests. The concluding section of the book on global prospects for the genuine universalization of human rights in the contemporary world raises profound issues regarding the beneficial and detrimental roles that religions can play in this process. Throughout the volume Dr. Gearon's editorial material provides an authoritative voice on the central issues at stake, their historical background, and appropriate conceptual nuance, as well as robust and insightful political analysis and commentary. The bibliographical suggestions for each section of the book are well-chosen, and, in combination with the references of the reprinted selections themselves, should enable any reader – whether student, scholar, advocate, or the general public – to pursue further inquiry that can only deepen his or her understanding of the interaction of religion and human rights in the contemporary world.

Sumner B. Twiss, Ph.D.
Distinguished Professor of Human Rights, Ethics, and Religion
Florida State University
Professor Emeritus of Religious Studies, Brown University
Co-Editor, *Advancing Human Rights*, Georgetown University Press Book Series

Acknowledgments

The Editor and Publishers wish to thank the following for permission to use copyright material:

Chapter 1: Jeff Haynes, "Religion" in *Issues in World Politics*, ed. B. White, R. Little, and M. Smith (Houndmills: Palgrave, 2001), pp. 153–70. Reproduced with permission of Palgrave.

Chapter 2: Stephen Ryan, "The United Nations" in *The United Nations and International Politics* (Houndmills: Macmillan Press Ltd, 2000), pp. 136–56.

Chapter 3: Nathan Lerner, "Religion and International Human Rights" in *Religion, Beliefs, and International Human Rights* (Maryknoll, NY: Orbis Books, 2000).

Chapter 4: Jocelyn Hellig, "Anti-Semitism: Judaism, Christianity and Islam" in John Witte Jr. and Richard Martin (eds.), *Sharing the Book: Religious Perspectives on the Rights and Wrongs of Proselytism* (Maryknoll, NY: Orbis, 1999), pp. 61–77. Copyright © 1999 by the Law and Religion Program at Emory University, Atlanta, Georgia.

Chapter 5: Charles Villa-Vincencio, "Theology and Human Rights" in *A Theology of Reconstruction: Nation Building and Human Rights* (Cambridge: Cambridge University Press, 1999), pp. 131–50.

Chapter 6: "Islam and Human Rights: Tradition and Politics" in *Islam and Human Rights: Tradition and Politics* by Ann Elizabeth Mayer. Copyright © 1998 by Westview Press. Reprinted by permission of Westview Press, a member of Perseus Books.

Chapter 7: Manochehr Dorraj, "Islam, Governance and Democracy" in Paul J. Magnarella (ed.), *The Middle East and North Africa: Governance, Democratization, Human Rights* (Aldershot: Ashgate, 1999).

Chapter 8: Sumner Twiss, "A Constructive Framework for Discussing Confucianism and Human Rights" in Wm Theodore de Bary and Tu Weimeing (eds.), *Confucianism and Human Rights* (New York: Columbia University Press, 1998), pp. 169–80. © 1998 Columbia University Press. Reproduced with the permission of the publisher.

Chapter 9: Damien V. Keown, "Are There Human Rights in Buddhism?" in Damien Keown, Charles Prebish, and Wayne R. Husted (eds.), *Buddhism and Human Rights* (London: Curzon, 1998), pp. 5–15.

Chapter 10: C. Joseph Barnabas, "Religious Freedom and Human Rights in India" in C.J. Nirmal (ed.), *Human Rights in India* (New Delhi: Oxford University Press, 2000), pp. 139–61. Reproduced by permission of Oxford University Press India, New Delhi.

Chapter 11: Carrie Gustafson, "Ghandi's Philosophy of *Satyagraha*: Cautionary Notes for the International Penal Lobby." Copyright © 1999 by M.E. Sharpe, Inc. In Carrie Gustafson and Peter Juliver (eds.), *Religion and Human Rights: Competing Claims?* (Armonk, NY: M.E. Sharpe, 1999), pp. 88–106. Reprinted with permission.

Chapter 12: Makau Mutua, "Returning to my Roots: African 'Religions' and the State" in Abdulla Ahem Naim (ed.), *Proselytization and Communal Self-Determination in Africa* (Maryknoll, NY: Orbis Books, 1999).

Chapter 13: Human Rights Watch, *Muslim–Christian Conflict in Sudan*. Used with the permission of Human Rights Watch. Not to be reprinted or republished without the expressed written permission of Human Rights Watch.

Chapter 14: Human Rights Watch, *Afghanistan*. Used with the permission of Human Rights Watch. Not to be reprinted or republished without the expressed written permission of Human Rights Watch.

Chapter 15: Human Rights Watch/Human Rights Watch Asia, *China: The State Control of Religion* (New York: Human Rights Watch, 1999), pp. 1–9. Used with the permission of Human Rights Watch. Not to be reprinted or republished without the expressed written permission of Human Rights Watch.

Chapter 16: Human Rights Watch India, *Politics by Other Means: Attacks on Christians in India* (London and New York: Human Rights Watch, 1999), pp. 1–10. Used with the permission of Human Rights Watch. Not to be reprinted or republished without the expressed written permission of Human Rights Watch.

Chapter 17: Human Rights Watch, *We Have No Orders to Save You: Hindu–Muslim Violence in India*. Used with the permission of Human Rights Watch. Not to be reprinted or republished without the expressed written permission of Human Rights Watch.

Chapter 18: Human Rights Watch, *Orthodox Christian Intolerance in Georgia*. Used with the permission of Human Rights Watch. Not to be reprinted or republished without the expressed written permission of Human Rights Watch.

Chapter 19: Human Rights Watch, *Israel, Gaza Strip, and Palestinian Authority Territories* (New York: Human Rights Watch, 2000), pp. 1–6. Used with the permission of Human Rights Watch. Not to be reprinted or republished without the expressed written permission of Human Rights Watch.

Chapter 20: Indigenous and Minority Traditions: Case Studies from Survival – Africa; Twa in Rwanda; People of the Niger Delta; Pygmies of Central Africa; Bushmen in Southern Africa; Aborigines in Australia; Indians in Amazonia; Indians in North America; Innu in Canada. Reprinted with permission.

Chapter 21: Paul Marshall, "The Current State of Religious Freedom" in Paul Marshall (ed.), *Religious Freedom Around the World* (Nashville: Broadman & Holman, 2000), pp.18–25. Used by permission.

Chapter 22: Tony Coates, "International Justice and Just War Theory" in Tony Coates (ed.), *International Justice* (Aldershot: Ashgate, 2000), pp. 46–60

Chapter 23: Carl Wellman, "The Proliferation of Rights: Moral Progress or Empty Rhetoric?" in *The Proliferation of Rights: Moral Progress or Empty Rhetoric?* by Carl Wellman. Copyright © 1999 by Westview Press, a Member of Perseus Books Group. Reprinted by permission of Westview Press, a member of Perseus Books.

The publishers apologize for any errors or omissions in the above list and would be grateful to be notified of any corrections that should be incorporated in the next edition or reprint of this book.

General Introduction

Liam Gearon

Human Rights and Religion Post-September 11

On September 10, 2001, the New York-based Human Rights Watch reported on the United Nations' World Conference on Racism, Racial Discrimination, Xenophobia, and Related Intolerance that had just ended in South Africa, a country once divided by state-sanctioned apartheid. Tensions had been evident between various factions for the duration of the conference. There was not full agreement on the proposal from Arab representatives that Zionism should be regarded as a form of racism. There was no consensus on the vexed question of reparation, especially by those presently rich, industrialized nations which had profited economically from the historical injustices of slavery. Yet there was seemingly broad agreement on the idea that discrimination on the basis of race, gender, culture, and religion was an infringement of a moral universal right. If all could not agree fully on how to compensate for the evils of the past nor agree on how to resolve present difficulties, this UN conference ended by at least giving an impression that disparate countries and cul- tures were in agreement about broad principles – ethical universals now commonly categorized as human rights. The heading of the Human Rights Watch press release on 10 September read: "Anti-Racism Summit Ends on Hopeful Note" (HRW, 2001). How different the world was to seem 24 hours later.

From New York, September 12, 2001, the heading of the Human Rights Watch response to attacks on the US read "Civilian Life Must Be Respected":

> We profoundly condemn yesterday's cruel attacks in the United States and express our condolences to the victims and their loved ones. This was an assault not merely on one nation or one people, but on principles of respect for civilian life cherished by all people. We urge all governments to unite to investigate this crime, to prevent its recurrence, and to bring to justice those who are responsible.
>
> Last night, President Bush said that the United States "will make no distinction between the terrorists who committed these acts and those who harboured them." Yet distinctions must be made: between the guilty and the innocent; between the perpetrators and the civilians who may surround them; between those who commit atrocities and those who may simply share their religious beliefs, ethnicity or national origin. People committed to justice and law and human rights must never descend to the level of the perpetrators of such acts. That is the most important distinction of all.
>
> There are people and governments in the world who believe that in the struggle against terrorism, ends always justify means. But that is also the logic of terrorism. Whatever the response to this outrage, it must not validate that logic. Rather, it must uphold the principles that came under attack yesterday, respecting innocent life and international law. That is the way to deny the perpetrators of this crime their ultimate victory. (HRW, 2001a)

The same tensions pervaded the annual global report by Human Rights Watch (2002) under the summary heading of "Anti-Terror Campaign Cloaking Human Rights Abuse: New Global Survey Finds Crackdown on Civil Liberties." Human Rights Watch here suggested that evidence pointed to "opportunistic attacks on civil liberties around the world" under the guise of a fight against terror. "Terrorists believe that anything goes in the name of their cause," said Kenneth Roth, Executive Director of Human Rights Watch. "The fight against terror must not buy into that logic. Human rights principles must not be compromised in the name of any cause." Roth claimed that, "for too many countries, the anti-terror mantra has provided a new reason to ignore human rights." Roth claimed too that the challenge to basic civil liberties in the United States and Western Europe under the guise of the campaign against terror could undermine the credibility of the governments of these countries to criticize abuses elsewhere in the world: "The fight against terror isn't just a matter of security," said Roth. "It's a matter of values." Human Rights Watch – an international monitoring organization based in New York which accepts no financial support from any government – suggested in the press release for this Report:

> The willingness of most Western governments to tolerate abuses by friendly governments in the Middle East and North Africa has tended to undermine the growth of a human rights culture there, Roth noted. The problems include the West's failure to rein in Israeli abuses against Palestinians, and its apparent disregard for grave civilian suffering caused by sanctions against Iraq. (HRW, 2002)

Such hypocrisy is highlighted by claims that a US report on global religious freedom was flawed. Thus on October 26, 2001, the US State Department's annual report on international religious freedom failed, according to Human Rights Watch, "to single out a number of egregious violators that are members of the US-led anti-terrorism coalition."

How You Might Use This "Reader"

This book is about the tensions that exist across the globe between ideas of universal human rights and religion. *Human Rights & Religion: A Reader* is based on the premise that religion remains an important factor in global politics. Indeed, after September 11 it would appear that such a statement is self-evident. Yet an examination of recent political and religious scholarship shows us that religion has been experiencing an ever-increasing resurgence in global significance ever since the fall of the Soviet Empire in the late 1980s (Casanova, 1994; Haynes, 1998). *Human Rights & Religion: A Reader* is an attempt to provide some initial guidance for the uninitiated and further insights for those knowledgeable of the complexities of religion and politics in a globalized world of increasing complexity but developing interrelationship. The book takes a particular angle here, one which has the most noticeable fault line in the world of both politics and religion: the rift, at times more evident than others, between universal value and cultural difference. This rift is nowhere more accentuated than in the human rights discourse of the international community at the United Nations.

The book is divided into four parts:

Part I   Generic Issues

The opening chapter by Jeff Haynes places religion in the context of world politics. Stephen Ryan's "The United Nations" sets forth the international framework for our consideration of universal human rights and the mechanisms by which they are maintained in international law. Nathan Lerner's "Religion and International Human Rights" develops this theme further and explicitly by looking at the precise place of religion in international human rights within the United Nations but also in various continental regional contexts.

The book as a whole does not deal at length with the vexed question of what constitutes a religion. The debate has a long history in the modern study of religions and there are numerous contexts where the reader might pursue the issue (see Smart, 1969; 1989). The term "religion" is seen to be self-designating. As the book is concerned with global traditions that have for millennia accepted this self-designation then this is not the place to problematize the term. For those unfamiliar with the discussions, scholars of religion often cite the Buddhist's lack of a belief in a God as a way of disallowing belief in God or even a supreme being as a universal designation. Smart (1989) suggested seven dimensions of religion as a way forward towards generic definition: the ethical, the doctrinal, the mythical, the experiential, the social, the ritual and the aesthetic. This is itself difficult as belief systems such as communism (or even football!) could well be squeezed into such a framework. For our part, the self-designation is the easiest path. There has also been some allowance for the fact that universal human rights and its encounter with conflict or compliance can arise from cultural forms that are not religious, either implicitly or explicitly.

This self-designation also mirrors the notion of human rights accepted in this book; namely, the common (if nominal) acceptance by the international community of a set of principles – initiated by the foundational Universal Declaration in 1948 – called "universal" rights. That these "rights" (let's say the 30 articles of the Universal Declaration) are far from universal in terms of their equitable distribution or their acceptance in certain religious, ideological or other cultural contexts is another, if important matter. It is precisely these tensions – controversy in terms of the discussion and implementation of "universal" human "rights" – that make

a book like this so necessary. The first section of the book is therefore designed to set the debate in an international context.

Part II Cultural and Religious Traditions

Part II provides a range of authoritative academic reflections from the world of human rights and religion. Recognizing that all the world's major faiths have a global and international presence and, therefore, not linked to a particular region or country, it recognizes that some traditions have close geographical and historical ties. Maintaining the distinctiveness and integrity of each faith, for this reason this section loosely groups "Judaism, Christianity and Islam" and "Confucianism, Buddhism and Hinduism." **Part II** is consciously headed "Cultural and Religious Traditions" rather than simply "Religious Traditions." This marks the fact that tension between universal human rights and the particularity of specific worldviews comes as strongly from cultural manifestations such as Confucianism which would not easily accept the self-designation of religion and yet, through the so-called "Asian-values" debate, surfaces strongly in the literature in potential conflicts with universal rights, and even the notions of right as opposed to duty. Interestingly, Confucianism is also a cultural tradition closely associated historically with a particular geographical area. One other dimension of human rights and cultural and religious traditions where the notion of a global presence is lacking is in indigenous traditions which tend not to translate into contexts beyond their physical homeland. The continent is presented here as a model of this notion, though of course there are many African traditions which have translated piecemeal through migration and the continued historical inheritance of colonialism and slavery.

Part III   Case Studies

Part III contains a wide range of regional case studies of actual conflicts between universal human rights and specific religious and cultural traditions. The publishers and editor are particularly grateful for the permissions granted by Human Rights Watch and Survival for allowing the numerous case study exemplars to be reproduced. The case studies add something distinctive to the volume's profile. Many books on human rights and religion focus on academic study – of the sort presented in **Part II** – while other studies emanate from the ground, from activists and human rights organizations; the former do not always give a sense of the immediacy of the conflict while the latter often lack the historical and analytical depth with which the problems have to be highlighted – for reasons of the same immediacy and urgency. A human rights organization does not necessarily have the time when campaigning to present a leisured academic reflection; an academic in a university will tend to be compelled by the pressures of scholarship to make sure the literature search and analysis are complete before making a judgment. This Reader attempts to combine the merits of both approaches.

Part IV   Global Prospects

The final part presents the volume's most speculative front, presenting some critical parameters for future discourse on human rights.

In terms of one famous example of speculation on rights, at the end of the Cold War, Francis Fukuyama (1992) elaborated a thesis famously known as "the end of history." Fukuyama's idea was that – after the victory of Capitalism over Communism – the world had entered a new and final phase in the organization of societies. Based on the acceptance of universal human rights, this "end of history" was manifested by the social and political realization of a new, collective moral consciousness. In practical terms, at least to Fukuyama, the "end of history" meant that all nation-states now universally accept a democratic model of governance as the right form of governance, and that such was based upon a value system of shared human rights. Democracy and universal human rights represented the end of ideological struggle. Thus Fukuyama confidently charted the number of countries around the world that have shifted from oppressive and dictatorial regimes to democracies – the United States taking the predictable lead.

Yet if human rights are to remain the benchmark for a world community otherwise divided by the political self-interest of nation-states and economic goals of multinational companies, key to successful implementation of genuinely universal human rights will be the extent of their equitable distribution. There is little doubt that the world community is far from achieving either universal or equitable distribution of rights. At the end of the twentieth century, the United Nations Commissioner for Human Rights, reviewing progress since the 1993 World Conference on Human Rights in Vienna, stated:

> The international community must conclude that five years after Vienna, a wide gap continues to exist between the promise of human rights and their reality in the lives of people throughout the world. At the beginning of the twenty-first century, making all human rights a reality for all remains not only our fundamental challenge but our solemn responsibility. (United Nations, 1998)

Scholars have also noted that the discourse of human rights has itself been open to abuse:

> A study of the discourse of human rights since the Second World War suggests that the rhetoric of human rights has been determined most clearly by the propaganda value it represented.
>
> The difference in the sort of human

rights different states proclaimed was dictated by the political ideology of each state.

International institutions with power tend to reflect the interests of powerful states.

International financial institutions have, by their operation, made the protection of economic rights almost impossible for poor states.

The economic interests of wealthy states have led indirectly but regularly to human rights abuse whether, for instance, through the export of tobacco, the export of pesticides or the export of subsidised food.

The aftermath of colonialism continues to bedevil colonial peoples in their attempts to promote and secure self-determination.

Finally, regardless of proclaimed international standards on human rights, there are some states which may regularly, persistently and blatantly ignore world opinion if their strategic or emotional importance is exceptional. (Mansell, 1999)

In terms of successful realization, the 1948 Universal Declaration of Human Rights falls far short of its high ideals.

On the one hand, evidence for the development of democracy and human rights as universal is fairly incontrovertible. On the other, emphasis upon these political developments – a sort of ideological globalization – masks the inequitable distribution of rights *and* the vast cultural differences behind such apparent universal conformity. Religious traditions are here both the model for such universalising tendencies – religions were the first systems to present moral codes as *universal* moral codes – as well as, simultaneously, the major potential obstacle to the implementation of such norms.

The tension between the universal and the particular has long been recognized by the United Nations. Ayton-Shenker's (1995) UN briefing paper "The Challenge of Human Rights and Cultural Diversity" encapsulates this concern. Cultural difference cannot be an excuse, the paper argues, for overriding universal human rights.

Religion is never mentioned explicitly in this context as a threat to universal human rights, yet their fundamentalist interpretations are the obvious target.

Such extremes are an integral part of the foundations of modern human rights discourse. The post-Holocaust context of the 1948 Universal Declaration of Human Rights meant that cultural difference was an *originating* force in the development of notions of modern human rights. Through Nazi persecution of religious, ethnic and other minorities, there is an historical relationship between religious persecution and genocide, and thus to the founding 1948 Universal Declaration.

Yet the broader relationship between religion and human rights is more complex. If the United Nations 1948 Universal Declaration arose from the quest to define basic human dignities in a world which had seen two global conflicts of unprecedented scale before the end of the first half of the twentieth century, the latter part of the same century saw the continued prevalence of violence based on ethnic identity in almost every continent of the planet. Indeed in the final years of the century the term genocide coined for the Holocaust had a linguistic partner in the term "ethnic cleansing." In a powerful analysis of the role of ethnic and cultural difference in nationalist struggles, Stephen Ryan highlights how – far from instigating an end to genocide – the decades after the 1948 Universal Declaration (the same year as the Genocide Convention) indicate a persistent pattern of its repetition. And ethnic, cultural and religious factors are often to the fore.

And we find now that the first year of the twenty-first century was marked with a date – September 11 – in which conflict will be in perpetuity associated with an ideological battle at least nominally "religious." However misguided the association and how far from the tradition's roots, religion as a cultural phenomenon continues to manifest itself as a force for social and political conflict, violence and

Table 0.1   *Major human rights abuses since the Second World War*

Date	State	Victims	Deaths
1943–1957	USSR	Chechens, Ingushi, Karachai	230,000
1944–68	USSR	Crimean Tartars, Meskhetians	57,000–175,000
1955–77	China	Tibetans	Not available
1959–75	Iraq	Kurds	Not available
196272	Paraguay	Ache Indians	90,000
1963–64	Rwanda	Tutsis	5,000–14,000
1963	Laos	Meo Tribesmen	18,000–20,000
1965–66	Indonesia	Chinese	500,000–1 million
1965–73	Burundi	Hutus	103,000–205,000
1966	Nigeria	Ibos in North	9,000–30,000
1966–84	Guatemala	Indians	30,000–63,000
1968–85	Philippines	Moros	10,000–100,000
	Equatorial Guinea	Bubi Tribe	1,000–50,000
1971	Pakistan	Bengalis of Eastern Pakistan	1.25–3 million
1971–9	Uganda	Karamajong	100,000–500,000
	Acholi, Lango		
1975–79	Cambodia	Muslim Cham	
1975–98	Indonesia	East Timorese	60,000–200,000
1978–	Burma	Muslims in border regions	Not available
1979–86	Uganda	Karamanjong, Nilotic Tribes	50,000–100,000
	Bagandans		
1981	Iran	Kurds, Bahais	10,000–20,000
1983–7	Sri Lanka	Tamils	2,000–10,000
1994	Rwanda	Tutsis	500,000–1 million
	Bosnia–Herzegovina	Mainly Bosnian Muslims	200,000

Source: Ryan, 2001.

repression. Yet religions also promote ideals of harmonious living with traditions that enrich contemporary understandings of international human rights with models of universal respect and justice.

If the world community has, to date, not seen genuinely *universal* human rights, how major world religions accept, reject or accommodate these essentially secular codes will be (along with factors highlighted by Mansell, 1999) central to their future realization in political actuality. If human beings have an historical propensity to fall short of stated ideals, are five decades or so long enough a period of time to make judgment on hope for the future? The 1948 Universal Declaration is in its infancy compared to the moral systems propounded by Jewish, Christian and Islamic or Confucian, Buddhist and Hindu traditions, all of which originally derive from ideas thousands of years old. The chapters in this

book unpack a selection of the important themes in the tension here: between the modern notion of universal human rights and moral codes that have existed on an altogether grander, even cosmological timescale.

In the context of this longer history, Jocelyn Hellig's chapter in this volume, a piece on the origins and contemporary manifestations of anti-Semitism, concludes with a chillingly predictive footnote of a very modern manifestation of this clash: Osama bin Laden, the man alleged to have been behind the bombings of the American embassies in Kenya and Tanzania, is reported to have invited "all Muslims to join his jihad against the Americans and against the Jews." (*The Sunday Independent,* August 23, 1998.)

Human Rights & Religion: A Reader reflects academic, political and religious debate on clashes of worldview. Such debate predates the events and aftermath of September 11 and, as **Part III** on Regional Case Studies shows, such clashes are likely to continue. Human history itself is in part the struggle between cultures. And one of the most powerful manifestations of human culture is religious belief. History did not end with Fukuyama's thesis. The clash of civilizations (Huntington, 1992) did not begin in the 1990s. Nor is the world suddenly unified by any post-September 11 crusade for democracy and universal human rights. Contemporary conflicts of worldviews are always best seen in the fuller context of the ancient traditions of religious belief and practice that yet survive in the modern world of contemporary politics.

Human Rights & Religion: A Reader is designed to encourage an historical perspective on the modern-day manifestations of the clash of worldviews that is as old as human society and human culture.

References

Ayton-Shenker, Diana. 1995. "The Challenge of Human Rights and Cultural Diversity." (Geneva: United Nations).

Casonova, José. 1994. *Public Religions in the Modern World*. Chicago: Chicago University Press.

Fukuyama, Francis. 1992. *The End of History and the Last Man*. London: H.Hamilton.

Haynes, Jeff. 1998. *Religion in Global Politics*. Harlow: Longman.

Human Rights Watch. 2001. 10 September 2001. "Anti-Racism Summit Ends on Hopeful Note." New York: HRW.

Human Rights Watch Human Rights Watch. 2001a. "Civilian Life Must Be Respected." New York: HRW.

Human Rights Watch Human Rights Watch. 2002. "Anti-Terror Campaign Cloaking Human Rights Abuse: New Global Survey Finds Crackdown on Civil Liberties." New York: HRW.

Huntington, Samuel. 1992. *The Clash of Civilizations*. Washington, D.C.: American Enterprise Institute.

Mansell, Wade. 1999. "Fundamental Human Rights Premises" in Christine Bell, ed., *Teaching Human Rights*. Warwick: University of Warwick.

Ryan, Stephen. 2001. Nationalism and Ethnic Conflict," in Brian White, Richard Little and Michael Smith, eds., *Issues in World Politics*, second edition. Basingstoke: Palgrave.

Smart, Ninian. 1969. *The Religious Experience of Mankind*. London: Fontana.

Smart, Ninian. 1989. *The World's Religions*. Cambridge: Cambridge University Press.

United Nations. 1998. *Report of the UN Commissioner for Human Rights*. Geneva: United Nations.

Further Reading/Research

See the Introduction to **Part III** for detailed guidance through the complexity of the United Nations machinery for human rights and Internet sources.

Generic Issues

Introduction to Part I

The range of available literature on religion and world politics is extensive. Jeff Haynes provides an overview of the major strands of thought that dominate under the following headings:

- The impact of religion on world politics
- Religion in contemporary world politics
- Religion and globalization
- Are hostile religious and cultural actors a threat to the West's security?
- Why has religion appeared as an issue on the world agenda?
- Confucianism and global order
- Islamic radicalism and the West

In a post-September 11 context one or two of the headings have something of a prophetic ring.

One distinctive aspect of the fall of Soviet Communism has been the rise in awareness of the place of religious factors in world politics. Indeed, Haynes comments that "the end of the Cold War was followed by an eruption of religious conflicts within a large number of countries which raised serious doubts about the possibility of moving from an old order rooted in bi-polarity, nuclear deterrence and ideological division to a new global order where the pursuit of peace, prosperity and coopera-tion would be paramount." Whether this is a direct result of the decline of an ideology once aspiring to global dominance might be contested. After all, the religious traditions concerned considerably predate Commun-ism. And religion here is part of a perceived "new agenda" for international relations in a post-Cold War world, an agenda which, according to Haynes "includes the environ-ment, illegal drugs, AIDS, terrorism, migration, refugees, human rights, new conceptions of security, democratization and religious actors with political goals." And while most of these issues are linked to cultural behaviour "they are also associated with religion as an aspect of cultural behaviour."

One of the notable features of the post-Cold War debate has been the discussion of potential religious and cultural threats to the new universals such as human rights presented by a supposed new world order. At the time of writing – the close of the twentieth century – Haynes identifies two main challenges to "the West": (1) cultural and political systems deriving from Con-fucianism, so-called "Asian values" and (2) a resurgence of Islamic fundamentalism. Haynes's language here somewhat inadver-tently exposes a well-developed critique of universal human rights. The claim that far from being universal understandings of moral, social, or political behavior they are, despite international representation at the UN, pronouncements arising from Geneva and New York and, only in part because of such, *Western* values. Yet his conclusions about the likelihood of this potential "threat" are, interestingly, not answered in the affirmative. He unsympathetically cites, for example, Fukuyama's claim that Islamic fundamentalism or the pejorative "Islamism," has "more than superficial resemblance to European fascism" (Fukuyama, 1992: 236). "It is one thing," argues Haynes "to argue that various brands of political Islam have qualitatively different perspectives on liberal democracy than some forms of Christianity, and it is quite another to claim that the Islamic countries *en masse* are poised to enter into a period of conflict with the West." In regard to perceived threats to world order traced to Islam, "such fears," claims Haynes, "are without firm foundation."

If Haynes's chapter sets the place for religion in global governance then Stephen Ryan's chapter sets modern conceptions of human rights within the organizational context of the United Nations. Ryan reminds us of the Preamble to the founding Charter of the United Nations that, "We the peoples of the United Nations determined . . . to reaffirm our faith in fundamental human rights, in the dignity and worth of the human person, in the equal rights of men and women and of nations large and small . . . to promote social progress and better standards of life in larger freedom." It is these larger freedoms with which most of the machinery of the United Nations is concerned – aside from, behind and indeed after the headlines. It is the bureaucracy of an ideal and, as Ryan comments, "No assessment of the contribution of the UN to international politics would be complete without a discussion of the Organization's work in the non-security realms. Because so much attention from the media and the academic community in the West has been directed at peace and security matters it is easy to forget that economic and social issues remain a vital concern for the majority of UN members. This is where most UN employees work and where most of the UN budget is spent. There is a plethora of specialized agencies and other UN bodies that have been working on an impressive range of economic, social, and cultural issues throughout the world." Ryan's overview here of the UN's mandate to better "the welfare of all

peoples" provides the context for any consideration of human rights. Here, the politics of human rights can never be entirely separate from the politics of poverty and wealth, issues of environment and sustainable development. As chapters in **Parts II** and **III** amply demonstrate, the lived, political realities of human rights are never neat. This is perhaps not something we should be surprised at when we remind ourselves how wide-ranging the original Universal Declaration was (see **box 1.1**), nor should it provide us with optimism when we reflect on the all too evident failings in the five or so decades since its inception.

Human Rights & Religion: A Reader in its opening chapters thus addresses two necessarily generic and general precursors to any particular and specific consideration of human rights and religion: religion *vis-à-vis* world politics and the international mechanisms for the definition and implementation of contemporary human rights. It is the United Nations that effectively dominates the public discourse of international human rights (Forsythe, 2001).

Lerner's chapter concludes **Part I** with an explicit examination of the place of religion within international human rights, with a particular focus upon religious human rights under the United Nations. Always a controversial topic, religion, as Lerner points out, has tended to have been made less than explicit whenever possible. The language is shifting though to an acceptance that religion might have positive connotations. But it was not until the 45th plenary meeting of the Economic and Social Council approved the Commission on Human Rights Resolution 2000/33 to incorporate belief more broadly. The title of the rapporteur changed from Special Rapporteur on religious intolerance to Special Rapporteur on freedom of religion or belief. The addition of the word "belief" adds a distinctive recognition that fundamental beliefs of a non-religious kind should be recognized in the same way as explicitly religious belief. **Part II** of *Human*

The UN Universal Declaration of Human Rights

THE GENERAL ASSEMBLY proclaims **THIS UNIVERSAL DECLARATION OF HUMAN RIGHTS** as a common standard of achievement for all peoples and all nations, to the end that every individual and every organ of society, keeping this Declaration constantly in mind, shall strive by teaching and education to promote respect for these rights and freedoms.

Article 1.
All human beings are born free and equal in dignity and rights.

Article 2.
Everyone is entitled to all the rights and freedoms set forth in this Declaration, without distinction of any kind, such as race, colour, sex, language, religion, political or other opinion, national or social origin, property, birth or other status.

Article 3.
Everyone has the right to life, liberty and security of person.

Article 4.
No one shall be held in slavery or servitude; slavery and the slave trade shall be prohibited in all their forms.

Article 5.
No one shall be subjected to torture or to cruel, inhuman or degrading treatment or punishment.

Article 6.
Everyone has the right to recognition everywhere as a person before the law.

Article 7.
All are equal before the law and are entitled without any discrimination to equal protection of the law.

Article 8.
Everyone has the right to an effective remedy by the competent national tribunals for acts violating the fundamental rights.

Article 9.
No one shall be subjected to arbitrary arrest, detention or exile.

Article 10.
Everyone is entitled in full equality to a fair and public hearing by an independent and impartial tribunal.

Article 11.
Everyone charged with a penal offence has the right to be presumed innocent until proved guilty according to law in a public trial.

Article 12.
No one shall be subjected to arbitrary interference with privacy, family, home or correspondence.

Article 13.
Everyone has the right to freedom of movement and residence within the borders of each state.

Article 14.
Everyone has the right to seek and to enjoy in other countries asylum from persecution.

Article 15.
Everyone has the right to a nationality.

Article 16.
Men and women of full age, without any limitation due to race, nationality or religion, have the right to marry and to found a family.

Article 17.
Everyone has the right to own property alone as well as in association with others.

Article 18.
Everyone has the right to freedom of thought, conscience and religion.

Article 19.
Everyone has the right to freedom of opinion and expression.

Article 20.
Everyone has the right to freedom of peaceful assembly and association.

Article 21.
Everyone has the right to take part in the government of his country.

Article 22.
Everyone, as a member of society, has the right to social security.

Article 23.
Everyone has the right to work.

Article 24.
Everyone has the right to rest and leisure.

Article 25.
Everyone has the right to a standard of living adequate for health and well-being.

Article 26.
Everyone has the right to education.

Article 27.
Everyone has the right freely to participate in the cultural life of the community.

Article 28.
Everyone is entitled to a social and international order in which the rights and freedoms set forth in this Declaration can be fully realized.

Article 29.
Everyone has duties to the community in which alone the free and full development of his personality is possible.

Article 30.
Nothing in this Declaration may be interpreted as implying for any State, group or person any right to engage in any activity or to perform any act aimed at the destruction of any of the rights and freedoms set forth herein.

Rights & Religion: A Reader therefore presents discussion of "cultural" (for example Confucianism) as well as explicitly "religious" traditions. Lerner's chapter is supplemented by a series of appendices at the end of this book which highlight key international documents pertinent to religion in relation to human rights which go back of course to Article 18 of the Universal Declaration and "the right to freedom of thought, conscience and religion."

Further Reading

Ayton-Shenker, Diana, "The Challenge of Human Rights and Cultural Diversity" (Geneva: United Nations Department of Public Information, 1995).

Baumann, Gerd, *The Multicultural Riddle: Rethinking National, Ethnic and Religious Identities* (London: Routledge, 1999).

Bloom, Irene, Martin, J. Paul and Proudfoot, Wayne L. (eds.), *Religious Diversity and Human Rights* (New York: Columbia University Press).

Forsythe, David P., *Human Rights in International Relations* (Cambridge: Cambridge University Press, 2001).

Lerner, Nathan, *Religion, Beliefs, and Human Rights* (Maryknoll, New York: Orbis, 2000).

Martin, Criselda S. (ed.), *Philosophy of Human Rights and Emerging Perspectives: Western versus Eastern Concepts of Human Rights* (Quezon City, Philippines: Institute of Human Rights, University of Philippines Law Center, 1999).

Niec, Halina (ed.), *Cultural Rights and Wrongs: A Collection of Essays in Commemoration of the 50th Anniversary of the Universal Declaration of Human Rights* (Paris: UNESCO, 1998).

Ryan, Stephen, *The United Nations and International Politics* (London: Macmillan, 2000).

Stahnke, Tad, Martin, J. Paul (eds.), *Religion and Human Rights: Basic Documents* (New York: Columbia University Press/Center for the Study of Human Rights, 1998).

The Declaration of the Parliament of the World's Religions, in Küng, Hans and Schmidt, Helmut *A Global Ethic and Global Responsibilities: Two Declarations* (London: SCM, 1998).

Religion

Jeff Haynes

I

◆ Religion in contemporary world politics ◆
◆ Tensions in international relations ◆
◆ Islam and the West ◆ Confucianism and global order ◆
◆ Religion and threats to global governance ◆

The end of the twentieth century was an era of fundamental political, social and economic change at the global level that continues to have a profound impact on the new century. Much of the change stemmed from, or at least was galvanized by, the ending of the Cold War, and it is now frequently associated with the multi-faceted processes known collectively as globalization. A truly global economy is now being consolidated and, some would argue, a global culture is also slowly emerging. At the same time, a number of crucial political developments, including a steady, if uneven, advance of democracy – from Latin America to Eastern and Central Europe, Asia and Africa – have taken place. In addition, many examples of the political involvement of religious actors around the world have occurred, leading the American commentator, George Weigel, to identify a global religious revitalization he refers to as the "unsecularization of the world" (quoted in Huntington, 1993: 26). This expression does not imply that the respiritualization of world politics is apolitical, but denotes, on the contrary, a new and widespread interaction between religion and politics. This chapter examines the nature and the extent of the interaction between religion and politics, assessing its significance both domestically and internationally for the twenty-first century.

The Impact of Religion on World Politics

Many recent events support Weigel's contention that the impact of religion on politics is occurring in areas where it was long thought to have left the public domain. This trend has not been confined to one or two countries, but is a prevalent feature of contemporary world politics. In Europe, a region frequently presumed to be inexorably secularizing, civil war in the early 1990s in Bosnia-Herzegovina among Croats, Serbs and Bosnians degenerated into a *de facto* religious conflict. Most combatants identified themselves in religious and cultural terms and, rather than finding ideological allies, they consolidated religious and cultural ties with, respectively, Germany, Russia and the Arab–Muslim world. In the late 1990s, the civil war in Kosovo between ethnic Albanians and Serbs could also be defined in terms of a conflict between Muslims and Christians. In Poland, Catholic prelates achieved considerable political importance in the post-Communist order. Pope John Paul II, a Pole, involved himself in political and social issues, including fierce denunciations of birth control. His aim was to stem the tide of what he saw as a serious "moral decline" and the rise of "evil." In Russia, the Orthodox Church emerged from communism as an actor of major social and political significance, while various constituent republics, including Chechnya and Dagestan, were subjected to serious attempts at Islamicization by Islamist radicals. In the United States, sustained attempts by Christian fundamentalists in the 1980s and 1990s to mould and drive the political agenda underlined the growing socio-political significance of religion. At the same time, in Israel, the expanding political influence of Jewish fundamentalist groups was marked by their membership of several governing coalitions (Moyser, 1991).

In the Third World, religious actors with political goals also appeared to be on the increase. Perhaps the most visible, encouraged by the 1978–9 Islamic revolution in Iran, was the widespread Islamic militancy in the Middle East and beyond. There was also the attempt by 'secular-socialistnationalist" Iraq to play the Islamic "card" both during and after the Gulf War in 1991. An explosion of militant Hinduism in officially secular India, focused on but not confined to the Babri Masjid mosque incident at Ayodhya in 1992, helped to transform that country's political landscape. During the 1990s, Hindu fundamentalists, located in the Bharatiya Janata Party (BJP), became politically important, as they helped to govern the country in several coalition governments. In Africa, Nigeria was polarized between Muslim and Christian forces, and Somalia lurched towards an Islamist government. Sudan was divided politically on religious grounds between Muslims and non-Muslims. From 1992, Algeria endured more than six years of civil war, with Islamist rebels fighting the government

forces and more than 100,000 people were killed in the conflict (see **box 1.3**). In Thailand, new Buddhist groups and parties emerged with their own political agenda. The list of examples can be extended, but hopefully the point is clear: since the 1990s it has become rather difficult to find any country where religion is not somewhere near the top of the political agenda, even in states that have long experienced secular principles and practices (Haynes, 1993, 1998).

Religion and Globalization

Many observers have argued that globalization and the renaissance of religion in world politics are strongly connected. McGrew suggests that globalization is the product of multiple "linkages and interconnections between the states and societies which make up the modern world system" (McGrew, 1992: 23):

> Although global interconnections have existed for centuries, their impact in the past has been comparatively minor, amounting to little more than "trade routes or select military and naval operations" that only affected "certain towns, rural centres and territories." (Held, 1993: 38)

Religion, of course, did have political consequences in the past. For example, Christianity and Islam grew to become world religions, conveying their associated civilizations around the world via colonization, conquest and the expansion of global trade. In the sixteenth and seventeenth centuries, during a period of sustained expansion of the international system, contending religious beliefs provided the chief motor for international conflicts and the main threat to international peace and security. But the development of the global state system after the Treaty of Westphalia in 1648 (which ended the religious wars in Europe between Catholics and Protestants) has largely reflected the history of clashing nationalisms, with each national group desiring its own state.

Before the rise of the European empires, religious globalization had been spearheaded by Muslims. For hundreds of years, prior to the late fifteenth century, Islam expanded from its Arabian heartland in all directions. The consequence was that vast territories in Africa and Asia and smaller areas of Europe (primarily parts of the Balkans and much of the Iberian peninsular) were Islamicized. The Moors' capital, for example, was Cordoba in Andalusia in southern Spain. But the demise of the Islamic European empire in the late fifteenth century was swift, a consequence of the rise of centralized European states with superior firepower and organizational skills.

Contemporaneous with the end of Islam as a cultural force in Western Europe was the beginning of the expansion of European influence across the globe. The search for gold in the Americas led in the early sixteenth century to the formation of European colonies there, and colonies were also established in the Caribbean and Asia. Between the fifteenth and nineteenth centuries, the spread of Christianity to Africa, accompanied by the extraction of millions of slaves, and to the Middle East and the Americas added to the emerging web of global interactions. Despite this global expansion of Christian Europeans, the social and cultural systems defined by Islam survived across Eurasia and the worldwide influence of Islamic beliefs persisted.

In the early years of the twentieth century, communism and fascism appeared as universal, secular ideologies with the propensity to attract converts across state boundaries. There was a process of global ideological differentiation, deepening after the Second World War, when the defeat of fascism led to the emergence of liberal democracy as the dominant but not yet global ideology. During the Cold War, one set of ideas – *communism* – was pitched against another – liberal democracy and its economic counterpart, capitalism – in a struggle for dominance that culminated in the defeat of Soviet-style communism at the end of the 1980s.

It is widely believed that the fall of the Soviet empire was due, in part, to the processes of globalization which ended the county's self-imposed isolation from the non-Communist world. These processes have been immeasurably facilitated by easy, widely available methods of interpersonal communications, such as the telegraph, telephone, the Internet, email, and fax. As Beyer puts it, we live in "a globalizing social reality, one in which previously effective barriers to communication no longer exist" (Beyer, 1994: 1). The development of *transnational* in conjunction with *national* religious communities has been greatly enhanced by the explosion of interpersonal and inter-group communications. Ease of communications has helped these communities to spread their message and to link up with like-minded groups. Links between religious and political actors both *in* and *between* countries have multiplied, as the contributors to Rudolph and Piscatori (1997) make clear. Primarily concerned with investigating the political consequences of cross-border interactions between Muslims and Christians, one of the book's findings is that transnational networks of religious groups feed off each other's ideas, often aid each other with funds, and form geographically extensive organizational bodies whose main priority is the well-being and advancement of the transnational religious community.

Religion in Contemporary World Politics

Developments since the end of the Cold War are said to have generated a "new agenda" for international relations. This agenda includes the environment, illegal drugs, AIDS, terrorism, migration, refugees, human rights, new conceptions of security, democratization and religious actors with political goals. Most of these issues are linked to cultural behaviour but they are also associated with religion as an aspect of cultural behaviour.

It is appropriate to make it clear at the outset what is meant by "religion" (**box 1.1**). It can be understood in two analytically distinct, yet related, ways. First, in a spiritual sense, religion provides a model of social and individual behaviour that helps believers to live their everyday lives. Religion is concerned with *transcendence* – that is, it relates to a supernatural reality; with *sacredness* – that is, to a system of language and practice that expresses the world in terms of what is deemed holy; and with *ultimacy* – that is, it relates people to the ultimate conditions of existence. In a second, more material, sense – the focus of this chapter – religion can defined by religious groups and movements. Several distinct kinds of religious groups and movements can be noted.

First, there are socially and politically conservative organizations like the Roman Catholic body, Opus Dei, which have a global reach. Second, there, are socially conservative religious groups, often regionally or nationally focused which, unlike Opus Dei, work to alter fundamentally the political scene, sometimes by resorting to terrorist tactics. Examples include India's Hindu chauvinist groups; American Christian fundamentalist organizations whose members have fire-bombed hundreds of abortion clinics and even murdered doctors who have performed abortions; and numerous Muslim bodies, including the Front Islamique de Salut (FIS of Algeria), the Islamic Party (Kenya), Balukta (Tanzania), Hamas (Palestine) and the Partai Islam (Malaysia).

A third category of religious groups is exemplified by the tens of thousands of Christian Base Communities (CBCs) that have formed in Latin America, the Caribbean (Haiti) and East Asia (the Philippines) with a combined membership of many millions of people. CBCs have a variety of religious and non-religious aims, but always with a strong developmental focus; they are almost entirely concerned with domestic issues and they do not have, or aspire to have, a global perspective. Finally, there are religious groups, such as the Association of Indonesian Muslim Intellectuals (Ikatan Cendekiawan Muslim se-Indonesia, known as ICMI), whose primary function, until the democratic changes in the country in the late 1990s, was to support the status quo by reinforcing the country's authoritarian political structure.

These examples demonstrate that religious groups have very diverse political and social aims in the contemporary world. The groups reflect not only their members' religious traditions and beliefs but also the complexities of their country's political culture(s) and system and, in some cases, external influences on the state. For example, Hamas has confronted Israel, in part because the political culture of the Palestinians in the Occupied Territories is rooted in decades of conflict with Israeli Jews.

Box 1.1 *Religion and Politics*

Religion is an important source of basic values. But it can have a powerful impact upon politics within a state or region, especially when it is linked to ethnicity and culture. Religious belief often reinforces both ethnic consciousness and inter-ethnic conflict, especially in the Third World (but not only there, think of Northern Ireland or the former Yugoslavia). Religious "fundamentalism," denotes a "set of strategies, by which beleaguered believers attempt to preserve their distinctive identity as a people or group" in response to a real or imagined attack from those who apparently threaten to draw them into a "syncretistic, areligious, or irreligious cultural milieu" (Marty and Scott Appleby, 1993: 3). Sometimes such defensiveness may develop into a political offensive which seeks to alter the prevailing social, political and, on occasions, economic realities of state–society relations.

To what extent are religious belief systems associated with political ideologies? The existence of a connection is not difficult to demonstrate. Close links exist, for example, between religion and nationalism in India, between Jewish and Christian fundamentalism and political conservatism, in Israel and the United States respectively, and between some of Thailand's new Buddhist movements and demands for a more just social, political and economic order. Religious groups now regularly express views on what constitute appropriate political and economic systems, on the nature of a country's inter-state relations, and on what social mores, customs and manners should prevail. Religio-political groups – religious groups with political aims – also endeavour sometimes to achieve their objectives by extending their field of operations from the domestic to the international field of action.

Why has religion appeared as an issue on the world agenda?

The Gulf War of 1990–1 was the defining moment in the debate about the post-Cold War global order when Islamic radicalism (or, pejoratively, "fundamentalism") became widely perceived as perhaps the most significant new threat to Western security. Before the Gulf War, the US President, George Bush, spoke confidently about the birth of a "new world order" emerging from the collapse of the Soviet Union and its Communist empire. But the Gulf War dashed such optimism. Thereafter, it seemed that the West's aim was to build and maintain global stability rather than strive for a qualitatively *better* world order, as Bush had initially proclaimed. The aggression of Muslim Iraq against Kuwait, a strong ally of the West, crystallized for many the threat to the global order posed by Islam.

The re-emergence of religion as an issue in world politics can be traced back to Iran's Islamic revolution in the late 1970s, a development which took many people by surprise. It went against the prevailing conventional wisdom that all societies would secularize as they modernized (see **box 1.2**). Most analysts presupposed that over time religion would lose much of its social and political importance. Third World or "developing" countries – emerging in great numbers from colonial status in Africa and Asia in the 1950s and 1960s – were predicted to follow the path taken by the economically developed countries of North America and Europe, where religion had lost a great deal of public significance and clout (Haynes, 1998).

Such views have proved erroneous: the evidence is now clear that societies do not necessarily secularize as they modernize; some do, some do not. But how do we explain the widespread "unsecularization" identified by George Weigel? There is no simple, clear-cut reason for this turn of events; no single theoretical explanation covers every case. However, it is apparent that as states have sought to develop by drawing on the processes of modernization, faith in the secular ideologies of change – such as socialism and communism – have declined, leaving many people with a sense of loss rather than achievement. This is because modernization undermines traditional value systems and yet at the same

Box 1.2   *Modernization*

For over 50 years, one of the most resilient ideas about societal development has been that nations will inevitably secularize as they modernize. The idea of modernization has been strongly linked to urbanization, industrialization and the elimination of "irrational" views associated with religion and ethnicity. Loss of religious faith and secularization dovetailed with the belief that technological development and the application of science would overcome the perennial social problems of poverty, environmental degradation, hunger and disease to bring about long-term human progress.

time allocates opportunities to people in highly unequal ways – both within and between nations. As a consequence, many people have begun to search for a new sense of identity, something to give their lives meaning and purpose during a period of historically unprecedented, diverse and massive change.

One consequence of the multiple political, social and economic upheavals that have occurred as the forces of modernization have swept so rapidly across the globe, affecting both developed and developing worlds, has been that large numbers of people now believe that they can most effectively pursue personal objectives by being part of a religiously oriented group or movement. By the end of the 1990s, there was a wave of politically oriented religiosity in the world – with serious implications for long-term social integration, political stability and international security. To complicate matters, politically-oriented religious groups and movements have not only attracted poor, marginalized segments of society. They cannot simply be thought of as contemporary manifestations of working class organizations using a religious ideology as a substitute for a secular one, such as socialism or communism. Many people with extensive education and high social status have also found religion to be attractive and fulfilling.

Are hostile religious and cultural actors a threat to the West's security?

Liberal democracy and capitalism have not been the only values projected after the Cold War. For each US President – from the triumphalist George Bush after the Gulf War to the self-satisfied Bill Clinton at the signing of the North American Free Trade Agreement (NAFTA) in 1994 – who has propagated the the virtues of liberalism, there have been other leaders, like the late Ayatollah Khomeini and his conservative heirs in Iran, the globally influential Christian fundamentalist preachers, such as Luis Palau and Benson Idahosa, the Hindu-chauvinists of the Rashtriya Swayamsevak Sangh and the BJP in India, and the Buddhist champions of socio-cultural renewal in Thailand, who have all advanced fundamentally different values and conceptions of the future from the ones espoused by Western leaders.

After the Cold War, two rival interpretations were put forward to account for the emerging trends appearing in world politics. An "optimistic" view, propounded by writers such as Bartley (1993) argued that the dominant flow of historical forces in the twenty-first century could well lead to more widespread economic development and to growing demands for democracy and individual (or familial) autonomy which authoritarian governments will be forced to grant as a result of popular and international pressure. Instant worldwide communications will reduce the power of oppressive governments, while the growth in numbers of democratic countries will diminish any potential for inter-state conflict.

A second, probably more influential, view is much more pessimistic. Associated with the works of Samuel Huntington (1993) and Francis Fukuyama (1992), both conservative American commentators, the "pessimistic" view identifies serious threats to global order from various non-Western religious and cultural sources. Huntington points to conflicting "civilizations," based on religious and cultural distinctions between blocs of rival national groupings. He believes that a "clash of civilizations" will be the primary source of conflict in the future. The main cleavage identified by Huntington establishes a "West versus the rest" dichotomy, with the particular "bugbears" being Middle Eastern Islam, East Asian Confucianism and "Asian values." All are said by Huntington to pose a serious threat to the West's security.

For Huntington, the West is identified in religious-cultural terms, coterminous with Christianity and a dominant democratic political culture emphasizing attributes of tolerance, moderation and consensus. Followers of Islam and Confucius, along with other East Asian authoritarians, on the other hand, are not seen to value such concepts and beliefs but, on the contrary, to hold worldviews that see no particular virtue in such ideas. The coming battle for global dominance will be between the West (especially North America and Western Europe) and its rivals in the Islamic and Confucian worlds. Israel, with its dominant Jewish population, is considered to be a staunch ally of the West, while Hinduism and Buddhism are dismissed by Huntington as anti-democratic, although probably irrelevant in the "battle." Africa, economically marginalized and culturally inchoate, is ignored. For Huntington, the invasion of Kuwait in 1990 and the ensuing struggle between Iraq's armed forces and the diverse troops brought together under the UN flag was a highly significant event, a catalyst in the formation of battle lines between the (Muslim) Arab world and the (Christian) West.

Huntington's concerns were endorsed by Francis Fukuyama (1992). For him, the triumph of liberal democracy and capitalism over communism marked the end of the Cold War, and "history," understood as a battle of ideologies, was over by 1989. No longer is there a plausible ideological alternative to the Western political-economic system. Henceforward, global political concerns (at least among Western states and emerging democracies elsewhere),will reflect shared political, security, economic and environmental goals. The "fly in the ointment" is the mass of culturally different, non-Western countries which not only fail to share the West's values but, worryingly, present alternatives of their own.

Fukuyama's earlier work (1989) exemplifies a shift from optimism to pessimism – from seeing "the enemy" as the Soviet Union to seeing it as the culturally alien "other." In 1989, Fukuyama was the epitome of optimism: the "end of history," he maintained, was marked by the ultimate and global triumph of liberal democracy and capitalism. For Fukuyama, the sudden collapse of East European communism indicated the passing of a particular phase of history, whereas the unequivocal victory of economic and political liberalism provided the final form of human government, and the arrival at the end-point of humankind's ideological evolution. The Western way of life represented for Fukuyama a pattern of universal validity, a ray of hope not only for the West but also for non-Western societies still struggling "in history."

In the Third World there would, no doubt, be "minor" internal conflicts within states which remain "in history" – because they are subject to "archaic" conditions fostering nationalist, religious or ethnic disputes – but in the longer run they too will tread the path of economic and political liberalism. In sum, the post-Cold War global order was seen to be a liberal order, only mildly and intermittently troubled by tiresome, yet essentially irrelevant, disputes between Third World peoples who had not (yet) developed the same levels of tolerance, consensus and uniformity of value systems as those in the West.

In *The End of History and the Last Man*, published in 1992, Fukuyama is much more circumspect about the prospects for a liberal post-Cold War global order; in this book he becomes a global-order pessimist. In 1989, he assumed that economic and political liberalism would govern the world in the long run; but by 1992, liberal democracy had become only a transitory historical form, the process of whose dissolution is already proceeding. This is because the "broad acceptance of liberalism, political or economic, by a large number of nations will not be sufficient to eliminate differences between them based on culture," differences which will "undoubtedly become more pronounced as ideological cleavages are muted" (Fukuyama, 1992: 233). "Culture" is a contested term, taken here to mean people's feeling of separateness based on ethnicity, nationalism, religion and/or language. The spectre of "clashing cultures" is also the theme of an article by John Mearsheimer, published in 1990. Mearsheimer argues that the end of the Cold War is leading to the revival of traditional state rivalries not only between Third World countries but also between the nation-states of Europe.

In sum, the chief post-Cold War threats to international stability, according to Huntington, Mearsheimer and Fukuyama, come from countries predominantly filled with non-Christian peoples, followers of Islam, Confucianism and other "Asian values." Christianity, on the other hand, is deemed to be a religion that has spawned cultures that promote the growth of liberal democracy and, by extension, global peace and security. The collapse of dictatorships in southern Europe and Latin America in the 1970s and 1980s, followed by the development of liberal democratic political norms (rule of law, free elections, civic rights), is regarded by Fukuyama and others as conclusive proof of the synergy between Christianity and liberal democracy, both foundations of global order. From this perspective, in the post-Cold War order, world conflict between the West and non-Christian Third World authoritarian countries is virtually certain, notwithstanding a trend towards the creation and consolidation of broadly democratic political systems in many areas of the world. Cultural and religious competition between countries emerges as the main area of international antagonism.

But are such "civilizations" as single-minded, undivided and uniform in the ways they act and perceive others as Huntington has asserted? Within most of the so-called great "civilizations," Said observes that there is in fact a great deal of dispute (1995: 32). This is as true of the United States as it is of the Islamic world. As Said asks rhetorically, "what is the real America"? Is it the mid-Western world of the moralistic Christian fundamentalists and televangelists? Or is it the gay communities of San Francisco and New York? Within "civilizations," moreover, new political voices –

often coming from the young and alienated – periodically emerge, demanding real changes, arguing that the dominant values and ideals of society are wrong. The point is that the main area of conflict is not necessarily *between* civilizations but could well be *within* them, as coreligionists present vying interpretations of what is "the" correct way to live a "proper" – that is, suitably religious – life. Some observers point to a generational element in contemporary religio-political struggles in some parts of the world. This is chiefly a question of relatively youthful people – often but not exclusively men – vying with older figures with higher levels of social, political and/or religious authority. The young pretenders employ differing religious interpretations in their struggle for recognition, status and socio-political domination over their older rivals.

Returning to the debate about whether non-Western cultural and religious systems pose significant threats to international (Western) peace and security, the next two sections assess the extent of the threat by examining, first, Confucianism and "Asian values" and, second, radical Islam.

Confucianism and Global Order

To what extent are the Confucian countries – and by extension those espousing "Asian values" – a threat to the West's security and well-being? Several countries in East Asia – China, Japan, South and North Korea, Singapore, Taiwan and Vietnam – have cultures rooted in Confucianism (Confucius was a Chinese philosopher who lived from 551–479 BC). China, North Korea and Vietnam are, of course, three of the few remaining Communist countries, while Japan, South Korea, Singapore and Taiwan are staunch allies of the West. What seems to be the chief shared cultural characteristic of these countries is that they are community orientated rather than individualistic. "[T]he community-orientedness of

Asian cultures," Fukuyama argues, "[often] originates in doctrines like Confucianism that have acquired the status of religion from being handed down through centuries of tradition"; it is "hierarchical and inegalitarian" (1992: 217, 325). Confucianism is often perceived by Western scholars as a "value system most congruent with Oriental authoritarianism" (King, 1993: 141).

Between the seventh and tenth centuries AD, a period when Confucianism flourished in Korea, it underpinned a "system of government and a religious or philosophical system which affected the social and cultural aspects of the nation's life" (Grayson, 1989: 153). In China, as Max Weber noted, "Confucianism was the status ethic of prebendaries, of men with literary educations who were characterized by a secular rationalism" (1969: 21). It was important to belong to the *cultured* stratum; if one did not, he (much less she) did not count. The Confucian status ethic, as a consequence, determined the Chinese way of life far beyond the cultured stratum and extended to those areas that came under Chinese influence, including many East Asian countries.

Over the last few years, two of the most economically important Confucian countries, Taiwan and South Korea, have democratized and improved their human rights record with the result that there is now meaningful competition for governmental power through regular elections. In both countries, there are significant opposition parties and extensive civil and political liberties. There is now freedom of expression and of the press as well as freedom to form organizations, to demonstrate and to strike. Thus, in three of the "Confucian" countries – South Korea, Taiwan and Japan – democratization and enhanced human rights seem increasingly entrenched. The tiny island state of Singapore is heavily pro-Western although by no means fully democratic, while Vietnam and China, still officially Communist, are increasingly open to

Western influence. Only North Korea retains its Communist aloofness, although even there things may be changing, as the country's increasingly dire poverty compels its leaders to deepen dialogue with former enemies. In sum, the differences between the "Confucian" states are more important than the alleged authoritarian similarities. There is very little – if anything – in the spectre of a "Confucian" threat to global order.

Other non-Christian countries in the region, such as Malaysia, have consistently put forward an alternative socio-political agenda. Espousing what leaders such as Prime Minister Mahathir Mohamad of Malaysia call "Asian values," this notion involves an "Asian model of democracy" reflecting a generalized conception of Asian cultural values which include harmony, consensus, unity and community before self. These have been contrasted with an (apparently) opposite set of "Western values" which are based on individualist ideas that support a mode of politics based on a conflictual or adversarial approach. According to proponents of "Asian democracy," such as the former president of Indonesia, General Suharto, these are not only inappropriate in an Asian setting but should also be a matter for reconsideration in the West where a significant decline in social standards is said to have taken place in recent decades. Dr Mahathir has pointed specifically to an "excess of democracy" as the root cause of these problems. The same criticisms have frequently been offered by Singaporean leaders, past and present.

Such thinking about democracy and human rights must be understood in the context of post-colonialism which has been a strong ideological force in domestic and regional politics in East Asia. Dr Mahathir's occasional remarks about British colonialism and racism indicate that memories of colonialism remain a salient factor. Resistance by Mahathir and other East Asian leaders to closer Australian involvement in regional bodies, such as ASEAN (Association of Southeast Asian Nations) has been justified explicitly by reference to Australia's "Western" culture, especially as this influences political approaches.

The Asian values debate became steadily more heated as the rate of economic growth increased, up to mid-1997, when the region was engulfed by a serious economic downturn. But before that juncture the spectacular economic successes in the region contributed to the great reverence for such forces as the "Confucian ethos," discussed above. The reputedly positive effects of Confucianism on the economy, however, were set, by Huntington, Fukayama and others, against the decidedly less progressive consequences of the belief system for human rights and democracy. Western liberals were unconvinced by the idea that "Asian democracy" based on Confucian principles of harmony, consensus and order were more appropriate for Asians than the adversarial practices associated with liberal democracy.

Far from underpinning a culturally attuned and dynamic form of local democracy, liberal critics see Asian and Confucian values as little more than an attempt by an influential set of authoritarian leaders to legitimate their power in the face of challenges from within, and criticisms from without. Yet there is very little evidence that the continuing debate about the nature and effects of Asian/Confucian values is likely to precipitate a major divide in world politics, as Huntington predicts. Of much greater concern to many East Asian leaders – in Malaysia, the Philippines and Indonesia, for example – is the spectre of Islamic radicalism. On this issue they are as one with Western governments; and this issue unites otherwise confrontational regimes in a shared fear of the "Muslim threat."

Islamic Radicalism and the West

One of the most serious threats to the West, according to Fukuyama, is Islamic "fundamentalism" or Islamism, the term used here because of the former's pejorative connotations. Fukuyama asserts that the values of Islam have a "more than superficial resemblance to European fascism" (1989: 236). But it is one thing to argue that various brands of political Islam have qualitatively different perspectives on liberal democracy than some forms of Christianity, and it is quite another to claim, as Huntington and others do, that the Islamic countries *en masse* are poised to enter into a period of conflict with the West. It is quite possible to argue that the alleged Muslim threat has more to do with the bigotry of some Western analysts than with Islam *per se*. Like "Asian values," Islam is often associated by Western analysts with a decidedly undemocratic set of ideas. The concept of an Islamic state, for example, suggests to many the clear antithesis of democracy. The West's response to the struggle for democracy in Algeria in the 1990s is a good illustration of this way of thinking (see **box 1.3**).

Despite Western fears, these struggles between groups in the Islamic world are directed primarily against their own rulers rather than against the West. It was the intransigent support of Western states – especially France – for the military junta in Algeria which served to export the civil war to Europe. Since the beginning of Islam over 1,000 years ago, Muslim critics of the status quo have periodically emerged in opposition to what they perceive as unjust rule (Mardin, 1993: 151). Contemporary Islamists can be seen as the most recent example, characterizing themselves as the "just" involved in a struggle against the "unjust." The dichotomy between "just" and "unjust" in the promotion of social change throughout Islamic history parallels the historic tension in the West between "state" and "civil society." The implication is that the "unjust" inhabit the state while the "just" look in from the outside, aching to reform the corrupt system.

Historically, the goal of the Islamically "just" has been to form popular consulta-

In December 1991, Algeria held legislative elections which most independent observers characterized as among the freest ever held in North Africa or the Arab Middle East. The following January, however, Algeria's armed forces seized power to prevent an overwhelming victory in the elections by the reformist Front Islamique du Salut (FIS). The assumption was that if the FIS achieved power then it would summarily close down Algeria's newly refreshed democratic institutions and political system. A respected London-based weekly news magazine posed the question which was on many people's lips "What is the point of an experiment in democracy if the first people it delivers to power are intent on dismantling it?" (*Economist*, 2 January 1992: 3). The answer might well be: this is the popular will, and it must be respected whatever the outcome. Algeria's army nevertheless had its own ideas. The FIS was summarily banned, thousands of supporters were incarcerated, and more than 100,000 people died in the ensuing civil war which spilled over into the streets of Paris in the mid-1990s with a bombing campaign carried out by the *groupe armee islamique*, the FIS armed wing (Webster, 1995).

tive mechanisms in line with the idea that the Muslim ruler was open to popular pressure and would seek to settle problems brought by his subjects. The concept of *shura* (consultation) should not be equated with the Western notion of popular sovereignty because sovereignty resides with God alone. *Shura* is a way of ensuring unanimity within the community of Muslims, "which allows for no legitimate minority position. The goal of the 'just' is an Islamically based society" (Dorr, 1993: 151). Thus, some – but not all – Islamists oppose Western interpretations of democracy, where sovereignty resides with the people, because it is seen as a system that negates God's own sovereignty. It is partly for this reason that Islamists (often in conflict with conservative, "unjust," Islamic establishments) have been conspicuous by their absence in demands for

Western-style democratic change in the Muslim world. Yet, despite an unwillingness to accept any sovereignty other than God's, some Islamic radicals have accepted the need for earthly rulers to seek a mandate from the people. For example, Dr Abdeslam Harras, leader of the Moroccan radical Islamic movement, Jama'at al-Da'wa al-Islamiyah, asserts that the ruler of an Islamic country should be elected by a majority of the people (Dorr, 1993: 152).

The rise of Islamism in virtually all of the world's Muslim states is primarily the result of the failure of modernization to deliver on its promises. Etienne and Tozy argue that Islamic resurgence carries within it "the disillusionment with progress and the disenchantments of the first 20 years of independence" (Etienne and Tozy, 1981: 251). Faced with state power which seeks to destroy or control the former communitarian structures and to replace them with an idea of a national citizenry based on the link between state and individual, popular (as opposed to state-controlled) Islam emerges as a vehicle of political aspirations. The Muslim awakening should be seen primarily in relation to its *domestic* capacity to oppose the state: "It is primarily in civil society that one sees Islam at work" (Coulon, 1983: 49). It does not translate into a wider threat to *global* order, except in isolated incidents, such as the bombing of the World Trade Center in New York in 1993.

To many people in the West, Islam is perceived monolithically as *dar Islam*, the undifferentiated "house of Islam." The rest of the world is understood as "the house of war," meaning that Islam is at war with everything outside it. But this by no means describes current realities within Muslim societies where there are energetic debates over the question of what Islam is and how it should express itself in fast-changing societies. In short, there is a battle over the definition of Islam and over who or what represents the voice of "authentic" Muslims. For example, governments in Algeria and Egypt have been for years opposed by the Islamists – *in the name of Islam*! Thus there are at least two broad interpretations of Islam vying for dominance in Egypt, Algeria and elsewhere in the Muslim world.

The issue of Islam and politics brings us to a further aspect of religion's recent involvement in world politics: its association with the global trend towards democracy. When we examine the role of non-Christian religious leaders in the demands for democracy in the Third World, a complex picture emerges. Huntington argues correctly that democracy is a trait often associated with Christian political cultures – both in the Third World and elsewhere; it is much less prominent in the Muslim world (Huntington, 1991: 73). Fukuyama contends that because Hinduism is rooted in "hierarchical and inegalitarian" religious teachings, Hindus have a rather ambivalent attitude towards democracy. By contrast, Buddhism, he asserts, "confine[s] itself to a domain of private worship centring around the family" but this also results in political passivity (Fukuyama, 1992: 217).

For both Huntington and Fukuyama, non-Christian political cultures in the Third World foster non-democratic political systems. But, to the extent that this position is valid, are Buddhist, Hindu and Muslim political cultures undemocratic because their followers have habitually lived in authoritarian political systems, or do their religious beliefs promote non-democratic cultures? Are authoritarian leaders in non-Christian countries unconcerned about democratic challenges because the religious beliefs of their subjects render them politically passive? Do spiritual cultures, in other words, discourage demands for political change? Answers to such questions are contested, but it is more important to acknowledge that the claims made by Huntington and Fukuyama are not universally valid. India, a nation of more than a billion people (over 80 per cent Hindus, and 11 per cent Muslims), has been a democracy (except for a two-year period between 1975 and 1977)

since 1947. Several Muslim-majority countries, such as Jordan, Lebanon, Kirghizstan and, most recently, Indonesia, the largest Muslim country in the world, have emerged as democratizing countries. Hindu/Buddhist Nepal has an elected government, while Buddhist-majority Thailand and Confucian Taiwan and South Korea also have democratically elected governments after decades of military rule. So it is not possible to defend the claim that all non-Christian cultures resist democracy and that, by extension, their political cultures will necessarily be authoritarian.

But we cannot leave it there. To complicate matters further, the impact of religion on democracy varies in another important respect. There is rarely consensus among co-religionists as to the precise nature or form of a desirable political regime. Gehad Auda outlines the nature of the broad Islamist political consensus in Egypt where there is wide agreement that liberal democracy is undesirable (Auda, 1993: 379–407). But despite years of *de facto* one-party rule, there is no agreement about either the precise nature of a desirable Islamic state or how to get one. Should the route taken by Iran, Saudi Arabia, Sudan or Afghanistan be followed or should a *sui generis* solution be established? By the same token, there is no consensus about whether violent revolution, the ballot box, or a mix of tactics and strategies is appropriate. Moreover, millions of middle-class Muslim Egyptians regard the notion of any form of Islamic state with horror, preferring perhaps a modern, Western-oriented, polity where religion plays no political role.

A similar divide is evident in Thailand where religious activists in the Palang Tham party were unable to rely on the ballot box in the 1990s to deliver their goal of a state built on Buddhist values. This was because so few Thais – 95 per cent Buddhist – supported this goal. As in Egypt, many among the burgeoning middle classes in Thailand desire a Western-oriented political system. In India, by contrast, Hindu nationalist parties, especially the electorally successful BJP, were able to win many millions of votes – and not only from poor, alienated people, but also from middle-class urbanites – by claiming that groups outside the Hindu "family" – especially Muslims and Christians – benefited disproportionately from the state's secular policies. By targeting non-Hindus as scapegoats, the BJP and its allies were able to gain impressive electoral successes, convincing many Hindu voters that Muslims and Christians were progressing "too fast" because of overly sympathetic state policies (Haynes, 1998).

These examples reveal that religious beliefs affect views on democracy, although not in any straightforward way. Yet the global trend towards greater democracy has been stimulated by a combination of international, transnational and domestic pressures. It is also apparent that the spread of democracy and its close corollary – market-oriented economic reforms – has been due in no small measure to the processes and imperatives of globalization acting upon local political cultures and religions.

Conclusion

What does the chapter tell us about the nature of contemporary world politics? From the evidence presented, it is clear that the contemporary involvement of religion in world politics poses significant analytical problems. Chief among them is that political religion cannot easily be explained by factors of traditional analytical importance to political science, such as the economy or class. The end of the Cold War was followed by an eruption of religious conflicts within a large number of countries which raised serious doubts about the possibility of moving from an old order rooted in bipolarity, nuclear deterrence and ideological division to a new global order where the pursuit of peace, prosperity and cooperation would be paramount.

New threats to world order were traced to both Confucianism and Islam. But such fears are without firm foundation. In the case of Islamism, domestically-orientated groups threaten the incumbency of their rulers rather than the global system; as for Confucianism, the differences between the "Confucian" states are more important than the alleged authoritarian similarities. There is little in the spectre of a "Confucian" or "Islamic" threat to global order.

While contemporary politico-religious movements display a number of broadly similar features across cultural and state boundaries, there are also differences both *between* and *within* them. But we should not be surprised by this. The world religions have always functioned as "terrains of meaning," subject to radically different interpretations and conflicts, often with profound social and political consequences. Islam, Hinduism, Christianity and Buddhism all have long traditions of reformers, populists and "protestants," seeking to give their religion contemporary meaning and social salience. The contemporary era is a period of wide religious reinterpretation, spurred by a plethora of changes at both the national and global levels. Those who neglect religion in analyses of world politics are likely to miss a highly dynamic feature of the global scene.

References

Auda, G. (1993) "The Islamic Movement and Resource Mobilization in Egypt: A Political Cultural Perspective," in L. Diamond (ed.), *Political Culture and Democracy in Developing Countries*. Boulder, CO: Lynne Rienner, 379–407.

Beyer, P. (1994) *Religion and Globalization*. London: Sage.

Coulon, C. (1983) *Les Muselmans et Le Pouvoir en Afriquee Noire*. Paris: Karthala.

Dorr, S. (1995) "Democratization in the Middle East" in R. Slater, S. Shutz and S. Dorr (eds.) *Global Transformation and the Third World*. Boulder, CO: Lynne Rienner, 131–57.

Etienne, B. and Tozy, M. (1981) "Le Glissement des Obligations Islamiques Vers Le

Phenomene Associatif a Casablanca" in Centre de Recherches et d'Etudes Sur Les Societes Mediterraneens, *Le Maghreb Musulman en 1979*. Paris, 251, quoted in C. Coulon, *Les Musulmans et Le Pouvoir en Afriques Noir*. Paris: Karthala (1983), 48.

Fukuyama, F. (1989) "The End of History," *National Interest*, 16: 3–18.

Fukuyama, F. (1992) *The End of History and the Last Man*. Harmondsworth: Penguin.

Grayson, J. (1989) "Korea" in S. Mews (ed.), *Religion in Politics*. Harlow: Longman, 153.

Haynes, J. (1993) *Religion in Third World Politics*. Buckingham: Open University.

Haynes, J. (1998) *Religion in Global Politics*. London: Longman.

Held, D. (1993) "Democracy from City-States to a Cosmopolitan Order?" in D. Held (ed.), *Prospects for Democracy*. Cambridge: Polity Press.

Huntingdon, S. P. (1993) "The Clash of Civilizations." *Foreign Affairs*, 71(3): 22–49.

King, A. (1993) "A Nonparadigmatic Search for Democracy in a Post-Confucian Culture: The Case of Taiwan, ROC" in L. Diamond (ed.), *Political Culture and Democracy in Developing Countries*. Boulder, CO: Lynne Rienner, 139–62.

Marty, M. E. and Scott Appleby, R. (1993) "Introduction" in M. Marty and R. Scott Appleby (eds.), *Fundamentalism and the State: Remaking Politics, Economies and Militance*. Chicago: Chicago University Press, 1–9.

McCrew, A. (1992) "Conceptualizing Global Politics" in A. McCrew and P. Lewis (eds.), *Global Politics*. Cambridge: Polity Press.

Moyser, G. (ed.) (1991) *Politics and Religion in the Modern World*. London: Routledge.

Rudolf, S. H. and Piscatori, J. (eds.) (1997), *Transnational Religion and Fading States*. Boulder, CO: Westview Press.

Said, E. (1995) "What is Islam?," *New Statesman and Society*, 10 February, 32–4.

Webster, P. (1995) "Capital of Terror," *The Guardian*, 6 September.

The United Nations

Stephen Ryan

2

- ◆ United Nations operations in non-security realms ◆
- ◆ Three generations of human rights ◆
- ◆ Welfare internationalism ◆ Human rights and the United Nations ◆
- ◆ The environment ◆ Global summits ◆

We the people of the United Nations determined . . . to reaffirm our faith in fundamental human rights, in the dignity and worth of the human person, in the equal rights of men and women and of nations large and small . . . to promote social progress and better standards of life in larger freedom. (Preamble of the UN Charter)

No assessment of the contribution of the UN to international politics would be complete without a discussion of the Organization's work in the non-security realms. Because so much attention from the media and the academic community in the west has been directed at peace and security matters it is easy to forget that economic and social issues remain a vital concern for the majority of UN members. This is where most UN employees work and where most of the UN budget is spent. There is a plethora of specialized agencies and other UN bodies that have been working on an impressive range of economic, social and cultural issues throughout the world, organized into what Claude (1984: 68) has described as a "kind of loose confederation."

Claude goes on to claim that the UN represents a move away from "the minimalist conception of the function of multilateral agencies to a kind of international New Dealism, an adaptation of the welfare state philosophy to the realm of world affairs" (Claude, 1984: 79). Armstrong, Lloyd and Redmond (1996: 66) agree with this assessment and claim that "whereas the League's roots lay in the nineteenth century liberalism of the night-watchman state, the UN reflected the twentieth century liberalism of the welfare state."

Welfare Internationalism

Each specialized agency has a separate relationship with the United Nations, though most are modelled on the agreement between the UN and the International Labour Organization (ILO), which was the first such document to be negotiated. The ILO was established in 1919 and was the only League of Nations body to survive the Second World War. From its base in Geneva it attempts to promote fair and humane conditions of labour. Some of the other specialized agencies, such as the Food and Agriculture Organization (FAO), also pre-date the establishment of the six principal organs of the UN. Coordination between the Secretary-General and the specialized agencies is made more difficult because many of them do not even have their headquarters in New York.

Many of the weakest and most vulnerable victims of conflict and exploitation have had the quality of their lives improved by the work of bodies such as the United Nations Children's Emergency Fund (UNICEF), which in 1994 had programmes in 149 states (United Nations, 1997: 43). The United Nations High Commissioner for Refugees (UNHCR) has assisted millions of refugees and displaced persons. The United Nations Disaster Relief Co-ordinator (UNDRO), established in 1972, has helped to provide authoritative reports of relief needs and to co-ordinate relief efforts by UN agencies. The World Heath Organization (WHO) sets standards and guidelines for drugs and vaccines and has played a major role in the elimination of smallpox, which affected 15 million people in 1967. It is now playing an important part in the global battle against AIDS and in 1987 began a global programme to combat this disease. Experts working for WHO, which is based in Geneva, estimate that there will be between 30 and 40 million cases of HIV in men, women and children by the start of the twenty-first century (Whittaker, 1995: 263) The United Nations Educational, Scientific and Cultural Organization (UNESCO) has been lighting against illiteracy and contributes to the search for peace from its Paris headquarters through programmes for education and understanding. The World Food Programme (WFP) assisted 57 million poor and hungry people in 1994 (United Nations, 1997: 47).

In this brief study we cannot describe all of this work in detail. So here we shall concentrate on the UN's work in two important areas, human rights and the protection of the environment. These are interesting areas because they reveal the extent of the divisions between the "North" and "South" on some key global issues. They seem to confirm the observation by Riddell-Dixon (1993: I) that in the 1990s the "dominant tension within the United Nations is between North and South – a development often conveniently overlooked by the North."

Human Rights

The League Covenant made no reference to individual human rights, but they are mentioned in the UN Charter in the preamble and articles 1, 53, 55, 56, 62 and 68. In the Assembly human rights issues are discussed in the third committee or in special committees established to examine, for example, Apartheid, Independence for Colonial Peoples or the Inalienable Rights of the Palestinian People to Self-determination. The Assembly has also passed numerous non-binding declarations and resolutions on the elimination of discrimination against women, the rights of the child, torture, the elimination of all forms of intolerance and of discrimination based on religion or belief, the treatment of prisoners, and the rights of prisoners facing the death penalty.

The most important human rights body within the UN system is the Human Rights Commission (HRC), and its establishment in 1946 as a subsidiary body of ECOSOC (Economic and Social Council) (in accordance with Article 68 of the Charter) signalled "the acceptance of human rights as a general part of the business of international society" (Vincent, 1986: 93). The HRC is now composed of 43 members who sit as representatives of governments. The Commission meets every year in February and March for six weeks, but its time is so limited that it rarely covers the whole of its agenda, which is packed with a wide range of items.

Alston (1992: 139) has noted that for 20 years the Commission insisted that it had "no power to take any action in regard to any complaints concerning human rights." However, in 1967 ECOSOC adopted Resolution 1253, which entitled the HRC to examine in public specific human rights violations by states. Many Third World states hoped that this could be used to criticize racist and colonial governments, though it has also been used to publicize human rights abuses in other circumstances. Special Rapporteurs or experts have investigated cases in, for example, Afghanistan, Albania, Bolivia, Chile, Guatemala, Romania, Iraq, El Salvador, Cuba, Israeli Occupied Territories, Poland from 1982 to 1984, Equatorial Guinea and Haiti.

In 1970 ECOSOC Resolution 1503 gave the HRC and its Sub-Commission for the Prevention of Discrimination and the Protection of Minorities the right to examine in confidence communications which revealed a consistent pattern of gross human rights violations. This became known as the 1503 procedure. At least 45 states have been reported to the HRC under this practice (Alston, 1992: 148). Even though this is a slow, secret mechanism open to political manipulation by states and blocs of states, it is, nonetheless, an important addition to the UN's human rights armoury. Nevertheless, it is important not to get carried away. Alston (1992: 173) comments that it is "difficult to accept that, after almost half a century of concerted efforts, the principal UN procedures for responding to violations are quite as embryonic, marginally effective and unevenly applied as they are."

The first major task of the HRC was to prepare the Universal Declaration of Human Rights, which was adopted by the General Assembly on 10 December 1948. It drew its inspiration from western texts on human rights and no state voted against it. However, Saudi Arabia, South Africa and the Soviet-bloc states abstained. The Declaration set out a number of basic rights such as the right to life, freedom of thought and conscience, the right to vote and the right to a fair trial. However, the Universal Declaration is not a legally binding document, and it took another 18 years for UN members to agree on how to give legal force to its principles. In the process, the initial idea of a single "international Bill of Rights" gave way in 1951 to two International Covenants. Eventually, in January 1966, the UN agreed on the Covenant on Civil and Political Rights and the Covenant on Economic, Social and Cultural Rights. They are "the most comprehensive statements of conventional human rights law yet adopted" (Hannum, 1995: 325). Both treaties came into force in 1976. The main reason why there were two covenants instead of one was that the superpower blocs could not agree on what to include in a single document. The western liberal democracies wanted to stress the classical liberal rights of the individual. The Marxist states wanted to stress group and class rights of a more economic and social nature.

The Covenant on Civil and Political Rights refers to the right to life and prohibits torture, inhuman and degrading treatment, and slavery. It also enshrines the right to a fair hearing, to freedom of thought, conscience and religion, and to freedom of expression and assembly. On the other hand the Covenant on Economic, Social and Cultural Rights emphasizes the right to work and to just and favourable conditions at work, the right to join a trade union, the right to social security and the right to education. Mower (1985: 3) has argued that economic and social rights are "rights to certain opportunities and conditions that are held to be essential if the individual is to be able to enjoy what is commonly referred to as a decent standard of living." Both Covenants refer to the right of national self-determination, a sign of the growing influence of Third World states at the UN.

A notable feature of the Covenant on Civil and Political Rights was the establishment of a Human Rights Committee, not to be confused with the Human Rights Commission. The committee is composed of 18 members chosen from states that have ratified the Covenant. Unlike the HRC representatives, these members are meant to serve in a personal capacity and are not meant to act as government delegates. This committee scrutinizes reports from states on how they have incorporated the Covenant into their own law. However, it tends to be rather cautious and it does not refer to any individual cases of human rights abuse. Also, there is no real incentive for states to take their responsibilities seriously and co-operation by states is entirely voluntary. Their representatives are not obliged to answer questions and the committee has no choice but to accept the answers given to it. Thus, although the committee may ask for additional information, "states actually provide only what they choose" (Donnelly, 1994: 207). However, states can sign an optional protocol which gives the committee the right to hear petitions from individuals in these states. Only about one-third of all states have signed this. Although the final decisions of the committee are made public, considerations of complaints from individuals take place in secret and the records of the committee's discussions are confidential.

In 1985 a Committee on Economic, Social and Cultural Rights was established as an independent expert committee. This followed several unsuccessful attempts by a working group to create an effective supervisory body for the 1966 Covenant on Economic, Social and Cultural Rights as part of ECOSOC's own machinery. The US was opposed to this committee, and has retained a consistent dislike of the whole idea of economic and social rights. Unlike the Human Rights Committee, the Committee on Economic, Social and Cultural Rights has no mandate deriving from the 1966 Covenants, since it is not mentioned there. However, in many other respects it works like the Human Rights Committee.

The UN is now trying to develop a "third generation" of rights, such as the right to development, the right to peace, and the right to a clean environment. In 1979 the Assembly agreed that every nation and every human being has "the inherent right to life in peace." In 1986 it adopted the Declaration on the Right to Development, with only the US voting against. These "peoples' rights" tend to be supported most fervently by Third World states, especially in Africa. In 1981, for example, the Organization of African Unity adopted the Banjul Charter on Human and Peoples' Rights. Peoples' rights include the right to exploit natural resources, the right to a life free from foreign domination, and the right to development (see Ferguson, 1986; Okoth-Ogenda, 1993).

At the same time as the General Assembly adopted the Universal Declaration it also agreed the International Convention on the Prevention and Punishment of the Crime of Genocide. This made it an offence to undertake actions with the intent to destroy in whole or in part a national, ethnic, racial or linguistic group. A number of acts were also identified as constituting genocide: killing members of a group; causing serious bodily or mental harm; deliberately inflicting conditions of life calculated to result in the physical destruction of the group; actions to prevent births within the group; and the transfer of children out of the group. Sadly, however, until recently the UN has been reluctant to invoke this Convention. This has led to some caustic criticisms of the UN, most notably by Kuper (1985). The reluctance to respond to genocide can be seen as a symptom of a more general indisposition to deal with the protection of ethnic minorities (Ryan, 1990).

After adopting the two 1966 Covenants the UN convened a major human rights conference at Tehran in 1968. Over 80 states attended and although they all voted that the 1948 Universal Declaration constituted an obligation for members of the international community, serious disagreements emerged between the North and the South. Third World states wanted to give much more prominence to racism, colonialism and self-determination and were intent on criticising South Africa and Israel. Many western governments wanted to focus on other human rights issues.

After Tehran the UN continued to expand its human rights remit. Discrimination against women received major attention. A Commission on the Status of Women had been created by ECOSOC in 1946, and this body worked on a number of issues relating to its mandate, which is to prepare recommendations and reports on "promoting women's rights in political, economic, civil, social and educational fields." A major step forward occurred in 1975, when the first international conference on women to be sponsored by the UN convened in Mexico City. The 8,000 delegates adopted the Mexico Declaration on Equality of Women and their Contribution to Development and Peace. The following year the Assembly adopted a Declaration on the Elimination of Discrimination Against Women and began work on the Convention Against All Forms of Discrimination Against Women. This was adopted by the Assembly on 18 December 1979 and came into force in 1981 (United Nations, 1993). The Convention recognizes that extensive discrimination against women still exists and commits signatories to take all appropriate measures to eliminate this discrimination in the fields of education, employment, health care, the law, and marriage and family relations. Article 17 created a Committee on the Elimination of Discrimination against Women to consider reports from states on how they are implementing the provisions of the convention.

Other UN conventions worthy of note include the 1969 Convention on the Elimination of all Forms of Racial Discrimination (CERD) arid the 1989 Convention on the Rights of the Child. Article 9 of CERD requires states to submit periodic reports to the UN Committee on the Elimination of Racial Discrimination and the Convention on the Rights of the Child has established a monitoring body

called the Committee on the Rights of the Child that also examines reports by states that have ratified the convention.

Tensions in the human rights system re-emerged at the huge World Conference on Human Rights held in Vienna in the middle of 1993. Five thousand delegates from about 170 states met to debate the UN's human rights role, though no analysis of individual cases of human rights abuses was allowed. Nonetheless there were squabbles between India and Pakistan over Kashmir, between Portugal and Indonesia about East Timor and between Israel and Palestine. A major fault line emerged between the developed West and several Third World states. These divisions had always been present in one form or another. In the 1980s, for example, Iran had criticized the two 1966 covenants because they were not fully consistent with Islamic doctrines (Quinn, 1992: 71). Now the divisions seemed wider than ever. Some Asian states such as China, Indonesia and Malaysia were wary of emphasizing universal rights because they feared that this could be characterized as a western attempt to impose alien values on their cultures. This argument was reflected in the 1993 Bangkok Declaration, where Asian and Pacific states claimed that human rights declarations should take account of national and regional particularities and different cultures and backgrounds.

At Vienna, however, the US led the resistance to such relativistic arguments and pushed strongly for a reaffirmation of universal rights. Thus the final document accepted that states had a solemn commitment to promote universal respect for human rights and fundamental freedoms and that the promotion and protection of human rights was a legitimate concern of the international community. A measure of relativism did appear in the final document in Section 1:5 of the Vienna Declaration and Programme of Action. This states that "the significance of national and regional particularities and various historical, cultural and religious backgrounds must be borne in mind." But the main thrust of the Declaration was to restate and defend the concept of universal rights. So the very first paragraph argues that the universal nature of human rights and fundamental freedoms is "beyond question."

Many states also wanted the human rights agenda to give a much more prominent place to "third generation" rights. One recalls here the comment of René Cassin that "the right to life, that's not only the right not to be condemned to death by arbitrary power or the right not to be murdered – it's also the right to eat!" (Best, 1983: 10). Some progress was made here and the 1986 General Assembly Declaration that development was a universal and an unalienable right and an integral part of fundamental human rights was unanimously armed at Vienna.

The idea of a High Commissioner for Human Rights was also discussed at Vienna. This was a proposal with a "long history" (Humphrey, 1984: 296–301) and although no agreement could be reached at Vienna the General Assembly was asked to consider this issue as a matter of priority. The post was approved by the General Assembly in Resolution 48/141 on 20 December 1993 and Jose Ayala Lasso of Equador was appointed the first High Commissioner with a mandate to promote and protect the effective enjoyment of all human rights and to co-ordinate the promotion and protection of these rights throughout the UN system. He tried to keep human rights issues on the international agenda through visits and his inputs at international gatherings. Lasso was also given the responsibility of co-ordinating the implementation of the UN Decade for Human Rights Education. The UN Secretary-General appeared to be opposed to this new post before it was created by the Assembly, but it had the strong support of the US and of many impartial observers who thought that the new office could raise the profile of human rights within the UN system. Despite these developments it is difficult to be too enthusiastic about the Vienna Conference. As one observer noted:

> While the World Conference did not collapse and managed to produce a final document with no apparent dissenters, it did not produce any new breakthroughs and it failed to confront many of the UN's shortcomings in promoting and protecting human rights. (Matthews, 1993: 34)

Another interesting development in the human rights field is the inclusion of human rights tasks in UN peacekeeping missions. Here special reference can be made to the UN mission to El Salvador (ONUSAL). This was the first peacekeeping operation to include human rights observers (about 120), who were mandated to engage in human rights monitoring through a network of regional and sub-regional offices throughout this central American state. However, this mission was criticized for being too timid because it seemed to be reluctant to criticize the government of El Salvador (Simons, 1994: 186).

Also worthy of note are the two *ad hoc* tribunals set up to investigate and prosecute war crimes in Rwanda and the former Yugoslavia. All the permanent members of the Security Council are suspicious of attempts to establish a more permanent institution to prosecute war criminals, but the US and France have expressed the most vocal opposition to a strong and independent International Criminal Court that could implement a more consistent response to breaches of the laws of war and the Genocide Convention.

The International Criminal Tribunal for the Former Yugoslavia (ICTFY) was established by Security Council Resolution 827 on 27 May 1993. It is authorized to investigate events in the former Yugoslavia since 1991 and has the power to prosecute suspects, though its jurisdiction has been rejected by Bosnian Serbs. After several years most war criminals remain unpunished, though there have been some arrests of those indicted at the Hague. In July 1997, for example, British soldiers attached to S-FOR arrested one Bosnian Serb and killed another in one such arrest operation. Yet many of those indicted remain at large including "big fish" such as Bosnian Serb leaders Radovan Karadzic and Ratko Mladic.

In the Rwandan case the international tribunal, based in Arusha in northern Tanzania and Kigali in Rwanda, was established after a commission of experts created by the Security Council decided months after the killings had started that genocide had been committed in Rwanda. However it has faced many difficulties. Many prosecution lawyers are young and inexperienced. There have been allegations of misconduct by some key officials at the tribunal, and some African states have been reluctant to co-operate. A lack of funding has created difficulties and disagreements have also arisen between the *ad hoc* tribunal and the government of Rwanda, which wants its own system for trying those accused of war crimes to have precedence over the UN body. The Rwandan government criticized a Security Council Resolution that prohibited the *ad hoc* tribunal from awarding the death penalty and thought that it should have been based in Kigali so that all Rwandans could have access to the proceedings. Whereas the UN tribunal has indicted only a few dozen suspected war criminals the Rwandan authorities are holding up to 90,000 suspects in gaol.

There is a clear strain between the UN's role in easing interstate diplomacy and its role in promoting an agenda based on international welfare and social justice. Member governments often give the impression that the promotion of human rights gets in the way of "normal" interstate activity. Why, for example, criticize China for its human rights record in Tibet if this will put at risk political and economic relations with Beijing? Outside UN meetings, where official representatives pay lip-service to high standards of behaviour, many states show little interest in human rights issues,

especially if turning a blind eye benefits their own national interest. For example, Maurice Abrams (1979), a US representative on the Human Rights Commission between 1965 and 1968, states that he was instructed by Washington not to condemn the human rights record of US allies such as Greece and Haiti during his period of service. Even when states do take up human rights issues partiality means there is always a danger that the debate becomes a "sinister farce" (Hoffmann, 1981: 117).

Nothing illustrates this more forcefully than the treatment of the Dutch Director of the UN's own Human Rights Division, Theo van Boven. He upset senior UN figures and some influential governments by his robust criticism of regimes guilty of serious human rights abuses. They were accustomed to bland and innocuous statements on human rights issues, but at the start of the 1982 Human Rights Commission meetings van Boven singled out seven governments for attack, including El Salvador and Guatemala. This not only upset many Latin American authoritarian regimes, but also infuriated the Reagan administration in the US, which supported these governments and was trying to argue that their human rights records were improving. The US government was already suspicious of van Boven because he had attended a human rights conference organized by the Sandinista administration in Nicaragua. The Dutchman's approach also upset Moscow, which did not want UN officials taking such a strong line against human rights abuses. So van Boven was removed from his post when his contract was not renewed by Secretary-General de Cuellar.

Human rights concerns are often downplayed when they clash with the interests of states. Hence the UN found itself unable to take a strong stand against major human rights abusers such as Pol Pot in Cambodia or Idi Amin in Uganda. Successive Secretaries-General have also tended to relegate human rights issues at the UN because they endangered the political work of the Secretariat in other areas. Hofmann (1981: 116) explains that states have a diverse range of important concerns. However:

> If one starts denouncing countries whose support one needs in all of those arenas, where will one be? But if one tries to balance off each of these concerns against human rights, what kind of crazy quilt will one get?

It may be that the UN does not yet have the balance right. Although Secretaries-General have taken up human rights issues in public and private, the UN tends to give priority to "peace" rather than "justice" (Ramcharan, 1987: 159).

The Environment

Unlike human rights, there is no mention of the environment in the UN Charter. Indeed, it was not until the 1970s that environmentalism became an important issue at the United Nations. As public unease rose about nuclear testing, the use of insecticides such as DDT, and the pollution of air, land and sea, a conference on the environment was convened in Stockholm from 5 to 16 June 1972. Although most Soviet-bloc states did not attend because of a dispute over whether the German Democratic Republic should be accorded a status equal to West Germany, 114 states and 200 non-governmental organizations participated in what one analyst called "the landmark event in the growth of international environmentalism" (McCormick, 1989: 88).

Several important initiatives did, indeed, emerge from this gathering. The United Nations Environmental Programme (UNEP) was established in Nairobi by the General Assembly in December 1972. A Declaration on the Human Environment, made up of 26 principles, was agreed after protracted negotiation, and 109 recommendations were included in a Plan of Action. The years from 1972 to 1982 were declared a decade for solving environmental problems.

However, certain doubts were also raised by poor states who feared that environmentalism, which they regarded as a rich state's disease, would restrict their economic growth, increase the cost of development and raise prices for their products in international markets. One of the Chinese delegation, for example, argued that "each country has the right to determine its own environmental standards and policies in the light of its own conditions, and no country whatsoever should undermine the interests of the developing countries under the pretext of protecting the environment" (McCormick, 1989: 99). Although there may indeed be only one planet earth, it seems that there are a number of different views about how we should treat it.

UNEP, under its first director Maurice Strong, initiated a series of programmes that attempted to monitor the global environment and educate people about the dangers of its degradation and pollution. An "earthwatch" network was established to monitor environmental conditions. In 1974 it also began a Regional Seas Programme that has addressed pollution in places like the Mediterranean, the Red Sea, the Persian Gulf and the Caribbean. Other issues tackled include desertification, deforestation, and the management of hazardous waste.

In June 1982 there was a major conference involving 105 states in Nairobi. It reaffirmed many of the principles endorsed at Stockholm. Yet again there were complaints voiced by the poorer states who wanted to place development above the environment. In 1987 the World Commission on Environment and Development (1987), also called the Brundtland Commission after its chairperson, issued its influential report. The commission had been created by the General Assembly and it attempted to reconcile the competing demands of "environmentalists" and "developmentalists" with the concept of sustainable development. It called for economic growth to be stimulated, claiming that poverty is a major source of environmental degradation; but also recommended that environmental resources should be preserved. This approach, which seemed to ignore significant differences of opinion between the two camps, was endorsed by the UNEP and by the World Bank. The same year a UNEP conference adopted the Montreal Protocol on Substances that Deplete the Ozone Layer. Indeed, in the 1980s atmospheric pollution emerged as one of the key environmental issues.

One manifestation of this concern was the creation of the International Panel on Climate Change in November 1988. This was made up of scientific experts who were to investigate the factors affecting climate change and to forecast and assess trends. In 1990 it produced a report that predicted that environmental damage, leading to changes in climate, would have a devastating effect on the lives of millions with a significant increase in desertification, agricultural disruption and shoreline erosion. The work of this International Panel, along with the Brundtland Report, played an important role in setting the agenda for the next major global environmental conference.

The 1992 United Nations Conference on the Environment and Development (UNCED) retained the link between environmental and development issues. This "Earth Summit," convened in Rio de Janeiro, was the largest conference ever held up to this date. Over 3,500 delegates attended and over 100 heads of state addressed the gathering. A number of initiatives emerged. The Earth Charter was a rather bland statement. The non-binding Agenda 21, signed by 178 states, was lengthier and was intended to be a blueprint for action. It called for an increase in growth, a reduction in poverty, a decline in population pressure, fairer use of the global commons, a reduction in the generation of waste and an increased centrality for environmental and development issues.

A Convention on Biological Diversity, which sought to preserve plant and animal species, was adopted by 140 states. A Convention on Climate Change, also known as the Framework Convention, obtained 155 signatories. This focused on "greenhouse gases" in the atmosphere and declared that emission levels would be held at 1990 levels until the year 2000. This was not a significant reduction because the US government, urged on by American businesses opposed to environmental regulation, insisted that more stringent controls were unacceptable. The UN's own independent Intergovernmental Panel on Climate Change challenged the low targets agreed at Rio in a major report in 1994. It doubted if stabilising emissions at 1990 levels would be enough to protect the atmosphere and predicted that further drastic action would be required.

A proposed convention on deforestation had to be abandoned when no consensus could be reached between northern and southern states. Instead a non-binding Declaration on Forest Principles was agreed. Finally, a new environmental body emerged as a result of the ruminations at Rio. In 1993 EQOSOC established a United Nations Commission on Sustainable Development based in New York. It is to monitor the implementation of the Rio agreements and serve as a forum for developing policies for sustainable development.

Limitations

Since the end of the Gold War more opportunities have arisen to raise both human rights and environmental issues at the global level. The growing significance of human rights issues at the UN can be seen in the debates about humanitarian intervention and the calls to apply the full force of international law to those guilty of genocide in Rwanda and Bosnia. Green issues are also now a significant component of the international agenda and the fear of environmental destruction is prompting a redefinition of security to include the protection of nature. Vogler (1997: 243) notes that summit meetings between the leaders of the G7 "now make declarations about forests and pollution alongside their more traditional preoccupations with interest rates and 'political' and 'security issues'."

Yet although both human rights and environmental issues are eroding the traditional distinction between "high" and "low" politics, that is, the distinction between security and welfare issues, we should not overstate their impact on inter-state relations or claim that they are of central importance even at the UN. We can feel the sense of disappointment in the analysis of many commentators in assessing the achievements in these two areas.

Amnesty International (1992), for example, points out that:

> the UN still has difficulty in confronting pressing human rights issues directly or taking effective action in response to urgent situations of gross violations, particularly when dealing with unresponsive or unco-operative governments.

Imber (1996: 150), assessing the contributions of the UN to the protection of "the environment, concludes that although the UN is the best place to conduct environmental diplomacy because it is the most important global forum for creating new norms, it is also the worst place, because it is just an organization of states and excludes many key actors.

We should note that work in these areas is not properly resourced. Both the UN Centre for Human Rights and the UNEP have suffered from lack of funding, which has led to understaffing. The secretariats of both UN bodies are located away from New York, with the Centre for Human

Rights based in Geneva and UNEP in Nairobi. Such arrangements make co-ordination between the Secretary-General and the specialized agencies more difficult and may reduce the influence of such agencies on UN policy. As the human rights agenda is becoming more significant, the geographic distance between the UN's political centre and its main human rights organ is becoming less defensible (van Boven, 1992: 578). Either the Centre for Human Rights should be moved to New York or its liaison office there should be upgraded. Furthermore, although the UN has set standards it lacks an effective independent monitoring system and fact-finding capability. Nor can it enforce these standards.

It is also important to note that great powers continue to shape the agenda for these issues. At Rio in 1992 the US opposed strict controls on the environment and so certain proposals had to be watered down. At Vienna the following year the US supported the idea of a High Commissioner for Human Rights, and such a post was created. This reminds us that the closing gap between high and low politics works both ways. It forces the great powers to take heed of economic and social issues, but it also thrusts the agendas of these powers into discussions of such matters.

Global Summits

The trend towards large, high-profile "world conferences" or "summits" is seen in other areas of the UN's social agenda. In 1994 there was the Cairo Conference on population and development. This adopted a plan of action to enable states to make reproductive health and family planning available to all by 2015 and reaffirmed that any form of coercion for family planning is unacceptable.

In March 1995 the World Summit on Social Development was held in Copenhagen. This issued a declaration aimed at reducing unemployment and poverty and focused on some of the negative aspects of globalization. In September the same year the UN Fourth World Conference on Women adopted the "Global Platform for Action." This was endorsed by all 189 delegations and identifies critical areas of concern and is supposed to promote equality for women. It suggests a number of strategic actions in areas such as poverty, education, health care, violence, employment, the portrayal of women in the media and the role of women in decision-making.

The question has sometimes been asked whether anything positive emerges from these international media events. Critics argue that these large UN conferences attract heads of government who see them only as photo opportunities and who offer no leadership or vision for the serious issues under discussion. Accusations of hypocrisy are, therefore, easy to make. Such meetings certainly bring to public attention the tensions that still exist between different states about social issues and all too frequently the fine words agreed at these meetings are never translated into political practice and few resources are made available to implement well-meaning plans. They therefore can illustrate, ironically, that the UN is a rather powerless body.

However such meetings help to institutionalize the notion of international responsibility and establish forums for non-governmental organizations (Forsyth, 1995). Fomerand (1996) also supports such events and argues that they serve three important functions: the creation, dissemination and sharing of knowledge; monitoring and early warning; and standard setting. He also emphasizes the opportunities these gatherings present for greater NGO involvement in these issues. They can therefore be viewed as part of a process of the social mobilization that is accompanying "globalization."

Article 71 of the Charter allows ECOSOC to "make suitable arrangements for consultation with non-governmental organizations which are concerned with matters within its competence." Such arrangements often involve placing NGOs into one of two categories. Category 1 NGOs are those that can claim to represent major segments of the population in a large number of countries. They can propose agenda items and may, on occasions, make oral interventions during ECOSOC meetings. Category II NGOs, like those in the first category, can send observers to ECOSOC meetings and submit written statements. They have an international reputation and a special competence in the areas covered by ECOSOC. One analysis of the growing importance of NGOs in the UN system has found that 92 UN agencies now have NGO liaison offices in many parts of the world (Alger, 1994: 308). Over 840 NGOs attended the Vienna Human Rights Conference, whilst at the Rio Earth Summit the NGOs convened a Global Forum to run parallel with the official meetings.

However, such gatherings also demonstrate that there is an absence of consensus on some key items. Tensions between the representatives of secular liberal states and those subject to Islamic or Catholic influences were obvious at the 1995 Women's Conference in Beijing over issues such as access to contraception and equal status. Many Third World states remain suspicious of the western emphasis on environmentalism, and are worried that the human rights issue could be used to legitimize intervention in their internal affairs. Therefore, as the UN becomes more active in social and cultural areas major disagreements can emerge about the significance to be given to cultural distinctiveness and to differences between rich and poor states. UN responses to issues such as human rights and environmental protection have often been inspired by western values. Perhaps Galtung (1994) is correct to call for a more balanced normative input into these global debates.

References

Abrams, Maurice B. (1979) Evidence to *House of Representatives Sub-Committee on Future Foreign Policy Research and Development*, 11 May–30 August, 1976. Washington: US General Printing Office.

Alger, Chadwick F. (1994) "Citizens and the UN system in a changing world," in Yoshikazu Sakamoto (ed.), *Global Transformation*. Tokyo: United Nations University Press.

Alston, Philip (1992) "The Commission on Human Rights," in Philip Alston (ed.), *The United Nations and Human Rights*. Oxford: Clarendon.

Amnesty International (1992) *Amnesty International Annual Report*, 1992. London: Amnesty International.

Armstrong, David, Lloyd, Lorna and Redmond, John (1996) *From Versailles to Maastricht: International Organizations in the Twentieth Century*. Basingstoke: Macmillan.

Best, Geoffrey (1983) *Humanity in Warfare*. London: Methuen.

Claude Jr., Inis L. (1984) *Swords into Plowshares*. 4th edition. New York: Random House.

Donnelly, J. (1994) "Human Rights and International Organizations," in Friedrich Kratochwil and Edward D. Mansfield (eds.), *International Organizations: A Reader*. New York: HarperCollins.

Ferguson, J. A. (1986) "The Third World," in R. J. Vincent (ed.), *Foreign Policy and Human Rights*. Cambridge: Cambridge University Press.

Fomerand, Jacques (1996) "UN Conferences: Media Events or Genuine Diplomacy," *Global Governance*, 2, 3: 361–75.

Forsyth, David P. (1995) "The UN and human rights at fifty," *Global Governance*, 1: 297–318.

Galtung, Johan (1994) *Human Rights in Another Key*. Cambridge: Polity.

Hannum, Hurst (1995) "Human rights," in Oscar Schachter and C. C. Joyner (eds.), *United Nations Legal Order, Vol. 1*. Cambridge: Cambridge University Press.

Hoffman, Stanley (1981) *Duties Beyond Borders*. Syracuse: Syracuse University.

Humphrey, John P. (1984) *Human Rights and the United Nations: A Great Adventure*. New York: Transnational.

Imber, Mark (1996) "The Environment and the United Nations," in John Vogler and Mark F. Imber (eds.), *The Environment and International Relations*. London: Routledge.

Kuper, Leo (1985) *The Prevention of Genocide*. New Haven: Yale University.

Matthews, Robert O. (1993) "United Nations Reform in the 1990s: North–South Dimensions," in Gerald Dirks et al., *The State of the United Nations, 1993: North–South Perspectives*. Providence, RI: Academic Council on the United Nations System.

McCormick, John (1989) *The Global Environmental Movement*. London: Belhaven.

Mower, A. Glenn (1985) *International Cooperation for Social Justice. Global and Regional Protection of Economic/Social Rights*. Westport: Greenwood Press.

Okoth-Ogenda, H. W. O. (1993) "Human and Peoples' Rights: What Point is Africa Trying to Make?," in Ronald Cohen et al., eds, *Human Rights and Governance in Africa*. Gainsville: University Press of Florida.

Quinn, John (1992) "The General Assembly into the 1990s," in Philip Alston (ed.), *The United Nations and Human Rights*. Oxford: Clarendon.

Ramcharan, B. (1987) *Keeping Faith with the United Nations*. Dordrecht: UNITAR/M. Nijhof.

Riddell-Dixon, Elizabeth (1993) "North–South Relations and the United Nations," in Gerald Dirks et al., *The State of the United Nations, 1993: North–South Perspectives*. Providence, RI: Academic Council on the United Nations System.

Rupesinghe, Kumar (1992) "The Disappearing Boundaries Between Internal and External Conflicts," in Elise Boulding (ed.), *New Agendas for Peace Research*. Boulder, CO: Lynne Rienner.

Ryan, Stephen (1990) "Ethnic Conflict and the United Nations," *Ethnic and Racial Studies*, 13, 1: 25–49.

Simons, Geoff (1994) *The United Nations*. Basingstoke: Macmillan.

United Nations (1993) *Yearbook of The United Nations*. New York: United Nations.

United Nations (1997) *Yearbook of The United Nations*. New York: United Nations.

Van Boven, Theo (1992) *Seminar on the Right of*

Restitution, Compensation and Rehabilitation for Victims of Gross Violations of Human Rights and Fundamental Freedoms. Utrecht: Netherlands Institute of Human Rights.

Vogler, Michael (1997) *South–North Refugee Migration: Lesson for Development Co-operation.* London: Centre for Economic Policy Research.

Vincent, R. J. (ed.) (1986) *Foreign Policy and Human Rights: Issues and Responses.* Cambridge: Cambridge University Press.

Whittaker, David J. (1995) *United Nations in Action.* London: UCL Press.

3

Religion and International Human Rights

Nathan Lerner

◆ Universal Declaration of Human Rights (1948) ◆

◆ The Krishnaswami Study (1959) ◆

◆ Covenants on Human Rights (1966) ◆

◆ UN Declaration on intolerance and Discrimination

based on Religion or Belief (1981) ◆

◆ UN Declaration on Minorities (1992) ◆ Other Relevant Instruments ◆

During the United Nations era four major instruments have responded globally to human rights issues related to religion and belief: (1) the 1948 Universal Declaration of Human Rights; (2) the 1959 Arcot Krishnaswami Study; (3) the 1966 International Covenants on Human Rights; and (4) the 1981 Declaration on the Elimination of All Forms of Intolerance and Discrimination Based on Religion or Belief. In addition, there have been several general texts and related instruments prohibiting discrimination. This chapter will analyze the religious human rights provisions in these instruments, with some reference to domestic legislation and jurisprudence.

The Universal Declaration of Human Rights

The Universal Declaration of Human Rights, adopted by General Assembly Resolution 217 A (III) of 10 December 1948, has a number of provisions relevant to religious human rights. Article 2 forbids

distinctions of any kind, including religion, in the enjoyment of the rights and freedoms set forth in the Declaration. Article 26 refers to religious groups and covers the right of education. Article 29, which addresses the limitations in the exercise of the proclaimed rights, is also relevant to those interested in protecting religious rights.

The most crucial provision of the Universal Declaration on religious rights is Article 18, which states:

> Everyone has the right to freedom of thought, conscience and religion; this right includes freedom to change his religion or belief, and freedom, either alone or in community with others and in public or private, to manifest his religion or belief in teaching, practice, worship and observance.

Article 18 greatly influenced the texts incorporated in the 1966 Covenants, and was influential in regional treaties and the 1981 Declaration, which will be discussed below. Nehemiah Robinson, in his classic commentary on the declaration, divided Article 18 into two parts: the first clause guarantees the right to freedom of thought, conscience, and religion; the second enumerates the specific rights included therein. This second part is not exhaustive. It only contains those rights that the United Nations thought essential to include because their observance might not be universal at present.[1]

Robinson understood that freedom of thought is a broad category. In his interpretation, it included the right to profess a religion or to profess none – in other words, the right to believe or not to believe. To Robinson, the freedom of thought included two other freedoms: freedom of conscience and freedom of religion, which were explicitly mentioned "in order to leave no doubts" in the minds of the peoples of the world, as it may be deduced from the *travaux preparatoires.* Freedom of conscience was not seen at the time as a strictly legal concept, and there was some opposition to its inclusion. On the other hand, the sacred and inviolable character of freedom of thought, in the words of René Cassin, allowed it to be understood as part of the vernacular of different legal systems.[2]

The term *belief* has a particular meaning in the declaration. Its inclusion in Article 18, and in similar articles in other instruments, should be interpreted strictly in connection with the term *religion.* It does not refer to beliefs of another character – whether political, cultural, scientific, or economic – all of which deserve protection according to law but do not belong to the sphere normally described as religion. The term *belief* was incorporated into the declaration to protect nonreligious convictions, such as atheism or agnosticism, and its meaning was clarified during the discussions on subsequent instruments dealing with religious rights.

Another difficult problem in the drafting of the Universal Declaration was the recognition of the right to change one's religion, a right that was denied by some religions and countries. The clause received opposition but, nevertheless, was adopted by a vote of 27 to 5, with 12 abstentions.

The acceptance was earned, according to Robinson, on the understanding that the declaration must be universal and that this clause did not represent a specific right but was the consequence of freedom of religion and thought. The drafters of the declaration were aware that there were many controversial issues involved, including apostasy; missionary activities; coercion and enticement; proselytism and its limits; the status of new or young religious movements struggling for recognition; and the social dangers inherent in the practices of certain sects using all kinds of manipulations to attract adherents.

Article 18 makes a mild concession to the rights of religious groups. It refers to everyone's right to manifest his religion or belief "alone or in community with others." The words "in community" do not involve a clear reference to religious bodies or institutions; such reference would have been outside the spirit prevailing in the United Nations at that time. Yet, these words suggest that religious rights are more than a strictly individual issue. A right to be exercised in community with others must therefore refer to something more than simply the collection of rights of individuals.[1]

The critical role of the Universal Declaration in the development of the legal and political philosophy of the second part of the twentieth century is beyond question. It is one of the most important single legal documents of our time, and most of its contents can now be seen as customary international law. Its impact on domestic law, in the West at least, remains powerful.

First Specific Steps: The Krishnaswami Study (1959)

It has been rightly asserted that the subject of religious human rights was shunned and neglected more than any other similar subject, perhaps as a consequence of the generally acknowledged fact that no topic has divided humankind more.[3] The

Subcommission on Prevention of Discrimination and Protection of Minorities decided that one of the first studies ordered by the subcommission should deal with this subject, including a program of action to eradicate religious discrimination. To that end, the subcommission appointed in 1956 a special rapporteur, Arcot Krishnaswami from India. He submitted in 1959 a careful and comprehensive report.[4]

The study was based on information that appeared in eighty-two country studies analyzed by the author. Krishnaswami was aware of the difficulties involved with such a comprehensive study of religious rights and emphasized that differential treatment meted out to individuals and groups is not always synonymous with discrimination. Sometimes discriminatory practices are to be found in countries where efforts have been made to eradicate discrimination.

Conscious of the difficulty in defining *religion,* Krishnaswami intended the phrase *religion or belief* to include various theistic creeds, as well as agnosticism, free thought, atheism, and rationalism. After recognizing freedom of thought, conscience, and religion as a legal right, he distinguished between the freedom to maintain (or change) religion or belief and the freedom to manifest religion or belief. It is the latter that engenders most of the legal problems.

Krishnaswami anticipated some of the problems emanating from the freedom to manifest religion or belief, and he therefore addressed permissible limitations upon the right, the individual and collective aspects of this right, and the public and private need to express this right. While the freedom to maintain (or change) a religion or belief is less prone to restriction, the right to manifest it is often the subject of state regulation and limitations.

Krishnaswami stressed that the followers of most religions and beliefs are member of some form of organization, church or religious community. Therefore, compulsion to join such bodies (or prevention from leaving) may become an infringement of the right to freedom of thought, conscience, and religion. Prescribed religious procedures or formalities do not necessarily involve such infringement. Nevertheless, Article 18 of the Universal Declaration attempts to guard against coercion. While sanctions against apostasy are rare today, some legal systems adopt the law of a particular religion, and this often leads to delicate legal questions.

Freedom to manifest religion or belief, Krishnaswami argued, includes protection of a religion's words, teachings, practice, worship, and observance. To be legitimate, such manifestations of religion must satisfy the criteria established in Article 29 of the Universal Declaration, should be respectful of religious minorities, and should work to ensure a greater measure of freedom for society as a whole.[5]

Krishnaswami concluded that the collective aspect of the freedom to manifest religion or belief in the form of freedom of assembly or the freedom of association and organization was especially important, as it was prone to state intervention and regulation. Minorities were, of course, vulnerable, especially when those minorities had religious affinities with those outside the state.

The Krishnaswami study included a detailed list of components of the freedom to manifest religion or belief. Some of these could be subject to permissible limitations, as in the case of human sacrifice, self-immolation, mutilation, slavery, prostitution, subversive activities, polygamy, and other practices that may clash with the requirements mentioned in Article 29 of the Universal Declaration. In such cases domestic legislation may only preempt norms adopted in international instruments when the minimum standard rule is not affected. The remaining list of freedoms related to the manifestations of religion or belief included worship, processions, pilgrimages, equipment and symbols, funeral arrangements, holidays and days of rest, dietary practices, marriage and divorce, dissemination of religion or belief, and training of personnel. Manifestation of religion or belief also included the freedom to forgo acts incompatible with prescriptions of a religion or belief, such as oaths, military service, participation in religious ceremonies, confession, and compulsory medical treatment.[6]

Krishnaswami devoted a short chapter to showing the possible relationships of a religion to the state. This category included states with either an established church or a state religion; states that recognize several religions; and states that mandate a separation of state and religion. Within this context Krishnaswami discussed the management of religious affairs; the financial relationship between the state and religion; and the duties of public authorities. This is also an area in which local constitutional law may prevail over international rules and where the relationship between the state and religion is profoundly influenced by cultural traditions.[7]

The study ended with a chapter on trends and conclusions that reflected the circumstances of the period in which it was prepared. In a final footnote Krishnaswami commented on the manifestations of anti-Semitism and other forms of racial prejudice and intolerance that have become the immediate cause of further measures adopted by the international community. He ended his report by enunciating sixteen rules he believed should be approved by the United Nations.[8] These rules were the basis of the Draft Principles on Freedom and Non-Discrimination in the Matter of Religious Rights and Practices. This draft was prepared by the subcommission.[9] It may be useful to summarize the contents herein.

The Draft Principles are divided into four parts that follow a preamble which proclaims the overall goal of promoting the freedom of thought, conscience, and religion (and eradicating discrimination on the ground of religion or belief). The principles follow very closely the text of the basic rules, with minor modifications.

Part I reaffirms: (1) the right of everyone to adhere, or not to adhere, to a religion or belief, in accordance with the dictates of his conscience; (2) the prior rights of parents or legal guardians to decide the religion or belief in which their child should be brought up – the best interests of the child serving as the guiding principle; and (3) that no one should be subjected to material or moral coercion to impair his freedom to maintain or to change his religion or belief. The wording of these three principles is slightly different from the wording used by Krishnaswami in his first rule, and it incorporates a fourth principle, the banning of any discrimination based on religion or belief.

Part II applies thirteen principles, which serve as a catalog of rights to be ensured to all. According to Part II, each person should be free to comply with the prescriptions of his religion or belief and free from performing acts incompatible with them, particularly as it concerns worship, places of worship, and objects necessary for the performance of rites. The thirteen principles reflecting these basic rules include the following rights:

1   to worship, with equal protection to be accorded to all forms of worship, places of worship, and objects necessary for the performance of rites;
2   to journey to sacred places;
3   to observe dietary practices prescribed by the religion or belief;
4   to acquire or produce materials and objects necessary for the prescribed practices, including dietary practices; when the government controls the means of production and distribution, it shall make those materials or objects available to the members of the religion or belief concerned;
5   to have marriage rites performed in accordance with his religion or belief and not to be compelled to undergo a religious marriage ceremony not in accordance with his convictions; and the right to seek marital dissolution and obtain it solely in accordance with the

applicable law, without any discrimination;

6 to have the prescriptions of the religion or belief of a deceased person followed in all matters affecting burial, cremation, or other methods of disposal of the dead, particularly concerning places, symbols, and rites, with equal protection against desecration and interference by outsiders;

7 to have due account taken of the prescriptions of each religion or belief relating to holidays and days of rest;

8 to teach or disseminate his religion or belief, in public or in private; and to be free from being compelled to take religious or atheistic instruction, contrary to his convictions or, in the case of children, to those of their parents or legal guardians;

9 to train personnel or bring teachers from abroad, and to be free from permanent limitations on training abroad;

10 to exemption from compulsory oath-swearing of a religious nature contrary to his convictions;

11 to exemption for genuine objectors to military service, where it is recognized, to be granted in such a manner that no adverse distinction based upon religion or belief may result;

12 to exemption on similar grounds from participation in certain public ceremonies; and

13 to exemption for priests or ministers of religion from having to divulge information received in confidence in the performance of their religious duties.

Part III addresses restrictions. The principles proclaimed in Part I and principles 10 and 13 of Part II shall not be subject to any restrictions. Other freedoms and rights shall be subject only to limitations prescribed by law solely for the purpose of securing the rights and freedoms of others or required by morality, health, public order, and the general welfare in a democratic society. These should be consistent with the principles of the United Nations.

According to Part IV, public authorities shall refrain from making distinctions with respect to the right to freedom of thought, conscience, and religion, and prevent individuals or groups from doing so. When there is a conflict between the demands of two or more religions or beliefs, public authorities should try to find solutions reconciling those demands in a manner ensuring the greatest measure of freedom to the whole society. No adverse distinctions should be made in the granting of subsidies or tax exemptions. But the state may impose general taxes to cover the cost of arrangements compensating the taking of property or of the preservation of religious monuments of historic or artistic value.

As pointed out, the rules prepared by Krishnaswami and the Principles drafted by the subcommission do not differ in substance and, in some cases, are identical. Rule 16, on the duties of public authorities, is more detailed than Part IV of the Principles, but generally is the same.

Many of the Krishnaswami principles have been incorporated into the 1981 UN Declaration and in the 1965 Draft Convention still pending before the United Nations. Without a doubt the Krishnaswami study was an important stage in the United Nations work on religious rights and was the first specific step to correct the neglect of religion by the international community. The study will be mentioned frequently in the following pages.

The 1966 Covenants on Human Rights

The International Covenant on Economic, Social, and Cultural Rights (ICESCR) and the International Covenant on Civil and Political Rights (ICCPR) were adopted by the UN General Assembly on December 16, 1966, by resolution 2200 A (XXI). They became effective on January 3, 1976, and March 23, 1976, respectively.[10] Despite the amount of time that passed between the adoption of the Universal Declaration and the covenants, the 1966 instruments reflect the thinking that inspired the declaration. The legal thought that predominated in the development of group rights in the 1965 Convention on Racial Discrimination, on the other hand, did not influence the covenants, probably, because of the modalities of the drafting process.

The most relevant provisions in the ICCPR are Articles 18, 20, and 27. Article 18 has four paragraphs. The first paragraph generally follows, with some minor changes, the wording of Article 18 of the Universal Declaration. The covenant does not refer to the right to change one's religion or belief. Instead it uses milder language, which reflects a compromise. Specifically, it proclaims that the right of everyone to freedom of thought, conscience, and belief shall include freedom to have or to adopt a religion or belief of his choice. There is no doubt, however, that the final text recognizes the right to change one's religion or beliefs or to abandon a religion and adopt a new one. This liberal interpretation is supported by the discussion made during the preparation of the covenant.[11]

Article 18(2) of the ICCPR states that no one shall be subject to coercion that would impair his freedom to follow or to adopt a religion or belief of his choice. The term *coercion* is not defined, but it seems reasonable to infer that it applies to the use of force or threats as well as more subtle forms of illegitimate influence, such as moral pressure or material enticement. Comparatively, the 1981 Declaration contained more detail about the notion of coercion.

Article 18(3) addresses limitations and should be read in conjunction with Article 4 of the covenant, which includes other articles that disallow derogation even in times of public emergency.[12] In addition, Article 18(3) should be compared with Article 29(2) and (3) of the Universal Declaration. Article 18(3) only permits limitations on the freedom to manifest one's religion or belief as are prescribed by law and are necessary to protect public safety, order, health, or morals or the fundamental rights and freedom of others. National security is not listed. Because religion is such a sensitive topic, the text must be interpreted in a restrictive way.

Only manifestations of religion, or religious practices, can be restricted. The freedoms of thought and conscience – and religious ideas not translated into practices – are beyond any restriction. There are virtually no problems regarding the religious practices of the major, well-established religions. Nevertheless, there have been some difficulties with *shehitah,* the slaughtering of animals according to Jewish tradition (and similar practices of the Santerian religion).[13] Also, issues involving the wearing of turbans, skullcaps, or veils or the growth of facial hair have required adjudication. Inevitably, certain religious rites, customs, and rules of behavior clash with public norms, health, or morals, and judicial intervention again becomes necessary. Morality is indisputably the outcome of cultural and historical factors that vary from society to society, and the determination of an international minimum standard may not be equally acceptable to all religions, civilizations, and countries.[14]

Article 18(4) addresses the liberty of parents and legal guardians to ensure that the religious and moral education of their children is in conformity with their own convictions. This is again a highly sensitive area. The United Nations has recognized that the interaction between religion and education is of great importance, but there has still been difficulty in reaching consensus among several international instruments, including the UNESCO Convention against Discrimination in Education, the 1981 Declaration, and the Convention on the Rights of the Child.[15] This area involves issues of both international and constitutional law, and adjudication at the national and international levels frequently has been necessary. For example, the Human Rights Committee in 1978 had to address a complaint submitted by the secretary of the Union of Free Thinkers in Finland against his country. The issue involved teaching history of religion in public schools.[16] The committee took the view that such instruction, if given in a "neutral and objective way" and respecting the convictions of parents and guardians who do not believe in any religion, does not violate Article 18 of the covenant.

Furthermore, Article 20(2) of the ICCPR provides: "Any advocacy of national, racial or religious hatred that constitutes incitement to discrimination, hostility or violence shall be prohibited by law." Article 20 does not require intent. Its wording was criticized, and several states entered reservations about it. The late Professor Partsch, discussing the changes introduced in the different drafts since 1953, stated that the final text abandoned a previous "balanced compromise" reached in the Commission on Human Rights.[17] The Human Rights Committee, on its part, in its General Comment on Article 20, made it clear that states are obliged to adopt the necessary legislative measures prohibiting the actions referred to therein. The prohibitions incorporated into Article 20 are fully compatible with the right of freedom of expression contained in Article 19, the exercise of which carries with it special duties and responsibilities.[18]

Article 20(2), and similar provisions incorporated in regional treaties and other recent instruments, should be compared with Article 4 of the Convention on Racial Discrimination.[19] This provision imposes clear-cut obligations on states to enact anti-incitement legislation, and many states have complied.[20]

A clash between rights may be involved, as some states fear that provisions prohibiting advocacy of racial or religious hatred may jeopardize other rights concerning freedom of speech and association.[21] This fear has manifested itself recently with the issue of hate crimes. The United

States Supreme Court for example, upheld the constitutionality of state legislation on enhancement of punishment for offenses motivated by racial or religious hatred.[22]

General Comment of the Human Rights Committees

The committee in charge of implementing the Covenant on Civil and Political Rights has also addressed issues related to religious rights. In 1993 the committee summarized its position by issuing a General Comment on Article 18, No. 22 (48).[23]

The committee felt the need to draw to the attention of state parties the fact that the freedoms of thought and conscience are protected equally with the freedom of religion and belief. Article 18 protects theistic, nontheistic, and atheistic beliefs, as well as the right not to profess any religion or belief. The committee stressed that the terms *beliefs* and *religion* are to be broadly construed, rejecting any tendency to discriminate against any religions or beliefs for any reasons, including the fact that they are newly established or represent religious minorities that may be the subject of hostility by a predominant religious community.[24] The committee intended to avoid situations in which well established religious groups enjoyed a broader legal recognition than newly formed groups. The committee also attempted to address the right to propagate religious ideas that do not enjoy support of the majority, provided that the propagation of these ideas does not exceed the limits imposed by law. Still, it is necessary to ask how broadly the term *belief* may be construed.

The freedoms of thought and conscience, and the freedom to have or adopt a religion or belief of one's choice, are protected unconditionally. No one can be compelled to reveal his or her thoughts or be made to adhere to a religion or belief. In this respect the rights proclaimed in Article 18 should be compared to the right to hold opinions without interference as recognized by Article 19(1) of the covenant. This is not the case with the freedom to manifest religion or belief, whether this freedom is expressed individually or in community with others. This freedom, as mentioned in this provision, encompasses a broad range of acts, including ritual and ceremonial acts and practices integral to such acts, such as the building of places of worship, the use of ritual formulas and objects, the display of symbols, and the observance of holy days and days of rest. It also encompasses dietary regulations, clothing requirements,[25] the use of a particular language, and rituals associated with certain stages in life. This freedom also includes the right to choose religious leaders and teachers, establish seminaries or religious schools, and prepare and distribute religious texts and publications. The committee considered it necessary to list the components of the right to manifest religion or belief following the 1981 Declaration and the Krishnaswami study. The detailed listing was not meant to be exhaustive and should be read in conjunction with the restrictions addressed in Article 18(3).

Paragraph 5 of the General Comment reiterates the notion that the covenant bars any coercion that would impair the right to replace one's current religion with another religion or atheistic views. This right to conversion has burdened all stages of the drafting of international instruments dealing with religion. In defining *coercion* the committe included (1) the use or threat of physical force or penal sanctions, and (2) restrictions on access to education, medical care, employment, or other rights guaranteed by the covenant. The same protection is enjoyed by holders of nonreligious beliefs.

The Human Rights Committee also clarified the reach of Article 18(4) with regard to education. Public school instruction related to the teaching of the general history of religions and ethics is permitted if it is given in a neutral and objective way. Public education that includes instruction in a particular religion or belief, on the other hand, is inconsistent with the covenant – unless a provision is made for nondiscriminatory exemptions or alternatives to those who want them. The guarantee of the freedom to teach a religion or belief includes the liberty of parents or guardians to ensure that their children receive a religious and moral education in conformity with their own convictions.

The 1993 General Comment refers to a former General Comment No. 11(19), which determines that state parties are obligated under Article 20 of the ICCPR to enact laws to prohibit advocacy of national, racial, or religious hatred that constitutes incitement to discrimination, hostility, or violence. The committee emphasized that the prohibition of incitement to religious hatred is fully compatible with other basic freedoms.

The committee also stressed that Article 18(3) should be interpreted strictly: restrictions not specified in the paragraph are disallowed, even if they are utilized to protect other rights. Additionally, limitations may be applied only for their specific purposes and must be directly related and proportionate to the specific need on which they are predicated. They should not be used for discriminatory purposes or be applied in a discriminatory manner. The freedom from coercion and the liberty of parents and guardians to ensure religious and moral education of their children cannot be restricted. Permissible limitations must be established by law and should be interpreted with a view to protect the rights guaranteed under the covenant.[26] Legitimate constraints, such as imprisonment, should not affect religious rights, as far as it is reasonably possible.

In the same paragraph, the committee dealt with the delicate notion of morals, a concept that derives from many social, philosophical, and religious traditions. When the freedom to manifest a religion or belief has the purpose of protecting morals, it must be based on principles not derived exclusively from a single tradition.

The fact that a religion is recognized as

an official state religion, or is the religion of the majority of the population, should not result in any impairment of rights for nonbelievers or adherents of other religions, according to the covenant. Privileges for the members of the predominant religion should be regarded as discriminatory. The committee expects state members to report on measures taken to protect the rights of religious minorities under the covenant and its Article 27. States are also required to provide information regarding practices that are punishable as blasphemy. Blasphemy is not mentioned in existing international human rights instruments but has caused controversy in domestic legislation.[27]

Paragraph 11 of the General Comment addresses conscientious objection, a right that is not explicitly mentioned in the covenant. The committee believes that such a right can be derived from Article 18, inasmuch as the use of lethal force may seriously conflict with the freedom of conscience and the right to manifest one's religion or belief. There shall be no discrimination against conscientious objectors on the ground that they have failed to perform military service. The question of conscientious objection in some cases falls outside the scope of religious rights. Pacifism may be considered a belief, but it is generally of a nonreligious nature. *Conscientious* and *religious* may or may not necessarily mean the same thing, as United States and European case law makes clear.[28]

I have dealt in length with the committee's General Comment for three reasons: (1) the comment's intrinsic importance; (2) the authority and influence of the members of the committee who wrote the comment; and (3) the likelihood that the comment will influence the incorporation of religious rights in other modern instruments.[29] In addition, the General Comment will likely play a part in determining the scope of domestic legislation and judicial interpretation. It already has played a part in influencing the Krishnaswami study and the 1981 Declaration.

The International Covenant on Civil and Political Rights is the only global human rights treaty dealing with religion that contains measures of implementation. As of June 1, 1999, 144 states had ratified or acceded to the covenant, and 95 states had become parties to the Optional Protocol on individual communications. The periodic reports submitted by state parties (plus complaints or commnications filed by individuals) permitted the Human Rights Committee (which is in charge of implementation) to cover a broad range of human rights issues related to religion. The 1993 General Comment on Article 18 summarized the principal views of the committee in this regard.

The yearly Reports of the Committee – issues as General Assembly Official Records (GAOR), Supplement No. 40 – contain salient information on religious rights. When examining the periodic state reports, members of the committee were able to ask questions and require additional information regarding the legislation concerning such rights from representatives of the states. For example, when the second periodic report of Morocco was discussed, members asked questions regarding procedures on the recognition of religious sects, the status of the Bahá'í faith, marriages between members of different religious groups, and the meaning of terms such as *religion of the state*, *revealed religions*, and *heretical sects*.[30] During the consideration of the second periodic report of Austria, members asked questions regarding the issues of conscientious objectors, status of Jehovah's Witnesses, and criminal-law rules concerning blasphemy.[31] The members also scrutinized Colombia's third periodic report, which provided information on the modifications of the concordat with the Holy See in order to adjust it to the new constitution.[32] The members also discussed blasphemy in the United Kingdom;[33] apostasy and discrimination against religious minorities in Sudan;[34] differences in the treatment of churches in Argentina, Lithuania, and

Israel;[35] and restrictions on religious rights in the former USSR.[36] Almost every country that submitted periodic reports was subjected to some scrutiny. When the initial report of Zimbabwe was considered in 1988, the members had to consider the clash between traditional practices and customary law, on one hand, and provisions of the covenant on the other.[37] The committee recommended that practices which were incompatible with the covenant should be prohibited by legislation. A similar discussion took place with regard to Tanzania.[38]

As for individual complaints or communications, the Human Rights Committee addressed relatively few cases involving religious rights, as compared with other rights. Out of 823 communications involving fifty-six states (submitted until 1998), only a few referred to alleged violations of religious human rights. Most of those related to conscientious objection, education, and equality among churches.[39]

The Covenant on Economic, Social, and Cultural Rights refers to religious rights, albeit in a more limited way.[40] Article 13(1) addresses the need to ensure "understanding, tolerance and friendship among all . . . religious groups." Paragraph 3 of the same article refers to the liberty of parents to ensure the religious and moral education of their children in conformity with their own convictions. Article 2(2) forbids discrimination of any kind, including religious discrimination.

The implementation system of the ICESCR has not been effective. Shortly after the creation of the ICESCR in 1976, a Committee on Economic, Social, and Cultural Rights (composed of independent experts) was established and has been meeting periodically to examine the reports submitted by state parties.[41] This committee so far has contributed little to the dialogue on religious rights and the abuse thereof.

The United Nations Declaration on Intolerance and Discrimination based on Religion or Belief

The Declaration on the Elimination of All Forms of Intolerance and Discrimination Based on Religion or Belief was proclaimed by the General Assembly of the United Nations by resolution 36/55 of November 25, 1981. It is presently the most important international instrument regarding religious rights and the prohibition of intolerance or discrimination based on religion or belief.[42] The declaration, as well as the draft convention still pending before the United Nations, originated in response to the outburst of anti-Semitic incidents that occurred in several places in 1959 and 1960. These were called the swastika epidemics, and many feared a revival of Nazism.

The United Nations response to those attacks and the resolutions adopted by the various UN organs culminated in General Assembly resolutions 1780 and 1781(XVII) of December 8, 1962. These resolutions asked for the preparation of twin but separate declarations and conventions addressing the manifestations of religious and racial discrimination and intolerance. The separation between the two subjects was the result of lobbying by Third World countries who wanted to adopt a document on racism, but were largely indifferent to religious discrimination, and of international politics, the Cold War, the Arab–Israeli conflict, and the issue of anti-Semitism in the Soviet Union.[43] Some delegates took the view that there was a theoretical difference between religious sentiments, on the one hand, and prejudice, hatred, or discrimination against people of a different race or color, on the other. In any case the result was a speedy preparation of the instruments on race and slow progress on issues of religious discrimination and intolerance.

In 1965 the General Assembly requested

that the relevant UN bodies try to complete the preparation of both a declaration and convention on religion. Some work was done on both, but in 1972 the General Assembly decided to give priority to the draft declaration. In practice, this meant postponing indefinitely the adoption of a mandatory treaty, despite the fact that a draft, which will be summarized below was in the process of being developed.

Additional work was slow to develop and consisted mainly of the activities of a working group appointed by the Commission on Human Rights. Finally, in 1981, after tenacious efforts, the Commission on Human Rights completed a draft, which was adopted by a vote of 33 to 0, with 5 abstentions. At the Third Committee of the General Assembly the vote in favor was 45 to 0, again with 5 abstentions. In both cases the abstentions were from the representatives of the Communist members of those bodies. Finally, the General Assembly adopted the draft, without a vote, after two decades of procrastination. The decision was preceded by intensive lobbying and pressure from nongovernmental organizations interested in religious human rights and was supported by several governments. Until the very last moment amendments were submitted, and complicated negotiations took place. This showed the inherent complexity and sensitivity of the issue.

One of the major problems surrounding the drafting of the declaration was the meaning of the term *religion*. Communist spokespersons argued that the use of the word *religion* did not explicitly extend the principle of tolerance to atheistic beliefs. They claimed that it was necessary to ensure full equality of treatment between believers and nonbelievers and that the proposed text was one-sided. On the other hand, Western delegates, in particular the United States representative, took the view that the declaration was intended to protect religious human rights, while the rights of persons without a religion, such as materialists, atheists, or agnostics,

could find adequate protection in the text. The face-saving solution, which was rather simplistic, was to insert in the Preamble and in Article 1(1) the word *whatever* before the word *belief,* yielding "whatever belief."

Another difficult issue was one which had already created difficulties during the preparation of the Universal Declaration and the covenants. Once more, the main opposition came from the Muslim delegations. The Iranian spokesperson rejected the related provision contained in Article 18(2) of the Covenant on Civil and Political Rights. Indonesia insisted on establishing a clear distinction between conversion resulting from persuasion and that which was the consequence of coercion. The matter was settled by way of a double compromise. Explicit references to the right to change one's religion were deleted from the text, both in the Preamble and in Article 1, thus representing a departure from the wording used in the Universal Declaration and the covenant. The result was a weakened text, but this was necessary in order to make the change acceptable to the West and avoid jeopardizing the progress achieved in two decades of protracted and difficult negotiations. As part of the accommodation, a new Article 8 was added. It states that nothing in the declaration shall be construed as restricting or derogating from any right defined in the Universal Declaration of Human Rights and the International Covenants on Human Rights. States that did not ratify the covenants may, after this compromise, claim that the right to change one's religion, although included among the clauses of the Universal Declaration, cannot be afforded the status of customary international law. Nevertheless, there was a great desire to see the draft adopted, and compromise was attainable, especially if it was clear that the right to conversion, although not mentioned explicitly, was not derogated or restricted in the new declaration.

Provision of the Declaration

The difficulties in the drafting of the declaration could already be seen in the discussion about its title. Originally, it was intended to be a Declaration on the Elimination of All Forms of Religious Intolerance, but in 1973 a change was made following an amendment proposed by Morocco in the Third Committee. The purpose of this change was to adjust the title of the draft declaration to that of the draft convention and make it consistent with the wording of the Universal Declaration. The two added words – *discrimination* and *belief* – became significant.

Discrimination, the term used in all the anti-discrimination treaties and declarations, has a clear legal meaning. This is not the case with *intolerance,* which is vague and lacks exact legal meaning. *Intolerance* has been used to describe emotional, psychological, philosophical, and religious attitudes that may prompt acts of discrimination or other violations of religious freedoms, as well as manifestations of hate and persecutions against persons or groups of a different religion or belief.[44] Nevertheless, the wording of definitional Article 2(2) of the declaration indicates that the terms *discrimination* and *intolerance* are actually employed as equivalent. This is not the only case of inadequate drafting in the declaration, but it can be explained, if not justified, by the long preparation process, the many amendments, and the search for compromise.

The addition of the word *belief* was intended to satisfy those who wanted to protect the rights of nonbelievers, such as rationalists, freethinkers, atheists, agnostics, and supporters of other nontraditional philosophies. There were also proposals to include explicit references to the right to conduct antireligious propaganda, but this issue was not pursued.

In addition to the change of title many modifications were introduced in the drafts of the Preamble. Many of these modifications were of a semantic nature, but some were meant to address controversial matters of principle and substance. The use of the terms *religion* and *belief* once again dominated the discussions. In response to those who tried to protect nonbelievers, some argued that the original purpose of the document was both to ensure equality among the different religions and to protect religious rights. Those who did not believe in any transcendental or normative religion, it was argued, were already protected by the general freedoms prevailing in a democratic society. There was consensus that coercion against nonbelievers must always be prohibited.

The final text did not include provisions on incitement. Such provisions existed in the preliminary drafts prepared by the Subcommission on the Prevention of Discrimination and Protection of Minorities and the Commission on Human Rights, but never made the final cut. Nevertheless, the pending draft convention contains a clause related to incitement.

The protected rights

Articles 1 and 6 of the declaration contain a catalog of rights that provide a universally agreed-upon minimum standard in the area of religious human rights. Article 1 generally follows the model of Article 18 of the Universal Declaration and the Covenant on Civil and Political Rights – except for the change of religion clause (as amended in the Third Committee) and the saving provision of Article 8 of the declaration: Consequently, authoritative interpretations of the covenant are applicable to the declaration.[45] The declaration uses the term *everyone* in Article 1, meant to protect nationals and aliens, as well as permanent and nonpermanent residents.[46] Paragraph 1 proclaims three fundamental freedoms: the freedoms of thought, conscience, and religion, including whatever belief one chooses. The external manifestations of religion, worship, observance, practice, and teaching – are guaranteed in terms identical to those of the covenant and should be interpreted in conjunction with the rights listed in Article 6 of the declaration.

Article 1(2) prohibits coercion that impairs freedom of religion. But Article 1(3) allows for limitations on the freedom to manifest one's religion or belief, if such limitations are prescribed by law and necessary to protect public safety, order, health or morals, or the fundamental rights of others, as understood in free societies. Serious difficulties may develop when religious rights clash with the notion of morals as interpreted by some countries, and the margin of discretion allowed may differ from country to country. General principles incorporated into human rights law regarding these limitations are also applicable to the declaration.[47] It should be kept in mind that Article 18 of the ICCPR, which is referenced by Article 4 of the covenant, represents one of the rights for which no derogation in time of public emergency is permitted.

Article 6 provides a a concrete list of freedoms of thought, religion, and belief. This list provides a detailed enunciation of the rights that fall within an accepted minimum standard. Some rights are missing, but, on the whole, the list is comprehensive. The list contains the following freedoms:

(a) the freedom to worship or assemble in connection with a religion or belief, and to establish and maintain places for these purposes;

(b) the freedom to establish and maintain appropriate charitable or humanitarian institutions;

(c) the freedom to make, acquire, and use to an adequate extent the necessary articles and materials related to the rites or customs of a religion or belief;

(d) the freedom to publish and disseminate relevant publications in these areas;

(e) the freedom to teach a religion or belief in places suitable for these purposes;

(f) the freedom to solicit and receive voluntary financial and other contributions from individuals and institutions;

(g) the freedom to train, appoint, elect, or designate by succession appropriate leaders called for by the requirements and standards of any religion or belief;

(h) the freedom to observe days of rest and to celebrate holy days and ceremonies in accordance with the precepts of one's religion or belief;

(i) the freedom to establish and maintain communications with individuals and communities in matters of religion and belief at the national and international levels.

All these rights are, of course, subject to the limitations mentioned in Article 1(3). Some of them are tied to the constitutional system of the country and are affected by the nature of the relationship between religion and state in that country.

Article 6 omitted some rights that the Subcommission on the Prevention of Discrimination and Protection of Minorities included in its early drafts. The omitted rights include the right to establish federations, which would complete the right mentioned in Article 6(b); the right to teach and learn the sacred language of each religion (and to bring teachers from abroad), which is not automatically included in Article 6(e); the right to receive state aid when the state controls the means of production and distribution, a right of crucial importance for those religions implementing dietary prescriptions; the right to obtain either inside the country or abroad; the right not to undergo a religious marriage ceremony that is not in conformity with one's convictions; and the right to a burial ceremony in accordance with the religion of the deceased person. The subcommission's draft also included provisions on the legal status of cemeteries, religious oaths, and discrimination by the state when granting subsidies or taxing constituents. Some of the missing rights are listed in the pending draft convention.

Article 6 should be compared with principles 16 and 17 of the Concluding Document of the 1989 Vienna meeting of the Conference on Security and Cooperation in Europe, which includes a few of the omitted provisions.

The original text of the declaration prepared by the subcommission was strongly influenced by Arcot Krishnaswami's principles. The final text was strongly affected by the amendments, compromises, and concessions that resulted from the long drafting process. Political considerations, as always, played a crucial role, and non-governmental organizations were active lobbyists. In particular, the issues of religious education and the preservation of certain rites and customs (such as blood transfusions) provoked lengthy discussions.

It is important to stress that Article 6 of the declaration addresses individual rights that can only be exercised by a group. Compared to previous instruments, it represents important progress, especially as it anticipates the needs of religious communities or congregations. Many previous UN instruments, which focused exclusively on individual rights, failed to address the fact that only groups can establish and maintain places of worship and religious institutions, or appoint religious leaders, or establish federations.

Prohibition of discrimination and intolerance

Articles 2 and 3 of the declaration address intolerance and discrimination based on religion and belief. These articles, influenced by the Declaration and Convention on Racial Discrimination, are affected by similar difficulties, particularly in the way in which the terms *discrimination* and *intolerance* are employed. It has already been pointed out that *discrimination* has a precise legal meaning under international and human rights law while *intolerance* does not. This leads to vague and inconsistent drafting. For example, Article 2(1) refers to *discrimination* only. Article 2(2) mentions *intolerance and discrimination.* The term *intolerance* is not used at all in Article 3 or Article 4(1), which address measures to be taken by states. Article 4(2) distinguishes between the need to prohibit discrimination and to combat intolerance, a distinction that tries to differentiate between both forms of behavior. As for the declaration, the Convention on Racial Discrimination again serves as the model for the definition of the two words. Under Article 2(2), *intolerance and discrimination based on religion or belief* means any distinction, exclusion, restriction, or preference based on religion or belief and having as its purpose or as human rights and fundamental freedoms on an equal basis. Religious discrimination and intolerance are not limited to public life, as was the case in the Convention on Racial Discrimination.

Overall, the text is deficient, particularly since Article 2(1) prohibits discrimination by the state and by institutions, groups of persons, or persons. As Krishnaswami's study reminds us, however, not every preference based on religion or belief can be considered discriminatory and thus prohibited. For example, a concordat between a state with a predominantly Catholic population and the Holy See may be appropriate. Additionally, many states declare as public holidays the days sacred to the majority of the population; this would not be discriminatory if observance of the holy days of the minorities is duly protected, as far as possible.[48] More difficult is the case of states that permit only members of a given religion to accede to certain public positions, such as president of the state. Some states, in fact, have an established church or even a state religion. When do such situations become discriminatory?[49] As a general rule, no impairment should attach to any person or group in the enjoyment of fundamental freedoms. Otherwise, preferences may constitute discrimination. The given facts and social reality – as well as common sense – are determinative factors.

The prohibition of discrimination by institutions or persons also creates problems. For example, religious institutions should be granted some leeway when hiring personnel, mandating dressing habits, or organizing the observance of particular customs. The granting of privileges to members of one religion in given circumstances does not necessarily curtail the basic human rights of others and would therefore not contradict the declaration.

Another concern is the possibility of a clash between the recognition of religious rights and societal norms. For example, the clash between religious rights and the prohibition of discrimination based on gender may be irresolvable – and, in fact, has resulted in frequent adjudication. In order to guarantee the observance of the rights proclaimed in the declaration, state action is often necessary. According to Article 4 of the declaration, all states shall take effective measures to prevent and eliminate discrimination on grounds of religion or belief in all fields of civil, economic, political, social, and cultural life, enacting or rescinding where necessary legislation to that effect. States should also take all appropriate steps to combat intolerance on the grounds of religion or belief.

Problems arising from the imprecise use of the terms *discrimination* and *intolerance* have already been mentioned. Although the meaning of *to combat* is not explained, it suggests an obligation to adopt criminal law measures against organizations that incite others to practice religious intolerance. Special Rapporteur Elizabeth Odio Benito, in fact, has recommended the adoption of penal laws.[50] This may be contrary to the policies of certain countries that are reluctant to limit in any way the freedoms of speech and association.

Article 7 refers to national legislation that would allow everyone to avail himself. or herself of the enunciated rights and freedoms. This article, which has been criticized for its vagueness, has been difficult to apply.

Article 5, which addresses the rights of the child, is among the most controversial provisions in the declaration. There is a close relationship between religion and education, and the attempt of a religion to influence the child may conflict with the attempt of the parents to raise that child. Article 5 is long, and it fails to clarify important points, such as who would qualify as a child. Article 5 does recognize the right of parents (or legal guardians) to organize their families in accordance to their religion or belief. Furthermore, Article 5 promotes the notion that children should have access to religious education in accordance to the wishes of their parents or legal guardians. The "best interest of the child" – an idea that appears in the Declaration on the Rights of the Child and the Convention on the Rights of the Child but is not mentioned in the covenants[51] – should be the guiding principle.

The proviso "best interest of the child" is intended to limit the freedom of action of parents and legal guardians. Nevertheless, the declaration does not deal with the many questions likely to be raised when the wishes of the parents conflict with the best interest of the child. Moreover, in totalitarian or ideological states, the best interest of the child may be interpreted differently by the educational authorities and the parents of the child. Limitations on parental authority have frequently required adjudication at the domestic and international levels.

In general, the child should be protected against religious discrimination. The practices of a religion or belief in which a child is raised should not be injurious to the child's physical or mental health (Article 5(5)). The limitations mentioned in Article 1(3) of the declaration, namely, public safety, order, health, or morals or the fundamental rights and freedoms of others, should be taken into account.

Evaluation of the Declaration

On the whole the 1981 Declaration was an important breakthrough in the struggle to extend international protection to religion. Of course, a declaration is not a treaty and is therefore not binding. Nevertheless, as a UN solemn statement it carries weight and gives expression to prevailing international trends. It does have certain legal effect, and it implies an expectation of obedience by members of the international community to the extent that it may be seen as stating rules of customary international law.[52]

The catalog of rights contained in the declaration is helpful although not complete. The explicit references not only to individual rights or rights to be exercised collectively but also to the rights of the group (or the religious community or congregation) is of monumental importance, especially when compared to other limited international texts. Compromise has been necessary, but Article 8 has made possible the universal acceptance of the declaration. The wording of several articles is unsatisfactory, reflecting the protracted negotiations. Nevertheless, the declaration unquestionably represents progress in a sensitive area of human rights that, in comparison with other rights, had been largely neglected.

The necessity or possibility of a convention

Some may ask whether the declaration makes unnecessary the preparation of a binding convention on religious human rights. The answer may be inconclusive, particularly if the end result is a treaty that does not fully address substantive rights respecting religion. Nevertheless, concerned nongovernmental organizations have advocated the adoption of a convention. A similar stand was taken by the special rapporteurs, the Subcommission on the Prevention of the Discrimination and Protection of Minorities, and a 1984 Seminar on the Encouragement of Understanding, Tolerance, and Respect in Matters Relating to Freedom of Religion or Belief.[53] The General Assembly of the United Nations, which deals every year with the

elimination of all forms of religious intolerance, has not directly addressed the issue of whether there should be a convention in its last resolutions before this writing, the General Assembly nevertheless urged states to take measures to combat hatred, intolerance, and acts of violence, including those motivated by religious extremism, and to guarantee freedom of thought, conscience, religion, and belief. The General Assembly also welcomed steps to implement the declaration and encouraged the Commission on Human Rights to do the same. Still, there was no reference at all to the question of a convention.[54] The 1993 Vienna Conference on Human Rights also remained silent on this issue.[55]

Theo van Boven, in a working paper prepared at the request of the Subcommission on Prevention of Discrimination and Protection of Minorities, has taken a cautious view on the question of a convention. He recommended that, prior to the drafting of such an instrument, solid preparatory work should be done.[56] Others, such as Yoram Dinstein, have stressed the singular contribution that a convention could make to the promotion of freedom of religion. Dinstein is, however, aware of the fact that the prospects for a convention are unlikely, and that there is very little enthusiasm for a new implementation mechanism.[57]

The draft convention presently pending, as elaborated by the Commission on Human Rights,[58] contains a preamble and twelve articles adopted by the commission. The draft reflects the prevailing mood when it was discussed simultaneously with the draft declaration. The major differences between the substantive articles of the declaration and those of the draft convention are the result of the amendments added in the latter stages of the preparation of the declaration. Also, the draft convention lists some rights not mentioned in the 1981 Declaration. For example, draft Article IX follows the pattern of Article 4 of the Convention on Racial Discrimination and is likely to result in controversy, if work on the draft convention should continue. The measures of implementation are similar to those incorporated into other anti-discrimination instruments, which are based mainly on a reporting system that encompasses individual petitions.

Implementation of the Declaration

Since continued work on a convention now seems doubtful, it may be more useful to examine the various ways that the 1981 Declaration has been monitored. (Non-governmental organizations may collaborate and do their own monitoring.) Because the Human Rights Committee has a duty to follow the relevant articles of the covenant, it has been suggested that working groups be established to make sure that it does so, although no formal proposals have been advanced in this regard. In any case, the principles listed in the declaration should provide governments with guidance to adjust their own legislation to the international minimum standard.

Both the Commission on Human Rights and the Subcommission on Prevention of Discrimination and Protection of Minorities appointed special rapporteurs to conduct studies and submit reports related to the implementation of the declaration. The special rapporteur of the commission, Angelo Vidal d'Almeida Ribeiro, was appointed in 1986 and submitted seven reports.[59] A new special rapporteur, Abdelfattah Arnor, was appointed in 1993. The special rapporteur of the subcommission, Elizabeth Odio Benito, was appointed in 1983, and her task was to undertake a comprehensive study of the scope of the problems related to intolerance on grounds of religion or belief. Odio Benito, using the declaration as a term of reference, was able to update the findings of the Krishnaswami study.[60]

The reports submitted by the special rapporteurs provide a global perspective on the state of religious rights. The special rapporteurs circulated questionnaires among many states and based their reports on the responses. In addition, they analyzed the present state of affairs in the various countries, commented on issues reflected in the individual responses, and formulated recommendations based on their conclusions.

In her study Odio Benito concluded that the phrase *intolerance and discrimination based on religion or belief* encompassed not only discrimination, but also included acts intended to stir up hatred against or persecution of persons or groups. She stressed the uniformity of the Universal Declaration, the Covenant on Civil and Political Rights, and the 1981 Declaration regarding the right to change one's religion or to remain without any at all. According to Odio Benito, full realization of all other human rights is closely linked to freedoms of thought, conscience, religion, and belief. Violations of religious rights frequently involve violation of many other basic rights, including the right to life. A listing of such violations, region by region, is included in the study, which also examined various church-state relationships. The author of the study did not draw a firm conclusion as to whether, and to what extent, any of the existing constitutional arrangements give rise, *per se* or in practice, to religious intolerance. She did, however, point out when, on the whole, the existing situation falls below the standards in the 1981 Declaration.

Furthermore, Odio Benito recommended that the international community continue its efforts to adopt a convention. This is consistent with the conclusions reached by the 1984 United Nations Seminar on the Encouragement of Understanding, Tolerance, and Respect in Matters Relating to Freedom of Religion or Belief. Odio Benito also suggested that several studies should be made concerning the following subjects: discrimination against women within churches and within religions; discrimination against centuries-old religions that do not belong to the group of major religions; and the emergence of new religions and practices of sects. Until the adoption of a convention containing implementation measures, these kinds of studies are critical in helping the appropriate bodies determine what human rights issues are most salient. In order to make these kinds of determinations, human rights bodies may resort to arrangements that the ECOSOC (Economic and Social Council) can make under Article 64 of the UN Charter.

Angelo Vidal d'Almeida Ribeiro, the former special rapporteur of the Commission on Human Rights, also filed reports addressing allegations against certain governments whose practices may have departed from the provisions of the declaration. He transmitted these allegations to the respective governments in seven detailed and documented reports. These reports also contained comments formulated by the affected governments. The special rapporteur aimed to identify factors that might impede the implementation of the declaration and the collection of specific information. He circulated questionnaires to the governments and established communication with them based on their replies. He also directly approached those governments against which allegations had been made. The reports contained information from nongovernmental sources, including religious groups and organizations.

The reported cases covered a wide range of situations involving persons of various religions under different legal and political systems. These cases came from most regions of the world. The special rapporteur highlighted the fact that the majority of allegations involved the right of religious choice; the right to change one's religion; the right to worship in public and in private; and the right not to be subjected to discrimination on any grounds. Violations of the declaration's provisions have also been a reflection and cause of violations concerning other fundamental freedoms and rights. Violence has frequently accompanied these violations. Sometimes this

violence has erupted on a massive scale, as has been the case in the former Yugoslavia.

Special Rapporteur d'Almeida Ribeiro noted some positive developments and stressed the importance of interfaith dialogue. In particular, he favored the preparation of a binding instrument, especially in the light of the recommendations submitted by Theo van Boven to the Subcommission on Prevention of Discrimination and Protection of Minorities.

Following the resignation of Angelo Vidal d'Almeida Ribeiro, the chairman of the Commission on Human Rights appointed Abdelfattah Amor as special rapporteur. Professor Amor has submitted reports since 1994.[61] In particular, he sent summaries of allegations made against certain countries (concerning religious rights) to those countries against which those allegations were made. Such allegations concerned various forms of harassment, arrest, torture, or ill treatment of victims of religious intolerance. Some of the reports referred to the desecration or destruction of religious sanctuaries or cemeteries. The special rapporteur, in order to support his views and observations, has also made visits *in situ* and has drawn on governmental and nongovernmental sources, taking into account any information received from religious groups. He also sent questionnaires to governments regarding the subject of his mandate and responded to urgent appeals made by Bangladesh, Iran, Iraq, Pakistan, and Saudi Arabia.

While conducting his work, Amor found and addressed numerous examples of religiously oriented persecution and discrimination. These include murders carried out by armed groups of Islamic militants; discrimination against groups such as the Church of Scientology in Germany; imprisonment due to expression of religious beliefs; discrimination against religious minorities, particularly Christians and Shi'ite Muslims in Saudi Arabia; restrictions against Jehovah's Witnesses in

Austria; persecution against writer Taslima Nassrin, and other acts of religious intolerance against the Hindu, Christian, and Buddhist minorities in Bangladesh; restrictions upon Protestant organizations in Belarus; persecution against Christians and Christian missionaries in Bhutan, where Buddhism and Hinduism are the only recognized religions; prohibition and persecution (including acts of physical violence) of many sects in Bulgaria; violation of the right to conscientious objection in Cyprus; restrictions on religious activities and attacks on the freedom of religion of Jehovah's Witnesses, Seventh-day Adventists, and Baptists in Cuba; violence, including assassinations, by Islamic fundamentalist groups in Egypt; violations of religious freedom in Ethiopia; restrictive legislation in the Russian Federation; imprisonment of conscientious objectors and harassment of religious groups in Greece; religiously oriented killings and violence in India; persecutions against Bahá'ís, Jews, and Christians in Iran; persecutions against Shi'ite Muslims in Iraq; incidents in the territories occupied by Israel, Kenya, Lebanon, and Liberia; anti-conversion laws in Malaysia and Morocco; anti-Protestant incidents in Mexico; discrimination against Christians in Mongolia; persecution against Christian and Muslim religious communities in Myanmar; persecution of religious minorities in Pakistan; killing of Christians in the Philippines; intolerance in Romania; massacres of clergymen in Rwanda; severe violations and violence in Sudan and Sri Lanka; violation of the rights of religious minorities in Turkey, Vietnam, Yemen, and Zimbabwe.[62]

In order to achieve as complete a picture as possible, Special Rapporteur Amor visited numerous countries, including China, Pakistan, Iran, India, Greece, Sudan, Australia, and Germany. Based on these visits, he submitted reports with conclusions and recommendations.[63]

As part of his work, Special Rapporteur Amor requested clarifications from the respective governments and suggested approaches that would address discrimination within the framework of the particular government. Amor took the view that the achievement of religious tolerance and nondiscrimination must go together with the achievement of human rights as a whole. He believed his goal of curbing religious extremism and terrorism could be achieved through education. He acknowledged that in certain cases it is difficult to establish a clear distinction between religious and ethnic conflicts, and between such conflicts and political persecution. Still, he devoted special attention to conversion and proselytism, blasphemy, attacks on places of worship and religious sites, and problems related to sects and conscientious objection. He also addressed in his conclusions and recommendations the issue of ethnic cleansing in former Yugoslavia and ethnically related events in Algeria. Along with addressing particular problems, Amor also invited the states he investigated to share legal texts related to the freedom of belief; his hope was to build a compendium of national enactments related to that freedom.

In his 1996 report[64] Amor divided the violations of religious rights into six categories. These categories, based on the communications he received, included (1) violations of the principle of nondiscrimination in religion and belief; (2) violations of the principle of tolerance, a category that reflected the concern about religious extremism; (3) violations of the freedom of thought, conscience, and religion or belief, including the freedom to change religion; (4) violations of the freedom to manifest one's religion or belief; (5) violations of the freedom to dispose religious property; and (6) attacks on the right to life, physical integrity, and security of person. He concluded that the elaboration of an international convention on the elimination of religious intolerance and discrimination was a necessary but premature step, given the present circumstances.[65]

In his 1998 report Amor paid special attention to the development of a culture of tolerance and stressed the role of education as an essential and priority means of combating intolerance and discrimination.[66] He surveyed the replies received from seventy-seven states to a questionnaire on problems relating to freedom of religion and belief from the standpoint of the curricula and textbooks of elementary and secondary schools. Among his preliminary findings Amor noted a marked difference between states based on secular principles and those based on a theocracy or official state religion. In particular, he highlighted the problems related to the compulsory nature of religious instruction; the imposing of a particular kind of religious instruction on members of another faith without giving them the right to be excused; the difficulties created when minority religions have no private religious institutions; and the limited teaching of comparative religion. In response, the rapporteur recommended further study of religious extremism, proselytism, freedom of religion and poverty, and sects and new religious movements.

The United Nations Declaration on Minorities

Religious rights include (1) individual rights; (2) collective rights (exercised by several persons jointly as prescribed by Article 27 of the Covenant on Civil and Political Rights); and (3) rights of the religious group or community. The last category contains the rights of what is usually described as a religious minority. It is difficult to analyze this subject because there is no generally accepted definition of religious minority. Many definitions have been proposed, and one enjoying support is that of Professor Francesco Capotorti, UN special rapporteur on minorities. According to Capotorti,

a minority is a group which is numerically inferior to the rest of the population of a state and in a non-dominant position, whose members possess ethnic, religious or linguistic characteristics which differ from those of the rest of the population and who, if only implicitly, maintain a sense of solidarity, directed towards preserving their culture, traditions, religion or language.[67]

There are as many definitions of minority as there are proposals to replace the term.[68] Self-perception and the perception of the surrounding society are of great importance, particularly in the case of religious minorities or groups. In general, states have been less reluctant to recognize the rights of an organized religious group or minority, believing that there will be few consequences of such recognition – except in the case of territorial concentration or political tension. Many states understand that it is virtually impossible to respect freedom of religion or belief without (1) permitting believers to organize their representative institutions; (2) granting them some authority to deal with the individual members of the faith; and (3) allowing them to maintain contact freely with similar organized groups outside the state. Much, of course, depends on the constitutional regime of the state, and there have been instances of special arrangements between states and certain churches or religions.

When analyzing the evolution of the status of religious minorities and other minorities, we need to consider four major stages: (1) an early period of nonsystematic protection of religious groups through the incorporation of special protective clauses in international treaties and through humanitarian intervention of influential powers; (2) the protective system under the League of Nations, based on special treaties, special clauses in general treaties, or unilateral undertakings; (3) the pattern followed by the United Nations as expressed in Article 27 of the Political Covenant (and slightly less so in the 1992 declaration on minorities), implying an almost total shift from group protection to a guarantee of individual rights and freedoms; and (4) modern trends, which acknowledge the necessity of harmonizing individual freedoms, the rights of the state and the needs of organized religious groups.

The early treaties granted protection to certain religious minorities, frequently as a consequence of territorial changes. Usually, the treaties were based on the link between one of the parties and a sector of the population of the other state. It was only after the Vienna Congress in 1815 that the scope of such treaties was expanded.[69] Humanitarian intervention produced positive results in some cases, but, without an articulated scheme, these treaties had obvious limitations.

The League of Nations system for the protection of religious and other minorities was far from perfect. Nevertheless, its failure was not the consequence of intrinsic defects but was due to the political turmoil in Europe after World War I, especially the assault by the Nazi and Fascist regimes against democracy and the rule of law. The League's Covenant did not incorporate any general article about minorities, and attempts to include a comprehensive article on religious persecution did not succeed. States that signed treaties or made declarations about minorities included Poland; Austria; Czechoslovakia; the Kingdom of the Serbs, Croats, and Slovenes; Bulgaria; Romania; Hungary; Greece; Turkey; Albania; Lithuania; Latvia; Estonia; and Iraq. Provisions on minority rights were also incorporated in treaties concerning Danzig, the Aland Islands, Upper Silesia, and Memel.[70]

Under the League of Nations system many rights were guaranteed. These included the free exercise (in public and private) of any creed, religion, or belief; equality of treatment in law and in fact, with a prohibition against discrimination; equal access to public employment and professions; the use of minority languages in religious ceremonies or activities; the right to establish institutions and schools;

and the right to have public funds allocated to religious, educational, and charitable needs. Such guarantees could not be derogated by domestic legislation without the approval of the Council of the League. The Council was entitled to consider violations and take appropriate action. Disputes were to be submitted to the Permanent Court of International Justice, which had compulsory jurisdiction. A mechanism for petitions by individuals or associations acting on behalf of a minority was established, and the Council could make recommendations based on the respective case. For example, under the Bernheim petition in 1933, which was based on the convention between Germany and Poland of 1922 regarding Upper Silesia, the Nazis were prevented for some time from implementing measures against Jews, who were considered a religious, ethnic, and linguistic minority.[71]

The Permanent Court of International Justice dealt on several occasions with issues related to minorities. Its *Advisory Opinion on Minority Schools in Albania*, although referring primarily to the linguistic rights of the Greek minority in Albania, became universally respected as it acknowledged the need for all minorities (especially religious minorities) to have suitable means for the preservation of their traditions and characteristics.[72]

In the United Nations period the prevailing opinion asserted that individual rights and the principle of nondiscrimination were the appropriate means of protecting everyone, including members of minorities. There was an overall reluctance to recognize any type of group rights, mainly for historical and political reasons. In fact, the Charter does not refer to minorities at all. A proposed inclusion of an article on minorities in the Universal Declaration of Human Rights was not accepted. Article 26 does refer to the promotion of understanding, tolerance, and friendship among racial or religious groups, but this reference is vague.

The Subcommission on the Prevention of Discrimination and the Protection of Minorities introduced Article 27 of the Covenant on Civil and Political Rights, a controversial and highly criticized article that nevertheless serves as the basis of the United Nations approach to the issue. Article 27 refers to religious and other minorities, members of which should not be denied the right, in community with other members of their group, to profess and practice their own religion.[73] The criticism of Article 27 exposed the shortcomings of the covenant's approach to minority rights and led to the 1992 United Nations Declaration on the Rights of Persons Belonging to National or Ethnic, Religious, and Linguistic Minorities, which represented some progress in the acceptance of minority rights.[74]

As its title indicates, the declaration embraces national or ethnic, religious, and linguistic minorities. But these terms are hard to define. The term *national minority* frequently includes minorities that represent a part of some other nation, or what some we describe as a parent state.[75] (This same kind of definition may apply to religious groups, too.) But in the declaration the term *national minorities* is equivalent to ethnic, religious, and linguistic minorities. While the preamble of the declaration promotes the principles mentioned in the Declaration on Intolerance and Discrimination Based on Religion or Belief, parts of the declaration require clarification.

Article 1 of the 1992 declaration urges states to take measures to protect the existence and identity of religious minorities. There is an implicit acknowledgment of group rights, or rights that go beyond the scope of individual rights. Article 2 grants to persons belonging to minorities the right to profess and practice their own religion and to participate effectively in religious life. These persons are entitled to establish and maintain their own associations and to establish and maintain free and peaceful contacts with other members of their group, including those who reside in other states. Otherwise, the relationship of the UN declaration on minorities to religious human rights is limited. Nevertheless, the declaration represents progress (with regard to freedom of religion and belief) from the development of the Political Covenant.

Religious Rights in Other Relevant Instruments

Several legal texts adopted separately during the United Nations era contain provisions on religious rights. Humanitarian law – consolidated in the four widely ratified Geneva conventions of 1949 – contains provisions prohibiting any adverse distinctions founded on religion or faith.[76] The Convention on Prisoners of War also addressed religiously oriented issues, such as the exercise of religious duties, attendance of services, the role of chaplains and ministers of religion, and the use of facilities for the performance of their duties. In particular, the Fourth Convention urged respect for the religious convictions and practices of the protected persons. This convention also referred to the work of ministers of religion, the use of books and articles for religious needs, and the need for adequate premises for the religious services.

The 1979 Convention on the Elimination of All Forms of Discrimination against Women contained provisions that clashed with practices of some religious traditions that were incorporated into general legislation.[77] Several states expressed reservations about the clauses that were perceived to conflict with religious traditions. Both the Human Rights Committee under the Political Covenant and the Committee on the Elimination of Discrimination against Women (CEDAW) addressed the issue of equality for women, especially in matters concerning family law. Judicial or quasi-judicial intervention has been required, most notably in Europe. In order to gain a full perspective, this clash between gender-oriented law and law that is grounded on religious traditions should be seen in the wider context of the discussion on the universality of human rights.

Because religious rights and education are closely related, international instruments addressing education are relevant for the analysis of religious rights. The freedom to teach one's religion (and ensure that parents' wishes for the religious education of their children are respected) and the degree to which the state supports religious instruction raise complicated issues that can only be resolved by careful balancing among differing human rights. The UNESCO Convention against Discrimination in Education, adopted in 1960 and in force since 1962, was one measure that tried to prohibit discrimination based on religion.[78] Under this measure separate educational systems for religious purposes were permitted, provided that participation in such systems was optional and conformed to authorized standards (Article 2). Overall, education was meant to promote understanding and tolerance among religious groups. Yet, it was important that religious and moral education was imparted in conformity with the convictions of the children, meaning that nobody should be compelled to receive religious instruction inconsistent with his or her convictions (Article 5).

In order to gain a full understanding of the relationship between education and religion, the provisions of the UNESCO Convention against Discrimination in Education should be read in conjunction with the relevant articles of the 1948 Universal Declaration of Human Rights and the 1966 Covenant on Social, Cultural, and Economic Rights. In addition, the Declaration on the Rights of the Child and the Convention on the Rights of the Child, which contain provisions related to religion and education, should be considered. These provisions also emphasize the need to give primary consideration to the best interest of the child. Despite the attempt to provide a suitable framework for addressing issues

pertaining to education and religion, however, provoked judicial intervention at the municipal, regional, and international levels.[79]

The International Labor Organization (ILO), which in 1958 adapted the Convention (No. 111) concerning Discrimination in Respect of Employment and Occupation (in force since 1960), attempted to prohibit discrimination on the basis of religion.[80] Specifically, the ILO organized bodies that addressed employee complaints that were based on denial of equality because of religion. These complaints often resulted when religious duties conflicted with working conditions, especially in regard to days of rest and holidays. There have also been many instances of judicial intervention.[81]

Another important ILO treaty addressing religious rights has been the 1989 Convention No. 169, concerning Indigenous and Tribal Populations and Peoples. This is a partial revision of the 1957 convention on this subject. The new convention is more group-oriented and recognizes the aspirations of indigenous peoples to maintain and develop their identities and religions, ensuring protection for their religious and spiritual values and practices. The United Nations has also addressed this subject and proclaimed 1993 as the International Year for the World's Indigenous Peoples. General Assembly Resolution 45/164 (1990) made reference to cultural identity and restrictions on religious customs.[82]

International instruments related to the condition of migrant workers have also considered their cultural and religious needs. The 1990 UN Convention on the Protection of the Rights of Migrant Workers and Their Families contained provisions guaranteeing the religious rights of such migrants. Article 12 of the convention was clearly inspired by Article 18 of the Political Covenant.[83]

Conclusions

Based on the foregoing, the following conclusions can be reached.

First, United Nations instruments dealing with religious human rights do not define the term *religion*. This is the result of a general trend to avoid ideological or philosophical definitions that may cause controversy and make it more difficult to reach agreement between states in such a delicate area of human behavior. It is, however, indisputable that, in United Nations law and in modern human rights law, the term *religion,* usually followed by the word *belief,* means theistic convictions, involving a transcendental view of the universe and a normative code of behavior, as well as atheistic, agnostic, rationalistic, and other views in which both elements may be absent.

Second, the United Nations system for the protection of religious human rights does not presently include any specific obligatory treaty regarding religious human rights. Article 18 of the 1966 International Covenant on Civil and Political Rights, and provisions related to religious issues in the covenant and in treaties prepared by the United Nations and other international bodies, significant number of those provisions are seen today as reflecting customary international law, and some, such as the prohibition of discrimination on religious grounds or the outlawing of genocide against religious groups, belong to the restricted category of *jus cogens.* Freedom of religion is one of the fundamental rights that cannot be derogated in states of emergency. The General Comment on Article 18 formulated by the Human Rights Committee constitutes an authoritative source for the interpretation of the covenant clauses.

Third, the discussion on the need and/or convenience of a mandatory treaty on religious rights and freedoms is inconclusive. The main argument in favor of a convention is, of course, the general desire to grant religious rights a protection similar to that extended to other basic rights. The example of the widely ratified Convention on Racial Discrimination, incorporating a relatively effective system of monitoring and implementation, is pointed out as justifying the treaty-oriented approach. Arguments against a treaty, neither new nor exclusive to the sphere of religion, are the risk of having to compromise on a very low common denominator of protection and the possible reluctance on the part of some states to ratify an instrument that may clash with long-established systems of law, mainly in the area of family law, personal status, and conversion.

Given this inconclusive debate over a mandatory instrument, the existence of a monitoring system, in the form of reports or studies by special rapporteurs appointed by UN organs, provides a modest degree of protection of religious rights, naturally not equivalent to conventional obligations assumed by states. There have been proposals, mainly from nongovernmental organizations, aimed at improving that system. These include suggestions to establish national bodies to monitor religious rights, in the spirit of the 1981 Declaration, the submission of periodic reports from member states to ECOSOC, and similar measures not implying a mandatory treaty.

Fourth, the 1981 Declaration on the Elimination of All Forms of Intolerance and Discrimination Based on Religion or Belief was a powerful step forward in the search for a system of protection of religious human rights. The declaration, which incorporated many – though not all – of the principles enunciated in the seminal study by Arcot Krishnaswami, includes a comprehensive and detailed catalog of rights related to freedom of conscience, religion, and belief, and their exercise in practice. The declaration progresses beyond the purely individualistic approach of the covenants and is nearer to some recent instruments that acknowledge the group dimension of religious human rights. Such rights cannot be adequately protected unless the rights of religious organizations, communities, and congregations as such are recognized and ensured beyond the purely individualistic freedoms. This may be of great importance for collectivities and communities of a religious origin in which the religious element may appear combined with ethnic and cultural characteristics.

Fifth, there are some particularly complicated problems that continue to arouse controversy. Examples of such problems include matters of conver-blasphemy, rights of women and children, and conscientious objection (which is not always a religious matter). A major controversy – not exclusively affecting religious rights – relates to the question of striking a balance between the prohibition of incitement against religious groups, as enunciated in Article 20 of the ICCPR, and the freedoms of speech or association. There have been different answers to this question, depending on the constitutional systems of the respective countries. The precedent of the Convention on Racial Discrimination and trends presently prevailing in connection with religious rights seem to indicate a growing understanding of the need to protect substantive social values against abuses of the freedoms of speech and association.

Sixth, in the 1990s tragic events affecting the life and welfare of millions of persons have taken place, involving population sectors defined by religion as well as ethnic identity. The need to ensure the protection of religious, ethnic, and cultural groups, irrespective of the nature of the group, was acknowledged by the judiciary of several countries. The shocking practices of "ethnic cleansing" in the former Yugoslavia and Rwanda have added urgency to the recognition of that need.

The protection of religious human rights during the United Nations era is thus quite limited. Provisions of a positive character do exist and have exercised a considerable influence on domestic legislation. The claim that they are not enough, particularly at times of high international and intra-national tension, seems to be supported by current events. Religious human rights deserve more than to remain a neglected chapter in the universal endeavors to ensure observance of and respect for human rights.

Notes

1 Nehemiah Robinson, *Universal Declaration of Human Rights: Its Origin, Significance, Application, and Interpretation* (1958), 128ff. See also Martin Scheinin, "Article 18," in *The Universal Declaration of Human Rights: A Commentary . . .* Asbjorn Eide et al. (eds.) (1992), 263–74; Karl J. Partsch, "Freedom of Conscience and Expression, and Political Freedoms," in *The International Bill of Rights*, ed. Louis Henkin (1981), 209–45; John P. Humphrey, "The Universal Declaration of Human Rights: Its History, Impact and Judicial Character," in *Human Rights: Thirty Years after the Universal Declaration*, ed. B. G. Ramcharan (1979), 21.

2 Scheinin, "Article 18," 266.

3 Warwick McKean, *Equality and Discrimination under International Law* (1983), 121.

4 *Study of Discrimination in the Matter of Religious Rights and Practices*, UN Sales No. 60.XIV.2 (1960).

5 *Ibid.*, 18.

6 *Ibid.*, 35ff.

7 John Witte Jr. distinguishes seven principal patterns regarding state and religion: (1) state religions; (2) established churches; (3) state neutrality; (4) state concordats with the Catholic Church (there are also a few similar agreements with other religions, as we shall see later); (5) no official religion; (6) separation of churches and state; and (7) protection of legally recognized religious groups. See, John Witte Jr., *The State of Religious Human Rights in the World: A Comparative Religious and Legal Study* (1993).

8 *Study of Discrimination*, 63–6.

9 *Ibid.*, 71–4.

10 For the text of both covenants, see United Nations, *Human Rights: A Compilation of International Instruments*, at 8, 20, UN Sales No. E.93.XIV.1 (1983) [hereafter *Human Rights*]. Among the many works

on the covenants, see generally Henkin, *The International Bill of Rights*; Theodor Meron, ed., *Human Rights Law-Making in the United Nations* (1986); Philip Alston, ed., *The United Nations and Human Rights* (1992); Dominic McGoldrick, *The Human Rights Committee (1991)*. See also the reports of the Human Rights Committee, published as *Official Records of the General Assembly (GAOR), Supplement No. 40*.

11 See further discussion in chapter 4 [of the original publication].

12 On limitations in the covenant, see Thomas Buergenthal, *"To Respect and to Ensure: State Obligations and Permissible Derogations,"* in Henkin, The International Bill of Rights, 72–89, and Alexandre C. Kiss, "Permissible Limitations on Rights," in *ibid.*, 290–310.

13 For a United States Supreme Court decision on animal sacrifices according to the Santeria rite, see *Church of the Lukumi Babalu Aye, Inc. v. City of Hialeah*, 508 US 520 (1993).

14 See, *inter alia*, Donna J. Sullivan, "Gender Equality and Religious Freedom: Toward a Framework for Conflict Resolution," *New York University Journal of International Law and Politics* 24 (1992): 795–856, at 819–20; Leon Sheleff, "Tribal Rites and Legal Rights," *Israel Yearbook on Human Rights* 18 (1988): 153–72; Aviam Soifer, "Freedom of Association: Indian Tribes, Workers, and Communal Ghosts," *Maryland Law Review* 48 (1989): 350–83.

15 For the three mentioned instruments, see Convention against Discrimination in Education, in *Human Rights*, 1: 101–7; Declaration on the Elimination of All Forms of Intolerance and of Discrimination Based on Religious or Belief, in *ibid.* 1: 122–5; Convention on the Rights of the Child, in *ibid.*, 1: 171–3.

16 *Hartikainen v. Finland*, Communication No. 40/1978, in *Selected Decisions of the Human Rights Committee under the Optional Protocol*, 1: 74–6, UN Doc. No. CCPR/C/OP/1, UN Sales No. E.84.XIV.2 (1985) [hereafter *Selected Decisions*].

17 Partsch, "Freedom of Conscience and Expression," 453–4 n.75.

18 Report of the Human Rights Committee, UN GAOR 38th Sess., Supp. No. 40, Annex VI, at 110, UN Doc. No. A/38/40 (1983).

19 For the text of the Convention, see International Convention on the Elimination of All Forms of Racial Discrimination, *Human Rights*, 1: 66–79.

20 See Committee on the Elimination of Racial Discrimination, Positive Measures Designed to Eradicate All Incitement to, or Acts of, Racial Discrimination, UN Doc. No. CERD/2, UN Sales No. E.85.XIV.2 (1983). See also Nathan Lerner, *The UN Convention on the Elimination of All Forms of Racial Discrimination* (1980). For a model national legislation against racial discrimination and incitement, see Elimination of Racism and Racial Discrimination, UN GAOR, 48th Sess., Agenda Item 107, UN Doc. A/48/558 (1993). Incitement on religious grounds is not specifically mentioned in this document.

21 See Colloquium, "International Colloquium on Racial and Religious Hatred and Group Libel," *Israel Yearbook on Human Rights* 22 (1992), especially articles by Nathan Lerner, "Incitement in the Racial Convention: Reach and Shortcomings of Article 4," in *ibid.*, 1–15, and Rudolf Bernhardt, "Human Rights Aspects of Racial and Religious Hatred under Regional Human Rights Conventions," in *ibid.*, 17–29. See also Kevin Boyle, "Religious Intolerance and the Incitement of Hatred," in *Striking a Balance: Hate Speech, Freedom of Expression and Non-discrimination*, ed. Sandra Coliver (1992), 61–71. In 1993 the Committee on the Elimination of Racial Discrimination stated that the prohibition of the dissemination of racist ideas is compatible with the right to freedom of opinion and expression. Report of the Committee on the Elimination of Racial Discrimination, UN GAOR 42nd Sess., Supp. No. 18, at 115–16, UN Doc. No. A/42/18 (1987).

22 *Wisconsin v. Mitchell*, 508 US 478 (1993).

23 Report of the Human Rights Committee, UN GAOR 48th Sess., Supp. No. 40, Annex VI, UN Doc. A/48/40 (1993).

24 *Ibid.*, para. 2.

25 These issues have engendered interesting judicial decisions in some countries. See Leon Shaskolsky Sheleff, "Rabbi Captain

Goldman's Yarmulke, Freedom of Religion and Conscience, and Civil (Military) Disobedience," *Israel Yearbook on Human Rights* 17 (1987): 197–221. In *Goldman v. Weinberger* 475 US 503 (1986), the United States Supreme Court decided that an Air Force regulation on the dress code took precedence over religious traditions. The issue was solved by legislative means. See 10 USC.A. sec. 774 (1988). See also the well-known Sikh cases *Mandla v. Dowell Lee*, 1108 All E.R. (Eng. C.A. 1982) and *Panesar v. Nestle Co. Ltd.*, 1980 I.C.R. 144 (Eng. C.A.). In France, after contradictory decisions of the Conseil d'Etat, the Ministry of Education, with the support of the teachers' unions, prohibited in 1994 in public schools the traditional head coverage used by Muslim girls. The ban includes all ostentatious religious identifications, as distinguished from discrete signs such as small crosses, stars of David, or the name of Allah. The issue was described in newspaper articles as a national pyschodrama. See Robert Sole, "Derrier le foulard islamique," *Le Monde* (September 13, 1994): 1. In Israel, the Supreme Court affirmed a decision of a Christian private school in Nazareth to reject a Muslim girl student who insisted on using the traditional veil. Some cases came before the European human rights bodies. In *X. v. United Kingdom*, App. no. 7992/77, 14 European Commission of Human Rights Decisions and Reports 234 (1978), the duty of a Sikh motorcyclist to remove his turban and wear a crash helmet was seen as interfering with his religious freedom justified for the protection of public health.

26   Report of the Human Rights Committee, para. 8.

27   *Ibid.*, para. 9–10. The issue of blasphemy, an offense in some legislations (Britain, Egypt, and Iran, for instance), caused public controversy as a result of the publication in 1988 of Salman Rushdie's *The Satanic Verses* in Great Britain. The author was condemned to death by the Khomeini regime in 1989. Restrictions on publications considered blasphemous against the Church of England were declared compatible with Article 10(2) of the European Convention on Human Rights by the European Commission of Human Rights.

See *Gay News v. U.K.*, 5 E.H.R.R. 123 (1983). The Bangladesh government has brought criminal charges against the writer Taslim Nasreem for blasphemy. On blasphemy generally, see Leonard W. Levy, *Blasphemy: Verbal Offense against the Sacred, from Moses to Salman Rushdie* (1993).

28   See generally, Rafael Palomino, *Las Objeciones de Conciencia* (1994); Chaim Gans, *Philosophical Anarchism and Political Disobedience* (1992); Kent Greenawalt, *Conflicts of Law and Morality* (1987); Joseph Raz, *The Authority of Law* (1979); Rafael Navarro-Valls and Javier Martinez Torrón, *Las Objeciones de Conciencia* (Torino, 1997). The European Commission on Human Rights dealt with the meaning of *conscientious objection* in, *inter alia*, *Grandrath v. Germany*, 1967 Yearbook of the European Convention on Human Rights 626. The European Convention on Human Rights refers to conscientious objection in Article 4 and not in connection with religion. The US Supreme Court granted exemptions not only on religious premises. In *Welsh v. United States*, 398 US 333 (1970), for instance, the Supreme Court granted such exemption on secular grounds.

29   While the General Comments are neither scholarly studies nor secondary legislative acts, and are crouched in general terms, they represent an important body of experience in considering matters from the angle of the covenant. Torkel Opsahl, "The Human Rights Committee," in Alston, *The United Nations and Human Rights* 369–443, at 415.

30   Report of the Human Rights Committee, UN GAOR 47th Sess., Supp. No. 40, at 15–16, UN Doc. No. A/47/40 (1994).

31   *Ibid.*, 24–5.

32   *Ibid.*, 89.

33   Report of the Human Rights Committee, UN GAOR 46th Sess., Supp. No. 40, at 100, UN Doc. No. A/46/40 (1991).

34   *Ibid.*, 127; also, Report of the Human Rights Committee, UN GAOR 53rd Sess., Supp. No. 40., at 25, UN Doc. No. A/53/40 (1998).

35   For Argentina, see Report of the Human Rights Committee, UN GAOR 45th Sess., Supp. No. 40, at 49, UN Doc. No. A/45/40

(1990); for Lithuania, see UN GAOR 53rd Sess., Supp. No. 40, at 32, UN Doc. No. A/53/40(40); for Israel, *ibid.*, 49. In this respect the committee expressed concern regarding the application of religious law to matters of personal status.

36 *Ibid.*, 26. In its last report before this writing the committee dealt with discrimination on religious grounds in Iraq. *Ibid.*, 21.

37 CCPR/C/74/Add.3.

38 A/53/40, pp. 38–9.

39 *Selected Decisions*, vols. 1 and 2, in Selected Decisions of the Human Rights Committee under the Optional Protocol, UN Doc. CCPR/C/OP/2, UN Sales No. E.89.XIV.1 (1990).

40 For the text, see *Human Rights*, 1: 8–19.

41 See generally, Philip Alston, "The Committee on Economic, Social and Cultural Rights," in Alston, *The United Nations and Human Rights*, 473–508.

42 For the text, see *Human Rights*, 1: 122–5. For an analysis of the declaration, see Nathan Lerner, *Group Rights and Discrimination in International Law* (1991), 75–96; Donna J. Sullivan, "Advancing the Freedom of Religion or Belief through the UN Declaration on the Elimination of Religious Intolerance and Discrimination," *American Journal of International Law* 82 (1988): 487–520.

43 Lerner, *Group Rights and Discrimination*, 46. For the reasons for the difference of treatment by the UN of the religious issue as compared to other human rights, see also Antonio Cassese, "The General Assembly: Historical Perspective 1945–1989," in Alston, *The United Nations and Human Rights*, 25–54, at 37.

44 *Webster's Third New International Dictionary* (1986) defines *intolerant* as "refusing to allow others the enjoyment of their opinion or worship," and as equivalent to bigoted. Elizabeth Odio Benito, *Study of the Current Dimensions of the Problem of Intolerance and Discrimination Based on Religion or Belief*, UN ESCOR 39th Sess., Agenda Item 13, at 3, UN Doc. E/CN.4/Sub.2/1987/26 (1986), states that manifestations of intolerance go in many cases much further than discrimination and involve the stirring up of hatred against, or even the persecution of, individuals or groups of a different religion or belief. In its resolution 48/126, of December 20, 1993, on the 1995 Year for Tolerance, the General Assembly described tolerance as the recognition and appreciation of others, the ability to live together with and to listen to others, and as a sound foundation of any civil society and of peace. UN Press Release GA/8637, January 20, 1994, at 382–4.

45 See, *inter alia*, Partsch, "Freedom of Conscience" and Reports of the Human Rights Committee and its authoritative General Comment on Article 18 of the Covenant, summarized above.

46 See Odio Benito, E/CN.4/Sub.2/1987/26, at 37.

47 On several occasions the Human Rights Committee and the European Court on Human Rights dealt with the scope of permissible limitations. The European Court clarified the notion of morals in the *Handyside Case*, 24 European Court of Human Rights (ser. A) (1976).

48 Difficulties arose in the case of elections taking place on days that are holy for some religious minorities in the country who prohibit work and traveling on such days. Flexibility and good will are necessary in such situations, which may be difficult to foresee.

49 Krishnaswami points out that an identical formal relationship between the state and religion may result in discrimination in some cases, but not in others. See the Krishnaswami study, 46. Odio Benito, on the other hand, mantains that the establishment of a religion or belief by the state amounts to preferences and privileges that may be discriminatory. E/CN.4/Sub.2/1987/26, at 21.

50. Odio Benito, E/CN.4/Sub.2/1987/26, at 25.

51 For the texts of the declaration and the convention, see *Human Rights* 1: 171 and 174, respectively. On the subject generally, see Geraldine Van Bueren, *The International Law on the Rights of the Child* (1995); Lawrence J. LeBlanc, *The Convention on the Rights of the Child: United Nations Lawmaking on Human Rights* (1995).

52 See Stephen Schwebel, "The Effect of Resolutions of the UN General Assembly on Customary International Law,"

American Society of International Law, Proceedings of the 73rd Annual Meeting (1979): 301. Odio Benito, E/CN.4/Sub.2/1987/26, at 49, refers to concrete obligations of conduct for states and individuals.

53 On the seminar, see the report by Kevin Boyle, United Nations Seminar on the Encouragement of Understanding, Tolerance, and Respect in Matters Relating to Freedom of Religion or Belief, UN Doc. ST/HR/Ser.A/16 (1984), particularly para. 102(q), on the possibility of a convention.

54 See, for instance, UN Doc. A/54/100 (June 15, 1999). Formerly, in its resolution 41/20 of December 4, 1986, the General Assembly stated that standard setting should proceed with adequate preparation.

55 For the Vienna Declaration and Programme of Action, see 32.I.L.M. 1661 (1993).

56 Theo van Boven, *Elimination of All Forms of Intolerance and Discrimination Based on Religious Belief: Working Paper*, UN SCOR 41st Sess., Agenda Item 11, UN Doc. E/CN.4/Sub.2/1989/32 (1989). Van Boven mentions suggestions to frame a new binding instrument in the form of a protocol to the ICCPR, in which case the Human Rights Committee would become the implementation machinery. He also points out the practical difficulties for the establishment of a new treaty body (*ibid.*, 27). See also Theo Van Boven, "Advances and Obstacles in Building Understanding and Respect between People of Diverse Religions and Beliefs," *Human Rights Quarterly* 13 (1991): 437–49, an adapted version of the Arcot Krishnaswami Lecture at a conference of experts on ways to promote the 1981 Declaration, Project Tandem, New Delhi, 1991.

57 Yoram Dinstein and Mala Tabory (eds.), *The Protection of Minorities and Human Rights* (1992), 179.

58 *Elimination of All Forms of Religious Intolerance: Note by the Secretary-General*, UN GAOR 25th Sess., Agenda Item 56, UN Doc. A/7930 (1970). See Appendix, p. 131 above.

59 For the seven reports, see UN Doc. E/CN.4/1987/35; E/CN.4/1988/45 and E/CN.4/1988/45/Add.1; E/CN.4/1989/44; E/CN.4/1990/46; E/CN.4/1991/56; E/CN.4/1992/52; E/CN.4/1993/62 revised by E/CN.4/1993/62/Corr.1 and E/CN.4/1993/62/Add.1.

60 Odio Benito, E/CN.4/Sub.2/1987/26.

61 Until this writing, UN Doc. E/CN.4/1994/79; E/CN.4/1995/91; E/CN.4/1996/95 revised by E/CN.4/1996/95/Corr.1 and E/CN.4/1996/95/Add. 1 and E/CN.4/1996/95/Add.2; E/CN.4/1997/91 and E/CN.4/1997/91Add.1; E/CN.4/1998/6 and E/CN.4/1998/6/ Add.1 and E/CN.4/1998/6/Add.2.

62 See UN Doc. E/CN.4/1995/91.

63 On the visits, see UN Doc. E/CN.4/1995/91, E/CN.4/1996/95/Add.1 and E/CN.4/1996/95/Add.2, E/CN.4/1997/91/Add.1, as well as Human Rights Questions, Including Alternative Approaches for Improving the Effective Enjoyment of Human Rights and Fundamental Freedoms: Note by the Secretary-General, UN GAOR 51st Sess., Agenda Item 110(b), Add.1, UN Doc. A/51/542/Add.1 and *ibid.*, Add.2, and UN Doc. E/CN.4/1998/6/Add.1 and E/CN.4/1998/6/Add.2.

64 UN Doc. E/CN.4/1996/95.

65 *Ibid.*, 14.

66 UN Doc. E/CN.4/1998/6.

67 UNP Sales No. E.91. XIV.2.

68 The bibliography on minorities is enormous. For an early list, see Definition and Classification of Minorities, at 26–51, UN Doc. E/CN.4/Sub.2/85, UN Sales No. E.50.XIV.3. For recent literature in addition to Capotorti's Study, see, *inter alia*, Felix Ermacora, "The Protection of Minorities Before the United Nations" 182, vol. 4, *Recueil des Cours* (1983): 247–370; Louis B. Sohn, "The Rights of Minorities," in Henkin, *The International Bill of Rights*, 270–89; Lerner, *Group Rights*, Patrick Thornberry, *International Law and the Rights of Minorities* (1991); Dinstein and Tabory (eds.), *The Protection of Minorities and Human Rights*; Catherine Brolman et al. (eds.), *Peoples and Minorities in International Law* (1993).

69 On this early period, see Thornberry, *International Law and the Rights of Minorities*, 25ff.; Malcolm D. Evans, *Religious Liberty and International Law in Europe* (1997), 42–74.

70 For an authoritative interpretation of the system and the context in which it worked,

see Jacob Robinson et al., *Were the Minorities Treaties a Failure?* (1943).

71 In relation to this interesting and rare case, see Stephen J. Roth, "The Impact of the Holocaust on the Legal Status of Jews and Jewish Communities," *Israel Yearbook on Human Rights* 9 (1979): 121–39, at 128.

72 *Minority Schools in Albania*, 1935 P.C.I.J. (ser. A/B) no. 64, at 17.

73 The interpretation of Article 27 provoked a debate among scholars. See Thornberry, *International Law and the Rights of Minorities*, 149ff.; Francesco Capotorti, "Are Minorities Entitled to Collective International Rights?" *Israel Yearbook on Human Rights* 20 (1990): 351–7; Lerner, *Group Rights*, 14ff.; Lerner, "The Evolution of Minority Rights in International Law," in Brolman et al., *Peoples and Minorities in International Law*, 88ff.; Yoram Dinstein, "Freedom of Religion and the Protection of Religious Minorities," in Dinstein and Tabory, *The Protection of Minorities and Human Rights*, 154ff.

74 On the declaration, see Nathan Lerner, "The 1992 UN Declaration on Minorities," *Israel Yearbook on Human Rights* 23 (1993): 111–28.

75 See Dusan Janjic et al. (eds.), *Democracy and Minority Communities, Theses for the Law on Freedoms and Rights of Minority Communities and Their Members* (1993), 34.

76 For the 1949 humanitarian law conventions, see International Committee of the Red Cross, *The Geneva Conventions of August 12, 1949* (1949), as well as Jean S. Pictet, *International Committee of the Red Cross, Commentary: Geneva Convention* (1952).

77 For the texts of the declaration and the Convention on the Elimination of All Forms of Discrimination against Women, see *Human Rights*, 1: 145–9 and 1: 150–63. On the convention generally, see Theodor Meron, *Human Rights Law-Making in the United Nations* (1986), 53–82; Donna J. Sullivan, "Gender Equality and Religious Freedom: Toward a Framework for Conflict Resolution," *New York University Journal of International Law and Politics* 24 (1991–2): 795–856; Kathleen E. Mahoney and Paul Mahoney (eds.), *Human Rights in the Twenty-First Century* (1993).

78 For the text, see Convention against Discrimination in Education, *Human Rights*, 1: 101.

79 For the American case law, see M. Glenn Albernathy, *Civil Liberties under the Constitution* (1993), 172–220, 345–76; for some of the European cases, see *Case of Kieldsen, Busk Madsen and Pedersen*, 23 European Court of Human Rights (ser. A) at 25 (1976), and *Angelini v. Sweden*, European Commission on Human Rights, App. No. 1049, 10 E.H.R.R. 123 (1988); on the global level, *Hartikainen v. Finland*, Communication No. 40/1978, in *Selected Decisions*, 1: 74. This case was also considered by the European Human Rights Committee.

80 For the text, see Discrimination (Employment and Occupation) Convention, *Human Rights*, 1: 96.

81 See, *inter alia*, the decision of the Court of Justice of the European Communities in Case 130/75, *Preis v. Council of the European Communities* [1976] 2 Common Market Law Reports 708 (1976). The court stated that if a candidate for a job or a religious organization applies in time for a change in dates for a job examination, for religious reasons, that should be taken into account, if possible. For a different stand by the European Commission, see *M. v. Austria*, 1993 CD 25. The commission rejected a complaint against the denial of an adjournment of a hearing for religious motives because of the complexity of the case.

82 For the 1989 convention, see Convention (No. 169) concerning Indigenous and Tribal Peoples in Independent Countries, *Human Rights*, 1: 471. For its analysis, see Lerner, *Group Rights*, 99–114. For the UN draft declaration, see Commission on Human Rights, *Discrimination against Indigenous Peoples: Technical Review of the United Nations Draft Declaration on the Rights of Indigenous Peoples: Note by the Secretariat*, UN ESCOR 46th Sess., Agenda Item 15, UN Doc. E/CN.4/Sub.2/1994/2 (1994) and UN Doc. E/CN.4/Sub.2/1994/2/Add.1; Work Group on Indigenous Populations, Commission on Human Rights, Discrim ination

against Indigenous Peoples, UN ESCOR 46th Sess., Agenda Item 5, UN Doc. E/CN.4/Sub.2/1994/30 revised by UN Doc. E/CN.4/Sub.2/1994/30/Corr.1 (1994).

83 For the text, see International Convention on the Protection of the Rights of All Migrant Workers and Members of Their Families, *Human Rights*, 1: 550. For its analysis, see Ved P. Nanda, "The Protection of the Rights of Migrant Workers," *Asian and Pacific Migration Journal* 2 (1993): 161–77.

Cultural and Religious Traditions

Introduction to Part II

Part II focuses upon particular cultural and religious traditions. It is divided into three subsections:

- Judaism, Christianity and Islam
- Confucianism, Buddhism and Hinduism
- Indigenous and Minority Traditions

It makes sense to have some degree of subdivision for this major section of the book. Judaism, Christianity and Islam are linked because, despite all the historical and contemporary conflict between them, their interaction has been based upon a tremendous amount of interrelatedness – geogaphically, politically and, as monotheistic religions, theologically.

In the section on Judaism, Christianity and Islam, Jocelyn Hellig's "Anti-Semitism: Judaism, Christianity and Islam" marks a useful opening here for a number of reasons. First, the 1948 Universal Declaration was motivated by the excesses of the Nazi era. The Holocaust was not only about the persecution and annihilation of the Jews but they were the Third Reich's principal target for destruction. And in terms of European Jewry the Nazis were largely successful. It is not by accident that the 1948 Genocide Convention was instigated in the same year as the Universal Declaration of Human Rights. Modern manifestations of anti-Semitism as a specific aspect of religious and cultural persecution were at the heart of the development of contemporary human rights. Second, in view of the volume's broader aims to take a longer historical view, Hellig's chapter sets anti-Semitism in a broader history of religions. Third, Hellig's chapter illustrates an important general point in a book on human rights and religion, namely that religions do not operate in isolation but through interrelatedness – especially in geography and theology – that is so often the cause not of harmony but of violent dispute. As box II.i illustrates, anti-Semitism is not something that has gone away.

Charles Villa-Vincencio's chapter on Christianity and human rights is drawn from his magisterial work on the role of theology and nation building (Villa-Vincencio, 1999). He cites the preamble of the United Nations Charter of 24 October 1945 to "save succeeding generations from the scourge of war, which twice in our lifetime has brought untold sorrow to mankind" and to "reaffirm faith in fundamental human rights, in the dignity and worth of the human person, in the equal rights of men and women" and "to promote social progress and better standards of life in larger freedom," fostering international cooperation in "promoting and encouraging respect for human rights and for fundamental freedoms for all without distinction of race, sex, language or religion." Villa-Vincencio then delves back into Christian history to examine how the traditions of Roman Catholicism and Protestantism have differently formulated ethical philosophies – in relation to the

Box II.i

Western Europe: Rights Groups Condemn Racist and Anti-Semitic Violence

(New York, May 9, 2002) Amnesty International and Human Rights Watch are gravely concerned by the sharp increase in Western Europe of violent attacks on persons and property prompted by intolerance of religious, racial, cultural, and national differences. In particular, the two international human rights organizations strongly condemn the wave of racist attacks against Arabs and anti-Semitic attacks against Jews, and call on West European governments to redouble their efforts to combat racism in all its forms and to bring to justice suspected perpetrators of hate crimes.

The recent increase in anti-Semitic attacks has unfolded in the wake of the Middle East crisis. They follow a general rise in racist and xenophobic violence in Western Europe, particularly against Arabs and certain ethnic and religious minorities, which spiked sharply in the aftermath of the 11 September attacks in the United States.

Recent anti-Semitic violence has included the posting of threatening hate mail, vandalizing of synagogues and Jewish cemeteries, and verbal abuse and physical assaults targeting Jews. The following examples highlight the rise in anti-Semitic violence in a number of West European countries:

- In France, hostility toward Jews has led to a particularly serious wave of attacks. The French police recorded 395 anti-Semitic incidents between 29 March and 17 April, 63 percent of which involved anti-Semitic graffiti. Between 1 January and 2 April, 34 "serious anti-Semitic actions" were recorded; e.g. attacks on Jewish persons or property, including synagogues and cemeteries. In April, several synagogues, in Lyon, Mont-pellier, Garges-les-Gonesses (Val d'Oise) and Strasbourg were vandalized, while a synagogue in Marseille was burned to the ground. In Paris, a crowd threw stones at a vehicle transporting pupils of a Jewish school, and the vehicle's windows were broken. The authorities are now investigating these attacks.
- In the UK, at least 48 attacks on Jews were reported in April, compared with 12 in March, seven in February, 13 in January and five in December. Some of the assaults resulted in the hospitalization of victims with serious injuries. Reportedly, the victims were mainly orthodox and Hassidic Jews. In an April attack on a London synagogue, a swastika was scrawled on the lectern.
- In Belgium, synagogues in Brussels and Antwerp were firebombed in April; the facade of a synagogue in Charleroi, southwest Belgium, was sprayed with bullets. A Jewish bookshop and delicatessen in Brussels were destroyed by fire. Criminal investigations have been opened in these incidents, as well as into a physical assault on the Chief Rabbi of Brussels in December 2001.
- In April, synagogues were attacked in Berlin and Herford in western Germany. In the same month in Berlin, a young Jewish woman was reportedly attacked in the underground rail system because she was wearing a pendant of a Star of David. Two Orthodox Jews were attacked and slightly injured by a group of people on a shopping street after visiting a synagogue.

Amnesty International and Human Rights Watch both have monitored racist and xenophobic violence in Western Europe, including against Arabs and Muslims in the wake of the 11 September attacks in the United States. The international human rights organizations condemned these attacks, which have included verbal abuse, physical assaults and attacks on mosques – and express alarm that they continue. In an attack in Brussels on 7 May, a Moroccan immigrant couple was shot dead and two of their children wounded by an elderly Belgian neighbor, reportedly expressing racist views.

Amnesty International and Human Rights Watch welcome the 25 April statement by the European Union's Justice and Home Affairs Council "condemning the racist acts perpetrated in various places in the EU in recent weeks." The Council urged joint EU action to combat discrimination and racist, anti-Semitic and xenophobic violence, and to raise public awareness. In its statement, the Council also stated that preventive action should be taken against all forms of intolerance aimed at persons of the Jewish or Muslim faith or any other faith. Earlier in April, the interior ministers of France, the UK, Germany, Spain and Belgium issued a joint declaration against racism and anti-Semitism.

Government and political leaders in various countries have not only condemned the attacks, but some have also taken measures to provide protection to Jewish cultural and religious centres. In France over 1,100 extra police have been deployed to protect synagogues. In addition, authorities have opened judicial investigations and in some instances, convicted perpetrators of racist violence. The Belgian government stated on 1 April that it would expedite bringing to justice the perpetrators of such attacks and take all measures to ensure the security of places of worship. The police in London have stepped up their presence in Jewish areas and the Attorney General has promised a crackdown on racially motivated hate crimes.

Amnesty International and Human Rights Watch urge all West European governments to take immediate and effective measures to prevent racist and anti-Semitic violence; and to vigorously investigate, arrest, and prosecute perpetrators of such violence. We also call on governments to make public the measures they are taking to combat racist and anti-Semitic violence, and to report to the public periodically the results of these efforts. (HRW, 2002)

individual and the state – and their respective accommodations with the modern discourse of universal human rights.

Of all world religions, Islam is arguably presented in the West most prejudicially in terms of international human rights and in relation to wider questions of democracy and state governance. Ann Elizabeth Mayer in her chapter on Islam and human rights argues that "Islamic law and Islamic thought have been treated as irrelevant by people involved in the development of international human rights law. Serious treatises by recognized specialists on the development of international human rights law have not produced evidence of Islamic inspiration for international human rights law or its historical antecedents." She presents a thorough examination of Islam's historical and contemporary relation to contemporary human rights as a discourse of the West. Manochehr Dorraj looks at a more specific aspect of this cultural dissonance on human rights in the political context of Islam, state governance and democracy.

In his opening chapter to the volume Haynes identified Confucianism and "Asian values" as another source of potential conflict with the West and "Western" values such as human rights. Confucianism

is distinctive in the context as it represents a system that has never designated itself as a religion. Confucianism is more likely to be seen as an ethical, social and political philosophy, in short, pragmatic rather than metaphysical in intent. As Haynes writes: "Several countries in East Asia – China, Japan, South and North Korea, Singapore, Taiwan and Vietnam – have cultures rooted in Confuc- ianism (Confucius was a Chinese philosopher who lived from 551–479 BC). What seems to be the chief shared cultural characteristic of these countries is that they are community-orientated rather than individualistic." Sumner Twiss presents in this context, "A Constructive Framework for Discussing Confucianism and Human Rights."

Buddhism and Hinduism have historical links through common origins in the Indian subcontinent. Geography itself raises interesting questions for world religions in an era of globalisation. Religions are less limited to particular geographical locations. Buddhism is practised widely and seriously in many Western countries and is a minority tradition in India, the country with which its development was first associated. Damien Keown's question, "Are There Human Rights in Buddhism?" has that analytical ring that has made Buddhism

Box II.ii

Caste

Discriminatory and cruel, inhuman, and degrading treatment of a vast global population has been justified on the basis of caste. In much of Asia and parts of Africa, caste is the basis for the definition and exclusion of distinct population groups by reason of their descent. Over 250 million people worldwide continue to suffer under what is often a hidden apartheid of segregation, modern-day slavery, and other extreme forms of discrimination, exploitation, and violence. Caste imposes enormous obstacles to their full attainment of civil, political, economic, social, and cultural rights.

Caste is descent-based and hereditary in nature. It is a characteristic determined by one's birth into a particular caste, irrespective of the faith practiced by the individual. Caste denotes a system of rigid social stratification into ranked groups defined by descent and occupation. Under various caste systems throughout the world, caste divisions also dominate in housing, marriage, and general social interaction-divisions that are reinforced through the practice and threat of social ostracism, economic boycotts, and even physical violence.

Among the communities effected are the Dalits or so-called untouchables of South Asia-including Nepal, Bangladesh, India, Sri Lanka, and Pakistan-the Buraku people of Japan, the Osu of Nigeria's Igbo people, and certain groups in Senegal and Mauritania. The prominence of caste as a social and economic indicator for the widespread South Asian diaspora is also notable. These communities share many features; features that have allowed even the most appalling practices to escape international scrutiny. In many cases, caste systems coexist with otherwise democratic structures. In countries such as India and Nigeria, governments have also enacted progressive legislation to combat abuses against lower-caste communities. Despite formal protections in law, however, discriminatory treatment remains endemic and discriminatory societal norms continue to be reinforced by government and private structures and practices, in some cases through violent means.

Lower-caste communities are almost invariably indistinguishable in physical appearance from higher-caste communities. This is not, as some would say, a black and white issue. For most outsiders then, the visual cues that otherwise accompany race or ethnicity are often completely lacking. Stark economic disparities between low and high-caste communities also get buried under a seemingly homogenous landscape of poverty. Poverty can be quite deceptive. It makes one conclude that all suffer from it equally. A closer look reveals the discrimination inherent in the allocation of jobs, land, basic resources and amenities, and even physical security. A closer look at victims of violence, bonded labor, and other severe abuses also reveals disproportionate membership in the lowest ranking in the caste order. A perpetual state of economic dependency also allows for abuses to go unpunished, while a biased state machinery looks the other way, or worse, becomes complicit in the abuse.

The language used to describe low and high-caste community characteristics in the examples that follow are striking in their similarity, despite the variation in geographic origin, with ideas of pollution and purity, and filth and cleanliness prevalent. In turn, these designations are used to justify the physical and social segregation of low-caste communities from the rest of society, their exclusion from certain occupations, and their involuntary monopoly over "unclean" occupations and tasks.

The exploitation of low-caste laborers and the rigid assignment of demeaning occupations on the basis of caste keep lower-caste populations in a position of economic and physical vulnerability. The triple burden of caste, class, and gender effectively ensures that lower-caste women are the farthest removed from legal protections. Only with the honest implementation of the International Convention on the Elimination of All Forms of Racial Discrimination (ICERD) and of domestic laws designed to abolish the vestiges of various caste systems and to protect the economic, social, cultural, civil, and political rights of all, can the process of attaining economic and physical security, and human dignity, begin.

In August 2000 the UN Subcommission on the Promotion and Protection of Human Rights passed resolution 2000/4 on Discrimination Based on Work and Descent.[1] The resolution, aimed at addressing the issue of caste, reaffirmed that discrimination based on work and descent is prohibited under international human rights law. The Subcommission also decided to further identify affected communities, examine existing constitutional, legislative, and administrative measures for the abolition of such discrimination, and make concrete recommendations for the effective elimination of such practices.

In August 2001, subcommission expert R. K. W. Goonesekere presented his working paper on work and descent-based discrimination to the subcommission's fifty-third session. The paper was submitted pursuant to Subcommission resolution 2000/4. Because of time and other constraints, Mr. Goonesekere limited the paper's focus to the Asian countries of India, Nepal, Pakistan, Sri Lanka, and Japan but stated that further study of African countries in particular was warranted. The presentation of the paper, and the ensuing debate amongst subcommission experts that followed, marked the first time that caste discrimination was discussed as a major source of human rights violations worldwide by a UN human rights body. The subcommission also determined by consensus to extend the study to other regions of the world where work and descent-based discrimination continues to be experienced.

This important resolution underscores the notion that caste systems are inherently economic and social in their consequences and that the exclusion of lower-caste communities extends to the economic and social realms of wages, jobs, education, and land. The report [of which this extract forms a preamble] discusses the manifestations of caste and descent-based discrimination and abuse in over a dozen countries. It is not meant to be an exhaustive review but an introduction to the prevalence and global dimensions of this underreported problem. It is also an appeal to governments to give close and systematic attention to the problem of caste discrimination at the World Conference Against Racism, Racial Discrimination, Xenophobia and Related Intolerance and beyond. Despite the magnitude of the problem, as of this writing, caste-based discrimination had been systematically cut out of the WCAR's intergovernmental process through the actions of a handful of governments. This has occurred despite the Committee on the Elimination of Racial Discrimination's repeated affirmations that caste, as a form of descent-based discrimination, falls within the definition of racial discrimination under article 1 of the ICERD.

Concerted international attention and the commitment of resources to assist national governments in this important work are also long overdue. In many parts of the world, the success of the World Conference will turn upon its commitment to effectively addressing the issue of caste. For at least a quarter-billion people worldwide, the end of apartheid in South Africa did not signal the end of segregation and servitude in their own lives. This important conference can and should bring us closer to this important global goal. (HRW, 2001)

Note
1   UN Subcommission on the Promotion and Protection of Human Rights, "Discrimination Based on Work and Descent," E/CN.4/SUB.2/RES/2000/4, August 11, 2000.

so popular in the West for its lack of dogmatism and its emphasis upon individual experience. Hinduism, while practised by populations around the world from the United Kingdom to the South Pacific, remains a religion integral to the life of India. A vast land renowned for its diversity of religious traditions (India possesses one of the world's largest Islamic populations), modern-day India has had its fair share of religious conflict. Since 1948 there have been decades of post-Independence Hindu–Muslim violence, seen most recently in and around Ayodhya. Hindu–Sikh violence was much in evidence after the assassination of Indira Ghandi in 1984. There has too been much intolerance at Christian minorities by Hindu nationalists (HRW, 1999). Joseph Barnabas outlines such developments in his chapter, "Religious Freedom and Human Rights in India." Carrie Gustafson's examination of

Gandhi's political philosophy – even if indirectly "Hindu" – assesses the potential for contemporary applications the philosopher-saint's thinking on human rights and political process beyond India. Although Gustafson's chapter focuses more on Gandhi-inspired non-violence as a means of political action, Gandhi was also famous for his struggle against the oppression of the untouchables of India's caste system. More than half a century after the death of Gandhi, the UN recognizes that around 250 million people around the world (not only in the Indian subcontinent) still suffer through some form of caste system. While specific case studies of religion in India will arise in the case studies of **Part III**, the issue of caste in the world today as summarized in **box II.ii** is worth highlighting as a reminder that even academic discussions of human rights and religion – for instance, talk of "Asian values" – has implications for individual human beings.

The third subsection of **Part II** briefly covers, via a consideration of Africa, some key issues pertinent to minority and indigenous traditions. Indigenous traditions have often been the subject of oppression and persecution by those religions which have as a matter of historical fact come to dominate the world's religious belief systems, at least numerically. Makau Mutua's chapter examines the domination of Christianity and Islam in African states' religious policy, often to the neglect of "indigenous" traditions. Mutua's chapter raises questions of power, authority and the political oppression by religions themselves against less powerful traditions, something of relevance to indigenous, especially tribal religions the world over. But Mutua's chapter also serves as a reminder that should inculcate a degree of guilt in former colonial powers, often those that today so often espouse the universality of human rights. Too often in the past, and arguably in some context still today, missionary religious activity went hand-in-hand with imperialism. More case studies of indigenous traditions are included in **Part III** of

Human Rights & Religion: A Reader. Indeed the present academic reflections in **Part II** here prepare the groundwork and highlight themes that are then developed through a series of regional case studies where, often in intense inter-religious conflict, human rights and religion surface in global politics.

References

Human Rights Watch. 1999. *Politics By Other Means: Violence Against Christians in India.* New York: HRW.

Human Rights Watch. 2001. *Caste Discrimination: A Global Concern.* New York: HRW.

Human Rights Watch. 2002. "Western Europe: Rights Groups Condemn Racist and Anti-Semitic Violence." New York: HRW.

Villa-Vincencio, Charles. 1999. *A Theology of Reconstruction: Nation-Building and Human Rights.* Cambridge: Cambridge University Press.

Further Reading

Afkhami, Mahnaz (ed.) *Faith and Freedom: Women's Rights in the Muslim World* (London: I.B. Tauris, 1995).

Anderson, Michael R., and Guha, Sumit (eds.) *Changing Concepts of Rights and Justice in South Asia* (Oxford: Oxford University Press, 1998).

An-Naim, Abdullahi Ahmed (ed.) *Proselytization and Communal Self-Determination in Africa* (New Jersey: Orbis, 1999).

Atkin, Bill and Evan, Katrine (eds.) *Human Rights and the Common Good: Christian Perspectives* (Wellington, NZ: Victoria University Press, 1998).

Beaumont, Paul R. *Christian Perspectives on Human Rights and Legal Philosophy* (Carlisle: Paternoster, 1998).

Charlesworth, Max *Religious Business: Essays on Australian Aboriginal Spirituality* (Cambridge: Cambridge University Press, 2000).

de Bary, William Theodore and Weiming, Tu (eds.) *Confucianism and Human Rights* (New York: Columbia University Press, 1998).

Gustafson, Carrie and Juviler, Peter (eds.) *Religion and Human Rights: Competing Claims?* (New York: M.E. Sharpe, 1999).

Hogan, Linda *Christian Perspectives on Development Issues* (London: CAFOD, 1998).

Keown, Damien V., Prebish, Charles S., and Husted, Wayne R. *Buddhism and Human Rights* (London, Curzon, 1998).

Keppley, Mahmood, Cynthia *Fighting for Faith and Nation: Dialogues with Sikh Militants* (Hawaii: University of Hawaii Press, 1996).

Magnarella, Paul J. (ed.) *The Middle East and North Africa: Governance, Democratization, Human Rights* (Aldershot: Ashgate, 1999).

Mayer, Ann Elizabeth *Islam and Human Rights: Tradition and Politics* (London: Westview, 1999).

Mendelsohn, Oliver and Baxi, Upendra (eds.) *The Rights of Subordinated Peoples* (Delhi: Oxford University Press, 1997).

Nirmal, C.J. (ed.) *Human Rights in India: Historical, Social and Political Perspectives* (Oxford: Oxford University Press, 2000).

Novak, David *Covenantal Rights* (Princeton: Princeton University Press, 2000).

Rouner, Leroy S. *Human Rights and the World's World's Religions* (Chicago, IL: University of Notre Dame Press, 1994).

Tanwar, Reicha *Women: Human Rights, Religion and Violence* (Kurukshetra: Nirmal, 1998).

Villa-Vincencio, Charles *A Theology of Reconstruction: Nation Building and Human Rights* (Cambridge: Cambridge University Press, 1999).

Witte, John and Bordeaux, Michael (eds.) *Proselytism and Orthodoxy in Russia: The New War for Souls* (New York: Orbis, 1999).

Witte, John and van der Vyer, Johan D. (eds.) *Religious Human Rights in Global Perspective: Religious Perspectives* (Grand Rapids, Michigan: Wm Erdmans Publishing Co., 2000).

Anti-Semitism: Judaism, Christianity and Islam

Jocelyn Hellig

4

◆ Defining anti-Semitism ◆ Christian anti-Semitism ◆

◆ Islamic anti-Semitism ◆ Anti-Zionism and anti-Semitism ◆

As this chapter will make clear, it was not only in Christianity but also in Islam that negative images of the Jew developed. Judaism, Christianity, and Islam each make absolute claims based on one core tradition, the Abrahamic tradition. Ironically, although the anti-Jewish stereotype of the Jew developed by Christian tradition was ultimately far more damaging and deep-rooted than that developed in Islam, today Muslim anti-Semitism (which is generally expressed in anti-Zionist terms) appears to be the more threatening of the two. This chapter will examine the dynamics inherent in this development, first with reference to Christianity and then to Islam.

Problems of Definition

Anti-Semitism, an imprecise word that is notoriously difficult to define, has as its irreducible meaning a dislike of Jews.[1] What makes definition so difficult is the fact that the term *anti-Semitism* can be applied to everything from vague feelings of dislike of or discomfort about Jews, at one end of the spectrum, to outright murder of them at the other. Between the two extremes one observes various forms of limitation on Jews' lives. These range from legislation

that denies immigration of Jews to various countries or limits their social, economic, or educational aspirations, to active, often violent, persecution of Jews. Since a level of anti-Semitism exists in all societies, particularly the type limited to negative feelings about Jews, or what may be termed "genteel" anti-Semitism, one of the ways of assessing the seriousness of anti-Semitism is to examine the way in which it serves to hinder the lives of Jews. A variety of factors – political, social, economic, and religious – determine the development, nature, and extent of anti-Semitism. Thus, anti-Semitism fluctuates from period to period and from region to region.

Added to the difficulty of definition is the fact that words like *anti-Israeli, anti-Judaic,* and *anti-Zionist* are constantly confused with the word *anti-Semitism.* These essentially different concepts are used interchangeably, sometimes as a result of simple linguistic imprecision, but sometimes by design, as a tactic for achieving specific political and ideological ends. Although anti-Zionism is not necessarily anti-Semitism – in that criticism of the government of Israel, or even opposition to the establishment of the secular State of Israel, finds adequate representation among Jews themselves – anti-Zionism may also be seen to be a transmuted anti-Semitism. Robert Wistrich has suggested that because, after the Holocaust, it became unacceptable to mouth antisemitic sentiments, anti-Semitism was expressed through anti-Zionism.[2]

Difficulty with regard to definition of the term *anti-Semitism* notwithstanding, there is an underlying quality to anti-Semitism that seems to separate it from all other forms of ethnic and racial prejudice and that goes beyond mere denigration or even persecution. Although all forms of racism are dehumanizing in that they treat racial groups as monoliths and endow all members of a racial group with permanent – usually negative – characteristics, it is the demonization of Jews and the attribution to them of a quality of cosmic and eternal evil that mark anti-Semitism. Anti-Semitism has, as its most influential roots, the mythic structure of Christianity in its relation to Judaism. A particular role is assigned to the Jews in the Christian drama of salvation. This designated role, according to Richard L. Rubenstein, reveals a logic in Christian theology that, when pushed to the extreme, ends with justification of, if not incitement to, the murder of Jews. The Holocaust of the Second World War was thus "the terminal expression of Christian anti-Semitism."[3] At this level dehumanization becomes so complete that it denies to Jews all human rightsthe rights to possession, dignity, citizenship, and ultimately the right to life itself.

The Holocaust was enacted under cover of war and was made possible by the fact that Jews were stripped, through legislation, of all power. Power, as Yehuda Bauer has defined it, is the "capability to influence decisions of others either through the implied or explicit threat of sanctions or through promise of political advantages deriving from military, economic, electoral, or other assets."[4] By this criterion the Jews of the Third Reich were absolutely powerless, and it was this experience and its disastrous entailments that made the Jewish return to Israel as an independent home-

land so essential. Jews were returned to political sovereignty for the first time in almost two thousand years. Some scholars, notably Emil Fackenheim, regard this as a return of the Jewish people to history itself.[5] No longer the objects of history, Jews, by being in a position to make their own power decisions, are now participants in history. The Holocaust and the reestablishment of the State of Israel, the two *kairoi* of modern Jewish history, have influenced all aspects of modern Jewish thought. No Jewish community can be examined in isolation from them.

Christian Anti-Semitism

Dislike of Jews seems as old as Judaism itself. There was a significant amount of Jew-hatred in ancient times, but it was vastly exacerbated by the Christian "teaching of contempt" against the Jews. Long before the inception of Christianity, in classical times, expression of anti-Semitism could take on quite vicious forms, as is evidenced in the diatribes of Apion of Alexandria. The source of Jew-hatred appears to be resentment of Jewish monotheism, the Jewish claim to chosenness, and the religious laws that maintained Jewish separateness. As David Berger points out, however, "if ancient paganism had been replaced by a religion or ideology without an internal anti-Jewish dynamic, it is likely that the anti-Semitism of the classical world would have gradually faded. Instead, it was reinforced. The old pedestrian causes of anti-Jewish animus were replaced by a new, powerful myth of extraordinary force and vitality."[6]

Christianity's anti-Jewish teaching became explicit in three areas: (1) the Jewish rejection of Jesus as the Messiah; (2) the doctrine of Jewish chosenness; and (3) the deicide accusation against the Jews. Each of these will now receive brief consideration.

Rejection of Jesus as the Messiah

Christian anti-Semitism, as Rosemary Ruether argues, is not peripheral but central to Christianity. Relating to Christianity's core doctrine of Christology, anti-Semitism is found in the New Testament itself. The New Testament becomes an "anti-Jewish midrash" of the Old Testament (itself a term of denigration of the Jewish scriptures), which sets out to prove that the church was the rightful heir to the promises of God, while the Jews were punished and rejected, and Judaism discredited.

Within the Hebrew Bible, there is an implicit promise of a Messianic Age; for Christians, the promise was fulfilled with the life, death, and resurrection of Jesus. However, since the Jews rejected the validity of that claim, they were seen to be blind to the true purport of their own scriptures, and the church developed a polemic against them in the form of an exegetical tradition that attempted to prove that Jesus was the messiah predicted in the Old Testament. Jewish blindness was to assume great significance, not only with regard to discrediting Judaism's religious law, leadership, and worship, but with regard to its history as a whole, dating back to the time of Moses. "The dialectic of judgment and promise is rendered schizophrenic, applied not to one elect people, but to two peoples; the reprobate people, the Jews, and the future elect people of the promise, the Church."[7] In divine intentionality, it now appeared, there had always been two peoples: the people of faith, who are the rightful heirs of the promise to Abraham; and the fallen, disobedient people, who never obeyed God or heard the prophets. The church becomes the true heir of the promises to Abraham, while the Jews are the heirs of an evil history of perfidy, apostasy, and murder. The result is that the Jews are cut off from their divine election. As a punishment, they were destined to be kept alive as witnesses to Christian verities, but they were to live a reprobate existence, outside of their Promised Land and scattered throughout the world. This interpretation often complicates Christian attitudes to the State of Israel.[8]

The doctrine of chosenness

The doctrine of Jewish chosenness is another potent cause of anti-Semitism. Never regarded by Jews as a doctrine of racial superiority, but rather as one of special responsibility, it has resulted in several difficulties. First, it has been consistently misunderstood and distorted by outsiders. Second, it has been emulated throughout the world in order to legitimate a host of racist theories. The most notable of these is Nazism, an ideology which, according to George Steiner, boomeranged catastrophically against the Jews themselves in a "hideous relationship of parody."[9] Third, in a dynamic not unlike sibling rivalry, it serves to alienate Jews and Christians in that both claim chosenness. Fourth, it plays an important role in the dehumanization of Jews.

With the lack of logic inherent in two peoples being chosen by the same God, the church saw itself as the "New" or "True" Israel, while the promises to the Jews were seen as abrogated. This resulted in a myth of "displacement" of, or of "superseding," the "old Israel" with the "new Israel." The idea that the mission of the Jewish people was finished with the coming of Jesus Christ is, for Franklin H. Littell, the cornerstone of Christian anti-Semitism. This writing off of the old Israel, he claims, rings a genocidal note. "To teach that a people's mission in God's providence is finished, that they have been relegated to the limbo of history, has murderous implications which murderers will in time spell out." The murder of six million Jews by baptized Christians, from whom membership in good standing was not (and has not been) withdrawn, raises, for Littell, the most insistent question about the credibility of Christianity.[10]

One of the most destructive entailments

of the doctrine of chosenness with regard to anti-Semitism is that it has thrust the Jews into an unwanted supernatural vocation as central actors in the salvation of the world. According to Richard Rubenstein, it may be impossible for Christians to remain Christians without regarding the Jews in mythic, magic, and theological categories. "Jews alone of all the people in the world are regarded as actors and participants in the drama of sin and innocence, guilt and salvation, perdition and redemption."[11] Unable to conceive of Jews as ordinary people, capable of the same virtues and vices as others, people dehumanize them. By condemning the Jews to the realm of the sacred, chosenness places them in a special category of expectation. Either praised as Jesus-like or condemned and murdered as Judas-like, Jews become the objects of decisive hatred.

So potentially damaging is the doctrine of chosenness that Rubenstein has called for its demythologization. Yet, this would not be an easy matter, as Judaism and Christianity are equally dependent on its retention. For Arthur Hertzberg, the doctrine is so central that he has claimed that "the essence of Judaism is the affirmation that the Jews are the chosen people; all else is commentary."[12] But the chosenness of the Jews is equally central to Christianity. "Unless Jews have a supernatural vocation," avers Rubenstein, "the Christ makes absolutely no theological difference."[13]

The deicide accusations

The dehumanization engendered by the doctrine of chosenness has been vastly exacerbated by the deicide accusation, which not only dehumanizes Jews but demonizes them. Although responsible theologians attempt to spread the blame for killing Christ to all humanity, Matthew 27: 25 confirms Jewish guilt for all generations. One who can kill God is not beyond the most heinous of crimes. This slander against the Jewish people acts as a justifica-tion for the persecution and murder of Jews and was a powerful motivating factor during the Holocaust.[14] Alice L. Eckhardt points out that the German churches, during the 1930s, generally emphasized the curse upon Israel. She cites the words of a Protestant bishop in 1936, the year after the issuing of the Nuremberg racial laws:

> When the Jews crucified Jesus, they cruci-fied themselves, their revelation and their history. Thus the curse came upon them. Since then that curse works itself out from one generation to another. This people has . . . become a fearful and divinely ordained scourge for all nations, leading to hatred and persecution.[15]

While the deicide accusation was not the cause of the Holocaust, Emil Fackenheim suggests that "had there been no two-thou-sand-year-old slander of Jews as a deicide people, the Holocaust could not have happened."[16]

The negative potential of the deicide accusation must be assessed against the power of the myth that encapsulates it. Hyam Maccoby regards the myth of the crucifixion of Jesus as the most powerful the world has ever known. In a breath-taking drama designed to lift the burden of guilt from those who believe, the Jews do *not* play the role of the scapegoats. Jesus himself is the scapegoat who takes upon himself the sins of the world. The function of the Jews was to bring about the necessary death of the scapegoat in order to save humankind from crisis. For Christianity, the cruel, sacrificial death of Jesus was a necessity, and the Jews were the evil instru-ments by which it was brought about. The Jews are thus the earthly agents of the cosmic powers of evil. They are the deicides who, by their wickedness, unwittingly save the world, but who are thus doubly damned in that the death of Christ is not efficacious for *them,* and because, with the deicide, they crown a long career of sin with the greatest of all sins, the murder of God. They become the embodiment of evil and excite a combination of awe and hate that, as the hallmark of anti-Semitism, separates it from all other forms of xenophobia.

Because the Jews were cast as cosmic villains in the Christian doctrine of atonement, their role demanded that any sign of happiness or prosperity among them should arouse anxiety for Christians, for if the Jews did not suffer, who would bear the guilt for the sacrifice of Jesus? As anti-Semitism is so ingrained in the central myth of Christianity, the only solution, according to Maccoby, is the return of the repressed, namely, a real understanding of Christendom's irrational prejudice against the Jews and its determination always to think of them in negative terms.[17] It is the idea that Jews are cosmic villains that makes views about world conspiracy, such as *The Protocols of the Elders of Zion,* so plausible. Without the decisive religious significance of Jews in Christianity's central drama, such theories would surely be dismissed by rational people as absurd.

When Christianity became the official religion of the Roman Empire in the fourth century, Christendom's negative perception of the Jews was translated into concrete legislation. The triumph of the church was interpreted as proof of divine favor, and Jews were seen as an anachronism, sustained merely by stubbornness. Jewish practice was circumscribed by law. In the medieval world Jews were an easily identifiable minority of nonconformists in a conformist world. This resulted in them being perceived and treated as alien to European society. Over the centuries a formidable anti-Jewish stereotype was developed, originally based on religiously inspired antipathy but later adapting itself around various foci. During the nineteenth century the focus was racial, and anti-Semitism was transmuted into a pseudo-scientific form. With emancipation Jews had become equals before the law in European society. In order to confirm their status as fundamentally and irrevocably alien to the rest of society, however, it became necessary to focus attention on allegedly permanent, unchanging characteristics such as race. Their equality could thus be delegitimated. This, in effect, meant that whereas escape from violent anti-Semitism had previously been allowed through conversion, no escape was now possible. Anti-Semitism was later to develop political ramifications and become fused with anti-Zionism.

Christian teaching had formed the basis for these developments and has had an ineradicable influence. As Claire Huchet-Bishop has suggested, the negative image of the Jew fostered by Christian teaching has "permeated our Western culture so thoroughly that even people wholly detached from the church, including atheists, are no longer unbiased in their reactions toward Jews, though they may think they are."[18] "What Christian teaching has done," she avers, "it has to undo; and it will take a long time."[19]

Islamic Anti-Semitism

Traditional views

Anti-Semitism, in the forms manifest in the Christian tradition, is not apparent in Islamic tradition. Yet, as Bernard Lewis points out, since 1945 certain Arab countries have been the only places in the world where hardcore Nazi-style anti-Semitism is publicly and officially endorsed and propagated.[20] When Islam arose in the seventh century of the common era, Jews were a homeless and powerless people. In accordance with its claims of superiority over Judaism and Christianity, Islam regarded the Jews and Christians as *dhimmi* (protected peoples). Judaism was a tolerated religion in the Muslim world, and Jews were to adopt a low profile and self-effacing attitude.

The Qur'an distinguishes between warfare against pagans, which is to be total and unrelenting, and toleration of Jews and Christians. Jews and Christians should be tolerated, provided that they pay a special tax and are humiliated. These Quranic teachings, Jane S. Gerber suggests, created a formula for religious pluralism in which Jews could survive and even prosper, but if they became too ostentatious in their success, there was no guarantee that the original relationship of contractual protection would be honored.[21] While the notion of "toleration-protection cum humiliation"[22] took varied and sometimes outrageous forms, the radical isolation of the Jew as an outsider in Christian Europe was never approximated in the Muslim world. "Jews were objects of officially legislated contempt, but they were not intended to be objects of officially instituted hatred."[23]

Traditional Islam, although it did display hostility against Jews, did not demonize them. Mohammed had a complex and ambivalent attitude to Jews. His conflict with the Jewish tribes of Medina, along with the bitterness that it engendered, is reflected in the Qur'an and in the Hadith. Jews were labeled corrupters of scripture (Q. 3:63), were accused of falsehood (Q. 3:71), and were seen as enemies of Islam. "Thou wilt surely find that the strongest in enmity against those who believe are the Jews and the idolaters" (Q. 5:85). Yet, Mohammed did not outlaw the Jews or remove them entirely from Arabia. His conflict with them ended in the destruction of the Jewish tribes, not in Mohammed's. Because there was no equivalent of the deicide myth in traditional Islam, the Jews were not demonized.[24] This made it possible for Muslims to adopt a more relaxed and less embittered attitude toward their Jewish subjects. In the Islamic world, Jews were one minority among several and, although the Qur'an favors Christians over Jews, they received equal treatment under Islamic law. Jews were never free of discrimination under Islamic rule but were only occasionally subject to persecution. Their situation, according to Lewis, was never as bad as in Christendom at its worst, nor ever as good as in Christendom at its best. While prejudice was always present, it was usually muted, rarely violent, and

mostly inspired by disdain and contempt rather than by the explosive mixture of hate, fear, and envy that fueled the anti-Semitism of Christendom.[25]

Modern views

"European-style" anti-Semitism among Muslims arose out of various political developments, most particularly out of the Jewish resettlement in Palestine, the establishment of the State of Israel in 1948, and the series of Arab–Israeli wars that followed. From a political perspective the first development was the rise to world domination of the European empires during the nineteenth and early twentieth centuries. Along with European ideas, such as liberalism, constitutionalism, and socialism that were conveyed to the Arab world came anti-Semitism.[26] At the same time, Muslim and other minorities were weakened by the breakdown and collapse of the old political structures and the loyalties and traditions associated with them. New patriotic and nationalist loyalties made it more difficult to tolerate any kind of diversity. Because it is easier to be tolerant from a position of strength than it is from a position of weakness, Muslims began to mete out far harsher treatment to religious, ethnic, and even ideological minorities.[27]

From a Muslim religious perspective the return of Jews to sovereignty in Israel, in the midst of the Islamic world, runs against the grain of the understanding of Jews as *dhimmi*. The most potent reason for the development of European-style anti-Semitism in the Muslim world, therefore, was the Jewish return to Israel. Starting out as marginal to the main Arab struggle, anti-Semitism started to become dominant after the 1956 Sinai War and was accelerated by the Six Day War of 1967 – both of which were swift and overwhelming Israeli victories.[28] While the war of 1948–9 was a hard-fought struggle that lasted many months and in which Israel won the prize of survival at high cost, these later defeats presented a terrible problem of explanation for the vanquished Arabs, particularly in that they had been thwarted by a people traditionally perceived as cowardly and lacking in all the military virtues. As the local media put it: "The Jew in his very soul and character has not the qualities of a man who bears arms. He is not naturally prepared to sacrifice for anything, not even for his son or wife . . . "[29] Imposed by "cowards," these more recent humiliating defeats demanded recourse to an explanation that was beyond the normal processes of rational thought and that invoked demonic, conspiratorial powers. Such an explanation had already been offered in Christendom and had gained wide currency, even in the Arab world. Islamic anti-Semitism thus departed from its traditional historic manifestation and demonized the Jew, taking as its model Christian-inspired documents, such as the *Protocols of the Elders of Zion.*

Anti-Semitism was now generally disguised as anti-Zionism, which postulated a dangerous, shadowy, international conspiracy with its Jewish center in the Middle East. While the geographic focus has changed, the content of the mythology remains familiar. In the view of Robert Wistrich, there is a continuity between Nazi anti-Semitism and current militant anti-Zionism. Hitler unleashed an attack on the Jews that has not yet been fully spent, in that it has been resuscitated by Arab nationalism.[30] The problem today lies not so much in the resurfacing of anti-Semitism, but in the reintroduction of anti-Semitism as a legitimate ideological tool, and its acceptance as part of "respectable" public discourse.[31]

Anti-Zionism and Anti-Semitism

It is a vexing question whether anti-Zionism is a new form of anti-Semitism, indeed, whether it is anti-Semitism at all. One has to distinguish between opposition to Israeli policy as a legitimate political criticism, and ideological anti-Zionism which persistently denies any legitimacy to a Jewish homeland in the Middle East. There is so much malevolence and sheer malice in the attack on Zionism that it is hard to see it as part of legitimate political opposition to a political movement. The word Zionist, as Dan Segre points out, has acquired an autonomous derogatory meaning of its own that transcends both time and space and is applied as an epithet to denote total evil. The term has, in the process, lost all rational connotation in relation to history or geography, and Zionists have ceased to be seen as human beings. Zionism is thus perceived not merely as a bad political phenomenon but as a cancerous growth. Thus, "the ongoing state of war with the Arabs does not imply – as it does for other states – a situation of military occupation so much as one of automatic colonial racism."[32] Unremitting hostility against the State of Israel in much of the Arab world and the Jewish involvement in the Middle East crisis serve merely to propel anti-Zionism but not to explain totally its nature.

So virulent is the denunciation of Zionism that some scholars believe that it is not merely an extension of anti-Semitism but that the roots lie, in part, elsewhere. They assert that there are other complex causative factors. Although anti-Semitism and anti-Zionism have common roots, anti-Zionism possesses a logic of its own. It can, according to Segre, be attributed in large part to deep-seated psychological fears that derive their logic from a need to exorcise threatening developments with which rationality cannot cope. One of these is the strength of separate Jewish identity, not only in the past but now also in the context of a nation-state. The dispersion of Jews was historically seen as divinely sanctioned. The growth of rationalism, historical criticism, and secularism, however, overturned this shielding interpretation. The Gentile world has always seen Jewish survival as an enigma. With the establishment of the

Jewish State in Israel, this enigma has now been transferred from the individual to the political plane and is exacerbated by the peculiar nature of Israeli nationalism. There is a widespread inability to come to terms with Israel as a transnational state – one whose affiliates or centers of identification lie outside of it.[33] This results in deep fears about a kind of "pan-Judaism" with its focus in Israel, and is one of the dynamics underlying the accusation that Zionism is racism, an accusation that continues to mitigate against the ultimate normalization of the State of Israel.

The charge that Zionism is racism, though an outrageous canard, contains, according to Nathan Glazer, a modicum of meaning. This meaning is based on the special relationship of Israel to the Jewish people. Because it was established under the ideology of Zionism as a home for the Jewish people, Israel must be a home for *all* the Jewish people. However, because of its internal politics – and possibly other considerations – Israel must accept the orthodox Jewish religious definition of who is a Jew. This results in a questioning of the Jewish status, for example, of the Falashas who were airlifted to Israel. The issue is, therefore, not one of racism, but results from this chain of religious, historical, and political circumstances. Zionism, an overwhelmingly *secular* movement for the *national* liberation of Jews, who are defined by *religious* criteria, opens itself to attack as racist.[34] Factors such as these arouse widespread hostility, which finds support in anti-Semitism. But these factors may now, themselves, serve to support anti-Semitism. The identification of Zionism with racism opened the way for another cruel twist. Jews, previously victims of racism, were now themselves seen as racists. This exonerated the world from any sense of guilt toward the Jews for the Holocaust and from any sense of commitment to a Jewish state. It allowed the Israeli Jews to be perceived as "Nazis," while the Palestinians were now perceived as the victims or "Jews."[35]

The fact that Israel has not managed to achieve normality is another factor that underlies the development of anti-Zionism. Although the State of Israel was established in order to normalize the life of the Jewish people, it has not managed to achieve this. The reasons underlying the world's inability to perceive Israel as a state like any other are the ongoing hostility to Israel of some of its neighbors; the continuing unwillingness of these neighbors to accord Israel legitimacy, in spite of early international legal recognition of the state; and the special relationship of the state to the Jewish people.

An important conduit of anti-Zionist sentiment in Africa is Third World ideology, the dynamics of whose development has been illuminatingly traced by Rivlin and Fomerand.[36] Though disparate, they point out, Third World countries are united by certain psychological and social predispositions that have a critical bearing on their perception both of Israel and the Arabs. Having been passive subjects of the politics of others rather than active participants themselves, Third World countries have in common their recent emergence on the international scene as independent actors. Generally lacking in industrialization and crippled by social and economic underdevelopment, their common experience of political subordination and economic poverty has implanted within them and their elites bitter memories of victimization by foreign exploiters. These provide the foundation for the emergence of anti-colonialism and anti-imperialism as the dominant motifs underlying their struggle for self-determination. Characteristic of this ideology is a concern for all the oppressed peoples of the world.

Israel originally shared many major attributes of the Third World states, and, with the heterogeneity apparent in the Third World, could have been – and in fact originally desired to be – part of it. It should be noted at the outset that Israel had originally hoped to pursue a policy of nonalignment with either the United States or the Soviet Union. Long victimized and oppressed, like Third World countries, Jews had fought a war of national liberation in Palestine against a colonial regime. Like countries of the Third World, Israel had to confront problems of economic development, social mobilization, political integration, and modernization. Its inhabitants, with the exception of its Ashkenazi leadership, had come largely from the Third World. These oriental Jews, like members of the Third World, had suffered the cutting of their traditional cultural moorings under the impact of modernism.

Despite all these similarities, Israel was not accorded Third World status. Its inhabitants were not viewed as natives but as foreigners, who, as exponents of Western culture, were agents of Western imperialism. Far from Israel's struggle against Great Britain being accepted as part of the struggle of dependent peoples in Asia, it was seen as thwarting a colonial people, the Arabs of Palestine, in their own fight for independence.[37] The ideological lens of anti-colonialism and anti-imperialism directed the Third World toward a pro-Palestinian Arab and anti-Israeli position. This was reinforced by the bourgeois style of life that developed in Israel, by Israel's treatment of the Arab minority, and by Israel's collusion with Great Britain and France (the arch-imperialists) in the 1956 Suez operation. Israel's heavy dependence on the United States for military and economic aid after the Six Day War of 1967 further honed this negative image of Israel.[38]

Much of this negative perception of Israel was engendered by Arab propaganda, which was aimed at alienating Africa from Israel and was aided by the dominant presence of Islam in the Third World. As African and Asian colonies attained independence, Islam experienced increased solidarity, which was reinforced by meetings of the Islamic elite at world Islamic meetings. Exchange of diplomatic representation, meeting at the United Nations, and general contact with the Islamic world, brought about through the *hajj* and the media, determined the preeminent place of Islam in the world view of much of the Third World and influenced it toward an anti-Israeli and pro-Arab stance.

The development of anti-Zionist attitudes in the Third World was facilitated by lack of contact with Jews and an unfamiliarity with their historical travail. This helped to impede sympathy for the return of Jews to Palestine and the establishment of the State of Israel. People of the Third World, who do not have large Jewish communities in their midst, do not share any guilt that the Western world may have for the Holocaust. They cannot, therefore, be expected to react as Westerners did. Major anti-Semitic events, including the Holocaust, were not part of their close experience. Given all these factors, it took a surprisingly long time for the Third World to become totally alienated from Israel.

In fact, there were, originally, and for over a decade, positive attitudes to Israel. Sharing with Israel the challenges of nation-building and changing the face of the land, and confident that they would not be dominated by a more powerful partner, African states turned initially to Israel for technical assistance. They had developed their own negative images of the Arabs, were grossly unfamiliar with the details of the Palestine problem, and were almost totally ignorant of the existence of a human tragedy involving the Arabs of Palestine. All these factors had provided a climate favorable to Israel in Africa.[39]

The shift in black Africa's attitude to Israel did not take place abruptly. Wanting to cultivate black support without risking the loss of continental unity, the Arabs' goal was to loosen the African states' ties with Israel and persuade them to accept the Palestine issue as a legitimate concern of black Africa. This strategy only gained its initial breakthrough in 1961 at the Casablanca Conference, where Israel, in addition to being viewed as siding with apartheid because of an influential Jewish population in South Africa, was condemned as "an instrument in the service of imperialism and neo-colonialism – not only in the Middle East but also in Africa and Asia." Deep concern was expressed over "depriving the Arabs of Palestine of their legitimate rights."[40] Even so, the Arab–Israeli dispute was not a matter of direct concern to black African states, and only became so in 1967. With Israel's spectacular victory in the Six Day War, black Africa could no longer avoid getting involved. Nor could it resist Egyptian pressure for support at Organization for African Unity meetings. The Six Day War saw the beginning of a change in the perceptual maps of Third World leaders. No longer perceived as a biblical David fighting against impossible odds, the Jewish state was now seen as a militarily invincible power. This view emerged just as the Third World was being transformed into a cohesive coalition of the underdog and underprivileged peoples of the world, and was fueled by the growing frustration at the Third World coalition's inability to bridge the gap with the rich, industrialized world. This led to an anti-imperialism and anti-colonialism directed primarily against the United States and its allies, most importantly, Israel.[41]

Israel's friendly relations with white Southern Africa at a time when the African community was mobilizing world opinion against the fascist and colonialist regimes of South Africa, Rhodesia, and Portugal simply added to its dereliction [42] There was also heightened suspicion of Israel because of its closeness to the United States, for whom disillusionment had set in among African leaders. With the 1973 occupation by Israel of a portion of Egyptian territory on the West Bank of the Suez Canal, the Arab–Israeli conflict was propelled from a purely regional problem to an African one. Because it was a "threat to African soil," it became an issue affecting the entire African continent.[43] By 1973, the estrangement reached its nadir with seventeen African countries breaking relations with Israel. Israel was now seen to exhibit close parallels with the hated South Africa. Both were

viewed as nations of alien settlers, oppressing indigenous populations and serving as outposts of imperialist ventures against the Africans.[44] These perceptions were exacerbated by economic realities, as could be discerned in the 1974 statement of President Senghor of Senegal: "The Arabs have the numbers, space and oil. In the Third World, they outweigh Israel."[45]

An essential part of all these developments is the Middle East conflict, which is just one part of the anti-Zionist picture. Its outcome will have an effect on the development of anti-Semitism. Future prospects with regard to Muslim–Jewish relations are inextricably tied with peace in the Middle East. Bernard Lewis maintains that "for Christian anti-Semites, the Palestine problem is a pretext and an outlet for their hatred; for Muslim anti-Semites, it is the cause. Perhaps if that cause is removed or significantly diminished, the hostility too may wane, not disappear, but at least return to the previous level of prejudice."[46] There is an awesome choice that confronts Jews, Arabs, and the world at the present day. This is the willingness for Israel and the Palestinians to enter into genuine dialogue and the preparedness by Israel to respond appropriately. If there is no solution or alleviation, Lewis avers, and the conflict drags on, there is no escape from an unending downward spiral of mutual hate, which will embitter the lives of Arabs and Jews alike. Any optimism concerning Arab–Jewish relations, however, has to be tempered by the possibility that the virus of a demonizing anti-Semitism may already have "entered into the bloodstream of Islam to poison it for generations to come as Christendom was poisoned for generations past. If so, Arab and Jewish hopes will be lost in the miasma of bigotry." [47]

Conclusion

This chapter has examined the ways in which two proselytizing religions – Christianity and Islam – negatively view

Jews. The relationship among Judaism, Christianity, and Islam is hostile precisely because the three religions share a common tradition. The anti-Semitic stereotype, which demonizes Jews and attributes to them cosmic powers for evil, finds its most potent origin in the mythic structure of Christianity as it relates to Jews. Though present in the ancient world, anti-Judaism was given a powerful new impetus by Christianity's central myth, the drama of the crucifixion, and the role that was assigned to the Jews therein. The Jews became the embodiment of evil, the alien "other," in Christian Europe. Although modern anti-Semitism has centered on other foci, such as race, the fact that its roots are religious and, hence, are located within an area of ultimate concern, accounts for its irrationality, depth, and pervasiveness.

The relationship between Judaism and traditional Islam is intrinsically far less problematic. Yet Muslim countries are today the only countries in the world in which Nazi-style anti-Semitism is officially endorsed and propagated. Traditionally, Judaism was a tolerated religion and Jews a minority among several others in Muslim lands. The notion of the *dhimmi* – a minority alternatively protected and humiliated – laid the basis for religious pluralism in Muslim society. While there was prejudice against Jews, it was inspired by disdain and contempt rather than by the explosive mixture of hate, fear, and envy that characterized the anti-Semitism of Christendom. Demonization of the Jews was not automatic in that traditional Islam lacks a deicide myth. This was, however, to undergo changes.

The active propagation of anti-Semitism does not occur in a vacuum. While continually present in its "genteel" form, the practical expression of anti-Semitism requires a disruption of political, economic, and social conditions. Accordingly, European-style anti-Semitism among Muslims arose primarily out of political developments, the most decisive of which was the return of the Jews to their home-land in Israel in 1948 and the Arab–Israeli wars that followed. This was especially true of those – such as the Six Day War of 1967 in which a humiliating defeat was imposed on the Arabs by a people hitherto perceived as powerless and "cowardly." Not only did a Jewish homeland in the Middle East fly in the face of the Muslim idea of the Jews as *dhimmi*,[48] but the humiliating defeats required an explanation inaccessible to ordinary logic. This was supplied by a recourse to the antisemitic stereotype that had developed in Christendom. With the rise to world domination of the European empires of the nineteenth century, and the attendant spread of European ideas into the Muslim world, came anti-Semitism. Christendom's anti-Semitic stereotype was ready for the taking. Presenting the Jews as global conspirators, it supplied an answer to such inexplicable occurrences.

Anti-Zionism has become a primary vehicle through which anti-Semitism is expressed in the Muslim world. It is sometimes indistinguishable from anti-Semitism. This chapter suggests that while anti-Zionism is sometimes identified as anti-Semitism or seen as an extension of it, it has its own complex causative dynamics. Employed in response to irrational, deep-seated fears, it could, of course, only find an object after 1948. A prominent factor in the spread of anti-Zionism is Third World ideology. This has had the effect of extending the antipathy against Jews and Zionism beyond the confines of inter-religious rivalry. But, in the case of Africa, it is also associated with the spread of Islam and an attempt to alienate African countries from Israel.

It is paradoxical that while anti-Semitism derives its pervasiveness and depth from interreligious rivalry, the religions themselves exercise some control through the moral restraints that inhere in them. Religions hold safeguards against wholesale slaughter of others. It is when the antisemitic stereotype is adopted into ideologies such as Nazism and the distorted religious ideas of Islamism (as contrasted with Islam), that all restraint is abandoned. Hitler, while mocking Christianity, took it seriously in the one aspect that demonized the Jews. In the absence of Christian moral restraints he enacted a program of mass destruction in which Jews were treated as subhuman and were therefore stripped of the most basic of human rights. In the new terrorist warfare promoted by fundamentalist Islam, the perceived enemy is not only America but Jews. They are also a stated target.[49] The random activity of terrorists infringes human rights on another level.

The aim of proselytization is positive, but there are always negative implications. One is the denigration of the target individual's previous religion. This is particularly so with regard to indigenous religions. The other, at least in the case of Christianity and Islam, is the spreading of an anti-Jewish stereotype. Anti-Semitism, even if only at the level of ill-feeling, will never disappear. In the modern world Jews have their greatest opportunity and freedom in democratic societies, which place controls on human rights abuses. In the face of anti-American (and hence anti-Jewish) terrorism, these may, however, prove to be ineffectual

Notes

1 The term *anti-Semitism* was coined in German in 1879 by Wilhelm Mart, a professed anti-Semite. In English, the word is often written with a hyphen, which is an absurd construction in that there is no such thing as "-Semitism" to which it might be opposed. In German and Hebrew the term has no hyphen, and it is therefore more accurate to write the English word without a hyphen (see Y. Bauer, "In Search of a Definition of Anti-Semitism," in *Approaches to Anti-Semitism*, ed. M. Brown (Jerusalem, 1994), 10.

2 R. Wistrich, "The Anti-Zionist Masquerade," *Midstream* (August/September 1983): 8–18.

3 R. L. Rubenstein, *After Auschwitz* (Indianapolis, 1966), 19.

4 Y. Bauer, *The Jewish Emergence from Powerlessness* (Toronto, 1979), 41.

5 See, e.g., Emil Fackenheim, *The Jewish Return into History Reflections in the Age of Auschwitz and a New Jerusalem* (New York, 1978).

6 D. Bergen (ed.), *History and Hate: The Dimensions of Anti-Semitism* (Philadelphia, 1986), 5.

7 Rosemary Radford Ruethen "Anti-Semitism and Christian Theology," in *Auschwitz: Beginning of a New Era*, ed. E. Fleischner (New York, 1977), 81.

8 When Herzl met Pope Pius X in 1904, he was received with theological hostility, because the Holy See found it difficult to conceive of the return of the Jews to Palestine or to accept that, if such an event were to take place, it would be carried out by secular Jews. See D. V Segre, "Is Anti-Zionism a New Form of Anti-Semitism?" in *Anti-Semitism in the Contemporary World*, ed. M. Curbs (Boulder, CO, 1986), 153n.

9 G. Steiner, "Jewish Values in the Post-Holocaust Future," *Judaism* 16, no. 3 (Summer 1967): 276–81.

10 F. H. Littell, *The Crucifixion of the Jews* (Macon, GA: Mercer University Press, 1986).

11 Rubenstein, *After Auschwitz*, 56.

12 *The Condition of Jewish Belief. A Symposium Compiled by the Editors of Commentary Magazine* (New York, 1966), 90.

13 Rubenstein, *After Auschwitz*, 186.

14 There is, for example, a haunting scene in Claude Lanzmann's film of the Holocaust, "Shoah," in which a group of Poles claims to have witnessed a rabbi interpreting the Jewish fate during the Holocaust as a "deserved" punishment for the crime of deicide.

15 Cited by A. L. Eckhardt, "The Holocaust, the Church Struggle, and Some Christian Reflections," in *Faith and Freedom: A Tribute to Franklin H. Littel*, ed. R. Libowitz (New York, 1987), 33.

16 E. L. Fackenheim, "Philosophical Reflections on Claude Lanzmann's 'Shoah,'" in Libowitz, *Faith and Freedom*, 13.

17 H. Maccoby, "Theologian of the Holocaust," *Commentary* 74, no. 6 (December 1982).

18 C. Huchet-Bishop, "Response to John Pawlikowski," in Fleischner, *Auschwitz*, 183.

19 *Ibid.*, 180.

20 Bernard Lewis, "Anti-Semitism in the Arab and Islamic World," in *Present-Day Anti-Semitism*, ed. Y. Bauer (Jerusalem, 1988), 57.

21 J. S. Gerber, "Anti-Semitism in the Muslim World," in Berger, *History and Hate*, 73–93.

22 *Ibid.*, 80.

23 *Ibid.*

24 Lewis, "Anti-Semitism," 60.

25 *Ibid.*, 61.

26 Awareness of the Dreyfus trial in France, for example, resulted in the first Arabic translations of specifically antisemitic books. These, however, had limited influence at the time.

27 Lewis, "Anti-Semitism," 62.

28 *Ibid.*, 63.

29 *Ibid.*, 65.

30 See R. Wistrich, *Hitler's Apocalypse: Jews and the Nazi Ideology* (London, 1985).

31 Lewis, "Anti-Semitism," 70.

32 Segre, "Anti-Zionism," 145–54.

33 *Ibid.*

34 N. Glazer, "Anti-Zionism – A Global Phenomenon," in Curtis, *Anti-Semitism*, 155–63.

35 I. Rabinovitch, "Anti-Semitism in the Muslim and Arab World," in Bauer, *Present-Day Anti-Semitism*, 265.

36 B. Rivlin and J. Fomerand, "Changing Third World Perspectives and Policies towards Israel," in *Israel and the Third World*, ed. M. Curbs and S. A. Gitelson (New Brunswick, NJ, 1976), 325–60.

37 *Ibid.*

38 *Ibid.*, 328.

39 *Ibid.*, 339.

40 *Ibid.*, 342.

41 *Ibid.*, 348.

42 *Ibid.*, 346.

43 *Ibid.*, 347.

44 *Ibid.*

45 *Ibid.*

46 Lewis, "Anti-Semitism," 65.

47 *Ibid.*

48 It should be noted that the Christian theology of the Jews as a reprobate people was also disturbed by this decisive historic event.

49 Osama bin Laden, the man alleged to have been behind the bombings of the American embassies in Kenya and Tanzania, is reported to have invited "all Muslims to join his jihad against the Americans and against the Jews" (*The Sunday Independent*, August 23, 1998), 4.

5

Theology and Human Rights

Charles Villa-Vincencio

◆ Theology and human rights ◆ Catholicism and human rights ◆

◆ Protestant traditions of human rights ◆

Political definitions and formulae often give rise to different theories. Jean Bodin's understanding of "political authority" in his *Les Six Livres De La Republique* (1577), was this kind of study. He defined a sovereign as someone capable of rising above the conflicting interests of society, and law as "nothing else than the command of the sovereign."[1] The later definition gave rise to the tradition of legal positivism. The debate which followed in the wake of this tradition, in turn, resulted in the quest for a set of fundamental values; a moral understanding of the rule of law, able to protect the general welfare of all people, without capitulating to the partisan demands of any one group and worthy of being a basis for effectual rule. In what follows attention is given to the values which have come to shape the moral understanding of law, and more especially the human rights debate as a basis for law-making.

Human rights, as we understand the concept today, emerged as part of a slowly evolving process, part of an idea whose time had come. *Magna Carta* had already been signed in England in 1215. The *Petition of Rights* followed four centuries later in 1628, and after the Glorious Revolution came the *Bill of Rights* in 1689. Almost a hundred years later, in 1791, came the *Bill of Rights*

of the United States Constitution, making America the first state to be in submission to a constitution which defines human rights "as the basis and foundation of government." It was preceded in 1789 by the French *Declaration of the Rights of Man and Citizen.*

Written within the epoch of the social establishment of the bourgeoisie, the major concern of the American and French constitution (which made liberal rights theory a part of established modern politics) was the defence of the interests of citizens as free individuals, free producers and free proprietors.[2] This resulted, almost from the time when they were written, in the twin concerns of these documents – socio-economic freedom and political equality on the one hand, and individual rights, due process of law and the right to own private property on the other – being interpreted with a bias in favour of individual rights. Subsequent centuries saw the emphasis on free choice and the protection of the individual from interference by the state and other people become the unquestioned dominant concern of liberal western political theory and praxis.

The 1918 Russian Revolution sought to correct this imbalance in a constitution which committed the Russian Socialist

Federated Congress of Republics "in struggle to destroy every, exploitation of man by man, every class division of society, unmercifully to crush the exploiters . . ." severing itself from the tradition of middle-class human rights which had become a part of the political pursuits of the West.[3] A *different* set of human rights was affirmed – not the rights of the merchant class revolting against the divine right of kings, but the rights of workers against those who owned the industries and exploited the poor.

Then came the Nazi and Fascist terror of the 1930s and again the need became obvious to protect the rights of individuals. On 24 October 1945 the United Nations Charter was established, with a Preamble giving expression to the determination of the new body to 'save succeeding genera-tions from the scourge of war, which twice in our lifetime has brought untold sorrow to mankind," to "reaffirm faith in funda-mental human rights, in the dignity and worth of the human person, in the equal rights of men and women," and "to promote social progress and better stan-dards of life in larger freedom." One of four main goals of the United Nations, as stated in Article I.I is to foster international coop-eration in "promoting and encouraging respect for human rights and for funda-mental freedoms for all without distinction of race, sex, language or religion." Three years later, on 10 December 1948, the *Universal Declaration of Human Rights* was adopted by the General Assembly of the United Nations. Forty-eight of the 56 member states of the United Nations voted in favour of the adoption of the Declaration, while 8 states abstained from voting. Subsequently 6 of the abstaining states have adopted the Declaration as well as over 100 of the states which became members of the United Nations after 1948. It took until 1966 before the *International Covenant on Economic, Social and Cultural Rights* and the *International Covenant on Civil and Political Rights* were adopted, and they were not ratified until 1976. They

then became legally binding on the states that voted for ratification.[4]

Despite the tardiness in making the Declaration a viable and binding means of protecting international human rights, Lourens Ackermann (the first occupant of a chair in human rights in South Africa) argues that "if anything, it (the Declaration) has achieved greater status because of the delays . . ." In the process people came to "feel a deep need for a universal human rights instrument to whose terms they can hold governments and societies to account." "The Declaration," he continues, "has become a standard by which to test state constitutions, a weapon in inter-national diplomacy, and a set of principles to which the UN organs refer when confronted by human rights issues." As such, he argues, the Declaration has become a source of "customary international law, very much like the customary domestic law, or 'common law' of a country."[5]

A number of additional international and regional covenants and treaties have, of course, followed in the wake of the *Universal Declaration of Human Rights* and the two International Covenents.[6] Each of these, like the *Universal Declaration of Human Rights* itself, have, to varying degrees stressed the importance of both individual and political rights on the one hand, and socio-economic rights on the other; recognising that the two different categories or generations of rights need to be protected in different ways. This has given rise to a growing international recog-nition of the need for the two generations (and more recently a third generation of developmental and ecological rights) to form a comprehensive whole.

The need for harmony between indi-vidual and political freedoms (the freedom of speech, religion, assembly and dissent) and socio-economic well-being (the right to work, housing, health-care and educa-tion) at the same time continues to tear at the heart of the human rights struggle. In Eastern Europe, for example, it could be argued that one set of human rights have recently been traded for another. People have demanded the individual rights denied to them by undemocratic socialist dictatorships, while at the same time being thrust into social and economic anxiety as the cost of living spirals and unemployment escalates. Poland, for example, is "caught in the vice of the International Monetary Fund and World Bank, which is creating unemployment, an inflation rate of 1,000 per cent and a foreign debt that has surpassed 45 billion US dollars."[7]

The need for an inclusive understanding of human rights is further accentuated by the bitter class distinctions and conflicts which characterise western society. This is a quest which remains unfulfilled despite the euphoria promoted in some quarters of capitalism concerning the "failure of socialism" in Eastern Europe. The question posed in what follows is *whether theology has a contribution to make toward transcending the historic contradiction between individual and socio-economic rights.* Does it provide a theoretical framework within which to move beyond the impasse of secular debate?

Why Theology?

Bodin's understanding of political sovereignty came in the wake of a succession of religious wars in sixteenth-century France. He saw the need to locate law-making above religious controversy. Liberal political thought, following Locke and others, has since turned this insight into the secular political tradition which characterises the western debate on politics and human rights. This important gain, earned in the wake of centuries of religious-motivated human suffering, has persuaded Leo Strauss, as a political philosopher, to argue that the quest for human rights "should be kept independent of theology and its controversies."[8] "A pluralistic society that tries to make its unifying political and moral principles religious in any nontrivial

sense is in for trouble," argues Frederick Olafson in similar fashion.[9] Some Christians have, in turn, rejected talk of the theology of human rights for very different reasons. Seeing it as a humanistic development, bordering on personal arrogance and pride, they argue that the image of God has been destroyed within humanity, leaving humankind irremediably sinful, deserving of no recognition and worthy of no intrinsic rights.

This is a theological argument that has on occasions been used politically to defend the most flagrant violations of human rights. J. M. Potgieter, professor of private law at the University of South Africa, employs the argument as a basis for rejecting all proposals for a Bill of Rights in South Africa intended to defend and promote the rights of all its citizens.[10] Insisting that the image of God can only be restored through conversion to Christ, he regards the masses as having no essential rights. Linked to an ideology of white (Afrikaner) Christian nationalism in South Africa, this of course, has the most serious moral and political implications. Similar arguments were used during the crusades to justify the slaughter of human beings seen as "infidels," less than fully human and worthy of extermination because they refused to submit themselves to the ideology of the medieval church. Potgieter's argument is but a small step from the reactionary kind of apartheid ideology which has traditionally located rights and privileges exclusively in the hands of whites as the carriers of the gospel and "civilised values," extendable by derivation only to those blacks who conform to white ("Christian") understandings of civilisation and government. The argument further lends itself to amoral and uncompromising notions of "law and order." Right-wing Christians have, for example, taken this argument to the point of absurdity in citing Potgieter's argument as a basis for attacking church leaders and theologians who have supported the call for a Bill of Rights in South Africa. Within the context of indiscriminate violations of the most basic human rights by the South African state, a rightwing Christian group has argued: "An honest person needs no special 'rights' in order to associate, disassociate, assemble, read, speak, perform or travel." "The rights [demanded by human rights activists] . . . for the arrested, accused and convicted," the statement continued, "seem to be aimed primarily at limiting the power of the police."[11]

So why theology? Would it not be better for theologians to learn the bitter lessons of history and leave politics to the politicians and human rights to those secular, "value-free" disciplines which best equip society to rise above what are too often the sectarian interests of religious and secular ideologues? To the extent theology is ideologically captive to one or another political agenda, the answer is an unqualified "yes." To the extent that it provides a basis for ideological critique, while contributing to a better understanding of humanity, as a basis for the promotion of such rights that sustain human dignity, a theological silence in the face of human rights violations can only be construed as morally repugnant and socially irresponsible.

The primary task of theology is not, however, to "reinvent the wheel," in reworking the list of human rights already defined and defended by countless human rights agencies around the world. There is consensus within the major Christian traditions that the rights identified in most human rights declarations are worthy of theological support, while emphasising the need for support to be given to socioeconomic (Second Generation) as well as developmental and ecological (Third Generation) human rights alongside more generally accepted First Generation rights. As such the consensus reflects a broad global perspective on human rights, incorporating the liberal values of western bloc countries and social values of eastern bloc countries as well as First and Third World perspectives. This is best seen in the "Common Ground on Human Rights" which emerged as part of the World Council of Churches' study on human rights at the St Polten, Austria, conference in October 1974.[12] With participation in the study project by representatives of socialist and Third World countries, the findings of the study reflect a priority concern for those whose rights were at the time seen to be most under threat in the world as a whole. The proposed list of human rights begins with the right to life. Then comes the right to cultural identity, followed by democracy, the right to dissent, personal dignity and freedom of religion.[13]

(a) There is a basic human right to life – inclusive of the entire question of survival, of the threats and violations resulting from unjust economic, social and political systems, and the equality of life.

(b) There is a right to enjoy and to maintain cultural identity.

(c) There is a right to participate in the decision-making process within the community – which comprises the entire issue of effective democracy.

(d) There is a right to dissent – which prevents a community or a system from hardening into authoritarian immobility.

(e) There is a right to personal dignity – which implies, for example, the condemnation of all torture and of prolonged confinement without trial.

(f) There is a right freely to choose a faith and a religion – which encompasses the freedom, either alone or in community with others, in public or in private, to proclaim one's faith or one's religion by the means of teaching, practice, worship and ritual.[14]

The listing of rights by the Roman Catholic *Magisterium* provides a similar, although slightly varied emphasis, stating:

(a) That all men are equal in nobility, dignity and nature, without any distinction of race, sex or religion.

(b) That everyone therefore has the same fundamental rights and duties.

(c) That the rights of the human person are inviolable, inalienable and universal.

(d) That everyone has a right to existence, to bodily integrity and well being, to everything necessary to maintain a decent standard of living, such as food, clothing and shelter, means of subsistence and any other services indispensable to social security.

(e) That everyone has a right to a good reputation and respect, to protection of privacy and to an honest representation.

(f) That everyone has a right to act in accordance with the right norms of his own conscience and to investigate the truth freely following the ways and means proper to man. This may in certain circumstances involve the right of dissent for reasons of conscience from some rules of society.

(g) Freely and to be correctly informed about public events.

(h) That everyone has the right to worship God according to the right norm of his conscience, to practise his religion both in private and public, and to enjoy religious liberty.

(i) That the person's fundamental right is to have all his rights safeguarded by law; namely, to a protection that is impartial, inspired by the true norm of justice, and at the same time effective. This means that all are equal before the law and any judicial procedure should give the accused the right to know his accusers and also the right to a proper defence.

(j) Finally, the *Magisterium* asserts that fundamental human rights are inseparably interconnected in the very person who is their subject with just as many respective duties; and that rights as well as duties find their source, their sustenance and their inviolability in the Natural Law which grants or enjoins them.[15]

There is general consensus among Christian churches on the rights affirmed in the WCC and the Roman Catholic declarations, although debate on the prioritising of rights necessarily continues. Some might even argue an ecumenical study on human rights would require both the St Polten and the Vatican priorities to be reshuffled. It would probably also be necessary to include an affirmative action clause concerning the participation of black people and/or women in most, if not all, nations on earth. The continuing debate that has not changed is the theological consensus on an *inclusive* perception of rights. The essential theological task is, however, at a deeper level. Jan Milic Lochman makes this point in arguing that, if the church is to make a serious contribution to the human rights struggle, it involves more than fine-tuning, or even over-hauling, the existing secular human rights debate. The church, he argues, is obliged rather to engage in "a deepened theological reflection in order to work out the specifically Christian contribution to the further development of the human rights issue."[16] Heinz-Eduard Todt goes further in arguing that while the St Polten conference produced a "new classification" of rights, more useful than the "bewildering mass of codified human rights conventions" in existence, "what was offered here was *not* a theological basis."[17] The plural character of contemporary society suggests that the primary task of the church is perhaps not so much to promote the "specifically Christian" (Lochman) contribution to human rights as much as to share with others in establishing a popular cultural, spiritual and theoretical basis which defines and promotes human rights. Briefly stated, from a theological perspective, human rights have to do with the realisation that all people are created in the image of God, enjoying equal human worth. In order to realise and fulfil their destiny as the bearers of God's image, the fundamental rights of all people are to be fully claimed and concretely appropriated, recognising that without certain basic rights (as outlined by the WCC and the Vatican) people are not able to realise their full God-given potential. To deny these rights to people is to oppose the work and purpose of God in the world. As such it is a sinful act requiring repentance and reparation. Popular ecclesial culture does not view the violation of human rights in this serious manner. The issue does not enjoy the kind of prominence nor the urgency that many other issues enjoy in the liturgy, teaching and witness of the Christian Church.

The church's primary task is clearly to facilitate *Christians* to promote and appropriate the values of a human rights culture. It is understandable (and correct) therefore that it is essentially the identifying of a Christian theological basis for human rights that has become the focus of most ecumenical and denominational human rights studies.[18] Because of the wide acceptance of the St Polten and Vatican cataloguing of human rights, the primary aim of the various ecclesial studies which have emerged in their wake has not been a listing of rights as much as the articulation of a political ethic grounded in a theological understanding of what it means to be human. In the words of Winston Ndungane:

> The doctrine of human rights is man's attempt at exercising his responsibility as God's steward on earth in that it seeks to challenge all the injustices that distort the image of God in man. It is an attempt to establish a social condition where there are harmonious and peaceful relations among the people of the world, and where people are able to realise their full potential as God created them. There is some kind of relation that exists between the notion of human rights and the Christian doctrine of man . . . [19]

The obligation of the church at the same time reaches beyond the confines of its own membership – it is to share in the promotion of a wider culture within which there is sensitivity to, and support for, human rights. It must be shown that these human rights claims are not merely theoretical "political options" or a set of moral values to which certain religious and/or moral people adhere. Indeed, until such time as it is acceptable that the pursuit and realisation of these rights are inherent to what it means to be human, the human rights agenda will never occupy its rightful place in political struggle. Addressing St Andrews University in 1934, the Rector of that university observed:

> Freedom is the most ineradicable craving of human nature. Without it peace, contentment and happiness, even manhood itself, are not possible. The declaration of Pericles in his great funeral oration holds for all time:
>
> "Happiness is Freedom, and Freedom is Courage."
>
> That is the fundamental equation of all politics and all human government, and any system which ignores it is built on sand.[20]

The Rector was General J. C. Smuts. Unable to interject this dynamic into his political vision for South Africa, he unwittingly predicted the inevitable outcome of the policy of apartheid.

Until such time as the human rights agenda is seen to be the ineradicable centre of human existence, it is likely to continue to function as no more than a rhetorical appendage to the more important political agenda of hegemony, national security and trade. It will continue to be picked up and dropped at the will and pleasure of rulers whose own "rights" (privileges) are too often realised at the cost of the fundamental rights of others. *The task of theology is help locate the human rights struggle at the centre of the debate on what it means to be human and therefore also at the centre of social and political pursuit.* It is to help invest the existing human rights agenda with a dynamic to fulfil its ultimate goals, by sharing (with other disciplines) in defining the nature and ultimate purpose of humanity.

Differently stated, unless human rights values are grounded in the cultural and political ethos of a nation and become a part of the motor that drives society, they tend to be little more than of decorative value, often used to conceal the harsh reality of human abuse and exploitation. Jeremy Bentham once referred to such moral ideal as "nonsense – nonsense on stilts." His words are sobering: "A reason for wishing that a certain right were established, is not that right – want is not supply – hunger is not bread."[21] At the risk of repetition, *the question is whether it can be shown that the pursuit of rights is inherent to what it means to be human.* If this is the case, the failure to have these rights fulfilled will necessarily result in social and political conflict. This, in turn, means that the pursuit of human rights could become the most essential and viable cultural and spiritual lever available to social reformers and ethicists in the mobilising of people for the pursuit of a more just world order.

Jürgen Moltmann poses a pertinent theological question in enquiring in what manner theology can serve this end. Its primary concern is not, he suggests, in some idealistic or abstract way simply to promote more sensitivity and awereness of human rights. It is rather a *revolutionary* task. It has to do with unleashing "the dangerous power of liberation," which is inherent to a theological understanding of what it means to be human, into the socio-political and economic structure of society.[22] In other words, it is the struggle for human rights that theology has its best chance to be materially grounded in the political and socio-economic struggle for a world that conforms more closely to the demands of the gospel.

A theology of human rights is an inherent part of theological anthropology. It gives expression to an understanding of humanity which transcends both the individualistic bias of the dominant forms of western liberalism and the unqualified collectivism of rigid Marxist notions of humanity. Neither have provided a satisfactory sense of what it means to be a person with inherent personal dignity realisable in relationship and community with other people. In the words of Max Stackhouse, the secular alternatives "leave us relying only on the *fluxus quo*" – with people torn between individual desire and social responsibility.[23]

The *inclusive* notion of human rights, inherent to a theological understanding of humanity, constitutes an important theological contribution to the human rights debate. Theology is at the same time obliged to take the criticism, coming from Iredell Jenkins and others, seriously. His concern is essentially that attempts to expand human rights to cover ever greater areas of social and economic needs ultimately undercut the legitimacy of a more limited list of political or First Generation rights which can and need to be immediately fufilled. The critique, of course, echoes the concern of Anthony Matthews that the broadening of the notion of the rule of law to include all social and political concerns ultimately transforms it into less than a minimum anterior principle against which to test all political ideologies, allowing it to become synonymous with a particular political agenda.[24] Jenkins writes:

> There is so much unnecessary suffering and wanton abuse and neglect of men in need that a doctrine that cries out against these conditions and demands their correction merits both our thanks and our attention . . . But there is also much in this doctrine [of human rights] that seems unsound and imbalanced, arousing doubts and reservations in the minds of many . . . The doctrine seems altogether devoid of internal restraints and controls. It is a dangerous doctrine because it advances no criteria, whether theoretical, empirical or practical, for determining its reach. It grounds rights in humanity, and then leaves the notion undefined, so that the content of rights is indefinite and indeterminate.[25]

The theology of human rights, which grounds rights in an understanding of what it means to be human, is essentially about contributing to the kind of theoretical control for which Jenkins asks. Correctly interpreted it circumvents ideological captivity, by providing an understanding of humanity which functions as a standard against which to measure all ideological systems. At the same time it lifts human rights claims above the level of mere rhetoric by focussing on praxis.[26] Theology is about ultimate meanings and the significance of these ultimates for daily living. As applied to human rights this has to do with a theological understanding of what constitutes the dignity and meaning of life, what it means to be truly human, and what essential rights are needed to protect this humanity.

Clearly theological answers to these questions will be "ideologically" or "contextually" coloured in the same way as answers that emerge from any other discipline. Theological and secular human rights declarations which have emerged from western liberal democracies are clearly different to those that have come out of socialist situations, and First World human rights priorities usually differ from those that come out of Third World situations. There is at the same time remarkable consensus regarding the very foundation of human rights, which can be reduced to the freedom and well being of people. It is this that ultimately places the human rights agenda above the desires of some to justify particular ideologies and/or legitimate the practices of their own nations.

The Ecumenical Debate

As a way of developing the theoretical basis asked for, and the communally based understanding of humanity sought after in the last chapter, attention is given to some of the important contemporary theological studies on human rights in the Roman Catholic and Protestant traditions.

Roman Catholic rights theory

Post-Vatican II Roman Catholic doctrine on rights is best characterised in a statement made by John XXIII in 1961. He describes the modern tradition of the church as "dominated by one basic theme – an unshakable affirmation and vigorous defense of the dignity and rights of the human person."[27]

This emphasis is developed in *The Pastoral Constitution on the Church in the Modern World (Gaudium et Spes)* published during the last session of Vatican I in 1965, and *Message Concerning Human Rights and Reconciliation* published by the Roman Synod of Bishops in 1974. It is further elaborated in a paper prepared by the Papal Commission, *Justitia et Pax*, entitled *The Church and Human Rights*, published in 1975.

The traditional Thomistic understanding of nature and grace is seen throughout these documents. The *Justitia et Pax* paper observes: "The teaching of the *Magisterium* on fundamental human rights is based in the first place or is suggested by the inherent requirements of human nature . . . within the sphere of Natural Law." What this means is that the affirmation of the *Magisterium* "that all men are equal in nobility, dignity and nature, without distinction of race, sex or religion," together with a series of related rights ranging from food, clothing and shelter to judicial procedure and the rights of women included in the *Justitia et Pax* document are seen to be part of the order of creation made known in natural law and discernible through reason.[28] These are rights which the *Magisterium* regards, in the language of liberal natural rights theory, to be self-evident – there to be seen by any fair minded person as made known and verified in common experience.

The document then goes further. It affirms what has always been part of the Thomistic and Catholic tradition, but often neglected prior to Vatican II. This is the insistence that it is ultimately through the revelation of Christ that the basic rights of humankind are made known in a fuller and more decisive manner. Echoing *Gaudium et Spes*, we read in *The Church and Human*

Rights: "The truth is that only in the mystery of the Incarnate Word does the mystery of man take on light . . . Christ, by the revelation of the mystery of the Father and His love, fully reveals man to man himself."[29] John Paul II's words to the Pueblo Conference in 1979 underscore this emphasis, giving the kind of Christological focus to Roman Catholic doctrine which has made post-Vatican II Catholic–Protestant dialogue so much easier:

> The truth that we owe to human beings is, first and foremost, a truth about themselves . . . Thanks to the Gospel, the Church possesses the truth about the human being. It is found in an anthropology that the Church never ceases to explore more deeply and to share.[30]

Hollenbach's important survey of the development of Roman Catholic rights theory shows why particular claims or human rights (which include such basic needs as food and shelter) have come to be regarded by the *Magisterium* as indispensable for the protection of the true identity of humankind.

> Human dignity is not an abstract or ethereal reality but is realized in concrete conditions of personal, social, economic and political life. The history of the papal teaching has been a process of discovering and identifying these conditions of human dignity. These conditions are called human rights.[31]

Locating John Paul II's social teaching within this broader framework, John Langan explains why he finds himself both attracted and disconcerted by a Pope whose moral and religious teachings tend to find little support among many people whose concern it is to promote social justice. Focussing mainly on *Sollicitudo Rei Socialis* (*On Social Concern*) (1988) as a major papal social encyclical, Langan identifies the theological significance of the way in which the document approaches the fundamental

structures of society which shape and determine the quality of human life.[32] Rejecting both liberal capitalism and Marxist collectivism as "imperfect and in need of radical correction," the encyclical regards both as "subject to the structures of sin."[33] John Paul II had already spoken of the structures of sin in the 1984 Apostolic Exhortation, *Reconciliatio et Paenitentis* (*Reconciliation and Penance*).[34] He importantly refuses "to draw a comforting line between a sinful social realm of powerful institutions and a private realm of passive innocents whose lives are occasionally marred by personal vices." Responsibility for socially significant sin is located not merely before "a relatively small number of "movers and shakers" who initiate harmful practices or who derive substantial benefits from them . . . Almost all who count as citizens or (social) agents" have a responsibility to do something about it.[35]

Personal sin remains a fundamental category for John Paul II, but in *On Social Concern* the power of the structures is seen to be such that they extend "far beyond the actions and the brief lifespan of an individual." They interfere "in the process of the development of peoples" and "work against a true awareness of the universal common good." "The sum total of these negative forces," he argues, constitutes "an obstacle which is difficult to overcome."[36] The Pope's sense of social and corporate sin, which strikes at the very identity of what it means to be human, has profound human rights implications. To say the least it requires the human rights agenda to reach into the socio-economic and political sphere precisely because these structures inescapably shape the very fabric of what it means to be human.

The full implications of the Pope's insights concerning the power of the structures of sin cannot be fully developed here. There are sentences in his encyclical which suggest that social structures can become so powerful that they become a demonic presence not only shaping the character of our lives, but also determining our perceptions of the common good, and therefore our understanding of good and evil. The tone and moral concern of the encyclical concerning the potentially destructive force imposed by social structures on people as moral agents is tantalising. It can provide the basis for a link with the work of writers like Trent Shroyer, Franz Hinkelammert and others who would take the insights of the encyclical a step further. For Shroyer cybernetics has become the dominant instrument shaping contemporary society, limiting the power of the individual as a moral agent and restricting social change.[37] Hinkelammert defines the interlocking synthesis of political, economic, military, scientific and technological as modernity's "ideological weapon of death." It virtually excludes the possibility of moral agency or debate.[38]

Against this background the Pope's suggested solution could, of course, be dismissed as simply inadequate. He calls for conversion and the emergence of new spiritual attitudes as a basis for transforming action. He at the same time strikes at the heart of what he regards as the controlling ideologies behind the structures of sin – "the all consuming desire for profit" and "the thirst for power." Without specifically identifying profit with the West and the ideology of state power with earlier manifestations of eastern bloc socialism, he sees these two forces as the controlling mechanisms of the modern world. More than that, "in today's world," he suggests, the two are "indissolubly united, with one or the other predominating." This sometimes results in human life being shaped by decisions that are inspired only by economics or politics. All this, he continues, results in "idolatry: of money, ideology, class and technology."[39] Here, of course, John Paul II's social teaching (ironically) finds common cause with *The Road to Damascus,* a document signed by oppressed Christians engaged in liberation struggles in South Africa, Namibia, South Korea, Philippines, El Salvador, Nicaragua and Guatemala, which argues that "the sin of idolatry lies at the heart of the imperialism of money" which motivates the exploitation and oppression of Third World countries by western imperial nations.[40] The Pope moves even further in the direction of liberation theology in calling for the empowerment of the poor and for solidarity with those who suffer as a consequence of the sinful structures which exemplify this idolatry. And solidarity, he insists, "is not a feeling of vague compassion or shallow distress at the misfortunes of so many people . . . It is a firm and persevering determination to commit oneself to the common good."[41] The empowerment of the poor, for the Pope, involves an ethic of non-violent self-assertion for the poor and an ethic of generous self-giving for the rich.[42]

The essential concern that Langan understandably has with *On Social Concern is* what he defines as "a profound tension between the affirmation of the possibilities for conversion and the recognition of the ways in which people are involved with or enmeshed in structures of sin."[43] Differently asked, is conversion and the generation of new spiritual attitudes (asked for by the pope) possible in the kind of world defined by Shroyer and Hinkelammert? Unless this fundamental tension is resolved, suggests Langan, the danger exists that the Pope's call to conversion will be "little more than the moralistic exhortations designed to convict all of us of sin and likely to produce in many a reaction of defensive or even derisive dismissal."[44] The failure of the encyclical to address all that is involved in this tension is what ultimately separates the social teaching of the Pope from liberation theology and the *Road to Damascus* document.

Having identified this tension, Langan shows the direction in which the church would be obliged to move for the implications of the Pope's demanding articulation of social living to be realised.[45]

1 The denial of the essential goods necessary for survival and for functioning as free and equal citizens would need to be

seen as an act of sinfulness, requiring the church to commit itself to a process of redistribution and reallocation of goods.

2   Rights (including, for example, the right to shelter, food and health care) that are necessary for survival with decency and for full participation in society as free and equal citizens would need to be regarded as primary. This means that the rights to private property and the rights to goods and services not included in the primary requirements would probably need to be restricted and/or renunciated in order to fulfil the primary rights.

3   A range of psychological, social and spiritual considerations facilitating the redistribution process would need to be devised.

The implication of John Paul II's teaching is to locate the struggle for human rights within the context of political economy. It recognises that in a world controlled and manipulated by dominant life-shaping social and economic structures, questions concerning full participation in life on the basis of freedom and equality involve more than the right to the freedom of expression and choice or even the right to food and shelter. They necessarily involve questions concerning which ideologies and structures allow for the possibility of these ideals being realised. The importance of *On Social Concern* for the human rights debate concerns its theological understanding of the inescapable social character of life and human behaviour. It contributes to a theoretical understanding that links liberal individual rights to a social agenda which includes socio-economic and political concerns. The Roman Catholic doctrine of rights further necessarily locates the human rights debate fully within the theological and pastoral ministry of the church. On *Social Concern* shows that the struggle against human rights violations on both the personal and the social level is synonymous with the

fight against sin. To share in the quest for human rights as the essential concrete requirements for decent human living is, in turn, an inherent part of the evangelical task of the church to proclaim personal and social conversion.

This comment on Roman Catholic rights theory, brief as it is, necessarily requires mention of John Paul's latest encyclical, *Centesimus Annus,* in which a similar argument is developed to that contained in *On Social Concern.* In responding to the collapse ofsocialism in the Soviet Union and Eastern Europe, the need is again stressed to transcend the limitations of both free-market capitalism and eastern bloc socialism. Without taking the debate significantly beyond what is already outlined, *Centesimus Annus* reiterates the essential challenge facing contemporary Roman Catholic social ethics as being the need to move beyond the existing social structures of both East and West. In so doing it unequivocally recognises the struggle for economic justice to be an inherent part of the church's evangelical calling. It also views democracy as a quest that stands central to the gospel. [46]

Protestant teaching on human rights

There is, of course, no one Protestant doctrine on human rights or anything else. There are a variety of different Protestant approaches. These differences can largely be traced back to the origins of Protestantism in the sixteenth century. In what follows attention is given primarily to two major emphases within Protestantism: Lutheran and Reformed or Calvinist theology, representative of two different theological ways of approaching social ethical questions.

The sixteenth century was, of course, a century within which the resourcefulness and responsibility of humanity had already been re-established in the events of the Renaissance. The Protestant Reformation was a different kind of celebration of the worth of humankind.[47] Turning away from any suggestion of a humanistic understanding of inherent human worth or basic rights was a celebration of salvation as a free and undeserved gift of God. It was soon realised, however, that a person liberated from the medieval preoccupation with earning his or her salvation through ecclesial restraints and obligations was a person spiritually emancipated to participate in society in a free and uninhibited manner. It had to do with learning "to live in Christ through faith and with one's neighbour through love."[48] Leaving aside the complicating question of some being chosen as recipients of God's grace and others not, those who understood themselves to be saved from forces of degradation and sin participated in life and made demands on society with a zeal that had not been witnessed in Europe for generations past.[49]

The Lutheran tradition   Martin Luther's primary concern was, of course, to reform the church, particularly regarding its audacious claims that the destiny of the human soul could be determined by the purchase of indulgences, with the wealth generated by this system being used for the benefit of the ecclesial and political elite. His objective was the rediscovery of a simple spirituality which linked the individual soul directly to God through faith, devotion and honest living. The far-reaching political implications of this gosepl soon, however, became obvious to everyone concerned. The church in Rome realised that it was striking at its established theological and political hegemony. The German princes saw it as an opportunity to wrench further power from Rome, relocating the spiritual centre of of the German people within the context of German nationalism. The poor in Germany and elsewhere, in turn, saw spiritual freedom to carry within it a host of different socio-economic and political rights, to which they laid claim through a series of peasants' revolts.

The outcome was that, within a decade

of Luther having proclaimed his message of justification by faith alone, he found himself drawn essentially onto the side of the princes. Like Augustine before him, Luther regarded history as, at best, a place of tentative peace to be endured while awaiting the dawn of God's kingdom. He believed there was a natural hierarchy in society, and that the German princes were the legitimate rulers equipped "to patch and darn as best we can while we live, punish the abuses and lay bandages and poultices over the sores."[50] Required to rely more and more on the supportive and benign Frederick the Wise and his immediate successors in Saxony, he was content to leave the direct political ordering of society to them. He theologically opposed the peasants and plebeian priests who promoted the cause of rebellion in the name of a God given freedom, and in similar fashion he opposed those within the Anabaptist movement who renounced involvement in the political realm. The task of the Christian, Luther taught, was to live in obedience to his or her conscience as informed by the Word of God, giving obedience to those who rule, except where their commands contradicted the Word of God. In brief, Luther's two kingdom doctrine stood at the heart of all that he had to say on human relations and social ethics. The task of the church, in the words of the *Augsburg Confession* (written by Melanchthon in consultation with Luther) "was to preach the Gospel and administer the sacraments," while "temporal authority is concerned with matters altogether different from the Gospel."[51]

This doctrine has been interpreted in different ways by separate Lutheran theologians, as it tended to be employed in different ways by Luther himself.[52] A balanced reading of the doctrine suggests that the " spiritual kingdom" (which is the concern of the church) and the "temporal kingdom" (which is the concern of civil authorities) are both manifestations of the "kingdom of Christ" over against the "kingdom of the devil." It is the understanding of the two kingdom doctrine which explains Luther's willingness to be politically involved, at least to the extent of counselling and criticising the princes, while persuading his followers to become involved in politics. For him there was no blueprint in scripture or special insight among Christians which provided a specifically "Christian" answer to the complexities of political reality. The Christian, renewed by the spirit of God, he believed, was nevertheless better equipped to deal with these problems than the person unexposed to the redeeming power of God. He never, however, tired of proclaiming: *simul justus el peccator* – those who are justified are at the same time still sinners. This, he thought, was what made politics such a messy business! Moltmann's summary statement on the two kingdom doctrine is worthy of special attention:

> Luther's two kingdoms doctrine is in truth a critical-polemical separation between God and Caesar. It permits neither a Caesaro-papalism nor a clerical theocracy. It intended to teach that the world and politics may not be deified, nor may they be religiously administered. One should give to Caesar what belongs to Caesar – no more and no less – and give to God that which is God's. One should turn the self-deified world into the world, and let God be God. One should deal rationally with the world, with the law and with force The world is not and it never will become the kingdom of God; rather it is a good earthly order against evil chaos. One should deal spiritually – which means with faith – with God and his gospel. The gospel does not create a new world but saves people through faiths.[53]

All this means, of course, that from a Lutheran perspective the human rights debate is a part of the temporal or secular agenda. A few examples are enough to make the point. Martin Honecker affirms a strong Lutheran distinction between theology (dogmatics) which he regards as deriving knowledge from revelation, and

ethics which is an exercise of universal reason in response to the revealed tenets of faith. To try to base human rights (as an exercise in ethics) on the special postulates of faith involves for him the danger of absolutising human endeavour while undercutting its universality.[54] Trutz Rendtorff takes a slightly different approach to the same end. He identifies a parallel between the concept of human rights and the Christian doctrine of justification by faith. In the same way that the doctrine of justification by faith affirms God's unconditional acceptance of the sinner, human rights must be conferred on all people unconditionally. The actual task of defining these rights, however, remains a secular phenomenon.[55] In brief, in Lutheran theology human rights must be taken seriously as a basis for creating the very best world possible. At the same time it needs to be recognised that it is not *the* ultimate solution to life's problems. This emphasis within Lutheran theology is jealously guarded as the exclusive realm of the gospel. Only as people are transformed by the power of the gospel are they truly able to love one another and live in harmony and community.

The Lutheran World Federation's (LWF) study, *Theological Perspectives on Human Rights,* published in 1977 is a thorough and insightful study which illustrates Lutheran social ethics at its best.[56] Having identified *freedom, equality* and *participation* as "the three inviolable basic elements of worldly rights," the document is careful to insist that there is, however, no simple identity between these rights and the gospel. Concepts such as "structural parallels" and "analogy" are used to describe the link and yet the difference between "the justice which applies in the kingdom of God and that in worldly law." In so doing the essential task of the gospel is underlined.[57] It is *constructively* and *critically* to challenge all human rights proposals from the perspective of faith and love, which should enable Christians to engage in the struggle for human rights with a level of hope and courage that surpasses what the law alone can generate within us. In so doing, we are at the same time to be conscious of boundaries of the gospel "and not seek to achieve by force of law things which can only emanate from spontaneity and love."[58] This, in turn, requires us to "promote in an unconstrained way" the best human rights proposals which appear at any given time.[59] That is, without reducing the social ideals of the gospel to any specific set of. This tension stands central to all theological debate. All human rights claims, the gospel requires us to commit ourselves without constraint to the goals of the current human rights endeavours.

In a study on human rights published at the same time as the LWF study, Heinz Eduard Todt and Wolfgang Huber focus attention on the same theological imperative. They perceive within human rights debate "elements of transcendence" which point to the content of the gospel.[60] Elsewhere Todt speaks of the human rights struggle as "a parable of the kingdom of God."[61] In so doing Todt and Huber address the immediate concern of Lutherans while at the same time, as will be shown shortly, giving expression to a concern that is central to the Evangelical Reformed tradition. As such (reflecting perhaps the encounter between Reformed and Lutheran theologies in the Heidelberg ecclesial context), they give expression to the heart of the ecumenical focus on human rights. This is a focus which gives clear moral support to the human rights agenda, while seeking constantly to subject this agenda to the renewing power of the gospel.

The similarities between the theological basis of Catholic rights theory and the Lutheran approach to human rights are extensive. Not least among these is the way within which transcendence is viewed in relation to human rights. Commenting on the approach of *Gaudium et Spes* to ethical commitment, Hollenbach identifies what he regards as a tension inherent to human existence – a tension between the drive of the human spirit toward a value worthy of absolute commitment and an awareness of the shifting and limited nature of all historical values. Two equally wrong consequences can follow:

> The quest for transcendence could be focussed on an historically limited value in a way that absolutises this value. The result would be idolatry and enslavement. On the other hand, a complete or premature withdrawal from historical engagement in the name of pure transcendence is also a temptation.[62]

This tension stands central to all theological debate. All human efforts to define or create the ethical ideal need to be assessed and critiqued from the perspective of the divine absolute which always demands more than human endeavour can deliver. The affirmation of the transcendent absolute can, however, never become an excuse not to commit oneself to the best human alternative available.

The Lutheran ethic can be (and has been) incorrectly read in support of both errors, by a distorted and one-sided interpretation of its content. By requiring the church to focus on the postulates of the faith, while recognising that human endeavour can never be more than sinful, the urgency of the human rights struggle has been seriously undermined. In its most extreme forms this approach has led to the church confining itself to the saving of souls, content to leave politics to the politicians. The other reading of Lutheran ethics (which is at the centre of the contemporary Lutheran human rights studies) requires *serious commitment to the best human rights proposals possible, while affirming that it is through the gospel alone that ultimate human harmony is achieved.* This ethic, Lutherans argue, ultimately injects the human rights debate with precisely the kind of critical urgency that is needed. In so doing it also provides an important incentive against allowing the human rights debate (and the theological question concerning the nature and identity of true humanity) from becoming captive to any particular ideological agenda.

The Reformed tradition The Reformed or Calvinist side of Protestantism was obliged to address a side of the theological tension (or dialectic) with an urgency that never imposed itself on Luther. Geneva was an independent city of refugees and social reform was a priority if it was to survive at all. John Calvin had been expelled from the city eighteen months after his arrival, and when he returned it was with a sense of reluctance. He did not enjoy the full confidence of he rulers, and he never fully trusted them. In this context his sense of covenant, with an obligation to fulfil God's will in every area of human existence in the face of a host of conflicting loyalties, ultimately gave his theology a dynamic and a sense of social urgency which Luther, operating essentially with the same theological principles, was not required to realise. Calvin insisted that the civil authorities were under divine mandate to deliver "legitimate and just government" providing for the essential needs of God's people.[63]

If for Luther politics was the *affairs of people* hammered out in debate and compromise, for Calvin politics was the *affairs of God* to be discerned within Scripture and rationally tested within the community of faith. If Lutheran theology can be criticised for containing the capacity to distract from the "religious" zeal required to save the world from human rights violations, Calvinism carries within it the capacity to assimilate religion and politics into an uncompromising theocracy.

Calvin's Geneva, consisting largely of exiles, was clearly a centre of social reform by the time Calvin's ministry drew to a close.[64] It also evidenced the first signs of popular participation in government.[65] At the same time it experienced its "moments of pronounced imperialism." This was, of course, equally true of Puritan Massachusetts in colonial America, and is still true of "hard-line heretical Calvinism in South Africa."[66] "Imperial Calvinism" soon hard-

ened into a dogmatic fundamentalism, which replaced the freedom inherent to the sovereignty of the biblical God with a God of undeviating order, whose unquestioned authority was given to an equally intractable chosen elect. Calvinist theology also spawned two very different kinds of Reformed thought: "Evangelical Calvinism" and "Free Church Calvinism" or Puritanism.[67] Affirming the absolute freedom of God in the building of human community and the reestablishing of the Kingdom of God on earth, Evangelical Calvinism has in recent times come to be associated with the theology of Karl Barth and its radical critique of all existing social structures as an incentive for what Paul Lehmann has referred to as Barth's theology of "permanent revolution."[68] Free Church Calvinism was, on the other hand, influenced by Protestant developments in Switzerland, Holland, France and elsewhere, but essentially emerged as a distinctive ecclesial type in England and later in America. Concerned essentially with the right ordering of the community of faith rather than society as a whole, this family of churches within the Reformed tradition unleashed a theological dynamic that eventually reached beyond ecclesial boundaries into secular politics. Its impact would come to be felt not only through the Congregational churches, the Baptists, Society of Friends (Quakers) and various "separatist" groups, but also indirectly through the Anglican Church and later the Methodists, as well as the English and American libertarian political traditions.

The unifying theme within the Reformed tradition is freedom through the grace of God to share in building a society that reflects the values and ideals of the gospel. Responding to the freedom of the gospel as understood by Luther, Calvinists developed the claim of God on their lives within an organised, disciplined and political ethic that has made Reformed theology a significant ingredient in the struggle for human rights within the western political tradition. Within the contexts of Geneva and Puritan Anglo-America, both of which demanded participation in the process of nation- and community-building, the appropriation of biblical symbols (the Exodus, the covenant, a calling to be saints and an obligation to share in building the Kingdom of God on earth) seemed a natural and obvious development. Max Weber's formative study, *The Protestant Ethic and the Spirit of Capitalism*, describes the political and economic sense of vocation central to this experience.[69]

The outcome was an ethic closely related to the secular liberal debate on natural rights, democracy and social contract. What distinguished Puritan ideas from those of Locke, John Stuart Mill, Rousseau and others was essentially a twofold emphasis[70]: *One*, the ethical ideal shaping the covenantal community is not merely socially *constructed* and *discerned* within the revealed will of God. Puritan spirituality taught that to the extent that individuals respond to and live in accordance with the "given" or revealed realities of life they experience fulfilment as persons. It brought a spiritual incentive to liberal politics, and, as Weber showed, those who committed themselves to the Puritan ideals came to understand their social and economic prosperity as a sign of God's favour and assurance of their election as the chosen people of God. This ultimately gave rise to a momentum which carried its adherents well beyond religion into a secular life style that held onto only the most distant rudiments of its historic origins. *Two*, the biblical symbols out of which Puritanism shaped its ethic carried within them communal values. Despite the strong sense of individualism which emerged within Puritanism as it reached toward ever more secular and material goals, the communal values grounded in its origins theoretically distinguished Puritan theology from liberal individualism. The Puritans and liberals shared the view that society should be governed according to "self-evident" truths.[71] For the Puritans this meant the laws of God (tested by reason

within the community of saints) such as the freedom of religion and the right to assembly. For liberals this meant ideas and values (seen to be self-evident within the experience of any hard-working individual) such as the right to own property.

In reality the encounter between Puritans and liberals was, of course, more complicated than this. Liberals shared many of the values affirmed by the Puritans, and the Puritans were able to find theological reasons for legitimating those values cherished by liberal individualists. Despite the "privatisation" of Puritanism and its eventual absorption into liberalism, the theological roots of Calvinism continue to challenge the individualism of the West. In contemporary debate it continues to operate as a potential "dangerous memory" ready to activate the communal and democratic ideals so desperately needed to bridge the chasm between liberal individualism and socialist collectivism. It symbolises a form of communalism being sought for on the social-democratic side of liberalism. It, in turn, finds common ground with people in Third World situations, theologically and in human rights declarations such as the *African Charter on Human and Peoples' Rights,* affirming communalism as the basis of human rights.

The "coming together" of traditions was seen in the meeting in Nairobi in 1970 of the World Alliance of Reformed Churches (WARC) which initiated a study programme on human rights as a "first step towards an ecumenical 'Christian Declaration on Human Rights'." The conscious response by the WARC to Third World demands and the early history of the Reformed tradition is explicit in the theme of the study, entitled a "Theological Basis of Human Rights and Liberation."[72] Like the WCC's St Polten report and the documentation of the Vatican, the WARC report reflects a consciousness of Third World demands in placing the right to life, to nourishment and to work at the beginning of the list of human rights. It locates the human rights struggle within the context of people breaking out of colonial dependence, cultural alienation and political oppression.

Within this context the theological point of departure for the WARC study is located in the liberating message of the Bible, as seen in an "original study paper" prepared for the study project by Jürgen Moltmann.

> In the Old Testament, theological thought begins with Yahweh's liberation-history with Israel in the Exodus and only afterward, and on this basis, comes to the confession that this God of liberation is the Creator of all things and the Redeemer of all people. In the New Testament, too, theological thought begins with the confession of Christ as the liberator and only then, and on this basis, comes to the doctrine of creation and eschatology.[73]

From this focus the parameters of the WARC study follow.[74]

1 *Christian theology is a theology of liberation.* "The sick, the possessed, the leprous, the humiliated and the godless" experienced Jesus as a concrete liberator from their concrete misery and they believed in this liberation."

2 *The theology of liberation is a theology of people.* Theologically speaking, the human rights debate is located within the doctrine of anthropology. Theologically people are to be understood and defined "in similitude [as a counterpart] to God." Created and redeemed by God, human beings have God-given rights. They also have certain ethical claims made on them.

3 *The theology of liberation is a theology of the future.* "How can there develop out of the ideal of human rights a concrete utopia which relates the intended human future of man to the specific political, social and racial injustice of the present in order to overcome opposition and resistance?" "Does the struggle for the realization of human rights not presuppose an inner break in the national egoism and the class intel-

lect or the racial mind-set? If Christians find their identity in the crucified Christ, then what relevance can national, cultural and economic identity still have for them?"

The study, located within the context of the quest for liberation, gives rise to certain fundamental theological insights concerning human rights. The struggle for liberation is not only inherent to what it is to be human, but the call to liberation is the call of God. This essential call teaches us what it means to be truly and fully human. Human beings, created in God's image have rights and responsibilities not only for the world within which they live but for future generations. The final document or "definitive study paper" presented at the conclusion of the WARC study develops this aspect under the rubric "God's Claim on Human Beings." The quest for basic rights is here directly related to an obligation to live a life that is befitting of one bearing the image of God, redeemed by Christ and empowered by the Holy Spirit to accomplish the will of God on earth. *This means that the pursuit of human rights comes to be seen as an inherent part of what it means to be human.* In the words of the "Resolution on Human Rights" adopted by the General Synod of the United Church of Christ in the USA, "human rights are the gift and demand of God." "The fundamental human right is the right to be responsible to God . . . to fulfil the fundamental task of becoming human persons . . . "[75] The implications of this theology for political systems and social practices within which women are marginalised and not permitted (let alone facilitated) to participate fully in society are significant. It similarly challenges many global situations where people are denied the fullest human participation in life on the basis of religion, class and race. Without explicitly addressing such particular concerns, the WARC report provides theological space within which contextual concerns can be addressed.

The Reformed emphasis on human rights is located in the vision of humanity made known in the scriptural doctrine of the covenant. It "involves the bonding of persons to others under God's law, for God's Kingdom, empowered by God's love." In an ecumenical sense it gives expression to what John Paul II defined as the "truth about the human being." In the WARC study this focus is developed in relation to both the implications of God's creation and the promise of the eschaton as a basis for engagement in the struggle for human rights.

What this means is that the WARC study locates the human rights doctrine decisively within the context of the evangelical task of the church. This ultimately is its strength. Todt asks a question, however, which all theology is obliged to address if its contribution to human rights is to go beyond the level of motivating people to commit themselves to a set of unrealistic ideals. "What," he asks, "is the relationship between the WARC 'Theological Basis of Human Rights' and the conventions which have recently become part of international law?" Todt's concern is to make a clear (Lutheran) distinction between "the universal postulates on human rights" which emerge from theological discussion and the "codified human rights agreements of the United Nations."[76] The challenge is twofold: Theology, he argues, has a responsibility to identify the difference between the rights and duties of the people of God inspired by faith in the ideals of the gospel and love of one's neighbour on the one hand and the values which form part of the various human rights declarations on the other. A theology which fails to do this carries within it not only the danger of reducing the demands of the gospel to the liberal and/or socialist ideals of the different human rights conventions, but in so doing it undermines the particular contribution of theology to the human rights debate, which includes a vision of a reality that transcends the present debate. This is a distinction which evangelical

Calvinism readily understands. It has to do with what Barth called God's "No" to human endeavour in order that God may say "Yes" through the gospel.[77] The second concern implied in Todt's question concerns the theological status of codified human rights agreements and international law. Representing a consensus of enlightened commitment to human rights, they deserve, in the words of the LWF study the support in "an unconstrained way" as "structural parallels" which anticipate the kind of society which the gospel requires us to strive for.[78] Differently stated, a concern to promote the ideals of the gospel should never cause us to deviate from promoting existing human rights declarations, as a step towards a more perfect social order.

Towards Theological Consensus on Human Rights

The debate between Lutheran and Reformed theology ultimately serves to stimulate and refine rather than undermine the respective approach of these two traditions. A consideration of other denominational studies on human rights also shows that the essential emphases of these traditions constitute the poles between which all Protestant human rights theologies are located.

Together with the Roman Catholic studies on human rights, they provide a basis for theological discussion which incorporates most doctrinal approaches to human rights. The Anglican and Methodist churches, for example, while showing theological tendencies which reflect the various strands of their respective histories, tend more toward the Catholic and/or Lutheran approaches. Affirming the *Universal Declaration of Human Rights,* the 1948 Lambeth Conference of the Anglican communion, for example, states:

> The Conference declares that all men, irrespective of race or colour, are equally the objects of God's love and are called to love

and serve Him. All men are made in His image: for all Christ died; and to all there is made the offer of eternal life. Every individual is therefore bound by duties towards God and towards other men, and has certain rights without the enjoyment of which he cannot freely perform those duties. These rights should be declared by the Church, recognised by the State and safeguarded by international law.[79]

The 1988 Lambeth Conference again endorsed the *Universal Declaration* of *Human Rights,* stressing the importance of "highlighting human interdependence and the need to eliminate exploitation," in a way (which accords with the ecumenical consensus) that allows for Second and Third Generation rights to take a more central location within the human rights struggle.[80]

In its recent publication on human rights, the United Methodist Church in the United States also affirms its support for the *Universal Declaration of Human Rights,* adopting a similar position to that of the Anglican church, in affirming the God-given worth and dignity of all people, while stressing that as a covenant people "we are called to responsibility rather than privilege." The statement continues: "As a people "committed to Christ" and "called to change" we are responsible for securing the integrity of our covenant in the midst of new imposing human rights developments." Special attention is drawn to the need to critically analyse trends and developments which may impinge on human rights in the modern world. These include the impact of capital intensive technology, the use of data banks to provide pervasive information, the growing phenomenon of an underclass of persons domestically and internationally excluded from full participation in society owing to educational, cultural, economic and political conditions, the technological and social displacement of these people, the escalation of militarism, the growth of racist movements, the rising expectations of developing countries and

the disproportionate sharing of global resources.[81] Again the focus is on Second and Third Generation rights without denying basic First Generation rights. In stressing the covenant relationship and responsibility within which the church finds itself, the Methodist declaration carries within it tones of a Reformed emphasis, while the concern for the captivity of humankind within the structures of the modern world reflects an analytical concern for structural sin as expressed in post-Vatican II social concerns. In brief, a variety of ecumenical influences are seen within the Methodist position on human rights (in much the same way that ecumenical factors shape most theological positions in most churches today) as is the theological eclecticism which has traditionally shaped the Methodist heritage.

Other churches, notably those in the Anabaptist tradition and, to some extent, some under the influence of Evangelical Calvinism have given attention to the "community of believers'" emphasis, over against the liberal emphases which eventually emerged in many churches within the Puritan tradition. Differences aside, the Roman Catholic doctrine of rights finds a point of departure in a Thomistic understanding of nature and grace, while the Lutheran–Calvinist tradition within Protestant teaching on human rights is located within a tradition of sin and grace. The former begins with a definition of humanity as given in creation and revealed in Christ. The latter begins with humanity as it is, bound in captivity, crying out for liberation, emphasising that it is only in redemption that the insights inherent to the doctrine of creation and eschatology can be fully appreciated. The point has, however, already been made. The effects of ecumenism have imposed what would once have been regarded as a Roman Catholic position on many Protestant churches while, as already noted, post Vatican II Catholic social teaching has come to include emphases readily acceptable to the churches in the Protestant tradition. The above analyses of the different theological approaches suggest sufficient common ground to project an ecumenical consensual statement on human rights.

Notes

1 Jean Bodin, *Les Six Livres De La Republique* (Paris: Chez I du Puis, 1583) . See discussion in Terry Pinkard, *Democratic Liberalism and Social Union* (Philadelphia: Temple University Press, 1987), p. 58. Also Stanley J. Berm, "Sovereignty," in *Encyclopedia of Philosophy* (New York: Macmillan Co. and Free Press, 1967).

2 C. B. Macpherson, "Natural Rights and Justice in Hobbes and Locke," and John W. Chapman, "Natural Rights and Justice in Liberalism," in D. D. Raphael (ed.), *Political Theory and the Rights of Man* (Bloomington: Indiana University Press, 1967), 1–15; 27–42. Also Zechariah Chafee, Jr., *How Human Rights Got into the Constitution* (Boston: University Press 1952) and Ernest Barker, "Natural Law and the American Revolution," in *Tradition of Ciaility* (Cambridge: Cambridge University Press, 1948), 263–355.

3 This development is outlined in the World Alliance of Reformed Churches' study on the theological basis of human rights. See Jürgen Moltmann, "The Original Paper: A Theological Basis of Human Rights and of the Liberation of Human Beings," in Allen O. Miller (ed.), *A Christian Declaration on Human Rights* (Grand Rapids: Eerdmans, 1977), 26–9.

4 Lourens Ackermann, "Introduction," to *Human Rights for South Africans,* edited by Mike Robertson (Cape Town: Oxford University Press, 1991), 1.

5 *Ibid.*, 3–5.

6 Some of the other major international human rights treaties are: the *Convention on the Elimination of All Forms of Discrimination Against Women,* the *Convention Against Torture and Other Cruel Inhuman or Degrading Treatment or Punishment.* The regional declarations include: *The European Convention of Human Rights, The American Convention of Hunan Rights, The African Charter of Peoples' and Human Rights.*

7 A speech by Erich Weingartner, former executive secretary of the World Council of Churches' Commission of the Churches for International Affairs. Published as an occasional paper by the Institute for Christian Ethics, Waterloo Lutheran Seminary, Waterloo, Ontario, Canada. 1990.

8 Leo Strauss, *Natural Rights and History* (Chicago: University of Chicago Press, 1953), 164.

9 Frederick A. Olafson, "Two Views of Pluralism: Liberal and Catholic," *Yale Review,* 51 (1962), 531.

10 J. M. Potgieter, "Gedagtes oor die nie-Christelike Aard van Menseregte," *Tydskrif Vir Hedendaagse Romeins Hollandse Reg,* 52: 3, August, 1989, 386–408.

11 *The Gospel Defence League Newsletter,* June 1989.

12 *Human Rights and Christian Responsibility,* vols 1–3 (Geneva: WCC-CCTW, 1975).

13 See Jürgen Moltmann, *On Human Dignity: Political Theology and Ethics* (Philadelphia: Fortress Press, 1984), 8.

14 Quoted in Jan Milic Lochman, "Human Rights from a Christian Perspective," in Allen O. Miller (ed.), *A Christian Declaration on Human Rights: Theological Studies of World Alliance of Reformed Churches* (Grand Rapids: Eerdmans, 1977), 17.

15 Pontifical Commission ("Justitia et Pax," *The Church and Human Rights* (Vatican City, 1975), 22.

16 Lochman, "Human Rights from a Christian Perspective," in Miller (ed.), *A Christian Declaration,* 17.

17 Heinz-Eduard Todt, "Theological Reflections on the Foundations of Human Rights," *Lutheran World,* 24: 1 (1977), 45.

18 See, *inter alia,* WARC study in Miller (ed.), *A Christian Declaration of Human Rights*; the Lutheran World Federation of Churches" study in Jorgen Lissner (ed.), *Theological Perspectives on Human Rights* (Geneva: Lutheran World Federation, 1978); The Pontifical Commission "Justitia et Pax," *The Church and Human Rights* (Vatican City, 1975); John Paul II, *On Social Concern (Sollicitudo rei socialis)* (Washington, D.C.: US Catholic Conference, 1988);

Theological Studies Department of the Federation of Protestant Churches in the German Democratic Republic, "Theological Aspects of Human Rights," *WCC Exchange*, 6 (December, 1977); United Church of Christ in the United States of America, "A Pronouncement on Human Rights," in Alfred Hennelly, SJ and John Langan, SJ (eds.), *Human Rights in the Aermicas: The Struggle for Consensus* (Washington DC: Georgetown University Press, 1982), 150–8.

19 Winston Njongo Ndungane, *Human Rights and the Christian Doctrine of Man*. A dissertation towards the degree of Master of Theology submitted to the Faculty of Theology, King's College, University of London, September 1979.

20 Quoted in M. M. Corbett, "Human Rights: The Road Ahead," *Human Rights: The Cape Town Conference*, C. F. Forsyth and J. E. Schiller (eds.) (Cape Town: Juta and Company, 1979), 2.

21 Jeremy Bentham, "Anarchical Fallacies," in Fredrick A. Olafson (ed.), *Society, Law and Morality* (Englewood Cliffs; Prentice-Hall, 1961), 347.

22 Moltmann, "The Original Study Paper: A Theological Basis of Human Rights and of the Liberation of Human Beings," in Miller, *The First Liberty: Religion and the American Republic* (New York: Paragon House Publishers, 1988), 32.

23 Max Stackhouse, "A Protestant Perspective on the Woodstock Human Rights Project," in Hennelly and Langan, *Human Rights in the Americas*, 146.

24 Anthony Mathews, *Law, Order and Liberty in South Africa* (Berkeley: University of California Press, 1972), 29.

25 Iredell Jenkins "From Natural to Legal to Human Rights," in Erwin H. Pollack (ed.), *Human Rights* (Buffalo: Jay Stewart, 1971), 213.

26 See also David Hollenbach, SJ, *Claims in Conflict: Retrieving and Renewing the Catholic Human Rights Tradition* (New York: Paul, 33.

27 Quoted in Hollenbach, *Claims in Conflict*, 42.

28 *The Church and Human Rights*, 21–8.

29 *Ibid.*, 28.

30 John Paul II, "Opening Address at Pueblo" in John Eagleson and Philip Scharper (eds.),

Pueblo and Beyond (Maryknoll: Orbis Books, 1979), 63.

31 Hollenbach, *Claims in Conflict*, 68.

32 John Langan, "Personal Responsibility and Common Good in John Paul II." A paper delivered at Claremont Graduate School, Claremont, California, 2–3 February 1990.

33 *On Social Concern*, pars. 21, 36, 41.

34 John Paul II, *Reconciliation and Penance (Reconciliatio et Paenitentis)* (Washington DC: US Catholic Conference, 1984).

35 Langan, "Personal Responsibility," 6.

36 *On Social Concern*, par. 36.

37 Trent Shroyer, *The Critique of Domination: The Origins and Development of Critical Theory* (New York: Brazilier, 1973).

38 Franz J. Hinkelammert, *The Ideological Weapons of Death* (Maryknoll: Orbis Books, 1986).

39 *On Social Concern*, par. 37.

40 *The Road to Damascus: Kairos and Conversion* (Johannesburg: Skotaville, 1989), 10

41 *On Social Concern*, par. 38.

42 *Ibid.*

43 Langan, "Personal Responsibility," 21.

44 *Ibid.*

45 *Ibid.*, 14–19.

46 John Paul II, *Centesimus Annus* (Vatican City, 1991).

47 For a discussion of these developments as they pertain to the human rights debate see Stackhouse, *Creeds, Society and Human Rights,* 54–65.

48 Martin Luther, "The Freedom of a Christian," *Works of Martin Luther* (Philadelphia: Muhlenberg Press, 1959), vol. III, 341.

49 Stackhouse suggest Protestantism was part of the same world of thought as conciliar Catholicism which the Council of Constance tried to crush in 1415. *Creeds, Society and Human Rights* (Grand Rapids: Eerdmans, 1984), 44–9.

50 See "Treatise on Good Works," *Works*, vol. 44, 95; "To the Christian Nobility," *Works*, vol XLIV, 212–15; "To the Nobels of Germany," *Works*, vol. XLV, 355–78.

51 Article 28, The Augsburg Confession, in T. R. Tapport (ed.), *The Book of Concord* (Philadelphia: Fortress Press, 1959).

52 See the discussions in Jürgen Moltmann, *On Human Dignity: Political Theology*

and Ethics (Philadelphia: Fortress Press, 1984), 63.

53 *Ibid.*, 70–1.

54 Discussed in Todt, "Theological Reflections," in *Lutheran World*, 52.

55 *Ibid.*

56 Lutheran World Federation, *Theological Perspectives on Human Rights* (Geneva: Lutheran World Federation, 1977). Also Jorgen Lissner and Aren Sovik (eds.), *A Lutheran Reader on Human Rights* (Geneva: Lutheran World Federation, 1978).

57 LWF, *ibid.*, 15.

58 *Ibid.*

59 *Ibid.*, 16.

60 Wolfgang Huber and Heinz Eduard Todt, *Menschenrechte. Perspektiven einer menschlichen Welt* (Stuttgart: Kreuz Verlag, 1977). Quoted in Moltmann, *On Human Dignity*, 12.

61 Todt, "Theological Reflections," 57.

62 Hollenbach, *Claims in Conflict*, 72.

63 John Calvin, *Commentaries on the Epistle of Paul the Apostle to the Romans* (Grand Rapids: Eerdmans 1948), 469.

64 Andre Bieler, *La pensee economique et sociale de Calvin* (Geneva: Librairie de l'Universite, 1959). Also Andre Bider, *The Social Humanism of Calvin* (Richmond: John Knox Press, 1964).

65 Paul Lehmann, *The Transfiguration of Politics* (New York: Harper and Row, 1975), 41. See John Calvin, *Institutes of the Christian Religion*, IV, XX, 31a; a passage Ernest Barker calls "the seedbed of modern democracy."

66 Stackhouse, *Creeds, Society and Human Rights*, 56.

67 *Ibid.*, 55–7.

68 This theme is discussed in Chapter 1 of Villa-Vincencio's book.

69 Max Weber, The *Protestant Ethic and the Spirit* of *Capitalism* (New York: Harper and Row, 1958).

70 Stackhouse, *Creeds, Society and Human Rights,* 62.

71 *Ibid.*, 70.

72 The documentation of the study which culminated in a meeting of the Theological Department of the WARC in London in 1976 is published in Allen O. Miller (ed.), *A Christian Declaration on Human Rights* (Grand Rapids: Eerdmans, 1977).

73 Jürgen Moltmann, "The Original Study Paper: A Theological Basis of Human Rights and of the Liberation of Human Beings," in Allen O. Miller (ed.), *A Christian Declaration*, 31.

74 *Ibid.*, 32–4. These directives are given here in summarised form.

75 Published in Hennelly and Langan, *Human Rights*, 150–8.

76 Todt, "Theological Reflections," in *Lutheran World*, 45–6.

77 Karl Barth, *Epistle to the Romans* (London: Oxford University Press), pp, 475–502.

78 LW, 15–16.

79 *Resolutions of the Lambeth Conferences*, 1867–1978, compiled by the Rt. Revd Philip Russell and the Revd Arthur Gosling. Published by the Secretary General of the Anglican Consultative Council for the Lambeth Conference, 1988.

80 *The Truth Shall Make You Free: Lambeth Conference 1988, the Reports, Resolutions and Pastoral Leiters from the Bishops* (London: Church House Publishing, 1988) 223–4.

81 *Faithful Witness on Today's Issues: Human Rights* (Washington, D.C.: The General Board of Church and Society, n.d.), 3–5.

6

Islam and Human Rights: Tradition and Politics

Ann Elizabeth Mayer

◆ Western civilization ◆ The United Nations ◆
◆ Islamic law ◆ Muslims and Western constitutionalism ◆
◆ Muslim ambivalence on rights ◆
◆ Persistence of traditional priorities and values ◆

To understand the contemporary problems of accommodating human rights within an Islamic framework, it is necessary to review the development of international human rights concepts.

The Contribution of Western Civilization

The human rights principles utilized in international law came from the West and are of relatively recent vintage. Although one can find ideas that anticipate human rights concepts in Ancient Greek thought, the articulation of human rights principles – though not necessarily labeled as such – came much later. Certainly, the development of the intellectual foundations of human rights was given an impetus by the Renaissance in Europe and by the associated growth of rationalist and humanistic thought, which led to an important turning point in Western intellectual history. This was the abandonment of premodern doctrines of the duties of man and the adoption of the view that the rights of man should be central in political theory.[1] It was during the European Enlightenment that

the rights of man became a preoccupation of political philosophy, and it was then that the intellectual groundwork for modern human rights theory was laid.

Eighteenth-century British and French thinkers put forward the precursors of modern human rights ideas and had great influence on the rights provisions in the American Declaration of Independence of 1776, the Virginia Declaration of Rights of 1776, and on the Bill of Rights that was added to the US Constitution in 1791. These, along with the Fourteenth Amendment of 1868, have in turn had great influence on subsequent rights formulations, as have the concepts of the 1789 *Declaration des droits de l'homme et du citoyen*, developed at the time of the French Revolution.

Common to the British and French philosophies that contributed to the production of rights doctrines was the idea that the rights of the individual should be of paramount importance in a political system. In a survey of the historical evolution of rights concepts, one scholar has said that the significance of the shift from concern for law to the concern for rights "derives from the fact that the concept of rights is individualistic in the sense that it is a from-the-bottom-up view of morality rather than one from the top down, and from the related fact that it generally expresses claims of a part against the whole."[2]

Long before international human rights law emerged, constitutionalism had been viewed as a means of placing legal limitations on the powers of governments, and the US Constitution and later European constitutions became models that were widely copied elsewhere. Central to these constitutions are curbs on governmental power and safeguards for individual liberty, which is to be insulated from governmental intrusions.

Recognizing that individual rights would sometimes need to be curtailed in the public interest or because of extraordinary circumstances, the drafters of constitutions sought to define and restrict the justifications that states could invoke to deprive people of freedoms. The desire to restrict the ability of the state to intervene in the area of freedom afforded to the individual was due to an awareness that if excessive qualifications were placed on these freedoms, they could render them nugatory, as the state would no longer be effectively restrained from infringing on individual freedoms.

It was on these Western traditions of individualism, humanism, and rationalism and on legal principles protecting individual rights that twentieth-century international law of human rights ultimately rested. Because of the linkage among individualism, humanism, and rationalism, a rejection of these values is tantamount to rejecting the premises of modern human rights.

The Role of the United Nations

Proponents of international human rights espoused the idea that rights should be guaranteed not just in constitutional rights provisions but also by an international law, binding on all nations. After World War II, the United Nations, as the preeminent international organization, took a leading role in formulating rights that had previously been left to domestic legislation. The UN Charter (1945) called for respect for human rights and fundamental freedoms but did not undertake the difficult task of specifying what these entailed. The UDHR, adopted by the General Assembly in 1948, specified the centrality of human rights issues in the mission of the United Nations. Its Preamble called on members to seek to construct a new world order on a sounder basis, one in which "recognition of the inherent dignity and of the equal and inalienable rights of all members of the human family is the foundation of freedom, justice, and peace in the world."

In the decades since its foundation, a major mission of the United Nations has been to secure protection for what came to be known as "human rights." Many rights instruments and conventions codifying international human rights' norms were subsequently produced under the auspices of the United Nations.[3] Doctrines have developed well beyond the negative rights referred to earlier, now encompassing many affirmative rights that require governments to take measures to meet people's needs, especially in the social and economic spheres. Although the patterns of ratification of international human rights conventions have been uneven, and there is much that remains controversial about international human rights law, on many human rights principles there is sufficient consensus to justify saying that international human rights law has come to be part of customary international law.

The Role of Islamic Law

Islamic law and Islamic thought have been treated as irrelevant by people involved in the development of international human rights law. Serious treatises by recognized specialists on the development of international human rights law have not produced evidence of Islamic inspiration for international human rights law or its historical antecedents. One person who has written extensively on Islam but is not a specialist in international law has suggested that there may have been indirect Islamic influences on the early stages of the development of international law itself,[4] but the case for an Islamic influence has not yet been documented in a convincing fashion.

In the case of the learned literature on international human rights by academic specialists, there is an indifference to the Islamic tradition: The idea of consulting Islamic law has clearly been dismissed by specialists in the field. This is hardly surprising, because, historically, international human rights law is closely linked with the Western legal heritage, within which Islamic law has no normative value and little prestige. Questions of Islamic law are only occasionally mentioned in scholarly writing on international human rights – for the sake of comparison with the international norms or to illustrate the problems of introducing international norms in areas of the developing world. Islamic law is treated, if at all, as a marginal, exotic phenomenon. The critiques offered by Muslims who object to international human rights norms on religious grounds do not seem to have provoked much consternation or interest on the part of Western scholars on the theory of international law, for the latter do not feel that the legitimacy of international law is in any way jeopardized by assertions that it fails to conform to Islamic norms. Underlying all of this is definitely a presumption in favor of the superiority of international law and its associated institutions and a belief in the relative backwardness or inappropriateness of any Islamic models with which they may conflict.

These perspectives of legal scholarship in the area of international law are connected to the relative positions of the West and the Muslim world today. One should recall that Islam is overwhelmingly the religion of Third World countries. Centuries ago it was Islamic civilization that was more advanced than Western civilization, and Europe borrowed extensively from Islamic culture, but now it is the Western world that has attained the model of civilization that other societies generally seek to emulate. Islamic culture no longer beckons as something to be studied and learned from; it seems at the moment to have little to teach the economically more highly developed and technologically much more advanced societies of the West.

To note that today the West has a legal tradition that is more modern than the Islamic one is not to say that Western law is by its nature superior and that Islamic law is by its nature inferior. Similarly, to indicate the historical lag in the development of human rights concepts in Islamic thought is also not the same thing as ascribing inadequacy to Islam. The lag in Islamic legal development *vis-à-vis* that of the West, leading to Muslims' belated attempts to construct Islamic versions of human rights, is the result of a complex interplay of political, economic, and cultural factors in which Islamic doctrines often were as much shaped by their environment as they were forces shaping that environment. Thus, to point out that there are anachronistic features that persist in some versions of Islamic law is not to blame Islam for the relatively underdeveloped state of legal institutions in contemporary Muslim countries.

This study in no way aims to establish that human rights could not have developed in an Islamic milieu, but it relies on the evidence that, as a matter of comparative legal history, Islamic human rights concepts developed after Western and international human rights models had been produced. The reasons for this lag must be taken into account. Without paying adequate attention to the historical circumstances that delayed the production of human rights in Islamic milieus, one cannot account for many of the peculiar features of Islamic human rights schemes. To understand what shaped the Islamic human rights schemes discussed here, it is essential to remember that aspects of Western rights concepts associated with a different level of political and legal development have been superficially imitated without their underlying tenets being fully examined or accepted and that these rights concepts have been combined with features of a legal culture that tends to express the very different values and experience of premodern societies.

The Premodern Islamic Heritage

As we have seen, the individualism characteristic of Western civilization was a fundamental ingredient in the development of human rights concepts. Individualism, however, is not an established feature of Muslim societies or of Islamic culture,[5] even though Sufism, or mysticism, which is a major component of the Islamic tradition, does have elements of individualism. Islamic civilization did not create an intellectual climate that was conducive to according priority to the protection of individual rights and freedoms.

Islamic doctrines were historically produced in traditional societies, where one would not expect individualism to be prized. Nonindividualistic and even anti-individualistic attitudes are common in traditional societies, where individuals are situated in a given position in a social context and are seen as components of family or community structures, rather than as autonomous, separate persons. Premodern Islamic thought naturally reflects these traditional values and priorities. When one says that Islamic doctrines formulated by Muslim thinkers in the past tend to be anti-individualistic, one is making an observation that relates more to the historical context in which these ideas were produced than to Islam as a religion. To describe such

doctrines is not to say that Islam is inherently incapable of accommodating principles of individualism.[6]

The connection of Islamic thought with the values of traditional societies has not, however, meant that Islamic culture lacks features that in the West contributed to the development of human rights. The Islamic heritage offers many philosophical concepts, humanistic values, and moral principles that are well adapted for use in constructing human rights principles. Such values and principles abound even in the premodern Islamic intellectual heritage. However, a variety of historical factors as well as the political ascendancy of an orthodox philosophy and theology that were hostile to humanism and rationalism – and, ultimately, hostile also to the liberal ideals associated with human rights – kept the exponents of such values and principles in a generally weak and defensive position over much of the history of Islamic civilization. If the adherents of rationalist and humanistic currents had had greater political power and influence, such thinkers might have directed intellectual development in ways that would have created a much more propitious climate for the early emergence of human rights ideas. As it is, despite their minority position, the views of rationalist and humanistic Muslim thinkers are definitely anchored in the Islamic tradition.

One of the most important rationalist currents in Islamic thought was that of the group known as the *mu'tazila*, whose members' influence in the Sunni world reached its zenith in the ninth century, after which they were largely suppressed.[7] Although since the crushing of the *mu'tazila* rationalist thinkers have generally been on the defensive in Muslim milieus, rationalist currents were never entirely extirpated, and in Twelver Shi'i Islam such currents have remained influential. There was an ongoing tension between the rationalist inclinations of Islamic philosophers, many of whom were influenced by Greek philosophy, and the tenets of the dominant philosophy of ethical voluntarism. Islamic thinkers who too openly espoused the idea of the supremacy of reason over Revelation and called for laws to conform to human notions of justice have always risked being branded heretical by staunch adherents of the view that both Islam and its divine law cannot be evaluated by reference to the tenets of human reason.

Some eminent Islamic philosophers, such as al-Farabi (d. 950) and Ibn Rushd (d. 1198) ["Averroës"], came close to saying that it is reason that determines what is right and true and that religion must conform to its dictates.[8] However, orthodox theologians in Sunni Islam were generally suspicious of human reason, fearing that it would lead Muslims to stray from the truth of Revelation. The prevailing view in the Sunni world, one that the *mu'tazila* unsuccessfully combatted, has been that because of their divine inspiration, *shari'a* laws supersede reason. They embodied God's will and were necessarily just. Human reason, in the orthodox Sunni view, was incapable of ascertaining what was just. Instead, the orthodox view was the Muslims should unquestioningly defer to the wisdom of God as expressed in divine Revelation and the example of the Prophet of God, the truth having been set forth in the texts of the religious sources.[9] Given the dominance of this mainstream Islamic view, it naturally became difficult to realize an Islamic version of the Age of Reason.

The ascendancy of ethical voluntarism and the relative weakness of rationalist currents in Sunni Islam had important consequences for Islamic thinkers' view of the relationship of ruler and ruled. Islamic thought tended to stress not the rights of human beings but, rather, their duties to obey God's perfect law, which, by its nature, would achieve the ideal balance in society. Since whatever God willed was *ipso facto* just, according to the orthodox Islamic view, perfect justice could be achieved if all God's creatures, both ruler and ruled, were obedient to his commands as expressed in Islamic law. Still today one

finds this emphasis on duties. For example, Ayatollah Khomeini insisted that man had no natural rights and that believers were to submit to God's commands.[10]

Since the pious Muslim was only supposed to understand and obey the divine law, which entailed abiding by the limits that God had decreed, demands for individual freedoms could sound distinctly subversive to the orthodox mind. Such demands might be taken to suggest that individuals did not consider themselves strictly bound to submit to the dictates of Islamic law and the commands of the authorities charged with its execution or that they were presuming to use their own fallible human reasoning powers to challenge the supremacy of religious teachings.[11]

The aim of Islamic law was to ensure the well-being of the Islamic community, or umma, as a whole, in a situation where both the ruler and the ruled were presumed to be motivated to follow the law in order to win divine favor and avoid punishment in Hell. In consequence, *shari'a* doctrines remained highly idealistic and were not developed to provide institutional mechanisms to deal with actual situations where governments disregarded Islamic law and oppressed and exploited their subjects.[12] Scholars of Islamic law did not traditionally address issues like how to curb abuses by the ruler or how to restrict oppressive governments: rather, they tended to think of the relationship between ruler and ruled solely in terms of this idealized scheme, in which rulers were conceived of as pious Muslims eager to follow God's mandate.[13] No need was perceived to protect the rights of the individual *vis-à-vis* society or the government – with the single exception of the area of property rights, where the *shari'a* did provide remedies for the individual wrongfully deprived of property by official action.[14]

These features of Islamic orthodoxy inhibited the growth of concepts of individual rights that could be asserted against infringements by governments, while never totally eclipsing other currents in Islamic thought that were hospitable to rights ideals. The rationalist current, though placed on the defensive, survived, notably in the minority Shi'i tradition. One can identify humanistic currents beginning in the early stages of Islamic thought and continuing to the present.[15] In addition, early Islamic thought includes precursors of the idea of political freedom.[16] Concepts of democracy very much like those in modern political systems can be found in the earliest period in Islamic history in the ideas of the Kharijite sect, which broke off from mainstream Islam in the seventh century over the tatter's refusal to agree to the Kharijite tenet that the successors to the Prophet Muhammad had to be elected by the community.[17] Adherents of the Kharijite sect have been castigated for their un-orthodox views and their literature is not familiar to most other Muslims; but it still might be said that the Islamic tradition from the outset has included ideas that anticipated some of the democratic principles that underlie modern human rights norms.[18] Sufi theology and poetry also comprise prototypes of modern principles of humanism and individualism.[19]

The premodern Islamic heritage was rich in ideas. The dominant currents were ones that did not provide a congenial setting for the early development of human rights concepts, but there were from the earliest stages features of the Islamic tradition that offered the potential for successful integration of the premises of modern human rights.

Muslim Reactions to Western Constitutionalism

Just as there is no unitary Islamic position on the merits of rationalism and humanism, so there is no unanimity on where Islam stands *vis-à-vis* constitutionalism, an institution closely tied to the development of legal protections for rights. The modern system of human rights, though formulated in international law, requires translations into rights provisions in national constitutions in order to afford effective legal guarantees for the rights involved. The reactions of Muslims to constitutionalism, which clearly came to the Middle East from the West, have historically run the gamut from enthusiastic endorsement to hostile rejection.

The hold of Islamic doctrines, which tended to support the maintenance of the existing order and to stress the duties of the individual rather than individual rights, started to weaken as Muslim elites became familiar with Western ideas of law and governance in the nineteenth century. When Muslims began seeking legal means for curbing despotic and oppressive rulers, they turned not to the Islamic tradition but to Europe for models. Constitutionalist movements, typically inaugurated in the Middle East by adherents of secular nationalist movements – led by Westernized elites and often by Western-trained lawyers – were formed.[20] These people perceived traditional Islamic institutions as unsuitable for Middle Eastern societies that were launching programs of modernization to remedy their military and economic weakness. New ideas about the proper relationship between government and citizens were borrowed from Europe, and establishing the political freedoms of citizens *vis-à-vis* the state became a major goal. Early constitutionalists moved in the direction of dismantling legally imposed inequalities among citizens, and the nation rather than the religious community became the focus of political loyalty.[21] New concepts of freedom percolated through Muslim societies in the nineteenth and twentieth centuries as Middle Eastern governments began to accede to mounting pressures for adopting constitutional forms of government borrowed from the West.

Muslims who advocated constitutionalism frequently found that conservative *'ulama*, or learned men of religion, were among their most determined foes. Often the *'ulama* fought constitutionalism in the name of preserving Islam because they were convinced that constitutional principles conflicted with *shari'a* law.[22] The historical pattern of *'ulama* resistance to constitutionalism endured longest in Saudi Arabia, the Muslim country where conservative *'ulama* have retained the greatest political influence. Despite decades of efforts by liberal members of the Saudi elite to win acceptance for the notion of constitutionalism, a basic law was not adopted until 1992.

However, there is no necessary opposition between Islam and constitutionalism, and there were many *'ulama* who worked closely with liberal and reformist movements and who favored the adoption of Western-style constitutions. The famous and extremely influential Islamic reformer Muhammad 'Abduh (d. 1905), who served as grand mufti of Egypt, was one of the latter. An Azhar graduate and Islamic legal scholar, 'Abduh was a strong supporter of Egyptian nationalism and constitutionalism. He and other like-minded clerics saw no fatal conflict between constitutionalism and fidelity to Islam or between political freedoms and the *shari'a*.

In sum, one can say that Islamic clerics were divided and have remained so on the merits of constitutionalism and whether the *shari'a* permits the adoption of constitutional safeguards for individual rights and freedoms like those in the West. As current events show, Muslims continue to dispute whether elements of constitutionalism are compatible with the *shari'a*; thus there is no unanimity of opinion on an institution that is of central importance for the protection of human rights.[23]

Muslim Ambivalence on Rights

As has been noted, there is demonstrable support among Muslims for international human rights. Obviously, these supporters find the values and priorities of international human rights congenial. One can presume that the majority of Muslims who embrace human rights have attitudes that are influenced by Islamic teachings and Islamic culture. The phenomenon suggests that currents of Islamic thought must provide conditioning that is favorable for the reception of human rights. But what of those Muslims who accept human rights only warily and with substantial modifications and restrictions? What influences from the Islamic tradition or the associated value system account for their attitudes?

The best evidence of the attitudes of the Muslim conservatives who wrote the Islamic human rights schemes examined here lies in the texts of the schemes and in comments that they and other persons associated with the production of Islamic human rights documents have made. Here, some general characterizations of the attitudes that have shaped the distinctive features of Islamic human rights schemes can be made. The perspectives of these Muslim conservatives *vis-à-vis* human rights issues are fundamentally at variance with the values of international human rights law. An attempt will be made to explain how the lack of awareness of the significance of these differences in perspectives has confused issues and has in turn affected features of Islamic human rights schemes.

The indifference of Western scholars concerned with human rights to Islamic law and to criticisms of human rights that are based on Islamic criteria has been mentioned. Unlike those scholars, who regard the international rights model as normative and Islam as irrelevant, the authors of Islamic human rights think in terms of two conflicting models simultaneously. Even while promoting Islamic versions of human rights, they seem to regard international human rights as the ultimate norm against which all rights schemes are inevitably measured and from which they fear to be caught deviating. There is Muslim sensitivity regarding criticisms leveled against the Islamic tradition by Westerners, which accounts for the defensive or apologetic tone that pervades much of the literature that defends distinctive Islamic schemes of human rights. On the evidence of the schemes analyzed here, the authors of Islamic human rights principles must feel torn between a desire to protect and perpetuate principles associated with their own tradition – in many respects a premodern one – and anxieties lest that tradition be assessed as backward and deficient if Islam is not shown to possess the kind of "advanced" institutions that have been developed in the West. They thus seek to accentuate the formal resemblance between their schemes and the international ones even where that resemblance is misleading in terms of the actual level of rights protections that they envisage.

The authors' apparent sense of cultural inferiority *vis-à-vis* Western legal culture is reflected in strained attempts to blur distinctions between Islamic rules and their Western counterparts. They make special efforts to disguise features of the schemes that are most likely to provoke the opprobrium of the West. As the following analysis of Islamic human rights schemes will show, the discussion of rights protections is often kept at a level of idealistic abstraction, and the individual provisions become vague, equivocal, and evasive when the authors address areas where the premodern *shari'a* rules deviate sharply from modern human rights norms.

The desire to produce human rights schemes that appear to correspond to internationally accepted norms correlates with a lack of coherence in the thinking behind Islamic human rights schemes. This lack of coherence would not have arisen if the authors were deriving their rights schemes from Islamic models following an explicit methodology. One would expect that Islamic rights schemes would be offered only after the authors had first identified the philosophical premises on which an Islamic approach to rights issues should be based and the methodology appropriate for developing internally consistent interpretations of the Islamic sources. Creating a human rights scheme in this fashion would

entail real confidence in the appeal and viability of resources within the Islamic tradition on rights questions. These authors do not in fact possess that confidence.

As will be illustrated by the analyses of Islamic human rights schemes, the authors lack any clear theory of what rights should mean in an Islamic context or principles for deriving their content from the Islamic sources in a consistent and reasoned manner. Instead, they merely assemble pastiches of ideas and terminology drawn from two very different cultures without determining a rationale justifying these combinations or a way to reconcile the conflicting premises underlying them. That is, the deficiencies in the substantive human rights principles are the inevitable by-products of methodological confusion and weaknesses.

It must be emphasized that neither these methodological inadequacies nor the problematical results are necessary consequences of resorting to the Islamic tradition for inspiration. One can see, for example, in the work of Abdullahi an-Na'im the recognition that methodological questions are central to resolving the problem of where Islamic law stands on human rights. Offering a methodology that allows a fresh approach to the Islamic sources, an-Na'im has been able to develop a coherent scheme of human rights principles that is, for those who accept the validity of the proposed methodology, also one that emanates from Islamic values and principles.[24]

The methodological failings that have so affected the quality of the Islamic human rights literature are just another manifestation of problems that afflict contemporary Islamic thought generally and that have seriously hampered its ability to keep pace with modern intellectual and scientific developments. Especially valuable critiques of the unscientific quality of contemporary Islamic thought have been provided by Mohammed Arkoun, a professor at the Sorbonne,[25] and also from a very different angle, by Sadiq Jalal al-'Azm, a professor at the University of Damascus.[26] It is impossible here to do justice to these critiques, but it is necessary to note that the methodological defects decried here reflect a much bigger problem that presently preoccupies some of the most outstanding Muslim intellectuals.

Authors also seem to worry that their Islamic human rights schemes, which emerged after those of international law were firmly established, will be perceived as basically derivative, as the schemes examined here obviously are. When they address the issue of what came first, the authors insist, against the weight of historical evidence, that Islam invented human rights and that the international standards are at best belated attempts to codify rules that Islam introduced in the seventh century. Examples of such assertions can be found in the literature under consideration here.[27]

In their attempts to support the contention that human rights originated in the Islamic tradition, the authors rely on strained readings of the Qur'an or the accounts of the custom, or *sunna*, of the Prophet Muhammad to establish the Islamic pedigrees of rights.[28] They cite passages that in their opinion mean that the Islamic sources had established the equivalents of modern human rights. By concentrating on the era of the Prophet and projecting human rights principles back to the start of Islamic history, and then jumping more than a millennium to the present, they largely avoid referring to the actual record of Islamic political and intellectual history. However, if one is arguing that the Islamic tradition has a much older set of human rights principles than those developed in the West, it is important to show how Muslims have historically interpreted the Islamic sources.

Traditionally, the learned expositions of *shari'a* rules in the juristic treatises have been consulted as the definitive statements of how the Islamic sources should be interpreted to apply to various problems. To answer the question of whether and when human rights concepts were produced in Islamic culture and to discover what Islamic jurists have traditionally

believed Islam provided in the area of rights and freedoms, a legal historian would turn first to the great legal treatises and possibly also the writings on theology and philosophy that were produced in the premodern period of Islamic civilization – very approximately, from the ninth century to the fourteenth – and that are still widely consulted as the most prestigious statements of premodern Islamic doctrine. Barring the discovery of a previously unknown document, the search for an authoritative text dealing specifically with the problems that modern Muslims face in the rights area would be in vain. There is really no documented Islamic authority dating from the premodern period that squarely addresses human rights issues as such or that anticipates the interpretations of the sources that are currently being advanced by authors of Islamic human rights schemes.

By ignoring many centuries of juristic elaborations of the Qur'an and *sunna,* authors of Islamic human rights schemes are in effect rejecting the bulk of the Islamic legal tradition, which one would expect them to examine and assess before asserting that Islam has a longer tradition of human rights than does Western culture. Even if the principles of Islamic human rights did inhere in the original sources, for purposes of legal history, one would want to know when Muslims first started perceiving the human rights implications of the sources. This, the record shows, did not happen until very recently. Thus, Islamic human rights principles are newly coined ones, much newer than rights principles in the West, which can be traced to the Enlightenment and to a certain extent even before that.

When one abandons the search for express treatments of human rights issues and looks instead in the writings of the premodern jurists, theologians, and philosophers for the elaboration of ideas that would either tend to accommodate human rights principles or to create obstacles to their reception in the Islamic tradition, one finds voluminous relevant material. The problem then becomes that there is too much authority and that it is conflicting in its implications for rights. After one surveys premodern Islamic intellectual history, one realizes that there was no settled Islamic doctrine on rights or proto-rights in that period, only currents of thought that would create either a more or a less propitious foundation for the as-similation of modern human rights concepts within an Islamic framework.

This complexity presents problems for authors of Islamic human rights schemes. Pressures for Islamization entail the extirpation of Western cultural influences and return to Islamic models in the area of government, law, social organization, and culture. A prominent feature of Islamiz-ation programs has been demands for decolonization in the legal sphere – a rejec-tion of Western legal models that were imposed or borrowed in a period when Muslims were ruled or dominated by Western powers. This legal decolonization in theory should mean the reinstatement of indigenous Islamic models. However, the Islamization programs rest on a false premise: that there exist in all areas settled Islamic legal countermodels of the Western models that are being repudiated. It is an article of faith to proponents of Islamiz-ation that Islam is a comprehensive ideol-ogy and scheme of life; they do not acknowledge its complexity or that there were major gaps in the *shari'a*.[29] But, as noted, there was no definitive Islamic model of human rights, whence the dilemma.

Under these circumstances, provisions of Islamic human rights schemes, to serve the ends of Islamization programs, must be given enough distinctively Islamic charac-teristics to satisfy the demands for Islamic versions of rights. Simultaneously, the schemes must stick close enough to Western models in order to cover essen-tially the same terrain as the Western schemes that are being rejected.

In general, in areas where the theory of Islamization requires the abandonment of Western law but where there are no juristi-cally elaborated Islamic models to be resuscitated from the premodern tradition, gaps are filled with newly minted Islamic rules. It is inevitable that the latter will be in some respects modeled after the Western rules that they are intended to supplant, even if they are given Islamic features and attributed to the Qur'an and *sunna*. The pressures to avoid acknowledging a debt to the Western human rights tradition entails recourse to strained interpretations of the Islamic sources, which, in reality, provide little express guidance for drafting specific rights provisions.

It is natural, therefore, that some authors of Islamic human rights schemes who have not developed an adequate methodology for constructing human rights on Islamic foundation should feel tempted to rewrite the historical record of the development of human rights in an attempt to cancel out in advance the intellectual debt that they owe to Western culture and to defend their schemes against charges that they are merely imitations of Western human rights concepts. The failure to examine honestly the historical evolution of human rights concepts in the West and to study their philosophical antecedents often seems to confuse the authors of Islamic human rights, who lack understanding of the philosophical underpinnings of interna-tional human rights and the meaning of "rights" in modern legal systems. This disregard for preliminary jurisprudential questions accounts, one presumes, for some of the incoherence in the way that the term *rights* is used in these schemes.[30]

The Persistence of Traditional Priorities and Values

Proponents of Islamic human rights schemes often do not comprehend the philosophical and logical problems involved in integrating schemes of indi-vidual rights and freedoms, which are inextricably bound to values originally emanating from Western civilization, in a matrix of values found in traditional societies and premodern Islamic thought, values that the proponents of Islamic human rights schemes are trying to preserve. Although there are currents in premodern Islamic thought that would mesh readily with modern human rights theories, the authors of the Islamic human rights literature tend to be influenced by the ideas and attitudes of traditional orthodoxy, such as ethical voluntarism, the supremacy of divine Revelation, and hostility toward rationalism and humanism. They have thus elected to adhere to the same intellectual framework within which the precepts of the premodern *shari'a* were elaborated. Historically, these positions impeded the development of human rights concepts.

Ideally, one would want complete expositions of the authors' philosophies of human rights appended to each of the schemes. Then the analysis of those philosophies could be correlated with a critical appraisal of the provisions of each scheme. Unfortunately, the authors have not provided such essays. In default of such, ideas that these authors and other Muslim conservatives who write on Islamic human rights have offered will be examined in order to show that traditional anti-humanistic, anti-rationalist, and anti-individualistic ideas are still influencing Muslim conservatives' perceptions of human rights. Ultimately, the persistence of these orthodox perspectives will be obvious in the features of the Islamic human rights schemes that they have shaped. The analysis will show how Islamic human rights schemes express and confirm the premodern values and priorities that have predominated in orthodox Islamic thought for more than a millennium. Meanwhile, Muslims who have been won over to international human rights have implicitly discarded these premodern perspectives as outmoded.[31]

Insofar as the schemes expressly indicate their priorities, they uphold the primacy of

Revelation over reason and none endorse reason as a source of law. For example, when one examines the Preamble to the English version of the UIDHR, one sees that it takes the position that divine Revelation has given the "legal and moral framework within which to establish and regulate human institutions and relationships." This idea is implicit throughout the text of the Arabic version, as texts of the Qur'an, God's Revelation, and the *sunna* of the Prophet, the practice of the divinely inspired messenger, are extensively quoted. It is thus clear that for the authors of the UIDHR divinely inspired texts enjoy primacy as the source of law. The status of reason is correspondingly demoted. In a later passage in the Preamble of the UIDHR, the authors proclaim in the Arabic version that they believe that human reason *(al-'aql al-bashari)* is insufficient to provide the best plan for human life, independent of God's guidance and inspiration. In the corresponding part of the English version, after stating that "rationality by itself" cannot be "a sure guide in the affairs of mankind," they express their conviction that "the teachings of Islam represent the quintessence of Divine guidance in its final and perfect form."

In such a scheme any challenges that might be made to Islamic law on the grounds that it denies basic rights guaranteed under constitutions or international law are ruled out *ab initio*; human reason is deemed inadequate to criticize what are treated as divine edicts. This affirms the traditional orthodox view, that the tenets of the *shari'a* are perfect and just, because they represent the will of the Creator, being derived from divinely inspired sources. In the Islamic human rights schemes proffered by Mawdudi and Tabandeh, there is also reliance on extensive quotes from the Islamic sources, which is an indication that they follow the traditional view that the texts of Revelation are the definitive guides for what law should be, not human reason.

The supremacy of Islamic law in Iran is confirmed in various provisions of the

Iranian Constitution in addition to Article 4, which has already been quoted. The primacy of Revelation is confirmed in Article 1, which calls for a government based on truth and Quranic justice, and in Article 2, which states that the Iranian Republic is based on belief in the acceptance of God's rule and the necessity of obeying his commands, affirming belief in "divine Revelation and its fundamental role in expressing his law" and the "justice of God in creation and in divine law." Also according to Article 2, these aims are to be achieved by "judgment made on a continuous basis by the eminent clergy, based on the Book [the Qur'an] and traditions of the saints," the last-named meaning the divinely inspired imams of Twelver Shi'ism. The Iranian Constitution thus professes to be anchored in principles derived from divine Revelation.

In a similar vein, according to the Preamble of the Cairo Declaration: "Fundamental rights and universal freedoms in Islam are an integral part of the Islamic religion" and "are contained in the Revealed Books of God and were sent through the message of the last of His Prophets." That is, Revelation is theoretically central to this scheme of human rights, as well. Moreover, after speaking of "basic human dignity" in Article 1(a), the Declaration claims: "True faith is the guarantee for enhancing such dignity along the path to human perfection," indicating that faith – as opposed to reason – is to guide Muslims in this connection. In a similar vein, the Saudi Basic Law in Article 7 affirms that the Qur'an and the *sunna* of the Prophet reign supreme over the Basic Law and all other laws of the state, thereby clearly subordinating rights to Islamic Revelation and prophetic inspiration.

In the Azhar draft Islamic constitution the evidence is less clear. One can, however, infer a similar emphasis on divine Revelation and conclude that a command of religious texts is deemed central to knowledge from individual provisions that incorporate Quranic language and concepts, the requirements in Articles 12 and 13 that call for the memorization of the Qur'an in schools and teaching the prophetic traditions, and the provision in Article 11 that religious instruction should be a main subject in education.

In addition to according Revelation a central role in their Islamic human rights schemes, the authors do not seem to accept the shift from an emphasis on human duties to an emphasis on human rights that characterizes modern thought on rights. In a passage in the English version of the Preamble to the UIDHR that has no obvious counterpart in the Arabic version, the authors indicate "that by the terms of our primeval covenant with God our duties and obligations have priority over our rights," thereby coming close to reaffirming the traditional idea that Islam provides a scheme of duties, not a scheme of individual rights. It is therefore obvious from the outset that the UIDHR will have the effect of denying rights, including ones that are guaranteed under international human rights law, in the guise of establishing Islamic duties. Should there be complaints that this Islamic scheme strips away protections afforded the individual under international human rights norms, the ready-made defense will be that the Islamic sources must be deferred to because they represent God's plan and that the purpose of Islam is not so much to secure rights as to ensure obedience to divine commands.

In the Azhar draft constitution one sees a similar concern for the fulfillment of Islamic duties. In Article 12 the government is required to teach Muslims their duties (al fara'id). In contrast, there is no mention of the existence of need to teach Muslims about freedoms.

The Cairo Declaration refers to duties and obligations and stresses the inferiority of humans *vis-à-vis* their Creator. For example, Article 1 provides in section (a) that all human beings "are united by submission to God" and "are equal in terms of basic human dignity and basic obligations and responsibilities," and states in section (b) that all human beings are God's children ['*iyal*]. Similarly, having declared in Article 1 that the government is Islamic and in Article 5 that it is a monarchy in the Saudi family, the Saudi Basic Law in Article 6 treats the duty to obey the monarch as being religious in nature, asserting that citizens are to pay allegiance to the king, "in accordance with the Holy Qur'an and the *sunna* of the Prophet, in submission and obedience," thereby linking obedience to the royal family to obedience to God. Section 5, labelled "rights and duties," contains precious few rights.

A. K. Brohi, a former minister of law and religious affairs in Pakistan, has written a number of pieces on human rights in Islam and exhibits a rights philosophy similar to the ones embodied in the schemes under discussion here. Brohi has been prominent enough in this field to be selected to give the keynote address at a major international conference on human rights in Islam held in Kuwait in 1980 under the sponsorship of the International Commission of Jurists, Kuwait University, and the Union of Arab Lawyers. Brohi's speech recapitulated points made in an earlier piece on Islam and human rights, published in the official Pakistani case law reporter in 1976, while Zulfikar Ali Bhutto, the prime minister whom Zia executed after his coup, was still in power. It is significant that the same points were incorporated in an article in the official Pakistani case law reporter in 1983, when President Zia's martial law regime and Islamization programs were in full force. Apparently the Zia government did not find anything in the article that would tend to undermine its position that military dictatorship and suspension of rights were compatible with Islamization. Excerpts from the seminar and the article show how Brohi rejects the philosophical underpinnings of Western human rights:

> Human duties and rights have been vigorously defined and their orderly enforcement is the duty of the whole of organized communities and the task is

specifically entrusted to the law enforcement organs of the state. The individual if necessary has to be sacrificed in order that the life of the organism be saved. Collectivity has a special sanctity attached to it in Islam. [35]

The Western man's perspective may by and large be called anthropocentric in the sense that there man is regarded as constituting the measure of everything since he is to be regarded as the starting point of all thinking and action. The perspective of Islam, on the other hand, is theocentric, that is, God-consciousness, the Absolute here is paramount; man is here only to serve His Maker . . . [In the West] rights of man are seen in a setting which has no reference to his relationship with God – they are somehow supposed to be his inalienable birthrights . . . Each time the assertion of human rights is made, it is done only to secure their recognition from some secular authority such as the state or some such regal power.[36]

[In Islam] there are no "human rights" or "freedoms" admissible to man in the sense in which modern man's thought, belief, and practice understand them: in essence, the believer owes obligation or duties to God if only because he is called upon to obey the Divine Law and such Human Rights as he is made to acknowledge seem to stem from his primary duty to obey God.[37]

Thus, it would appear, there is a sense in which Man has no rights within a theocentric perspective; he has only duties to His Maker. But these duties in their turn, give rise to all the rights, Human Rights in the modern sense included . . . There can, in the strict theory of the Islamic law, be no conflict between the State Authority and the individual – since both have to obey the Divine Law.[38]

Human Rights conceived from the anthropocentric perspective are treated by Western thinkers as though they were no more than an expedient mode of protecting the individual from the assaults that are likely to be made upon him by the authority of the State's coercive power by the unjust law that may be imposed by that authority to deny man the possibility of self-development through the law-making power of the brute majorities. Islam, on the other hand, formulates, defines and protects these very rights by inducing in the believers the disposition to obey the law of God . . . and showing obedience to those constituted authorities within one realm who themselves are bound to obey the law of God . . . Furthermore, affirmation of these rights is to enable man not only to secure the establishment of those conditions in terms of which the development of man as an individual on earth may be possible, but also to enable man so to conduct himself, inwardly as well as outwardly, as to be able to obey the Divine Law . . . By accepting to live in Bondage to this Divine Law, man learns to be free. [39]

The tenets of Western individualism are unacceptable in Brohi's scheme, in which man is clearly not meant to be the measure of all things. The idea that individuals enjoy certain inalienable rights is dismissed. In Brohi's comments one sees again the emphasis on duties. The individual is expected to obey the duly constituted authorities, who, in their turn, should obey God. The idea that human rights standards would need to be fashioned to protect the individual from oppression by the government is rejected, as it was in the idealistic visions of the structure of society that were presented by premodern Islamic thinkers and that precluded the development of modern concepts of individual rights. Like the premodern theorists of Islamic government, Brohi assumes that when Islamic law is in force, the government will necessarily obey the dictates of the *shari'a*, so the individual will have no cause to complain of government misconduct.

In Brohi's treatment of rights one sees both a strong affirmation of the idea that the individual is bound by the duty of obedience and, withal, a carelessness regarding the issue of to whom or to what the individual owes obedience. One notes that Brohi is sometimes speaking of subordination to God and Islamic law, which is

clearly required in the Islamic tradition, but that at other times he means the subordination of the individual to organized communities, a collectivity, political authorities, or the state. Regarding the latter, there is much less in the way of unequivocal Islamic authority justifying claims that obedience is owed. Brohi does not seem to perceive that the Islamic warrant establishing the duty of a believer to obey the commands of God should not necessarily be extended to cover the obligations of a citizen of a contemporary country to obey the commands of the state. Like many other Muslim conservatives who write on rights, Brohi fails to appreciate that the model of communal solidarity that one finds in traditional societies in the Muslim world is in no way distinctively Islamic but reflects the features commonly found in societies before the intrusions of industrialization and urbanization. Brohi does not analyze the significance of the original linkage between the lack of support for individualism in premodern Islamic thought and the situation of the individual in traditional societies, where the lack of individual rights and freedoms did not have the same nefarious consequences that the lack of protection for individual rights has had under the modern nation-state. From the fact that premodern Islamic thought was not anthropocentric, he leaps to the conclusion that in the twentieth century, the anthropocentric perspective should be treated as unacceptable by Islamic criteria. Brohi goes from a description of the subordination of the individual to group interests that was widely accepted in traditional societies – regardless of whether Islam was or was not the dominant religion – to the unwarranted conclusion that Islamic doctrine calls for such subordination even in the drastically changed circumstances of contemporary states, where the power of the central government is immeasurably enhanced. [40]

The idea that in the modern state there will naturally be conflicts between the competing interests of individual citizens and the government is rejected by Brohi. His notion that in an Islamic system one cannot separate the individual and the government reflects adherence to the premodern jurists' views that the ruler and ruled stood together, united in their duties of obedience to the *shari'a*.[41] Where there is reliance on such anachronistic views, it is not surprising that denials of individual rights and freedoms by governments are seen as a nonexistent problem. It is conclusively presumed that in an Islamic setting individual–state tensions do not arise.

Mawdudi's main political concern with regard to duties seemed to be how to preserve the power of the state. In his book *The Islamic Law and Constitution*, Mawdudi, who inaccurately quoted the Prophet as saying that "the state" (not referred to in the original) "shall have to be obeyed, in adversity and in prosperity, and whether it is pleasant or unpleasant to do so," opined:

> In other words, the order of the State, be it palatable or unpalatable, easy or arduous, shall have to be obeyed under all circumstances [save when this means disobedience to God] . . . a person should, truly and faithfully and with all his heart, wish and work for the good, prosperity and the betterment of the State, and should not tolerate anything likely to harm its interests . . . It is also obligatory on the citizens of the Islamic State to cooperate wholeheartedly with the government and to make sacrifices of life and property for it, so much so that if any danger threatens the State, he who willfully refrains from making a sacrifice of his life and property to ward off that danger has been called a hypocrite in the Qur'an.[42]

This is obviously an attempt to provide an Islamic rationale for total subjugation of the individual to the state although assuming that the Prophet was referring to the modern state involves a definite anachronism. One can see how similar Mawdudi's formulation of the individual's obligations to obey the government is to that offered by President Zia in justifying his military dictatorship in Pakistan. The only excuse for disobeying the government is in cases where obeying the government would entail violating Islamic law, thereby constituting disobedience to a command of God. Of course, a government that purports to follow Islamic law, as President Zia's did, would not concede that it was giving the citizenry any grounds whatsoever for disobedience, so it is unlikely that such a government would accept any excuse for disobedience. In fact, many members of the political group that Mawdudi founded as well as others who shared his outlook were among the mainstays of support for President Zia's program of Islamization in Pakistan. They were clearly at ease with the loss of rights and freedoms attendant on the coming to power of Zia's military dictatorship.

The authors just cited may take the position that there exist such things as Islamic human rights; their comments, however, reveal that they are philosophically at odds with the ideas that the rights of the individual should be accorded central importance and deserve legal protection from interference by governments. The authors are hostile to individualism and the idea that individual rights and freedoms deserve strong protections against government infringement. Given their position, one would expect these authors to say that modern human rights concepts according primacy to individual rights and freedoms cannot be accommodated within an Islamic framework. Instead, many Muslims writing in this area have been inclined to try to preserve traditional anti-individualistic, communitarian values and priorities while paradoxically trying to insert human rights provisions in that unsuitable matrix. But rights in the context of a value system so inimical to individual freedom will not mean rights as commonly understood in international law.

In contrast, the international human rights standards rest on the assumption that the rights of the individual are the primary concern of civil and political rights and that they must be protected against infringements, particularly by governments, but also by society.[43] If one accepts Ronald Dworkin's definition of a "right" as a claim that it would be wrong for the government to deny an individual even though it would be in the general interest to do so, one could say that it would be impossible for authors with such attitudes to conceive of rights in the Western sense, since they consistently accord priority to the interests of the collectivity, the community, or the state.

A person unfamiliar with Islamic history might assume that special circumstances or unique institutions in Islamic civilization may have compensated for the lack of formal legal safeguards for individual rights and freedoms and that this lack had less nefarious consequences in the Muslim world than it had in Western societies prior to the imposition of legal restraints on governments' ability to infringe human rights. One might speculate that special forms of social solidarity within the community meant that the relationship of the state and the individual was less adversarial than it was in the West, so that the authors of Islamic human rights were justified in downgrading the significance of protections for individual rights in terms of their own cultural experience.

In fact, in the Middle East the absence of legal protections for human rights has correlated with patterns of misrule, oppression, and denials of rights by despotic rulers that are very similar to those historically experienced in the West. The idealized schemes of Muslim ruler and Muslim ruled both acting in concert and in common obedience to the divine law that are invoked in the cited passages were not realized in practice. Although some Muslims would say that the feasibility of the Islamic model was illustrated by the harmonious collaboration of ruler and ruled in the era of the Prophet and under some of his immediate successors – to which the Shiʿis would add the era in which they were ruled by divinely inspired imams – these reports of saintly rulers in the earliest period of Islamic

history by no means signify that the dictates of Islamic piety have normally proved adequate to constrain the behavior of the despotic regimes that have dominated most societies in the Muslim world. The historical record shows that religious scruples rarely deterred governments in Muslim countries from oppressing their subjects. Although Muslim rulers had at their disposal the mechanisms to impose obedience on their subjects, individual subjects had few ways other than the risky course of overt rebellion to challenge cruel and tyrannical rulers.

In reality, the individual and the state in the Muslim world have had conflicting interests that have most often been resolved at the expense of individual rights and freedoms. The authors of these Islamic human rights schemes must be aware that this pattern has continued in the Muslim world today and now has more serious consequences, given the enormous increase in the powers wielded by central governments. Nonetheless, such writers are disposed to ignore the significance of the vast disparity in power between the individual and the modern nation-state.

Since most current theorists of Islamic human rights persist in talking exclusively in terms of an idealized vision of Islamic social harmony, even though the record of centuries as well as the acts of current governments have manifestly demonstrated the inadequacy of the very scheme that they propose, one may doubt that their Islamic human rights schemes were actually devised to address the rights situation in contemporary Middle Eastern societies. Because of their otherworldly, idealistic focus, it is not surprising that the authors of Islamic human rights schemes produce rights provisions that seem grossly inadequate by the standards of international human rights and that fail to call for human rights protections that could address and remedy the real problems of human rights deprivations in contemporary Middle Eastern societies.

It is entirely consonant with their

mistrust of the ability of human reason to ascertain what is right and just and their inclination to rely on Revelation as the true source of law that these authors of Islamic human rights schemes neglected the philosophical exercise of working out a coherent theory of what rights mean. Instead, they have in some instances simply appropriated ideas from texts on Islamic law and ethics, treating them as if they offered authoritative statements of rights, irrespective of whether these involve principles deserving of the status of rights according to the international criteria or whether they would even be susceptible of legal enforcement. The consequence is the inclusion of many trivial or meaningless "rights" that in international law would not rise to the level of human rights. The authors have apparently no grasp of what freedoms are fundamental in terms of the contribution that they make to the happiness and well-being of the individual and what freedoms most need protection in light of the patterns of governmental human rights abuses prevalent in modern political systems in general and in contemporary Middle Eastern societies in particular.

In consequence, the priorities implicit in these schemes are not those of international law. Failing to offer protection for what international law deems fundamental rights, they do cover issues unrelated to conventional rights principles. The Iranian Constitution is a noteworthy exception in this respect. It appears that Iran's established tradition of constitutionalism inhibited its drafters from abandoning the familiar categories that are normally used in formulations of rights.

Examples of the inadequate rights formulations show frivolous notions of entitlements. Some inadequate formulations seem to have resulted from an author gleaning from the Islamic sources the idea that certain conduct is censured and drawing the conclusion that human beings have "rights" not to be affected by such conduct. Thus, Islamic human rights include the "right" not to be made fun of or

insulted by nicknames,[44] which is obviously taken from the Qur'an 44: 11, "Let not a folk deride a folk who may be better than they . . . neither defame one another, nor insult one another by nicknames." Other "rights" that have been derived from Islamic texts include the right of the women of the household not to be surprised by a male family member coming in suddenly and unannounced,[45] and the "right" not to be tied up before being killed.[46] In addition, one encounters a "right" not to have one's corpse mutilated,[47] which seems to envisage that human rights protections should be extended to corpses, even though human rights concerns ordinarily presuppose that the rights claimant be living, not dead.[48]

Indeed, when one thinks about the rights provisions involving women, one realizes that, far from affording protection for freedoms, they contain implicit restrictions on women's rights. There is an assumption that the world is sexually segregated and that women stay at home in seclusion from men. So strict is this segregation meant to be that even male family members should not ever intrude on women's quarters without giving women warning so that they can cover themselves in a suitably modest manner. Thus, the provision implies that even in the home there will be female seclusion and veiling, which in turn is connected with the woman's duty to avoid indecency. There is really nothing connecting this supposed right of women not to be surprised by men of the family coming in unannounced with any principle of international human rights, only with traditional notions that women's obligations under the *shari'a* include the duties to stay segregated, secluded, and veiled.

As a kind of corollary to the development of "rights" not to be subjected to behavior censured in the Islamic sources, behavior that is treated as good or proper in those sources may create a related right. "Rights" that fall within this category include "the obligation of believers to see that a deceased person's body is treated with due solemnity"[49] and the "right" to safety of life – meaning that people should come to the aid of a person in distress or danger.[50] It is hard to see how any "right" can be involved, since the beneficiaries are either dead or in a state of peril where they are helpless to vindicate the "right" that is being afforded to them.

These and other "rights" provisions that are included in these Islamic human rights schemes do not belong in compilations of human rights because they concern offenses dealt with by tort or criminal law, which involve the conduct of private actors. Generally, international human rights law, because it is concerned with governmental conduct, does not set rules for cases where injury or death is caused either due to negligence or as a result of criminal conduct by a private individual. Such cases are normally regulated through tort or criminal law, as most legal systems consider tort and criminal sanctions adequate for the purposes of compensation, retribution, and deterrence. In contrast, in Islamic human rights schemes, there are provisions that guarantee the "right" not to be burned alive,[51] the "right" to life – which turns out to be a right not to be murdered [52] and a woman's "right" to have her chastity respected and protected at all times.[53] Although murder or rape does violate international human rights law if it is practiced as a matter of state policy, if it is no more than a criminal act by a private actor, it is left to domestic criminal legislation to impose a penalty. The "right" set forth in the Islamic scheme does not appear to be directed against state policy, but only against the criminal. Furthermore, the woman's right to have her chastity respected is a very ambiguous one, since, in the context of the contemporary Middle East, protection of chastity is often associated with regimes of sexual segregation and seclusion and female veiling – all practices which can be justified on the grounds that they are necessary to protect women's chastity. So, the "rights" just discussed do not offer meaningful protections for individual freedoms, and at least one could be

utilized to deprive women of freedoms.

A similarly insignificant "right" is the right of ex-spouses to strict confidentiality on the part of their former spouses with regard to information that the latter have obtained that could be detrimental to them.[54] This belongs to the realm of evidentiary privilege or private tort claims, which are not normally the concern of human rights law.

Another "right" stipulated is that of unbelievers to recover the corpses of their fellows who have fallen in battle against the Muslims without having to pay for the privilege.[55] The question of whether a fee could be assessed from unbelievers in these circumstances is hardly one that any serious advocate of enhanced human rights protections in the Middle East would choose to place on an agenda of important contemporary human rights problems.

This category of rights that have no international counterparts also includes the "right" to cooperate (in the cause of virtue – presumably, Islamic virtue) and not to cooperate (in the cause of vice and aggression – presumably, as defined by Islam)[56] and the "right" to propagate Islam and its message.[57] These "rights" are different from international norms, where religious freedoms are protected regardless of one's religion; here it appears it is only Muslims who would benefit from these "rights."

After examining the vague and confused concepts that the authors of Islamic human rights include in their lists of Islamic human rights, one sees that they have no sure grasp of what the concerns of human rights are. Their efforts to incorporate elements from the Islamic sources, relying on Revelation rather than reason to find rights principles, lead them to include provisions that would be totally out of place in a scheme that shared common philosophical premises with those of international human rights.

Other consequences of the failure by Islamic human rights schemes authors to adopt a concept of what a right means that is philosophically coherent and truly comparable to the way that "right" is used in international law are illustrated in subsequent chapters. In summary, the distinctive features of the Islamic human rights schemes do correlate in a general way with the authors' decisions to try to graft rights terminology on a body of concepts and values casually appropriated from the premodern Islamic tradition without first rethinking that tradition in terms of its compatibility with modern human rights norms.

Notes

1   Leo Strauss, *Natural Right and History* (Chicago: University of Chicago Press, 1953), 181–2.

2   J. Roland Pennock, "Rights, Natural Rights, and Human Rights – A General View," in *Human Rights: NOMOS 23*, J. Roland Pennock and John W. Chapman, (eds.) (New York: New York University Press, 1981), 1.

3   A compilation may be found in *International Human Rights Instruments of the United Nations, 1948–1982* (London: Mansell, 1983).

4   Marcel Boisard, "On the Probable Influence of Islam on Western and International Law," *International Journal of Middle Eastern Studies* 11 (1980), 429–50.

5   For a general account, see A. J. Arberry, *Sufism: An Account of the Mystics of Islam* (New York: Macmillan, 1950). Notwithstanding Sufis' concentration on dissolving the individual and achieving spiritual oneness with God, their focus on the perfection of the individual soul and their common disregard for Islamic law and ritual does tend to link them with currents of thought that would challenge authority.

6   This is not to say that this distinction is always made by Muslims. A review of anti-individualistic perspectives maintained by proponents of Islamic human rights schemes shows (chapters 5–8 of Mayer's book), contemporary Muslims often confuse features of premodern culture that are reflected in medieval Islamic thought with Islam itself, concluding that individualism is incompatible with the Islamic religion.

7   The ideas of the *mu'tazila* are discussed in George Hourani, *Islamic Rationalism: The Ethics of 'Abd al-Jabbar* (Oxford: Clarendon Press, 1971); Majid Khadduri, *The Islamic Conception of Justice* (Baltimore: Johns Hopkins University Press, 1984), 41–53.

8   Khadduri, *The Islamic Conception of Justice*, 78–105.

9   The struggles between proponents of reason and Revelation in Islamic intellectual history are described in A. J. Arberry, *Revelation and Reason in Islam* (London: Allen & Unwin, 1957; Khadduri, *The Islamic Conception of Justice*, 39–58, 64–70; Mohamed El-Shakankiri, "Lot divine et lot humaine et droit dans l'histoire juridique de l'Islam," *Studia Islamica* 59 (1981), 161–82.

10 Khomeini's views are presented in Farhang Rajaee, *Islamic Values and World View: Khomeyni on Man, the State, and International Politics* (Lanham, MD: University Press of America, 1983), 42–5.

11 These points are made in Noel Coulson, "The State and the Individual in Islamic Law," *International and Comparative Law Quarterly* 6 (1957), 49–60.

12 In this, Islamic legal thought resembles aspects of the natural law approach to rights in Western civilization. See Myres McDougal, Harold Lasswell, and Lung-chu Chen, *Human Rights and World Order: The Basic Policies of an International Law of Dignity* (New Haven: Yale University Press, 1980), 68–71.

13 A useful introductory survey of this topic is Erwin J. Rosenthal, *Political Thought in Medieval Islam: An Introductory Outline* (Cambridge: Cambridge University Press, 1962).

14 Coulson, "The State and the Individual," 50.

15 Examples of works that document the humanism that was and continues to be part of the Islamic tradition are Mohammed Arkoun, *L'humanisme Arabe au ive/ve siècle: Miskawayh, philosophe et historien* (Paris: J. Vrin, 1970), and *Rethinking Islam. Common Questions, Uncommon Answers* (Boulder, CO: Westview Press, 1994); Marcel Boisard, *L'humanisme de l'Islam* (Paris: Albin Michel, 1979); Hisham Djait, *La*

Personnalite et le devehir arabo-islamiques (Paris: Albin Michel, 1974); Joel Kraemer, *Humanism in the Renaissance of Islam. The Cultural Revival During the Buyid Age* (Leiden: Brill, 1986); Fazlur Rahman, *Islam and Modernity: Transformation of an Intellectual Tradition* (Chicago: University of Chicago Press, 1982); and Roy Mottahedeh, "Toward an Islamic Theology of Toleration," in *Islamic Law Reform and Human Rights. Challenges and Rejoinders,* Tore Lindholm and Kari Vogt, (eds.) (Oslo: Nordic Human Rights Publications, 1993), 25–36.

16 Some examples are given in Franz Rosenthal, *The Muslim Concept of Freedom Prior to the Nineteenth Century* (Leiden: Brill, 1960), 100–1, 105, 144.

17 Elie Adib Salem, *Political Theory and Institutions of the Khawarij* (Baltimore: Johns Hopkins University Press, 1965); Khadduri, *The Islamic Conception of Justice,* 2023.

18 The general ignorance of Kharijite doctrines is partly linked to the fact that the remnants of the original community fled under persecution to remote parts of the Muslim world. Thus, one finds them in places like Oman and in the mountains or isolated settlements in Algeria. Because so much of the writing by Kharijites was destroyed by their foes, the source materials on their ideas are quite limited.

19 A relationship between Sufi and feminist perspectives has been proposed in a work on Islamic feminism. See Leila Ahmad, *Women and Gender in Islam. Historical Roots of a Modern Debate* (New Haven: Yale University Press, 1992), 95–100.

20 For an examination of the case of Egypt, see Farhat Ziadeh, *Lawyers, the Rule of Law, and Liberalism in Modern Egypt* (Stanford: Hoover Institution, 1968).

21 A classic account of the changing political views of the Arab elite at the time that constitutionalist ideas were percolating through Muslim societies is in Albert Hourani, *Arabic Thought in the Liberal Age, 1798–1939* (Oxford: Oxford University Press, 1967).

22 Examples can be found in Abdol Karim Lahidji, "Constitutionalism and Clerical Authority," in *Authority and Political Culture in Shi'ism,* Said Arjomand, (ed.)

(Albany: SUNY, 1988), 133–58; and Haiti, *Shi'ism and Constitutionalism.*

23 An example of the uncertain status of constitutionalism is the fact that, to avoid offending Muslims who believe that constitutions are un-Islamic, the 1992 Saudi Basic Law in its own text disavows any intention to be a constitution. Instead, it modestly calls itself *al-nizam al-asasi li'l-hukm,* or "basic regulation for government." Article 1 of the Basic Law reaffirms the primacy of the Islamic sources, maintaining that the country's "constitution," or *dustur,* is the Qur'an and the *sunna* of the Prophet Muhammad.

24 Examples of Professor An-Na'im's work can be found in "A Modern Approach to Human Rights in Islam: Foundations and Implications for Africa," in *Human Rights and Development in Africa,* Claude Welch, Jr., and Roland Meltzer, eds. (Albany: SUNY Press, 1984), 75–89; his study of the religious reformer Mahmud Muhammad Taha, along with the translation of Taha's major work, *The Second Message of Islam,* Abdullahi an-Na'im, trans. (Syracuse: Syracuse University Press, 1987); and his *Toward an Islamic Reformation: Civil Liberties, Human Rights and International Law* (Syracuse: Syracuse University Press, 1990).

25 Arkoun, *Rethinking Islam.*

26 Sadiq Jalal al-'Azm, *Naqd al-fikr al-dini* (Beirut: Dar al-tali'a, 1972).

27 See, for example, Abu'l A'la Mawdudi, *Human Rights in Islam* (Leicester: Islamic Foundation, 1980), 39; Sultan Hussein Tabandeh, A *Muslim Commentary on the Universal Declaration of Human Rights,* F.J. Goulding, trans. (Guildford: F. J. Goulding, 1970), 1, 85; and the first page of the English-language pamphlet version of the UIDHR [Universal Islamic Declaration of Human Rights].

28 This is particularly true in the case of the UIDHR, Tabandeh, and Mawdudi. They cite sources without attempting to show how the rights they purport to see in the text have been derived. Examples will be offered subsequently.

29 The writings of Mawdudi epitomize these characteristics.

30 This methodological deficiency is not peculiar to Islamic legal thought. Following

the natural law approach to rights in the Western tradition has led to similar confusion and arbitrariness in deriving rights principles. A treatise on human rights concludes that "the abiding difficulty with the natural law approach is that its assumptions, intellectual procedures, and modalities of justification can be employed equally by the proponents of human dignity and the proponents of human indignity in support of diametrically opposed empirical specifications of rights." McDougal, Lasswell, and Chen, *Human Rights and World Order*, 70–1.

31 For a discussion of the tensions between these value systems as they are embodied in the current political struggle in Morocco, see Ann Elizabeth Mayer, "Moroccans – Citizens or Subjects? A People at the Crossroads," *New York Journal of International Law and Politics* 26 (1993), 63–105.

32 A. K. Brohi, "The Nature of Islamic Law and the Concept of Human Rights," in International Commission of Jurists, Kuwait University, and Union of Arab Lawyers, H*uman Rights in Islam, Report of a Seminar Held in Kuwait, December 1980* (International Commission of Jurists, 1982), 43–60.

33 A. K. Brohi, "Islam and Human Rights," *PLD Lahore* 28 (1976), 148–60.

34 A. K. Brohi, "The Nature of Islamic Law and the Concept of Human Rights," *PLD Journal* 1983, 143–76.

35 Brohi, "The Nature of Islamic Law" (Kuwait seminar), 48.

36 Brohi, "Islam and Human Rights," 150.

37 *Ibid.*, 151.

38 *Ibid.*, 152.

39 *Ibid.*, 159.

40 For similar perspectives, see Abdul Aziz Said, "Precept and Practice of Human Rights in Islam," *Universal Human Rights* 1 (1979), 73–4, 77; M. F. al-Nabhan, "The Learned Academy of Islamic Jurisprudence," *Arab Law Quarterly* 1 (1986), 391–2; Taymour Kamel, "The Principle of Legality and Its Application in Islamic Criminal Justice," in *The Islamic*

Criminal Justice System, Cherif Bassiouni, ed. (New York: Praeger, 1982), 169; and Cherif Bassiouni, "Sources of Islamic Law and the Protection of Human Rights," in *The Islamic Criminal Justice System,* 13–14, 23.

41 This failure to accord significance to the question of the rights of the individual *vis-à-vis* the state has a counterpart in the *Shari'a* classification of rights in only two categories, those of the rights of God (to obedience from Muslims), *huquq Allah,* and the rights of the slaves (of God), or *huquq 'ibad.* The latter are rights that give individuals legal claims against other individuals. Coulson, *The State and the Individual in Islamic Law,* 50.

42 Abu'l A'la Mawdudi, *The Islamic Law and Constitution* (Lahore: Islamic Publications, 1980), 252. The original, in a more accurate translation, reads: "Hearing and obeying are the duty of a Muslim man both regarding what he likes and what he dislikes." *Mishkat Al-Masabih,* English Translation with Explanatory Notes, James Tobson, trans. (Lahore: Muhammad Ashraf, 1963), vol. 2, 780.

43 Jack Donnelly, "Human Rights as Natural Rights," *Human Rights Quarterly* 4 (1982), 391.

44 Mawdudi, *Human Rights,* 24.

45 *Ibid.*, 24–5.

46 *Ibid.*, 36.

47 *Ibid.*, 37.

48 It is not unheard of, but highly unusual, to claim that the dead have human rights. If one adopted the view, based on a coherent philosophical approach, that the dead have human rights, one would be likely to propose other rights as well. See Raymond Belliotti, "Do Dead Human Beings Have Rights?" *Personalist* 60 (1979), 201–10.

49 Article 1.b, UIDHR.

50 Mawdudi, *Human Rights,* 18.

51 *Ibid.*, 36.

52 *Ibid.*, 17.

53 *Ibid.*, 18.

54 Article 20.e, UIDHR.

55 Mawdudi, *Human Rights,* 38.

56 *Ibid.*, 22.

57 Article 14, UIDHR, Arabic version.

Islam, Governance and Democracy

7

Manochehr Dorraj

◆ Islam and democracy ◆ Muslim modernists and traditionalists ◆

◆ Islam and human rights ◆

> To declare God's sovereignty means: the comprehensive revolution against human governance in all its perceptions, forms, systems and conditions and the total defiance against every condition on earth in which humans are sovereign which the source of power is human. *Sayyid Qutb*

> The state is not something from God but from the people . . . the state has to serve the benefit of the Muslims. *Rashid al-Ghannoushi*

The recent intellectual interest in civil society and democratization throughout the Middle East and North Africa has reinvigorated the debate on the compatibility of Islam and democracy. This chapter assays the historical and theological genealogy, the nuances, and the complexities of this debate.

There is no consensus among scholars of Islam as to the relationship between Islam and democracy. While some see Islam as an obstacle to democracy (Tibi, 1990), others perceive of a liberal interpretation of Islamic heritage as the only hope for the success of democracy in the Muslim World (Binder, 1988). Most of the ideological appraisals of Islam that either discard it as "reactionary" or conservative, or those that dub it as inherently "revolutionary" or

radical overlook the fact that Islam is not a monolithic faith. Throughout its turbulent history, Islam has been interpreted to legitimize the status quo as well as to rebel against it. Therefore, this chapter addresses the following pertinent questions: What are the nuances of Islamic precepts and how do they influence the development of Islamic polity? What is the state of discourse on the compatibility or incompatibility of Islam and democracy? What is the perspective of Islam on human rights? What are the outstanding theoretical issues in these debates among Muslim theologians and Western scholars?

Islam and Democracy: Postulating the Problem Theoretically

The longing for social justice and opposition to autocratic rule has captured the imagination of Muslim intellectuals and progressive theologians throughout recent history. After the western encroachment on Muslim lands and the ensuing ideological challenge, these issues found a new urgency. Facing Western dominance, Muslim scholars and leaders had to grapple with new political and cultural issues. One distinct challenge for Muslim intellectuals was coping with Western dynamism and the vitality of its democratic political institutions. This awareness brought to bear the necessity of reform and renewal of Islam. Hence, Muslim thinkers had to address the question of the compatibility of Islam and democracy.

There are at least two contending concepts of democracy: procedural and substantial. Robert Dahl, for example, defines procedural democracy as "polyarchy," a system characterized by free competition among groups and individuals, selection of leaders through popular and competitive elections, and existence of civil and democratic liberties. This concept of democracy is concerned with a series of democratic processes and procedures designed to safeguard a participatory republican system (Dahl, 1971).

The roots of substantial democracy can be attributed to Aristotle, who related the idea of democracy to social and structural issues in society, such as the existence of small territory, self-governing units, and a large middle class. He conceived of self-governance in a Greek city-state as the major cornerstone of democracy. Aristotle defined democracy as the rule of the majority (Aristotle, 1972). The later development of the concept emerged from the social revolutions that swept Europe in the seventeenth and eighteenth centuries. Whereas during the Middle Ages Christianity and Judaism were used to legitimize monarchies and the divine rule of kings, by the seventeenth century, under the influence of the Renaissance, rationalism, and the Reformation, both of these religions were reinterpreted to accommodate nascent democratic ideals. Thus, religious reformation played a significant role in the development of the Western world. Likewise, historically, Islam has been used to legitimize political absolutism and monarchies as well as to mobilize the people against monarchies and arbitrary rule. However, much of the Muslim world never experienced a religious reformation

that separated the sacred from the secular. Thus, rationalization of the sacred and its adaptation to the needs of industrial growth and development that were prerequisites to the democratic revolutions of Europe had no corollary in the Muslim world.

The formative origins of democracy are to be found in intellectual and institutional traditions of the Western world and its concern with defining the nature of legitimate government, the limits of its power, and the rights and obligations of its citizens. As such, democracy refers to a system of government with certain legal and institutional structures and processes to define the parameters of social and political life. Democracy is also based on rule by consent of the governed, political accountability, right to dissent, separation of state and "church," freedom of conscience and religion, and a legal code based on secular law. Islam, by contrast, is based on immutable principles. As a politicized faith recognizing no separation between state and "church," Islam encompasses the personal, the social, as well as the political realms of life. As a "total religion," it has specific provisions for social and personal affairs.

There are numerous tensions between Islam and democracy. The word *Islam* means submission to the will of God. Orthodox Muslims believe that God is the only true sovereign on earth. While believers are granted certain political rights, in general, liberties and democratic rights that may challenge "the rightful" Islamic authority and order, tolerating social permissiveness, are regarded as unnecessary and even dangerous for salvation. Since Islam is the source of individual and collective identity and it permeates both realms of life, the interest of *ummah* (the Muslim community) always takes precedence over that of the individual. Therefore, the very existence of the individual as an autonomous being separate from the community, with certain inalienable rights, is alien to mainstream Islamic orthodoxy. Hence, *Shari'a* (the Islamic holy law) is not born out of communal consensus, open contestation of ideas, or deliberation. It is perceived as the divine law to be interpreted by the highest religious authorities in the community in order to guide the faithful toward the ultimate goal of creating a community of the righteous. Virtuosity is defined in terms of individual conformity to *Shari'a*. There is, however, some room for flexibility, in so far as the decree of one doctor of law or a high-ranking cleric can be annulled by another.

The two major sects of Islam have elitist origins. After the death of Muhammad, the Sunnis held that only members of his tribe (Quraysh) were eligible to succeed him. The Shi'ites insisted that only the members of the Prophet's immediate family who had inherited his knowledge and innocence could rule. There is an unresolved tension between the Shi'ites' belief in Imamat (the charismatic rule of the seven or twelve male descendants of the prophet, depending on which sect, Ismai'lis or Ithna'sharis) and the notion of popular sovereignty. In the absence of the twelfth Imam, who is said to be in occultation, the mantle of Imamat is passed down to the *Ulama* (the learned clergy) as the intermediaries between humans and God. This partially explains why, for example, the leaders of the Iranian revolution of 1979 opted for *Valayat-i Faqih* (the rule of the jurisconsult) and the charismatic leadership of Ayatollah Khomeini. So far as the orthodox Shi'ites are concerned, without the necessary religious leadership and supervision, the community will deviate from the righteous path. It is incumbent on devout Shi'ites to obey the commandments of the leading cleric of the day (the Ayatollah), because he is regarded as "the source of emulation." Secular rule, the devout Shi'ites hold, can only usher in moral decay and corruption.

The Sunni doctrine of *khalifah,* in contrast, regards the community as the vice-regents of God and allows for limited input by the community in the process of political decision-making. Nevertheless, as the head of a centralized state, the power of the khalif remains supreme with extensive judicial and executive powers and more limited legislative power. These conflicting interpretations of Islamic doctrine have been carried to modern time. Whereas Ayatollah Khomeini, for example, argued for the necessity of the rule by jurisconsult, which would effectively put the clergy in charge of state power, Sayyid Qutb, the leading Egyptian traditionalist (who was executed by Jamal Abdul Nasser in 1966) opposed the need for the stewardship of professional clergy. He argued that,

> the kingdom of God on earth will not be established when religious leaders supervise sovereignty on earth as was the case under the power of the church, nor by men who pontificate in the name of God as was the case under "theocracy" or divine rule . . . (Tamadonfar, 1989: 106)

This is only a small indication of the immense diversity in Islam. If democracy is viewed merely in its formal and constitutional dimensions, then it is incompatible with Islam. If the definition is broadened to encompass the broader essence of democracy, then there are possibilities for reconciliation and accommodation despite the profound differences. Democracy, for example, is closely linked with equality. In the Greek concept of equality, individuals were equal only if they owned slaves or property. The Islamic concept of equality, on the other hand, is not contingent upon property or ownership. Theoretically, Islam considers all believers equal members of the community despite their race, origins, or status. The only criterion for superiority is the piety of the believer (Enayat, 1982: 126–8). Despite early Islam's discrimination between believers and non-believers, Arabs and non-Arabs *(Ajams* and *Mawalis),* Muslim men and women and its acceptance of slavery as an institution (Rosenthal, 1960: 29–34), the teachings of early Islam bore a distinct strain of egalitarianism (Marlow, 1997). The roots of this egalitarianism can be detected in the pre-Islamic Arab Bedouin culture. Both the sharing of wealth with kin and the Arab tradition of valuing hospitality and generosity point to a sense of raw equality and the cooperation necessary for survival in the harsh life of the desert (Anderson, Seibert and Wagner, 1990: 25). Islam's moral code incorporated these social realities.

Pristine Islam was impacted by two egalitarian elements: monotheism and tribalism. Belief in oneness of God can reinforce a sense of brotherhood of all believers. Tribalism may reinforce a sense of communitarianism. This egalitarian spirit can be found in the Qur'an and the Hadith (alleged utterances and conducts attributed to the prophet Muhammad) as well as the statements of Umar and Ali, the two "rightly guided" khalifs who succeeded him.

Those who advocate the compatibility of Islam and democracy attempt to demonstrate how the seeds of accountable government were already present in Islamic tradition. They point out that Islam is against arbitrary rule, and they see in the paradigmatic example of the prophet the precedent against tyranny. To strengthen the political solidarity of the community, they assert, the prophet developed a delicate definition of political power: authority of the ruler stems from the ummah, through their *shura* (consultation) and must be accountable to them through *ijma* (consensus) (Esposito and Piscatori, 1991: 434). Muhammad also refused to name a successor, thus leaving the decision to the community at large. To prevent a profound rift between the rich and poor in his community, Muhammad encouraged *saddaqah* (contribution to the needy) and *zakat* (legal alms). He also created *bait al mal* (public fund) to finance communal needs (Watt, 1962: 252–3). The electoral process in the Muslim world is traced to the seventh century rule of Ummar, who succeeded the prophet as one of the four rightly guided khalifs. Ummar, it is said, appointed a shura, or electoral committee,

to choose his successor, the third khalif (Uthman) (Goldschmidt, 1991).

As the Islamic conquest ushered in new wealth and power and the society became more stratified and hierarchical, a distinct tension developed between the professed egalitarianism of pristine Islamic theology and the existing disparity of wealth and power. This tension remains unresolved and is an animating force in the present Islamic revival and the pervasive populist interpretation of the faith. As the Abassid dynasty incorporated some of the Persian tradition of kingship, administration, and statecraft, the new Arab khalifs became increasingly defensive, attempting to justify the pervading social inequalities in Islamic terms. The egalitarian spirit of early Islam was a major motif in popular rebellion against state power in many parts of the Islamic empire from the eighth to the thirteenth centuries (Marlow, 1997).

This relatively raw egalitarian tradition lacked any trace of individualism, a crucial component of Western democracy. In the hierarchical tribal society of bedouin Arabs, the concept of "citizens" as autonomous individuals with certain inalienable rights never developed – as it did not in the West until the emergence of commercial capitalism in the eighteenth century. The harsh life of the desert made individual survival dependent on collective cooperation. The reliance on the tribe for sustenance and security firmly established the primacy of the community over the individual.

Most Muslim khalifs considered the people living in their domain as subjects who owed them "complete and immediate obedience" (Lewis, 1988: 94). In the formative stages of *Shari'a* in the seventh century, slavery was an acceptable institution; women were generally regarded as unequal to men; and religion was the main source of cultural identity. Therefore, the source of discrimination between slaves and free men, men and women, and Muslims and non-Muslims was historically grounded. Close scrutiny of the Qur'an reveals that property and natural and individual rights are subordinate to the collective interest, sanctity and security of the community. The injunction *Al-amri bi ma'ruf Valnahi al-munkar* (rejoicing the good and forbidding the evil) makes it incumbent upon Muslims to watch over public morality.

Preserving the sanctity of the community of the faithful requires leaders with legitimate authority. Muslim traditionalists believed that if the power of the leader were contingent upon a system of checks and balances, the charisma and consequently the authority of the leader would erode. Such was the justification for obeying the authority of charismatic kings and khalifs (Khajeh Nezam al-Mulk, 1960). It is, however, misleading to surmise that Islam supports arbitrary rule. To the contrary, the Qur'an encourages the rule of law (*Shari'a*) and exhorts the faithful to obey legitimate and just Muslim rulers. Enticing "sedition" (*fitnah*), however, carries a heavy penalty in the Islamic legal code. Since it is not often clear what constitutes "sedition" and what is rightful criticism, Muslim leaders have much latitude to define *fitnah* as political expediency would dictate. Muslim lands throughout history have seen their share of autocratic rulers who have charged their opponents with enticing fitnah, thus justifying their annihilation.

In regard to racial and ethnic relationships, however, the Islamic world has fared relatively better throughout modern history than has the Western world. Islam recognizes Jews and Christians as "the people of the book." It respects their faith as the two monotheistic religions, and it respects Moses and Jesus as prophets of God. Christianity, by contrast, (perhaps partially because it emerged earlier), does not grant the same recognitions to Islam and Muhammad. Muslim treatment of Jews also demonstrates that the anti-Jewism manifested in Europe never was as extensive in the Muslim world. The mass expulsion and genocide of Jews witnessed in Germany, Poland, Russia and France, for

example, has no equivalent in Muslim lands (Enayat, 1982: 129–30). To be sure, the Ottoman government's attacks on Armenians in the early part of the twentieth century, the violation of human rights of Sudanese Christians by the Islamic government of Sudan, and the persecution of the Bahai community in Iran evince that Muslim governments have engaged in abuse and persecution of religious minorities. But this has been done on much smaller scale than under Fascism.

To summarize, scholars who argue for the compatibility of Islam and democracy refer to the following five attributes of Islam: (1) The practice of consultation (*shura*) by the Prophet and the four rightly guided khalifs in pristine Islam. Whereas the traditional notion of *shura* referred to the ruler asking other members of the court for advice, the modern revisionist concept as formulated by a leading Muslim modernist, Fazlur Rahman, for example, reinterprets *shura* to mean "mutual advice through mutual discussions on an equal footing" (Esposito and Voll, 1996: 28) (2) Closely related to *shura* is the concept of *ijma* (consensus) or the collective judgment of the Ulama that is binding on the Muslim community. Whereas the traditional concept of *ijma* referred to the consensus of the leading *Ulama* regarding the application of Islamic law to social and religious issues, the modern revisionist concept of *ijma* calls for the popular consensus of the community. (3) *Ijtihad* (independent judgment) is said to endow the believers with freedom to interpret Islam for themselves, thus challenging the monopoly of the clerics (the doctors of law) on interpretation of holy law. (4) Closely related to the concept of *ijtihad* is *qiyas* (analogical reasoning). Muslims can use *qiyas* to interpret holy law on the basis of rationalism. This potentially renders theirs a reasoned faith that is not based on fear, dogma, or blind obedience. (5) The concept of *bay'ah* is presented as another pillar of democratic governance. Whereas the traditional conservative notion of *bay'ah* refers to the mandatory allegiance of subjects to the khalifs, the modern reformist interpretation implies the people's approval of a ruler's right to govern and the necessity for free elections. The reformist account also projects *bay'ah* as a social contract between the ruler and the ruled. If the ruler abuses his or her power, then the community has the right to withdraw its support and oppose him/her. Reformists define *bay'ah* as the principle of rule by the consent of the governed. (6) The right to criticize the unjust ruler is derived from the duty of the believers "to rejoice the good and forbid the evil." This predisposes Muslims to take an active role in the implementation of social justice in their communities. (7) The respect for the life, private property and equality of all believers is presented as other indications of the compatibility of Islam and democracy. (8) Finally, it is argued that just as democracy emerged from Christian legal canons, so to is it possible for a future democratic legal framework to emerge from reformist interpretations of the *Shari'a* (Enayat, 1982; Esposito and Piscatori, 1991; Esposito and Voll, 1996).

"Democratic" interpretations of Islamic precepts are more common among Muslim modernists of the late nineteenth and twentieth centuries who favored a representative government and a parliamentary political system. Modernists such as Assad Abadi (Afghani), Abduh, Iqbal, Shariati, Bazargan, Ghannouchi, and Soroosh were inspired by Western rationalism and the dynamism of Western democratic institutions. They abhorred the spirit of fatalism prevalent among many Muslim traditionalists. They used their power of interpretation of the holy law and the Qur'an to reform and revitalize Islam, to encourage participatory politics and to end political absolutism and tyranny. By emphasizing the principle of free will *(ikhtiar)*, *ijtihad*, and *qiyas*, they argued that Muslims can become masters of their own destiny by educating themselves and becoming engaged in political affairs of their respective communities (Esposito, 1984: 44–60).

Below I present some of the leading Muslim modernists and traditionalists and briefly explore their divergent ideas on Islam, governance, and democracy.

Muslim Modernists and Muslim Traditionalists

Jamal al-Din al-Afghani (1838–97), who was born in Iran but lived in various parts of the Muslim world and Europe, aspired to reconcile Islam with the modern world. In contrast to the traditionalists, Afghani called for the revival of Islam based on a new interpretation that would accommodate Western philosophy, science, and rationalism. Afghani's opposition to Western colonialism was complemented by his admiration for Western democracy and its constitutional system. He believed that the archaic members of the *Ulama* who resisted modernization and social progress were as much responsible for the stagnation of Islam and Muslim societies as were the Western colonialists.

As he put it,

> The Westerners have conquered the world, not because of their belief in Jesus or Mary, but because of their capacity to build railroads; to create the telegram system. We have lost, because we have become the prisoners of our own superstitions and ignorance. (Dorraj, 1990: 89)

His advocacy of pan-Islamism was based on a dynamic reform and renewal of the faith. Afghani favored the synthesis of religion and science, faith and reason. He promoted enlightened religiosity. He used pedagogical as well as clandestine activities, persuasion of political leaders and called on the masses to revolt in order to instigate social change. He saw tyrants as obstacles to constitutional government and popular sovereignty. Therefore, he urged Muslim leaders to reform their governments and put an end to repression and corruption (Keddie, 1968: 52–62).

Muhammad Abduh (1849–1905), the Egyptian disciple of Afghani, was another influential modernist. He led a reform movement known as *salafiyya* throughout the Arab world. Early in his career he joined Afghani in his anti-colonial struggle against British and French domination of Egypt. This rebellion culminated in Urabi Pasha's unsuccessful nationalist revolt in 1882. After British occupation of Egypt, Abduh was exiled to Paris. Upon his return to Cairo in 1888, he abandoned the path of revolution and opted to transform his country through the reform and renewal of Islam. He advocated the selective adaptation of Western values and institutions and strove to demonstrate the compatibility of Islam and Western rationalism. After he became the head of the *Shari'a* law court system and a member of the legislative council of Egypt in 1899, he initiated a series of reforms in Islamic law, education, and theology. Recognizing the weaknesses of traditional Islamic law regarding equal treatment of women, Abduh opposed polygamy and advocated legal and educational reforms that enhanced the status of women (Esposito, 1984: 49, Dorraj, 1992: 96–7). In his ceaseless attempts to find precedents for representative government, he innovatively reinterpreted the Islamic past. Thus *maslah* (public good) was interpreted as utilitarianism, *shura* became parliamentary democracy, and *ijma* was presented as the necessity to respect public opinion. His ideal government, however, was a constitutional monarchy (Mortimer, 1982: 175–87).

Muhammad Iqbal (1873–1938) was a prominent modernist whose influence reached as far as India, Pakistan, Egypt and Iran. Like his modernist predecessors, he was also exposed to and influenced by Western civilization and rationalist philosophers. He received his doctorate in philosophy from Heidelberg and Munich. Iqbal considered Islam a complete faith that was superior to both capitalism and communism. An advocate of participatory politics and representative government, he favored modern legislative assemblies over the Ulama. Iqbal presented a critical, rationalist, and democratic reinterpretation of Islam. He admired Western intellectual traditions and democratic institutions as well as some aspects of socialism. He attempted to find precedents for both in Islam (Esposito, 1983: 175–87). Iqbal believed in the absolute inseparability of religion and politics. As he asserted,

> In Islam, God and universe, spirit and matter, Church and state are organically linked to each other. Whatever may emerge, imperialism or democracy, if religion is separated from politics, there remains tyranny, aggression, lawlessness, and exploitation. (Iqbal, 1973: 103–4)

Iqbal's ideas on democracy were ambiguous and contradictory. On the one hand, he opposed Western democracy, declaring it to be a cosmetic on the face of imperialism which with "iron feet ... tramples down the weak without remorse." He also believed that democracy "lets loose all sorts of aspirations and grievances" which may lead to anarchy. He criticized democracy because it "counts" rather than "weighs." He contended that while in a democracy the individual and individualism are valued, the spiritual well-being of individuals is ignored (Abbott, 1971: 155–75). But Iqbal also regarded democracy as one of the most important aspects of Islam. Individual rights, however, must be subordinate to the welfare of society and the interests of Islam are more significant than those of the Muslim (Hassan, 1971: 157 and Dorraj, 1995: 275). Such prevalent ambiguities and contradictions reflect the dual world of Muslim modernists who were caught between their admiration for Western rationalism and democratic institutions, on the one hand, and their abiding loyalty to Islamic authenticity, on the other.

One modernist who was deeply influenced by Iqbal and harbored his ambivalence and ambiguities toward democracy is Ali Shariati (1933–77). Born in Iran and educated at the Sorbonne, France, where he received a doctorate in sociology, Shariati was influenced by such diverse philosophers and sociologists as Durkheim, Hegel, Marx, and Sartre, and such Third World activists and scholars as Franz Fanon. He applied an innovative approach to Quranic exegesis, which enabled him to draw activist conclusions. His politicized interpretation of Shi'ite Islam galvanized and mobilized Muslim youths, many of whom participated in or led the Iranian revolution of 1979. In the eyes of many of his followers he was "the Luther of Iran" and the leader of Islamic Protestanism (Dorraj, 1990: 140–1). One of Shariati's major contributions was to present a social analysis of Islam and impart social consciousness to his audience. He asserted that, "It is only through a social struggle that human beings can really grow. In isolation one can become a philosopher, a poet, a virtuous and pious man, but one cannot become a Muslim" (Shariati, 1973: 28). Shariati's concept of democracy is linked to his perception of leadership in the Islamic community. He interpreted imamat as the necessity for revolutionary leadership. Imamat should not be confused with a democratic government. As Shariati explains,

> Imamat is not dependent on choice, but recognition. For example, in a democracy the people are the source of power and they are the deciding factor. The government mediates between the leader and the people. In Islam, however, the relation of the people to the Imam is mediated by "the truth." People are not the deciding element, they are the recognizing element. (Shariati, 1972: 127)

Shariati does not say who determines the truth. But he makes it clear that without the leadership of the Imam the individual is lost, like a sheep without a shepherd. As for the duty of community, Shariati clearly states:

> The members of the ummah, despite their race or color, think alike and believe in a single leadership to guide them towards progress and perfection. The goal of society must be progress and not necessarily happiness. It is the duty of the ummah to choose the former over the latter. (Shariati, 1972: 62)

To dispel possible illusions that any members of the community may have about the nature of the Imam's leadership, Shariati states:

> The Imam need not be democratic in the formal sense of the word. He is not obliged to act according to the wishes of the members of the community. Neither must he consider the well-being and happiness of the masses as his primary goal. The most important duty of Imam is to guide the ummah in the most direct and efficient way toward perfection, even if it would mean great suffering for the community. (Shariati, 1973: 63)

Only a Muslim's understanding of this necessity, held Shariati, would set him/her free and prepare him/her for the unity with God. Shariati regarded Western democracy as unsuitable for Muslim societies. Because of the low rate of literacy, asserted Shariati, the majority of the people are not yet in a position to decide what is best for them. He also believed that in so far as democracy is based on maintaining the status quo, it was incompatible with the goal of Islamic societies for revolutionary change (Tamadonfar, 1989: 41). Thus, Shariati's theory of leadership possesses a distinct totalitarian streak that jeopardizes the humanitarian bent of his political ideology and his agenda for social change. Because of his sudden death in 1977, he did not see the Iranian revolution and he did not leave us an evaluation of its leader.

A Muslim modernist and a contemporary of Shariati who participated in the revolution and was, for a brief period, the first prime minister of the Islamic Republic of Iran, was Mehdi Bazargan (1907–94). His liberal interpretation of Islam quickly put him at odds with the traditionalists who dominated the government. Like Shariati, he was a French-educated Muslim lay intellectual, but with a degree in engineering. Compared to the radical inclinations of Shariati, however, Bazargan was more liberal and moderate in his political temperament. He held that Islam is not based on coercing individuals into compliance with its rule. All individuals, Muslims and infidels alike, must be granted equal protection and equality before the Islamic law (Bazargan, 1982: 27). Unlike Shariati, who emphasized the primacy of the community and collective action, Bazargan shifted the emphasis to the inviolability of the individual and individual rights. Since individuals constitute the basis of society, social progress must begin with the transformation of individuals. Thus, individual welfare takes precedence over the collective. Hence, Bazargan regarded Islamic edicts and ordinances as a matter of private values and conscience not to be regulated by the state. No government should legislate morality or persecute people on the basis of their alleged religious deviation (Bazargan, 1982: 28). Bazargan opposed a totalitarian interpretation of Islam. He favored popular sovereignty and pluralism, and regarded a synthesis of Islam and democracy as the most desirable form of government. He was also active in the defense of human rights. In 1986, he established the Society for the Defense of Freedom and the Sovereignty of the Iranian People. The society's goals were "to struggle against despotism, for political and social freedom, and for the equality of all before the law, and to defend Iran's honor in world public opinion" (Chehabi, 1990: 302). Toward the end of his life, he opposed theocracy and advocated the separation of religion and politics. He called on the clergy to go back to the mosque and leave politics to the technocrats and politicians. He believed that subjecting a spiritual faith, such as Islam, to mundane politics in a corrupt world, denudes it of its spiritual essence. Ideologization of Islam as an instrument of power politics ultimately diminishes Islam and Muslims (Chehabi, 1990: 278–304).

In the contemporary Muslim World several prominent Muslim leaders have also advocated the compatibility of Islam and democracy. Among them are Sheikh Muhammad al-Ghazali and Sheikh Yusuf al-Qaradawi of Egypt, Rashid al-Ghannouchi, head of Tunisia's Islamist movement, and Abdol Karim-i Soorosh of Iran. Ghazali perceives democracy as a system that prevents arbitrary rule and protects citizens from the abuse of power by government. Prevention of arbitrary rule and making government accountable, holds Ghazali, is something that Islam and democracy have in common.

Ghannouchi considers the struggle against oppression and for such democratic principles as free elections, majority rule, peaceful transition of power, and the protection of the rights of minorities as universal principles that can and must be respected under an Islamic democracy. According to him, there are no contradictions between the spirit of Islamic precepts and these democratic rights and procedures. He also supports a pluralist electional system in which Muslims are in the minority.

Qaradawi polemicizes against those traditionalists who perceive of democracy as unIslamic and unpious. He considers democracy a system in which people can freely elect their leaders, question them, and depose them if they abuse power. The virtue of democracy, asserts Qaradawi, lies in its opposition to despotism (Ghadbian, 1997: 78–80).

In the same vein, Abdolkarim-i Soroosh, a philosophy professor and one of the leading ideologues of the Islamic Republic in the early years of the revolution, argues for primacy of reason and freedom as the necessary precondition of human development. Having witnessed the suppression of democratic rights and the use of Islam as an instrument of power politics in Iran, he became concerned with the diminishing spiritual essence of Islam and with religious despotism. He has become an advocate of separation of religion and politics. He asserts that religion must not stand as a dominating force above society; it must serve human welfare and well-being. Hence, justice must not be subordinate to the requirements of Islamic doctrine or political expediency. Rather, Islam must meet the standards of social justice and adhere to the universal declaration of human rights. To remain legitimate, religious governments must democratize and respect and protect human rights (Soorosh, 1994: 235–83).

The Muslim traditionalists, on the other hand, such as Sheikh Fadlallah Nuri and Ayatollah Khomeini of Iran and Sayyid Qutb of Egypt opposed democracy and the idea of popular sovereignty and secular law. The attitude of Mawdudi, the leading traditionalist theologian of Pakistan, was too complex and nuanced to fall into this category. Mawdudi was more sympathetic to democratic institutions and ideals than most of the other traditionalists of the twentieth century.

Sheikh Nuri (d. 1909) of Iran perceived a constitutional democracy as a threat to the rule of *Shari'a*. He was an ardent opponent of the constitutional revolution of 1906–9 in Iran that sought to end monarchial absolutism. Nuri and his cothinkers opposed the opening of schools for women and the building of factories and "European" industries. To delegitimize the constitutional movement to adopt a secular constitution modeled after the constitution of Belgium, Nuri emphasized its "alien" and European origins. Nuri's major objection to constitutionalism and parliamentarism centered around such issues as:

> the inauguration of the customs and practices of the realm of infidelity . . . the intention to tamper with the sacred law which is said to belong to 1300 years ago and not to be in accordance with the requirements of the modern age, the ridiculing of the Muslims and insults directed at the *Ulama*, the equal rights of nationalities and religions, the spread of prostitution,

and freedom of the press which is contrary to our sacred law. (Arjomand, 1983: 179)

As the perceived guardians of cultural authenticity and religious sanctity, Nuri and his followers felt threatened by the intelligentsia's adoption of Western secular values. Perceiving the constitutionalists as the agents of Western influence in Iran, they vehemently attacked them.

Another prominent traditionalist who opposed democracy was Ayatollah Khomeini (1902–89), the leader of the Iranian revolution of 1979. Khomeini was raised in a traditional religious household and received a traditional Shi'ite education in theological seminaries. He came to political prominence by leading the 1963 uprising against the Shah's regime. His subsequent exile put him out of the reach of the monarchy and allowed him to take a more militant political position against the Shah. In order to arouse the masses to political action against monarchy, he developed a populist interpretation of Shi'ism. This increased his popularity and strengthened his stature as a leader. In his treatise on government and Islam, *Valayat-i Faqih* (the rule of the jurisconsult), Khomeini polemicized against both monarchy and Western democracy and called for the creation of an Islamic government. The governments that the Prophet Muhammad and Imam Ali (the first Shi'ite *Imam*) created were theocracies, argued Khomeini, and it is the duty of Muslims to follow their paradigmatic model. Only such Islamic government and the seizure of power by *Ulama* can ensure the rule of *Shari'a* and safeguard the sanctity and the salvation of the Muslim community. In an Islamic government a legislative body in the Western sense of the word is not necessary, Khomeini argued; in the Islamic government God alone is the ruler and the legislator. However, a consultative assembly is necessary to conduct consultation among Muslims according to the principle of *shura*. Thus, he referred to this consultative body (Tamadonfar, 1989: 47).

Khomeini explains that the rule of the jurisconsult in Islamic government is not arbitrary: "Those who govern are subject to a set of conditions that are specified in the Qur'an and the traditions of the most noble prophet, God's benedictions be upon him" (Khomeini, 1978: 52–3). The rule of the juriconsult is tantamount to a neo-Platonic idea of the Philosopher King. Since ordinary people lack the wisdom and the necessary religious knowledge to guide the community toward eternal salvation, it is argued, only the jurisconsult can provide a leader who knows what is best for his subjects. The title of *Faqih* (the cleric who is the most knowledgeable of *Shari'a*) bestowed upon him the mantle of the deputy of the Prophet in the absence of the twelfth Imam. This endowed him with great power as the judge, the arbiter and the prosecutor of the holy law. But Khomeini was more than a *faqih*. He was also a grand Ayatollah (the source of emulation) whose commandments and decrees were binding on his followers, who owed him loyalty and obedience. As such, Khomeini's charisma was rooted both in Shi'ite tradition of folk religion as well as his political legitimacy as the leader of the 1979 revolution. This potent combination of religious sanctity and political authority rendered Khomeini's power supreme.

Khomeini regarded Islamic government as the guardian of Islamic ideals and sanctity. Thus, any opposition to the Islamic Republic was tantamount to treason. He exhorted the necessity for the "unity of words and deeds" among Muslims. He admonished that pluralism and a multi-party system were deadly for the nation. All factions and groups "should merge into one united Islamic front: the party of God (*Hizballah*)" (Tamadonfar, 1989: 46–9). It is not then surprising that both the leftists (the Marxists and the Islamic Mujaheedin) and the rightists (monarchists) opponents of the Islamic Republic were persecuted.

Abul A'la Mawdudi (d. 1979), the founder of *Jama 'at-i Islamic* (Islamic League) in Pakistan conceived of Islam as a complete system that is the antithesis to Western democracy. He asserted that Islam is opposed to the idea of popular sovereignty; sovereignty belongs to God only. But in so far as humans are regarded as the vice-regents of God, some divine power is relegated to them. Mawdudi considered separation of religion and politics as a dangerous phenomenon. When religion is relegated to the personal realm, it gives rise to "bestial impulses and men perpetrate evil upon one another. In fact, it is precisely because they wish to escape the restraint of morality and the divine guidance that men espouse secularism" (Tamadonfar, 1989: 37). Mawdudi also perceived the seizure of state power as an instrumental step in the implementation of *Shari'a* and the creation of the "kingdom of heaven." As he puts it,

> the reforms which Islam wants to bring about cannot be carried out merely by sermons. Political power is essential for their achievement . . . the struggle for obtaining control over the organs of the state when motivated by the urge to establish the *din* (religion) and the Islamic *Shari'a* and to enforce the Islamic injunctions, is not only permissible but is positively desirable and as such obligatory. (Tamadonfar, 1989: 39)

Mawdudi regarded the authority of the Islamic state as all-encompassing, penetrating social and personal realms. This Islamic totalitarianism is, however, perceived to be different from Fascist or Communist totalitarianism, because it rejects dictatorship and grants liberties. In so far as democracy can be reconciled with the rule of Islamic law and subordinated to it, he entertained the possibility of it in a new synthesis he termed a totalitarian "theo-democracy" (Esposito and Piscatori, 1991: 436; Esposito and Voll, 1996: 23–9). Mawdudi regarded the Islamic polity as the kingdom of God (a theocracy). But Islamic theocracy is different from the theocracies in Europe prior to the eighteenth century. According to him,

The theocracy built by Islam is not ruled by any particular religious class but by the whole community of Muslims including the rank and file. The entire Muslim population runs the state in accordance with the book of God and the practice of his prophet . . . The executive under this system of government is constituted by the general will of the Muslims who have also the right to depose it. (Esposito and Voll, 1996: 24)

While every Muslim who is capable is entitled to interpret the *Shari'a*, no one, not even the entire community, has the right to change an explicit command of God (Esposito and Voll, 1996: 24). Mawdudi's thoughts on Islam and democracy, like those of many other Muslim theologians and theorists of the twentieth century, were full of ambiguities, contradictions, and ambivalence. For Mawdudi, as long as the leader is "just" and "right," his authority remains uncontested and he can disregard the political voice of the legislature. Only Muslims have the right to govern because only they are capable of upholding Islamic law and guiding the Muslim community toward the righteous path (Tamadonfar, 1989: 49–54). Therefore, political contestation and free access to political power, despite one's religious convictions or affiliation, which are constituent elements of the democratic process, are discarded. Moreover, if the Islamic state is the guardian of the divine truth, as many Muslim traditionalists hold, then alternative interpretations of truth and tolerance of diverse ideas become impossible. In Mawdudi's doctrine it is not clear who defines what a "right" and "just" leader is, or to whom the community owes allegiance and obedience.

A disciple of Mawdudi who became one of the prominent voices of militant Islamic traditionalism was Sayyid Qutb (d. 1966) of Egypt. Unlike Mawdudi's mild political temperament and his desire to reconcile Islam and democracy, Qutb considered all terrestrial powers, secular or religious, as illegitimate. He believed in divine sovereignty and opposed theocracies and rule by professional clergy as the usurpation of power under the name of religion. He also regarded Jamal Abdul Nasser's secular regime as the new *jahalia* (ignorance and barbarism). Since human beings were sinful, argued Qutb, in any government that is based on a group of people legislating for others, equality and absolute dignity, cannot be realized (Esposito and Piscatori, 1991: 435). Qutb considered both capitalism and socialism as flawed systems that were particularly unsuitable for the Muslim World. He also opposed communism for its preoccupation with materialism and its. disegard for human spiritual needs. As Qutb asserted, "communism in itself is an insignificant idea which deserves no respect from those who think humanely, above the level of food and drink" (Tamadonfar, 1989: 42). According to Qutb, Islamic government is a 'system that provides us with the bread that communism provides, and frees us from economic and social disparity, realizing a balanced society while sustaining us spiritually" (Tamadonfar, 1989: 42). Qutb's intransigent attitudes brought him early death at the hands of Nasser's regime in 1966. But his impact proved to be resilient especially on the left flank of the Muslim Brotherhood movement in Egypt, inspiring many Muslim militants and their leaders who have opposed Sadat's and Mubarak's governments, often with violence.

Many other contemporary leading traditionalist theologians also oppose democracy. Shiekh Muhammad Mutawwali al-Sha'rawi, a traditionalist religious leader from Egypt, declared in 1982 that *shura* does not connote simple majority rule, and Islam and democracy are incompatible. Likewise, in Algeria, Ali Benhadj, another traditionalist religious leader, objects to majority rule on the grounds that "rights and justice cannot be quantified; the greater number of votes does not translate into the greater moral position" (Esposito and Piscatori, 1991: 436).

Most Islamic states from Pakistan to the Sudan seem to have opted for a semblance of divine and popular sovereignty. The traditionalists' negation of Western democracy must be perceived in terms of the defensive position of Muslims in the post-colonial era of Western cultural and economic domination. Steeped in tradition and entrenched as the guardians of the Islamic past, they find themselves unable to fully embrace the idea of democracy with its roots in Judeo-Christian tradition. Yet, aware of the appeal of the concept of popular sovereignty to contemporary Muslims, they have opted for a compromise. By reinterpreting the Islamic past to find precedents for participatory politics and a parliamentary political system, they have attempted to respond to the popular sentiment for political participation.

This brief overview of the political thoughts of some leading Muslim modernists and traditionalists is an indication of the complexities involved in analyzing the compatibility and incompatibility between Islam and democracy. This debate is not confined to Muslim theologians. It has been a topic of controversy and polemics among academics as well.

Some academics consider Islam and its patrimonial culture as incompatible with democracy (Huntington, 1991). Others argue that since Islam owes its formative development to a pre-industrial age, it is structurally incapable of coping with the demands of the modern world. One such scholar is Bassani Tibi, who argues that any successful cultural accommodation of social change – including democracy – is dependent upon two central issues. First, there must emerge a democratization of access to science and technology and an elimination of the North–South gap. Second, Islamic monism must be replaced by intellectual pluralism. Muslim societies must desacralize their politics and depoliticize their religion. Only then can they successfully secularize their societies and democratize their political culture (Tibi, 1990: 1–5, 45–55, 179–96). Tibi asserts that

Islamic culture is particularly handicapped in the areas of law, language, and education to come to terms with change and accommodate new social realities. Because Quranic truth is regarded as eternal and immutable, and the *Shari'a* is all-encompassing, covering the private as well as the social realms of life, its jurisdiction over Muslims' lives is unlimited. A system of law viewed as immutable is extremely hard to change (Tibi, 1990: 74). The second element of Islamic culture that Tibi regards as an obstacle to democratic change is the Arabic language. The sources of Islamic law, the Qur'an and Hadith are Arabic proclamations.

Like Islamic law, the Arabic language is not open to change. Arabic is regarded as a sacred language. Thus, it has failed to accommodate new expressions and words. Finally, Islam in its all-encompassing nature also dominates education. Islamic education is not concerned with investigation and inquiry, but with learning in a sacred sense; it is a place for the cultivation of Islamic science and the teaching of the Qur'an and Hadith and branches of knowledge stemming from them. The access to rational science (natural science and philosophy), so critical to the development and growth of democracy in the West, has been obstructed in the Middle East. Thus, the creativity essential to the development of new ideas and the fostering of democratic growth has been limited. Hence, many universities in Muslim states are "rote-learning" institutions that encourage memorization of material instead of understanding and research (Tibi, 1990: 58, 104–10).

While parts of Tibi's critical assertions bear some merit, other parts can be disputed on several grounds. First, Tibi totally ignores the principle of *ijtihad*, which allows the Muslim clergy to reinterpret the *shari'a* and adapt to changing conditions. Indeed *ijtihad* has made the continuous vitality and relevance of Islam possible over the years. Second, language is the medium of articulation of human perception and the tool of human communication; it evolves with changing human conditions. Therefore, it is both analytically as well as factually wrong to declare Arabic an immutable language. Indeed, both French and English influences in Arabic have abounded since the dawn of the colonial era. Third, Tibi's contention that many universities in the Muslim world are "rote-learning" institutions is contradicted by his earlier observation in regard to the universalization of science. Hence, his contention that no research takes place in these universities seems an exaggeration. To be sure, research facilities are limited in the Muslim world, but in this age of the transfer of knowledge and technology, no country can close its borders to scientific method and the flow of information. This includes the most conservative of them all, Saudi Arabia.

Other scholars such as Richard Norton are more optimistic about the prospects for civil society and democratization in the Muslim world. He sees the development of an incipient civil society and the strengthening of the middle class as hopeful signs that the chances for democratization in the region are better than generally assumed (Norton, 1995). Yet, others such as Leonard Binder, contend that without a rigorous Islamic liberalism, political liberalism will not succeed in the Middle East, despite the emergence of bourgeois states (Binder, 1988). Unlike some who counterpose the Western intellectual tradition of rationalism to Islamic traditionalism, Binder attempts to find precedence for liberal thought in Islamic intellectual tradition itself. Having witnessed the ideological retreat of secular liberalism in the 1980s, he concludes that the only way liberalism can emerge as a viable ideological alternative is through the rediscovery or reinterpretation of the Islamic sacred past. While Binder's argument for the most part seems compelling, given the preeminent role of Islam in the process of political socialization and cultural life in general, he does not provide a satisfactory response to the assertion made by such scholars as Bar rington Moore, who holds that the social conditions that produced Western democracy are not present in the Third World (Moore, 1966).

The fact that some of the alternatives proposed by Muslim liberals seem to be out of touch with the pervading political realities of the Muslim world and, consequently unrealistic, poses an additional problem. For example, the Egyptian liberal Muslim theorist Abd al-Raziq's contention that "Islam has nothing to do with state" (Binder, 1988: 147), a clear attempt to depoliticize Islam, stands little chance of winning wide support among the masses entering the political arena with their traditional Islamic values. Islam not only competes with secular creeds to win the hearts and minds of the people, it also struggles for survival as a vital and relevant cultural medium in the wake of the global hegemony of Western culture. It may well be that liberalization of politics in the Muslim world will not flourish without separating religion from politics and desacralizing the political arena. But for that to happen, fundamental changes in the political landscape must take place to accommodate a vibrant civil society, tolerance, and pluralism. Closely related to the prospect for an Islamic liberalism in the region is the issue of human rights.

Islam and Human Rights

Many educated people throughout the Muslim world are concerned that while the Islamists, as persecuted opposition groups, may appear as advocates of democratic values and human rights, when they seize power they may impose their own variant of totalitarianism under the pretext of protecting Islamic sanctity and truth. There is also concern and trepidation that if an Islamic state is expected to be the guardian of divine truth and sacred principles, then the free competition of ideas which lies at the heart of pluralism becomes impossible.

While the spirit of Islamic tenets can be interpreted to conform with many elements of democracy and human rights, there are serious tensions between Islam as a political project and democracy and human rights. Since the present phase of Islamic revivalism is, for the most part, dominated by Muslim traditionalists rather than modernists, anxieties about the protection of human rights by Islamic governments run high, particularly among intellectuals and artistic communities.

The skeptics who see Islam and democracy as incompatible emphasize that *Shari'a* is the word of God. It is not a legislated law, but a *revealed* one. As such, there are serious limitations on its reinterpretation, elasticity, and malleability. In the eyes of orthodox Muslims, *Shari'a* has all the necessary requirements to guide them in this life and prepare them spiritually for the hereafter. Therefore, it has achieved perfection and any fundamental change or reinterpretation will compromise its sanctity and authenticity. It is also argued that human rights are given only by God; they are not inherent to humans. In so far as rights are acknowledged, they are defined as the obligations of the faithful, defined by the dictum, "rejoicing the good and forbidding the evil." In this rigid perception of Islam, human logic, rationality, and reason, which are perceived as fallible and ultimately inferior to divine wisdom, take a back seat to the unassailable sanctity of the holy law.

Not surprisingly, the Islamic notion of human rights is very different from its Western counterpart. First, rights are defined as religious duties and obligations rather than inalienable rights of the individuals in the Western sense. For example, freedom of expression is tolerated, but only in so far as it does not negate the *Shari'a* or question sacred Islamic principles. Second, the right of the community takes precedence over the right of the individual. Third, Islamists define rights more broadly to encompass social and economic rights.

While medieval Islamic law, like medieval Christian law, had some elements incompatible with human rights, the more modern interpretations of it are not necessarily so. The traditional Islamic penal code as interpreted and executed in Saudi Arabia and Sudan, for example, is clearly incompatible with the universal declaration of human rights. To be sure, many conservative apologists and some Muslim authoritarian regimes have evoked the sanctity of the *Shari'a* to suppress human rights. They may also violate or disregard the principle of Islamic law itself when political expediency or *raison d'état* (reason of state) requires (Sisk, 1992: 26–9).

Certain Muslim scholars, such as Ali abd al-Raziq, Farag Fawdah, and Muhammad Sa'id al-Ashmawi, consider the separation of religion and politics as a necessary prerequisite for democratization and the protection of human rights in Islamic societies. Can an Islamic order tolerate freedom of speech, association, and the contestation of political power by non-Muslims, communists, and liberals who may be regarded as "apostates," "renegades," "atheists" and the "enemies of Islam"? If not can we speak of the compatibility of Islam, human rights and democracy? (Kramer, 1995: 117–18). Human rights refer to universal inalienable rights of the people to be free from the coercion of a lawless state. The harsh punishment of political dissidents in Saudi Arabia, the persecution of Bahais in Iran and Christians in Sudan provide a few examples of human rights violations in the Muslim world. In many parts of the Muslim world, the authoritarian state, be it secular or Islamic, regards the people as subjects, whose life, liberty, and property can be trampled on if "the reason of state" requires it.

Violation of the rights of women and gender inequality also remain rampant in the Muslim world. Patriarchy and a patrimonial political system have proven to be resilient. The rate of political participation of women in the Arab world is among the lowest in the Third World, and female occupations are limited to such traditionally defined roles as nursing and teaching. Women's representation in positions of power also remains meager. In certain countries women are even denied such elementary rights as freedom to travel. In Saudi Arabia, for example, women are barred from traveling alone. Therefore, an essential element of democratization of the political system and expansion of human rights is gender equality and the empowerment of women.

Other scholars, while noting the profound tensions between Islam and human rights, seem more optimistic about the possibility of a reconciliation. In her study of Islam and human rights, Ann Mayer (1991) demonstrates how Islamic acceptance of civil and human rights is always circumscribed and confined by the *Shari'a*. Through a textual analysis of the Islamic Republic of Iran, Pakistan, and Sudan (under Numeiri) and an analysis of the writings of Mawdudi and Tabandeh, she discerns a pattern in all three countries:

> they borrow substantive rights from international human rights documents while reducing the protections that they actually afford. This is accomplished by restricting them so that the rights can only be enjoyed within the limits of *Shari'a*, which are unspecified. These emendations leave virtually unlimited discretion to states in deciding what the scope of the affected rights should be. (Mayer, 1991: 76)

Mayer is aware of the political, historical and cultural contexts of the Islamic response to human rights, especially in the modern era. By raising such pertinent issues as the impact of colonialism and the concomitant rise of cultural nationalism, she puts the Muslims' reaction and their defensive embrace of *Shari'a* in its proper historical and political context. By doing so, she separates herself from both conservative Muslim apologists, whose retrograde ideas perpetuate autocratic rulers and the patrimonial political culture that nurtures them, and their conservative Western coun-

terparts, who intellectually attack and denigrate anything Islamic. This attribute renders Mayer's analysis more balanced. She concludes that,

> The patterns of diluted rights in Islamic human rights schemes should not be ascribed to peculiar features of Islam or Islamic culture but should be seen as a part of a broader phenomenon of attempts by beneficiaries of undemocratic and hierarchical systems to legitimize their opposition to human rights by appeals to supposedly distinctive cultural tradition. (Mayer, 1991: 213)

Mayer sees the solution in a "synthesis of Islamic and international human rights norms" (Mayer, 1991: 207), a synthesis that could be realized if the Muslim world overcomes its present defensive posture. This could happen if the present global power arrangements change in favor of the Muslim world or if the present adversarial relation between some Western nations and parts of the Muslim world are replaced by more accommodating policies.

Conclusion

There is no yes or no, categorical answer to the question of the compatibility of Islam and democracy. To present a balanced response, one must ask which Islam? Who interprets it? And in what historical and social context? The lay and intellectual interpretations of Islam differ profoundly, as do the modernist and traditionalist accounts. The traditionalists have argued that Muslim societies have fallen behind in the race for progress and development because they have deviated from the fundamental teachings of the Prophet and the sanctioned traditions of Islam. Muslims can regain their past glory only if they embrace their tradition and emulate the paradigmatic example of pristine Islam. Imitation of the West can only contaminate the spirit of true Islam and bring moral decay and decline. The modernists, on the other hand, assert that Muslims have fallen behind because they have stagnated, embracing obsolete ideas of the past and refusing to accommodate the realities of the modern world, including rationalism and scientific thought. Only a modernized Islam and a reasoned faith can remain relevant in this rapidly changing world. Such divergent outlooks on how Islam must confront the intellectual and political challenges of the West partially explain the disparate responses of the two schools in regard to democracy and human rights. This also illuminates why the traditionalists, for the most part, harbor a rejectionist attitude toward democracy, while the modernists are, by contrast, more accommodating.

Western democracy evolved out of the Renaissance, the Reformation, rationalism, the industrial revolution and the development of commercial capitalism. These developments decimated the decrepit feudal social structure and the monarchial system associated with it, thus ushering in the democratic revolutions of the eighteenth century that swept western Europe and the United States. Democratic revolutions gave birth to parliamentary republics, put an end to the divine rule of kings, separated state and church and inaugurated open participation of the masses in the political process. It took the Western world two centuries of struggle, trial and error, progress and retrenchment to resolve the conflict between the forces of tradition and modernity, religion and secularism, and competing economic and social interests.

By contrast, the Muslim world has neither had a Renaissance and Reformation nor an industrial or democratic revolution. In many parts of the region feudal structures and norms still persist, as do monarchies, notably among the Persian Gulf Arab states and in Jordan. If posing the question of compatibility of Islam and democracy is intended to ask whether the Western prerequisites of democracy can be replicated in the Muslim world, the answer is emphatically no. "Islamic democracy" is going to have its own unique attributes and characteristics. Muslim societies have to go through their own process of resolving the contradictions and tensions that emerge on the path to political and economic development, carrying their particular history and cultural baggage. In the process, they will have to define their own variant of "democracy."

While democracy is culture bound, human rights are universal. All human life is inviolable and the right to live free from the coercion and abuse of a lawless state is longed for around the globe. Abuse of human rights in the Muslim world may not have as much to do with Islam as it does with social and economic forces that foster authoritarianism. The general conditions of poverty, the high rate of illiteracy, the presence of intrusive militaries, the pervasiveness of military governments, the lack of any longstanding democratic traditions and the weaknesses of civil society are perhaps more significant than Islamic culture in determining the fate of human rights.

As the source of cultural identity, authenticity, and consciousness for a majority of Muslims, Islam plays a preeminent role in social life. Therefore, the following questions raised by Kramer deserve serious thought and debate: Does political democracy presuppose not just economic, but also intellectual, liberalism? Can Islam allow for liberal thought without losing its true essence? (Kramer, 1995: 113). Furthermore, can Muslims regard Islam as another ideology, competing in the market place of ideas? Can they concede to intellectual pluralism as liberals do? In the final analysis, given the diversity, contradictions, and nuances inherent in Islam, these fateful questions cannot be answered philosophically, but only practically, in the realm of political life and through the mass action of millions of Muslims inspired by the new dreams through the mass action of millions of Muslims inspired by the new dreams and ideals of their age.

References

Abbott, Freeland (1971) "View of Democracy and the West" in Malik, Hafeez (ed.), *Iqbal: Poet Philosopher of Pakistan* (New York: Columbia University Press).

Anderson, Roy, Robert Seibert, and Jon Wagnor (1990) *Politics and Change in the Middle East: Sources of Conflict and Accommodation* (Englewood Cliff, NJ: Prentice-Hall).

Arjomand, Said Amir (1983) "The Ulama's Traditionalist Opposition to Parliamentarism, 1907–1909," *Middle Eastern Studies,* Vol. 17: 171–86.

Aristotle (1972) *The Politics,* Book 6 (Cambridge, MA: Harvard University Press).

Bazargan, Mehdi (1982) *Bazyabi-i Aneshha (Re-evaluation of Values),* Vol. 3 (Tehran: Liberation Movement of Iran).

Binder, Leonard (1988) *Islamic Liberalism: A critique of Development Ideologies* (Chicago: University of Chicago Press).

Chehabi, H.E. (1990) *Iranian Politics and Religious Modernism: The Liberation Movement of Iran under the Shah and Khomeini* (Ithaca : Cornell University Press, NY).

Dahl, Robert (1971) *Polyarchy: Participation and Opposition* (New Haven, CT: Yale University Press).

Dorraj Manochehr (1990) *From Zarathustra to Khomeini: Populism and Dissent in Iran* (Boulder, CO: Lynne Rienner).

—— (1992) "The Politics of Islamic Revival and Counterculture Mobilization in the Middle East: A Comparative Analysis," in Lehman, Cheryl R., and Moore, Russell M. (eds.), *Multinational Culture: Social Impacts of a Global Economy* (Westport, CT: Greenwood Press), 91–105.

—— (1995) "The Intellectual Dilemmas of a Muslim Modernist: Politics and Poetics of Iqbal," *The Muslim World,* Vol. 85, No. 3–4: 266–79.

Enayat, Humid (1982) *Modern Islamic Political Thought* (Austin, TX: University of Texas Press).

Esposito, John L. (1983) "Muhammad Iqbal and the Islamic State" in Esposito, John (ed.), *Voices of Resurgent Islam* (Oxford: Oxford University Press).

—— (1984) *Islam and Politics* (Syracuse: Syracuse University Press).

Esposito, John L. and Piscatori, James P. (1991) "Democratization and Islam," *Middle East Journal* Vol. 45 No. 3: 427–40.

Esposito, John L. and Voll, John O. (1996) *Islam and Democracy* (Oxford: Oxford University Press).

Ghadbian, Najib (1997) *Democratization and the Islamist Challenge in the Arab World* (Boulder, CO: Westview Press).

Goldschmidt Jr, Arthur (1991) *A Concise History of the Middle East* (Boulder, CO: Westview Press).

Hassan, Riffat (1971) "The Development of Political Philosophy," in Malik, Hafeez, (ed.), *Iqbal: Poet Philosopher of Pakistan* (New York: Columbia University Press), 136–58.

Huntington, Samuel (1991) *The Third Wave: Democratization in Late Twentieth Century* (Norman: University of Oklahoma Press).

Iqbal, Muhammad (1973) "The Reconstruction of Religious Thought in Islam" in *Kulyah E. Iqbal (The Collected Works of Iqbal)* (Lahor: Javid Iqbal), 95–117.

Keddie, Nikki R. (1960) *An Islamic Response to Imperialism* (Berkeley: University of California Press).

Khajeh, Nezam al-Mulk (1960) *The Book of Government or Rules for Kings* (London: Routledge Kegan Paul).

Khomeini, Ruhollah (1978) *Velayat-i Faqih, (The Rule of the Jurisconsult)* (Tehran: Amirkab Publisher).

Kramer, Gudrun (1995) "Islam and Pluralism" in Brynen, Rex, Korany Bahgat, and Noble, Paul (eds.), *Political Liberalization and Democratization in the Arab World,* Vol. I (Boulder, CO: Lynne Rienner) 113–28.

Lewis, Bernard (1988) *Language of Islam* (Chicago: University of Chicago Press).

Marlow, Louise (1997) *Hierarchy and Egalitarianism in Islamic Thought* (Cambridge: Cambridge University Press).

Mayer, Ann E. (1991) *Islam and Human Rights: Tradition and Politics* (Boulder, CO: Westview Press).

Moore, Jr., Barrington (1966) *The Social Origins of Democracy and Dictatorship* (Boston: Beacon Press).

Mortimer, Edward (1982) *Faith and Power: The Politics of Islam* (New York: Vintage Books).

Norton, Augustus R. (1995) *Civil Society in the Middle East,* Vol. 1 (Leiden: E. J. Brill).

Rosenthal, Franz (1960) *The Muslim Concept of Freedom* (Leiden: E. J. Brill).

Shariati, Ali (1972) *Qasetin, Mareqin, Nakesin (Oppressors, Deceivers, Betrayers)* (London: League of Muslim Students in Europe).

— (1973) *Iqbal: Ma'mar-e Tajdid Bana-ye Tafakor-e Islami (Iqbal: The Architect of the Renewal of Islamic Thought)* (Tehran: Forugh Publication).

— (1973) *Ummat Va Immamat (Community and Leadership)* (Houston, TX: Association of Muslim Students in the United States and Canada).

Sisk, Timothy (1992) *Islam and Democracy: Religion, Politics and Power in the Middle East* (Washington, D.C: United States Institute of Peace Press).

Soroosh, Abdolkarim (1994) *Farbeh Tar Az Ideology (More Potent than Ideology)* (Tehran: Saral Cultural Institute).

Tamadonfar, Mehran (1989) *The Islamic Polity and Political Leadership. Fundamentalism, Sectarianism, and Pragmatism* (Boulder, CO: Westview Press).

Tibi, Bassam (1990) *Islam and Cultural Accommodation of Social Change* (Boulder, CO: Westview Press).

Watt, Montgomery W. (1962) *Muhammad at Madina* (Oxford: Oxford University Press).

8

A Constructive Framework for Discussing Confucianism and Human Rights

Sumner Twiss

◆ Confucianism and human rights ◆

◆ Historical and pragmatic approaches ◆

◆ Intercultural human rights dialogue ◆

I write this paper from the perspective of one who works in the field of comparative ethics and who has been involved in recent intercultural dialogues on the relationship between international human rights and the ethics of religious and philosophical traditions.[1] In the latter context, I have focused especially on recent debates about whether human rights are relative only to particular cultural moral traditions, or whether they are properly conceived as universal and interculturally applicable. In these debates three issues have arisen as dominant concerns: (1) how international human rights and their justification ought to be construed within intercultural moral dialogues; (2) whether the perception of some scholars about an incompatibility between universal human rights and particular cultural traditions is sound; and (3) how one ought to respond to the difficult hermeneutical and moral issues likely to arise when quite different cultural moral visions and idioms confront each other in dialogue about human rights. These issues establish the parameters for the remarks that follow. My goal can be simply put: to develop a constructive framework for intercultural human rights dialogue and to

illustrate its utility with respect to the Confucian tradition.[2]

For the purposes of this discussion, human rights are to be understood as the set of rights articulated in the 1948 Universal Declaration of Human Rights and in the two subsequent and related covenants that came into force in the mid-1970s (jointly known as *The International Bill of Human Rights*), as well as in subsequent treaties and conventions.[3] The Covenant on Civil and Political Rights guarantees rights such as freedom of thought and expression, freedom from arbitrary arrest and torture, and freedom of movement and peaceable assembly. The Covenant on Economic, Social, and Cultural Rights provides for such rights as the right to work and receive fair wages, to protection of the family, to adequate standards of living, to education, to health care, to people's self-determination regarding their political status and economic, social, and cultural development, and to ethnic and religious minorities' enjoyment of their own culture, language, and religion. International human rights have been further expanded and elaborated by treaties on prevention of genocide, elimination of racial discrimination, elimination of discrimination against women, protection of refugees, rights of children, elimination of discrimination based on religious identity, and the rights of indigenous peoples (the latter is pending action). Although many of the rights articulated in these conventions are uncontested and accepted as universally normative, others are contested in the international arena, a fact which partially accounts for intercultural human rights dialogues.

These conventions are often interpreted as projecting a characteristic understanding of the conceptual features of human rights, which are worth introducing at the outset.[4] Human rights are typically regarded as moral (and legal) claims with such high priority that they are construed as entitlements to certain conditions and goods which must be socially guaranteed. Moreover, these priority claims or entitlements are conceived as being held by all human beings, who, particularly under adverse circumstances, can legitimately assert them against specified others, usually states or state representatives, who have correlative duties to satisfy their claims. Adapting a well-turned phrase from Ronald Dworkin, human rights are internationally recognized "trumps" held by all persons against specified others. Furthermore, it is also typically asserted that human rights must be claimed, recognized, and responded to as rights if they are to be fully functional as priority claims.

I take some exception to this typical characterization of the conceptual features of human rights, for I do not think it is sufficiently nuanced to account for other features which I discern in the international practice of human rights. Let me offer a few examples. First, as we will see later, there is an entire generation of developmental-collective human rights, some of which are cited above, that address the priority claims of entire peoples and communities, and these appear to be excluded by the standard characterization. Second, this characterization clearly holds that the priority claims of human rights must be recognized as rights

in order to be effective, but this seems to discount cases where the conditions and goods enjoined are guaranteed in a strong way by means other than explicit rights in certain traditions and societies – for example, as systemic requirements of a morally legitimate government or political system; as prerequisites for the appropriate fulfillment of people's socio-moral responsibilities in pursuit of the common good. It strikes me that the priorities identified by the subject matter of human rights can be normatively guaranteed by systems and traditions that lack or otherwise resist the explicit conceptuality of rights.[5] Third, although this is not a point that I discuss further in this paper, the typical characterization of human rights appears overly oriented to conceiving of human rights as priority claims against states or state representatives, but increasingly a large bulk of human rights problems – particularly those being addressed by social–economic human rights – stem from the practices of nonstate entities such as transnational corporations, which may be largely beyond the control of states. This is an important issue that is only now being recognized, and addressing it may well entail further nuances in a proper understanding of international human rights.[6]

Revised Understanding of Human Rights and Their Justification: A Historical and Pragmatic Approach

In order to explore the aforementioned issues and to develop a heuristic framework, we need at the outset to attend closely to a concern that arises when representatives of certain cultural traditions and scholars of those traditions consider international human rights.[7] The concern is this: human rights appear to many to represent a Western moral ideology intended to supplant the moral perspectives of diverse cultural, religious, and philosophical traditions. This perception has become a serious obstacle to progress in both intercultural dialogue and comparative ethics when considering human rights. Addressing this concern head-on may have the salutary effect of not only removing an obstacle to intercultural and scholarly work but also permitting us to develop a revised understanding of human rights that may benefit such work in the future.

The fundamental question raised by this perception is: What is the relationship between the universal claims of human rights conceived as a kind of "minimal morality" and the more particular, usually richer and more extensive moralities advanced by cultural traditions?[8] In particular, many cultural representatives and comparative philosophers worry that a typical liberal understanding of human rights, conceived as a set of core principles that ground moral judgments about behavior in diverse cultural settings, means that human rights are implicitly imperialistic.[9] More precisely, they worry that a human rights based core morality oriented to the rights of individuals is designed to supplant those moral traditions oriented to (for example) more communitarian visions and categories, implying the end, or at least the irrelevance, of the particular moral traditions that have emerged in the context of various cultures. And, they ask in a pointed way, would such replacement really be a moral advance for the peoples of the world, or rather (for example) a regression and entrenchment into a myopic social atomism?

In addition to this concern about hegemony over and replacement of rich and thick moralities by a thin morality, questions are raised about the metaphysical and epistemological assumptions seemingly associated with the promotion of human rights as a foundation for universal moral judgments. Here we encounter charges of an outmoded theory of moral knowledge (foundationalism), of narrow and myopic conceptions of human nature (e.g., as principally and narrowly self-interested), or truncated conceptions of persons and communities (e.g., as, respectively, isolated individual monads and market societies of unrelated strangers), and of loveless visions of the world stripped of interdependency, thick relationships, and compassion.[10] If, as many assert, claims about human rights are based on problematic conceptions of human nature, personhood and community, and moral knowledge, then cultural representatives at human rights dialogues may well wonder whether they are being asked to accept invalid ideas, notions that are no longer accepted even by many in the West.

These concerns and questions, however, betray a serious misunderstanding of the nature, source and function of human rights, and it is crucially important to set the record straight in this regard. Despite the common perception that human rights are simply an outgrowth and entailment of Western assumptions about human nature and moral rationality, it is a fact that the Universal Declaration of Human Rights (1948) was reached through a pragmatic process of negotiation between representatives of different nations and cultural traditions.[11] While it may be true that Western representatives had the upper hand in this process, the simple fact remains that pragmatic negotiation between differing views about the subject-matter was the process of choice, not theorizing about matters of moral knowledge, political philosophy, or even jurisprudence. Moreover, this pragmatic approach has continued to characterize the drafting and adoption of subsequent human rights covenants, conventions and treaties. We need to ask, therefore, what this process signifies or suggests about the nature, status and justification of human rights, and the answer may be reassuring to those who worry about the hegemony of a particular ideology in human rights.

The framers of human rights declarations, conventions, and treaties explicitly take – for better or worse – a pragmatic approach to the relationship between human rights norms and particular cultural traditions. This approach starts with the facts of moral plurality and cultural particularity and finds that in situations of crisis people of quite different traditions are able to acknowledge their mutual respect for certain basic values. The Universal Declaration was, for example, the historical product of a very particular crisis brought about by the genocide and brutalization of persons and communities during the Second World War. In the face of this crisis, representatives from a number of cultural traditions were able to recognize their mutual agreement in the judgment that such acts are antithetical to each and all of their traditions, and through a process of pragmatic negotiation, they were able to agree on incorporating this judgment in the language of specific human rights. The fact that rights-language was employed was doubtless due to the dominance of the Western legal tradition in the international arena, but the mutually agreed upon judgment about the proscription of certain acts was not exclusively a "Western" moral judgment.

Similarly, the subsequent human rights covenants of the 1970s were born from the mutual recognition that the oppression and material disadvantages suffered especially by peoples in developing countries were incompatible with moral sensibilities contained in a number of particular cultural moral traditions. Significantly, the influence of non-Western (or at least non-First World) cultural representatives was more prominent here, accounting in part for negotiated agreements to give greater emphasis to social and economic rights as well as collective rights of self-determination and development. A similar process led to the 1979 convention on the protection of women's human rights, and more recently, the 1993 UN Draft Declaration on the Rights of Indigenous Peoples. The point is that far from preempting or replacing the rich moral teachings of various cultural traditions, specific expressions of human rights concerns have arisen from the mutual recognition by adherents of these traditions

that they have a shared interest in the protection of certain values. Brutality, tyranny, starvation, discrimination, displacement, and the like are recognized by adherents of all traditions as their common enemy. This recognition implies that despite cultural differences many, if not all, traditions do in fact share important substantive moral values. At least in certain critical moments, participants in otherwise diverse traditions find that they have a shared set of aspirations as well as a shared capacity to suffer at the hands of those who violate the dignity and well-being of human persons and communities.

On pragmatic moral grounds, then, participants in particular cultural traditions and in the community of those concerned for human rights might consider specific expressions of human rights as products of successive recognitions by diverse peoples of a set of values embraced by their own distinctive cultural moral traditions. No one cultural tradition is the sole source of human rights concerns. Human rights are, from this point of view, the expression of a set of important overlapping moral expectations to which different cultures hold themselves and others accountable. Moreover, since there is as yet no end to the suffering that human beings impose on one another, we can expect to see additional moments of recognition, the addition of new human rights to those already recognized and the emergence of new types of human rights emphases.

One implication of this record of human rights negotiations and recognitions is that it is most appropriate to take a historical perspective on the emergence and formulation of human rights norms. The intercultural recognition of human rights has a history, and, as pointed out by Burns Weston (following Karel Vasak), this history marks at least three distinctive generations (types) of human rights, with each successive generation not supplanting the earlier one(s) but rather adding to, as well as nuancing, the earlier.[13] The first generation, emerging most definitively in the aftermath of World War II, is generally comprised of civil–political rights or liberties, although also touching on certain social and economic rights, as influenced by the background of Franklin D. Roosevelt's "Four Freedoms" speech and the identification of "freedom from want."[14] The second generation, emerging most definitively in the human rights covenants of the 1970s, adds a new emphasis on social and economic rights to crucial goods and services and their just allocation, though this generation is also clearly linked with the first and looks forward to the third (by identifying the rights of peoples to self-determination and their cultural rights). The third generation, which is now most definitively emerging amidst Third and Fourth World claims for global redistribution of power, wealth, and the common heritage of humankind (e.g., ecosystem, peace), adds yet another new emphasis on developmental–collective rights to peoples' self-determination and development (e.g., political, economic, cultural) as well as to a more just distribution of material and nonmaterial goods on a local and planetary scale. This generation also is linked with the preceding ones, inasmuch as it is concerned not only with the collective rights of peoples but also the liberties and material welfare of their individual members. The international human rights community recognizes all three generations or types of human rights as important and interrelated and needing to be pursued in a constructive balance or harmony. These three generations are, in a word, indivisible, though in a given situation or context, one or another generation may merit special emphasis.

Now, it is important to note that in some quarters there appears to be a tendency to correlate strongly these three generations with distinctive assumptions about human nature, persons, and community, in such a way as to seemingly undermine the contention that all three generations are interrelated and indivisible.[15] Weston associates civil–political human rights with the philosophy of liberal individualism,

social–economic rights with the socialist tradition, and developmental–collective rights with the philosophy of holistic community.[16] Inasmuch as different cultures and traditions make their own distinctive contributions to international human rights, there is something to this contention, but it could also be misleading as well, for, as argued by Weston, it deflects attention away from the fact that successive generations not only add new human rights emphases to the earlier generations but also modify our understanding of the nature and import of earlier generations. There is, in effect, a recursive and spiraling hermeneutical process at work here that needs to be taken into account – recursive in the sense of returning to and interpreting the earlier generations in light of the succeeding, and spiraling in the sense of interpreting the later generations in the light of the recursive move. International human rights constitute, in short, a dynamic tradition in their own right that may mitigate the effects of perceived internal incoherence.

For example, in baldly characterizing civil–political human rights as the "negative" liberties (or "freedoms from" oppressive political authority) advanced by liberal individualism, one might risk deflecting attention away from the fact that these liberties are also understood as "enablements" or "enpowerments" for persons' to function as flourishing members of a polity or community where they try to convince others of their ideas about the best way to live together in their society.[17] That is to say, civil–political liberties are not simply the negative "freedoms-from" associated with a caricatured liberal individualism concerned with protecting the privacy of radically autonomous, isolated, selfinterested, ahistorical and acultural selves, but rather are positive enpowerments to persons' involvement in a flourishing community that are compatible with, for example, communitarian traditions of moral and political thought. The subsequent generation of social–economic human rights, with its concerns about exploitation of certain classes and colonial peoples, helps to highlight this positive function of civil–political rights, by driving home the point that certain minimal social–economic conditions are necessary for people to flourish fully as politically involved members of their societies. By the same token, however, we can also see the wisdom behind the thesis that civil–political liberties may be crucially important to the enhancement of peoples' social and economic situation: for example, exercising civil–political rights may result in pressures for change in social and economic conditions.[18] Thus do these two generations change our understanding of both, beyond the traditional philosophies and assumptions often associated with them, enabling us to appreciate their interdependence and mutual effects.

A similar point can be made about the effects of the third generation of human rights (developmental–collective) on the other two. To associate these third-generation rights with the philosophy of holistic community on a planetary scale without further adumbration could run the risk of permitting these rights to be seen as in dramatic tension with, for example, the civil–political rights generally ascribed to individual persons. While it is certainly true that collective rights of self-determination and development of material and non-material goods are primarily ascribable to communities and people, it is not true, as Weston indicates, that these need be construed as incompatible with the other generations.[19] With respect to social-economic rights, we can easily interpret collective human rights as an emphatic and more just generalization of social and economic benefits to the oppressed and suffering peoples of the world (conceived both collectively and individually). Indeed, the collective rights of, for example, the peoples of the Fourth World are in principle compatible with civil–political liberties – the Iroquois Six Nations Confederacy being a prime historical example,

and the Draft Declaration of the Rights of Indigenous Peoples being another, more contemporary example.[20]

My point in this discussion should not be lost: all three generations of human rights in fact identify and forward a wide range of enpowerments, both individual and collective, that are crucial to individual and community flourishing on a local and wider scale. And, insofar as they do this, they are interdependent and mutually influential and compatible all the way down, so to speak. Furthermore, under this understanding, human rights in general are compatible in principle not only with cultural traditions that emphasize the importance of individuals within community (which is a more apt characterization of Western liberalism) but also with cultural traditions that may emphasize the primacy of community and the way that individuals contribute to it – that is *both* more liberal individualist *and* more communitarian traditions. Rigid dichotomies as well as static understandings of the historical sources of human rights may be quite misleading with regard to the conceptual flexibility and development of international human rights.[21]

Now, some may think that I am glossing over necessarily large differences between liberal and communitarian interpretations of, for example, civil–political rights or liberties. In particular, they may contend that in liberal traditions these rights are held by individuals against the state, whereas in communitarian traditions they are granted by the state only so long as they are exercised in the interests of the state. While such a contention may be applicable in some cases, it is not true for all, and it may not be necessarily true for any, pending clarification of the social ideals of the traditions in question. Insisting on the supposed gap between liberal and communitarian traditions runs the risk of identifying traditions with states. It also overlooks those cases in which civil–political liberties are regarded as constitutive and defining elements of both liberal and communitarian ideals of a flourishing community that can be used to critique deviations of respective states from those ideals. There may indeed be a large difference between, on the one hand, liberal and communitarian social ideals incorporating civil–political liberties in their traditions of moral and political thought, and, on the other, the actual constitutions and practices of states in measuring up to those ideals. This is an unfortunate fact of our less-than-ideal world, but it does not undermine my claim that both liberal and communitarian traditions can recognize and value the importance of civil–political liberties in their respective ideals of community flourishing. The differences between liberal and communitarian traditions would then devolve on the differences in the content of their respective ideals of communal flourishing apart from their shared commitment to civil–political liberties. It is this understanding of a shared commitment to the role of civil–political liberties in diverse social ideals that is forwarded by international human rights.[22]

A second important consequence of this historical and pragmatic conception of human rights involves a revised understanding of their status and justification. Human rights identify and specify conditions that are crucially important for a life worthy of human persons and communities as negotiated and agreed upon by representatives from diverse traditions.[23] In effect, human rights represent a common vision of central moral and social values that are compatible with a variety of cultural moral anthropologies – a unity within moral diversity. At one level their justification depends on a practical moral consensus amongst diverse traditions which have acknowledged their mutual recognition of the human importance of these values. This recognition is grounded in shared historical experiences of what life can be like without these conditions, as well as in a negotiated agreement and commitment to see these conditions fulfilled. Moreover, this negotiation, consensus, and commitment are open

and public: made by, to, and before the peoples of the world.

At a second level of justification, each of these traditions may justify its own participation in the consensus by appealing to its own set of moral categories as appropriate to its particular philosophical or religious vision of human nature, person and community, and moral epistemology. Thus, internal to a cultural moral tradition, the subject matter of particular human rights (what they are about or what they address) may be justified as, for example, divinely ordained precepts, implications of natural law or natural reason, self-evident moral truisms, systemic moral assumptions about appropriate relations between state and citizen, entailments of certain virtues, etc. (the list is open-ended precisely because of the rich variety of cultural moral traditions). This distinction between levels or arenas of human rights justification makes possible the recognition that a tradition may have the resources to justify its agreement to participate in and abide by international human rights without necessarily being compelled to forge its own internal human rights categories. Even if they lack the internal conceptuality of rights and human rights, most (if not all) traditions have the internal moral resources at least to recognize the importance of the subject matters being addressed by international human rights and to justify on internal cultural moral grounds, pertaining to their own visions of human nature and welfare, their agreement to abide by the pragmatic international consensus on human rights. This may constitute a different, possibly more attainable, burden of justification for some traditions than that of having to develop their own internal human rights subtraditions. While these traditions would presumably develop internal understandings of how their moral visions and idioms relate to the subject matters addressed by international human rights (i.e., a "theory" of relationship), they are not compelled to adopt or develop an internal human rights subtradition in any stronger sense (e.g., the active internal deployment of the language and discourse of human rights).[24]

Recognition of a two-level approach to the source and justification of human rights has a number of advantages, not the least of which is that it appears to capture the actual state of affairs about how human rights are justified. Moreover, it permits us to acknowledge in a reasonably sophisticated manner both commonalities and differences among cultural moral traditions – they share a set of core values while at the same time articulating and living by the richer and more variegated moral visions appropriate to their historical circumstances and cultural settings. Furthermore, it allows us to acknowledge that while human rights may be justified on grounds of pragmatic agreement at the point where moral traditions may overlap in their shared insights and commitments, they may also be justified and even construed within different moral idioms as appropriate to cultural moral diversity. Additionally, this approach permits us to appreciate the historical specificity and development of human rights norms at the international level as the result of reciprocal interactions among diverse traditions, while still being able to respect internal variations among different conceptions of human nature and corresponding moral conceptualities, languages, and epistemologies. Moreover, inasmuch as this approach is founded on a historical and pragmatic vision of the source of human rights, it allows us to appreciate more thoroughly the specific contributions that different moral cultures might make to the recognition and formulation of human rights norms. Finally, the two-level approach permits us to handle some of the epistemological controversies about human rights by resisting the imposition of one culture's moral epistemology on all the rest. Human rights need not be justified monolithically by one particular epistemology, entailing the rejection of all other epistemic approaches, precisely because we can

distinguish between levels of appeal – pragmatic and negotiated con- sensus for all at the international level, but tolerance for a variety of approaches at the cultural level.[25]

I admit that this two-level approach will not resolve all problems about the moral epistemology of human rights, much less all tensions between the universality of human rights and the particularity of cultural moral traditions. But it may mitigate these problems and tensions for the purposes of intercultural human rights dialogues. If, for example, cultural representatives, or scholars on their behalf, can see that they are not being asked to relinquish their epistemic appeals and moral idioms, but only to confine their use to the context or level where they would have the greatest effect, then they may be somewhat freer to operate pragmatically and consensually at the international level and in intercultural dialogues. Moreover, the two-level approach may assist cultural representatives and scholars in seeing and dealing with the big issues of crucial conditions for human well-being rather than getting bogged down in smaller issues of cultural nuance, in a context that calls for pragmatic negotiation between cultures rather than cultural proselytization aimed at the wholesale conversion of others. Furthermore, the two-level approach may well prompt cultural representatives and scholars to deal explicitly with issues of how to translate their internal cultural views into a language and idiom that is more broadly persuasive at the intercultural or international level: for example, Buddhist dependent co-origination or Confucian one-bodiedness with heaven, earth, and the myriad things may only have "moral bite" for other Buddhists or Confucians, respectively, but insofar as these notions can be translated into terms of shared responsibility for the ecosystem and possibly recognition of the claims of all sentient beings, they can in fact function to greater effect at the intercultural level.[26]

Issues will remain about how to adjudicate contestable human rights norms that fall outside the agreed-upon international consensus, especially when these norms may appear to conflict seriously with particular cultural visions of social relations. But, again, the two-level approach may assist the adjudication process by encouraging cultural representatives and scholars to consider whether there might not be correspondences between the positions of other cultures and more submerged voices within those traditions that have not been heard or taken seriously enough. Thus the level of pragmatic negotiation can direct attention to the question of internal cultural moral diversity and possibly bring new resources into human rights dialogues.

To summarize: The facts, as I have represented them, of an international pragmatic moral consensus regarding human rights and of the history of their three successive generations, inspired by the socio-moral visions of diverse cultural traditions, contradict the simplistic claim that human rights represent a hegemonic Western moral ideology. Furthermore, the fact of three generations of human rights, together with their recursive and spiraling hermeneutical interaction, contradicts also the myopic perception that human rights are exclusively civil–political liberties. Moreover, the two-level approach to human rights justification, together with the historical and pragmatic perspective I have provided on the background of international human rights, implies that these rights are not strongly associated with or grounded in problematic metaphysical and epistemological assumptions. On the contrary, they are in a significant sense "theory thin" at the international level, permitting wide diversity at the internal cultural level and mitigating the temptation to locate human rights within any one moral or political theory.[27] Finally, I might observe that while it is an open question as to whether certain cultural traditions may lack, either explicitly or even implicitly, their own internal human rights subtraditions, it seems more than likely that all cultural traditions have the resources necessary to justify on internal grounds and in

their own moral idioms, their agreement to abide by the international human rights consensus, for this constitutes a lesser burden of justification that does not require cultural traditions to employ the conceptuality of human rights at the cultural level.

Applying This Revisionary Understanding to the Confucian Tradition's Role in Intercultural Human Rights Dialogue

To clear the way for this application, I need first to consider some contemporary scholarly debate about universality versus relativism in human rights. This debate appears to take place on two levels. The first level involves explicit debate between competing conceptions of human rights, one of which emphasizes their universality as legal norms and the other emphasizing their particularity as moral norms (with the suggestion of their ideological adventitiousness as legal norms in the world community).[28] This level of debate is conducted among scholars of human rights per se. The second level of debate is more implicit coming as it does from scholars of particular cultural traditions who take differing positions about whether human rights are or can be compatible, conceptually and morally, with these traditions. At this second level, one encounters scholars who tend toward an incompatibility thesis as well as scholars who are open to finding compatibilities between human rights norms and culturally particular moral norms and idioms.[29]

While it is not possible to discuss in detail the work of scholars engaged in these debates, I do want to discuss certain general traits of their work that will help us to identify significant shortcomings in our consideration of human rights *vis-à-vis* the Confucian tradition. For convenience, I will use the simple labels of "universalists" and "particularists" to refer to the two camps that predominate at both levels of scholarly debate. Universalists tend to emphasize the universality of human rights as legal and moral norms as well as some sort of foundationalist epistemology to ground their status as universal moral rights.[30] Particularists, by contrast, tend either to deemphasize the legal status of human rights norms or to stress their roots in Western moral ideology (e.g., liberal individualism) as well as resisting the supposed legitimacy and persuasiveness of moral epistemology traced to and linked with the seventeenth- and eighteenth-century Enlightenment period in the West.[31] In the latter case, they see moral norms and modes of reasoning as more significantly conditioned by historical and cultural context than may be admitted by universalists. Particularists also tend (1) to emphasize, in order to resist, the ideological individualism supposedly associated with civil–political human rights, and (2) to contrast the communitarian moral visions of non-Western societies and cultures with this ideological individualism.

In my view there are problems with the positions of both camps. With respect to the universalist position, there are dangers implicit in trying to justify tout court human rights by appealing to a contestable moral epistemology (e.g., Western foundationalism) in the international arena. Such a move not only undercuts the benefits attained by a two-level approach, but it also deflects attention away from the power and function of justification through negotiated pragmatic consensus, and enmeshes human rights in what could be endless epistemic uncertainty and debate. Moreover, such a monolithic approach to human rights justification runs the serious risk of interfering with the processes of both pragmatic negotiation and human rights dialogue among diverse cultural moral traditions.

For their part, human rights particularists can be charged with significant myopia about the complexity and historical development of human rights. The myopia stems from the failure to recognize that there are three, not just one, generations of human rights – civil–political, social–economic, and developmental–collective – and that the latter two generations significantly modify the ideological individualism that particularists associate with civil–political rights. Thus particularist arguments about tensions and incompatibilities between non-Western communitarian traditions, on the one hand, and civil–political individualist human rights, on the other, overlook possible (and I believe likely) compatibilities between these same traditions and social–economic, collective, and even civil–political rights (under our revised understanding). Some particularist comparisons between supposedly radically individualistic human rights and communitarian traditions may suffer from a further problem: some of the materials employed in the comparisons tend to emphasize rather exclusively classical texts from very ancient periods of those traditions, without giving proper attention to later texts and periods which might provide relevant data about the diversity of views internal to the traditions in their more modern form.

An example of a particularist comparison that illustrates these problems is provided by Henry Rosemont's article critiquing the relevance of human rights to the Confucian tradition.[32] In this article Rosemont not only assumes that human rights are exclusively civil and political individual rights – overlooking social–economic and collective rights as well as the nuances I have suggested with regard to a more communitarian understanding of civil–political rights – but also confines his comparison to ancient Confucianism, rather than including within his scope of comparison later neo-Confucian developments as well. Strongly contrasting with this tendency toward problematic comparison is Wm. Theodore de Bary's article where, after taking an explicitly historical view of "human rights as an evolving conception," de Bary identifies a range of neo-Confucian thinkers, principles, and recommended reforms that seem to be plausibly compatible with selected first- and second-generation human rights: e.g., humane governance (nontorture, penal reform), fairness in taxation and charitable granaries (reform of social–economic conditions and allocation of material goods), legal reform and recognition of "the inherent worth of the individual" as well as "the essential voluntarism of the political and social order (tendency in the direction of civil–political liberties understood as enpowerments to community involvement)."[33] While I admire Rosemont's work in Chinese philosophy generally, I am inclined to regard de Bary's approach as the more valid and useful when it comes to examining the possible place of human rights in the Confucian tradition.

I now want to offer a sketch of how human rights under my revised understanding can fit within the Confucian tradition. I shall do this in five steps. First, especially since I am not a scholar of Confucian tradition, it seems appropriate for me to outline my general understanding of those parameters of the tradition that may have a particular bearing on human rights. Second, in order to provide some hope and relevant background for this project, I shall mention briefly a historical contribution of the Confucian tradition to the Universal Declaration of Human Rights that appears to be little known. Third, I shall propose that all three generations of human rights, with varying degrees of emphasis, can be compatible with Confucian moral and political thought; that is, I shall offer as hypotheses for other's consideration how I regard human rights as fitting within this tradition. Fourth, in conformity with my two-level approach to human rights justification, I shall further suggest that it is fully open to the Confucian tradition to justify on its own terms, to its own participants, its agreement to participate in human rights consensus at the international level. Finally, I shall conclude by proposing that the two-level approach permits us to chart interactions in the future between the Confucian tradition and the international human rights community. My

understanding of the parameters of the Confucian tradition relevant to human rights is as follows: Confucian moral and political thought is basically communitarian in outlook: (1) emphasizing the fact that the human person is essentially a social being; (2) giving primacy of place to the duties that persons have to the common good of the community and the virtues needed for the fulfillment of these duties; and (3) casting reciprocal social relationships and roles (especially the Five Relationships) as fundamental to communal flourishing and its shared vision of the good. At the same time, the tradition also emphasizes the importance for all its participants, ranging from rulers to ordinary people, of moral self-cultivation, predicated on an innate moral potential to develop virtues of benevolence, righteousness, propriety, and discernment, and guided by paradigmatic moral exemplars (sages) who are themselves guided by the tradition's basic texts and the moral and political compasses contained therein. This strong orientation to persons in community is grounded in a vision of the interdependence of all beings in the universe, which in turn sustains a basic sympathy for the whole and its constitutive parts, in the image of extending care from family relationships into ever larger concentric circles of care. When one reviews the range of Confucian thinkers, from Confucius himself, through Mencius, to the neo-Confucians such as Zhu Xi, Wang Yang-Ming, and Huang Zongxi, one gains the sense that the Confucian moral and political tradition is greatly concerned about all those conditions – for example, social, economic, educational – that have a bearing on people's cultivation of their moral potential to flourish as responsible members of an organic community in a harmoniously functioning universe.[34]

Pier Cesare Bori, referring to records of the debates surrounding the drafting of the Universal Declaration of Human Rights, reports that the Confucian tradition, as represented by the Chinese delegate Chang, influenced the formulation of Article I.[35] As reported by Bori, the first version of this article stated: "All men are brothers. As human beings with the gift of reason and members of a single family, they are free and equal in dignity and rights." With respect to this article, Chang argued for the inclusion of "two-men-mindedness" (the basic Confucian idea of ren) in addition to the mention of "reason." At the forefront of Chang's mind, suggests Bori, was the idea of a fundamental sympathy, benevolence, or compassion (as represented by Mencius) as constitutive of human beings generally. The wording finally adopted included "conscience" in addition to "reason," with the understanding that "conscience" was not the voice of an internal moral court but rather the emotional and sympathetic basis of morality, "a 'germ' objectively present" in all persons, "which reason must cultivate." Thus was a basic Confucian concept inscribed in the opening article of the Universal Declaration, a fact that ought to suggest to us (1) international human rights are not, contrary to the common perception, simply an ethnocentric Western construction, and (2) the Confucian tradition may well be compatible with and have more to contribute to a proper understanding of these rights.

Given the Confucian tradition's historical emphasis on the responsibility of the ruler to ensure the subsistence, livelihood, and education of the people as a qualification of political legitimacy (stemming from the Mencian notion of righteous revolt against an emperor who, in oppressing the people, loses the mandate of Heaven) it seems a further short step to contend that the tradition supports the second generation of human rights.[36] And in fact we can see this at work in the background of a long-standing openness of twentieth-century Chinese regimes to social and economic human rights as well as their efforts to better the material conditions of the people. The influence of Marxism may be in the foreground here, but there is evidence of Confucian influence as well.

Ann Kent, a particularly sensitive interpreter of human rights in the contemporary Chinese context, argues persuasively that both Confucianism and Marxism tend to emphasize an organic society oriented to the primacy of the collective good over the individual and the responsibility of the ruler or state to ensure social stability and the material welfare of the people, as well as informal social mechanisms for adjudicating conflict.[37] And she relates the first two of these parallels or elective affinities in part to the Chinese openness to second generation human rights. My first hypothesis, then, is that the Confucian tradition is quite properly open to the recognition of socio-economic human rights. Whether or not it chooses to employ the language of human rights, the tradition's emphasis on the importance of this subject matter indicates that its representatives can sensibly participate in an international consensus on their formulation.

My second hypothesis is that the Confucian tradition, at least in some of its phases, is also compatible with first-generation civil–political human rights. In his *Liberal Tradition in China,* de Bary argues persuasively that a number of neo-Confucian thinkers put forward ideas of, respectively, the moral nature of humankind and individual perfectibility (Zhu Xi), autonomy of the moral mind and individual conscience (Cheng-Zhu), generalized human potential for sagehood (Cheng Yi, Zhu Xi), personalism understood as the concept of the person's flourishing in community with others (Cheng Yi, Zhu Xi), self-governing community and voluntarism at the local level (Zhu Xi, Wang Yang-ming), and even a reformed conception of the law as a check on political abuse as well as a conception of public education for enhancing people's political participation (Huang Zongxi).[38] While these ideas do not support a radically individualistic interpretation of civil–political rights since the true person is construed as a thoroughly social being they are quite compatible with such rights conceived as positive enpowerments for persons' involvement in and contribution to social and political processes aimed at communal flourishing. Moreover, there is no gainsaying the judgment by de Bary that Huang's ideas in particular "could have provided a framework for what we call today 'human rights,'" which I interpret to refer primarily but not exclusively to civil–political liberties. In sum, the Confucian liberal tradition seems in principle compatible with first generation human rights under the communitarian-open interpretation of those rights that I advanced earlier.

It also seems relevant to point out that some Confucian-influenced human rights activists appear to agree with this second hypothesis. For example, Kim Dae Jung, a Korean human rights activist, has publicly rebutted the challenge by Lee Kuan Yew, former prime minister of Singapore, to the relevance of human rights to East Asian societies.[39] In so doing, Kim Dae Jung self-consciously represents Confucian political philosophy as a tradition that incorporates a heritage of ideas and practices compatible with and open to civil–political human rights. As Confucianism reemerges as an increasingly important factor in the Chinese context, one can envisage internal cultural dialogues about, for example, the relative balance of civil–political and social–economic human rights that might result in a more explicit commitment to the former as well as the latter.

As a third hypothesis, I want to suggest that the Confucian world view also seems compatible with the third generation of developmental–collective human rights. This hypothesis is supported in part by the aforementioned notion of righteous rebellion by the people and by the neo-Confucian emphasis on the principle of voluntarism in self-government in community structures, which taken together appear but a short step from collective rights to self-determination and development. But an even deeper consideration

stems from what Tu Weiming has called "the highest Confucian ideal" – namely, "the unity of Man and Heaven, which defines humanity not only in anthropological terms but also in cosmological terms," extending Confucian humanism and its sense of moral responsibility to a planetary or even universal scale.[40] I wager that combining these elements – self-governance and the unity of Man and Heaven – would support not only Third and Fourth World developmental claims to participate in the power, wealth and common heritage of humankind, but also their rightful claims to peace and harmony on a total world scale. The Confucian moral and metaphysical vision – its one-bodiedness with Heaven and Earth and myriad things – is clearly intended to advance the welfare of the entire holistic community of interdependent beings, covering the subject matters of human rights and even extending these to "green" rights as well.

I suggested earlier that a two-level approach to human rights justification permits particular moral cultures to justify on their own terms to their own constituencies their agreement to participate in human rights consensus at the international level, where that consensus is itself justified on pragmatic moral grounds. This means that the recognition of particular human rights may be justified at the internal level in terms of Confucian moral categories and idioms. Some scholars of the Confucian tradition have maintained that, internally, this would not be possible because the tradition lacks the conceptual resources to do so.[41] The reason given is that the Confucian tradition is a virtue-based communitarian morality that can have no room for the concept or recognition of rights, human or otherwise. There are at least three lines of counter-response to such a contention. One is to show that communitarian traditions do not, simply by virtue of their community-orientation, lack the conceptual resources for handling human rights. A second is to show that the Confucian tradition in particular does not lack such resources. And a third is to show that even if the tradition lacked rights conceptuality per se, it could nonetheless use its resources to justify its agreement to participate in international human rights consensus.

The first line of counterresponse is demonstrable in light of a number of considerations. First, there are communitarian moral traditions which do in fact recognize the categories of rights and human rights (for example, varieties of Christian moral traditions, including most prominently Catholic social teachings, which simultaneously reject radical individualism, advance a thoroughly social understanding of the person and the importance of community as well as duties and virtues oriented to the common good, and yet accept human rights in their three generations) and varieties of indigenous cultural moral traditions, which are thoroughly communitarian in outlook and yet build in recognitions of all three types of human rights (otherwise the draft declaration of indigenous peoples' human rights would not be possible as it stands).[42] Second, there appears to be no logical reason for contending that rights-discourse is incompatible with communitarian traditions, so long as we resist asservations that such discourse must presuppose assumptions about the radical autonomy of persons abstracted from communal bonds, social roles and historical and cultural traditions.[43] As I have suggested, such assumptions seem manifestly inapplicable when considering the meaning and history of human rights. Moreover, as Seung Hwan Lee has pointedly argued, referring to the work of Joel Feinberg, it is difficult to conceive of any moral tradition which incorporates practices of property, promises, contracts, loans, marriages, partnerships, etc. as devoid of conceptual counterparts (to duties) that have the function of rights.[44] As he says, "in this sense, the concept of rights is indispensable for our moral life regardless of social ideals (whether communitarianism or liberalism)

and regardless of the types of morality (whether virtue-based or rights-based) we adopt." Indeed, I know of no cultural moral tradition which lacks a sense of claims that can be made against others in the context of cooperative social practices relying upon interpersonal or intergroup expectancies produced by the behavior they regulate.[45]

In the particular case of the Confucian tradition, Lee also convincingly argues that there are "plentiful instances from Confucian literatures" of "the substantive content of rights," ranging from Mencius' examples of entrustments of the care of one's cattle or one's family to another (with implicit duties and rights) and his defense of a people's apparent "right to revolt against tyrannies," to Chung-ying Cheng's and Hyung I. Kim's interpretations of yi (though I concede that there may be interpretative issues with regard to these examples).[46] And I believe that de Bary's lectures on neo-Confucian liberalism and its openness to human rights categories reinforce the persuasiveness of a compatibility between Confucian thought and human rights. This suggests to me that the Confucian tradition does have the conceptual and moral resources to recognize and even justify internally international human rights. Even if this were not the case, I think that de Bary's discussion makes it clear that, even without the conceptuality of rights per se, the tradition has the resources to recognize and justify the subject matters of human rights, that is, to support the importance of meeting people's social and economic needs and to support the civil and political enpowerments that people need for communal self-governance and personal self-cultivation. That is, even if the tradition itself preferred not to use the languages of rights or human rights, those resources seem more than adequate to support the tradition's agreement to participate in and abide by, on pragmatic moral grounds, an international human rights consensus. On the matter of explicit procedures and appeals within the Confucian tradition for justifying internally its agreement to participate in international human rights consensus, I suspect that there are myriad possibilities, and I am content to let representatives of the tradition handle that matter. My own sense of those possibilities ranges across appeals to the moral compasses and standards contained within classical texts (e.g., *Analects, The Mencius),* to various sages, teachers, and advisers who exemplify the Way (i.e., appeals to the behavior and thought of paradigmatic characters), to the normative content of Confucian virtues as expressive of human moral destiny, to the *li* (principles, patterns) revealed by the innate heart/mind or its intuitive practical moral knowledge, etc. With any of these appeals, it is important to be clear that the tradition need not derive and justify human rights per se from its own moral categories (though that may be possible as well, as I have suggested), but only use them to justify its agreement to participate in and abide by the pragmatic intentional consensus for reasons pertaining to its own vision of human moral nature and welfare.[47] This constitutes a different and possibly more attainable burden of justification than that of having to forge its own internal human rights tradition (though the resources seem to be present for this as well).

Let me now recapitulate the three theses proposed in this section of the paper: (1) that the Confucian tradition has moral content overlapping with international human rights in their three generations; (2) that this overlapping content can be plausibly framed internally in the idiom of human rights; and (3) that this overlapping content, even if not framed in human rights language, is sufficient for the tradition to justify internally its agreement to participate in an international human rights consensus.[48] Much of what I have argued supports all three theses. Confucian parallels to the three generations of human rights are intended to support at least thesis (1), though they have some bearing on theses (2) and (3) as well. The points about

communitarian traditions in general and the Confucian tradition in particular being compatible with idioms of rights and human rights are intended to support thesis (2). And the point that even if thesis (2) were resisted for some reason, the Confucian tradition has resources sufficient for justifying its participation in an international human rights consensus is an articulation of thesis (3) that combines thesis (1) with my earlier discussion of a two-level approach to human rights justification.

Finally, I think it important to point out that the two-level approach to justifying human rights permits us in principle to chart past and future interactions or reciprocal influences between the Confucian tradition and the international human rights community.[49] The historical contribution of the Confucian tradition to the Universal Declaration of Human Rights illustrates one influence of the tradition on an international human rights negotiation. I see no reason why Confucian moral and political thought could not make further contributions – for example, strengthening a more communitarian-receptive understanding of civil–political liberties as enpowerments aimed at community involvement and flourishing; strengthening the thesis about the interdependence and indivisibility of the three generations of human rights; advancing the cause of those developmental–collective human rights particularly concerned with matters of peace, harmony and ecological responsibility. Moreover, I believe that the tradition's further involvement in human rights dialogues, at national and international levels, might result in its gaining clarity on its own commitment to the subject matters of human rights. Nascent and prescient resources of the tradition that bear on human rights may well be highlighted and brought into promising intercultural dialogue. With the ever-increasing awareness of global diversity, the recognition that a greater number of voices need to be heard at a higher degree of participation might lead to more subtle accounts of human rights at both of the levels that I have discussed here.

Notes

1   See, for example, John Kelsay and Sumner B. Twiss (eds.), *Religion and Human Rights* (New York: The Project on Religion and Human Rights, 1994), and Sumner B. Twiss and Bruce Grelle, "Human Rights and Comparative Religious Ethics: A New Venue," *The Annual of the Society of Christian Ethics,* 1995, 21–48.

2   This framework is more extensively elaborated in my concurrent essay, "Comparative Ethics and Intercultural Human Rights Dialogues: A Programmatic Inquiry," in Lisa S. Cahill and James F. Childress (eds.), *Christianity: Problems and Prospects* (Cleveland: Pilgrim Press, 1996), ch. 21, an essay which was inspired in part by my experience at the 1995 Conference on Confucianism and Human Rights. A few of my reflections in that essay are incorporated in the present paper.

3   See *The International Bill of Human Rights* (New York: United Nations, 1993), which is also reprinted in many volumes dealing with the subject matter of international human rights. This summary characterization is drawn in part from "Terms: 'Human Rights' and 'Religion,'" worked out in consultation with Kusumita Pedersen (former Executive Director of the Project on Religion and Human Rights), in Kelsay and Twiss (eds.), *Religion and Human Rights*, iii–iv.

4   This characterization is articulated by many human rights scholars; see, for example, Henry Shue, *Basic Rights: Subsistence, Affluence, and US Foreign Policy* (Princeton: Princeton University Press, 1980), ch. 1, and Jack Donnelly, *The Concept of Human Rights* (New York: St. Martin's Press, 1985), chs. 1–2. The source for the subsequent reference to Ronald Dworkin's notion of rights as trumps is his justly famous *Taking Rights Seriously* (Cambridge, MA: Harvard University Press, 1977).

5   This point contrasts strongly with the approach of Henry Rosemont developed in his "Why Take Rights Seriously? A

Confucian Critique," in Leroy S. Rouner (ed.), *Human Rights and the World's Religions* (Notre Dame, IN: University of Notre Dame Press, 1988, 167–82), and rearticulated in his contribution to the present volume.

6   For some recent illuminating and provocative discussions of this issue, see Neil Stammers, "Human Rights and Power," *Political Studies* 41 (1993): 70–82, and "A Critique of Social Approaches to Human Rights," *Human Rights Quarterly* 17 (1995): 488–508.

7   This section of the present paper is drawn in part from Twiss and Grelle, "Human Rights and Comparative Religious Ethics," 30–5. The entire discussion is now more extensively developed and refined in my "Comparative Ethics and Intercultural Human Rights Dialogues."

8   The following reflections were inspired in part by Michael Walzer, "Moral Minimalism," reprinted in his *Thick and Thin: Moral Argument at Home and Abroad* (South Bend, IN: University of Notre Dame Press, 1994), 1–19. This issue was discussed in a preliminary way in "Concluding Reflections by the Editors," in Kelsay and Twiss (eds.), *Religion and Human Rights,* 113–23; see esp. 118–20.

9   This worry was quite pointedly articulated by some participants at a Conference on Religion and Human Rights, sponsored by the Project on Religion and Human Rights and held in New York City, May 22–4, 1994, as well as some participants at the 1995 Conference on Confucianism and Human Rights.

10 Henry Rosemont makes such criticisms in his contribution to the present volume.

11 For a revealing discussion of this pragmatic process of negotiation by one of its participants, see John Humphrey, *Human Rights and the United Nations: A Great Adventure* (Dobbs Ferry, NY: Transnational Publishers, 1984).

12 See Walzer, "Moral Minimalism," esp. 17–18.

13 Burns H. Weston, "Human Rights," reprinted in Richard Pierre Claude and Burns H. Weston (eds.), *Human Rights in the World Community: Issues and Action* (2nd edn.; Philadelphia: University of

Pennsylvania Press, 1992), 14–30, see esp. 14–21.

14 I am indebted to Louis Henkin, a participant at the 1995 Conference on Confucianism and Human Rights, for reminding me of this background influence of F. D. R.'s "Four Freedoms" speech. See also Louis Henkin, *The Age of Rights* (New York: Columbia University Press, 1990), 16–18.

15 See, for example, Adamantia Pollis, "Human Rights in Liberal, Socialist, and Third World Perspective," in Claude and Weston (eds.), *Human Rights,* 146–56, which is a revised version of her original essay published in Peter Schwab and Adamantia Pollis (eds.), *Towards a Human Rights Framework* (New York: Praeger, 1982), 1–26.

16 Weston, "Human Rights," 18–20.

17 See David Hollenbach, "A Communitarian Reconstruction of Human Rights: Contributions from Catholic Tradition," in R. Bruce Douglas and David Hollenbach (eds.), *Catholicism and Liberalism: Contributions to American Public Philosophy* (Cambridge: Cambridge University Press, 1994), 127–50. Weston himself says that "What is constant in this first-generation conception . . . is the notion of liberty, a shield that safe-guards the individual alone *and* in association with others, against the abuse . . . of political authority" ("Human Rights," 18, my italics).

18 For empirical data on this thesis and connection see, for example, Han S. Park, "Correlates of Human Rights: Global Tendencies," *Human Rights Quarterly* 9 (1987): 405–13, including references.

19 As Weston says, while these rights project "the notion of holistic community interests," each right also "manifests an individual as well as collective dimension." "Human Rights," 20.

20 See Consultation Group on Universality vs. Human Rights, Sumner B. Twiss as principal coordinating author, with Abdullahi A. an-Na'im, Ann Elizabeth Mayer, and William Wipfler, "Universality vs. Relativism in Human Rights," in Kelsay and Twiss (eds.), *Religion and Human Rights,* 30–59; see esp. 56–7; and Twiss and Grelle, "Human Rights," esp. 39–46.

21 Weston puts the point this way: "Essentially individualistic societies tolerate, even promote certain collectivist values; likewise, essentially communitarian societies tolerate, even promote certain individualistic values. Ours is a more-or-less, not an either-or, world." "Human Rights," 21.

22 The issues addressed in this paragraph are much more extensively developed and refined in my "Comparative Ethics and Intercultural Human Rights Dialogues." In that paper I argue that international human rights incorporate intercultural agreement on the importance of a sort of "homeostatic balancing" (in the words of Erich Loewy) of communal and individual interests for both liberal and communitarian societies and traditions. See Erich H. Loewy, *Freedom and Community: The Ethics of Interdependence* (Albany: State University of New York Press, 1993).

23 Strictly speaking, only states make formal human rights agreements, but arguably these states represent diverse cultural moral traditions.

24 For a similar approach to human rights justification, see Tore Lindholm, "Prospects for Research on the Cultural Legitimacy of Human Rights: The Cases of Liberalism and Marxism," in Abdullahi an-Na'im (ed.), *Human Rights in Cross-Cultural Perspectives: A Quest for Consensus* (Philadelphia: University of Pennsylvania Press, 1992), 387–426 (see esp. 395–401). Although Lindholm's justificatory strategy and my own two-level approach share significant similarities in aim and logic, there are also important differences.

25 I suspect that more could be done to develop the logic of this pragmatic and negotiated international consensus along the lines of, for example, John Reed. A version of neo-pragmatism, but I save this task for another occasion. See John P Reeder, Jr., "Foundations Without Foundationalism," in Gene Outka and John Reeder, Jr. (eds.), *Prospects for a Common Morality* (Princeton: Princeton University Press, 1993), 191–214.

26 For a critical assessment of the agenda of eco-Buddhism, see Ian Harris, "Causations and *Telos:* The Problem of Buddhist Environmental Ethics," *Journal of*

Buddhist Ethics 1 (1994), an electronic journal available at *http://www.psu.edu/jbe/jbe.html*. For contrasting perspectives on the uses of human rights discourse *within* Buddhism, see Damien Keown, "Are There Human Rights in Buddhism?" and Kenneth Inada, "A Buddhist Response to the Nature of Human Rights"; both in *Journal of Buddhist Ethics* 2 (1995).

27 During the 1995 Conference on Confucianism and Human Rights, a number of participants tended to interpret the international human rights consensus – which I regard as intentionally theory-thin – exclusively in terms of contemporary political philosophies in the American context (e.g., Rawls, Dworkin) and their strong commitments to certain understandings of the nature of the self, the meaning of rationality, and the priority of the right over good. From the point of view developed here, however, these latter philosophies are no more than expressions of one particular cultural moral tradition's understanding of human rights at an internal level. It is a mistake to view this understanding as necessarily inscribed and operative at the international level. Such a view threatens to disrupt at the outset the attempt to investigate how the Confucian tradition might relate itself to the international human rights consensus understood as a theory-thin pragmatic moral agreement among diverse cultures.

28 The initial paragraphs of this section are drawn from Twiss and Grelle, "Human Rights," 36–9. The first level of scholarly debate is represented in many anthologies, for example, Adamantia Pollis and Peter Schwab (eds.), *Human Rights: Cultural and Ideological Perspectives* (New York: Praeger, 1979), and an-Na'im, *Human Rights in Cross-Cultural Perspectives.*

29 The second level of debate is well illustrated by the contributions in Rouner, *Human Rights and the Worlds Religions.*

30 See, for example, Alan Gewirth, *Human Rights: Essays on Justification and Applications* (Chicago: University of Chicago Press, 1982), and his more recent "Common Morality and the Community of Rights," in Outka and Reeder (eds.) *Prospects for a Common Morality*, 29–52, as well as the illuminating discussion and

critique of foundationalist approaches to human rights in Michael Freeman, 'The Philosophical Foundations of Human Rights," *Human Rights Quarterly* 16/3 (August 1994): 491–514.

31 For illuminating examples of particularist approaches, see Adamantia Pollis and Peter Schwab (eds.), "Human Rights: A Western Construct with Limited Applicability," in Pollis and Schwab (eds.), *Human Rights*, 3–18, and Alison Dundes Renteln, *International Human Rights: Universalism Versus Relativism* (Newbury Park, CA: Sage Publication, 1990).

32 Henry Rosemont, "Why Take Rights Seriously? A Confucian Critique," in Rouner (ed.), *Human Rights*, 167–82; see also his "Interlude: Modern Western and Ancient Chinese Concepts of the Person," in Henry Rosemont, *A Chinese Mirror: Moral Reflections on Political Economy and Society* (La Salle, Ill.: Open Court, 1991), ch. 3.

33 Wm. Theodore de Bary, "Neo-Confucianism and Human Rights," in Rouner, *Human Rights*, 183–98; the following quotations are from 184 and 197, respectively. See also de Bary's *The Liberal Tradition in China* (Hong Kong: Chinese University Press, 1983; reprint New York: Columbia University Press, 1983) and his *Waiting for the Dawn: A Plan for the Prince* (New York: Columbia University Press, 1993).

34 My gratitude to my colleague Harold D. Roth for our discussions and courses together, which have focused in part on Confucian materials, especially Confucius, Mencius, and Wang Yang-ming, as well as excellent secondary sources, some of which I cite here.

35 Pier Cesare Bori, *From Hermeneutics to Ethical Consensus Among Cultures* (Atlanta, GA: Scholars Press, 1994), ch. 7 ("Human Rights and Human Nature"); the following quotations are from 67, 69, and 70, respectively. In her contribution to the present volume, Irene Bloom discusses a functionally similar example with regard to a Confucian contribution to the 1950 UNESCO "Statement on Race."

36 *Mencius*, trans. D. C. Lau (London: Penguin Books, 1970), iB:8 and iB:12; see also A:7, 4A:1, 7B:14. If interpreted as a

right, this notion of righteous revolt would appear to be a collective right regarding social and economic conditions.

37 Ann Kent, *Between Freedom and Subsistence: China and Human Rights* (Hong Kong and New York: Oxford University Press, 1993), ch. 2.

38 See de Bary, *The Liberal Tradition in China*, esp. 12, 20, 27, 32–3, 49–50, 85, for succinct summaries of these points; the following quotation is found on 85.

39 Kim Dae Jung, "Is Culture Destiny? The Myth of Asia's Anti-Democratic Values" *Foreign Affairs* 73/6 (November/December 1994): 189–94.

40 Tu Wei-ming, *Confucian Thought: Selfhood as Creative Transformation* (Albany: State University of New York Press, 1985), 171–81; quotation from 180.

41 For example, Roger T. Ames, "Rites as Rights: The Confucian Alternative," in Rouner (ed.), *Human Rights*, 199–216 (see esp. 203–9); Rosemont, "Why Take Rights Seriously?" esp. 175–6, and *A Chinese Mirror*, ch. 3; Tu Wei-ming, *Way, Learning, and Politics: Essays on the Confucian Intellectual* (Albany: State University of New York Press, 1993), 30–31i and Tu Wei-ming, Milan Hejtmanek, and Alan Wachman (eds.), *The Confucian World Observed: A Contemporary Discussion of Confucian Humanism in East Asia* (Honolulu: The East–West Center, 1992), 17. From their contributions to the 1995 Conference on Confucianism and Human Rights and to the present volume, I gather that Tu may have changed his mind about this matter, while Rosemont has not.

42 See, for example, Hollenbach, "A Communitarian Reconstruction of Human Rights," and Alexander Ewen (ed.), *Voice of Indigenous Peoples: Native People Address the United Nations* (Santa Fe, NM: Clear Light, 1994), Appendix B, 159–74, which reprints the text of the UN Draft Declaration of the Rights of Indigenous Peoples.

43 This is an indirect response to Henry Rosemont's paper in the present volume. I question the accuracy of the assumption that autonomy as Rosemont describes it is a strong premise of international human rights. Does the insistence on the impor-

tance of people's civil and political liberties presuppose a radically autonomous person? Cannot such rights construed as social enpowerments be compatible with a society based on a relational conception of the self? Though I agree that in a communitarian society there will be issues of how to balance civil–political liberties against social–economic rights, it strikes me that significant civil–political liberties can serve very well the pursuit of the social good in a communitarian society. This entire matter is discussed much more extensively in my "Comparative Ethics and Intercultural Human Rights Dialogue."

44 See Feinberg's justly famous and influential essay, "The Nature and Value of Rights," reprinted in his *Rights, Justice, and the Bounds of Liberty: Essays in Social Philosophy* (Princeton: Princeton University Press, 1980), 143–55. Seung-Hwan Lee is one philosopher who makes excellent use of Feinberg in Seung-Hwan Lee, "Was There a Concept of Rights in Confucian Virtue-Based Morality?" *Journal of Chinese Philosophy* 19/3 (September 1992): 241–61; see esp. 241–5; the following quotation is from 245.

45 I am perfectly willing to concede that claims implicit in social practices of the sort mentioned here are a far cry from recognizing international human rights. In order to close this gap a bit more, we need only to consider the functional requisites that must be addressed by any cultural moral tradition which hopes to maintain itself over time and serve its members in trying to lead a decent life: for example, security of the person, satisfaction of basic social and economic needs, some notion of fair procedure in dispute settlement, protection of "natural" interpersonal relations, etc. Whether or not these are given the status of explicit rights, a viable tradition will need to treat such items as deserving of priority, and that, combined with implicit rights or conceptual counterparts to rights in social practices, seems sufficient to permit a cultural moral tradition to at least make sense of the point and subject matter of human rights.

46 Lee, "Is There a Concept of Rights?" 246–50; quotations from 246 and 248, respectively. See also Mencius, 213:4 and

7A:33. Mark Unno has suggested to me that as a further response to those who find human rights discourse incompatible with Confucian thought, I mention the pragmatic situations faced by individuals who participate in social and cultural practices that bring together more than one set of moral discourses. One of his examples was that of a Chinese government official working in international trade who must at some level implicitly accept the discourse of human rights, since, for example, "most favored nation status" is inseparable from human rights issues. If this same official embraces or appeals to Confucian morality, then he or she must think about how human rights as a historical discourse is related to Confucianism. Prescinding from issues of using human rights in American foreign policy, I think that the general point is well-taken: namely, that real-life situations often compel consideration of how moral discourses can be negotiated in such a way that one acknowledges the fact that one may already be subscribing to the validity of these discourses in a practical sense. This point broadens and at the same time makes more vivid the importance of identifying compatibilities between the Confucian tradition and international human rights, as well as seeking a modus vivendi for how this tradition can participate on pragmatic grounds in international human rights consensus.

47 Randall Peerenboom's interpretation of Confucius's philosophy as "anthropocentric pragmatism," as contrasted with the foundationalism of Huang-Lao, may lend some support to the acceptability of this pragmatic line of justification within the Confucian tradition; see R. P. Peerenboom, *Law and Morality in Ancient China: The Silk Manuscripts of Huang-Lao* (Albany: State University of New York Press, 1993), ch. 4. Here it might be appropriate to mention that this particular strategy diverges from Peerenboom's own attempt to project a Chinese theory of rights in his "What's Wrong with Chinese Rights? Towards a Theory of Rights with Chinese Characteristics," *Harvard Human Rights Journal* 6 (1993), 29–57.

48 My thanks to my colleague John P. Reeder for suggesting that I develop this recapitulation.

49 Here it is appropriate to cite Andrew Nathan's judgment that "there are common points between the Western and Chinese conceptions of rights, such as a belief in the social usefulness of free speech . . . [which] do constitute a basis for dialogue and possible mutual influence," as well as his view that, "This Chinese intellectual tradition contains many of the building blocks of a more liberal, pluralistic theory of rights, and the new opening to the West has made many of the resources of foreign intellectual traditions available for fresh consideration." Andrew J. Nathan, "Sources of Chinese Rights Thinking," in R. Randle Edwards, Louis Henkin, and Andrew J. Nathan, *Human Rights in Contemporary China* (New York: Columbia University Press, 1986), 125–64; quotations from 163–4.

9 ▶ Are There Human Rights in Buddhism?

Damien V. Keown

♦ Concepts of rights ♦ Buddhism and rights ♦

♦ Human rights ♦

In the autumn of 1993 the Parliament of the World's Religions met in Chicago to determine whether a consensus on basic moral teachings could be found among the religions of the world. The meeting was attended by representatives of the major world religions as well as ethnic and other minority groups. Representatives of many Buddhist schools, including Theravada, Mahaydna, Vajrayana, and Zen were present and the main closing address was given by the Dalai Lama in Grant Park on September 4th.

One of the major fruits of this interfaith convention was a document known as the *Declaration towards a Global Ethic*.[1] The *Global Ethic* sets out the fundamental moral principles to which it is thought all religions subscribe. Many of these principles concern human rights, and the *Global Ethic* sees the universal recognition of human rights and dignity by the religions of the world as the cornerstone of a "new global order."

A related aim of the *Global Ethic* was to provide "the basis for an extensive process of discussion and acceptance which we hope will be sparked off in all religions."[2] The present paper is a contribution to this process from a Buddhist perspective. Its aims are limited to an exploration of some of the basic issues which must be addressed if a Buddhist philosophy of human rights is to develop. I say "develop" because Buddhism seems to lack such a philosophy at present. Buddhism is a latecomer to the cause of human rights, and for most of its history has been preoccupied with other concerns. It might be suggested, in defense of Buddhism, that concern for human rights is a postreligious phenomenon which has more to do with secular ideologies and power-politics than religion, and it is therefore unreasonable to accuse Buddhism of neglect in this area.[3] I will suggest below that such an understanding of human rights is mistaken, but leaving the specific issue of human rights to one side there is no doubt that Buddhism lags far behind religions such as Christianity and Islam in developing the framework for a social gospel within which questions of this kind can be addressed. For such an intellectually dynamic tradition Buddhism is a lightweight in moral and political philosophy. A fig-leaf of a kind may be found in the suggestion that since much Buddhist literature remains untranslated there may be hidden treasures in these areas awaiting discovery. Such appeals. to the unknown, however, lack credibility. For one thing, it would be curious if only texts on *these* subjects had been lost to history while literature on all manner of other topics abounds. Nor can it be a coincidence that these subjects are absent from the traditional monastic curricula. The absence of a discipline of philosophical ethics in Indian culture as a whole makes it much more likely that Buddhism simply invested little time in questions of these kinds.[4]

Political events in the course of this century, however, have forced the issue of human rights to the top of the agenda.[5] The Chinese invasion of Tibet, the bitter ethnic conflict in Sri Lanka, and the experience of military dictatorship in countries such as Burma have all provided contemporary Buddhism with first-hand experience of the issues at stake. Another development which has done much to focus attention on social and political themes is the emergence of "socially engaged Buddhism," a movement whose very name implies a critique of the more traditional (presumably "disengaged") forms of Buddhism. Leading Asian and Western Buddhists now routinely express their concern about social injustice in the Western vocabulary of human rights. What I wish to consider here is how appropriate this language is for Buddhism, and what grounds there are for supposing that Buddhism is committed to the cause of "human rights" or has any clear understanding of what the concept means. Given the lack of intellectual effort down the centuries in articulating, promoting and defending rights of the kind which the world (and especially the West) is now called upon to secure for oppressed groups like the Tibetans, the more cynical might suggest that this late conversion to the cause is born more of self-interest than a deep and long-standing commitment to social justice. In calling for respect for human rights today, then, is Buddhism simply riding on the coat-tails of the West or is there, after all, a commitment to human rights in Buddhist teachings?

My theme here may be summed up as the conceptual and doctrinal basis for human rights in Buddhism. I am concerned with the intellectual bridgework which must be put in place if expressions of concern about human rights are to be linked to Buddhist doctrine. There are many aspects to this problem, but three related issues will be considered here: the concept of rights, the concept of *human* rights, and the question of how human rights are to be grounded in Buddhist doctrine. I ask first if the concept of "rights" is intelligible in Buddhism. To answer this question it will be necessary to gain some understanding of the origin of the notion in the West. Next I ask whether the Buddhist concept of *human* rights (if such a thing exists) is the same as the Western understanding. Finally I consider in what specific area of Buddhist teachings a doctrine of human rights might be grounded.[6] Since the discussion is essentially theoretical, detailed reference will not be made to particular Buddhist cultures or schools, to specific human rights "abuses," or to the human rights "record" of particular regimes.[7]

Before turning to these issues a preliminary point must be made about Buddhism itself. In speaking of "Buddhism" I should make clear that I am writing with reference to an abstraction which might be termed "classical" Buddhism. This abstraction is neither the same as nor different from Buddhism in any historical or cultural context. It is not meant to represent the views of any sect and is broad enough to include both Theravada and Mahayana schools. The justification for this fiction lies in the belief that whatever concept of human rights we regard Buddhism as holding must be one which is universal in form. The essence of any doctrine of human rights is its unrestricted scope, and it would be as strange to have distinct "Theravada," "Tibetan" and "Zen" doctrines of human rights as it would be to have "Catholic," "Protestant" and "Eastern Orthodox" ones. To insist on the priority of cultural and historical circumstances would be tantamount to denying the validity of human rights as a concept.

Rights

The concept of a "right" has a long intellectual history in the West, and the contemporary notion of a right as an exercisable power vested in or held by an individual has its antecedents in a more impersonal understanding of what is objectively true or right. Etymologically, the English word "right" is derived from the Latin *rectus* meaning straight. *Rectus*, in turn, can be traced to the Greek *orektos* which means stretched out or upright. As Richard Dagger notes, "The pattern . . . is for the notion of straightness to be extended from the physical realm to the moral – from rectos to rectitude, as it were."[8] In other words, the property of a physical object, namely that of being right, straight or upright, is applied metaphorically in a moral context. Dagger suggests:

> By analogy with the physical sense, the primary moral sense of "right" was a standard or measure for conduct. Something was right – morally straight or true – if it met the standard of rectitude, or rightness . . .

Once the idea of "rightness" had been transferred to the moral domain, the next development was to view it as denoting a personal entitlement of some kind. Dagger continues:

> From here the next step was to recognize that actions taken "with right" or "by right" are taken as a *matter of right*. The transition is from the belief that I may do something because it is a right, in other words, to the belief that I may do something because *I have a right* to do it . . . Thus the concept of rights joins the concept of *the right*.[9]

The metaphorical moral usage of terms such as "right," "straight" and "upright" (in opposition to "crooked," "twisted" and "bent") readily suggests itself to the mind. The rationale for the transition from the moral use of "right" to the notion of a right as a personal entitlement, however, is less obvious. Indeed, this development which took place in the West during the late Middle Ages, and which has been described as the "watershed"[10] in the history of "right," may be a phenomenon which is culturally unique. The evolution of the concept in this direction occurs sometime between Aquinas in the thirteenth century and the jurists Suarez and Grotius in the seventeenth. The modern usage appears clearly in Hobbes, writing in the middle of the seventeenth century, and the idea of a right as a personal power occupies center stage in political theory from this time on.

As part of this evolution in the concept of a right the notion of natural rights comes to prominence towards the end of the seventeenth century, notably in the writings of John Locke. The belief that there are natural rights flows from the recognition of human equality, one of the great ideals of the Age of Revolution. Natural rights are inalienable: they are not conferred by any judicial or political process nor can they be removed by these or other means. These natural rights of the seventeenth and eighteenth centuries are the forerunner of the contemporary notion of human rights.

Two questions might be asked concerning the evolution of the doctrine of natural rights in the West. First, why did it take so long for the concept of natural rights to appear? The answer seems to lie in the fact that for much of Western history "rights" were closely tied to social status, and were essentially a function of position or role in society. A hierarchical social structure, such as was predominant in Roman and medieval society, is antithetical to the notion of natural rights. In these circumstances a person's duties and responsibilities are determined fundamentally by the office they hold (lord, citizen, slave), offices which are to a large extent hereditary. It was only when the hierarchical model was challenged and replaced by an egalitarian one that the idea of natural rights began to gain ground.

The second and more important question for our present purposes is: Does the part played by the unique cultural matrix of social political and intellectual developments in the Enlightenment mean that human rights are essentially a function of the historical process? This conclusion need not follow, for while it may be said that in the seventeenth and eighteenth centuries the notion of natural rights was "an idea whose time had come," the idea itself was not entirely new. The influence of Christian doctrine can be seen in several respects,[11] such as the belief (ultimately deriving from Judaism) of a "universal moral law rooted in the righteousness of God."[12] Since human beings are created in the image of God and loved by him as individuals each is worthy of dignity and respect. Furthermore, since each is a member of the human community under God, all other memberships (tribe, state, nation) are secondary.[13] Apart from Christianity, ideas about the just treatment of individuals on the basis of their common humanity are found in a secular context in Stoicism and the writings of Cicero and Seneca.[14] The philosophical justification for a doctrine of human rights has thus always been available, although the ground in which this seed might flourish – a particular combination of social, political and intellectual developments – has not.

So much for historical background. What of contemporary theories of rights? The concept of a right has been analyzed in a number of ways, as evidenced by the extensive interdisciplinary literature on the subject spanning diverse fields such as politics, law, philosophy and history. Within this discourse of rights there is no single definition of a right which commands universal assent. For our present purposes, however, a basic understanding of the concept will suffice. We noted above that a right is something personal to an individual: it may be thought of as something an individual *has*.[15] What the holder of a right *has* is a benefit or entitlement of some kind, and at the most general level this is an entitlement to justice. This entitlement may be analyzed into two main forms for which there are corresponding rights: rights which take the form of a claim (claim-rights), and rights which take the form of a liberty (liberty-rights).[16] A *claim-right* is the benefit which A enjoys to impose upon B a positive or negative requirement. A *liberty-right* is the benefit which A enjoys of being immune from any such requirement being imposed by B.[17] This basic understanding of a right may be summed up in the following working definition: *a right is a benefit which confers upon its holder either a claim or a liberty*. One important feature of any right is that it provides a particular perspective on justice, in that the right-holder always stands in the position of beneficiary. This subjective aspect of the entitlement, which, as we have seen, appeared early in the history of the concept, remains crucial to the modern understanding of a right. This is brought out in the following definition by Finnis:

> In short, the modern vocabulary and grammar of rights is a many-faceted instrument for reporting and asserting the requirements or other implications of a relationship of justice *from the point of view of the person(s) who benefit(s)* from that relationship. It provides a way of talking about "what is just" from a special angle: the viewpoint of the "other(s)" to whom something (including, *inter alia*, freedom of choice) is owed or due, and who would be wronged if denied that something.[18]

The above brief review of the Western concept of a right was required as a preliminary to an assessment of its relevance to Buddhism. We are now in a position to ask whether the concept of a right is found in Buddhism. If it is, then talk of *human rights* in Buddhism seems legitimate.[19] If it is not, there is a danger of anachronistically foisting onto the tradition a concept which is the product of an alien culture.[20]

Buddhism and Rights

We took our cue for the discussion of rights in the West from etymology, and perhaps we can glean something further from this source. Above it was noted that the English word "right" is derived from the Latin *rectus* meaning straight. Both "right" and *rectus* themselves, however, have a more remote ancestor in the Sanskrit *rju* (straight or upright). The equivalent form in Pali is *uju* (or *ujju*) meaning "straight, direct; straightforward, honest, upright."[21] It would therefore appear that both the objective sense ("straight") and the metaphorical moral sense ("rectitude") of the word "right" referred to earlier occur in Buddhist as well as Western languages. Despite a common Indo-European etymology, however, there is no word in Sanskrit or Pali which conveys the idea of a "right" or "rights," understood as a subjective entitlement. [22]

Does this mean that the concept of rights is alien to Buddhist thought? Not necessarily. Alan Gewirth has pointed out that cultures may possess the concept of rights without having a vocabulary which expresses it. He suggests that it is "important to distinguish between having or using a concept and the clear or explicit recognition and elucidation of it . . . Thus persons might have and use the concept of a right without explicitly having a single word for it."[23] Gewirth claims that the concept of rights can be found in feudal thought, Roman law, Greek philosophy, the Old Testament, and in primitive societies. In connection with the last Finnis points out that anthropological studies of African tribal regimes of law have shown that "the English terms a 'right' and 'duty' are usually covered by a single word derived from the form normally translated as 'ought.'" He suggests that the best English translation in these cases is "due" because "'due' looks both ways along a juridical relationship, both to what one is due to do, and to what is due to one."[24]

It seems, then, that the concept of a right may exist where a word for it does not. Could this be the case in Buddhism? In Buddhism what is due in any situation is determined by reference to Dharma. Dharma determines what is right and just in all contexts and from all perspectives. With respect to social justice the Rev. Vajiragnana explains:

> Each one of us has a role to play in sustaining and promoting social justice and orderliness. The Buddha explained very clearly these roles as reciprocal duties existing between parents and children; teachers and pupils; husband and wife; friends, relatives and neighbors; employer and employee; clergy and laity . . . No one has been left out. The duties explained here are reciprocal and are considered as sacred duties, for – if observed – they can create a just, peaceful and harmonious society.[25]

From this it would seem that Dharma determines not just "what one is due to do" but also "what is due to one." Thus through A's performance of his Dharmic duty B receives that which is his "due" or, we might say, that to which he is "entitled" in (under, through) Dharma. Since Dharma determines the duties of husbands and the duties of wives,[26] it follows that the duties of one correspond to the entitlements or "rights" of the other. If the husband has a duty to support his wife, the wife has a "right" to support from her husband. If the wife has a duty to look after her husband's property, the husband has a "right" to the safe-keeping of his property by his wife. If under Dharma it is the duty of a king (or political authority) to dispense justice impartially, then subjects (citizens) may be said to have a "right" to just and impartial treatment before the law.

Should it be concluded, then, that the notion of a right is present in classical Buddhism? The answer depends on the criteria adopted for "having" a concept. Dagger sets out the options:

> If one is willing to look primarily for the idea or the notion, however it may be

expressed, then one can confidently say that the concept of rights is virtually as old as civilization itself.

On the other hand:

If one insists that the form of expression is crucial . . . so that a concept cannot be said to exist unless there is a word or phrase that distinguishes it from other concepts, then one would have to say that the concept of rights has its origin in the middle ages.[27]

I think our conclusion should be that the concept of rights is implicit in classical Buddhism in the normative understanding of what is "due" among and between individuals. Under Dharma, husbands and wives, kings and subjects, teachers and students, all have reciprocal obligations which can be analyzed into rights and duties. We must qualify this conclusion, however, by noting that the requirements of Dharma are expressed in the form of duties rather than rights. In other words, Dharma states what is due in the form "A husband should support his wife" as opposed to "Wives have a right to be maintained by their husbands." Until rights as personal entitlements are recognized as a discrete but integral part of what is due under Dharma, the modern concept of rights cannot be said to be present. In this respect, however, Buddhism is far from unique, and a similar comment could be made about many other cultures and civilizations. Finnis points out with respect to Roman law:

[I]t is salutary to bear in mind that the modern emphasis on the powers of the right-holder, and the consequent systematic bifurcation between "right" . . . and "duty," is something that sophisticated lawyers were able to do without for the whole life of classical Roman law.[28]

He also suggests, rightly I think, that "there is no cause to take sides as between the older and the newer usages, as ways of expressing the implications of justice in a given context."[29] A right is a useful concept which provides a particular perspective on justice. Its correlative, duty, provides another. These may be thought of as separate windows onto the common good which is justice or, in the context of Buddhism, Dharma. It would therefore be going too far to claim that the notion of rights is "alien" to Buddhism or that Buddhism denies that individuals have "rights."

In sum it might be said that in classical Buddhism the notion of rights is present in embryonic form although not yet born into history. Whether anything like the Western concept of rights has, or would, appear in the course of the historical evolution of Buddhism is a question for specialists in the various Buddhist cultures to ponder. In many respects the omens for this development were never good. Buddhism originated in a caste society, and the Asian societies where it has flourished have for the most part been hierarchically structured. MacIntyre, citing Gewirth, mentions that the concept of a right lacks any means of expression in Japanese "even as late as the mid-nineteenth century."[30] The preconditions for the emergence of the concept of rights would seem to be egalitarianism and democracy, neither of which have been notable features of Asian polity before the modern era. On the other hand a justification for the rejection of hierarchical social structures is not hard to find in Buddhism – one need only look at the Buddha's critique of caste.[31] Buddhism also holds, in the doctrine of no-self, that all individuals are equal in the most profound sense.[32] Like the Christian doctrine that all men are created equal before God this would appear to be fertile ground for a doctrine of natural rights. What seems to have been lacking in both faiths, but perhaps more so in Buddhism, was the will to incarnate this theoretical vision of man in the flesh of historical institutions.

Human Rights

In the preceding section attention was focused on the concept of a right. Here we consider what it means to characterize certain rights as *human* rights,[33] and pursue further the discussion initiated in the preceding section as to whether Western notions of human rights are compatible with Buddhism.[34]

The point has already been made that what are today called human rights were originally spoken of as "natural" rights, in other words, rights which flow from human *nature*. In the seventeenth century philosophers and statesmen began to define these rights and enshrine them in early constitutions such as the "Fundamental Orders of Connecticut" as early as 1639. Documents of this kind inspired the publication of other declarations, charters and manifestos in a tradition which has continued into modern times. As an example of a modern charter of human rights we may take the Universal Declaration of Human Rights proclaimed by the General Assembly of the United Nations in December 1948. Since its promulgation this thirty-article code has been used as a model for many subsequent human rights charters.

What is the Buddhist position with respect to declarations of this kind? It may be useful to begin by asking whether Buddhism would endorse the Universal Declaration of Human Rights. The repeated calls by the Dalai Lama for respect for human rights give some reason to think that it would. The signing of the *Global Ethic* by many Buddhists also suggests that Buddhism has no reservations about subscribing to charters or manifestos which seek to secure universal human rights. Moreover, there seems to be nothing in any of the thirty articles to which Buddhism would take exception. Perera's commentary on each of the thirty articles of the Universal Declaration shows them to be in harmony with early Buddhist teachings

both in letter and in spirit. In his Foreword to the commentary Ananda Guruge writes:

> Professor Perera demonstrates that every single Article of the Universal Declaration of Human Rights – even the labour rights to fair wages, leisure and welfare – has been adumbrated, cogently upheld and meaningfully incorporated in an overall view of life and society by the Buddha.[35]

But how are these rights to be justified with reference to Buddhist teachings? In asking this question I am not seeking justification by reference to textual passages which seem to support the rights claimed. There are many passages in the Pali Canon, as Perera has ably demonstrated, which support the view that early Buddhist teachings were in harmony with the spirit of the Declaration. The justification required at this point has more to do with the philosophical presuppositions underlying these passages and the overall Buddhist vision of individual and social good.

The various declarations on human rights themselves rarely offer a justification for the rights they proclaim. MacIntyre observes dryly how "In the United Nations Declaration on Human Rights of 1948 what has since become the normal UN practice of not giving good reasons for any assertion whatsoever is followed with great rigor."[36] A gesture towards justification is sometimes made in recital clauses by reference to the "inherent dignity. . . of all members of the human family" or some similar form of words. The *Global Ethic*, which provides a fuller statement than most, echoes the Universal Declaration in its call for "the full realization of the intrinsic dignity of the human person."[37] It states: "We make a commitment to respect life and dignity, individuality and diversity, so that every person is treated humanely." This is amplified as follows:

> This means that every human being without distinction of age, sex, race, skin, color, physical or mental ability, language, religion, political view, or national or social origin

possesses an inalienable and *untouchable* dignity. And everyone, the individual as well as the state, is therefore obliged to honor this dignity and protect it.[38]

Elsewhere, as part of his dialogue with world religions, Küng makes a constructive suggestion on this point that students of Buddhism might do well to pay heed to:

Should not Buddhist thinkers, as they critically assess their own and alien traditions, make a more direct effort to establish an anthropology centered around *human dignity* (which the Buddha himself deeply respected)? Buddhists are fully aware that man can be adequately understood only as conditioned in every way, as a relational being within the totality of life and the cosmos. But should they not reflect more earnestly, especially in an ethical vein, on the problems of the unique, inviolable, noninterchangeable human self, with its roots in the past and its future destiny?[39]

It is by no means apparent, however, how human dignity is to be grounded in Buddhist doctrine. The very words "human dignity" sound as alien in a Buddhist context as talk of rights. One looks in vain to the Four Noble Truths for any explicit reference to human dignity, and doctrines such as no-self and impermanence may even be thought to undermine it. If human dignity is the basis of human rights Buddhism would seem to be in some difficulty when it comes to providing a justification for them. The theistic religions, on the other hand, seem much better equipped to provide an account of human dignity. Christians, Muslims and Jews typically refer to the ultimate source of human dignity as divine. Article one (paragraph 1,700) of the most recent *Catechism of the Catholic Church*, for instance, states: "The dignity of the human person is rooted in his creation in the image and likeness of God." Buddhism, clearly, would not wish to make such a claim. Küng notes how leading Buddhists at the Parliament of the World's

Religions felt called upon to protest at calls for "a unity of religions under God," and at references to "God the Almighty" and "God the Creator" in invocations during the proceedings. He suggests, however, that these differences are reconcilable since the Buddhist concepts of "Nirvana, Shunyata and Dharmakaya . . . fulfil analogous functions to the concept of God" and can be regarded by Christians as "parallel terms for the Absolute."[40]

It may or may not be the case that Mahayana schools recognize a transcendent reality which resembles the Christian concept of God as the Absolute, and there are those better qualified than myself to address such a question. Here I will make only three brief points regarding the problems which arise in regarding these things as the source of human dignity. The first is that since these concepts are understood differently by the main Mahayana schools they are unlikely to provide the common ground which is required as a foundation for human rights. The second is that it is difficult to see how any of these things can be the source of human dignity in the way that God can, since no school of Buddhism believes that human beings are created by them. The third point is that even if some metaphysical ground of the above kind can be identified in Mahayana Buddhism it still leaves the problem of how human dignity is to be grounded where Theravada Buddhism is concerned. For the Theravada, *Nirvana* is not a transcendent Absolute, nor do the concepts of *Sunyata* and *Dharmakaya* have anything like the meaning or significance they attain later. No grounding for human rights can be truly satisfactory, I would suggest, unless it unambiguously forms part of the core teachings of classical Buddhism as a whole.

One suggestion as to how human rights can be grounded in Buddhist doctrine has been made by Kenneth Inada. In a discussion of "The Buddhist Perspective on Human Rights," Inada suggests "there is an intimate and vital relationship of the Buddhist norm or Dhamma with that of human rights."[41] He explains the relationship as follows:

> Human rights is indeed an important issue, but the Buddhist position is that it is ancillary to the larger or more basic issue of human nature. It can be asserted that the Buddhist sees the concept of human rights as a legal extension of human nature. It is a crystallization, indeed a formalization, of the mutual respect and concern of all persons, stemming from human nature. Thus, human nature is the ultimate source, the basis from which all other attributes or characteristics are to be delineated. They all have their respective *raison d'être* in it. They are reflections and even byproducts of it. The reason for assigning human nature the basic position is very simple. It is to give human relations a firm grounding in the truly existential nature of things: that is, the concrete and dynamic relational nature of persons in contact with each other, that which [sic] avoids being caught up in rhetorical or legalistic tangles.[42]

Few would disagree with the proposition that human rights are grounded in human nature. Towards the end of the extract, however, Inada seems to move away from his initial suggestion that *human nature* is the "ultimate source" of human rights towards the view that the ultimate ground is the "dynamic relational nature of persons in contact with each other." In other words, it is in the *interrelatedness* of persons rather than in the persons themselves that the justification for human rights is to be found. This is confirmed a little later:

> Consequently, the Buddhist concern is focused on the experiential process of each individual, a process technically know as relational origination (*paticca-samuppada*). It is the great doctrine of Buddhism, perhaps the greatest doctrine expounded by the historical Buddha. It means that, in any life-process, the arising of an experiential event is a total, relational affair.[43]

How is the link between dependent-origination and human rights to be forged?

The argument reaches its conclusion in the following passage:

> Like a storm which consumes everything in its wake, an experience in terms of relational origination involves everything within its purview. Hence, the involvement of elements and, in our case, human beings as entities should not be in terms of mere relationship but rather a creative relationship which originates from the individual locus of existence. In other words, each individual is responsible for the actualization of an "extensive concern" for everything that lies in his or her path of experience. So, we may say that the sum total of the "extensive concerns" can be referred to as a mutually constituted existential realm, and it thereby becomes a fact that there will be mutual respect of fellow beings. It is on this basis that we can speak of the rights of individuals. These rights are actually extensions of human qualities such as security, liberty, and life.[44]

In simple language, the argument seems to be as follows. Human beings, like everything else, are part of the relational process described in the doctrine of dependent-origination; since no-one exists independently we should look out for one another; looking out for one another means respecting each other's rights; examples of the rights we should respect are security, liberty and life.[45]

Although I have described this as an "argument" it is little more than a series of assertions. Working backwards, it is difficult to know what sense to give the concluding sentence: "These rights are actually extensions of human qualities such as security, liberty and life." It is unclear what is meant by "human qualities" here. In what sense is security a "human quality" (perhaps a "need")? Why is life described as a "quality" of a human being? Even granted that these things are "human qualities," what does it mean to say that rights are extensions of "human qualities?" In the first extract quoted above, Inada suggests that "the Buddhist sees the concept of human rights as a legal extension of human nature." What is left unexplained, however, is how human nature (or "human qualities") become legal rights. Do all "human qualities" extend into rights or only some? If so, which and why? Finally, if "human qualities" are what give rise to rights, why invoke the doctrine of dependent-origination?

The derivation of human rights from the doctrine of dependent-origination is a conjuring trick. From the premise that we live in "a mutually constituted existential realm" (we all live together) it has "thereby become a fact" that there will be "mutual respect of fellow beings." In the twinkling of an eye, values have appeared from facts like a rabbit out of a hat. However, the fact that human beings live in relationship with one another is not a moral argument about *how they ought to behave*. By itself it offers no reason why a person should not routinely abuse the rights of others. Inada's suggestion that human rights can be grounded in the doctrine of dependent-origination turns out to be little more than a recommendation that people should be nice to one another on the ground that we are "all in this together."[46]

The approach adopted by Perera is rather different. Perera's main concern is to demonstrate that the articles of the Universal Declaration are adumbrated in early Buddhist teachings, rather than explore their philosophical foundations. He acknowledges that "Buddhism credits the human personality with a dignity and moral responsibility"[47] but does not explain fully whence this arises or how it provides a foundation for human rights. In a number of places he suggests certain possibilities regarding the source of human dignity, not all of which seem to be compatible. At one point he defines "the ethical assumption on which the Buddhist concept of human rights is founded" as the "fundamental consideration that all life has a desire to safeguard itself and to make itself comfortable and happy."[48] Basing rights on desires, however, is problematic. One reason is that certain people, for example those who seek

to end their lives through suicide, seem to lack the desire in question. Nor is it difficult to conceive of a justification for human rights abuses along the lines that the victims "no longer cared what happened to them." If they themselves had no interest in their future, whose rights would have been violated? A deeper problem is that the mere existence of desires establishes nothing from a moral point of view. Desires are many and varied and can be met in manifold ways. Moral questions arise both at the level of whether a desire should be met and how it should be met. The identification of a desire may be a starting point for moral reflection, but it is certainly not its end.[49]

On the preceding page Perera suggests an alternative foundation for human rights, one which links it to human dignity. He writes: "Buddhism posits, as Jean Jacques Rousseau did much later, that the essence of human dignity lies in the assumption of man's responsibility for his own governance."[50] No Buddhist sources are cited in support of this claim, and I believe it is unlikely that Buddhism would wish to link human dignity quite so closely to politics. Perhaps if this suggestion were developed a little further it would make reference to underlying human capacities such as reason and autonomy which enable men to constitute themselves into orderly societies, and then point to these as the underlying source of human dignity. While political institutions may be produced through the exercise of distinctively human capacities, however, it is unlikely that Buddhism would locate "the essence of human dignity" in their creation. According to the *Aggannasutta*, the evolution of political societies is the consequence of depravity and decline, which makes them a dubious testament to human dignity.

Where then, should the foundations for a Buddhist doctrine of human rights be sought? The proper ground for a doctrine of human rights, I suggest, lies elsewhere than in the doctrine of dependent-origination, as suggested by Inada, or in either the desire for self-preservation or the acceptance of responsibility for self-government, as proposed by Perera. Perera, in fact, comes closest to what in my view is the true source of human rights in Buddhism in his commentary on Article 1.[51] In discussing the first sentence of the Article ("All human beings are born free and equal in dignity and rights") he comments that "Buddhahood itself is within the reach of all human beings. . . and if all could attain Buddhahood what greater equality in dignity and rights can there be?" To focus attention upon the goal, I believe, is more promising than any of the other approaches considered thus far. Perera seems to grasp its significance in a remark towards the end of his commentary on Article 1. He writes:

> It is from the point of view of its goal that Buddhism evaluates all action. Hence Buddhist thought is in accord with this and other Articles in the Universal Declaration of Human Rights to the extent to which they facilitate the advancement of human beings towards the Buddhist goal.[52]

I believe the above statement provides the key to understanding human rights from a Buddhist perspective. What is missing in Perera's commentary, however, is the explicit linkage between the goal and human dignity, and it is this which I will now try to establish. What I will suggest in general is that the source of human dignity should be sought not in the analysis of the human condition provided by the first and second noble truths (the area where Buddhist scholarship has myopically focused its attention) but in the evaluation of human good provided by the third and fourth. Human rights cannot be derived from any factual non-evaluative analysis, of human nature, whether in terms of its psycho-physical constitution (the five "aggregates" which lack a self), its biological nature (needs, urges, drives), or the deep structure of interdependency (paticca-samuppada). Instead, the most promising approach will be one which locates human

rights and dignity within a comprehensive account of human goodness, and which sees basic rights and freedoms as integrally related to human flourishing and self-realization.[53] This is becuase the source of human dignity in Buddhism lies nowhere else than in the literally infinite capacity of human nature for participation in goodness.[54]

The connection between human rights and human good can be illustrated by asking what the various declarations on human rights seek to secure. Documents which speak of human rights commonly announce a list of specific rights and freedoms and proclaim them to be inviolable. The rights proclaimed by the Universal Declaration include the right to life, liberty, security of person, equality before the law, privacy, marriage and protection of family life, social security, participation in government, work, protection against unemployment, rest and leisure, a minimum standard of living, and enjoyment of the arts. The exercise of these rights is subject only to such general limitations as are necessary to secure due recognition and respect for the rights and freedoms of others and the requirements of morality, public order and general welfare (Article 29.2). Otherwise, the rights are expressed in categorical forms such as "Everyone has. . ." and "No-one shall. . ." For example, Article 3: "Everyone has the right to life, liberty and security of person." And Article 4: "No one shall be held in slavery or servitude; slavery and the slave trade shall be prohibited in all their forms." The document thus understands the rights it proclaims as both "universal" and exceptionless. Using the terminology introduced earlier it can be seen that some of these rights are claim-rights while others are liberty-rights. Article 2 confirms this when it speaks of an entitlement to both the "rights and freedoms set forth in this Declaration."[55]

What do these rights and freedoms amount to? It might be said that they map the parameters of human "good-in-community." In other words, these rights and freedoms are what is required if human beings are to lead fulfilled lives in society. Article 29.1 recognizes this when it observes "Everyone has duties to the community *in which alone the free and full development of his personality is possible.*"[56] In the absence of human rights the scope for human development and fulfillment through social interaction is drastically reduced. The rights specified define and facilitate aspects of human fulfillment. The right to life is clearly fundamental since it is the condition for the enjoyment of all other rights and freedoms. The right to "liberty and security of person" (Article 3) is also basic to any understanding of human good. Without these minimum conditions the scope and opportunity for human fulfillment would be intolerably restricted. The same would apply in the case of slavery (Article 4), torture (Article 5), and the denial of rights before the law (Article 6). It can also be seen that many of the detailed rights identified are actually derived from more fundamental ones. Article 3, for example, "No one shall be held in slavery," is clearly implied in Article 2, "Everyone has the right to . . . liberty." It might thus be said that many of the thirty articles articulate the practical implications of a relatively small number of fundamental rights and freedoms which are the basis of the common good.

It may be noted that the Universal Declaration itself and modern charters like it do not offer a *comprehensive* vision of human good. This is not intended as a criticism, for the purpose of such charters is to secure only what might be termed the "minimum conditions" for human flourishing in a pluralistic milieu. The task of articulating a comprehensive vision of what is ultimately valuable in human life and how it is to be attained falls to the competing theories of human good found in religions, philosophies and ideologies. Buddhism provides one view of human nature and its fulfillment, Christianity another, secular philosophies a third. To pursue any of these different paths, however, requires the

substructure known as "human rights," a complex of fundamental rights and liberties which are the preconditions for the realization of the particular opportunities made available by the competing ideologies.

If the aim of human rights declarations is understood in the way outlined above then human rights is fundamentally a moral issue. Where there is no right to life, liberty and security of person, and where torture is routine, the opportunities for the realization of human good are greatly reduced. Freedom of religion (Article 18), for example, is vital to the Buddhist vision of individual and social good, and the consequences of the loss of these rights are all too obvious in Tibet. Human rights is thus an area in which religions have a legitimate and vital stake, and there is every reason why it would be proper for Buddhism both to endorse the Universal Declaration and call upon others to respect and implement it.[57]

If religions have a legitimate stake in human rights, we might expect to find many of the rights and liberties spelled out in human rights charters present in either an express or implied form in their moral teachings. These typically include commandments or precepts forbidding killing, stealing, adultery, and lying, as do the first four of the Five Precepts. These evils are prohibited because it is immediately apparent that they are antithetical to human flourishing-in-community. The rationale for these prohibitions, I suggest, coincides to a large extent with that of the various human rights manifestos.[58] These manifestos, indeed, may be regarded as a translation of religious precepts into the language of rights. The process of casuistry can be seen at work in both. Just as a limited number of moral precepts can be expanded to meet the needs of different social situations (many of the extensive Vinaya rules, for example, have their source in a handful of moral precepts),[59] so the many articles in human rights charters are extrapolated from a comparatively small number of basic rights and freedoms.

It must be admitted there are grounds

for skepticism towards the parallel which has just been suggested since it cannot be denied that the Buddhist precepts look and sound very different from contemporary declarations on human rights. The Buddhist precepts make no reference to "rights" at all, and are couched instead in the form of undertakings.[60] Let us examine what these undertakings involve. On the basis of our earlier analysis it would seem that "taking the precepts" in Buddhism is actually the formal acknowledgment of a subsisting duty, a duty which arises from Dharma. The person who takes the precepts is saying in effect "I hereby recognize my Dharmic duty not to do x,y, and z." Since duties have their correlative in rights, however, rights must also be implicit in the good the precepts seek to promote. We saw earlier that rights provide a way of talking about what is just and unjust from a special angle. We noted further that a person who has right has a benefit, a benefit which can be described as either a claim or a liberty. In the context of the precepts, then, the right-holder is the one who suffers from the breach of Dharmic duty when the precepts are broken. In the case of the first precept this would be the person who was unjustly killed. The right the victim has may therefore be defined as a negative claim-right upon the aggressor, namely the right not to be killed. In simple terms we might say that the victim has a right to life which the aggressor has a duty to respect.

That the translation between precepts and rights is accurate, and that the agreement between the two formulations is more than superficial or accidental, is supported by the authenticity with which the Dalai Lama was able to affirm the *Global Ethic*. Kuschel comments as follows:

> Something else seems decisive to me: authenticity and humanity. The reason why the Dalai Lama's speech was so convincing, and indeed seized people's hearts, so that it was often interrupted by spontaneous applause, was that this man simply wanted to be an *authentic Buddhist*. His plea for mutual respect, dialogue and collaboration, for understanding between peoples and respect for creation, was not an adaptation to Christian or Western values, but came from the depths of his own Buddhist spirituality.[61]

Further evidence of the linkage between the Buddhist precepts and social justice is found in the Theravada tradition. Writing on the theme of "Justice in Buddhism" Vajiragnana states:

> Man is responsible for society. It is he who makes it good or bad through his own actions. Buddhism, therefore, advocates a five-fold disciplinary code for man's training in order to maintain justice in society. These five . . . precepts are extremely important fundamental principles for promoting and perpetuating human welfare, peace and justice.[62]

I suggest, then, that the apparent differences between the moral teachings of Buddhism and human rights charters is one of form rather than substance. Human rights can be extrapolated from Buddhist moral teachings in the manner described above using the logic of moral relationships to illumine what is due under Dharma. A direct translation of the first four precepts yields a right to life, a right not to have one's property stolen, a right to fidelity in marriage, and a right not to be lied to. Many other human rights, such as the rights to liberty and security can either be deduced from or are extant within the general corpus of Buddhist moral teachings. A right not to be held in slavery, for example, is implicit in the canonical prohibition on trade in living beings.[63] These rights are the extrapolation of what is due under Dharma; they have not been "imported" into Buddhism but were implicitly present.

If modern conceptions of human rights and Buddhist moral teachings are related in the way I have suggested, certain conclusions follow for our understanding of the Buddhist precepts. If there are universal and exceptionless rights, as human rights charters affirm, there must be universal and exceptionless duties. If human rights such as a "right to life" (by which I understand a right not to have one's life taken unjustly) are exceptionless, there must also be an exceptionless duty to abstain from unjustly depriving a human being of life. The First Precept in Buddhism, therefore, should be understood as an exceptionless duty or moral absolute.

Is this reverse translation, from absolute human rights to absolute moral duties, supported by textual sources? There is every reason to think that it is. Such an understanding of the precept is clearly evident in classical Buddhism, which tirelessly reiterates the principle of the sanctity of life found in the pan-Indian teachings on non-harming (*ahimsa*), and which gives no reason to suppose that its moral precepts are to be understood as anything other than exceptionless norms. If, on the other hand, it is thought that the precepts are not to be understood as moral absolutes, then it is difficult to see what justification there can be for Buddhists to hold that there are universal and exceptionless human rights. It would be inconsistent to affirm the latter but deny the former.

The above account of human rights in Buddhism has been given entirely within the context of an understanding of human good which has its apex in nirvana-in-this-life. Reference to the transcendent dimension of human good and its ground has been avoided for several reasons. The first is that no reference need be made to transcendent realities in order to ground human rights. That this is so can be seen from the absence of any reference to such realities in contemporary human rights charters, and the fact that many atheists are vigorous defenders of human rights. Where Buddhism is concerned, the vision of human good set out in the third and fourth noble truths provides the necessary basis for a doctrine of human rights. Human rights turn out in essence to be what justice requires if human good is to be fulfilled. The second reason for avoiding reference to

transcendent realities is that my aim has been to suggest a basis for human rights acceptable to classical Buddhism as a whole. Since all schools of Buddhism affirm the third and fourth noble truths and the vision of human good they proclaim, the required common ground for a pan-Buddhist doctrine of human rights is present.

The above should not be read as a *denial* that there can be a transcendent ground for human rights in Buddhism. Because the transcendent dimension of human good is left obscure in Buddhist teachings, however, the transcendent ground for human rights is also obscure. In terms of the account given here, the transcendent ground for human rights would be post-mortem nirvana, not in the sense of an absolute reality (as suggested by Küng) but as the universalization of human good on a transcendent plane. The twin axes of human good are knowledge (*prajñā*) and moral concern (*karunā*) and on the graph defined by these axes can be plotted the soteriological coordinates of any individual. Through participation in these twin categories of good, human nature progressively transcends its limitations and becomes saturated with nirvanic goodness. Eventually, in post-mortem nirvana, this goodness attains a magnitude which can no longer be charted. If a transcendent ground for human rights is desired, this is where it should be sought.

To sum up: it is legitimate to speak of both rights and *human* rights in Buddhism. Modern doctrines of human rights are in harmony with the moral values of classical Buddhism in that they are an explication of what is "due" under Dharma. The modern idea of human rights has a distinctive cultural origin, but its underlying preoccupation with human good makes it at bottom a moral issue in which Buddhism and other religions have a legitimate stake. The *Global Ethic* endorses the view that the principles it sets forth on human rights are neither new nor "Western" when it states: "We affirm that a common set of core values is found in the teachings of the religions, and that these form the basis of a global ethic."[64]

A final thought. Above I have spoken only of human rights, and in the context of Buddhism this perspective may be unduly narrow in that it seems to preclude the universe of sentient non-human beings from any entitlement to rights. Buddhists may feel, therefore, that it is less prejudicial in discussions of this kind to revert to the older terminology of "natural" rights. Whether or not animals have rights, and whether these are the same rights as human beings, is a matter which requires separate discussion. If human rights flow from human nature, as suggested, it may be that rights of different kinds flow from natures of different kinds. Such would seem to be the understanding of classical Buddhism.

Notes

1   The text of the Declaration, along with commentaries and supplementary information is available in Küng and Kuschel (eds.) (1993).

2   Küng and Kuschel (eds.) (1993: 8).

3   For a range of cultural and ideological perspectives on human rights see Pollis and Schwab (1979).

4   On the absence of ethics in Hinduism see Creel (1977: 20ff).

5   In spite of its contemporary importance, however, little appears to have been written on the subject from a specifically Buddhist perspective. The only monograph on the subject appears to be Perera,1991, and I am grateful to the Ven. Mahinda Deegalle for bringing it to my attention. Panikkar (1982: 76n) refers to a UNESCO Symposium which took place in Bangkok in 1979 entitled *Meeting of Experts on the Place of Human Rights in Cultural and Religious Traditions*, which apparently included discussion of Buddhism. I have as yet been unable to obtain a copy of the Final Report SS-79/CONF. 607/10 of 6 February 1980.

6   On the analogous question of whether there is an "African" doctrine of human rights see Howard (1986).

7   For information on these empirical questions see Humana (1992), Hsiung (1985),

Rupesinghe (et al.) (1993), de Silva (1988), also *Human Rights in Developing Countries*, Yearbook 1993 (Copenhagen, 1993: Nordic Human Rights Publications).

8   Dagger (1989: 293). I am indebted to Dagger's excellent paper throughout this section.

9   Dagger (1989: 294), original emphasis.

10 Finnis (1980: 206).

11 Stackhouse lists five (1984: 35ff). Little (1988) shows the dependency of the modern Western secular and liberal ideology on Christian theology by tracing the historical connection between the Christian concept of conscience and the intellectual framework within which the American doctrines of liberty and religious freedom emerged in the eighteenth century in the writings of Thomas Jefferson and James Madison. He suggests that this Western framework applies relatively unproblematically to Buddhism and Islam, and notes in general: "Thus, current human rights formulations, along with the important notions that underlie them, are by no means necessarily irrelevant to cultures outside the West" (1988: 31). For perspectives on human rights from the world's religions see Rouner (1988) and Swidler (1982). Issues concerning religion and rights are discussed by Bradney (1993). A commentary on the Universal Declaration from the perspective of Buddhism, Hinduism, Christianity and Islam may be found in *Human Rights and Religions in Sri Lanka*, published by the Sri Lanka Foundation (Colombo, 1988). The Buddhist commentary by Perera was republished separately in 1991.

12 Stackhouse (1984: 35)

13 Stackhouse (1984: 36).

14 For a survey see Carlyle and Carlyle (1950).

15 Finnis (1980: 208).

16 The most influential modern analysis of rights is that by Hohfeld (1964).

17 Finnis (1980: 199–205).

18 Finnis (1980: 205), original emphasis.

19 Perera's discussion of Buddhism and human rights does not address these questions, and seems to assume that the concept of rights and human rights as understood in the Universal Declaration are directly applicable to canonical Buddhism.

20 For the view that moral values are deter-

mined by culture, as maintained by many anthropologists, see Ladd (ed.) (1983). The defensibility of a specific cultural custom (female circumcision) from a human rights perspective is discussed by James (1994).

21 *Pali Text Society Pali–English Dictionary, uju and ujju.*

22 On the concept of rights in Hinduism and the meaning of adhikcira, see Bilimoria (1993), also Creel (1977: 19). In Buddhist languages the notion of rights may be distributed among a variety of terms, as perhaps, in Latin among the words auctoritas, potestas, dominium, iurisdictio, proprietas, libertas and ius (Dagger, 1989: 291).

23 Quoted in Dagger (1989: 286).

24 Finnis (1980: 209).

25 Vajiragnana (1992).

26 See, for example, the *Sigalovadasutta.*

27 Dagger (1989: 297).

28 Finnis (1980: 209) 29. Finnis (1980: 210) 30. MacIntyre (1981: 69). Cf. de Bary on the Chinese neologisms which have been coined to express these concepts (1988: 183).

29 Finnis (1980: 210).

30 MacIntyre (1981: 69). Cf. de Bary on the Chinese neologisms which have been coined to express these concepts (1988: 183).

31 The institution of caste is criticized in numerous early discourses, notably the *Sonadandasutta.*

32 Carrithers (1985) suggests that the Buddhist concept of the "self" (which he relates to Mauss's concept of the "moi") is one which is easily transportable across cultural frontiers. This enhances the prospects for a Buddhist doctrine of universal human rights.

33 Useful discussions of the philosophical basis of human rights may be found in Donnelly (1985) and Nickel (1987).

34 On how far the Western concept of human rights is relevant or applicable to other cultures see Panikkar (1982), Teson (1985), Milne (1986), Welch (et al.) (1990).

35 Perera (1991: xi).

36 MacIntyre (1981: 69).

37 *A Global Ethic*, 14.

38 *A Global Ethic*, 23, original emphasis.

39 Küng (1986: 383f), original emphasis.

40 *A Global Ethic*, 62f.

41 Inada (1982: 71)

42 Inada (1982: 70), paragraphs joined.

43 Inada (1982: 70).

44 Inada (1982: 700.

45 An earlier attempt to ground Buddhist ethics in dependent-origination can be found in Macy (1979). Macy offers the Sarvodaya Shramadana, a self-help movement in Sri Lanka, as "A notable example of the ethics of *paticca-samuppcida*," but, like Inada, fails to explain how a moral imperative arises out of this doctrine. Also drawn to the seemingly magnetic doctrines of no-self and dependent-origination is Taitetsu Unno, whose 1988 article, supposedly about rights, is taken up almost entirely in providing a Pure Land perspective on these two doctrines. While these doctrines offer a congenial metaphysical backdrop for Buddhist ethics, they cannot provide a moral ground for rights. Harris (1994) expresses doubts that dependent-origination can provide a satisfactory basis for Buddhist ecology.

46 In a second essay on the subject (1990) Inada gives much less emphasis to dependent-origination and seems to want to ground human rights in compassion. However, the nature of the argument, and in particular the concluding paragraph, are far from clear.

47 Perera (1991: 28, cf. 88).

48 Perera (1991: 29).

49 A further problem, although I believe it is ultimately a pseudo-problem, is that Buddhism sees desire as the cause of suffering. Desire would therefore seem an unlikely foundation for human rights.

50 Perera (1991: 28).

51 Article 1: "All human beings are born free and equal in dignity and rights. They are endowed with reason and conscience and should act towards one another in a spirit of brotherhood."

52 Perera (1991: 24).

53 A discussion of human nature and human good in Buddhism will be found in my *Buddhism & Bioethics* (Macmillan, 1995).

54 A more familiar way of making the same point in Buddhist terminology would be to say that all beings are potential Buddhas or possess the "Buddha-nature."

55 Emphasis added.

56 Emphasis added.

57 In the view of Perera: "From the religious angle, it is possible to state that in this Declaration lie enshrined certain values and norms emphasized by the major religions of the world. Though not directly expressed, the basic principles of the Declaration are supported and reinforced by these religious traditions, and among them the contribution of the Buddhist tradition, to say the least, is quite outstanding" (1991: xiii). Though not wishing to deny that the early teachings support the principles of the Declaration, I do not agree that the contribution of the Buddhist tradition to the cause of human rights is in any way "outstanding."

58 In certain areas (such as the prohibition on alcohol and matters of sexual morality) the precepts go beyond the more limited aims of human rights charters. This is because Buddhism provides a particular vision of human good and also defines the practices required for its fulfillment.

59 Keown (1992: 33).

60 Sometimes a contrast is drawn between the "voluntary" nature of the Buddhist precepts and the "commandments" of Christianity. While the format of the Buddhist precepts is certainly more appealing to liberal tastes, the distinction has little real meaning. The precepts apply whether or not they are formally "undertaken," and are commandments in all but name.

61 Küng and Kuschel (eds.) (1993: 104), original emphasis.

62 Vajiragnana (1992).

63 A.iii.208

64 Küng and Kuschel (eds.) (1993: 14).

References

Bilimoria, Purushottama. 1993. "Is 'Adhikara' Good Enough for 'Rights'?" *Asian Philosophy* 23, 3–13.

Bradney, A. 1993. *Religions, Rights and Laws.* Leicester: Leicester University Press.

Carlyle, R. W. and A. J. Carlyle. 1950. *A History of Medieval Political Theory in the West.* Edinburgh: Blackwood and Sons.

Carrithers, Michael. 1985. "An alternative social history of the self," in M. Carrithers, S. Collins, and S. Lukes (eds.), *The Category of the Person. Anthropology, Philosophy, History,* Cambridge: Cambridge University Press, 234–56.

Dagger, Richard. 1989. "Rights," in Terence Ball (et al.), *Political Innovation and Conceptual Change,* Cambridge: Cambridge University Press, 292–308.

de Bary, W. Theodore. 1988. Neo-Confucianism and Human Rights," in *Human Rights and the World's Religions,* ed. Leroy S. Rouner, Indiana: University of Notre Dame Press, 183–98.

de Silva, K. M. (et al., eds.). 1988. *Ethnic Conflict in Buddhist Societies: Sri Lanka, Thailand and Burma.* Boulder, CO: Westview Press.

Donnelly, Jack. 1985. *The Concept of Human Rights.* London and Sydney: Croom Helm.

Finnis, J. M. 1980. *Natural Law and Natural Rights.* Clarendon Law Series, H. L. A. Hart (ed.). Oxford: Clarendon Press.

Harris, Ian. "Causation and Telos: The Problem of Buddhist Environmental Ethics," *Journal of Buddhist Ethics* 1: 45–56.

Hohfeld, Wesley. 1964. *Fundamental Legal Conceptions.* New Haven: Yale University Press.

Howard, Rhoda. 1986. "Is there an African concept of human rights?," in R. J. Vincent (ed.), *Foreign Policy and Human Rights,* Cambridge: Cambridge University Press, 11–32.

Hsiung, James C. 1985. *Human Rights in East Asia: A Cultural Perspective.* New York: Paragon House.

Humana, Charles. 1992. *World Human Rights Guide.* Oxford: Oxford University Press.

Inada, Kenneth K. 1982. "The Buddhist Perspective on Human Rights," in Arlene Swidler (ed.), *Human Rights in Religious Traditions,* New York: Pilgrim Press, 66–76.

——. 1990. "A Buddhist Response to the Nature of Human Rights," in Claude E. Welch Jr. and Virginia A. Leary (eds.), *Asian Perspectives on Human Rights,* Boulder, CO: Westview Press, 91–103.

James, Stephen A. 1994. "Reconciling International Human Rights and Cultural Relativism: the Case of Female Circumcision," *Bioethics* 8: 1–26.

Keown, Damien. 1992. *The Nature of Buddhist Ethics.* London: Macmillan.

Küng, Hans and Karl-Josef Kuschel (eds.). 1993. *A Global Ethic. The Declaration of the Parliament of the World's Religions.* London: SCM Press.

Küng, Hans, Josef Van Ess, Heinrich Von Stietencron, and Heinz Bechert. 1986. *Christianity and the World Religions.* 2nd edn. London: SCM Press.

Ladd, John (ed.). 1983. *Ethical Relativism.* Lanham, MD: University Press of America.

Little, David, John Kelsay, and Abdulaziz Sachedina (eds.). 1988. *Human Rights and the Conflict of Cultures.* Columbia, SC: University of South Carolina Press.

MacIntyre, Alasdair. 1981. *After Virtue. A Study in Moral Theory.* London: Duckworth.

Macy, Joanna Rogers. 1979. "Dependent Co-Arising: The Distinctiveness of Buddhist Ethics," *Journal of Religious Ethics* 7: 38–52.

Milne, A. J. M. 1986. *Human Rights and Human Diversity.* London: Macmillan.

Nickel, James W. 1987. *Making Sense of Human Rights.* Berkeley: University of California Press.

——. 1982. "Is the Notion of Human Rights a Western Concept?," *Diogenes* 120: 75–102.

Perera, L. H. H. (ed.). 1988. *Human Rights and Religions in Sri Lanka. A Commentary on the Universal Declaration of Human Rights.* Colombo: Sri Lanka Foundation.

Perera, L. N. 1991. *Buddhism and Human Rights. A Buddhist Commentary on the Universal Declaration of Human Rights.* Colombo: Karunaratne and Sons.

Pollis, Adamantia and Peter Schwab. 1979. *Human Rights: Cultural and Ideological Perspectives.* New York: Praeger.

Rouner, Leroy S. 1988. *Human Rights and the World's Religions.* Notre Dame, IN: University of Notre Dame Press.

Stackhouse, Max L. 1984. *Creeds, Society, and Human Rights.* Grand Rapids, Michigan: William B. Eerdmans Publishing Company.

Swidler, Arlene (ed.). 1982. *Human Rights in Religious Traditions.* New York: Pilgrim Press.

Teson, Fernando R. 1985. "International Human Rights and Cultural Relativism," *Virginia Journal of International Law* 25: 869–98.

Tyagi, Yogesh K. 1981. "Third World Response to Human Rights," *Indian Journal of International Law* 21: 119–40.

Unno, Taitetsu. 1988 "Personal Rights and Contemporary Buddhism," in Leroy S. Rouner (ed.), *Human Rights in the World's Religions,* Notre Dame, IN: University of Notre Dame Press, 129–47.

Vajiragnana, Rev. "Justice in Buddhism," *Vesak Sirisara* (unpaginated version from the Electronic Buddhist Archive).

Welch, Claude. E. Jr. and V. Leary. 1990. *Asian Perspectives on Human Rights.* Boulder, CO: Westview Press.

Religious Freedom and Human Rights in India

C. Joseph Barnabas

10

- ◆ Overview of rights and religion ◆
- ◆ Religious tolerance and intolerance in India ◆
- ◆ Statutory limits on religious freedom ◆ Christians and other minorities ◆
- ◆ Human rights legislation in India ◆ Hinduism and Indian national identity ◆

Man is basically a religious animal. Attempts to show religion as an aspect of some animal species have collapsed, and now it is generally conceded that only humans are religious. In providing satisfaction of biological drives, animals appear to have a good life, but for humans biological needs are not everything. "A conscious relation to the wider human world, including the world of ideal possibilities, becomes a fundamental need for man."[1] This is precisely the function of the ultimate values of religious experience. Through religious tradition, humankind in the past experienced and communicated humanism to the younger generation. For example, among the Anglo-Saxons, certain religious traditions were followed in order to give weightage to human life or human values. If a family lost an adult because of murder, the man who killed was to pay the dead man's price to the bereaved family: a nobleman's price was fixed at 1,200 shillings, a lesser nobleman at 600 shillings, and a peasant at 200 shillings.[2] The 200 shillings of the late seventh century works out to an average value of Rs 1 lakh today. For that amount, one could buy one hundred sheep and sixteen bulls. It is in these aspects that the

idea of protection of human rights and freedom as a whole developed and over time was identified as religious freedom based on texts. From religious freedom gradually evolved ideas of personal, political and social freedom.

Freedom has meant not only "freedom from" but also "freedom to" and "freedom for." It is also defined as "the absence of hindrances to individual, whether those of political, ecclesiastical or other origin."[3] For instance, if a person is sent out of prison, but not allowed to go where he wants or do what he wants, it may not be called "freedom," it is only a release from prison.

The denial of freedom in various forms has led not only to untold misery, but also to persecution directed against entire groups of people. Wars have been waged in the name of religion or belief either with the aim of imposing upon the individual or as a pretext for extending economic or political domination. The Treaty of Westphalia concluded in 1648 after the Thirty Years' War in Europe represented an important step toward ensuring toleration both for Protestants in Catholic states and for Catholics in Protestant states. The

Declaration of the Rights of Man, issued in 1789 during the French Revolution, specified freedom of religious expression as one of the human rights entitled to protection.[4] Another landmark was the Treaty of Berlin (1878), through which the newly established states of Bulgaria, Montenegro, Romania and Serbia were given complete independence by the Ottoman Empire. Consistent with it, states undertook to ensure religious freedom to all their inhabitants. At the beginning of the twentieth century, transnational efforts were taken towards eliminating religious discrimination with the establishment of the League of Nations. The Covenant of the League in Article *22(5)* held a mandatary responsible for the administration of the territory under conditions that would guarantee freedom of conscience and religion.[5] After World War II, the realization of the need for a forum of human rights became widespread and hence the United Nations and other world forums emerged as centres for communicating and implementing human rights.

In the UN Charter, religion is specified, along with race, sex and language, as an impermissible ground of differentiation. Initially efforts were made to incorporate the freedom of religion into the UN Charter as a fundamental right. However, the Charter refers only to "human rights and fundamental freedoms" in general.[6] The UN Charter of Human Rights contains a right to freedom of religion. It is guaranteed in Article 2(1) that "every man is entitled to all the rights and freedoms set forth in this declaration, without distinction of any kind such as race, colour, sex, language, religion, political or other opinion, national or social origin, property, birth or other status." A further guarantee in Article 18(1) of the Charter clearly states that "every one has the right to freedom of thought, conscience, and religion." This right includes the freedom to change one's religion or beliefs and freedom either alone or in community with others and in public or private, to manifest one's religion or

belief in teaching, practice, worship and observance.[7] So the right to have or to adopt a religion or belief is no longer subject to limitations. Only the freedom to manifest one's religion or belief may be. When religious freedom comes in conflict with non-discrimination on grounds of religion, tolerance has to be respected. This was incorporated in Article 20, which stated that "any advocacy of religious hatred, that constitutes incitement to discrimination, hostility or violence, should be prohibited by law.[8]

Provisions to safeguard religious freedom were incorporated in the Special Declaration and Convention for the Elimination of All Forms of Religious Intolerance, and in the Declaration and Convention on the Elimination of All Forms of Racial Discrimination. The Vienna Declaration and Programme of 25 June 1993, declares and reaffirms in Article 19(1):

> the obligation of the States to ensure that persons belonging to minorities may exercise fully and effectively all human rights, and fundamental freedoms without any discrimination and in full equality before the law in accordance with the Declaration on the rights of persons belonging to the national or ethnic, religious and linguistic minorities.

The same opinion is being expressed in *consecutive* forums[9] insisting that:

> persons belonging to minorities have the right, to enjoy their own culture, to profess and practise their own religion and to use their own language in private and in public freely and without interference or any form of discrimination.

At Barcelona in 1995, a declaration on the role of religion in the promotion of peace was adopted at a meeting organized by UNESCO and the Centre UNESCO de Catalunya. The declaration recognized religion as an important component for human life. While admitting that "religion is not the sole remedy for all the ills of humanity" it acknowledged the "indispensable role" religion has to play in this critical time.[10] Under these circumstances, one tends to accept that religion has an object and functions in different ways. It offers ultimate meaning to one's culture. It is also a way of life to another culture, and for some it represents the highest aspiration of human existence. Moreover, religions claim to carry a message of salvation and have, through history, willy-nilly contributed to world peace.

The recognition of the procedural status of an individual before international human rights agencies is not an innovation. Individuals were recognized by religion even before the state recognized individuals. When struggles for freedom and conscience occurred in Europe, it was then that the individual was empowered with courage and insight. This insight ultimately paved the way for the formal incorporation of the principles of religious tolerance that were embedded in the national law in Switzerland and Transylvania, two relatively small, multi-religious communities bordering the great empires.[11] Religious sentiments and religious reformations did have an impact on the world bodies, because religion itself had raised consciousness of human rights. All religions basically in some form uphold human values and human rights.

What prompted the world to emphasize human rights? While the main stress of international law has evolved out of the predominance of the state and of the state system, the notions of rights evolved within the context of domestic political struggle. It is commonly accepted that only through Greek, Stoic and Christian roots came the ideas of human governance."[12] However, it was Christian-inspired thought that was responsible for stressing human rights in the western world. The three basic principles of Christianity that ultimately justify human rights value are human dignity, human equality and human responsibility.[13]

According to Christianity, human dignity was manifest when God created man in his own image. By doing so, God established a relationship with human beings. Jesus Christ called God his heavenly father. He also called his disciples friends. In this respect, the rational, moral and spiritual qualities of God were granted to human beings, and as a result man was projected from animal state as a creature of God.

The concept of equality of human beings is evident in the Book of Deuteronomy in chapter ten. It states:

> For the Lord your God . . . shows no partiality and accepts no bribes. He defends the cause of the fatherless and the widow and loves the alien, giving him food and clothing. And you are to love those who are aliens, for yourself were aliens.

Jesus Christ himself, through his teachings and parables, condemned favouritism and differentiation between rich and poor.

Human accountability is stressed in the Bible in terms of helping the needy and poor. When an expert of law tested Jesus Christ by questioning, "Teacher, which is the greatest commandment in the law?" Jesus replied, "To love the Lord your God with all your heart and with all your soul and with all your mind This is the first and greatest commandment. The second is like it; love your neighbour as yourself, all the law and the prophets hang on these two commandments" (Matthew 22: 34–40). While defining who the neighbour was, Jesus replied, "he who is in need" (Luke 10: 25–37). As far as human responsibility is concerned, it rests in forgiving others who work against us, knowingly or unknowingly. Jesus said, "for if you forgive men when sin against you, your heavenly father will also forgive you. But if you do not forgive men their sins, your father will nor your sins" (Matthew 6: 14–15).

The thrust of missionary zeal was the freedom to which seemed a logical consequence of the freedom to propagate as quoted in the Indian Constitution. Yet in 1968 and in 1963 respectively the states of Madhya Pradesh and Orissa passed a "Freedom of Religion Act" which explicitly denied that freedom. The Constitution as interpreted by the Supreme Court upholds them, granting that those who follow Christ may express their conviction, but are restrained from following it up in terms of that belief, which would naturally lead to conversion. This is all the more controversial in that converts who were disadvantaged were denied the benefits of state welfare schemes and other benefits as they had not demonstrated the degrees of suffering exhibited and documented by those who did not convert. The standpoint of Islam in respect of human rights (equality and freedom) revolves around three points: (1) equality in the value of human beings, (2) equality before law and order and in the right to speak, and (3) equality in economic affairs. The Qur'an states,

> Oh mankind, we created you from a single pair of male and female and made you into nation and tribes that you may know each other, not that you may despise each other. Verily the most honoured of you in the sight of God is, he who is the most righteous.

The Qur'an also states, "Oh mankind, your God is one, your father is one. All of you are related to Adam and Adam was made of dust."[14]

In Islamic territory, the person, property, and honour of every individual are fully protected and thereby equality before law and order is ensured. Islam insists on paying attention to the condition of the protected (non-Muslims) and treating them securely. The right to speak is explicitly found in the "safeguard of the rights of non-Muslims in the Islamic territory." It has gone so far as to give them the liberty of practising customs entirely opposed to those of Islam. It is understood that a Muslim man has the right to marry a

"developed" non-Muslim, a Christian or Jew but giving her the right to retain and practise her own faith.[15]

In the question of equality in economic affairs, the Qur'an lays "special emphasis on the uplifting of the economically depressed, toward which a state levy was to be collected from the rich."[16] Islam, through its moral injunctions, aimed at creating feelings of mutual love and affection among people, under which they may help their weak and poor brethren and at the same time create permanent institutions in society to guarantee help and assistance to those who are lacking means of survival. What the Qur'an actually means is "that this wealth may not circulate among the rich." The controversial belief that the disadvantaged will be naturally converted is central to Islam. It desires that "no legal, functional or traditional handicaps should exist to prevent an individual according to his capacity and talent, nor should any social distinctions operate in protecting the privileges of a certain class, race, dynasty or group of people."[17] When the Universal Declaration of Human Rights was announced, a renowned Muslim leader commented that "to a student of Qur'an not one word in the preamble or in the objectives of the Charter, and not a single Article in the text of the Universal Declaration of Human Rights will seem unfamiliar."[18]

In these terms, one would find the ideology of human rights values in Islam. The problem in some of the Semitic religions is that the degree of intolerance increases in relation to correct representations or communications of the truth. The arguments of Caliph Omar and the Nazi book burnings are not without explanations. The only fear is that intolerance is extended to writers and not just their work, for example, Hypatia, Ken Saro Wiwa, and Salman Rushdie in our time. The question is, does protection of minority rights cover those who dissent and protest against the practices of their own religions as evident in traditions, rituals and beliefs, such as

Tabari, one of the great commentators of the Qur'an, who tried to explain different meanings as visualized by different people? The idea that most religions are monolithic and intolerant of dissent is not part of remembered religious experiences. So long as one is not compelled to uphold beliefs, there is still hope for human rights in religious practices, as our religious freedom still remains open. However, in the mind of the true believer, blasphemy as practised makes human rights difficult to defend. The temptation to play God, as Calvin did, is evident in the case of Michael Servetus (1511–53). Servetus, who had in his work "on the Errors of the Trinity" accused traditional scholastic theology of Greek philosophical terms and the introduction of non-biblical categories into the definitions of the Trinity, was condemned by the Inquisition and later burnt to death by Calvin, in spite of a promise of safe passage at Geneva. What the Ayatollah Khomeini intended to do to Salman Rushdie is a continuation of such a trend. From pronouncing death to the writer, the reader is also sentenced. Human rights continue to be violated even as we march towards the twenty-first century.

The practice of Hinduism, in mostly Asian countries and from ancient times, was flexible enough to accommodate people of other faiths. The goal of ancient Indian religion was to give humanity spiritual consolation as well as to point the path to final release from worldly life. The ancient sages of India seem to have thought of such issues as reflecting the problems that beset humanity everywhere in the world. Therefore, they were mainly concerned with solving problems throughout the world. It was universal peace (*visva santhi*) that they aimed at. In order to achieve this goal, the sages never gave themselves to any national or religious identity as such. The word they preferred and the concept they cherished was *dharma*, which has a world-wide application, and which included in its sweep almost all the religions of the world.[19] As we know it,

dharma is for respecting all religions, and according to dharma, every religion is good. Dharma is, basically, the order inherent in man.

The effort of every individual must be to make out this order and apply it in practice in order to bring about unity throughout the world. It gives freedom to every individual but advocates, at the same time, that one should not misuse one's freedom because the order of life, which dharma insists on, must not be disturbed. It exhorts humanity to follow the examples of those who have cultivated virtues such as equipoise, equanimity and equivalence, of those who recognize the fundamental human dignity of every created being, and those who look on all with an equal eye.

The scheme of life devised by ancient sages of India was a dharmic scheme in which religious freedom is granted to every individual. Religious rites and rituals were meant only to acquire mental, emotional and spiritual stability, by being one with the environment. In this scheme, therefore, there was no discontinuity between the world of man and the world of God on the one hand, and the world of man and the world of animals and plants on the other. The whole universe was looked upon as one unit that included all these worlds. Keeping this in mind, the sages declared that their idea was to see the whole universe in its essential unity and not in its disintegrated format. The dharmic scheme made room for all human beings (*samvomanawsi janatam*): such human rights and values are certainly embedded theoretically in the principles of Hinduism. In India, particularly in Hinduism as understood in the ancient and medieval period, was preserved the right to free discussion and dissent. No Inquisitions marked religious developments, though "fundamentalists" persecuted, and still do, those "who did not belong." The important point for those intellectuals who seek the right of religious freedom is that the books embodying the principal *nastika* philosophies have been preserved over two thousand years, though the works of the more extreme materialist school, the *lokayatika,* were only known from quotation.[20]

While all religions insist in their doctrine on the value of human rights, no religion seems to recognize them in practice. Religion as such is based on positive values, but religious orthodoxy alone produced counter-values to religious tolerance. One is often reminded of how religious fundamentalism caused religious oppression, through churches, temples and Scriptures. Persons who left the officially recognized religion were often deprived of certain rights. They were excommunicated, exiled or given major punishments. On the other hand, the clerics of the official religion were regarded as officials of the government, while other groups did not enjoy such status.[21] It was against this background that religious reformers largely based their struggle against traditional ecclesiastical rulers. These struggles induced national and international leaders to think about human rights. Today in every nation we see a multiplicity of religions that have naturally made possible religious freedom. In the same way, the liberalization of religious faith and practice led to a more openly observed religious freedom. The choice to conform or to deny one's traditional religious faith and practice is part of a religious freedom that has been activated and is now accepted. The constitutions of nearly all modern states have incorporated more or less elaborate guarantees for freedom of religion and conscience and for protection against discrimination on grounds of religion or belief.[22] But the reality is disheartening. Religion, instead of promoting harmony, creates disharmony; instead of curtailing violence, it induces violence.

Idols or icons were used to expose the qualities of God in action for the common and illiterate laymen. But they are sometimes misused to incite violence. During and after the destruction of the Babri Masjid, the image of Ram has transformed "from a tranquil, tender and serene God to an angry, punishing one, armed with several weapons."[23] Anuradha Kaput, in an article titled "Deity to Crusader: The Changing Iconography of Ram," portrays how the images of Ram are published through posters:

> The images now available show Ram pulling his bowstring, the arrow poised to annihilate. The God wears an armour or a breastplate, and is sometimes pictured over a diva (lamp), the Sri Ram Jyoti, and sometimes within it. The Jyoti has a photograph-like image of a temple on it – the temple that is to be built in Ayodhya. In another poster, Ram is shown standing alone alongside the model of the selfsame temple. He is very heavily armed, far more heavily than in any earlier representation. Apart from his customary dhanush, he appears carrying a trishul (trident), a sword, and an axe.[24]

In view of the manipulative impact of idols, E. V. Ramaswami in the 1960s and 1970s opposed fundamentalism and promoted freedom by propagating atheism and by smashing idols. From Ingersol to Gora, rationalist thought had free access on the Indian highway. Almost all the religions are being criticized for their inability to protect human values within their purview. Eligibility for high governmental posts, including the head of the state, either by law or tradition is confined to those who seemingly hold officially sanctioned religious beliefs. Acts of discrimination appear to consist for the most part in the imposition of religious tests in selecting candidates for public appointments and the granting of preferences to members of particular faiths. Educational opportunities are *sometimes determined* by religious background lack of it. In some countries, the religious bias in the form religious instruction indoctrinates education, precipitating a "constructed" communal tension and conflict.[25]

Religious barriers not only have an effect upon the shaping and sharing of affection and values but also, on a more general level, tend to stifle the growth of congenial personal relationships.[26] Religion figures in the class structure of community, especially where it is highly rigid and hierarchical. Another danger emerging in recent years in theocratic states is forcing people to have faith in the state or in the government rather than in religion itself. This is mainly because the state propagated a particular religion initially and then lost faith in the religion but believed in religiosity. This is what is being done in some Islamic countries and what had been done earlier in Catholic Spain. Religious freedom as a basic human right is guaranteed through the constitution in many countries, but in democracy there should be a conducive climate where human rights can be affirmed among multi-religious groups. When such a climate is not there, how can loyalty to the state be expected?

The basic issues of religious freedom have been discussed and demanded since the sixteenth century, but they are not practised everywhere, even today.[27] In the name of religion, poets, writers and freedom fighters are murdered. Salman Rushdie and Tasleema Nasreen are threatened with death. Nobel laureate Aung San Suu Kyi is under house arrest for demanding democracy for her people.[28] Use of religious and quasi-religious symbols as coded messages is characteristic of public life. In Pakistan, two mentally unbalanced persons were held for insulting the Prophet. So was an unlettered 13-year-old, Salamat Masih, who was accused of writing blasphemy. Exploitation and harassment of the labouring Hindu and Kohli community of Sindh and discrimination against them continued. In Bangladesh, 1993 can be marked as one of the worst years in terms of human rights for religious minorities.

In India, human rights assumed importance when the Constitution was drafted. Article 25 granted the rights to propagate and disseminate religious beliefs. Article 26 provided a religious institution the right to manage its own affairs. Even then the human rights situation is not better. Criticism of erosion of human rights in

Kashmir, Punjab and the north-eastern states is universal. When Prime Minister Indira Gandhi was assassinated more than three thousand Sikhs were massacred in Delhi alone. In the name of religion, the 300-year-old Babri Masjid was demolished on 6 December 1992. Followed by this, curfew was imposed at 213 places and spread over nearly fifteen states. More than four hundred fifty people were killed and crores of people suffered for months from its impact in cities and towns. Simultaneous attacks were made on Hindus in Bangladesh after the destruction of the masjid. In Bombay, bomb attacks were made on innocent people by religious fanatics.

Between 1981 and 1992, about 11,538 people died in the Khalistan violence in Punjab, of which 61 per cent were Sikhs. In Kashmir, 2,272 unarmed civilians died during the violence in 1988–92, among which Muslims constituted 78 per cent. The riots in Bangalore in October 1994, over the broadcast of Urdu news, took many innocent lives, as did the publication of an English translation of a Malayalam short story, "Mohammad the Idiot," in the *Deccan Herald* (7 December 1986), which led to riots in Mysore and Bangalore. Foreign tourists are taken hostage and sometimes even killed in the name of religion. All this demonstrates the vulnerability of the Indian people today.

These atrocities and communal actions prove that many Indians do not recognize the basic principles of the Indian Republic. It is not established on the basis of religion. The Constitution in the matters of educational institutions, personal laws and of these rights granted to minorities include the right to open and run educational institutions of their own. Article 29 provides that any section of the citizens residing in the territory of India or any part thereof having a distinct language, script or culture of its own shall have the right to conserve the same. Article 30 granted rights to all religious or linguistic minorities to establish and administer institutions of their own choice for certain historical reasons, especially against the background of the partition of India and Pakistan and its after-math.[29]

Today, that right to establish minority educational institutions opened the flood-gates to mercenaries and enterpreneurs, who set up or work in educational factories. The institutional heads for all practical purposes treat students and teachers as second-class citizens, though they also belong to the same minority community. Fundamental rights enshrined in the Constitution are denied to them in the name of minority rights. The institutional heads often move the courts to establish their fundamental as well as unalterable right to administer their institutions.[30]

The Supreme Court in *Frank Anthony School Employees Association v. Union* of *India and Others* pronounced that "for the purposes of ensuring educational standards certain restrictions by way of regulations can be validly prescribed and that such. a regulation cannot be construed as interfer-ence in the affairs of minority institutions."[31] In *Christian Medical College Hospital Employees Union v. Christian Medical College, Vellore Association and Others,* the court held that:

> rights that are enforced through the several pieces of labour legislations in India have to be applied to every workman irrespective of the character of the management. Even the management of the minority educa-tional institutions has got to respect these rights and implement them. If such laws are made inapplicable to the minority educa-tional institutions, there is every likelihood of such institutions being subjected to maladministration.[32]

There was criticism of preferential treat-ment to minority institutions on the ground that they get aid from the state and thus are not entitled to claim any preferen-tial right or reservation in favour of students of the Christian community. Nevertheless, the Supreme Court held, in the case relating to admissions in St

Stephen's College, Delhi, that:

> Minority aided educational institutions are entitled to prefer community candidates to maintain their minority character in their institutions, and also to introduce subjects of their choice in conformity with University standards. The State may regu-late the intake in this category with due regard to the need of the community in the area which the institution is intended to serve. But in no case such intake shall exceed fifty per cent of the annual admis-sion. For the remaining portion, admission of other community candidates shall be done purely on the basis of merit.

Whether the 50 per cent reservation is a step in the right direction or not depends on how effectively and positively it is used by minority educational institutions.[33]

The All India Association for Christian Higher Education and the Commission for Education and Culture, Catholic Bishops' Conference of India, published *Judgements on Minority Rights* in 1996 focusing on Supreme Court judgements from 1951 to 1995. In their introductory note, the editors said:

> A striking feature of India is that several language and religious groups are minority in some states and majority in others. Educational institutions, irrespective of their religious and linguistic background are to develop both the individuality of persons and the unity of the nation. Institutions and communities are not to build up ghettoes and dose the doors to other language and religious groups. The last word as the Supreme Court is still involved in defining who is a minority

Even the Bharatiya Janata Parry, which has all along campaigned against discrimi-natory treatment to minorities has been and demanding abrogation of Article 30 of the Constitution, is now demanding for Hindus the right to establish and admin-ister educational institutions of their choice.[34]

The personal laws of the minorities are

complicated and attempts by governments to change them are interpreted as interfering in the rights of minorities. The personal laws regarding marriage, divorce and succession are very varied among the Muslims, Christians and Parsis. The whole of India knows about the case of Shah Bano, who claimed maintenance from her divorced husband under the provision of Section 125 of the Criminal Procedure Code. Muslim leaders created such a stir that Parliament enacted that the section did not apply to Muslims. So also a Christian claims today that he need not pay maintenance to his wife on the ground that she is mentally retarded and his church has annulled the marriage. Under the Indian Succession Act (1925), a Christian widow inherits only one-third of her husband's or son's property if he dies intestate. Similarly, under the Christian Divorce Act (1969), it is a fairly straightforward process for a man to get a divorce.[35] Such is the condition of the rights of a section among these minorities. Unless minority leaders look into the complicated situation of those sections and agree to some extent to a common civil code, these disparities cannot be removed.

Another obvious disparity is the policy implications for Dalit Christians of treatment by the government and by "upper caste" Christians. John C. Webster in his book *The Dalit Christians* says "between ten and fifteen per cent or all Dalits in India are Christians. Between two-thirds and three quarters of all Christians in India are Dalits." This huge segment is not treated on par with the Scheduled Castes and Tribes by the Government of India or by other Christians. Tribal Christians are eligible for Scheduled Tribe benefits, whereas Dalit Christians are ineligible for Scheduled Caste benefits.[36] Politically also, Dalit Christians have few opportunities to gain power because they are excluded from reserved opportunities. The various Acts and rules passed by Parliament to give special protection to Dalits are not applicable to Dalit Christians. These include the Protection of Civil Rights Act, 1955,

the Protection of Civil Rights Rule, 1977 and the SC and ST (Prevention of Atrocities) Act, 1989.[37]

Given this situation, Dalit Christians are denied protection of life and personal liberty. One glaring example is of Dalit Christians who could not get any protection during mass killings in the village of Karamchedu, Andhra Pradesh, on 17 July 1985. On 15 August 1996, the Church of South India, Rayalseema Diocese, sent a letter to the Collector and the Superintendent of Police about untouchability openly practised by tea-shop-owners at Arekal, who used separate glasses for Dalit Christians and charged them higher prices for food items.[38]

Upper-caste Christians are also guilty of treating Dalit Christians as inferior. Though caste does not affect the Christians' worship or rites, it affects the places Dalit and non-Dalit Christians occupy, and the roles they play in regular worship. In some areas of south India, Dalit Christians were given separate places of worship and separate burial places.[39] As a consequence Dalit Christians, who are unable to bear such humiliation and unable to protest, move to other churches where they think such disparities do not exist.

From colonial times, instead of enforcing children's right to read in common schools, the government followed the policy of providing special schools for them. Harijan welfare schools and hostels in Tamil Nadu are offshoots of such policies. In such schools, only SC and ST students are enrolled and SC and ST teachers teach. Such a policy promotes and strengthens the identity of caste. Instead of treating untouchability as an inhuman social custom like sati and infanticide, the British preferred to treat it as an article of Hindu religion and considered its removal beyond the purview of the government. Even Mahatma Gandhi with all his sincerity and earnestness as a crusader, his participation in the Vaikom Satyagraha in 1924 and his countryside tour against untouchability in 1924, failed to change the hearts of orthodox Hindus, and of many Congressmen on the question of the uplift of the depressed classes. The high hopes of Gandhi in the 1930s for the eradication of untouchability were belied in a short time. The conservative Hindus started organizing opposition to the anti-untouchability movement. The result was the denial of the right to enter temples, use wells and even buy a residential site in an upper-caste colony. The Constituent Assembly, on 29 April 1947, passed a resolution that "untouchability in any form is abolished and the imposition of any disability on that account shall be an offence."[40] But it has been proved beyond doubt that the caste system and untouchability are two aspects of a continuing traditional Hindu society that can be eradicated not through constitutional amendments and enactments, but only through convictions that reverse our behaviour.

Jawaharlal Nehru, India's first prime minister, was forthright in his approach to religion. Ainslee T. Embree stated that Nehru was of the opinion that one should have freedom to denounce ignorance and superstition, even though they may be cloaked in religious garb. In his writings, Nehru quoted Voltaire as saying "a man who accepts his religion without examining it is like an ox which allowed itself to be harnessed." At the same time, he pointed out that religion welds people into groups to face three brute facts of life: "contingency, powerlessness and scarcity." He added that though religion "enabled them to overcome guilt and alienation, yet it had a tendency to check change and progress inherent in human society."[41] For example, Christian groups of the nineteenth century opposed slave trade yet Christians had promoted slave trade for many centuries. Nevertheless, though religion is not the primary and major agent of change and modernization, it is a minor and at the same time an important source as well as a constituting element in India's modernization.

In India, it is known that a local segement of Muslims or Islamic nationalists created the concept of the nation of Pakistan, and that Sikh communalism appeared in the name of Sikh nationalism to make a similar demand for Khalistan. Any similar Christian nationalism or Hindu nationalism would be a disastrous end to the Indian Republic. In order to bring some change, the format of religious education, first of all, should be without fanaticism and exclusivism. All should convert religion into a source of helpful energy and disown killing in the name of religion.

Similarly, the state should give freedom to the people in matters of religion and conscience. In the erstwhile Communist countries, the state ignored the rights granted under Article 22(5) of the Covenant of the League, which held it to be the responsibility of the state to guarantee freedom of conscience and religion. The guarantee under Article 18(1) of the UN Universal Declaration of Human Rights, i.e. that everyone has the right to freedom of thought, conscience and religion, was rarely granted, especially in dictatorships. In the Chinese-controlled Tibet Autonomous Region, Buddhist monks and nuns are ill-treated and imprisoned. The reciting of "the Boundless Wisdom," a prayer written by the Dalai Lama that refers to the freedom of Tibet, is banned. The monks and nuns cannot keep the Dalai Lama's picture. They cannot even pronounce his name. A monk who had a book containing the prayer of Dalai Lama was expelled from his monastery in 1996. Monks are not allowed to listen to any broadcasts from India or to the Voice of America programmes. The Chinese authorities have taken measures to limit the growth of religion since the 1980s. The monasteries are not allowed to have more than a stipulated number of monks or nuns. The excess number of monks are removed and expelled. The Chinese government considers the spending of money, material and manpower on religion a waste. Above all, every monk or nun is required to draw a clear line of demarcation with the "Dalai Lama clique" in order to formally declare his or her opposition to the Dalai Lama and his politics. The statistics available to the Human Rights Watch document how much religious leaders and supporters are suppressed. Of the total number of prisoners released during 1995, about 44 per cent (562) monks and about 23 per cent (289) were nuns. And of the 610 in detention in 1995, more than half were monks (346) and nuns (156). Though the population of nuns in monasteries is estimated between 3 per cent and 4 per cent they represent 25 per cent of the total prison population.[42]

In India, the NHRC and local human rights groups often seem to be insensitive to atrocities committed against Christians. Fr. Christudas was paraded naked at Dumka on 2 September, 1997. Beside the case registered in this connection, was one about atrocities on tribals at Sendhwa in Madhya Pradesh. Action was initiated with reference to atrocities against tribals, whereas the case of Christudas was sidelined as a "Christian" issue. An unexamined allegation of sexual misconduct was cited as a factor in not acting on this particular case. On 24 October 1997, Fr A. T. Thomas was murdered near Hazaribagh as he was actively supporting the rights of the Dalits. In 1995, Sister Maria Rani was murdered in broad daylight at Indore, because she was organizing bonded labourers against local moneylenders. In the eyes of human rights activists it was only a case of the murder of a missionary. The fact that she acted in the interests of the poor was bypassed. In several cases of rape of Christian nuns, few women's organizations responded. This indifference is indeed disturbing in secular India. The issue is whether such a communal bias will mean that rights are only for certain segments of society. Violations of human rights need to be challenged equally by all for all citizens. The freedom to suffer "alone" is not peculiar to Christianity; it has happened to the Jews, Unitarians, Muslims and non-conformists.[43] In some places, attacks on property and on growing commercial ventures of the emerging Muslim entrepreneurs continue. There have been campaigns to boycott goods produced by Muslim entrepreneurs.[44]

In some states, in order to pacify minorities, governments at times announce policy programmes. After the demolition of the Babri Masjid in December 1992, there was a new urgency in the Congress to establish secular credentials. It announced an increase in the quota for Haj pilgrims, along with an increase in the emoluments of Imams.[45] It also preferred an ordinance before the President of India to grant Scheduled Caste benefits to converted Christians who had been from the Scheduled Castes. That ordinance was, however, returned by the President just before the Lok Sabha elections in 1996. Any territorial settlement of the minority population by granting them separate statehood is a dangerous proposition.[46] The right to self-determination in principle implies the right of all people, i.e. both majority and minority, and not either of them. Article 27 of the Covenant of Civil and Political Rights does not imply state action for the benefit of minorities. And the rights of minorities may not be universal rights since the groups may not exist in all states. The minorities in one state may be a majority in another state or in a nation. Further, the article does not make any mention of the right to self-determination of minorities. The declaration of the UN General Assembly's resolution 47/135 of 18 December 1992 does mean the following:

A positive duty is cast on states to take appropriate measures to protect the existence and identity of minorities under Article 1. The members of the minorities have a right to maintain contact with other minorities as well as with kin groups across frontiers. National policies and programmes shall be planned and implemented with due regard for the legitimate interests of persons belonging to minorities under Article 5.[47]

So, equality means relative equality,

namely the principle to treat equally what are equal and unequally what are unequal. To treat unequals differently according to their inequality is not only permitted but required.

The International Convention on Civil and Political Rights (ICCPR) 1986 stated in Article 27 that "in those States in which ethnic, religious or linguistic minorities exist, persons belonging to such minorities shall not be denied the right to enjoy their own culture, to profess and practise their own religion or to use their own language." Similarly, to exercise vigilance in the subcontinent, a SAARC Human Rights (Minority) Commission, which ensures reasonable stability of laws in each country, seems necessary for the political and social stability of our states.

All problems are being grappled with on a world front. We may manage to achieve solutions that offer greater stability, but experiences disclose an unceasing continuance of problems. Eternal vigilance and unremitting labour are our mortal lot. Commitment to any one faith does not always require us to search for truth in all religions. Differences have often brought conflict and increased intolerance. From such a background, the Inter-Faith movement has presented opportunities for new understandings that would mutually uphold freedom of religion.[48] It is this climate that would be conducive to realizing human rights. While religious freedom may be acceptable to S. Radhakrishnan, Maulana Abul Kalam Azad and A. J. Appasamy, Bishop of Coimbatore, we need to be wary about writers who poison the wells of knowledge of the common man by being hypercritical of the religion of minorities. However much theology in the past may have been a consequence of persecution, there are a number of points involved in this matter of essentials and non-essentials. One view is that in case of difference both sides cannot be right, but there is no infallible way of telling which is right and which is wrong. Since the point is not vital, each may leave the other to follow its own preference. The other view is that both views may be right because truth is varied, just as God is diversified.[49]

In the words of M. Ingham, freedom of religion, freedom of speech and freedom of the press are properly associated, whereas

civil liberties scarcely thrive where religious liberties are disregarded, and the reverse is equally true. Beneath them all is a philosophy of liberty which assumes a measure of variety in human behaviour, honours integrity, respects the dignity of man, and seeks to exemplify the composition of God.[50]

Religion provides the energy, vision and goodwill essential to building worldwide harmony.

The fellowship of man cannot be achieved where there are inequalities and discriminations. It has to be built upon the basis of respect for human dignity, to which all religions are witness. The circle of fellowship can be enlarged only when religionists are ready to serve the weak, the needy, the poor, the lonely in our society.[51]

Over many generations, different religions have existed side by side without generating conflicts, except that ther politicization of religions did not always augur well for the human rights of all. In our constitutional love of secularism, we find that most minorities suffer from a persecution complex. Human rights under these circumstances survive like germs in a poison. Ghalib in the nineteenth century, and foreign missionaries like C. F. Andrews and Mother Teresa in the twentieth century are not only examples of survival in communal constructs, but a sign of hope against hope in realizing all human rights for all. Optimism about this fulfilment needs to be based on evidence that the human rights of one are not achieved at the expense of the other.

Notes

1   J. A. Hutchison, *Paths of Faith* (New York: McGraw-Hill Book Company, 1975), 7.

2   T. Cairns, *Cambridge Introduction to the History of Mankind* (Cambridge: Cambridge University Press, 1971), 39.

3   Hutchinson, 1975, 594.

4   Myres S. Mc Dougal, Lasswell and Chen, *Human Rights and World Public Order* (New Haven: Yale University Press, 1980), 655, 668, 671.

5   *Ibid.*, 671.

6   K. Vasak, *The International Dimensions of Human Rights,* vol 1 (Connecticut: Greenwood Press, 1958), 83.

7   S. C. Khare, *Human Rights and UnitedNations* (New Delhi: Metropolitan Book Co., 1977), 220.

8   K. Vasak, *The International Dimension of Human Rights,* 8; 84.

9   *International Commission of Jurists Review,* Special Issue on the UN Conference on Human Rights, Vienna, 1993, 118.

10 *University News,* Association of Indian Universities, 3 July 1995, 27–8.

11 Myres S. Mc Dougal, Lasswell and Chen, *Human Rights and World Public Order,* 665.

12 R. A. Falk, "Theoretical Foundations of Human Rights," *Legal Perspectives,* LRSA, Chen.gleput, 1994, 2.

13 J. Stott, *Issues Facing Christianity Today* (Bombay: Gospel Literature Service, 1988), 144–51.

14 S. A. B. Habiz, "Human Rights in Islam," Al-Islam (Singapore), 5(e), July/September 1974, 39.

15 M. Hamidulah, *Introduction to Islam* (Paris: Centre Culturel Islamique, 1957), 141–3.

16 A. K. Brohi, "Islam and Human Rights," in A. Gauher (ed.), *The Challenge of Islam* (London: Islamic Council of Europe, 1978), 184.

17 S. A. A. Maududi, *Islamic Way ofLife* (Delhi: MMI, 1981), 71.

18 A. K. Brohi, "Islam and Human Rights," 186.

19 Interview with Dr Vishnu Bhat, Department of English, Madras Christian College, 25 August 1995.

20 J. B. S. Haldane, "A Rationalist with a Halo," *Rationalist Annual,* London, 1954, 15.

21 Myres et al., *Human Rights and World Public Order,* 656, 658.

22 K. Vasak, *The International Dimension of Human Rights,* 31.

23 In G. Pandey (ed.), *Hindus and Others* (New Delhi: Penguin Viking, 1993), 74–107.

24 *Ibid.,* 74–5.

25 Myres et al., *Human Rights and World Public Order,* 568.

26 *Ibid.*

27 R. H. Bainton, *The Travail of Religious Liberty* (New York: Harper and Brothers, 1958), 253.

28 M. Reddy, "Human Rights Today," *University News,* New Delhi, 1 January 1995, 9.

29 B. C. Moses, in Foreword to K. Chandru (ed.), *Two Bills and Two Schools* (Madras: Education and Legal Aid Society, 1992), 111.

30 *Ibid.*

31 *Ibid.*

32 *Ibid.*

33 V. Vijayakumar, "Minorities and the Law," *March. of the Law, III,* 1992, 190–1, 193.

34 K. Chandru (ed.), *Two Bills and Two Schools,* 2.

35 V. Thampu, K. Nicholls and C. Raj, *Kristiya Drishtanta* (The Theological Research and Communication Institute, New Delhi, 1989), 39–41. Sections 10, 17 and 21 of the Indian Divorce Act, 1896 as applicable to the Christian community were struck down in a Bombay High Court judgment, making divorce easier for Christian women (*Times of India,* 8 May 1997).

36 J. C. B. Webster, *The Dalit Christians: A History* (ISPCK, Delhi, 1994), 60–3, 172.

37 J. Massey, "The Constitution (Scheduled Castes) Order 1950 and Dalit Christians," *Peoples Reporter,* Bangalore, 16–30 September 1996, 5.

38 *Ibid.,* 4.

39 J. C. B Webster, *The Dalit Christians: A History,* 179, 180.

40 A. C. Pradhan, "'Depressed Classes' Uplift in the Gandhian Era: A Critique of Three Approaches," *Indian Historical Review XIX* (1 & 2), July 1992 to January 1993 (New Delhi: ICHR, 1996), 37, 40–1, 45, 49.

41 A. T. Embree, "Nehru's Understanding of the Social Function of Religion," *India International Centre Quarterly,* Spring & Summer issue, XX (1 & 2), 1993, I68, 173.

42 *Cutting off the Serpent's Head. Tightening Control in Tibet 1994–95* (Tibet Information Network Human Rights Watch/Asia, New York, 1996), 25, 29, 93, 116–17.

43 Walter Fernandes, "No Rights for Wrong Indians," *Times of India,* 3 February, 1998.

44 Javeed Alam, "The Changing Grounds of Communal Mobilization" in G. Pandey (ed.), *Hindus and Others,* 148.

45 M. Godbole, "Besieged Minorities," Times of *India,"* 23 February 1996, G.

46 *Ibid.*

47 Q. M. Maarij-Uddin, "Minority Rights in International Law: Problems and Perspectives," *National Law School Journal,* vol. 8, National Law School of India University, Bangalore, 1996, 109, 112–13.

48 M. Ingham, *Mansions of the Spirit* (Norwich: Canterbury Press, 1997).

49 *Ibid.,* 357.

50 *Ibid.,* 360.

51 Yoshiaki Tisaka, "Human Rights," Position Paper III, in Homer A. Jack (ed.), *Religion for Peace,* Proc. Kyoto Conference on Religion and Peace (New Delhi: Gandhi Peace Foundation, 1973), 372.

II

Gandhi's Philosophy

Carrie Gustafson

> ◆ Violence, power and systems of criminal justice ◆
> ◆ Deterrence theory ◆ Retributive theory ◆
> ◆ Reprobative theory ◆ International Criminal Court ◆
> ◆ Local initiatives ◆ Punishing for peace ◆
> ◆ Victims and survivors ◆ Indigenous values

In the end we see that it is better to tolerate the thieves than to punish them . . . But whilst we may bear with the thieves, we may not endure the infliction . . . Since we regard the thieves as our kith and kin, they must be made to realize the kinship. And so we must take pains to devise ways and means of winning them over . . . The thief is bound in the end to turn away from his evil ways and we shall get a clearer vision of truth. *Mahatma Gandhi* [1]

For the true believer, the one who sees human rights activism as always directed against power, as always operating on behalf of those who dwell "on the bottom," the intersection of international law and criminal law merits close inspection. As for the accused, there is no lower bottom. As for mechanisms to wield power, there is none more potent than the power to punish, save that of war.

As human rights activists lobby daily for a permanent international criminal court (ICC), their oratory is eerily reminiscent of former cold warriors, and hints at an emerging class of global interventionists bent on "doing something" to stem the world's horrors. Regarding human rights

atrocities as the work of an evil few operating apart from the ordinary Us, they propose a simple solution: hunt Them down, put Them away, and peace will again be ours.

Gandhi's philosophy of *satyagraha** provides an alternative. In combination with social theory, *satyagraha* offers an ethical and practical response to disorder, suffering, and injustice that eschews inflicting or threatening to inflict violence on others. Further, it serves to remind us that violence and power are inherent features of any system of criminal justice; that an expanded power to punish is not universally regarded as a sign of moral progress or the achievement of "justice"; that punishment is not the inevitable or the pre-eminent response to deviant behavior; and that strategies to resolve conflict and to strengthen social norms should reflect the inherent dignity and potential for moral responsibility in all persons – they should humanize, rather than degrade their participants.

For those who would dismiss *satyagraha* as "religious," a few brief remarks about the part played by religion and religious belief.

Many of the world's organized religions aspire to truth and non-violence, the central values of *satyagraha*. Yet few endorse the principled renunciation of coercive threats at its core, and their dogmatic, exclusionary tendencies made them frequent targets of Gandhi.[2] Gandhi wrote and said a great deal about religion, yet *satyagraha* cannot be ascribed to any particular orthodoxy. Indeed, a great strength of *satyagraha* is its universality – neither religion nor religious belief is sufficient or necessary. To the extent faith enters in, it is a faith rooted in non-violence and truth that even an atheist could endorse. Yet Gandhi's life-work, like that of Bishop Dinis Singulane in Mozambique, Martin Luther King in the United States, Aung San Suu Kyi in Burma, and Nelson Mandela in South Africa, is a testament to the religious values that inspire these and other individuals working to combat injustice without violence.[3]

For those who would dismiss *satyagraha* as "womanly," a fete brief remarks. Much could be said about the prominence of women in the practice of non-violence in India, Japan, Eastern Europe, Latin America, and elsewhere.[4] As a strategy to fight injustice that requires human commitment rather than military might, that aims to transform rather than to subvert human relations, that distributes power away from traditional centers to "ordinary" persons, non-violence is often associated with "feminine" values.[5] Conversely, systems of criminal justice – hierarchical, adversarial, remote, rule-oriented, and dispassionate – are commonly associated with men and "masculine" values. Yet human beings and human values are not so easily divided into gendered camps. Men have figured prominently among non-violent theorists and practitioners, and women have at times been vocal supporters of punitive justice. Moreover, for those aiming to reverse the historical tendency to marginalize "feminine" values like care and empathy in conflict resolution, such compartmentalization is of dubious value.[6]

Violence, Power, and Systems of Criminal Justice

As a practicing lawyer in colonial South Africa and India, Gandhi well appreciated that violence *and* power inhere in systems of criminal justice.[7] Punishment must involve pain, suffering, deprivation, or other unpleasant consequence or it ceases to be punishment. Often veiled in the garb of non-violence, the nature of criminal justice is unmistakable to those on the receiving end – whether a suspect gunned down by arresting authorities, an individual "put away for life," or an abandoned spouse or child.

The ICC lobby has been remarkably candid about law's violence. It is not uncommon to hear casual talk of the number of lives worth sacrificing for a criminal prosecution, calls for a commando force to "hunt down" alleged criminals, and declarations that "the only way to be decisive is to take casualties."[8] To this must be added reasonably foreseeable deaths that result from retaliatory strikes and the murder of prosecution witnesses and their families, so tragically familiar in Rwanda.

For those who would cite among the virtues of ICCs a splendid isolation from power politics, Gandhian thought and ongoing crises in Bosnia offer a reminder that systems of criminal justice are inextricably linked to strategies of power. By definition, the balance of power rests with those who do the punishing. In the words of peace activist Thomas Merton, the example of criminal justice is based on force, and it carries the message that "you

Satyagraha is the term Gandhi coined to describe his philosophy of active non-violence. Comprising the words satya (truth) and agraha (holding firmly), it literally means the firm grasping of or holding on to the truth. The core elements of *satyagraha* are truth, broadly defined to encompass factual and moral or metaphysical truth, and ahimsa, meaning not injuring and, more broadly, doing good even to the evil-doer.

get what you have the power to take."[9]

It has been said that a standing ICC holds the promise of universal justice that permanence will take power politics out. This is myth. For any foreseeable future, the permanent five members of the UN Security Council cannot be forced and will not submit to an effective, independent mechanism to enforce international criminal law. No matter how an ICC is established – by Security Council resolution, by treaty, or by the UN General Assembly – without the enforcement powers of the Security Council and its members, it would be an impotent entity. The gatekeeper and lead role played by the "permanent five" is and will remain secure no matter how an ICC is packaged.

The Burden of Legitimizing Law's Violence

Precisely because an expanded power to punish involves certain suffering and violence, the architects of ICCs are morally obliged to identify the specific aims they expect to achieve, and the mechanisms by which their progress will be assessed. Without a clear conception of appropriate and achievable aims, a firm basis in reality, and a critical understanding of their endeavor, ICC proponents risk costly failure. For Gandhi, who viewed ethics and politics as equally and fundamentally concerned with the pragmatic, the delict is double.[10] The apparent risk of doing more harm than good makes blind guesses and laundry lists of speculative ends unacceptable. The supposed aim of "achieving justice," having no empirical referent, is also a wholly inadequate response.

Deterrence theory

Virtually all theories of criminal justice can be characterized as either retributive or utilitarian. Among utilitarian schemes, the ICC lobby relies particularly on deterrence theory, and does so with a level of confi-

dence matched only by theorists' disaffection.[11] Positive criminology has accumulated masses of evidence testifying to the failure of deterrence. Described by Karl Menninger, it is an "utter failure," "primitive," "antiquated, expensive, and disappointing."[12] For James Miller, our deterrence-based system is "distinguished mostly by its failure to make communities safer and its alienation of large segments of our population."[13]

According to deterrence theorists, persons commit atrocities when the expected value of doing so exceeds the cost of punishment. Their solution? Simply raise the price for committing them by imposing certain and harsh penalties. Harvard psychologist James Gilligan identifies four problems with this model in the real world: "It is totally incorrect, hopelessly naive, dangerously misleading, and based on complete and utter ignorance of what violent people are actually like." The US imprisonment fiasco shows how misguided the behaviorist faith of ICC advocates is in times of ostensible peace. How the findings of myriad scholars on the exaggerated part played by rational calculus in deviant behavior translate in humanitarian crises remains, lamentably, wholly unexamined.[14]

Retributive theory

The liberal vision of reducing crime by attacking its social causes was all but supplanted in the 1980s by retributive schemes reflecting the belief that it is morally fitting that offenders be made to suffer, that something "in the souls of men" requires vengeance, and that society ought to respect and provide an institutional home for that urge. ICC discourse is imbued with like sentiment and the characteristic self-righteous tenor of those striving to secure the "deserved" punishment of others.

Before its renaissance, retribution was widely considered a dead letter, particularly among liberal theorists like H. L. A. Hart.[15]

In the words of Hannah Arendt, "We refuse, and consider as barbaric, the propositions that 'a great crime offends nature, so that the very earth cries out for vengeance; that evil violates a natural harmony which only retribution can restore; that a wronged collectivity owes a duty to the moral order to punish the criminal."[16] At the domestic level, the pendulum is again swinging slowly away from politically expedient appeals to vengeance. That historically progressive human rights advocates now move contrariwise is startling. If our true aim is to restore order and human dignity, *satyagraha* offers an approach vastly superior to the proverbial pound of flesh, as evidenced daily in transitional South Africa.

Reprobative theory

What ICC proponents ultimately seek through pain infliction is an authoritative expression of moral condemnation. They propose that life be risked – elsewhere, of course – so that we might emphatically demonstrate our abhorrence of the *unlawful* destruction of life. H. L. A. Hart, among others, assailed such expressive justice, depicting it as "uncomfortably close to human sacrifice as an expression of religious worship."[17] Reprobation and denunciation are important aspects of social ordering. But remote, atomized, violence-based international penal institutions are a dubious means to this end.

Gandhi, like Primo Levi and others, observed that evil in the world results largely from humanity's tendency to deny and disregard injustice and suffering *in toto*.[18] In the words of Auschwitz survivor Sarah Berkowitz, "silence is the real crime against humanity."[19] To recite Hitler's reputed quip – "Who after all remembers the Armenians?" – to legitimate prosecutions is thus inapt. Far from a failure to initiate criminal proceedings, the world largely ignored the Armenians' plight. Ongoing revelations about World War II indicate how tragically unexceptional such

indifference was. Then and now, the absence of *any* response to human suffering, not simply a punitive one, demands our attention.

Equating criminal prosecutions with justice

No claim of ICC lobbyists is more common or questionable than their equation of punishment and justice. Gandhi, like Plato, recognized that criminal punishment signifies *not* the triumph of justice and morality, but its antithesis.[20] Any so-called peace attained through punitive measures, Gandhi regarded with disdain, dismissing an international police force as "a concession to human weakness, not by any means an emblem of peace."[21] It may be pragmatic to punish wrongdoers, but doing so is an act of violence that no amount of justification can make intrinsically good or indicative of virtue.

Above all, a puritanical equation of justice and punishment is conducive to violence. The wisdom of *satyagraha* rests in its recognition that when ideals pertaining to ends gain ascendancy – when lives are to be sacrificed in the name of an abstract principle like justice – violence is more probable. Attempts to achieve justice or to undo injustice, whether pursued by individuals or groups, constitute *the one and only universal cause of violence*.[22] Once associated with movements for *social* justice, the slogan "no peace without justice" has been transformed overnight by ICC advocates into a recipe for perpetual war. Based on twenty-five years' work with the most violent individuals in US penal institutions, James Gilligan concludes:

> The purpose of both forms of violence, crime and punishment is the same: to restore justice to the world by replacing shame with pride. And the means by which that is accomplished is the same. The very same acts of violence and mutilation (by which one prevents one's victim from shaming oneself further) serve to shame

one's victim . . . [F]or it is shameful to suffer violence (regardless of whether it is called crime or punishment), just as it is a source of pride and honor to be the one who dispenses violence to others.[23]

The concept of justice is inextricably contextual and presupposes a local set of conditions and considerations. Different societies have distinct notions of what is fair and "right," as do their members.[24] It is not uncommon, therefore, for a verdict in a criminal trial to ameliorate one group's sense of injustice while provoking that of another. The varied responses given by Hutu and Tutsi to the question "Was justice served?" hours after a Rwanda court sentenced a Hutu to death provide a classic illustration.[25]

Should there be any doubt whether former warring parties are likely to consider ICCs productive of justice, a simple thought experiment should suffice. Imagine that defendants before ICCs are entitled to have their guilt determined by a jury of peers representative of their community, whether Chilean, Bosnian, Chechen, Canadian, or Nicaraguan. At present, and contrary to US jurisprudence, they have no such right. Were it otherwise, we might at least get a clear, if discomforting, glimpse at the underlying reality not unlike that bared in the O. J. Simpson proceedings, where "blacks 'got' the criminal verdict and the whites 'got' the civil one."[26] Due partly to the ubiquity of situationally rooted expectations and norms prevalent in armed conflict, "ordinary" members of an offender's community are best suited to understand and to judge deviant conduct alleged to have been committed in this context.

In a deeply divided society – arguably the only type of society likely to produce the types of crimes for which ICCs are intended – criminal prosecutions do not have a conciliatory effect; rather, they manifest and exacerbate division. This follows in part because those who occupy the dock are inevitably and widely seen as symbolic representatives of their group. As Court TV anchor Raymond Brown remarked of the trial of Dusko Tadic, such proceedings are *nothing but metaphor.* The association is even greater when "big fish" like Maurice Papon, P. W. Botha, General Pinochet, or Winnie Mandela are to be judged. Given their significance as metaphor, one can hardly expect ICCs to ameliorate collective guilt. On the contrary, they actually revive and inflame antagonistic sentiment, as Chancellor Adenauer foresaw of the Eichmann trial.

Disinterring Community, Decentering the Monstrous Few

Despite a veritable cottage industry of ICC literature and conferences, there is scant evidence of serious thought being given to *specifically who* is the intended beneficiary and target audience of international prosecutions. The omission bolsters suspicions voiced by a Rwandan delegate to the UN that they exist to appease the conscience of the international community, not to provide enduring value to a ravaged community.[27] For reasons given below, the subject and object of humanitarian efforts in the wake of human rights disasters must be the community directly affected by and implicated in the events. It is what Alex Boraine presumptively meant by "common," when he spoke of the "common good" of South Africa.

If champions of ICCs rather intend the amorphous "international community," they have yet to examine, even to identify, myriad derivative questions. If, for instance, a government's prerogative to punish rests, as some claim, on the reciprocal benefits and burdens constituting the social contract, on what does the international community base its prerogative? Individual Kurds, Bosnian-Serbs, Greek- Cypriots, and Palestinians would likely be hard-pressed to name the benefits they receive from the international community for which they are obliged. The mere occurrence of serious human rights violations is itself indicative of the inadequacy of international recourse and remedies.

ICC proponents also overlook the central question of what *units,* individuals or groups, should be the target of efforts to restore order to a badly fractured society. Backing a remedy designed to socialize *individuals,* they envisage a society disintegrated into an amoral, Hobbesian war of all against all, rather than *rival moral communities.* Deftly noted by Dennis Wrong, for group-level conflict to occur, the individual group members must already have been socialized to correctly gauge the expectations of others, to internalize at least some norms, and to possess selves sensitive to the appraisal of others.[28]

Like justice, crime is embedded in community and it is the ultimate concern of community. Gandhi well appreciated this and other commonplaces of modern criminology, like the need to focus on the character of society that engenders depraved acts, rather than fixating on a supposed base few. Repudiating the fashion of ascribing crime to isolated individuals, Gandhi declared:

> It hardly becomes us to take refuge in that moral alibi. Who are the hooligans after all? They are our own countrymen and, so long as any countryman of ours indulges in such acts, we cannot disown responsibility for them.[29]

Familiar to students of Nazi Germany, a Hitler – like a Stalin, a Karadzic, a Tudjman, a Mao – is only as strong as the power of mass obedience and support.

However, it is a mistake to confuse the notion of corporate responsibility with collective guilt or excusable impulses. As Gandhi reiterated time and again, life circumstances do not remove individual responsibility. Indeed, to hold otherwise is tantamount to denying the very foundation of human dignity.

The Heart of Normative Order: Punitive Sanction or Social Embeddedness?

The ICC lobby presupposes that formal institutions are integral to uphold group life and to stem deviant behavior. Reminiscent of presociological thought, this view overlooks the informal network of social ties that spontaneously create expectations and norms that predate and exist independently of legal institutions.[30] *Satyagraha* presupposes otherwise. The cooperation and consent of the governed is a *sine qua non* of long-term crime control and good government; soldiers or police may be able to "retake" a community, but they cannot hold it without the assent of its members. For lasting peace, Nelson Mandela proclaimed, "we do not rely on laws, we rely purely on persuasion."[31] For Gandhi, where society instead depends on law, law ceases to be law and society ceases to be society.[32]

To understand why people commit heinous acts, it helps to appreciate what motivates combatants to face the threat of death and mutilation in battle and to perform familiar heroic acts in gratuitous defiance of fate. Time and again, military historians and professionals dwell *not* on the coercive power of the army or state, but on what Dennis Wrong calls the "merely mental stuff that binds like chains of steel."[33] Like heroic deeds, deviant behavior stems from expectations of what is acceptable, even laudable behavior, which are borne out because others are aware of and live up to them. As modem Israeli soldiers attest, what most concerns combatants is "what others would think of them, or what their families or friends would feel about them when they came home."[34]

In conflict or cooperation, the major spring of human action is the desire to win the good opinion of family, friends, and close associates.[35] Indeed, the priority human beings place on honor and self-respect (our own and that of our group) over survival may be our most unique and our most dangerous attribute.[36] If we understand that fear of shame or ridicule is *the most common reason* human beings engage in violent behavior, the advantages of *satyagraha* over penal threats as a means to elicit right conduct become manifest.

Supporting and Yielding to Local Initiatives

Because the determinative response to deviancy occurs locally, communities that treat crime as something best left to institutions and professionals at far remove risk costly error. The requests of Cambodian and Burundi officials for an international tribunal to try certain of their nationals exemplify a dangerous abdication of responsibility that international mechanisms ought not to condone, let alone encourage. In the spirit of *satyagraha,* such requests ought to be rejected in favor of constructive, local action. Where, for instance, a state's judiciary is in such disarray that fair and impartial trials are not possible, rather than spending scarce resources on a stop-gap measure of dubious efficacy, the overriding aim should be to assist and encourage local efforts to remedy that situation as expeditiously as possible.

All but ignored in Cambodia, Bosnia, and Rwanda, the development of an effective and impartial local judiciary is vital to stabilize society. In Cambodia, an inept and corrupt judiciary remains after an unprecedented amount of humanitarian funds were spent on other projects. In Rwanda, limited capital (tangible and otherwise) expended on a comparatively opulent and ineffectual ICC should have been invested in local judiciary devastated by genocide and overwhelmed with approximately 120,000 individuals awaiting trial in squalid prison conditions.[37]

Where local leaders are *unwilling* to pursue a national remedy, and the international community is unwilling to spend the needed blood and treasure to assume de facto control à la Nuremberg, the best that can be done is to systematically collect and catalogue evidence. Whether "justice" comes quickly or not at all in such cases, events in Indonesia, Argentina, Ethiopia, South Korea, France, Cambodia, and so on indicate that changes in government, venue, and popular opinion disqualify the pat answer.

Punishing for Peace: The Unity of Means and Ends

A signal challenge to the ICC enterprise is the core precept of *satyagraha* that ends pre-exist in the means. In Gandhi's words:

> It's a great mistake to believe that there is no connection between the means and the end . . . The means may be likened to a seed, the end to a tree; there is just the same inviolable connection between the means and the end as there is between the seed and the tree.[38]

Gandhi's insistence on the inviolability of means derived in part from man's ability to exercise control over means, but never to command results. Transitional societies in particular, an ethically responsible policy is one that reflects a world where unintended consequences are the rule. An ends-oriented strategy like criminal justice, however well-intended, falls short of the mark.

The indivisibility of means and ends follows also from the axiom that violence, even where seemingly justified, only leads to more violence.[39] Hunting down "international criminals" does not deter violence. Rather, as an example of violence, it teaches what it would deter. The destructive strategies and war mentality integral to the pursuit of criminal justice only fuel revolt, engender martyrs, and harden resistance in the defeated "enemy" as confirmed by events in Somalia, Rwanda, and Bosnia. By choosing not to retaliate, *satyagrahis* undermine the target and throw him off balance in what is described as "moral *jiajitsu*."[40]

Above all, means are expressive and fused with values like human dignity and respect that signal the type of society we envision and presage the outcome we seek.[41] Here, the ICC enterprise is inapposite. Profoundly undemocratic, it is antithetical to responsible, local self-determination and accountability; it communicates that threats are considered constructive of social order, that the dominant party is willing to use force to achieve that end, and the imbalance of power that enables it to do so.[42] Like the Hegelian man who lifts a stick to his dog, to "civilize" others by force is to treat human beings as innately antisocial, amoral calculators, and to deny the spiritual unity of humankind envisioned by Gandhi.

A great strength of *satyagraha* is its inherent appeal to the Other as a moral agent endowed with reflective consciousness and concern for justice and other people's needs. No matter how depraved a person might appear to be, *satyagraha* reflects the dignity and potential for good in him or her. In the words of Gandhi, "Who can dare say that it is not in their nature to respond to the higher and finer forces? They have the same soul that I have."[43] The unparalleled success of Nelson Mandela, who "pinned the label 'man of integrity' to de Klerk's breast," demonstrates the efficacy of treating an adversary as a morally responsible agent capable of responding to reasoned normative appeals.[44]

Lasting stability is possible only when both sides to a conflict recognize they cannot *force* the other to submit, whether on the battlefield or the courtroom. For this, hope rests with those situated in the middle. Unlike a threat-based strategy, which dissipates the will of otherwise indispensable, well-intended persons, *satyagraha* is practiced *with* the opponent and avoids methods likely to humiliate, harass, or engender opposition. So that "ordinary" persons are given every chance for a decent response, *satyagrahis* ensure that the case is set out as clearly as possible, and that there is ample opportunity for the opponent to reflect and to respond. Here again, a punitive approach is inapt.

Practical Discourse and the Search for Truth

For Gandhi, truth was but another name for God, envisaged by everyone "in fragment and from different angles."[45] "Truth is my religion," he declared, "and *ahimsa* [non-violence] is the only way of its realization."[46] Gandhi's insistence on nonviolence and man's incompetence to punish derived from his belief that no human being is capable of knowing absolute truth. Conflict, he observed, is the result of misperceptions and competing relative truths, and its resolution requires a willingness to hear and to consider the opponent's position and to communicate one's own.[47] In particular, those on the margins of society – "criminal" and otherwise – must have an opportunity to be heard.

A core strength of *satyagraha* rests in the harmonizing, socializing, educative power of dialogue, increasingly recognized by contemporary social theorists. Like the Navajo strategy of "talking things out," *satyagraha* treats crime and conflict as a starting point for dialogue, wherein all are given an opportunity to express the truth as they see it and to offer solutions.[48] Like Willem de Haan's conception of practical discourse, it is an open, elaborative process that begins with the admission that there are no simple or categorical answers.[49] In contrast, administering "justice" by judicial fiat from above is anathema to the republican sense of a shared, participatory life.

A particularly misguided claim of ICC proponents is that criminal prosecutions are productive of "the truth." Nothing so belies this as the paucity of information about the Rwandan genocide generated by *hundreds* of criminal prosecutions, relative to the wealth of information about apartheid South Africa uncovered through non-prosecutorial means. Manifest in the trial of O. J. Simpson, criminal trials are anything but a search for the truth. On the contrary, their reductionist, bipolar logic and inherent barriers to the truth conceal, distort, and even reinvent history.[50] Remarked by Hannah Arendt following the Eichmann trial:

> [J]ustice for the accused necessitates that all the other questions of seemingly greater import – of "How could it happen?" and "Why did it happen?," of "Why the Jews?" and "Why the Germans?," of "What was the role of other nations?" . . . be left in abeyance.[51]

In post-World War II Germany, Japan, and France, judicial processes effectively absolved the general populace and overlooked the mass collaboration and institutional support by *unavoidably* ascribing responsibility to a select few individuals. Instead of stimulating serious moral deliberation and self-scrutiny, Mark Osiel concludes on the basis of exhaustive research that the trials hindered an open debate on the far more complex reality. [52]

Causal Understanding, Exculpations, and Forgiveness

Once a hallmark of conservative thinking, the degree of disinterest ICC proponents show in causal theory is striking. Of equal concern are their related efforts to steer thinking about complex conflicts into criminal stereotypes, exemplified by one journalist's recent appeal to portray "news" from Africa in criminal terms.[53] Declining his invitation, BBC correspondent Lindsey Hilsum observed:

> We refuse to allow conflicts in Africa to have any politics. We always report them as "crimes." They are not crimes. It's politics. We have to understand that, and if we don't we're nowhere.

Not unlike religious dogma Gandhi scorned, the popular appeal of criminal stereotypes emanates from the security of binaries – good and evil, guilt and innocence, right and wrong, Us and Them – that shield us from the uncomfortable and complicated realities that yield atrocities. Criminal prosecutions serve as substitute for understanding – a way to label, think, and talk about the adversary, rather than having to listen to her. The wisdom of *satyagraha* rests in a commitment to understand why people commit heinous acts. If our aim is prevention, nothing is more important.[54]

The popular notion *tout comprendre, c'est tout pardonner* – to understand everything is to forgive everything – is a moral fallacy and the bogeyman of every serious effort to understand violence. Primo Levi, occasionally cited as its key proponent, repeatedly acknowledged the importance of understanding, for "what could be perpetrated yesterday could be attempted again tomorrow."[55] The aim of causal understanding is not to obliterate, pardon, or justify the past, but to achieve primary prevention. As a witness to genocide in Rwanda avowed, "you have to try to understand, because if you don't try to understand, you get nowhere."[56]

Those who counsel against vengeance and retaliation are also often labeled "forgivers." Yet evident in the work of Gandhi, retaliation and forgiveness are not inversely related, nor do they exhaust the world of possible responses to injustice. Clearly one may forswear retaliation, but withhold forgiveness. Forgiveness, on the other hand, presupposes that any plans to punish or otherwise retaliate have been forsworn – for, once one has retaliated, what remains to forgive? It is nonsensical to assert that "unless justice is done it's difficult to think about forgiving,"[57] if by "justice" one means punishment.

For policymakers concerned with prevention and restoring order, the question of forgiveness may simply be beside the point except to the extent that they may not wish to foreclose individual acts of forgiveness. Above all, forgiveness is a matter of individual conscience that no institution or authority can demand or effect in another's name. It is thus not surprising to hear expressions of dissent when Desmond Tutu, for instance, offers forgiveness on behalf of all South Africans.[58]

Working to Identify and Satisfy the Particular Needs of Victims and Survivors

Any serious effort to deal with a legacy of human rights violations must include a commitment to confront and constructively respond to victims' suffering and sense of injustice. The extent of modern society's failure in this regard has been widely remarked by Gandhi and innumerable others. Given the profound and varied experiences of victims, as well as the disparate coping mechanisms within and across cultures, any singular "right" approach is untenable.[59] Satyagraha appropriately demands constructive remedial action, but abjures a one-size-fits-all managerial solution.

To the extent it is humanly possible to mitigate the suffering of survivors of atrocities, this can be accomplished as effectively, if not more, without inflicting or threatening to inflict suffering on other human beings. To the extent persons derive solace from seeing an enemy-oppressor "get what they deserve" – defeated or humiliated in the courtroom, if not on the battlefield – it is an end at which criminal law should not aim. The notion that penal institutions provide an essential outlet for innately violent and vengeful human beings has been thoroughly debunked by modern social science as dangerously unhelpful, pseudo-biology.[60]

The punishment as collective therapy model – the idea that peaceful coexistence requires a clean slate that only punishment can deliver – has been similarly discredited as bad socio-psychology and based on an exaggerated and misguided fear of vigilan-

tism.[61] Despite outrageous acts and levels of crime throughout history, vigilantism and vengeance remain extremely rare. In post-Civil War America, post-Stalinist Russia, post-Maoist China, post-Vichy France, colonial Congo, as well as present-day Cambodia, El Salvador, Argentina, Nicaragua, and Chile, victims and victimizers have coexisted in relative peace.[62]

There is perhaps no greater canard than the idea that punitive justice provides needed therapy for individuals – that nothing can assuage anger or restore dignity like punishment. Accounts of scholars who have worked extensively with survivors reveal that the urge for vengeance is far from universal.[63] Empirical studies indicate further that the emphasis on victimhood, blame, and powerlessness may actually undermine recovery from violent crime.[64] In Gandhi's experience, confirmed in the work of Bruno Bettelheim and Viktor Frankl with Holocaust survivors, individuals who neither submit passively nor retaliate to violence find in themselves a new sense of strength, dignity, and courage.[65]

What victims typically seek is the restoration of order, meaningful restitution and rehabilitative services, a thorough inquiry into the events that is recorded and publicly acknowledged, and an opportunity to participate in decision making and to recount their experiences. Echoed in the words of emancipated slaves – "Give us some land and you can keep your apology" – restitution and rehabilitation are especially vital, yet wholly ignored by the criminal justice model. Above all, meeting the day-to-day emotional challenges that result from the sheer terror of being victimized may be the greatest need, and the most daunting task. Faced with such pressing needs, the expenditure of untold sums *merely debating* the mechanics of prosecuting a handful of culpable elites perilously approaches malfeasance.

Avoiding Blueprints, Accommodating Indigenous Values and Needs

For the sake of appearing resolute, we risk putting an iron grip on diverse problems that demand local solutions. International criminal prosecutions exclude myriad values like mercy, shaming, recompense, forgiveness, compassion, and repentance that may be regarded locally as valuable, even imperative, to alleviate suffering and to restore order. By assuming that a serious disturbance of social order is first and foremost a criminal matter that demands a legal solution, we overlook and underrate indigenous values and practices like *satyagraha* or *ubuntu*, as practiced in South Africa.[66]

The cautionary words of Justice Richard Goldstone, former prosecutor of the International Yugoslav Tribunal, spoken at a time when the fate of his native South Africa was at stake, are instructive:

> A solution successful in one country may fail in another. The correct approach to the past will depend upon myriad political, economic, and cultural forces . . . The manner in which violations are handled, whether perpetrators are punished, lose office or are granted indemnities are issues will depend on political considerations which will differ from country to country.[67]

After the fashion of economic developmental assistance, will decades of costly error pass before the international community reawakens to the value of decentralization, discretion, and local initiative? Rather than indulge the notion that we have a corner on the universal meaning of justice, we should seek out and support local initiatives to restore human dignity and a semblance of order in the wake of human rights disasters. In striking contrast with events in Latin America and Southern Africa, those in the Balkans and the Great Lakes region of Africa suggest that a fixation on formal justice may be irrelevant *at best* to the ends of peace and stability.

Notes

1   Mahatma Gandhi, *The Moral and Political Writings of Mahatma Gandhi*, Volume 2: *Truth and Non-Violence*, Raghavan Iyer, ed. (Oxford: Clarendon Press, 1986), 229.

2   *Harijan*, May 30 1936. Quakers and Anabaptists provide notable exceptions. Mike Yarrow, *Quaker Experiences in International Conciliation* (New Haven: Yale University Press, 1978); *War and Its Discontents: Pacifism and Quietism in the Abrahamic Traditions*, J. Patout Bums, ed. (Washington, DC: Georgetown University Press, 1996).

3   The role of spiritual and religious factors in conflict resolution is discussed in *The Missing Dimension of Statecraft*, Edward Luttwak, ed. (Washington, DC: Center for Strategic and International Studies 1994); and *Justice Without Violence*, Paul Wehr, Heidi Burgess, and Guy Burgess, eds. (Boulder, CO: Lynne Rienner, 1994).

4   For example see *Bringing Peace Home: Feminism, Violence, and Nature*, Karen Warren and Duane Cady, eds. (Bloomington, IN: Indiana University Press 1996); and *Reweaving the Web of Life: Feminism and Nonviolence*, Pam McAllister, ed. (Philadelphia: New Society, 1982).

5   This distinction was most notoriously drawn in Carol Gilligan's *In a Different Voice* (Cambridge, MA: Harvard University Press, 1982).

6   Of note, studies on non-violence are ongoing at the US Institute for Peace, the Albert Einstein Institution, the Center for Strategic and International Studies, and the Program on Nonviolent Sanctions at Harvard University.

7   "The *Satyagraha* Way with Crime," in *Satyagraha (Nonviolent Resistance)*, Bharat Kumar, ed. (New York: Schocken, 1951).

8   See, for example, "Finding an Unlikely Ally in Bosnia," *Washington Post National Weekly*, September 8, 1997 14; "New Line in Bosnia? Raid to Seize Serbs Bolsters NATO Image," *Herald Tribune*, July 14, 1997.

9   Thomas Merton, *Faith and Violence* (South Bend, IN: Notre Dame University Press, 1968), 246.

10 George Orwell, "Reflections on Gandhi," in *The Collected Essays: Journalism and Letters of George Orwell*, Sonia Orwell and Ian Angus, eds. (New York: Harcourt, Brace and World, 1968), 84.

11 For scholarly critiques of deterrence theory, see John Brathwaite and Philip Pettit, *Not Just Deserts: A Republican Theory of Criminal Justice* (Oxford: Clarendon Press 1990); Adrian Howe, *Punish and Critique: Towards a Feminist Analysis of Penality* (London: Routledge, 1994); Barbara Hudson, *Justice Through Punishment: A Critique of the Justice Model of Corrections* (New York: St. Martin's Press, 1987); and Andrew Rutherford, *Criminal Justice and the Pursuit of Decency* (New York: Oxford University Press, 1993).

12 Karl Menninger "Therapy, Not Punishment," in *Philosophy of Punishment*, ed. Robert Baird (New York: Prometheus, 1988), 489.

13 James Miller, *Search and Destroy: African-American Males in the Criminal Justice System* (Cambridge: Cambridge University Press, 1996), 136.

14 James Gilligan, *Violence: Our Deadly Epidemic and Its Causes* (New York: Grosset-Putnam 1996), 94–5.

15 Brathwaite and Pettit, *Not Just Deserts*, 3, 6–7; Willem de Haan, *The Politics of Redress: Crime, Punishment and Penal Abdition* (London: Unwin Hyman, 1990), 115; Igor Primoratz, *Justifying Legal Punishment* (London: Humanities Press International, 1989), 70.

16 Hannah Arendt, *Eichmann in Jerusalem: A Report on the Banality of Evil* (New York: Penguin Books, 1992), 277.

17 Cited in Dan Kahan, "What Do Alternative Sanctions Mean?" *University of Chicago Law Review* 63 (Spring 1996), 591, 596.

18 Gandhi, *The Moral and Political Writings*, 624; Primo Levi, *Afterword*, trans. Ruth Feldman (New York: Collier-Macmillan, 1965), 214.

19 Sarah Berkowitz, *Where Are My Brothers?* (New York: Helios, 1965), 43.

20 V. S. Hegde, "The Practice of Law and Gandhi," in *New Dimensions and Perspectives in Gandhism*, V. T. Patil, ed. (New Delhi: Inter-India Publications, 1989), 411–25; Dennis Dalton, *Mahatma Gandhi: Nonviolent Power in Action* (New York: Columbia University Press, 1993), 127.

21 Gandhi, *The Moral and Political Writings*, 498.

22 Gilligan, *Violence: Our Deadly Epidemic*, 11–12.

23 *Ibid.*, 185.

24 For example, whether a disaster qualifies as misfortune or injustice may be determined largely by local sensibilities and the proclivity to respond with indifference, blame, punishment or relief. Judith Shklar, *The Faces of Injustice* (New Haven: Yale University Press, 1990), 38, 110.

25 Alan Zarembo, "Judgment Day," *Harper's*, April 1997.

26 See Laura Mansnerus, "Truth in the Simpson Trials: The Devil is in the Details," *New York Times*, January 12, 1997, 4; David Shipler, "Living Under Suspicion: Why Blacks Believe Simpson and Not the Police," *New York Times*, February 7, 1997.

27 Xinhua News Agency, November 26, 1996. See also "Justice for Genocide: Rwandan-Style," *The Economist*, January 11, 1997; "Rwanda: Punishing the Guilty, Maybe," *The Economist*, October 12, 1997.

28 Dennis Wrong, *The Problem of Order: What Unites and Divides Society* (New York: Free Press 1994), 161, 176, 182.

29 Gandhi, *The Moral and Political Writings*, 252.

30 Wrong, *The Problem of Order*, 49, 170, 222.

31 Patti Waldmeir, *Anatomy of a Miracle: The End of Apartheid and the Birth of a New South Africa* (New York: W.W. Norton, 1997), 261.

32 V. C. Hegde "The Practice of Law and Gandhi," 424.

33 Wrong, *The Problem of Order*, 45. See, for example, James McPherson, *For Causes and Comrades: Why Men Fought in the Civil War* (New York: Oxford University Press 1997); *The Laws of War: Constraints on Warfare in the Western World*, Sir Michael Howard, ed. (New Haven: Yale University Press, 1995); Samuel Hynes, *The Soldier's Tale: Bearing Witness to*

Modern War (New York: Penguin Books, *1997*); Richard Holmes, *Acts of War: The Behavior of Men in Battle* (New York: Free Press, 1985).

34 Holmes, *Acts of War*, 283.

35 John Brathwaite, *Crime, Shame and Reintegration* (New York: Cambridge University Press, 1989), 21.

36 Gilligan, *Violence: Our Deadly Epidemic*, 77, 197.

37 Madeline Morris, "Trials of Concurrent Jurisdiction: The Case of Rwanda," *Duke Journal of Comparative & International Law 7* (Spring 1997), 349; "Justice to Prevail?" *Washington Post,* February 2, 1997.

38 Dalton, *Mahatma Gandhi*, 9.

39 Johan Galtung, *Peace by Peaceful Means: Peace and Conflict, Development and Civilization* (Oslo: International Peace Research Institute, 1996), 7.

40 Orwell, "Reflections on Gandhi," 79. *Satyagrahis* are practioners of *Satyagraha*.

41 H. J. N. Horsburgh, *Non-Violence and Aggression: A Study of Gandhi's Moral Equivalent of War* (London: Oxford University Press, 1968), 44.

42 Wesley Cragg, *The Practice of Punishment: Towards a Theory of Restorative Justice* (London: Routledge, 1992), 196.

43 Gandhi, *The Moral and Political Writings*, 488.

44 Waldmeir *Anatomy of a Miracle*, 158.

45 Gandhi, *The Moral and Political Writings*, 252.

46 *Harijan*, April 30, 1938.

47 Madan Gandhi, "Metaphysical Basis of Gandhian Thought," *Dimensions*, 197, 206.

48 Robert Yazzie, "'Life Comes from It': Navajo Justice Conceptions of Criminal Justice," *New Mexico Law Review 24* (Spring 1994), 175.

49 de Haan, *The Politics of Redress*, 1590, 168.

50 Mark Osiel offers a comprehensive assessment of the efficacy of criminal trials to illumine events in the aftermath of human rights disasters in "Ever Again: Legal Remembrance of Administrative Massacre," *University of Pennsylvania Law Review* 144 (December 1995), 463.

51 Arendt, *Eichmann in Jerusalem*, 5.

52 Osiel, "Ever Again."

53 Roy Guttman, Reporting from the Killing Fields, conference at the University of California, Berkeley, May 1997.

54 Gilligan, *Violence: Our Deadly Epidemic*, 183, 258, 267.

55 Primo Levi, *The Drowned and the Saved* (New York: Summit Books, 1988), 53.

56 Lindsey Hilsum, Reporting from the Killing Fields, conference at the University of California, Berkeley, May 1997.

57 Tina Rosenberg, "Recovering from Apartheid," *New Yorker*, November 18, 1996.

58 Timothy Garton Ash, "True Confessions," *New York Review of Books*, July 17, 1997, 33–8.

59 Lynn Henderson, "The Wrongs of Victim's Rights," *Stanford Law Review* 37 (April 1985), 937, 997.

60 Gilligan, *Violence: Our Deadly Epidemic*, 210–11.

61 George L. Kelling and Catherine M. Coles, *Fixing Broken Windows: Restoring Order and Reducing Crime in Our Communities* (New York: Simon and Schuster, 1997), 108–56.

62 See, for example, "Cambodian Aesop Tells a Fable of Forgiveness," *New York Times,* June 28, 1997; David Rieff, "The Big Risk," *New York Review of Books,* October 31, 1996; Alan Zarembo, "Judgment Day," *Harper's,* April 1997.

63 See Thomas Buergenthal, "The United Nations Truth Commission for El Salvador," in *Transitional Justice: How Emerging Democracies Reckon with Former Regimes,* Neil Kritz, ed. (Washington DC: United Institute for Peace 1995), 292; Jose Zalaquett, "Confronting Human Rights Violations Committed by Former Governments: Applicable Principles and Political Restraints," in Kritz, ed., *Transitional Justice*, 3.

64 Henderson, "Wrongs of Victim's Rights," 955, 965.

65 Gandhi, *The Moral and Political Writings,* 293' Nina Sutton *Bettelheim: A Life and a Legacy,* David Sharp trans. (New York: Basic Books, 1996), 61, 65, and 104 Viktor Frankel, *Man's Search for Meaning,* Ilse Lasch, trans. (New York: Simon and Schuster, 1984).

66 *Ubuntu is* a term shared by a number of African languages, meaning humanity in Xhosa and human nature in Zulu, for

example. As described by one South African legal scholar

Ubuntu is a culture which places some emphasis on communality and on the interdependence of the members of a community. It recognizes a person's status as a human being, entitled to unconditional respect, dignity, value and acceptance from the members of the community such person happens to be part of. It also entails the converse, however. The person has a corresponding duty to give the same respect, dignity, value and acceptance to each member of that community. More importantly, it regulates the exercise of rights by the emphasis it lays on sharing and co-responsibility and the mutual enjoyment of rights by all.

Cited in Peter N. Bouckaert, "The Negotiated Revolution: South Africa's Transition to a Multiracial Democracy," *Stanford Journal of International Law* 33 (Summer 1997), 375.

67 Richard Goldstone, "Exposing Human Rights Abuses – A Help or Hindrance to Reconciliation," *Hastings Constitutional Law Quarterly* 23 (1995), 607, 615.

Returning to my Roots: African "Religions" and the State

12

Makau Matua

- ◆ Africa and Human Rights ◆ Civilization clash ◆ Identity reconstruction ◆
- ◆ Postcolonialism ◆ Counterpenetration ◆ Benin ◆

Four decades after physical decolonization, the African state is today mired in crises of identity (Zartman, 1995a; Mutua, 1995b; Nyong'o, 1992; Jackson and Rosberg, 1982; Schatzberg, 1988; Cohen et al., 1993; Irele, 1992: 296–302).[1] Multidimensional and complexly dynamic, these crises primarily feed from the traditional troughs of culture and religion, ethnicity and race, history and mythology, and politics and economics[2] (see also Mutua, 1995b: 505; Richardson, 1996: 1, 11; Zolberg, 1992: 303–11). In the quicksand known as the modern African state, this potent and volatile alchemical mix has all too frequently either been cataclysmic or fostered political dysfunction (Zartman, 1995b: 1–11; Human Rights Watch, 1995: 39–48; French, 1997: 9).[3] The realm of religion, together with its essential linkage to philosophy and culture, has been one of the pivotal variables in the construction of the identity of the modern African state (Munro, 1975: 147–8; Mbiti, 1970: 300–17).[4] Religion has been one of the critical seams of social and political rupture in several African states (Pobee, 1996: 402–6).[5]

Due to the centrality of religion in the construction of social reality, this critical examination of the treatment of African religions within the African state will necessarily probe the intersection of Islam, African religion, and Christianity – the three dominant religious traditions in Africa – and the role of the state in the establishment or disestablishment of one or other tradition (Mazrui, 1986).[6] Thus, the favor or prejudice of the state toward these traditions lies at the heart of this inquiry. Within the crucible of the African state, this chapter primarily argues that the modern African state, right from its inception, has relentlessly engaged in a campaign of the marginalization, at best, or eradication, at worst, of African religion (Barrow, 1900; see generally Mbiti, 1970).[7] Further, it argues that the destruction and delegitimation of African religion have been actively effected at the urging, or with the collusion and for the benefit of, either or both Islam and Christianity, the two dominant messianic traditions.

It is the contention of the chapter that

Author's Note: I qualify African religions in the subtitle of the chapter because I do not think that the term captures – if it ever could – the phenomenon under discussion. *Religion*, as a word, was unknown to many African languages; hence the difficulty of unpacking the African cosmology, segregating the "religious" aspects of it, and translating that universe in a Western idiom.

the conscious, willful, and planned displacement of African religion goes beyond any legitimate bounds of religious advocacy and violates the religious human rights of Africans. This orchestrated process of the vilification and demonization of African religion represents more than an attack on the religious freedom of Africans; it is in fact a repudiation, on the one hand, of the humanity of African culture and, on the other, a denial of the essence of the humanity of the African people themselves (Mbiti, 1970: 8–13).[8] In other words, at the core of the attempts to subjugate Africans to the messianic traditions is a belief not only in the superiority of the missionary and his or her messianic dogma but also in the sub-humanity of the missionary's subjects and their cosmology. Finally, the chapter explores, through the case of The Republic of Benin, the *raison d'être*, pressures, and tensions that attend the state-directed attempt at protecting and returning to the African past.

This inquiry does not rigidly draw an "us" and "them" dichotomy because cross-cultural penetration and counterpenetration will occur regardless of the insular impulses of cultural guardians. In fact, contact with "otherness" can be a spur for positive social change and progressive development. Societies that prevent the entry of "foreign" values or the export of their values into other cultures deny themselves the benefits of cross-fertilization. Closing off avenues for intercultural exchanges may preserve negative aspects of tradition to the detriment of the group. "Insiders" or those who map the margins of culture need to continually interrogate themselves about the effects of intercourse with "outsiders" and whether, how, or at what pace the exchange should occur. But the strategies employed in creating or managing that contact, as well as its form and content, require constant vigilance to avoid, as much as possible, dehumanizing, degrading, or destroying the "other." Culture should not be essentialized because people, time, and place conspire to construct it. But it represents the accumulation of a people's wisdom and thus their identity; it is real and without it a people is without a name, rudderless, and torn from its moorings.

It is not the argument of this chapter, therefore, that there is a purity to African religion. The genesis of ideas and cultures is always difficult to establish. What a culture has borrowed and the extent to which dynamics internal to it are the engines of change must largely remain fluid questions. At least one respected scholar has argued that even Islam and Christianity can be seen as indigenous African religions (King, 1971: 1–35).[9] This point is only interesting because even Mbiti distinguishes Islam and Christianity from African religion.[10] Each religious tradition has its own signature, a religious DNA or "genetic" fingerprint, so to speak. Semitic religions, such as Islam, Judaism, and Christianity, share certain core characteristics such as belief in the afterlife and conceptions of heaven and hell (Many and Greenspahn, 1988: ix).[11] Thus, one can identify, as Mbiti does, the distinguishing characteristics of African religions, although some scholars have questioned the normative framework he has employed to construct African religions (see generally, Mbiti, 1970: 19–20; Mutua, 1996: 417, 431; Shaw, 1990: 339; Hackett, 1990: 303, 305; Hackett, 1996: 9–10).[12] The important point here is the recognition of the existence of an African religious universe, a spiritual space, separate and distinct from either Islam or Christianity, and the role of the state in contracting or eradicating that sphere and promoting the messianic faiths in its stead. This chapter is therefore an attempt to unmask the perverted role of the state and to argue for its reorientation in addressing African religions. This chapter does not pretend to be what it is not. Its scope is very narrow in that it only seeks to underline the denigration of African religions in the context of modernity. In addition to pleading for the better understanding of African religions, it asks that political space be created to allow the expression of that cosmology.

Civilizational Clash: Identity Reconstruction

No African country has officially allocated a national holiday in honor of the gods of indigenous religions. All African countries, on the other hand, have a national holiday that either favors Christian festivals (especially Christmas), Muslim festivals (such as Idd el Fitr [sic]), or both categories of imported festivals. The Semitic religions (Christianity and Islam) are nationally honored in much of Africa; the indigenous religions are at best ethnic rather than national occasions. (Mazrui, 1991: 69–70)

The official suppression of African religions from public visibility throughout Africa, with the recent exception of The Republic of Benin, speaks volumes about identity reconstruction in Africa (*Chicago Tribune*, 1996: 8).[13] Indeed, the status of indigenous religions within African states cannot be understood without resort to the nature and purposes of the colonial state. More specifically, the relationship between religion and the state has hinged on the ideological, cultural, and philosophical outlooks of the African intellectual, political, and civil service classes germinated during colonial rule.

There is no doubt that colonization was primarily motivated by economic reasons (Young, 1991: 19).[14] As a process, colonization deployed racist dogma, religious penetration, military force, and commerce to subject Africa to Europe (Davidson, 1991a; Davidson, 1991b). The role of mission Christianity, with its near exclusive delivery of services in formal Western education and health, was central in coercing conversion from African religions (Munro, 1975: 148).[15] Missionaries saw themselves as agents for Westernization, and made little distinction between the church and the colonial state. According to one European author whose mission was in

Africa, the entire colonial project had to involve all those responsible for the "development of a primitive people" (Shropshire, 1938: xiii). He used the term *primitive* to define "all peoples who, in the main, are in the barbaric and pre-literary stage of sociological and cultural development" (Shropshire, 1938: xiii). He likened the Bantu child (the name given to most African peoples inhabiting eastern, central, and southern Africa) to a marsupial cub, the species of "lowly" mammals like the kangaroo (67).[16]

These racist misconceptions and attitudes toward Africans and their religions found fertile ground in the interpretations, dogma, and philosophy of Christianity and other Semitic religions. The view, held by many adherents of these traditions, that monotheism is the critical difference "between advanced (Western) religion and primitive paganism" has long been a basis for the treatment of other beliefs as satanic or devilish (Marty and Greenspahn, 1988: ix). Monotheistic religions thus sit at the top of the hierarchy while *polytheism* and *animism*, the terms used to describe African religions, dwell at the bottom of the evolutionary process (Mbiti, 1970: 9–12). This theory of religious evolution, which asserts the upward, single-directional track of development from so-called animism to monotheism allows the missionary to believe in the superiority of his or her faith (8–9).[17] These exclusive claims of a final, inflexible truth provide the foundation for proselytization and spur zealotry and missionary activity.

In contrast, African religions are communal and non-universalist; unlike Christianity or Islam, they do not seek to convert or remake the "other" in their image (Mazrui, 1991: 77). The notion of converting the "other" is alien because the religion of the people is their identity and being; as one author has put it, it is redundant and tautological to talk of the religion of the Yoruba, for instance, because their identity is their religion, their way of life (Long, 1988: 3–4). Mbiti has written that in traditional society there was no dichotomy between the secular and the religious, no distinction between the religious and the irreligious, and no separation between the material and the spiritual (Mbiti, 1970: 2). He writes, further, that:

> Wherever the African is, there is his religion: he carries it to the fields where he is sowing seeds or harvesting new crop; he takes it with him to the beer party or to attend a funeral ceremony; and if he is educated [formal Western education], he takes religion with him to the examination room at school or in the university; if he is a politician he takes it to the house of parliament. Although many African languages do not have a word for religion as such, it nevertheless accompanies the individual from long before his birth to long after his physical death. (2–3, emphasis added)

That is why the degradation of African religions should be seen as the negation of the humanity of the African people. In the internationally acclaimed novel *Things Fall Apart*, Nigerian writer Chinua Achebe tells the story of this civilizational clash, and the simultaneous deconstruction and reconstruction of the African identity by mission Christianity and the agency of the colonial state (Achebe, 1959). This meeting of cultures is captured through the tragic life of Okonkwo, a pre-colonial Igbo man whose world literally disintegrates before his eyes. A man of status and a guardian of Igbo culture and religion, Okonkwo and other Igbo resist the new faith and the authority of the colonial state; but when the resistance is almost certainly crushed, Okonkwo kills a meddling local collaborator of the colonial regime and then hangs himself rather than accept physical and spiritual surrender to the church and the colonial state (207).

Okonkwo had watched with bitterness as the missionaries mocked the Igbo religion (146),[18] converted some of his people, including his son, to Christianity, and then used them against Igbos opposed to the new dispensation (148–67). In one telling moment, an Igbo who had become a missionary himself congratulates Okonkwo's son for running away to study at a mission school. The missionary tells him: "Blessed is he who forsakes his mother and father for my sake" (152). When Okonkwo and his Igbo resisters burn down a church, they are arrested and physically beaten on orders of the local colonial administrator (189–97). Here, the church fuses with the state. According to an elder, the white man "has put a knife on the things that held us together and we have fallen apart" (176). In *Things Fall Apart*, the colonial administrator decides to write *The Pacification of the Primitive Tribes of the Lower Niger*, a book based on Okonkwo's life and death, which he sees as symbolic of Europe's victory over the Igbo (208–9).

In history, Achebe's fiction was played out repeatedly throughout Africa. The encounter between Christianity and the Igbo religion has been characterized as a four-part process: the establishment of a mission; recruitment of converts, usually from among the social "rejects"; attack or "persecution" of the mission by elders and guardians of Igbo religion; and the imposition of colonial rule, and its protection and promotion of the mission (Isichei, 1970: 209, 212). As put clearly by Isichei:

> Towns [African] felt an urgent need for allies and advocates in the face of the violence with which it [colonial rule] was established. They had to learn the language of the invader, to communicate with their new rulers. Large numbers of employment opportunities existed, and there was an obvious benefit to be gained from education. (212)

Education in missionary schools was perhaps the most decisive weapon in the reconstruction of African identity. The mission usually preyed on the youth, capturing them and tearing them from their cultural moorings. The colonial state financially supported the mission schools, thus enhancing the capacity to transform social reality (Shropshire, 1938: 431).[19] Isichei writes, again:

> The missionaries succeeded in maintaining their virtual monopoly of education, and obtained adherents, not through dialogue with adults, but by cutting children off from their traditional culture and placing them in the artificially unanimous environment of the school. Today most Igbo have been baptized, and traditional religion is the preserve of a small aging minority. (Isichei, 1970: 212; see also Debrunner, 1967: 103; Beidelman, 1982: 198)[20]

Without regard to which agency was the first to penetrate an African community, both the colonial state and the church worked hand in glove in the civilizing mission. In Ghana, for example, the colonial state paternalized African rulers for their "good relations" with missionaries but attacked what it called "fetishism" and "fetish priests" (Debrunner, 1967: 175). The colonial government's disapproval and attack on African religions and customs further encouraged new converts to reject the ways of their forebears (189).[21] For instance, female circumcision, which Christians denounced as satanic, was one such custom (Kenyatta, 1965; Lewis, 1995).[22] Most significantly, the colonial state passed laws and implemented policies designed to purge the continent of African religions (see, for example, Fasuyi, 1973). In Nigeria, for instance, African religions, dances, education, and art were banned (21).

> The early missionaries came to introduce a new religion; all the former religious rites and manifestations (including the dance and music) were banned, and new converts were encouraged to dispose of any art works which had been used in religious rites. (see also Young, 1991: 31)[23]

The processes of social transformation and identity reconstruction set in motion by the invasion of Africa by both Christianity and Islam, and particularly the former, dislocated and distorted the African worldview almost in its entirety. The colonial state buttressed that process through the delegitimation of African religious beliefs, and the legitimation, at the political and social levels, of the spiritual and religious cosmologies of the invaders. In the span of several decades, the peoples of Africa were largely reconstructed, never to be the same again.

Postcolonialism and the Culture of Silence

In most of Africa, the current states do not predate colonialism, but were created by European imperial powers. The governing classes in Africa – both intellectual and political – are the products of the colonial state or its uncritical successor, the postcolonial state (Hansen, 1993: 160–2). Though formally independent, the postcolonial state is conceptually much like its predecessor. According to Hansen:

> African leaders have adopted and continued to use political forms and precedents that grew from, and were organically related to, the European experience. Formal declarations of independence from direct European rule do not mean actual independence from European conceptual dominance. (161)

The uncritical acceptance by many African leaders of the postcolonial state is not surprising considering the conceptual aspirations of the African elite. Many of the new rulers were forged in the mission and colonial schools, a process that almost certainly entailed the ideological renunciation of African religions, traditions, and beliefs, on the one hand, and the embrace of Christianity and the traditions of the Europeans, on the other. Even as the new converts straddled the fence, as many inevitably did, and mixed the "old" with the "new," there was little doubt that the new was expected, as a matter of course, to overcome the old. The new religious, cultural, and educational structures were designed to create local servants of colonialism.

> The West European educational system was introduced, replacing the informal traditional system; it was geared to the needs of the colonial administration. This objective was stated in a 1921 speech by the first [British] Governor of Nigeria: "The chief function of Government Primary and Secondary Schools . . . is to train the more promising boys from the village schools as teachers for those schools, as clerks for the native courts, and as interpreters." (Fasuyi, 1973: 21; Nduka, 1965)

The new curriculum was usually conceived in the metropole, either in England or France, and required the study of political, cultural, and literary forms which were alien to Africa. The British Empire, its language, and the English themselves were presented as the agents of civilization, replacing African worldviews (Fasuyi, 1973: 21).[24] It was these "products" who would lead their countries to formal independence and become its rulers. In Ghana, Kwame Nkrumah, who led the country into formal independence from Britain, invoked his Christian and Western educational background when he proclaimed, "Seek ye first the political kingdom and all other things shall be added to you" (Isichei, 1995: 339). Little wonder that Ghana was one of the earliest conquests of the church on the continent (Debrunner, 1967).[25]

Elsewhere on the African continent, mission-educated men took power as Africa emerged from direct European colonial rule. The list is long. Leopold Senghor, the first president of Senegal, now a member of the *Academie Française* (Vaillant, 1990),[26] is a former seminarian and a leading Catholic intellectual (Isichei, 1995: 339). The late Felix Houphouet-Boigny, the Ivorian president who constructed the world's largest Catholic basilica in the country's interior, was obviously another devout Catholic (339–40).[27] Others share similar backgrounds: Julius

Nyerere of Tanzania was a Catholic; Kenneth Kaunda of Zambia was Presbyterian; and General Ignatius Acheampong of Ghana had been born into a Catholic family (338–40). With the possible exception of the king of Swaziland, the head of one of the few African states that predates colonialism, to my knowledge there is no African leader who openly professes African traditional religions. Note, however, that 77 percent of the population of Swaziland is Christian but only 20.9 percent adheres to African religions (*1996 Britannica Book of the Year*, 1996: 721). Virtually all African heads of state or government are Christian or Muslim. The religious affiliation of the leadership greatly influenced the character of the nascent black-governed African state, and provided a smooth conceptual continuum between itself and its predecessor, the colonial state.

There is little doubt that over the last century Christianity has expanded enormously in Africa. It is estimated that the number of African Christians will have risen from 10 million in 1910 to 393 million in 2000, making one in every five Christians an African (Isichei, 1995: 1; Moreno, 1996: 13).[28] Although European colonial powers saw Islam as a threat to their cultural hegemony, many writers now agree that Islam prospered during the colonial period (Hiskett, 1984; King, 1971). Once colonial conquest was established, the British, for example, instituted indirect rule, using or inventing local rulers to act as the agents of the new state. A good example of indirect rule was the governance of the northern Nigerian emirates for the British by the emirs (Hiskett, 1984: 276–301). Both the French and the British supported Koranic schools throughout most of Africa, and used them to train civil servants and teachers to serve the colonial state (Oliver, 1991: 202). Needless to say, Islam was favored over African religions.

> In situations where Muslim towns supplied the local government services for a countryside that was still in practice pagan

[African religions], colonial support for the Islamic authorities helped greatly to consolidate Muslim observance among the country people. (Oliver, 1991: 202)

While both messianic religions grew, there was a corresponding decline in African religions (Isichei, 1995: 324). The position of African religions and cultures has not differed, either substantially or qualitatively, under the postcolonial state. The combination of colonial norms and structures – which were deliberately conceived as hostile to African heritage – survived intact into the independent, African-ruled states and continued to be the conceptual basis for those new states. In essence, the new elites took over the civilizing mission of the departing colonial power and have generally sought the re-creation of Africa in the image of Europe, even in those states which were ruled by Islamic elites. The constitutional and legal norms adopted on the eve of independence, as well as subsequent laws and policies, continued to suppress African cultures and religions, in spite of demagogic overtures by some rulers to the contrary (Mutua and Rosenblum, 1990).[29]

African constitutions and laws are generally either openly hostile to African religions and culture or they pretend that such religions do not exist. Such pretense is a tacit hope that African religions have either been eliminated or marginalized and so fundamentally delegitimized that they warrant no attention. The independence constitutions, which were largely written by Europeans for Africans on the eve of independence, sought to transplant a formal liberal state to the continent, an entity whose continued survival would be guaranteed by the metropolitan power and would therefore be subservient to it (Nkrumah, 1965; Jackson, 1992). None of the independence constitutions, as far as this author knows, make any mention of indigenous African religions (Mutua, 1996: 434). Instead, they offer liberal generic protection of religious freedoms. The

language used strongly suggests that "received" and not indigenous religions are the target for such protection.

A survey of several independence constitutions will suffice. Kenya's 1963 independence constitution, for example, guaranteed to each person freedom of religion, including the "freedom to change his religion or belief, and freedom, either alone or in community with others, and both in public and private, to manifest and propagate his religion or belief in worship, teaching, practice and observance" (section 22(1), Constitution of Kenya, 1963). It defined religion as inclusive of a "religious denomination, and cognate expressions" (section 22(6)). Further, it limited religious freedom to the interests of public morality and health, and guaranteed individuals the right to observe and practice any religion without the "unsolicited intervention of members of any other religion" (section 22(5)).

The limitations placed on religion for reasons of "public morality" and "public health" were most likely aimed at elements of indigenous African religions which many colonial states regarded as abominable (Shropshire, 1938). Significantly, these provisions protect the right to proselytize, a feature common to Christianity and Islam. The constitutions of Malawi (section 19, Constitution of Malawi, 1964), Nigeria (section 24, Constitution of Nigeria, 1963), Zambia (section 24, Constitution of Zambia, 1964), and Congo (Leopoldville) (article 25, Constitution of Congo (Leopoldville) [Zaire], 1964) offer similar, if not identical, rights and protections to those granted by the Constitution of Kenya. None attempts to protect or reclaim African religions. Interestingly, the Constitution of Guinea (article 41, The Constitution of the Republic of Guinea, 1958) tersely and barely protects religious freedom while the Ivory Coast (article 6, Constitution of the Ivory Coast, 1960) and Mali (article 1, Constitution of the Republic of Mali, 1960) only mention religion with reference to the nondiscrimination clause.

In the three decades since independence, African constitutions have not assumed a different posture toward African religions. The constitutional silence and the absolute refusal to acknowledge the existence of African religions or cultures has continued to this day. For instance, no changes have been made to the religious clause of the Constitution of Kenya (section 78, The Constitution of Kenya, 1988).[30] Similarly, no substantial changes have been made to the constitutions of Nigeria (section 37, Constitution of the Federal Republic of Nigeria (Promulgation) Decree, 1989),[31] Zaire (now the Democratic Republic of Congo) (article 17, Constitution of the Republic of Zaire, 1990),[32] and Zambia (section 20, Constitution of Zambia, 1991).[33] They do not even make vague references to African religions or cultures. This silence has, additionally, been given negative meaning by government policies and laws in a number of states.

The current regime in Sudan is perhaps one of the clearest examples of the active use of the state and its resources to destroy non-Islamic religions, including African religion (see generally, Lawyers Committee for Human Rights, 1996; *1996 Britannica Book of the Year*, 1996: 719).[34] Attempts by the state to impose Islam on Christians and adherents of African religions in the south of the country have escalated the civil war, leading to the killing of an estimated 1.3 million southern, non-Islamic civilians. There have been widespread reports of enslavement and forced conversions of black African southerners and their indoctrination to Islam (Hentoff, 1995: A17; Moreno, 1996: 36–7). A report by a right-wing Christian group terms the process "cultural cleansing" which "seeks to eliminate a cultural group by forcibly stripping these children [adherents of Christianity and African religions] of their names, language, freedom, families, and religion" (Moreno, 1996: 36).

There are numerous examples of other African states that favor or promote the Semitic religions. President Frederick Chiluba declared Zambia a Christian nation, although there are substantial numbers of believers in African religions, Hinduism, and Islam (US Department of State, 1994: 330; *1996 Britannica Book of the Year*, 1996: 754; Mwalimu, 1991: 233).[35] In Zaire (now the Democratic Republic of Congo) a state decree in 1971 declared the Catholic church, some Protestants, and the Kimbanguists (an independent Zairian church) the only legally recognized churches (Moreno, 1996: 41). Elsewhere, African postcolonial states have banned elements of African religions (Munro, 1975: 106; Kenyatta, 1965: 261). The colonial state and church, and later the postcolonial state, banned important elements of African culture and religion. Among the Akamba of Kenya, for example, the colonial rulers abolished the recognition of Kamba shrines, the consultation of medicine men, work on Sundays, beer and tobacco consumption, dancing, polygamy, bridewealth, and use of the oath. A number of African states, including Algeria (article 2, Constitution of Algeria, 1989), the Comoros (Preamble, Constitution of the Federal Islamic Republic of the Comoros, 1992), Egypt (article 2, Constitution of the Arab Republic of Egypt, 1971),[36] Libya (article 2, Constitutional Proclamation of the Socialist People's Libyan Arab Jamahiriya, 1969), Mauritania (article 5, Constitution of the Islamic Republic of Mauritania, 1991), Morocco (article 6, Constitution of the Kingdom of Morocco, 1992), and Tunisia (article 1, Constitution of the Tunisian Republic, 1959) are either constitutionally Islamic or proclaim Islam to be the religion of the state. Other states substantiate their commitment to Islam by providing for certain religious institutions or requiring that senior officials be Muslims (article 21, Constitution of the Kingdom of Morocco, 1992; article 23, Constitution of the Islamic Republic of Mauritania, 1991; articles 38, 40, Constitution of the Tunisian Republic, 1959; van der Vyver, 1997: 1–2).[37] But in an unusual turn, the 1996 South African Constitution expressly recognized the "institution, status, and role of traditional leadership, according to customary law" subject to the Constitution (1996 South African Constitution, chapter 12, sections 211–12). While there is no explicit mention of African religions, this provision openly recognizes African values in the governance of the state. What most of these examples point to, however, is the delegitimation of African religions, and that spiritual universe, through the implementation by the state of norms and policies in education and other arenas of public life that are based on European, American, or Arab conceptions of society or modernization.

The Myth and Reality of Counterpenetration

There can be no doubt that over the last century Africa has undergone one of the most dramatic and fundamental transformations ever witnessed in human history. Crawford Young has written that the indelible imprint of Europe on Africa is unique among world regions (Young, 1991: 20).[38] The fact of the displacement, transformation, and reorientation of African norms by European values has been documented and is not a source of much controversy. What is contested is the qualitative effect of those processes on the African universe. At the extremes, some cast the encounter as completely detrimental to Africa, while other apologists of colonial rule see it as the unquestioned redemption of the "dark" continent. In the middle there is a multiplicity of "moderate" characterizations of the encounter, a kind of a sliding judgmental scale which sees the benefits as well as the costs of the culture clash. This section explores these dichotomous views and probes the claim of counterpenetration.

Although the delegitimation of African cultures and religions has proceeded apace over the last century, there are still substantial numbers of Africans who adhere to them or use some of their conceptions to construct new identities. The process of incorporating European normative frameworks in addressing the changing reality started at the outset of the encounter with the West. Among the Akamba of Kenya, for example, politico-religious movements which have been termed a worldwide phenomenon at the revitalization and reorganization of indigenous societies arose in the wake of colonial expansion (Munro, 1975: 110). Many of the movements utilized African religious thought although they combined it with elements of Islamic and Christian theology (Munro, 1975).

In the early years of colonial penetration, resistance was widespread. For example, Syokimau, the Kamba priestess, prophesied the detrimental effects of the culture clash (Munro, 1975: 11). Others in Kamba society, such as Siotune Kathuke and Kiamba Mutuavio in 1911 used Kamba religious conceptions to mobilize resistance to the missions and colonial rule, actions for which they were deported to distant parts of the country by the colonial authorities (Munro, 1975: 114–17). But frustration with colonial rule among the Akamba was heightened because of the economic pressures of taxation, forcible conscription into the colonial armed forces, and the imposition of new justice and religious orders (Munro, 1975: 114–17).

Once the earlier, more indigenous protest movements were crushed, others arose in their stead, this time identifying themselves more explicitly with Christian theology. In 1921, Ndonye Kauti led one such movement, with the promise of delivering the Akamba to a Golden Age after expelling the missions and the "evil" Europeans (Munro, 1975: 118–21). Like his predecessors, Kauti was arrested and deported (Munro, 1975: 120). The successful establishment of colonial rule vanquished these protest movements but left space for more "benign" and less "political" African Christian sects. Among the Agikuyu of Kenya, for example, Watu wa

Mngu [Kiswahili for People of God] arose as a response to the opposition of clitoridectomy by Christian missions (Kenyatta, 1965, 263). Christianity, which was now the establishment religion, selectively allowed the incorporation into its liturgy and ritual only those African conceptions which legitimized the church within Africa. The Zaire Rite, which "Africanized" worship in the Zairian Catholic church, and the use of African names for African Christians where previously missionaries insisted on European names, are some examples of the "Africanization" of the church (Isichei, 1995: 2–3). However, this model of counterpenetration is superficial and symbolic; it does not exert meaningful normative or conceptual African influence on the church.

Between 1880 and 1920, more serious attempts to "Africanize" Christianity took place in the movement called Ethiopianism (Idowu, 1975: 206). Although based largely on Christian theology, these churches born of Ethiopianism have been described as utilizing more conceptions of African traditional religions. According to Idowu, the Nigerian scholar of African religions, elements of Ethiopianism sought to recover Africa's "enslaved soul." He writes:

> "Ethiopianism" has taken various forms, ranging from attempts at the indigenization of the Christian Church, the founding of churches by charismatic, Christian African leaders, and the establishment of splinters from European-dominated churches as separatist churches which are completely free from any form of foreign interference. (Idowu, 1975: 206)

Idowu regards some aspects of the "Ethiopian" churches as "positive repudiations of Christianity" because they only used the "scaffolding of the Christian church to erect new structures for the self-expression of the traditional religion" (Idowu, 1975: 206). But another scholar downplays the "Africanity" of such churches; she notes that although the new religious organizations were established by

Africans, they "differed only in detail from the mission churches from which they had separated themselves" (Isichei, 1995: 3).[39] Whatever the case, there has been a complex process of innovation and interaction between African churches – both European and African separatist churches – and forms and conceptions of African religions (see generally, Olupona, 1991). Many of the "Ethiopian" churches appear to have been more interested in political and financial autonomy, with lesser degrees of conceptual independence from Christian theology and philosophy. This is not to say that the Christian church in Africa has not been concerned with the vexing questions of inculturation and identity. These are important issues because of the European origin of the church and the inherent white racism within it (Isichei, 1995: 3). Even the most devout African Christians or Muslims at best remain either as "insider-outsiders" or "outsider-insiders," because the religions they profess are anchored and mediated through other cultures, in this case either European or Arab. Africans remain the bearers of a suspended and distorted identity, because the adopted religions cannot fully express their history, culture, and being.

In any event, it is the contention of this chapter that whatever "spin" is given to Christian penetration and its conquest or delegitimation of the African spiritual world, the process of Christianization cannot be isolated from Westernization and the consequent devaluation of the cultural identity of Africans and their humanity. It is not possible, as Sanneh contends, to legitimately consider the Christian penetration of Africa as not being part of the imperial cultural package of the West, and its ideological and conceptual repudiation of Africa (Sanneh, 1993: 15–17). Sanneh asks for the transcendence of the view that

> [c]onverts [African] have capitulated to Western cultural imperialism, and that their sins have been visited on their children who are condemned to an ambiguous

identity, being born, as it were, with a foreign foot in their native mouth. Converts may, for that reason, be considered cultural orphans and traitors at the same time. (Sanneh, 1993: 16)

Sanneh further contends that there was a "vital compatibility" between African cultures and Christianity, although he admits to the distortion of that relationship (Sanneh, 1993: 16). Moreover, he emphasizes the "assimilation" of Christianity into local idioms and cultures, and suggests a "benign" encounter with the West (Sanneh, 1993: 16). This characterization of the meeting of the two cultures decontextualizes Christianity from the entire colonial project and the violence with which it was accomplished. Such violence was not always physical; it was also the psychological, emotional, and cultural denigration of African peoples and cultural norms.

The fact that Christianity emerged victorious in this cultural contest, and has been "embraced" by the majority of Africans today, does not make the process less violent or more humane. Others say that Christianity has been "translated" through African languages and cultures, as if to suggest that such a process authenticates or humanizes the encounter. It is clear that conversion, for example, was one-dimensional: the African converted to either Christianity or Islam, never the reverse. I need not abstract my views about the encounter with the West; I witnessed the schism between my parents and my grandparents as the encounter played itself out in their lives. On the one hand, my parents converted, thereby forsaking their identity and cutting themselves off from my grandparents. My parents presented their "choice" as "enlightened" and "progressive." To them, my grandparents represented a past without a future in the new society. But that "choice" had a lot to do with managing the new colonial dispensation. Based partially on my family history, I have concluded that the peoples of Africa have been spiritually enslaved, as

it has become impossible for them to carry their cultures forward in the new global normative order. Later in life, my parents could not articulate to my inquiring mind why they had forsaken the past so completely. In my view, the programmatic agenda of the African postcolonial state demands an immersion into Eurocentric norms and forms of culture and society.

Benin: a Return to the Roots?

On January 10, 1996, the Republic of Benin became the first African state to officially recognize a traditional religion when it declared a National Voodoo Day (*Chicago Tribune*, 1996; *Africa News*, 1996). Unlike many Africans in other states, the majority of Beninois are open adherents of the African religion known as voodoo, a fact which made it easier for the government to recognize the religion (*1996 Britannica Book of the Year*, 1996: 565). Sixty-two percent of Beninois practice voodoo as opposed to only 23 percent and 12 percent who profess Christianity and Islam respectively. These numbers, together with the history and politics of Benin, were instrumental in the state's official recognition of voodoo.

The territory now constituting The Republic of Benin, also known at other times as the Kingdom of Dahomey, was a firmly established state five centuries ago, before the advent of colonialism (Elias, 1988: 11).[40] Benin was conquered and declared a French colony in the late nineteenth century (*Constitutions of Nations*, 1965: 1: 149). One of the country's earlier independence constitutions made no mention of voodoo although it protected religious beliefs in its nondiscrimination clause (article 13, Constitution of Dahomey, 1964).[41] In a departure from earlier constitutional jurisprudence, the 1990 constitution of The Republic of Benin creates a secular state but protects the "right to culture," and puts the duty on the state to "safeguard and promote the national values of civilization, as much material as spiritual, as well as the cultural traditions" (article 10, Constitution of The Republic of Benin, Law No. 90–32, 1990).[42] Elsewhere, the constitution allows religious institutions to operate parochial schools (article 14) and protects the freedom of religion (article 23). The 1990 Constitution, the most democratic in the country's history, resulted from the popular defeat of the repressive Marxist regime of Mathieu Kerekou, the dictator who had ruled The Republic of Benin since the 1972 coup d'état (US Department of State, 1992).

Benin has been viewed by many as the birthplace of voodoo although until recently the religion was suppressed by the state (Cowell, 1993: 11). The colonial state equated voodoo with witchcraft and banned it (*Africa News*, 1996: 108). The first indication that the state would rehabilitate voodoo and remove the stigma associated with it came in 1993 when the first festival of voodoo culture and arts was held in Ouidah, only forty-five miles outside Cotonou, Benin's capital. At the festival, also attended by invitees from Haiti, Trinidad and Tobago, and other west African states, President Nicephore Soglo, the former World Bank economist and the first democratically elected leader in two decades, underscored the importance of voodoo to the majority of Beninois and to descendants of Africans in the diaspora sold to captivity in the Americas. Critics called Soglo's recognition of voodoo a ploy to pander to the electorate in the 1996 presidential elections, which he lost to Kerekou, the former dictator (*Phoenix Gazette*, 1996: A2; Aplogan, 1996).

There is little significance to whatever political motivations lay behind the official recognition of voodoo in Benin. What is important is the acknowledgment by the state of the religion of the overwhelming majority of its citizens. The Republic of Benin recognized facts on the ground and started the process of restoring dignity to the identity and humanity of voodoo, and of the human beings who practice it.

Benin's example should be emulated elsewhere in Africa to end the culture of silence and repression of the identity of millions of Africans.

At the continental level, African states took an important step in reclaiming part of the past when in 1981 they adopted the African Charter on Human and Peoples' Rights, the basis for the regional human rights system (The African Charter on Human and Peoples' Rights, 1981; Mutua, 1995a: 339).[43] Although critics have pointed out numerous problems with the African Charter (Shivji, 1989; Okoth-Ogendo, 1993; Mutua, 1995a; Flinterman and Ankumah, 1992: 159), the instrument claims to be inspired by the "virtues" of African "historical tradition" and the "values of African civilization" (African Charter, 1981: Preamble). It prohibits discrimination based on religion (article 2) and guarantees the freedom of religion (article 8). Most significantly, it burdens the state with the "promotion and protection of morals and traditional values recognized by the community" (article 17). It also requires the state to assist the "family which is the custodian of morals and traditional values" (article 18(2)) and enlists the state in popular struggles against foreign cultural domination (article 20(3)). Although these provisions raise questions about the states' understanding of tradition and culture, the African Charter makes a radical statement: African traditions, civilization, and cultural values must be part of the fabric of a human rights corpus for the region.

The African Charter officially rehabilitates African philosophy and norms and may very well contribute to the reclamation of Africa's spiritual universe. This could be an essential part of the solution to the crises of identity wracking Africans and the states they claim as theirs. A return, a recognition, and a coming to terms with the African past – both cultural and religious – would help heal the spirit and lead to the creation of more stable and humane societies. I believe that this is one of the essential means through which the humanity stolen from

Africa by the imperial religions can be restored.

Notes

1 For the analyses and descriptions of the crises which threaten the survival of the postcolonial African state and have occupied scholars and academics since decolonization, see those listed.

2 Although these traditional sources of friction beset virtually all states, their centripetal and centrifugal forces have tended to lay bare the high vulnerability of the African state, and on occasion, to cause its implosion. See generally, *Collapsed States,* edited by I. William Zartman (identifying and analyzing the reasons for, and process of, the collapse of a number of African states, including Chad, Uganda, Ghana, Somalia, Liberia, Mozambique, and Ethiopia).

3 While over the last decade a number of African states have failed, many of them have been reconstructed. The collapse of the Rwandan state in 1994 has been the most dramatic to date. The latest casualty has been the Zairian state (now renamed the Democratic Republic of the Congo) of Mobutu Sese Seko, which in May 1997 unraveled under military pressure from forces loyal to Laurent Kabila, now the head of state.

4 The modern African state (started as the colonial enterprise known as the colonial state), the proselytization of Christianity, and the imposition of European social, economic, and political values and structures were interwoven in a continuum of cultural divestiture and alienation from pre-colonial African values. The church, the flag, and formal European education were all closely intertwined.

5 Two African states, Nigeria and Sudan, have particularly been ravaged by religious conflict between Muslims and Christians in the contexts of the struggles for group autonomy and the control of the political state.

6 Africa's domination by Islam, Christianity, and African religions has been seductively termed its *triple heritage,* terminology which may suggest peaceful coexistence and mutual enrichment.

7 Although I recognize the plurality of African religious expressions, I will often use the singular terminology of *African religion* to emphasize the near-total uniformity of assault and denigration of African religions by messianic faiths. In addition, the term also points to the similarities in cosmology and philosophy amongst different African religions.

8 Discussing early missionary attitudes toward Africans and their religions, and concluding that most missionaries regarded African religions as primitive and savage, Mbiti notes further that:

> African religions and philosophy have been subjected to a great deal of misinterpretation, misrepresentation and misunderstanding. They have been despised, mocked and dismissed as primitive and underdeveloped. One needs only to look at earlier titles and accounts to see the derogatory language used, prejudiced descriptions given and false judgments passed upon these religions. In missionary circles they have been condemned as superstition, satanic, devilish and hellish. (Mbiti, 1970: 13)

9 Mbiti has noted that "Christianity in Africa is so old that it can rightly be described as an indigenous, traditional and African religion" (Mbiti, 1970: 300). But Mbiti here distinguishes between early Christianity in north Africa, Egypt, and Sudan (which he dubs indigenous) and mission Christianity beginning in the fifteenth century but particularly toward the end of the eighteenth century (according to him, this latter version is not indigenous) (300–3). Mbiti notes that Islam, too, is traditional, indigenous, and African in northern Africa, the Horn of the continent, and southward along the east coast (317). See King 1971 (describing the entry of both Christianity and Islam into Africa in pre-modern times).

10 According to Mbiti, Africans have their own religious ontology, which he groups into four categories: god as the supreme being responsible for humans and all things; spirits, the superhuman beings of the dead; human beings, the living as well as the unborn; and objects and phenomena without biological life (Mbiti, 1970: 20).

11 Semitic religions often distinguish themselves from other beliefs by the emphasis they place on monotheism.

12 More particularly, Mbiti paints the following picture of African religions:

For Africans, the whole of existence is a religious phenomenon; man is deeply a religious being living in a religious universe. Failure to recognize and appreciate this starting point has led missionaries, anthropologists, colonial administrators and other foreign writers on African religions to mis-understand not only the religions as such but the peoples of Africa.

Elsewhere, I have defined *indigenous* as all African religious expressions whose cores predate Islamization and Christianization. Such religions denote the beliefs of native, non-settler peoples and exclude Islam and Christianity.

Several scholars have charged Mbiti and other African writers with employing Judeo-Christian templates to translate African religions into a Western idiom. Some have argued that his and similar works, which they see as perpetuating a hegemonic version of African religions, are inspired by "theological" cultural nation-alism. This prevalence of Western Christian discourse has remained normative within African religious studies, resulting in distortions of that universe.

13 On January 10, 1996, the government of The Republic of Benin inaugurated National Voodoo Day, officially recog-nizing for the first time in post-independent Africa the importance of indigenous religion.

14 Describing pre-colonial Africa on the dawn of colonialism as a "ripe melon" with "sweet, succulent flesh" awaiting carving by European imperial powers.

15 Munro notes the use of education to "attract" converts in the Machakos district of Kenya. He writes, further, that:

Christian missionaries gained an edge over their rival proselytizers. Islam, which seemed less appro-priate than Christianity as a religion for those seeking to use a colonial system controlled by European Christians, made few new converts in the 1920s and the Haji [Muslim community] remained peripheral on the Kamba [Akamba, the indigenous people of Machakos district] scene. (Munro 1975, 148)

16 Shropshire asserts that like marsupial cubs, the children of the Bantu are more depen-dent on their mothers than children of "civilized" [European] parents (Shrop-shire, 1938: 67).

17 According to Mbiti, animism was coined by Europeans to describe the beliefs of "primitive" peoples who consider all objects to have a soul, hence the presence in their cosmology of countless spirits.

18 In one particular incident, a missionary tells a crowd of Igbos:

All the gods you have named [Igbo gods] are not gods at all. They are gods of deceit who tell you to kill your fellows and destroy your children. There is only one true God and He has the Earth, the sky, you and me and all of us.

19 Shropshire writes: "The education of the Bantu is largely in the hands of the mission-aries whom the Government support with special grants."

20 This view was captured by another Christian imperialist who wrote: "Let the Missionaries and the schoolmasters, the plough and the spade, go together. It is the Bible and the plough that must regenerate Africa." In Tanzania, mission schools were recognized as the "most important means by which the mission attracts converts and promotes its message."

21 Emboldened by the government's rejection of African customs, Christian schoolgirls, for example, refused to undergo the "dipo" custom, which culminated in initiation into womanhood.

22 For a description and analysis of female circumcision or *irua,* and its role in the construction of an individual's social iden-tity within the Agikuyu, one of the African nations in modern-day Kenya, see gener-ally Kenyatta, 1965. For a thoughtful exploration of feminist debates on the prac-tice, see Lewis, 1995.

23 Young has written:

African culture was for the most part regarded as having little value, and its religious aspect – outside the zones in which Islam was well implanted – was subject to uprooting through intensive Christian evangelical efforts, which were often state-supported. European languages supplanted indigenous ones for most state purposes; for the colonial subject, social mobility required mastering the idiom of the colonizer. In innumerable ways, colonial subjugation in Africa brought not only political oppression and economic exploitation but also profound psychological humiliation.

24 One writer notes:

Students [African] had to learn things which had little bearing on their own way of life, e.g., the geography and the political, social and economic history of Britain and the British Empire. Foreign literature was studied. English became the official language, in which all transactions were affected. Indigenous languages were neglected; oral poetry gave way to Shakespeare and English literature.

Those who managed to study abroad frequently came back alienated from their own society.

25 Christianity was brought to Ghana as early as the fifteenth century.

26 The *Academie Francaise,* the pinnacle of French culture, has forty "immortals," persons whose contribution to French culture and statecraft is unparalleled. Senghor was the first African to achieve the honor.

27 Pope John Paul II opened the basilica in person, even though it was attacked as unconscionable and wasteful spending in the midst of human poverty and suffering in a country that is only 10 percent Catholic (Isichei, 1995: 339–40).

28 According to another count, in 1993 Africa was 57.3 percent Christian, 26.7 percent Muslim, and 15.4 percent African religions. For more comprehensive statistics on religious affiliations by country, see *1996 Britannica Book of the Year,* 783–85.

29 An example of such cynicism and manipulation of African culture as a veil for a despotic regime is that of Mobutu Sese Seko, the former Zairian president, and his "authenticity" campaign through which he forbade the use of European names and dress while running one of the most corrupt and abusive regimes with the support of France, Belgium, and the United States.

30 Albert P. Blaustein and Gisbert H. Flanz, eds., *Constitutions of the Countries of the World,* Binder X (1988).

31 *Ibid.,* Binder XIV (1990).

32 *Ibid.,* Supplement Binder (1991).

33 *Ibid.,* (1992).

34 The National Islamic Front (NIF) government in Sudan came to power in 1989 following the overthrow of the democratically elected government of Saddiq Al-Mahdi. The NIF has sought to impose an extreme version of *shari'a* or Islamic law on all citizens, including non-Muslims. It is estimated that Sudanese are 74.7 percent Islamic, 17.1 percent African religions, and 8.2 percent Christian.

35 Zambia is 72 percent Christian, 27 percent African religions, and 0.3 percent Muslim.

36 As amended in 1980.

37 In Morocco, for instance, a council of religious leaders has responsibility over certain executive functions. In both Mauritania and Tunisia, the president must constitutionally be a Muslim.

38 Crawford Young notes:
The cultural and linguistic impact [of Europe on Africa] was pervasive, especially in sub-Saharan Africa. Embedded in the institutions of the new states was the deep imprint of the mentalities and routines of their colonial predecessors. Overall, colonial legacy cast its shadow over the emergent African state system to a degree unique among major world regions.

39 Isichei notes that in any event such churches are in a "state of relative, and sometimes absolute, decline, overtaken by the immense proliferation of 'prophetic' or Zionist churches" (Isichei, 1995: 3).

40 For example, the Oba [king] of Benin sent envoys to Portugal in 1514 to procure arms.

41 *Constitutions o f Nations,* 1965: 1: 151.

42 Blaustein and Flanz, *Constitutions of the Countries of the World,* Binder II (1993).

43 OAU Doc. CAB/LEG/67/3/Rev.S (1981). Reprinted in 21 LL.M. 59 (1982). The African Charter came into force in 1986.

References

1996 Britannica Book of the Year.

Achebe, Chinua. 1959. *Things Fall Apart.* Anchor Books, 1994 edition.

Africa News. 1996. "Benin Voodoo Receives Official Nod" (January). Available in LEXIS, News Library, CURNWS File.

The African Charter on Human and Peoples' Rights. 1981. OAU Doc. CAB/LEG/67/3/Rev.S (June 27). Reprinted in 21 LL.M. 59 (1982).

Aplogan, Jean-Luc. 1996. "Benin's President's Camp Acknowledges Poll Defeat" (April 2), *Reuters.* Available in LEXIS, News Library, CURNWS File.

Barrow, A. H. 1900. *Fifty Years in Western Africa.* Reprinted in 1969.

Beidelman, T. O. 1982. *Colonial Evangelism.* Bloomington, IN: Indiana University Press.

Chicago Tribune. 1996. "In Benin, Government Gives Voodoo New Respect" (February 15).

Cohen, Ronald et al. (eds.) 1993. *Human Rights and Governance in Africa.* Gainesville: University Press of Florida.

Constitutions of Nations. 1965. Volume 1, *Africa* (ed.) Amos J. Peaslee. The Hague: M. Nijhoff.

Constitutions of the Countries of the World. 1993, ed. Albert P. Blaustein and Gisbert H. Flanz. Dobbs Ferry, NY: Oceana Publications.

Cowell, Alan. 1993. "Pope Meets Rivals in the 'Cradle of Voodoo'," *New York Times* (February 5).

Davidson, Basil. 1991a. *Africa in History*. New York: Collier Books.

—— 1991b. *African Civilization Revisited*. Trenton, NJ: Africa World Press.

Debrunner, Hans W 1967. *A History of Christianity in Ghana*. Accra: Waterville Publishing House. *The Memoirs of Sir T. F. Buxton* are quoted therein.

Elias, T O. 1988, *Africa and the Development of International Law* 11. Dordrecht and Boston: M. Nijhoff.

Fasuyi, T A. 1973. *Cultural Policy in Nigeria*. Paris: UNESCO.

Flinterman, Cees, and Evelyn Ankumah. 1992. "The African Charter on Human and Peoples' Rights," in *Guide to International Human Rights Practice*. Philadelphia: University of Philadelphia Press.

French, Howard. 1997. "In Congo, Many Chafe under Rule of Kabila," *New York Times* (July 13).

Hackett, Rosalind I. J. 1990. "African Religions and I-Glasses," *Religion* 20.

—— 1996. *Art and Religion in Africa*. London and New York: Cassell.

Harbeson, John W, and Donald Rothchild, eds. 1991. *World Politics*. Boulder, CO: Westview Press.

Hansen, Art. 1993. "African Refugees: Defining and Defending Their Human Rights," in Cohen 1993.

Hentoff, Nat. 1995. "Slavery and the Million Man March," *Washington Post* (November 28).

Hiskett, Mervyn. 1984. *The Development of Islam in West Africa*. New York: Longman.

Human Rights Watch. 1995. "Genocide in Rwanda: April–May 1994," *World Report* 1995, 39–48.

Idowu, E. Bolaji. 1975. *African Traditional Religion*. Maryknoll, NY: Orbis Books.

Irele, Abiola. 1992. "The Crisis of Legitimacy in Africa," *Dissent* (Summer).

Isichei, Elizabeth. 1970. "Seven Varieties of Ambiguity: Some Patterns of Igbo Response to Christian Missions," *Journal of Religion in Africa* 3.

—— 1995. *A History of Christianity in Africa*. Africa World Press.

Jackson, Robert H. 1992. "Juridical Statehood in Sub-Saharan Africa," *Journal of International Affairs* 46.

Jackson, Robert H., and Carl C. Rosberg. 1982. *Personal Rule in Black Africa*. Berkeley and Los Angeles: University of California Press.

Kenyatta, Jomo. 1965. *Facing Mt. Kenya*. New York: Vintage Books.

King, Noel Q. 1971. *Christian and Muslim in Africa*. New York: Harper & Row.

Lawyers Committee for Human Rights. 1996. *Best by Contradictions: Islamization, Legal Reform and Human Rights in Sudan*.

Lewis, Hope. 1995. "Between 'Irua' and 'Female Genital Mutilation': Feminist Human Rights Discourse and the Cultural Divide," *Harvard Human Rights Journal* 8.

Long, Charles H. 1988. "Religions, Worlds, and Order: The Search for Utopian Unities," in Marty and Greenspahn 1988.

Marty, Martin E., and Frederick E. Greenspahn, eds. 1988. *Pushing the Faith: Proselytism and Civility in a Pluralistic World*. New York: Crossroad.

Mazrui, Ali A. 1986. *The Africans: A Triple Heritage*. Boston: Little, Brown.

—— 1991. "Africa and Other Civilizations: Conquest and Counterconquest," in Harbeson and Rothchild 1991.

Mbiti, John S. 1970. *African Religions and Philosophy*. New York: Praeger.

Moreno, Pedro C. (ed.) 1996. *Handbook on Religious Liberty around the World*.

Munro, F 1975. *Colonial Rule among the Kamba: Social Change in the Kenya Highlands* 1889–1939. Oxford: Clarendon Press.

Mutua, Makau. 1995a. "The Banjul Charter and the African Cultural Fingerprint: An Evaluation of the Language of Duties," *Virginia Journal of International Law* 35.

—— 1995b. "Why Redraw the Map of Africa: A Moral and Legal Inquiry," *Michigan Journal of International Law* 16.

—— 1995c. "Putting Humpty Dumpty Back Together Again: The Dilemmas of the Post-Colonial African State," *Brooklyn Journal of International Law* 21 (book review).

—— 1996. "Limitations on Religious Rights: Problematizing Religious Freedom in the African Context," in *Religious Human Rights in Global Perspective: Legal Perspectives*, ed. Johan D. van der Vyver and John Witte Jr. Boston: M. Nijhoff.

Mutua, Makau, and Peter Rosenblum. 1990. *Zaire: Repression as Policy* (Lawyers Committee for Human Rights).

Mwalimu, Charles. 1991. "Police, State Security Forces and Constitutionalism of Human Rights in Zambia," *Georgia Journal of International and Comparative Law* 21.

Nduka, Otinki. 1965. *Western Education and the Nigerian Cultural Background*.

Nkrumah, Kwame. 1965. *Neo-colonialism: The Last Stage of Imperialism*. New York: International Publishers.

Nyong'o, Peter Anyang' (ed.) 1992. *Thirty Years of Independence in Africa: The Lost*

Decades. Nairobi, Kenya: African Association of Political Science.

Okoth-Ogendo, H.W.O. 1993. "Human and Peoples' Rights: What Point Is Africa Trying to Make?" in Cohen 1993.

Oliver, Roland. 1991. *The African Experience.* London: Weidenfeld & Nicolson.

Olupona, Jacob K. (ed.) 1991. *African Traditional Religion in Contemporary Society.* New York: International Religious Foundation.

Phoenix Gazette. 1996. "Voodoo Day Called Play to Get Votes" (January 11).

Pobee, John S. 1996. "Africa's Search for Religious Human Rights through Returning to the Wells of Living Water," in *Religious Human Rights in Global Perspective: Legal Perspectives*, ed. Johan D. van der Vyver and John Witte Jr. Boston: M. Nijhoff.

Richardson, Henry J. 1996. "'Failed States,' Self-determination, and Preventive Diplomacy: Colonialist Nostalgia and Democratic Expectations," *Temple Int'l & Comp. L. J.* 10.

Sanneh, Lamin O. 1993. *Encountering the West.* Maryknoll, NY: Orbis Books.

Schatzberg, Michael G. 1988. *The Dialectics of Oppression in Zaire.* Bloomington, IN: Indiana University Press.

Shaw, Rosalind. 1990. "The Invention of 'African Traditional Religion,'" *Religion* 20.

Shivji, Issa. 1989. *The Concept of Human Rights in Africa.* London: CODESRIA Book Series.

Shropshire, Denys. 1938. *The Church and Primitive Peoples.* London: Society for Promoting Christian Knowledge; New York: The Macmillan Company.

US Department of State. 1992. *Country Reports on Human Rights Practices for 1991.*

US Department of State. 1994. *Country Reports on Human Rights Practices for 1993.*

Vaillant, Janet G. 1990. *Black, French, and African: A Life of Leopold Sedar Senghor.* Cambridge, MA: Harvard University Press.

van der Vyver, Johan D. 1997. "Religious Freedom in African Constitutions." Maryknoll, NY: Orbis Books.

Young, Crawford. 1991. "The Heritage of Colonialism," in Harbeson and Rothchild 1991.

Zartman, I. William. 1995a. "Introduction: Posing the Problem of State Collapse," in Zartman 1995b.

Zartman, I. William, ed. 1995b. *Collapsed States: The Disintegration and Restoration of Legitimate Authority.* Boulder, CO: L. Rienner Publishers.

Zolberg, Aristide R. 1992. "The Specter of Anarchy: African States Verging on Dissolution," *Dissent* (Summer).

Regional Case Studies: Human Rights Watch and Survival

PART

III

Introduction to Part III

Part III presents a series of regional case studies from human rights organizations, principally Human Rights Watch and Survival. **Part III** is divided into subsections, as detailed on p. 243.

The regional case studies in **Part III** add a sense of what **Part II**'s theoretical reflections mean "on the ground." If at times the case studies seem harrowing, organizations like Human Rights Watch and other governmental and non-governmental human rights organizations do nevertheless present a hope that international pressure by individuals as well as nation-states can make a difference to self-evident human suffering and injustice.

It should also be remembered when reading these case studies, of which only excerpts are given here, that these are the extremes of human rights abuses in relation to religion. And while one might be surprised at the global extent of religious intolerance, many countries value and are enriched by cultures of religious freedom and tolerance. Marshall's (2000) study deriving from Freedom House – one of America's oldest human rights organizations and an extract of which is reproduced in Part IV – presents a measured if at times still disturbing picture of religious freedom around the world. Situations also change. A case study is not a comprehensive, definitive study of a region or in this case a religion or religions in regional context. A case study here presents an historical snapshot of religion in conflict. The situation portrayed will be one in which human rights are at peril – rights to freedom of religion and belief as well as other fundamental civil and political rights.

Many case studies presented in **Part III** represent a political context in which a dominant force – religious or ideological – within a regime represses less powerful alternative views of the world: political, social, economic and here especially religious worldviews are repressed, often with and through violence. One of the merits of Human Rights Watch is its impartiality. An independent organization, it does not take funds from any government. New York based, a strong sense of the impartiality of Human Rights Watch is clear from its frequent criticism of the United States, though where merited it does offer support. Survival has a similar degree of independence. It must be said however that the views represented by Human Rights Watch or Survival are not necessarily specifically those held by the editor or publisher. And as with any political situation, one portrayal is likely to be challenged by another. Contexts and government change.

A good measure of accuracy in human rights reports holds to good journalistic practice in terms of veracity of reporting. Can information be corroborated? Does a regional assessment of human rights and religion in a government-sponsored report find support with NGOs' (non-governmental organizations) reports or international sources such as the United Nations? The worldwide web is increasingly the source of up-to-date information

Box III.i

Human Rights and Religion: Of Particular Concern?

Among those countries not named [by the US State Department Report on Religious Freedom (October 2001)] is Uzbekistan, where several thousand non-violent Muslims have been arrested in the last three years for practicing their faith outside state controls. Uzbekistan is hosting US forces involved in operations in Afghanistan.

The State Department report acknowledges that the Uzbek government has committed "abuses against many devout Muslims for their religious beliefs" – arresting people for proselytizing, for private teaching of religious principles, for wearing of religious clothing in public, and for distributing religious literature. It also acknowledges that authorities systematically torture religious prisoners.

"By not designating Uzbekistan a 'Country of Particular Concern,' the Administration missed an easy opportunity to show that the war on terrorism cannot be a campaign against Islam," Malinowski [an HRW spokesperson] said.

Saudi Arabia was not designated, although, as State Department spokesman Richard Boucher said today, "there is essentially no religious freedom" there. Christians working in the country are forbidden to conduct any form of public worship. The country's Shi'a Muslim minority faces severe discrimination. Conservative Sunni clerics associated with the government have publicly denigrated Shi'a as "apostates" and "non-believers" because some of their religious practices are at odds with the strict Wahhabi doctrine imposed by the country's rulers. In few countries in the world is the denial of religious freedom so integral to the self-conception and ethos of the government.

Also not designated was Turkmenistan, which suppresses all forms of religious practice other than state-sanctioned Islam and Russian orthodoxy. Hundreds of Protestants, followers of Hare Krishna and other minority religions have been harassed, questioned by police, and threatened with arrest for exercising their religious convictions. Turkmenistan is the only state in the former Soviet Union where authorities have confiscated and destroyed houses of worship (Seventh Day Adventist, Hare Krishna, and Muslim).

China was designated a "Country of Particular Concern," and the report's analysis of abuses of religious freedom is generally accurate, with one exception: The reporting on Xinjiang, the mainly-Muslim region of northwest China, is strikingly less critical than last year's. The government's "Strike Hard" anti-crime campaign, launched nationwide in April 2001, has led to many arbitrary arrests and summary executions in Xinjiang. Separatism and religion appear to be as much the targets as ordinary crime. Under "Strike Hard," people have been arrested, for example, for having "illegal religious publications" in their possession. Last year's State Department report accurately described a "harsh crackdown on Uighur Muslims . . . that failed to distinguish between those involved with illegal religious activities and those involved in ethnic separatism or terrorist activities." Today's report, by contrast, merely notes that "government sensitivity to Muslim community concerns is varied . . . and (in areas where there has been violence attributed to separatists) police crackdown on Muslim religious activity and places of worship accused of supporting separatism" in Xinjiang. The "Strike Hard" campaign isn't even mentioned.

Also designated were Burma, Iran, Iraq, North Korea, Sudan and the Taliban. Under the International Religious Freedom Act, when a country is named to this list, the Secretary of State must choose from an optional menu of steps, from diplomatic pressure to the imposition of sanctions. Most of the designated governments, however, are already subject to US sanctions. (HRW 2002)

on rapidly changing situations though annual reports on human rights and religion are presented by all major NGOs in the field, by the United Nations or through national governments. In the United States, for example, since the late 1990s, the US Department of State has produced an "Annual Report on

Box III.ii

Human Rights on the Internet: A Selective List

Amnesty International	www.ai.org.uk
Anti-Slavery International	www.antislavery.org
Centre for Research in Human Rights	www.roehampton.ac.uk/crhr
Charter 88	www.charter88.org.uk
Citizen 21	www.citizen21.org.uk
Human Rights Watch	www.hrw.org
International PEN (Poets, Essayists, Novelists)	www.oneworld.org.uk/intpen
Survival	www.survival.org.uk
United Nations	www.un.org
United Nations High Commission for Human Rights	www.unhchr.org

International Religious Freedom." **Box III.i** gives a good instance of where views between an NGO like Human Rights Watch and an official view – here the US Department of State Annual Report on International Religious Freedom for 2001 – differ. Readers can make their own assessment of the reasons for any such apparent discrepancies.

References

Human Rights Watch. 2002. *Human Rights and Religion: Of Particular Concern*. New York: HRW.

Marshall, Paul, ed. 2000. *Religious Freedom in the World*. Nashville, Tennessee: Broadman and Holman.

United Nation. 2002. *United Nations Documentation: Research Guide*. New York: UN.

Further Reading/Research

Box III.ii presents a selective list of starting points for human rights on the internet.

Box III.iii presents a United Nations Documentation Research Guide. While of more generic significance the Research Guide presents a pathway through the complexity of the United Nations machinery for human rights. The home page of the UN (*http://*www.un.org) is a good general starting point but **Box III.iii** presents an advanced research guide for academics, researchers and journalists.

The Research Guide is adapted from the United Nations Dag Hammarskjöld Library. For a research guide tailored to human rights specifically follow the links to "Special Subjects" and from there the link to "Human Rights." Of recent and most current concern in the United Nations on the theme of cultural and religious diversity – including minorities and indigenous peoples – are the pages devoted to the World Conference Against Racism (WCAR: *http://*www.un.org/WCAR/). For commentary on human rights and religion in the United Nations and related international instruments, see Nathan Lerner's chapter in **Part I**.

Box III.iii

United Nations Dag Hammarskjöld Library
Last updated: 31 March 2002
United Nations Documentation: Research Guide

Retrospective Research

The United Nations is a major publisher. Over the more than five decades of its existence, it has published hundreds of thousands of documents (reports, studies, resolutions, meeting records, letters from Governments, etc.) on topics of key interest (disarmament, the environment, human rights, international law, peacekeeping, etc.).

Under the circumstances, it might initially seem impossible to track down precise information in view of the overwhelming amount of data available, but a systematic approach to your research will always yield results.

Given the vast number of UN documents and publications and the non-uniqueness or similarity of many titles – a nebulous request for the report of the Secretary-General, for example, will yield thousands of hits – it is helpful to pinpoint your research to a specific time-frame and, preferably, to limit it to a particular organ or subsidiary body. The beginner may be at a loss in this regard, but a number of basic reference tools are available to provide help.

The various editions of *Everyone's United Nations* concisely summarize major events in the Organization's history. The researcher is given the forum (e.g., Security Council, General Assembly) before which and the year(s) during which the matter was discussed.

With these important pieces of information at hand, the next logical step might be to consult the *Yearbook of the United Nations* for the year(s) in question. The *Yearbook* will give a more detailed account, bibliographical citations to core documents available for consultation in *depository libraries* and *UN Information Centres* (or on the UN homepage for more recent years) and the full text of key resolutions.

For some researchers, the Yearbook may provide all the information required; others may prefer to exhaust the topic by going one level further: to the *Index to Proceedings* of the major organs (*General Assembly, Security Council, Economic and Social Council, Trusteeship Council*) to which the matter was presented. These highly specialized indexes are produced annually/sessionally and are comprehensive, including citations to every document relating to that organ's consideration of the topic.

The Encyclopedia of the United Nations also comes in handy for providing quick access to information of a general nature. Like the Yearbook, it very often cites the United Nations bodies involved and provides a time-frame, thereby enabling the reader to pinpoint his research more precisely should a more in-depth study be required.

The contents of *Basic Facts about the United Nations* are self-explanatory. This frequently updated handbook serves as a very handy, concise guide providing a condensed overview of United Nations activity in major spheres.

Current Research

As a first step in researching a current topic, it is often helpful to conduct a search in the United Nations press releases database which gives access to the full text of releases issued since October 1995. Three search options exist: *Last 30 days, Archives* and *Full text. Press releases* are not considered to be official documents but will in many cases yield valuable leads about, e.g., which bodies are currently discussing a particular topic and what actions have been taken. With this information in hand, a search for the official documentation relating to a specific topic can be facilitated.

If the body involved is known, it is useful to go directly to the website of that body in order to obtain more information on the issue on hand. The *Official Web Locator for the UN System* will guide users to the appropriate location.

http://www.un.org/Depts/dhl/resguide/basic/htm **Copyright © United Nations**

Muslim–Christian Conflict in Sudan

Human Rights Watch

13

- ◆ Historical background ◆ Repression in Northern Sudan ◆
- ◆ The Nuba ◆ Apostasy and the law ◆
- ◆ Status of women ◆ Update on human rights in Sudan ◆

Repression Continues in Northern Sudan

Gross human rights violations continue in Sudan five years after a military coup overthrew the elected civilian government on June 30, 1989, and brought to power a military regime dominated by the National Islamic Front (NIF), a minority party that achieved only 18.4 percent of the popular vote in the 1986 elections. The Sudanese have suffered under military rule and single-party dictatorship for twenty-seven out of the thirty-eight years since independence in 1956; they succeeded in overthrowing oppressive regimes twice in the past, in October 1964 and April 1985. Southern Sudanese continue to struggle against the present regime, as they have done against previous northern-dominated regimes for all but eleven of the thirty-eight years of independence. Massive violations of human rights and humanitarian law in the context of this civil war in southern Sudan are detailed in our July 1994 report, *Civilian Devastation: Abuses by All Parties to the War in Southern Sudan*. This report highlights human rights abuses in northern Sudan, focusing on individual testimonies to supplement the evidence of violations in the south detailed earlier.

As the current regime completes its fifth year in power [1994], all forms of political opposition remain banned legally and through systematic terror. The regime has institutionalized changes in the character of the state through extensive purges of the civil service and by dismantling any element of civil society that disagrees with its narrow vision of an Islamic state. Political power over the whole country has been entrenched in the hands of a tiny ideological elite.

Human Rights Watch does not question the right of a people to adopt any system of law and government through the genuinely free choice of the population. This is integral to a people's right to self-government. A military regime, however, is by definition not the choice of the citizens, who had no voice in its coming to power, no participation in the formulation and implementation of its policies, and no ability to change it. Any military regime is necessarily the negation and repudiation of the national right to self government. Here the loss is more total because military rule is coupled with an exclusivist ideology, alleged to be founded on religion, that flouts minority rights.

The government of Sudan is bound by the many international human rights treaties that it has ratified or to which it has acceded. According to standards set in these treaties, the right to self-government does not mean that the majority is entitled to violate the fundamental rights and freedoms of minorities. For example, Article 26 of the International Covenant on Civil and Political Rights (ICCPR) provides:

All persons are equal before the law and are entitled without any discrimination to the equal protection of the law. In this respect, the law shall prohibit any discrimination and guarantee to all persons equal and effective protection against discrimination on any ground such as race, color, sex, language, religion, political or other opinion, national or social origin, property, birth or other status.

The government of Sudan is in clear violation of this principle. In addition, it has taken extraordinary measures to prevent the world from learning the specifics of its abysmal human rights record, harshly punishing dissidents and excluding or restricting independent observers, journalists, human rights monitors, and humanitarian organizations. After granting a visa to Human Rights Watch in June 1993, the government twice, at the last minute, postponed the visit, which, as a result, could not be made.

Sudanese who attempt to speak out on human rights issues are subjected to threats or arrest, even when seeking to meet with the United Nations' own representatives, such as the UN Human Rights Commission's Special Rapporteur on Sudan, Gáspár Biró. Father Aliaba James Surur reported that he was picked up at his home on September 13, 1993, the morning after his meeting with Mr. Biró, and taken to the security headquarters; there he was warned that Mr. Biró would leave in two weeks and "'you will remain here.'" Four women who met with Mr. Biró were arrested in front of the UN office in Khartoum immediately after they left the meeting. The special rapporteur witnessed two of them being dragged down the street and forced into a police vehicle. Then the police arrested a group of about twenty-five persons, mostly women, who were waiting in the same place to meet Mr. Biró, beating up some of them. These arrests took place despite government assurances that the peaceful assembly of petitioners would be allowed.

As of the date of the special rapporteur's report, the Minister of Justice had not made good on his promise to the special rapporteur to send him a detailed report on these events.

Despite government efforts to deter scrutiny, it has become obvious that a large second-class citizenry has been created by the regime's version of an Islamic state. Public dialogue in Sudan has been silenced, even for those who share a commitment to the implementation of *shari'a* law but disagree with the policies and practices of the present government. All political parties remain banned, and arrests of their members continue unabated whenever they attempt any organized civic activity.

Armed conflict in the south of the country has provided the backdrop for particularly appalling abuse. The conflict has spread north over the last few years; the peoples of the Nuba Mountains of southern Kordofan have been suffering the combined effects of the cruelties of the army, government-sponsored militias and the insurgent Sudan People's Liberation Army (SPLA) which the government seeks to crush. The effect has been to turn the once peaceful and prosperous Nuba Mountains into a battlefield where villages are destroyed and people are driven from their land, herded into government camps or wantonly killed, while their educated community leaders are targeted for arrest or assassination. The entire area has been sealed off by the government from foreign eyes while its counterinsurgency campaign continues, since the government is sensitive to the bad publicity arising from the wholesale displacement campaign.

This report highlights excerpts from the

diary kept by a resident of Kordofan from late 1992 to April 1993 that describes the large-scale displacement of Nubans, their forcible relocation under intolerable conditions, the abduction of children, the forced recruitment of boys as young as thirteen into military services, the destruction of churches, the abuse of women in displaced persons' camps, and the manipulation of relief for Islamic proselytization purposes, among other abuses. This diary reinforces the findings on the situation in the Nuba Mountains presented in the February 1994 report of the UN Special Rapporteur on Human Rights in Sudan.

This report also covers the plight of displaced persons and squatters in urban areas of northern Sudan, including Nubans and southerners displaced by the war. In 1992 hundreds of thousands of the displaced and urban squatters were summarily evicted from their homes in urban areas. Their property was destroyed under a purported urban renewal campaign which targeted the large non-Arab and non-Muslim population of the capital. This campaign continued in 1993, and in 1994 an estimated 160,000 more people were similarly displaced from Khartoum and moved to unprepared sites far from water, work, or education.

One group of displaced has been especially targeted by the government: boys. On the pretext of taking care of street children, hundreds of boys, mostly southerners, are rounded up in the markets and on the streets and summarily dispatched to camps run by Islamists. No attempt is made to contact their families or to follow the Juvenile Welfare Act's procedure for removing a child from his family. The boys are beaten for small breaches of discipline and given a religious (Islamic) education regardless of their or their families' prior beliefs. At age fifteen they are incorporated into the government militia.

After political parties were banned in 1989, the top-ranking leaders of all opposition parties still in the country were arrested repeatedly, a pattern that continued in 1994. Detentions of others believed to be or to have been political activists continue to be carried out in a manner designed to terrorize and intimidate through mistreatment and torture while in detention or in unacknowledged unofficial detention centers called "ghost houses." A retired army brigadier was severely tortured after his detention in 1991 and periodically over the next two years; his testimony is reprinted in part in this report. Hundreds of other Sudanese continue to be subject to incommunicado detentions without charge or trial.

The efforts of the NIF, which guides the government in reshaping society, have resulted in a series of laws which place women and non-Muslims in a legally inferior relationship to men and Muslims. The death penalty is now expressly mandated for the crime of apostasy, the repudiation by a Muslim of his faith in Islam.

Among the recommendations Human Rights Watch makes is that the UN Security Council institute an arms embargo on the warring parties in Sudan and authorize a full-time contingent of UN human rights monitors with access to all parts of the country. The report also recommends that other countries use their votes in international financial institutions to freeze Sudanese requests for loans or disbursements on the grounds of gross human rights abuses. Recommendations directed to the government include abolishment of the crime of apostasy, the death penalty, flogging, the use of shackles, and the *hudud* punishment; cease torture; and cease imposing *shari'a* on non-Muslims.

A Nuban Diary

The Nuba number about one million. Their traditional home is in southern Kordofan, a part of northern Sudan which is almost the exact geographic center of the country. Anthropologists have noted that "the Nuba" is a term which encompasses a bewildering complexity of ethnic groups who speak more than fifty languages and dialect clusters. Well-known aspects of the Nuba culture include music, dance, body-painting and ritual wrestling. Some traditional religions survive, but most Nubans have been converted to Islam or Christianity.

The Nuba are mostly farmers in a fertile area. Their traditional rivals have been the cattle-herding Sudanese Arabs known as Bagarra, who live in southern Kordofan. The Bagarra have been allies of power centers in Sudan since the nineteenth century, while the Nuba have been peripheral to the main currents of Sudanese politics, neither aligned with the Arab-dominated northern parties nor belonging to the south. The Bagarra were aligned with the Umma Party of former Prime Minister Sadiq al-Mahdi and were essential elements in his government's counterinsurgency strategy against spla activity in the Nuba mountains. The Bagarra were armed by the transitional government (1985–86), then by the governing Umma Party (1986–89), and then by the government of the NIF. Their traditional raiding activities thus were diverted to strike at the SPLA and the lives and assets of its supposed followers among the Nuba in south Kordofan and the Dinka in adjoining northern Bahr el-Ghazal. The Bagarra's militia, the *Murahaliin*, began raiding Nuba communities in 1985 in the context of the counterinsurgency war.

The war in the Nuba Mountains escalated markedly in July 1987 when the New Kush Battalion of the spla, headed by Nuba commander Yousif Kowa Mekke and consisting mainly of Nuba fighters, infiltrated the area. The New Kush Battalion occupied the area around Talodi and grew in size by late 1988 to an estimated 3,000. It systematically assassinated or kidnapped community leaders and government officials who did not cooperate. In 1989 the SPLA made military gains in the area close to Kadugli town and Tuleishi, while the Murahaliin carried out increasing attacks on Nuba civilians.

After the NIF took power, the Popular Defense Act (1989) legitimized the Murahaliin militia as part of the paramilitary Popular Defense Force (PDF), which stepped up raids, now in conjunction with the army. While the SPLA continued to commit abuses such as raiding villages for food, kidnapping or forcibly conscripting youths for military service, killing civilians suspected of lack of sympathy, and indiscriminate attacks during raids, the violence by the Murahaliin and army escalated to an even higher level.

Opting for local solutions to local issues, in February 1990 some Bagarra leaders and commanders negotiated a truce with the spla to gain access for the Bagarra to traditional grazing lands in SPLA-controlled Dinka areas of the southern region of Bahr el Ghazal.

In response, the central government intensified its efforts to inflame the Bagarra's historical competition with the Nuba, with the objective of ridding the Nuba land of its Nuba inhabitants. Col. Husseini Abd El-Karim, then state commissioner of Kordofan, was assigned to carry out a policy of "eradication" and replacement of the Nuba with Bagarra Arabs, who were said to covet Nuba lands. The army, reinforced by the PDF, first targeted for arrest, torture, and summary execution the leaders and educated members of the Nuba. Then it confiscated land, evicted entire communities, destroyed entire villages, and tortured and murdered Nuba people.

In January 1992 the provincial government of Kordofan declared a jihad – a holy war – in the Nuba Mountains to rout the "remnants" of the SPLA.

On October 19, 1993, defecting 1st Lt. Khalid Abd al-Karim Salih denounced the government mobilization against the Nuba. At a press conference in Bern, Switzerland, he described the scorched earth campaign conducted by the government and estimated that between 40,000 and 50,000 Nuba were killed as a result of aerial and ground attacks on villages, especially in the areas around Um Dorain, El Takama,

Kartal, El Jilad, and Katla between May 1992 and February 1993. Salih, who was at the time a senior security officer in Kordofan with access to casualty figures, reported that the attacks were part of what he called the government's policy of "ethnic cleansing." He reported that young men were killed on the spot, while children often were removed from their mothers and sent to work as farm laborers.

A US government report cited "credible reports that human rights abuses are taking place throughout the transition zone, including massacres, kidnapping, and forced labor, conscription of children, forced displacement, and Arabization." While such outrages may be carried out by poorly-controlled militia without the approval and perhaps against the authorities' wishes, the US report concluded, "other abuses are occurring with a frequency and on a scale that makes it difficult to believe that they are happening without the knowledge and tacit complicity of the government authorities."

At the same time there was evidence that the SPLA was also responsible for abuses in the region. The UN special rapporteur on Sudan received testimony in the Kadugli area alleging SPLA atrocities. Local chiefs and emirs said that the spla was responsible for "all atrocities" committed in the Kadugli area in the past few years. They claimed that because of SPLA attacks seventy-three of 176 villages were empty in September 1993. The emirs charged the SPLA with killings and torture of unarmed civilians, rape, kidnapping, and forced military training of children. They also cited burning of homes and looting, and provided names of victims.

The UN Special Rapporteur for Human Rights in Sudan, Gáspár Biró, in his November 1993 and February 1994 reports, also concluded that the government was committing serious violations in the Nuba Mountains, among other findings, stating that

> The abduction of children, as well as of women, from southern Sudan and the Nuba Mountains is routinely practiced by members of different armed units, such as the Popular Defense Forces or mujahidin. A former high-ranking official of Darfur State admitted that abduction and traffic of children takes place routinely on a tribal basis in the conflict area of the Dinka and Rizeigat tribes.

> The situation of Christians in the government of Sudan-controlled areas in the Nuba Mountains remains particularly difficult, although since May 1993 some improvement has been reported; during the years 1990–94 a large number of cases of harassment of ordinary Christian citizens, as well as church personnel, were reported and well documented, as were cases where the right to freedom of religion was violated.

A diary kept from 1992 to 1994 by a resident of El Obeid, Kordofan, illustrates how the counterinsurgency war has shattered the lives of Nubans and southerners. The diary tells of the forced displacement of large numbers of people pushed out of the Nuba Mountains, northern Bahr el-Ghazal, and southern Kordofan by the counterinsurgency campaign, relocation of civilians without any provision whatsoever for housing or food, the government's forced recruitment of boys as young as ten, the destruction of churches, summary executions of displaced persons by soldiers, allegations of abuse of women in the government's centers for the displaced in Nuba areas called "Peace Camps," abduction of children, possibly for transfer out of the region and the country, manipulation of relief for Islamic proselytization purposes, cheating seasonal southern agricultural workers out of their wages by accusing them of sympathy for the SPLA, and many other abuses, including SPLA looting.

Reshaping the Law

The law has been radically reshaped in the important areas of apostasy, discrimination against Sudanese citizens on grounds of gender and religion, among other things.

Apostasy

In *shari'a*, the crime of apostasy, the repudiation by a Muslim of his faith in Islam, is punishable by death. This punishment was not explicitly codified as part of the Islamic *hudud* punishments when they were first introduced by former President Nimeiri in the 1983 Penal Code. It was nevertheless enforced in the case of Mahmoud Mohamed Taha by way of judicial construction of section 458(3) of the Penal Code, which stated that the lack of legislative provision does not preclude the imposition of any *hudud* punishment. This was a flagrant violation of the requirements of Article 15 (1) of the ICCPR:

> No one shall be held guilty of any criminal offense on account of any act or omission which did not constitute a criminal offense, under national or international law, at the time when it was committed. Nor shall a heavier penalty be imposed than the one that was applicable at the time when the criminal offense was committed. If, subsequent to the commission of the offense, provision is made by law for the imposition of the lighter penalty, the offender shall benefit thereby.

Thus the execution of Taha on January 18, 1985, not only violated the fundamental right of freedom of belief and conscience, but also due process of law, and clearly illustrated the inherently vague and arbitrary nature of the crime of apostasy. Taha was in fact executed for his political opposition to the Nimeiri regime, and not for his beliefs and views on Islamic reform that he had held and advocated openly since the early 1950s.

Section 126 of the 1991 Penal Code now expressly mandates the death penalty for apostasy that "is committed by any Muslim who advocates apostasy from Islam or openly declares his [her] own apostasy expressly or by categorical action." Unless an apostate recants his apostasy within the time stipulated by the court, the Penal Code mandates execution except where the apostate is a recent convert to Islam.

Although the definition of the offense of apostasy does not exempt a recent convert from conviction, the Code does not specify the punishment for recent converts. Presumably, that determination is left to the discretion of the court, which has the power to impose any punishment it deems fit according to the *shari'a* principle of *ta'zir* (reforming the offender) when no specific punishment is provided for by law.

The apostasy provision is open to abuse. The death penalty may be imposed for what the court deems to amount to repudiation of belief in Islam, regardless of the actual beliefs of the accused.

The provision is also open to political manipulation. As illustrated by the case of Taha, political or religious opposition by a Muslim that questions the government's interpretation of Islam or its establishment of a *shari'a* state can be construed as opposition to the "law of God," and warranting the death penalty as "constructive" repudiation of belief in Islam.

Section 126 of the 1991 Penal Code violates freedom of belief even under a most restrictive interpretation. It gives the government's interpretation of Islamic principle an absolute status, preventing Sudanese from freely exchanging views within an Islamic framework and from holding and changing personal beliefs. This contravenes Article 18 of the ICCPR, to which Sudan is a party.

The status of women

The NIF regime is committed to an interpretation of *shari'a* law that is particularly repressive and discriminatory against women, in violation of internationally recognized standards of human rights.

The regime's practice at the present time, however, is not fully consistent with its own declared ideological position and legal system in that a few women are appointed to high-ranking office and there are some instances of women's participation in public life. These exceptions, however, should not be allowed to hide the fact that the vast majority of Sudanese women suffer systematic discrimination, repression, and degradation every day simply because of their status as women.

Thus, during the early purges following the 1989 coup, thousands of women were dismissed from their jobs in accordance with statements of President al-Bashir, who described the ideal Sudanese woman as one who took care of herself and her reputation, cared for her husband and her children, did her household duties, and was a devout Muslim.

Following the 1989 coup, the rights of women in public life and employment began to be restricted. In Khartoum state, a number of decrees and local orders were issued to control women's appearance and behavior in public: Decree number 47 of 1989, for example, prohibits women from working in coffee and cafeteria premises. Public Transportation Regulation Order number 78 of 1991 requires women to take the back seats in transport to avoid sitting in front of men. Section 11 of a 1991 Public Order Decree requires anyone dealing with the public to separate men and women, and section 17 forbids women from selling food or tea after 5:00 p.m.

In December 1991, the governor of Khartoum decreed that Sudanese women should appear in public only in dress that meets public standards of decency, which was later defined by an all-male committee as a requirement to cover the entire body and head with loose opaque garments and forbidding trousers.

The Popular Police Force Act of 1992 gives wide-ranging powers to those appointed to serve as the guardians of morality, including the Public Order Police, Popular Police Forces, Popular Committees, and members of the officially-sanctioned Guardians of Morality civic group. Determination of what constitutes an offense to public morality or offends the public feeling enough to warrant arrest is almost always made by men untrained in law. A Khartoum-based Public Order official interviewed in November 1993 said that in the previous year his office had charged 150 women with "scandalous conduct" and 271 with "immodest dress" under the Popular Police Force Act of 1992. Another fifty were charged with practicing marginal economic professions such as the sale of tea, and thirty-eight women were lashed for this offense, mostly southerners.

A young Sudanese woman described her January 1, 1991, experience:

> On first January 1991, when I was on my way to the university about 8 o'clock p.m., I stopped . . . waiting for the bus. I was wearing white trousers and a white shirt. A police officer came to me and asked me about my nationality. I told him that I'm a Sudanese and showed him my identity card. He claimed that if I were a Sudanese, I would not wear such clothes because, as he claimed, they were not Sudanese clothes. I told him that there are no specific dresses for Sudanese women and that there are many Sudanese women wearing trousers. He said that the country is in the state of Islamic orientation. I told him that the Islamic dress would be applied after six months but not now. He took me to the police station of Nasser's Extension.
>
> There in the station I saw another officer and a police man to register my words. In addition there were two security men. The police man asked me to apologize so as to diffuse tensions. I told him I did no wrong and I did not know of the application of this law. The two officers were looking at me and laughing loudly.

An officer asked her whether anti-epilepsy medicine she had in her purse were birth control pills; both officers looked at her and commented about her body. One of them suggested they take off her trousers to identify her sex. They berated her and laughed, taking her to a dirty cell, and threatening her with sexual abuse:

The officer was laughing and repeating words I will never forget; I sat on the ground crying.

The chief officer came in and talked to me politely about the Islamic veil. . . . He actually wanted me to pay the cost of releasing me in bed. Of course I refused . . . He asked me to choose between his demand and going to the court. Of course he took me to the southern court in the Khartoum police station. In the court the judge asked [me] to agree [with] the officers [and plead guilty]. They showed me many women – prostitutes and sellers of local beer – and [the police were] hitting them. I fell to the ground and fainted.

When she recovered, the judge asked her again to agree with the charges, but when she persisted in her refusal he changed his tone and became very harsh, asking her why she wore such dress under the umbrella of Islamic rule.

She was sentenced to be lashed, a sentence that was carried out immediately.

They took the shirt off my back and then lashed me. When I kept silent and [was] not affected, the judge said I defied him and ordered them to lash me in excess.

Finally, he asked me whether my father and brothers knew that I wear trousers. I told him that they knew. Then he damned my father and brothers. He said that if I showed myself to him again, he would arrest me for six months.

The special rapporteur on human rights in Sudan noted several laws which contained provisions discriminating against women on account of their sex, so notably that, with regard to witnessing a marriage contract and to *hudud* offenses, the testimony of a woman is not equal to that of a man.

He also observed that

together with children, the people most affected by the phenomenon of displacement all over the Sudan are the women. A striking example is the fact that the majority of the women in Omdurman prison are women from the south convicted of

brewing, possessing or selling alcohol on the streets of Khartoum or around the camps for displaced persons. Sentenced to imprisonment and fines which they cannot pay for activities which for them are the only means of earning a miserable existence, these women are likely to become regular inmates of these prisons. It is to be noted that before the prohibition of alcohol there were only a few female inmates in this prison.

The main prison for women is in Omdurman, with another temporary one in Kober. In 1991 and 1992, women in Kober prison lived and slept in the open; that temporary prison is reportedly now closed.

Omdurman Prison for Women holds hundreds more than it was designed to hold. In late 1992, a social worker who visited the prison estimated that 700 women were there, northerners and southerners, with 200 children. Another study later in the year found the total number of women in Omdurman Prison was 825; the majority were convicts from the south and Nuba Mountains, 35.7 percent and 32.3 percent, respectively, of the women's prison population. Over 60 percent of the women prisoners were illiterate, and 58 percent had been convicted for liquor law violations.

Non-Muslims

Non-Muslims in Sudan continue to hold a tenuous position under a regime that has declared its intention of building an Islamic state according to its version of Islam, which discriminates against non-Muslim citizens in the most fundamental ways. Non-Muslims are theoretically excluded, for example, from high-level government office, the judiciary, the military, and any position in which a non-Muslim would exercise authority over a Muslim. More restrictions and discrimination apply to believers in non-scriptural religions than to Christians and Jews, but even the status of the latter groups is totally inconsistent with the requirements of international human rights law.

As in the case of women, the regime's practice at the present time is not fully consistent with its own declared ideological position and legal system, in that a few non-Muslims are appointed to high office and there are some instances of non-Muslim participation in public life. The vast majority of non-Muslim Sudanese, however, suffer systematic discrimination, repression, and degradation every day simply because of their status as non-Muslims.

The Khartoum area alone is populated by nearly two million displaced southerners, most of whom practice their traditional African religions and tens of thousands of Arab Copts and other Christians. In the Nuba Mountains there are hundreds of thousands who practice traditional African religions or Christianity as well as various forms of Islam. Non-Muslim Sudanese are not only subjected to *hudud* criminal punishments that are alien to their religion and culture, but also suffer various discriminatory and repressive policies.

Restrictions on Sudanese Christian churches date back to the Foreign Missionary Society Act of 1962, which treats churches as foreign rather than domestic entities and forbids the construction of churches without government permits. Repeatedly, authorities in many areas have refused to issue building permits for churches and church centers. In contrast, Muslim groups are not subject to these limitations, and mosques and Islamic centers are freely constructed.

The protestant Sudan Council of Churches and the Sudan Catholic Bishops' Conference regularly protest the discrimination against their membership, including the continuous relocation of the displaced persons, the privileges given to Islamic relief organizations in contrast to the tight limitations on Christian church relief activities, the harassment of non-Muslim citizens by the Popular Police Force, and the lack of equality in religious matters.

In late 1991, two bishops and two diocesan administrators issued a pastoral letter to encourage Christian resistance to recent acts against Church institutions and pastoral agents; in particular, the letter supported Christian sit-ins in the town of Ad-Damazin where the state tried to confiscate Church land and expel pastors. The central security administration on January 13, 1992, claimed that the letter violated national security and provoked civil strife, and ordered the bishops to hand over all copies of the letter. The signatory bishops, including Archbishop Gabriel Wako of Khartoum, were called to a meeting with security officers in Khartoum on January 15.

In the north and transition zones, the Sudan Council of Churches' efforts to deliver humanitarian relief are impeded. All missionary personnel were expelled from South Kordofan, and mass arrests and torture of local priests and catechists occurred in 1992. The Sudan Catholic Bishops' Conference condemned the open attack by the government on Christian churches, denial of the right of association and religion, and a "monumental and all-pervading security system which controls all aspects of public and personal life."

Note

Detailed notes and sources related to the above text can be found at *http://www.hrw.org*, following links to Africa and Sudan.

An Update on Human Rights Developments in Sudan (2000)

Despite openings in the political arena, the human rights situation in Sudan was grim. The government kept in force a state of emergency to suppress Islamist and other opposition to the ruling Islamist party. It was increasingly aggressive in pursuing the eighteen-year civil war, particularly in southern oil fields where its militias and army forcibly displaced thousands of residents. The war reflected a failure among Sudanese to agree on the role of religion in government, tolerance of diversity, and sharing of resources between the marginalized majority and the politically dominant Arab–Muslim minority. As Sudan comprised 35 million people divided into nineteen major African and Arab ethnic groups, about 70 percent Muslim and the rest Christian and traditional believers, lack of tolerance was an invitation to strife.

President Omar El Bashir's ruling National Congress (NC) party won the December 2000 presidential and legislative elections, which were boycotted by all the main opposition parties and excluded those living in rebel-held areas. That month the government amended the National Security Act permitting suspects to be detained indefinitely without charge and denied judicial review for up to six months. It extended the state of emergency through a second year, until December 31, 2001.

In late December 2000, security forces arrested seven civilian members of the opposition National Democratic Alliance (NDA) while they met with a US diplomat. The NDA had not registered a political party registration required an oath of allegiance to the ruling party's goals. The NDA civilians in Khartoum had ties to the military wing of the NDA, operating from exile, but their presence and low-key meetings in Khartoum were usually ignored by the authorities, who sought to woo the entire organization and its component parties back from exile. Charges of treason (carrying the death penalty) and threatening the existing government were brought against the NDA members. Defense lawyers protested numerous violations of fair trial rights.

Government opponents in the People's National Congress (PNC), a NC splinter party founded by Islamist political leader Hassan Turabi in 2000, were also harassed and jailed, but not charged with any crime.

In February 2001, Turabi signed a memorandum of understanding with the rebel Sudan People's Liberation Movement/Army (SPLM/A), and called on Sudanese to rise against El Bashir. Security forces arrested Turabi and at least twenty other PNC leaders. Turabi was charged with crimes punishable by death or life imprisonment, and authorities periodically rounded up PNC members.

After September 11, the Sudan government dismissed the charges against the NDA members, Turabi, and other PNC members, and freed all but Turabi – who remained under house arrest. Some thirty-five PNC activists were rearrested at their post-release press conference.

Reports of torture and ill-treatment continued. A Sudatel employee fleeing the July 2001 SPLA capture of Raga reportedly was beaten daily and was given little food or water after his detention by government forces. Security forces reportedly pulled out the fingernails of another man detained during the same exodus. Security forces in Juba reportedly continued to use a large metal shipping container as a detention cell, a years-long practice that subjected detainees to life-threatening heat.

The two English-language newspapers in Khartoum, *Khartoum Monitor* and *Nile Courier,* provided a political forum for southerners. The *Khartoum Monitor* was periodically suspended by security forces or by the Press National Council, however, and on April 12, 2001, security forces briefly detained its editor-in-chief Alfred Taban at a church-called news conference. In February 2001, a Sudanese court fined the independent *Al Rai Al Akhar* newspaper an astounding US $390,000, and fined the editor and a journalist another $5,800 or three months in jail each, for libeling local government. A government censor was permanently based in all newspaper offices. Censorship of English-language newspapers was tightened during the visit of the ACP–EU mission, and papers were forbidden to publish blank spaces indicating where censorship was imposed.

The government harassed and discriminated against Christians. In April 2001, police injured and briefly detained Christians demonstrating against a government order transferring an Easter service (convoked by a visiting German evangelist) from Khartoum to a suburb. The following day police teargassed students protesting these arrests outside All Saints' Episcopal church, then stormed the protest meeting inside the church, damaging windows and chairs, and tear-gassing the interior; three were seriously injured and fifty-seven arrested on this second day of disturbances. They had no legal representation at their trial the following day, which lasted less than one hour. The six girls detained and several boys were flogged; the rest were sentenced to twenty days in jail each.

Half of the Omdurman headquarters of the Episcopal Church of Sudan was illegally occupied by the ministry of health of Khartoum State, which continued its two-year battle to take over the other half of this church's freehold plot. Churches complained that Christian students undergoing obligatory military training in camps near Khartoum were denied their right to worship, in contrast to Muslim students. The law against apostasy – banning Muslims from conversion to another religion – was enforced on several occasions. In June 2001, security arrested an alleged convert to Christianity and held him incommunicado for three months, while reportedly torturing him and demanding that he reconvert to Islam.

In the north, destitute southern women continued to brew and sell traditional southern alcoholic drinks, for which they were arrested. More than nine hundred women were held in the Women's Prison in Omdurman (designed for two hundred) as of December 2000 in grossly poor conditions. The prison also housed southern women with twenty-year sentences for dealing in cannabis, and women sentenced, sometimes for indeterminate periods, for financial crimes.

On June 23, 2001, the authorities raided a workshop on "Democracy and Gender Issues" organized by the Gender Centre in Khartoum. Four speakers were arrested and released the same night. All participants in the workshop were interrogated about their political affiliations and their addresses were taken.

The most severe abuses occurred in the civil war fought in the south, the central Nuba Mountains, and the east. The Sudan government and its ethnic militias continued to displace, starve, abduct, rape, and kill civilians outright – while burning, and bombing, villages, churches, hospitals, and schools.

The rebel-held Nuba Mountains were hit especially hard in 2001. In May 2001, the government attacked the region, bombing extensively and burning down six villages, resulting in the displacement of more than 15,000 people. According to the Nuba relief office, an estimated 400,000 people were in SPLA-controlled territory as of June 2001, cut off from rest of rebel-held Sudan, with the lives of more than 50,000 displaced and 30,000 others unable to harvest crops at risk because of government attacks. The government persistently denied humanitarian access to civilians in the SPLA-held Nuba Mountains, through flight denials and shelling of airstrips used for unapproved relief deliveries. After years of negotiations, the UN in October 2001 succeeded in making the first-ever delivery there of relief with government permission. Another month of delivery was promised by the government, with no guarantee of access on an as-needed basis.

Following the brief capture of Kassala in eastern Sudan by opposition NDA forces (mostly SPLA) in November 2000, security forces arrested and reportedly tortured hundreds of southerners living in Kassala, in some cases extrajudicially executing them, according to the exiled Sudan Human Rights Organization.

Oil exploration and development in concession areas in Upper Nile exacerbated the conflict, with continuing displacement of civilians. Some 40,000–55,000 Nuer were displaced from the oilfields in the first half of 2001, according to two different reports, by government and its Nuer militias which were fighting the SPLA and its Nuer commanders. Often fighting resulted from government efforts to claim and to clear the people from the land, using its Nuer militias to push fellow Nuer out of the oilfields. More dependable government soldiers and *mujaheeden* then guarded construction equipment for roads, pipelines, drilling, and other oil infrastructure. Each oil facility was given a twenty-four hour guard of soldiers; up to four hundred soldiers were at Timsa, a location attacked by the SPLA in early 2001. The government imposed a long-term relief flight ban on most oil field areas in inaccessible Western Upper Nile (except for garrison towns), making the situation for civilians there even more acute.

Government use of new, heavier arms, including surface-to-surface missiles and helicopter gunships, and high-altitude Antonov bombing of southern and Nuba operations took a toll on the civilian population. Government aerial bombing destroyed the Episcopal Cathedral in Lui, Eastern Equatoria on December 29, 2000. Despite government pledges to stop bombing civilians and civilian structures, more bombing raids occurred: Tali, a center for relief food distribution in Eastern Equatoria, was bombed three times in December 2000, twice in January 2001, and again in May 2001. In June 2001, government Antonovs bombed three towns in Bahr El Ghazal, including one in which a World Food Program (WFP) relief operation was underway. Such attacks targeting relief deliveries in progress were increasing. Although bombing seemed to decline in September 2001, government planes bombed the little civilian village of Mangayat, twenty-five miles outside of rebel-held Raga in October on three different days, while WFP deliveries were in progress to aid an estimated 20,000 displaced people. The WFP gave up its attempt to distribute food.

Although the government of Sudan signed the 1997 Mine Ban Treaty, it did not ratify it and had not begun to destroy its stockpiled antipersonnel land mines. There were strong indications that both government and rebel forces in Sudan continued to use antipersonnel mines, but the government denied its forces did so. In October 2001, the SPLA signed an agreement at an NGO conference in Geneva to ban the use, production, storage, or transfer of antipersonnel land mines in its territory. Small arms and ammunition were produced by three new arms factories near Khartoum in partnership with Chinese companies, using government oil revenue.

Recruitment of boys aged sixteen and seventeen into the Popular Defence Force, a government Islamist militia, proceeded as government policy, and occasional press-gangs seized even younger children for this military service. The government-backed ethnic militias also recruited child soldiers in the south, sometimes forcibly, as did rebel groups. The SPLA admitted in 2000 it had about 10,000 child soldiers. Following an agreement with the SPLA, in February 2001 UNICEF began demobilizing some 3,000 SPLA child soldiers from northern Bahr El Ghazal. The children were disarmed and given schooling in transition camps, and by late August returned to their villages of origin. Some NGOs questioned the effectiveness of the program because, with no real job or school opportunities, the demobilized boys were likely to go back to the SPLA to survive. In late October, UNICEF said it was ready for another phase of demobilization, involving 1,000 children. The SPLA said it still had more than 7,000 child soldiers within its ranks.

Government army and militia forces continued to abduct women and children during ongoing raids in the south, mostly in northern Bahr El Ghazal and often in connection with the military train they accompanied to Wau, a garrison town. The Committee to Eradicate the Abduction of Women and Children (CEAWC), created by the government, was ineffective: the government admitted that abductors, even from among their own forces, were seldom prosecuted, although it announced in November 2001 its intention to set up a tribunal to try the abductors. UNICEF said 670 children were reunited with their families and 270 retrieved children were in CEAWC transit facilities, but retrievals had stalled. The Geneva-based solidarity organization Christian Solidarity International (CSI) claimed that between 1995 and 2001 it had "bought back" 56,000 enslaved Sudanese during sporadic CSI visits to SPLA territory. CSI estimated that there were an additional 200,000 enslaved in northern Sudan. (The CSI estimates doubled from 100,000 in 2000, without explanation.)

The Sudan government stopped supplying the Lord's Resistance Army (LRA), a Ugandan rebel group with a horrendous human rights record, in 2001 pursuant to an agreement with Uganda. The LRA subsequently began forcibly looting food from southern Sudanese, thousands of whom took refuge in Nimele and in northern Ugandan refugee camps. An LRA ambush on a relief agency vehicle traveling from northern Uganda to southern Sudan killed six Sudanese.

The SPLA openly opposed a broadening of civil society when it prevented civilians in its territory from attending two south-south peace and reconciliation conferences convened by the New Sudan Council of Churches (NSCC) in 2001. The NSCC and others condemned the SPLA's violations of freedom of movement, association, and speech. The Africa–Caribbean–Pacific–European Union (ACP–EU) mission noted that the SPLA's record on human rights was "far from being acceptable." The UN special rapporteur also criticized the SPLA.

In late February 2001, Nuer SPLA commander Peter Gatdet attacked and set fire to Nyal in Western Upper Nile, the base of the Riek Machar Nuer faction and a UN relief hub. The SPLA sponsored the attack. The US government forcefully condemned the attack. Abuses proliferated as the forces of Nuer leader Riek Machar, lacking material support, allied themselves alternatively with the government or the SPLA, and sought to reestablish their control over their home territory.

Note

Detailed notes and sources related to the above text can be found at http://www.hrw.org, following links to Africa and Sudan.

14

Afghanistan
Human Rights Watch

- ◆ War in Afghanistan – historical background ◆
- ◆ Religious aspects ◆
- ◆ Legal conduct of military campaign in Afghanistan post-September 11 ◆

The US-led military intervention in Afghanistan marks the fourth phase in the country's twenty-three year-old civil war. In every phase foreign powers have intensified the conflict by supporting one side against another.

The First Phase: The Saur Revolution and Soviet Occupation

Before civil war erupted in 1978, Afghanistan was a monarchy under Muhammad Zahir Shah, who had come to power in 1933. After World War II, both the US and the Soviet Union used economic assistance to compete for influence. After the US established military ties with Pakistan in 1954, Afghanistan increasingly turned to the Soviet Union support. In 1964 Zahir Shah convened a Loya Jirga, or Grand Council, of tribal leaders to debate a draft constitution that would provide for a more representational government. However, Zahir Shah did not relinquish any power; political parties were permitted to organize but not to contest elections. Zahir Shah was overthrown by his cousin Daoud Khan in 1973; the king has remained in exile in Rome

ever since. In staging the coup, Daoud had allied himself with the Parcham faction of the People's Democratic Party of Afghanistan (PDPA), a Marxist–Leninist party that had been formed in 1965. In 1967 the PDPA split into two factions, Parcham ("flag") which drew its support from urban, educated Pashtuns along with other ethnic groups, and Khalq ("masses") which had the support of educated rural Afghans, also predominantly Pashtun. Pashtuns comprise the largest ethnic group in Afghanistan and have dominated the government for centuries. Other major ethnic groups in Afghanistan include Tajiks, Hazaras and Uzbeks. [For more on Afghanistan's ethnic groups, see Human Rights Watch backgrounder, *Armed Conflict Poses Risk of Further Ethnic Violence*.] After gaining power, Daoud tried to marginalize the Parchamis and distance the government from the Soviet Union. The two factions of the PDPA reunited in 1977 and launched a coup on April 27, 1978, killing Daoud and seizing power. The PDPA government, under Khalq leadership, then embarked on a campaign of radical land reform accompanied by mass repression in the countryside that resulted in the arrest and summary execution of tens of thousands. Those targeted included political figures, religious leaders, teachers, students, other professionals, Islamist organizations, and members of ethnic minorities, particularly the Hazaras, a Shi'a minority that has long been subject to discrimination by Afghanistan's ruling elite. The government's repressive measures, particularly its attempt to reform rural society through terror, provoked uprisings throughout the country. Alarmed by the deteriorating situation, especially the collapse of the army and the prospect that a disintegrating Afghanistan would threaten its security on its southern border, the Soviet Union airlifted thousands of troops into Kabul on December 24, 1979. The Khalq president, Hafizullah Amin, was assassinated after Soviet intelligence forces took control of the government and installed Babrak Karmal, a Parchami, as president. The Soviet occupation force of some 115,000 troops and the Karmal government sought to crush the uprisings with mass arrests, torture, and executions of dissidents, and aerial bombardments and executions in the countryside. Some one million Afghans died during this period, most in aerial bombardments. These measures further expanded the resistance to the communist government in Kabul and fueled a flow of refugees out of the country that soon reached five million out of a population of about sixteen million. Islamist organizations that became the heart of the resistance – and collectively became known as the jihad fighters or *mujahidin* – based themselves in Pakistan and Iran. Seeing the conflict as a cold war battleground, the United States and Saudi Arabia, in particular, provided massive support for the resistance, nearly all of it funneled through Pakistan. The arms pipeline gave Pakistan a tremendous ability to bolster parties in Afghanistan that would serve its own interests. Joining the resistance forces were thousands of Muslim radicals from the Middle East, North Africa and other Muslim countries. Most fought with Pashtun factions that had the strongest support from Pakistan and Saudi Arabia, the

Hizb-i Islami of Gulbuddin Hikmatyar and Ittihad-i Islami of Abdul Rasul Sayyaf. Among them was Osama bin Laden, who came to Pakistan in the early 1980s and built training facilities for these foreign recruits inside Afghanistan.

The Second Phase: From the Geneva Accords to the Mujahidin's Civil War

Negotiations to end the war culminated in the 1988 Geneva Accords, whose centerpiece was an agreement by the Soviet Union to remove all its uniformed troops by February 1989. With substantial Soviet assistance, the communist government held on to power through early 1992 while the United Nations frantically tried to assemble a transitional process acceptable to all the parties. It failed. In the aftermath, the US and its allies abandoned any further efforts toward a peace process until after the Taliban came to power. The UN effort continued. but suffered from the lack of international engagement on Afghanistan. Donor countries, including the US, continued to support the relief effort, but as the war dragged on, aid donor fatigue and the need to respond to other humanitarian crises left the assistance effort in Afghanistan chronically short. In early 1992, the forces of Tajik leader Ahmed Shah Massoud, Gen. Abdul Rashid Dostum, head of a powerful Uzbek militia that had been allied with Najibullah, and the Hazara faction Hizb-i Wahdat, joined together in a coalition they called the Northern Alliance. On April 15, non-Pashtun militia forces that had been allied with the government mutinied and took control of Kabul airport, preventing President Najibullah from leaving the country and pre-empting the UN transition. Najibullah took refuge in the UN compound in Kabul, where he remained for the next four years. On April 25, Massoud entered Kabul, and the next day the Northern Alliance factions reached an agreement on a coalition government that excluded the Hizb-i Islami led by Gulbuddin Hikmatyar – the protégé of Pakistan. Rejecting the arrangement, Hikmatyar launched massive and indiscriminate rocket attacks on Kabul that continued intermittently until he was forced out of the Kabul area in February 1995. [For more on the Afghan parties, see Human Rights Watch backgrounder, *Poor Rights Record of Opposition Commanders*]. In June 1992 Burhanuddin Rabbani, the Tajik leader of Jamiat-i Islami, became president of the Islamic State of Afghanistan (ISA), while Hikmatyar continued to bombard Kabul with rockets. In fighting between the Hazara faction, Hizb-i Wahdat, and Sayyaf's Ittihad-i Islami, hundreds of civilians were abducted and killed. After ensuring that the governing council (*shura*) was stacked with his supporters, Rabbani was again elected president in December 1992. In January 1994, Hikmatyar joined forces with Gen. Abdul Rashid Dostum, head of a powerful Uzbek militia that had been allied with Najibullah until early 1992, to oust Rabbani and his defense minister, Ahmad Shah Massoud, launching full-scale civil war in Kabul. In 1994 alone, an estimated 25,000 were killed in Kabul, most of them civilians killed in rocket and artillery attacks. By 1995, one-third of the city had been reduced to rubble.

The Third Phase: The Taliban's Conquest of Afghanistan

During this period, the rest of the country was carved up among the various factions, with many mujahidin commanders establishing themselves as local warlords. Humanitarian agencies frequently found their offices stripped, their vehicles hijacked, and their staff threatened. It was against this background that the Taliban emerged. Former mujahidin who were disillusioned with the chaos that had followed their victory became the nucleus of a movement that coalesced around Mullah Mohammad Omar, a former mujahid from Qandahar province. The group, many of whom were *madrasa* (Islamic school) students, called themselves *taliban*, meaning students. Many others who became core members of the group were commanders in other predominantly Pashtun parties, and former Khalqi PDPA members. Their stated aims were to restore stability and enforce (their interpretation of) Islamic law. They successfully attacked local warlords and soon gained a reputation for military prowess, and acquired an arsenal of captured weaponry. By October 1994 the movement had attracted the support of Pakistan, which saw in the Taliban a way to secure trade routes to Central Asia and establish a government in Kabul friendly to its interests. Pakistani traders who had long sought a secure route to send their goods to Central Asia quickly became some of the Taliban's strongest financial backers. In September 1995, the Taliban took control of Herat, thereby cutting off the land route connecting the Islamic State of Afghanistan with Iran. The Taliban's innovative use of mobile warfare appeared to indicate that Pakistan had provided vital assistance for the capture of Herat. In September 1996, the Taliban took control of Kabul after Massoud was forced to retreat to the north. Sometime after Massoud's loss of Kabul, he began to obtain military assistance from Russia as well as Iran. The Northern Alliance was reconstituted in opposition to the Taliban. Osama bin Laden, who had left Afghanistan in 1990, returned in 1996, living first under the protection of the Jalalabad *shura* (tribal council), until the Taliban took control of Jalalabad and Kabul. In 1997 bin Laden moved to Qandahar where he developed a close relationship to Mullah Muhammad Omar, the head of the Taliban. His fighters fought alongside Taliban troops. In 1997, the Taliban renamed the country the Islamic Emirate of Afghanistan; Mullah Omar assumed the title *amir-ul momineen* (commander of the faithful). In areas under their control, Taliban authorities enforced their version of Islamic law, enacting policies prohibiting women from working outside the home in activities other than health care, and requiring corporal punishment for those convicted of certain crimes. They prohibited women from attending universities and closed girls' schools in Kabul and some other cities, although primary schools for girls continued to operate in many other areas of the country under Taliban control. The Taliban also enforced a strict dress code for women, and required men to have beards and to refrain from Western haircuts or dress. Arguably the most powerful agency within the Islamic Emirate of Afghanistan, as the Taliban renamed the country, was the Ministry of Promotion of Virtue and Prevention of Vice, which was responsible for the enforcement of all Taliban decrees regarding moral behavior. Through 1997 and 1998, the Taliban made repeated attempts to extend their control to the north of Afghanistan, where Dostum had carved out what amounted to a mini-state comprising five provinces which he administered from his headquarters in Shiberghan, west of the important city of Mazar-i Sharif. In Mazar-i Sharif, Dostum's forces controlled the city through an uneasy alliance with Hizb-i Wahdat, which had a stronghold in the large Hazara population in Mazar-i Sharif. On May 19, 1997, one of Dostum's deputies, Gen. Abdul Malik Pahlawan (generally known as "Malik"), who had a grievance against Dostum, struck an agreement with the Taliban and arrested a number of Dostum's commanders and as many as 5,000 of his soldiers. As the Taliban entered Mazar-i Sharif, Pakistan was quick to seize the opportunity to recognize the Taliban as the government of Afghanistan, as was Saudi Arabia and the United Arab Emirates. But the alliance with Malik quickly disintegrated when the Taliban attempted to disarm local Hazaras. Hundreds of Taliban soldiers were killed in the streets of Mazar-i Sharif, and some 3,000 were taken prisoner

by Malik, and allegedly also by Hizb-i Wahdat, and summarily executed. In August 1998 Taliban finally took control of Mazar-i Sharif and massacred at least 2,000 people, most of them Hazara civilians, after they took the city. In the aftermath, Dostum left Afghanistan for exile in Turkey; Malik also fled and has reportedly lived in exile in Iran since 1997. Shortly after taking control of Mazar-i Sharif, the Taliban took control of the town of Bamian, in the Hazara-dominated central highlands. Some time after this the erstwhile Northern Alliance enlisted the support of factions from outside their ethnic constituencies, including the Council of the East, a Pashtun group led by formers members of the Jalalabad *shura* (council), and renamed themselves the United Islamic Front for the Salvation of Afghanistan, or United Front, for short. Rabbani remained the president of the Islamic State of Afghanistan. Dostum continues to command forces within the United Front; as does Muhammad Karim Khalili, head of Hizb-i Wahdat. Harakat-i Islami, another Shi'a party with significant Hazara support, is also part of the United Front. Sayyaf retains a leadership position within the United Front; many of his forces are believed to have joined the Taliban. In August 1998, the United States launched air strikes against bin Laden's reputed training camps near the Pakistan border. The strikes came in the wake of the bombings of the US embassies in Nairobi and Dar es-Salaam. In October 1999 the U.N. imposed sanctions on the Taliban to turn over bin Laden, banning Taliban-controlled aircraft from takeoff and landing and freezing the Taliban's assets abroad. The Taliban's failure to hand over bin Laden led to an expansion of the sanctions regime on December 19, 2000, including an arms embargo on the Taliban, a ban on travel outside Afghanistan by Taliban officials of deputy ministerial rank, and the closing of Taliban offices abroad. Through 2000 and 2001, fighting continued in the northeast between Massoud's forces and the Taliban, with the Taliban taking control of Taloqan in September 2000, and driving the United Front further east to Faizabad. Fighting in the area, combined with the effects of a severe drought across the country, drove thousands of civilians into relief camps and into Pakistan. In the central province of Bamian, the forces of Hizb-i Wahdat and Harakat-i Islami, briefly took control of the town of Yakaolang in late December 2000, but lost it to the Taliban on January 8, 2001. After retaking the town, the Taliban massacred at least 178 civilians in reprisal. The town changed hands several times between January and June; during their last retreat from the area, Taliban troops burned down the town and many other villages in the district. In early 2001, Dostum returned to Afghanistan to meet with Massoud; his forces resumed guerrilla operations against the Taliban in mid-2001. At about the same time, the forces of Ismael Khan, the former Jamiat-i Islami governor of Herat who escaped from Taliban custody in 2000, also undertook guerrilla action against the Taliban in the center-west of the country. On September 9, 2001, Massoud was assassinated when suicide bombers disguised as journalists detonated a device hidden in a video camera. United Front leaders have claimed that the assassins were linked to bin Laden, and many observers believe that the assassination was designed to deprive the United Front of its most effective leader in the aftermath of the September 11 attacks on the World Trade Center and the Pentagon.

Legal Issues Arising from the War in Afghanistan and Related Anti-Terrorism Efforts

The horrific attacks of September 11, 2001 on the World Trade Center and the Pentagon that claimed the lives of thousands of civilians constituted criminal acts under both United States and international law. In particular, as acts of murder

committed deliberately as part of a widespread attack against a civilian population, they constitute crimes against humanity which can be prosecuted by any nation on earth. Chief among suspected perpetrators is Osama bin Laden, a Saudi exile in Afghanistan, who is said to have inspired, organized, trained and bankrolled a network of militants. Allegedly included in this network are groups dedicated to covert attacks on US targets, both military and civilian, as well as armed forces affiliated with bin Laden that operate under the overall command of Taliban armed forces in Afghanistan.

In response, a US-led military force has now attacked Taliban armed forces and targets associated with bin Laden and his network. This new international conflict comes on top of a longstanding civil, or internal, war between the Taliban and a group of opposing military forces known as the United Front or the Northern Alliance.

As this paper explains, governments may not use unlimited methods and means to pursue war, even a war against indistinct enemies. International humanitarian law, also known as the "laws of war," is designed, in principal part, to protect civilians and other non-combatants. Warring forces must distinguish combatants from non-combatants. As discussed below, these forces are required to minimize harm to civilians and civilian facilities and to refrain entirely from attacks that would disproportionately harm the civilian population and from attacks whose effects would be indiscriminate as between combatants and civilians.

Despite the existence of an armed conflict, certain aspects of international human rights law also remain in force. Even in a state of emergency, it is unlawful to suspend some rights, such as the prohibition on arbitrary deprivation of life, the prohibition of torture, freedom of religion, and trial *ex post facto*. Other civil and political freedoms may be derogated in an emergency, but under highly restricted conditions: the derogation must be for a limited period of time, in a way that involves no invidious discrimination, and only to the extent strictly required by an emergency so severe that it threatens the life of the nation.

The two bodies of law – humanitarian and human rights – can simultaneously govern different geographic areas. For example, an armed conflict raging in one country would be governed primarily by humanitarian law while in another country the pursuit of criminal networks through traditional law-enforcement means would be governed by human rights law, with full rights protections regulating the use of force and the fairness of trial, even if those networks had links to one of the parties in the armed conflict in the first country. Whether those who become the targets of the United States and its allies in the emerging anti-terrorism coalition are viewed as criminals or as an enemy in wartime is not merely a rhetorical distinction, since it affects such basic matters as when lethal force can be used. This paper addresses various questions about the requirements of international humanitarian and human rights law and the interplay between the two.

Q: Is the US military response to the September 11 attacks lawful? The question of whether it is lawful to wage war on states that are complicit in or tolerant of acts of terror is a complex one that is engendering considerable debate. See, for example, *http://www.crimesofwar.org* and www.asil.org/insights. The United Nations Charter restricts the use of force by states in their international disputes. Under the Charter, a state may lawfully employ force as a matter of individual or collective self-defense or when authorized by the Security Council to address acts of aggression or other threats to international peace and security.

Human Rights Watch avoids evaluating whether the launching of a given war is either lawful or just, in order to maintain our neutrality and authority in analyzing the way wars are fought under international humanitarian law. Like the International Committee of the Red Cross, our mandate in wartime focuses on the conduct of war, or *jus in bello*, rather than the legitimacy of war, or *jus ad bellum*. The only exceptions that Human Rights Watch has made to this policy is to call for military intervention where massive loss of human life, on the order of genocide, can be halted through no other means, as was the case in Bosnia and Rwanda in the 1990s. This paper addresses *jus in bello* questions under international humanitarian law.

Q: What is international humanitarian law? International humanitarian law governs the conduct of parties to international and internal armed conflicts. It comprises, among other treaties, the four Geneva Conventions of 1949 and their two protocols of 1977, the Hague Conventions of 1907 regulating the means and methods of warfare, and those principles that, because of their wide acceptance by the community of nations, have become customary international law binding on all states and belligerents. For most of the last decade through October 7, 2001, Afghanistan was embroiled in a civil war governed by the laws relating to internal armed conflicts. The US-led military action against Afghanistan beginning on October 7 is governed by the laws of international armed conflict, which provide the strongest and most developed protections to civilians and soldiers alike.

The cornerstone of international humanitarian law is the duty to protect the life, health and safety of civilians and other non-combatants such as soldiers who are wounded or captured or have laid down their arms. It is prohibited, for example, to attack or deliberately injure.

The distinction between combatants and non-combatants is fundamental in international humanitarian law. While it is legitimate under this law to target and use lethal force against enemy combatants and their commanders, it is never legitimate to target civilians and other non-combatants. In addition, as described below, the anticipated harm to noncombatants in any given attack may never be disproportionate to the expected military advantage.

Q: What are some of the main differences between international humanitarian law and international standards on law enforcement? Under the "combatant's privilege," international humanitarian law does not prohibit soldiers from killing enemy combatants – even if the opposing fighters are in retreat – so long as they are not wounded, captured, or otherwise out of combat (*hors de combat*). In contrast, international standards on law enforcement prohibit officers from using lethal force against criminal suspects except where strictly necessary to defend themselves or others from an imminent threat of death or serious injury. Criminal suspects, once in custody, may be prosecuted for any act of violence, whereas captured enemy combatants in international conflicts are normally entitled to specific protections as prisoners of war and may not be tried for their mere participation in hostilities against other combatants, although they may be prosecuted for other offenses, including common crimes, war crimes, and crimes against humanity.

Q: What international humanitarian law governs a war against non-state actors? As noted, the most developed part of international humanitarian law is the law governing armed conflict between states. The hostilities between the forces of the US-led coalition and the Taliban government in Afghanistan fit into this category. The same law governs armed conflict insofar as one government has been joined by a paramilitary organization that has been integrated into the government's armed forces. The military portion of al-Qaeda in Afghanistan, sometimes referred to as the 55th Brigade, appears to have such an integrated relationship with Taliban

military forces. But what law governs potential US efforts to pursue al-Qaeda or other alleged terrorist groups outside of Afghanistan, particularly if they are not integrated into the military forces of a government?

"War," of course, has been invoked rhetorically to describe campaigns against criminal groups such as drug cartels or the Mafia. However, such campaigns in fact are generally coordinated efforts at law enforcement, even where military means are employed, and not the launching of combat operations outside the context of criminal justice. Traditional human rights law applies to such efforts.

However, international humanitarian law does apply to certain armed conflicts between states and non-state actors, such as insurgents in a civil war. The International Committee of the Red Cross, in its Commentaries on Article 3 Common to the four Geneva Conventions of 1949, describes the understanding in this regard of the states that negotiated this provision. They believed, according to the ICRC, that a conflict with a rebel group would amount to an armed conflict governed by international humanitarian law insofar as the group is organized, has a responsible command, acts on a determinate territory, and is capable of respecting and ensuring respect for humanitarian law. As a loose network of individuals and groups said to be operating in some sixty countries, al-Qaeda appears unlikely to meet these requirements, at least outside Afghanistan. Even when military force is used against non-state actors that lack these attributes, Human Rights Watch maintains that the basic principles enshrined in international humanitarian law should still be upheld as a minimum standard. The Commentaries of the International Committee of the Red Cross also state that the fundamental guarantees of Common Article 3 of the 1949 Geneva Conventions would apply even if non-state combatants lacked all the hallmarks of classic rebel forces. Although the ICRC commentary addresses civil wars against insurgents, the same rationale should apply to an international conflict against non-state actors.

Q: Where there's a choice between pursuing criminal suspects through law enforcement or military action, what should the United States or its coalition partners do? As explained above, Human Rights Watch takes no position on the legitimacy or justness of any particular military intervention. However, in the absence of armed conflict against a particular country, Human Rights Watch insists on respect for that country's ordinary criminal justice guarantees so long as law-enforcement cooperation is feasible. Similarly, we oppose governments using military force against an internal enemy when it is feasible to employ available criminal justice remedies. Otherwise, the use of military force effectively subverts criminal justice guarantees such as the rights to life, liberty and a fair trial.

Q: Is it lawful to assassinate persons suspected of terrorist acts? International humanitarian law allows the targeting of opposing troops and commanders – even top commanders – in the course of armed conflict, provided that such attacks otherwise comply with the laws that protect civilians. However, it is a war crime to execute prisoners or to target non-combatants. In situations that fall short of armed conflict, international policing standards are more restrictive. They allow law enforcement agents to use lethal force only to protect themselves and others from the threat of imminent death or serious injury- and not, for example, to kill a suspect fleeing arrest in the absence of such a threat. These rules under international humanitarian and human rights law apply not only to government security forces but also to proxy forces whom they might engage.

Since 1976, successive US presidents have endorsed an executive order banning political assassinations. This order followed revelations of earlier US assassinations and assassination attempts of various world leaders. Consonant with the rules outlined above, this order does not prohibit targeting opposing combatants and their commanders in an armed conflict, and it does not prohibit the use of lethal force by law enforcement agents when necessary to avoid imminent death or serious injury. But it rightfully prohibits summary execution in any circumstance and the targeted killing of people (other than combatants in armed conflict) in lieu of invoking available criminal justice remedies.

Q: President Bush said that Osama bin Laden is "wanted, dead or alive." Can the United States put a bounty out for the killing of bin Laden or other suspects? No. The placing of a bounty for anyone's death is an invitation to his extrajudicial execution, which is prohibited.

Q: Can those captured in a war be prosecuted for crimes? What is the effect if they are found to be prisoners of war? Prisoners of war (PoWs) are certain categories of combatants in an international armed conflict who "have fallen into the power of the enemy." They may not be tried for the mere act of being combatants- that is, for taking up arms against other combatants. However, they may be prosecuted for the same offenses for which the forces of the power that detains them could be tried-including common crimes, war crimes, and crimes against humanity. Even if convicted, prisoners of war retain the detailed protections of the Third Geneva Convention of 1949 governing humane treatment.

The United States and its allies have not made clear their intentions with respect to affording PoW status or treatment to every combatant they may capture in Afghanistan. In international conflicts, captured members of a state's armed forces are prisoners of war. Although the Taliban's armed forces control most of Afghanistan, the United States (as well as the United Nations) does not recognize the

Taliban as the legitimate government of the country. In the past, US officials have affirmed the rule of international humanitarian law that if there is any doubt as to whether a captured person is entitled to PoW status, he will be treated as a PoW until a competent tribunal determines otherwise. Given that both the United States and Afghanistan are parties to the Third Geneva Convention governing the treatment of PoWs, both should be bound to respect these treaty provisions regardless of whether they view their opponent's armed forces as commanded by a lawful government.

"Irregular" troops such as volunteers or militia members – including any units affiliated with al-Qaeda – must be treated as PoWs only if they fulfill certain conditions. Under the Third Geneva Convention, those conditions include having a responsible commander, carrying arms openly, having a fixed distinctive sign recognizable at a distance, and conducting military operations in accordance with the laws and customs of war. Again, if questions arise about whether given troops meet these requirements, they should be afforded presumptive PoW status until a competent tribunal makes a determination to the contrary.

The First Additional Protocol to the Geneva Conventions (Protocol I) eased these requirements by allowing troops who as combatants do not bear a fixed, distinctive mark, such as a uniform (so long as they bear their arms openly) still in certain circumstances to be eligible for PoW status. Although some coalition states are parties to Protocol I, the United States is not, and this provision is not considered customary international law that would bind nonparties.

Captured combatants who are found not to meet the requirements for treatment as PoWs are considered to be detainees. Detainees do not receive the protections provided for PoWs; for instance, they may be tried for taking part in hostilities. However, they must be treated as civilians

in custody and are entitled to the protections for such civilians found under international humanitarian and human rights law.

International humanitarian law governing internal armed conflicts does not accord combatants captured by an opposing side PoW status.

Q: For what crimes could those who participated in the September 11 attacks be prosecuted? Persons who planned, aided or abetted the September 11 attacks could be prosecuted by US authorities for the domestic crimes of murder and hijacking. In addition, the hijacking of the planes could constitute offenses under various international terrorism treaties. Finally, these atrocities could be considered crimes against humanity.

Under the most recent definition of crimes against humanity as set forth in the statute of the International Criminal Court, acts such as murder and "other inhumane acts of a similar character intentionally causing great suffering, or serious injury to body or to mental or physical health" qualify as crimes against humanity "when committed as part of a widespread or systematic attack directed against any civilian population, with knowledge of the attack." Human Rights Watch believes that the deliberate hijacking of passenger planes and their use as explosives against office buildings causing some 5,000 deaths [subsequently realised as 3,000] would constitute a "widespread" attack. Although most adjudicated cases address crimes against humanity that were committed in the context of ongoing war and were organized under state authority, recent jurisprudence allows for the commission of such crimes in peacetime and by non-state actors.

Q: Where can suspects be prosecuted? Crimes against humanity, war crimes, and violations of treaties such as the Hague Convention for the Suppression of Unlawful Seizure of Aircraft give rise to universal jurisdiction, meaning that any state may try suspected perpetrators, regardless of the nationality of the suspect or the location of the crime. Whether a state can take advantage of universal jurisdiction depends on whether its domestic law gives such powers to its courts. However, if a state fails to prosecute a suspected perpetrator, it is obligated to extradite the suspect to another state that is willing and able to do so.

The continued existence of the death penalty in United States law has created difficulties in extradition from countries in Europe that have abolished it. Human Rights Watch opposes the death penalty in all forms and notes that the overwhelming trend of state practice is towards abolition. Before extraditing suspects, European countries have typically required assurances from the United States that the death penalty will not be applied, and such assurances have become relatively routine.

Some commentators have suggested an international forum to try those accused of the September 11 attacks. Because these crimes give rise to universal jurisdiction, an international forum could be given jurisdiction. However, because the International Criminal Court has not yet come into being, and by its founding statute has only prospective jurisdiction, it would not be able to take these cases. However, a new international tribunal could be constituted for this purpose. One option would be an ad hoc tribunal created by the U.N. Security Council and patterned on the international tribunals for former Yugoslavia and Rwanda. Another would be an international panel created by all or some of the various states whose citizens were victims of the attack.

Q: Exactly what provisions of international humanitarian law apply to the conflict in Afghanistan? The United States and Afghanistan are both parties to the Geneva Conventions of 1949. They are also bound by those provisions of the laws of war that, through wide state recognition and practice, have become customary inter-

national law. Many NATO and other possible coalition countries are also parties to Protocol I to the Geneva Conventions. Although neither the United States nor Afghanistan is party to Protocol I, the United States recognizes many of its provisions as reflective of customary international law. In addition, by virtue of having signed (but not ratified) Protocol I, the United States is obligated under international law to avoid actions that would undermine the guarantees of that treaty.

Q: What are the restrictions that international law places on targets of attack? A fundamental precept of international humanitarian law is that of "civilian immunity." At all times, it is forbidden to direct attacks against civilians; indeed, to do so intentionally amounts to a grave breach of humanitarian law, or a war crime. It is thus an imperative duty to identify and distinguish non-combatants from combatants in every situation and not to rely on inadequate reconnaissance or intelligence. A notable example of inadequate efforts to make this distinction was the NATO bombing of a refugee convoy on the Djakovica–Decane road in Kosovo during the 1999 air campaign in the mistaken belief that it was a military convoy.

Non-combatants include soldiers who are wounded or captured or otherwise removed from a combat role; however, regular combatants are still legitimate targets of attack even when "off-duty." Civilians lose their protected status when they are engaged in hostilities; however, when they return to civilian life their protection resumes. Political leaders would not be legitimate targets of attack unless their office or direct participation in military hostilities renders them effectively combatants. According to the International Committee of the Red Cross, direct participation in hostilities means "acts of war which by their nature and purpose are likely to cause actual harm to the personnel and equipment of enemy armed forces" and includes acts of defense. Thus, political leaders who are effectively commanders of a state's forces would be legitimate targets, but absent some unusual circumstance, officials of, say, a ministry of education would not.

It is also generally forbidden to direct attacks against what are called "civilian objects," such as homes and apartments, places of worship, hospitals, schools, or cultural monuments, unless they are being used for military purposes. Military objects are those that make an "effective" contribution to military action and whose destruction, capture or neutralization offers a "definite" military advantage. Where there is doubt, the object must be presumed to be civilian.

The mere fact that an object has civilian uses does not necessarily render it immune from attack if it meets the above-noted test: it makes an "effective" contribution to military action and its destruction, capture or neutralization offers a "definite" military advantage. However, such "dual use" objects might also be protected by the principle of proportionality, described below.

Even when a target is serving a military purpose, precautions must always be taken to protect civilians. One such precaution is effective warning of an attack where "circumstances permit" (discussed below). Another is taking steps to avoid attacks that threaten disproportionate harm to civilians – that is, "an attack which may be expected to cause incidental loss of civilian life, injury to civilians, damage to civilian objects, or a combination thereof, which would be excessive in relation to the concrete and direct military advantage anticipated."

Q: But isn't it lawful to attack targets that will demoralize the civilian population or weaken its support for the war effort? Lawful targets of attack are only those which by their "nature, location, purpose or use make an effective contribution to military action" **and** whose total or partial destruction, capture or neutralization, in the circumstances ruling at the time,

offers "a definite military advantage." Human Rights Watch takes the position that attacks directed at civilian morale do not meet this test – indeed, that they are inimical to international humanitarian law's purpose of protecting civilians. While there is no doubt that military attacks aimed at civilian morale can undermine one side's willingness to carry on hostilities, such a practice would also completely undermine the aim of protecting civilians. The logic of attacking civilian morale opens the door to attacking civilians and civilian objects themselves. In addition, international humanitarian law explicitly prohibits attacks whose primary purpose is to instill terror in the civilian population.

That said, there is no international law prohibition on targeting civilian morale or political will through non-military means, such as propaganda, diplomacy and the like. Attacks on military targets designed to harm military morale are not unlawful so long as they are not disproportionately harmful to civilians.

Q: What about the specific targets of the airstrikes in Afghanistan? The initial information is that the airstrikes of the US-led coalition have targeted, aircraft and air defense systems, military headquarters, military command and communications facilities, military training camps, front-line military positions, and airports. All except for the last are unambiguously military objects which may be lawful targets of attack, so long as the military advantage in destroying or harming them is not outweighed by the prospective harm to civilians.

Airports, roads and bridges may be dual-use targets, in that they might be used both for military purposes and to deliver humanitarian assistance to civilians. Electrical facilities also may serve both a military and civilian purpose. Although most of the Afghan population lacks electricity, certain urban facilities for civilians depend on electricity for long-term function, such as hospitals.

When a target is dual-use in nature, the impact on civilians must be carefully weighed against the military advantage served; all ways of minimizing the impact on civilians must be considered, and attacks should not be undertaken if the civilian harm outweighs the definite military advantage.

Q: *What are the legal constraints on methods of attack?* A corollary to the principle of civilian immunity is the basic prohibition of indiscriminate attacks. An attack is "indiscriminate" when its effect is not or cannot be limited to military targets and so it harms military targets and civilians or civilian objects without distinction. Typical examples would be the carpet-bombing of populous areas where military targets are interspersed, or the laying of anti-personnel landmines, which cannot distinguish between civilian or military feet. Indiscriminate attacks also include those which, as noted above, may be expected to cause incidental loss of civilian life, injury to civilians, or damage to civilian objects which would be excessive in relation to the "concrete and direct military advantage" anticipated from the attack. Human Rights Watch considers that the evaluation of whether an attack may cause excessive harm to civilians must be conducted for each attack and potential target, and not with regard to the conflict as a whole.

The law requires precautions and choices where civilians are at risk from attacks. The duty to take all feasible steps to minimize injury to civilians and civilian objects requires commanders to choose the means of attack that will minimize incidental harm to civilians. Where a party to the conflict has precision weapons at its disposal, it is under a duty to use "smart" rather than "dumb" bombs in or near populated areas. Likewise, where various military targets offer a similar military advantage, commanders must choose the target that threatens the least danger to civilian lives and civilian objects. Each party to the conflict also has the duty to provide "effective advance warning" of attacks that may affect the civilian population, "unless circumstances do not permit," such as where the element of surprise is critical to the success of the attack. So, for example, if a bridge or major highway is useful to the military as well as civilians, the opposing military is obliged to determine whether there are alternative targets whose destruction offers a similar advantage but less risk to civilians, or whether warnings are feasible before bombing, or whether there is a time of day for attack that would minimize potential harm to civilians. Finally, where an attack would be indiscriminate, or the target questionable, the attack must be cancelled or suspended.

Q: *What about the use of civilians as "shields" for military targets?* Parties to the conflict are required to take precautions against the effect of attacks on civilians to the maximum extent feasible. Among these precautions are removing the civilian population from the vicinity of military objectives and avoiding locating military objectives within or near densely populated areas.

Should one party violate this rule by using the presence of civilians to shield military targets, the opposing force is not excused, in calculating the legality of an attack, from taking the risk to civilians into account. That is, it is still necessary to weigh the concrete and direct military advantage of any attack against the prospective harm to civilians.

Q: *What about the prospect that thousands of Afghans who are fleeing their homes will starve or freeze this winter? Is that a violation of humanitarian law?* Deliberate starvation of the enemy's population is prohibited as a tactic of war, as are any methods designed to cause extremely severe damage to the environment or the destruction of objects on which civilians depend for survival, such as food or water sources. The population of Afghanistan has for years suffered extreme deprivation of food and health care due to political repression and the interrelated effects of war, conflict-related violence, and drought. Now, war-induced fear has exacerbated what was already a crisis, putting thousands of civilian lives at risk as foreign aid workers leave and humanitarian assistance is scaled back. There is no evidence that the US or any of its allies sought to cause such a grim humanitarian consequence. However, attacking forces must still remain conscious of the precarious situation and take it into account when calculating the effect on the civilian population of attacks on any potential military target. For example, certain roads, bridges and airports may ordinarily be legitimate military targets, but if they are also essential to the delivery of humanitarian relief throughout the winter, their attack may yield more harm to civilians than definite military advantage, and so would be forbidden.

In addition to making military decisions with the fragility of the civilian population in mind, Human Rights Watch believes it is morally incumbent on the US and its allies, as well as the international community at large, to provide humanitarian aid and take other effective and proactive measures to alleviate the prospect of starvation and mass civilian deaths.

Q: What types of weapons, or means of attack, are violations of international humanitarian law? A fundamental principle is that weapons and means of warfare must not cause "superfluous injury" or "unnecessary suffering." Dum-dum bullets were an early category of weapon found to violate this principle; blinding lasers are a more modern example. This principle, and the norm against weapons that harm civilians and soldiers indiscriminately, underlie the prohibition of a variety of weapons. Among these are biological and chemical weapons, and weapons such as anti-personnel landmines.

Cluster bombs, employed widely in the Gulf War as well as in the early stages of the NATO air war in Kosovo, present a hazard to civilians similar to anti-personnel landmines. The "bomblets" they release have been shown to have a high initial dud rate, leaving highly volatile explosives on the ground that cannot distinguish between combatants and civilians who might encounter them. The high initial dud rate is magnified by the large number of submunitions used. In addition, cluster bombs are difficult to target precisely and thus can also be an indiscriminate weapon if used near populated areas. Human Rights Watch urges the United States and its allies to refrain from using anti-personnel landmines entirely and from using cluster bombs in circumstances where they pose a deadly menace to civilians.

Q: If the Taliban or its allies violate international humanitarian law, does that absolve the United States and its allies from the duty to comply with this law? No. Non-respect for humanitarian law by one side to a conflict, however deplorable, does not excuse the opposing party from obeying the law.

Q: What responsibility does the United States bear if its allies violate these rules of warfare? The United States is directly responsible for any forces over which it exercises effective control. In addition, Human Rights Watch has long advocated that no security assistance be given to forces whose conduct displays a consistent pattern of gross violations of human rights and humanitarian law. In particular, Human Rights Watch urges that no such assistance be given to any group or coalition that includes commanders with an unremedied record of serious violations of international humanitarian law standards, including but not limited to General Abdul Rashid Dostum, the head of the Uzbek militia known as the Junbish; Haji Muhammad Muhaqqiq, a senior commander of the Shi'a Hazara party Hizb-i Wahdat; Abdul Rasul Sayyaf, leader of the now defunct Sunni Islamist party, Ittihad-i

Islami; and Abdul Malik Pahlawan, a former senior Junbish commander. In addition, we urge the establishment of mechanisms to hold abusers accountable as a way of serving justice and marginalizing these figures from any future Afghanistan government.

Note

Detailed notes and sources related to the above text can be found at _http_://www.hrw.org, following links to Asia and Afghanistan.

Other sources

Maley, William (ed.), _Fundamentalism Reborn: Afghanistan and the Taliban_ (Lahore, Pakistan: Vanguard Books, 1988).

Rashid, Ahmed, _Taliban: Militant Islam, Oil and Fundamentalism in Central Asia_ (New Haven: Yale University Press, 2000).

Roy, Olivier. _Afghanistan: From Holy War to Civil War_ (Princeton: Princeton University Press, 1995).

Rubin, Barnett R. _The Fragmentation of Afghanistan: State Formation and Collapse in the International System_ (New Haven: Yale University Press, 1992).

15

China: the State Control of Religion
Human Rights Watch

◆ Developing importance of religion in China ◆

◆ Religious diversity in China ◆ State control of religion ◆

Religion is becoming more and more important in China. In a country that remains officially atheist, conversions to Christianity have risen sharply, the country's 19 million Muslims are attracting the attention of their co-religionists elsewhere, and Buddhism is the fastest growing religion of all. The Chinese government acknowledges 100 million believers of all faiths out of a population of 1.2 billion, but it has been using the 100 million figure since the mid-1950s.

As interest in religion has increased, so has state control over religious organizations, in part because the Chinese government believes that religion breeds disloyalty, separatism, and subversion. Christianity and Islam in particular are seen as vehicles for foreign influence and infiltration by "hostile foreign forces," and religion is a critical element of the nationalist movements in Tibet and Xinjiang, where opposition to Chinese rule appears to be growing. Chinese authorities are keenly aware of the role that the church played in Eastern Europe during the disintegration of the Soviet empire. As a 1996 government document titled "Some Hot Issues in Our Work on Religion" illustrates, the Chinese government believes that Western countries are aiming to "achieve pluralistic political

beliefs through pluralistic religious beliefs" and that they have used religion since the 1980s to subvert socialist countries.

Government control is exercised primarily through a registration process administered by the State Council's Religious Affairs Bureau through which the government monitors membership in religious organizations, locations of meetings, religious training, selection of clergy, publication of religious materials, and funding for religious activities. The government also now undertakes annual inspections of registered religious organizations. Failure to register can result in the imposition of fines, seizure of property, razing of "illegal" religious structures, forcible dispersal of religious gatherings, and occasionally, short term detention. In Tibet, control takes the form of political vetting of monks and nuns and strict supervision of their institutions.

While long-term imprisonment, violence, and physical abuse by security forces against religious activists still occur, they appear to be less frequent than they were at the time of the first Human Rights Watch study of religion in China in 1992. In 1997, we found isolated cases but no evidence of widespread or systematic brutality. When reports of these harsher measures do surface, they are increasingly denounced by central government officials as examples of the excesses of local officials and their failure to implement policy directives correctly. (It should be noted, however, that verifying reports of persecution and crackdowns remains very difficult, given restricted access to China.)

Every important Chinese leader and religious official has stressed that

> no one in China is prosecuted for his or her religious beliefs but rather for suspected criminal acts. Tightening of control over religion, they maintain, has come only at the expense of illegal groups and illegal activities. There are two problems with that argument, however. One is that refusal to register and submit to the kind of intrusive monitoring outlined above is precisely what renders an organization illegal. The second is that for Chinese officials, religious belief is a personal, individual act, and they distinguish between personal worship and participation in organized religious activities. It is the latter that they go to great lengths to control, not the former. The whole concept of religious freedom, however, involves not only freedom of the individual to believe but to manifest that belief in community with others.

The government's argument that its control of religion is strictly in accordance with the law is not new; it argues the same when confronted with protests over its treatment of political dissent. But several elements of its policy on religion have changed. While lessening its reliance on arrests and detention, the government is enforcing requirements on registration more strictly than ever before. It has narrowed the criteria it uses for identifying "authentic" religious groups, distinguishing between the five officially-recognized religions – Buddhism, Daoism, Catholicism, Protestantism, and Islam – and cults or sects practicing "feudal superstition." As illegal entities with no claim to protection, the latter are subject to a distinct set of penalties. Popular religion, a

syncretic blend of Daoism, Buddhism and polytheistic elements that is central to the lives of millions of Chinese, is not even acknowledged as a religion. The government is also increasingly engaged in carefully planned mass campaigns promoting "socialist spiritual civilization" and inculcating patriotism as an antidote to religion. Political reeducation for the public at large is a prominent feature of the campaigns. Another new tactic is the government's increasing tendency to target the China-based representative of an "illegal" religious network (usually a foreign proselytizing organization) rather than individual members. It used to be that any local pastor or lay leader of an underground church linked to a foreign movement faced arrest; more and more, the Chinese government seems to be looking for an organizer at the district or provincial level.

In the kind of intrusive control the Chinese government exercises over religious activities, it violates the rights to freedom of association, assembly, and expression as well as freedom of religion. Article 19 of the Universal Declaration of Human Rights provides for the right to hold and express opinions and receive information and ideas "regardless of frontiers"; and Article 20 grants the right to peaceful assembly and association.

Article 18 of the Universal Declaration of Human Rights states:

> Everyone has the right to freedom of thought, conscience and religion; this right includes freedom to change his religion or belief, and freedom, either alone or in community with others and in public or private, to manifest religion or belief in teaching, practice, worship and observance.

The only limitations that a government can impose, according to the declaration, are those necessary to secure "due recognition and respect for the rights and freedoms of others" and protecting "morality, public order and the general welfare in a democratic society." The peaceful gathering of unregistered groups is no threat to morality, public order, or general welfare; China's onerous registration requirements are clearly an unnecessary limitation on freedom of religion, particularly when failure to register results in some of the penalties outlined above.

China's narrow interpretation of freedom of religion as equivalent to freedom of private belief is contrary to the much broader international standard. In 1991, the UN General Assembly passed a resolution called "Declaration on the Elimination of All Forms of Intolerance and of Discrimination Based on Religion or Belief." The declaration in Article 6 elaborates on the right to religious freedom, noting that it includes the following elements:

(a) to worship or assemble in connection with a religion or belief, and to establish and maintain places for these purposes;
(b) to establish and maintain appropriate charitable or humanitarian institutions;
(c) to make, acquire, and use to an adequate extent the necessary articles and materials related to the rites or customs of a religion or belief;
(d) to write, issue and disseminate relevant publications in these areas;
(e) to teach a religion or belief in places suitable for these purposes;
(f) to solicit and receive voluntary financial and other contributions from individuals and institutions;
(g) to train, appoint, elect or designate by succession appropriate leaders called for by the requirements and standards of any religion or belief;
(h) to observe days of rest and to celebrate holidays and ceremonies in accordance with the precepts of one's religion or belief;
(i) to establish and maintain communications with individuals and communities in matters of religion and belief at the national and international levels.

Thus, the Chinese government's distinction between legal and illegal religious activities based on either willingness to register with the Religious Affairs Bureau and accept government control or on the nature of the beliefs themselves (the five recognized religions as opposed to "sects") is a violation of freedom of religion. Its efforts to restrict organized religious activities, vet the selection of religious leaders and location of meetings, ban "unauthorized" materials, break up "illegal" gatherings, and hamper communication with co-religionists outside China are also in violation of this right.

In a place like Xinjiang, wracked by political violence, where China may have a legitimate concern about Islamic radicals from Afghanistan, Kashmir, or the Middle East providing military training and arms to Uighur separatists, Chinese authorities have reasonable grounds for arresting those suspected of violence or, under some circumstances, searching homes or religious institutions. A violation of religious freedom takes place, however, when people are forbidden to gather for prayers, when mosques deemed to be "illegal" because they are not registered are razed, or when the distribution of purely religious material is halted.

Religion must Serve the State

There is nothing trivial about religion. The management of religious problems is deeply concerned with politics, government policy and the masses . . . We must definitely adopt Lenin's attitude on such questions: "Be especially cautious," "Be most rigorous," and "Think things over carefully." (Ye Xiaowen, Head of the Religious Affairs Bureau, March 14, 1996)

Since early 1996, Chinese leaders, in government and party documents, speeches, and articles in official publications, have consistently reiterated the three guiding principles for management of religion: adaptation to socialist society, supervision according to the law, and correct and comprehensive implementation of the party's religious policy. At the same time, they have made repeated reference to China's official atheism, its policy of separation of church and state, and the need for religion to serve economic development.

Adaptation to socialist society

The Chinese government insists that religion must serve the state and adapt – or be adapted – to socialist society. According to one analysis, this means highlighting moral teachings and curbing religious "extremism." It also means a religion must adjust its "theology, conception, and organization" and interpret its canon and doctrine "in the interests of socialism." According to Li Ruihuan, the Politburo member in charge of culture, this means that religious groups should help promote economic reform, or as a senior government official in Xinjiang put it, "Ancient traditions and religions cannot become obstacles to development."

The principle of adaptation undermines freedom of religious belief by insisting that any principles and doctrines of the five recognized religions that do not conform to socialism should be changed. Expressions of faith that the government does not recognize as "normal" are subject to punishment.

Supervision according to the law

Increasingly the government is citing violations of Chinese law as its pretext for dismantling churches, monasteries, mosques, temples or congregations that refuse to adapt, especially targeting those individuals and organizations that attempt to operate outside official bureaucratic control.

The emphasis on law – including the Chinese constitution, the criminal code, and various administrative regulations and policies – to control religion is a relatively new development that emerged in the 1990s. Broadly worded laws, such as those on "counterrevolution," were, of course, in place long before and used against religious activists. But it was only in 1994 that a series of regulations on registration procedures for religious organizations and management of their activities was promulgated by the State Council.

The emergence of these regulations may have been a response to what was seen by the government as a growing danger. It may have reflected an awareness on the part of the Chinese leadership that violence and force would neither succeed in preventing the growth of religion in China nor destroy religion's influence in society. It may also have been designed to appeal to the international community, which had generally applauded China's tentative steps toward legal reform. But the government appears to have concluded as well that the regulations work, and that their enforcement is a feasible alternative to harsher methods of repression. The stress during the last two or three years thus has been less on punishment of individual offenders than on "lawful supervision" and strict regulation of religious organizations. There has been an emphasis as well on strengthening officially approved religious organizations and workers, with particular focus on the need to build up a younger generation of patriots.

This is not to suggest that the central government has succeeded in eradicating the use of extra-legal means to limit religious activity or that the laws in place are in accord with international human rights standards. But with surveys indicating that the faith of Chinese in the party and trust in a socialist future have declined, and with more and more people turning to religion, the government appears to be changing its methods of control and allowing its citizens to express their faith within the confines of the "law." The laws themselves, however, are the problem.

Dangers of destabilization

The Chinese leadership argues that religion must "conduct its activities so as to safeguard the unity of nationalities and national unification and resist "exploitation of religion by hostile domestic and foreign forces." In 1991, well aware of the declining force of Marxism and the social dislocations brought about by economic reform, it launched a five-year "socialist spiritual civilization" campaign, with an emphasis on ideological education, patriotism, self-abnegation, dedication to the party, and rejection of bourgeois-liberal values. In November 1994, Zhao Puchu, president of the official Chinese Buddhist Association, noted at a seminar that by "guid(ing) everyone to set up correct ideals, convictions and beliefs, a world view, and a set of values," the party hoped to check discontent brought on by discrepancies in economic development and by the center's demands on the provinces. Zhao noted that "patriotic education" was the means for "inspiring the national spirit" so as to overcome obstacles and to "strengthen national cohesion."

On August 11, 1996, Wang Zhaoguo, the director of Party Central's United Front Work Department, not only warned against splittism but inveighed against the use of religious issues by hostile international forces as "a breakthrough point" to "westernize" China. While stressing that the religious situation in China was stable, he tied "recent" problems to changes in domestic and international relations. The same viewpoint was expressed in the same language in an article analyzing China's religious problem which appeared in 1996 in a restricted circulation (*neibu*) magazine, one of the publications of *Qiushi*, the Chinese Communist Party's official theoretical journal. Wang's remarks followed a ten-day conference in northeastern China at which religious leaders discussed measures to strengthen patriotism among believers and to replace the aging clergy and religious staff with young and middle-aged well-trained leaders. In May 1997, an article in *Tianfeng*, the magazine of the official Chinese Christian Church, called on all Chinese believers to see patriotism as their Christian duty.

The danger that religion poses does not just come from the West in the view of Chinese leaders. On June 14, 1997, in a listing of seven factors that could destabilize the country, top party officials included "foreign radical religious forces (which) have greatly enhanced their influence in some areas occupied by minority nationalities." One such area is Xinjiang Autonomous Region in the northwest, with a majority Muslim population and a good percentage of party members openly professing adherence to Islam. The region, once known as East Turkestan, has an armed separatist movement led by members of the Uighur ethnic group. While the movement is primarily nationalist and not religious, the Chinese government believes the rebels are receiving support from radical Muslim groups abroad. The Xinjiang government chairman clearly believes religion and disunity are linked. "The biggest danger threatening stability," he said, "comes from separatism and illegal religious activities."

Similar charges have been made with respect to Tibet, where the Chinese leadership has put a high priority on preventing collusion between the "Dalai clique" and "international reactionary forces." Again and again, Tibetan and Chinese officials accuse the Dalai Lama, Tibet's exiled leader, of using religion to engage in "political infiltration" and to sell his separatist ideas. The Chinese government likewise views the Catholic church as a potential destabilizing force, given its role in the overthrow of communism in Eastern Europe. It is deeply suspicious of Protestantism, officially called Christianity in China, because of the overseas connections of its missionary organizations, not only to the West but to Taiwan and South Korea as well.

The Bureaucracy: An Instrument of Control

As early as the 1950s, the Chinese government began to set up an elaborate bureaucratic supervisory structure so that religion might better serve the political ends of the state. With some shifts in emphasis, that structure remains. All key policy decisions are taken by the Standing Committee of the Politburo, the highest organ of the Chinese Communist Party. The United Front Work Department, a party organ, is responsible for implementing that policy. On the government side, the State Council's Religious Affairs Bureau (RAB), organized according to administrative levels with offices at the provincial, municipal, district and sometimes county levels, executes policy. Each of the recognized religions has a "patriotic association" to help manage the relationship between church and government, seeing to it that directives are implemented on the local level and that any relevant information is transmitted to the center. The structure of these associations parallels that of the RAB.

Catholicism and Protestantism have two monitoring bodies, one concerned with politics, the other more involved in ecclesiastical issues. The Chinese Catholic Bishops Conference, the leading national structure, is charged with implementing the "three-self" policy and approving the selection and ordination of bishops. The three-self policy, designed to remove foreign influence from religious affairs, maintains that all religious organizations should be self-administering, self-supporting, and self-propagating. The appointment of bishops goes to the heart of China's dispute with the Vatican, since it directly challenges the Pope's authority. The Chinese Catholic Patriotic Association (CCPA) is a mass organization of laity and clergy. Its purpose, under the leadership of the party and government, is to unite all Catholics in patriotism and to assist the Catholic Church in implementing the three-self policy.

All Protestants in China are united under one "post-denominational" church, on the theory that ideological, doctrinal, and ritual differences are secondary to the unity of Protestants insofar as patriotism

and adherence to the three-self policy are concerned. The two organizations responsible for Protestant affairs are the China Christian Council (CCC), which is directly involved in internal pastoral affairs, and the Three-Self Patriotic Movement (TSPM), concerned with the relationships between individual churches and the Chinese government. According to its 1997 constitution, the TSPM's objectives are to foster patriotism among believers, strengthen unity among Christians, and protect church independence and autonomy. It is also charged with protecting the unity and stability of the nation and building spiritual and material civilization, all under the leadership of the Communist Party and the people's government. According to one of its officials, the TSPM was not established to control Christianity's development but to defend it against imperialist control.

In recent years, Chinese officials appear to have promoted the importance of the China Christian Council at the expense of the Three-Self Patriotic Movement, in part to assuage the historical antipathy of the Protestant community to the latter. Many believers suspect TSPM leaders of being atheistic, committed to promoting the party's interests rather than those of rank-and-file church members. In addition, believers resent the role the TSPM has played in persecuting congregations that have resisted registration. Church officials, on the other hand, stress the accomplishments of both organizations, such as arranging for Bible printing and distribution, helping negotiate the return of church property expropriated during the Cultural Revolution (1966–76), easing registration requirements, and bringing local level persecution to the attention of central authorities.

Major splits have developed between the "official" or "open" and the "underground" Catholic churches and between the official or open Protestant meeting sites and so-called house churches. Although there is no hard and fast line dividing the two sets of Catholics, members of the underground church recognize the authority of the Vatican, refusing either to register their churches or to obey the dictates of the Religious Affairs Bureau or the Chinese Catholic Patriotic Association. In some areas, the divisions are sharp and bitter; in others, official and underground clergy openly cooperate. In some cases, members of the officially-recognized clergy have secretly made their peace with Rome.

On the Protestant side, the division is between established denominations, such as Anglicans, Methodists, Lutherans, Presbyterians, and Baptists, who have agreed to supervision by a lay bureaucracy and who aim to moderate Chinese religious policy by working from within the system, and a more conservative, aggressively evangelical wing. Those working from within the system are pushing for clear and comprehensive religious law. They argue that as the registration regulations have proven, a comprehensive law will protect them from arbitrary actions on the part of the state. It is far easier, they say, to fight for what is promised in writing.

As vindication of their policy, they point to the growth in the number of Christian converts, although no one knows for certain how many there are. (The late chairman of the Chinese Catholic Bishops Conference put the number of Catholics at 4 million, but the Holy Spirit Study Center in Hong Kong estimates that in 1996, China's Catholic population numbered 10 million. Sources close to the China Christian Council estimate the number of Protestants at between 10 million and 13.3 million, but some estimates go up to 35 million and even higher.)

Some aspects of the argument that working within the system creates space for growth, however, are flawed. To demonstrate growth, proponents compare current estimates of believers with the estimates from the Cultural Revolution period, a time when the government attempted to dismantle the entire religious infrastructure and persecute all believers. Moreover, much of the recent increase in numbers is attributable to the proselytizing efforts of conservatives willing to sabotage the government's "three-fix" policy that limits approved religious leaders to a fixed geographical location designated by the government. The evangelicals are much more wary of the registration process and of a legal system that remains tightly under the control of the party.

Note

Detailed notes and sources related to the above text can be found at *http*://www.hrw.org, following links to Asia and China.

Politics by Other Means: Attacks on Christians in India

16

Human Rights Watch

- ◆ Religious minorities in India ◆
- ◆ Persecution of Christians ◆
- ◆ Patterns of religiously-motivated violence and repression ◆
- ◆ Context of anti-Christian violence ◆

India's inter-religious violence now extends to Christians, and its underlying causes are the same as those promoting violence against Muslims, Dalits ("untouchables"), and other marginalized groups in the country – political and economic power struggles linked rhetorically to the creation of a Hindu nation. Attacks against Christians, which have increased significantly since the Hindu nationalist Bharatiya Janata Party (Indian People's Party, BJP) came to power in March 1998, point to a disturbing trend of the assertion of Hindu nationalism by governments in power at the state and central level. They are part of a concerted campaign of right-wing Hindu organizations, collectively known as the *sangh parivar*, to promote and exploit communal tensions to stay in power – a movement that is supported at the local level by militant groups who operate with impunity. The number of Christians being attacked is still relatively small but has increased in the months preceding national parliamentary elections in September and October 1999. Corresponding closely to particular election contests in which Hindu nationalist

groups have pursued major strategic goals, the attacks have continued in the periods following electoral victory.

A majority of the reported incidents of violence against Christians in 1998 occurred in Gujarat, the same year that the BJP came to power in the state. In April 1999 Human Rights Watch visited the Dangs district in southeastern Gujarat, site of a ten-day spate of violent and premeditated attacks on Christian communities and institutions between December 25, 1998, and January 3, 1999. Human Rights Watch was able to document patterns there that are representative of anti-Christian violence in many other parts of the country. These include the role of sangh parivar organizations and the local media in promoting anti-Christian propaganda, the exploitation of communal differences to mask political and economic motives underlying the attacks, local and state government complicity in the attacks, and the failure of the central government to meet its constitutional and international obligations to protect minorities.

Between January 1998 and February 1999, the Indian Parliament reported a total of 116 incidents of attacks on Christians across the country. Unofficial figures may be higher. Gujarat topped the list of states with ninety-four such incidents. Attacks have also been reported in Maharashtra, Kerala, Madhya Pradesh, Bihar, Orissa, Andhra Pradesh, Haryana, Tamil Nadu, Karnataka, Manipur, West Bengal, Uttar Pradesh, and New Delhi. Attacks on Christians have ranged from violence against the leadership of the church, including the killing of priests and the raping of nuns, to the physical destruction of Christian institutions, including schools, churches, colleges, and cemeteries. Thousands of Christians have also been forced to convert to Hinduism.

Jamuna Bhen, a thirty-year-old agricultural laborer in Dangs district, Gujarat, told Human Rights Watch, "The Hindus removed the ornamentation from our church on December 25 [1998]. They threatened us by saying that they will set the church house on fire. Then they started taking down the roof tiles . . . There were one to two hundred people who came from other villages. They said, 'We will burn everything.' We begged them not to. We said, 'Don't do this,' and said we will become Hindu." Along with twenty-four other Christians, Jamuna was taken to a hot springs that night to undergo a "reconversion" ritual to Hinduism: "They took us to Unai hot springs, they took twenty-five people and converted us . . . They took our photos and gave us photos of Hanuman [a Hindu deity] and gave us a saffron-colored flag. Then they forced us into the water, all twenty-five of us. Then we were brought home. I started feeling sick in my stomach; I had a fever. They said, 'You are now Hindu,' but we remain Christian." In a pattern similar to the response to organized violence against lower castes, the tendency is for local officials under pressure to arrest a few members but not the leaders of the groups involved. The communities affected represent some of the poorest in the country and include Dalits and members of local tribal communities, many of whom convert to Christianity to escape abuses under India's caste system. In many cases, Christian institutions and individuals targeted were singled out for their role in promoting health, literacy, and economic independence among Dalit and tribal community members. A vested interest in keeping these communities in a state of economic dependency is a motivating factor in anti-Christian violence and propaganda.

These recent attacks fall into a pattern of persistent abuse against marginalized communities. They represent a clear failure on the part of both the central and state governments to ensure that such communities enjoy the full protection of their constitutional rights to freedom of religion and equal protection under the law. Despite the existence of comprehensive legislation to address the problem of religious intolerance and communal violence, the government has failed to prosecute offending individuals and organizations; instead, it has in many cases offered tacit support and indirect justification for the attacks.

Christians are not the only minority to be targeted by the sangh parivar. Violence against Sikhs in northern India in 1984 and against India's Muslim community nationwide in 1992 and 1993 also stemmed from the activities and hate propaganda of these groups. Members of the sangh parivar include the Rashtriya Swayamsevak Sangh (National Volunteer Corps, RSS), the Vishwa Hindu Parishad (World Hindu Council, VHP), and the VHP's militant youth wing, the Bajrang Dal. In the state of Maharashtra, the Shiv Sena political party has also been implicated. The RSS seeks to promote a Hindu ethos within India and among Indians living abroad. Although an ostensibly cultural organization, RSS cells are involved in supporting political candidates for government, trade unions, and student organizations. The VHP was established in 1964 to unite Hinduism's regional and caste divisions under a single ecumenical umbrella. It is actively involved in Sanskrit education, the organization of

Hindu rites and rituals, and the converting of Christians, Muslims, and animists to Hinduism. These organizations, although different in many respects, have all promoted the argument that although India is a democracy, because Hindus constitute the majority of Indians, India should be a Hindu state.

In the words of a sangh parivar activist in Gujarat, "The VHP is for the promotion of religion, the Bajrang Dal is for the protection of Hindus, and the BJP is for politics. The work systems are different, but the aim is the same. We all want *akand bharat*: all nations under India. We want what we had before independence, minus the British. We should have a Hindu nation. Other religions can do whatever they want, but they should not insult Hinduism. We also don't want them to distribute their vote but to give it to the Hindus. Everyone will come together to support against [the] Congress [party]."

Despite this ideological position, the VHP has denied any involvement in the attacks on Christians; instead, it has repeatedly accused Christian missionaries of converting the poor by force, a charge that the Christians have rejected. The Christian community also asserts that the situation has worsened since the Hindu nationalist BJP came to power in Delhi in March 1998. Although Prime Minister Atal Behari Vajpayee has publicly dissociated himself from the VHP and given assurances of safety to all Christians, his position has been ambiguous: while officially condemning the killing of Australian missionary Graham Staines in January 1999, for example, the prime minister called for a "national debate on conversions." Human rights groups criticized the move as legitimizing the motives behind the Staines attack.

The response of other BJP officials has been to echo the VHP and blame the violence on a conversion campaign by the Christian community. A Christian conspiracy, some argue, exists on a global scale. In February 1999, BJP national General Secretary K. N. Govindacharya alleged that the church has set a target to turn at least 51 percent of the world's population to Christianity by the dawn of the twenty-first century. After having converted large populations in Africa, he added, evangelists had now made Asia the prime target. Govindacharya added that Christian missionaries use "fraud, allurement and fear to bring about religious conversions." In response to a question on the reconversions of Christians to Hinduism, Govindacharya asserted that the reconversions were merely a homecoming process.

In Gujarat's Dangs district, local officials, including police officers, have given outright support to rallies organized by groups that have fomented the violence. State and local officials have also attempted to downplay the destruction of Christian property, dismissing the burning of churches as attacks on mere temporary structures. Though authorities have characterized the violence as spontaneous eruptions or communal clashes between local groups, there is much evidence to suggest that they have been carefully organized by the leadership of extremist Hindu groups.

Local police have not provided adequate protection to villagers in the affected areas, even though there have been early warnings of violence. In some cases, police have refused to register complaints by members of the Christian community, whereas they have registered complaints by others against Christians. Some Christians who have filed charges with the police have been pressured to withdraw their complaints. Officers who have taken action in response to anti-Christian attacks have been threatened with transfers. India's National Human Rights Commission has taken notice of recurring attacks in various states and has also issued notices to the chief secretaries of Orissa, Madhya Pradesh, and Gujarat, and to the Union home secretary seeking immediate and effective measures to prevent such events in the future. The

National Commission for Minorities has also submitted several reports to state and central governments recommending prosecutions and accusing the government of wilful neglect at all levels.

This report documents the gang rape of four nuns in Madhya Pradesh in September 1998 and the killing of an Australian missionary and his two sons who were trapped in their car and burned alive in the state of Orissa in January 1999. The follow-up to the killings revealed serious irregularities in official treatment of anti-Christian violence. A government appointed commission of inquiry accused Bajrang Dal activist and BJP member Dara Singh of leading the attack in the Orissa killings. The commission exonerated the Bajrang Dal as such, insisting that Singh acted alone, and blamed the Congress Party-led state government for allowing the murders to take place under its watch. Despite Singh's numerous television interviews following the attack, police claimed that they were unable to find him.

With India's national parliamentary elections in September and October 1999, the situation deteriorated recently as the Hindu right sought to form a BJP-led single-party government at the center. On August 26, 1999, Bajrang Dal activist Dara Singh struck again, chopping off the arms of Sheikh Rehman, a Muslim trader, before setting him on fire before a crowd of 400. One week later, Rev. Arul Doss was shot in the chest with an arrow and beaten to death by a group of unidentified assailants. Just days before the national parliamentary elections, both attacks took place within twenty miles of the Graham Staines killing in the state of Orissa, and each one coincided with a major Hindu festival. The BJP charged the Congress-led state government with criminal negligence, while Congress sought to blame the incidents on the policies and activities of sangh parivar organizations. While communal tensions in the state were exploited by political parties on all sides, as of this writing, the main perpetrators of the attacks were still at large.

The Context of Anti-Christian Violence

Amounting to 2.3 percent of the nation's population, Christians nonetheless constitute the third-largest religious group in India after Hindus and Muslims. Though characterized by Hindu nationalist leaders as an alien faith or the religion of India's colonial rulers, Christianity took root in India almost 2,000 years ago when St. Thomas the Apostle evangelized in the south – home today to a majority of India's twenty-three million Christians. In more recent years, missionaries have converted sizable majorities in three small north-eastern states: Nagaland, Mizoram and Meghalaya. Today, close to 70 percent of India's Christians are Catholic.

Attracted by the church's emphasis on social service and equality, many tribals and Dalits ("untouchables") have converted to Christianity in an effort to escape their impoverished state and abusive treatment under India's caste system. Most of the attacks against Christians have taken place in the country's "tribal belt," which runs from the Pakistani border in the west to Burma and Bangladesh in the east. The belt is home to 81 million indigenous people, whose ancestors inhabited India before the Aryan invasions of about 2000 BC brought the country its dominant ethnic group. Animists or spirit worshippers by nature, many tribals do not practice Hinduism. Much like Dalits, they traditionally fall outside the Hindu fold. Dalits, a population of nearly 160 million people, continue to suffer from extreme social discrimination, segregation and violence because of their rank at the bottom of India's caste system. Upon converting to Christianity, Dalits lose all privileges previously assigned to them under their scheduled caste status.

Until recently, Christians enjoyed a relatively peaceful coexistence with their majority Hindu neighbors. In the past several years, however, Christians have become the target of a campaign of violence and propaganda orchestrated by Hindu nationalist groups attempting to stem the tide of defecting low-caste and tribal voters. In 1996, two Catholic priests were killed in Gumla district, Bihar, their skulls crushed. In October 1997, the decapitated body of a third Catholic priest was found in a forest in Bihar. Rev. A. T. Thomas was apparently targeted for aiding Dalits in the area. Earlier in the month, Father Christudas was forced to parade naked through the town of Dumka after being accused of sexually assaulting one of his students. The string of attacks sent shock waves throughout the country and prompted Christian groups to demand increased protection of Christian communities in a state notorious for its lawlessness and ongoing caste wars. The incidents also foreshadowed the deterioration of Hindu–Christian relations in 1998 and 1999.

According to the Indian Parliament, a total of 116 incidents of attacks on Christians took place across the country between January 1998 and February 1999. Most of the attacks have taken place in the north and the west where the Christian populations are smaller and Hindu nationalist sentiments are stronger. The increase in violence has paralleled the rise of the Hindu right in India's political arena and the undermining of communal harmony by Hindu extremists, a trend that had been noted by the United Nations special rapporteur on religious intolerance in a 1997 report.

United Nations Special Rapporteur on the Question of Religious Intolerance

At the invitation of the Indian government, the United Nations special rapporteur on the question of religious intolerance, Abdelfattah Amor, visited India in December 1996. In the report resulting from his investigation, Amor warned of rising Hindu extremism and the effect it was having on India's secular democratic structure. While investigating the situation of Christians in India, Amor's attention was drawn to "the existence of Hindu extremism, encountered in varying degrees within ultra-nationalist political parties or parties attracted by ultra-nationalism (RSS, VHP and BJP)." Amor found that in some states, "proselytizing activities are sometimes hampered by abusive official interpretations of legislation prohibiting all forced conversion, or by accusations of obtaining conversions by offers of material benefits, and thus of exploiting hardship." The report also cited administrative obstacles encountered by foreign missionaries seeking Indian entry visas, as well as restrictions on transfers of foreign funds destined for Christian institutions in certain states.

At the time of his visit, Amor found that "Hindu extremists occasionally attempt to stir up trouble within Christian institutions," though the incidents were limited. He noted that Christians had complete freedom to disseminate religious material, including the Bible, and with the exception of a few administrative obstacles, they were able to construct places of worship without restriction. The report went on to state that the situation of Christians was generally satisfactory but added:

> Mention must . . . be made of the activities of the extremist Hindu parties, which are attempting to undermine the communal and religious harmony which exists in India by the political exploitation of religion. Occasionally the militantism of these extremists significantly (although marginally) affects the situation of Christians in the religious field and within society in general. The Special Rapporteur was informed of isolated cases of murders of and attacks on members of religious orders, including nuns in Bihar and Kerala.

After the rapporteur's visit in December 1996, the situation deteriorated significantly.

The National Commission for Minorities

In 1998 the National Commission for Minorities conducted numerous investigations into attacks on Christian communities. The majority of its investigations took place in the states of Gujarat (see below), Madhya Pradesh and Orissa. Human Rights Watch spoke to Tahir Mahmood, the chairperson of the National Commission for Minorities. He claimed that the commission had been flooded with complaints from all over the country:

> Similar atrocities have taken place against Muslim communities in the past fifty years. Now there is a shift of focus to Christians. These are deeply sentimental issues. Stories of coerced conversions of low-caste and tribal Hindus to Christianity are doing much harm. Society has been poisoned and the central government has been a silent spectator

Although the commission has submitted numerous reports on the incidents investigated, the government has done little to implement the commission's recommendations. As explained by Chairperson Mahmood:

> We have sent eighteen special reports to the states. If they concern entire communities or the union territories then they also go to the central government . . . Since 1992 our annual reports have not been tabled in Parliament. In 1996, I cleared the arrears, and the reports are now up to date. Soon after the reports were finally tabled, the government fell [in April 1999] . . . The BJP uses its status as a caretaker government as an excuse not to do anything – unless it is something they want to do; then they say they have all the powers. The government is not barred from taking action in the absence of tabling the reports. They can take action and then report to Parliament. But they will sleep over it.

Commenting on the nexus between political parties and communal attacks, the chairperson added:

> The BJP talks of distancing itself from guilty bodies, but no action is taken in that direction. These are the very bodies that helped them come to power. How can they dissociate themselves from them? . . . This is what they said they would do before coming to power. Now they say they are secular. But they cannot stop state governments . . . In Madhya Pradesh, Orissa, and Gujarat, even criminals are becoming communally selective thanks to the policies of the central government. There is a nexus between criminality and communalism, and the credit goes exclusively to the policies of the BJP. Someone has to take responsibility. Communalization of politics is not new. Communalization of crimes is a new phenomenon.

The *Sangh Parivar*

The Hindu organizations most responsible for violence against Christians are the VHP, the Bajrang Dal, and the RSS. According to a former RSS member, these groups cannot be divorced from the ruling BJP party: "There is no difference between the BJP and RSS. BJP is the body. RSS is the soul, and the Bajrang Dal is the hands for beating." The RSS was founded in the city of Nagpur in 1925 by Keshav Baliram Hedgewar with the mission of creating a Hindu state. Since its founding, it has propagated a militant form of Hindu nationalism as the sole basis for national identity in India. According to the RSS, both the leaders of India's nationalist movement and those of post-independence India failed to create a nation based on Hindu culture. More than fifty years later, the RSS still sees itself as the antidote to what it considers the dangerous tendencies of modern-day India: "the erosion of the nation's integrity in the name of secularism, economic and moral bankruptcy, incessant conversions from the Hindu fold through money-power, ever-increasing trends of secession, thought patterns and education dissonant with the native character of the people, and State-sponsored denigration of anything that goes by the name of Hindu or Hindutwa." Western thought and civilization are perceived as enemies of Hindu culture. Religions such as Islam and Christianity are depicted as alien to India, as they are the religions of foreign invaders – the Mughals and the British.

The RSS believed that the liberation of the Hindu state required what it termed *sarvangeena unnati,* or all-round development of the nation. The RSS wanted "the entire gamut of social life" to be designed "on the rock bed of Hindu nationalism," a goal that inspired the creation of RSS political, social, and educational wings, a family of organizations that is now referred to collectively as the *sangh parivar.*

The Vishwa Hindu Parishad (VHP) was formed in 1964 to cover the social aspects of RSS activities. The VHP organizes and communicates the RSS message to Hindus living outside India and holds conferences for Hindu religious leaders from all over the country. The most publicized of the VHP's activities was its campaign to build a temple to the Hindu god Ram at the site of the Babri Masjid, a mosque in the city of Ayodhya in Uttar Pradesh. The VHP, along with the other sangh organizations, claimed that the site of the mosque was actually the birthplace of Ram and that a temple at that site had been destroyed in order to build the mosque. On December 6, 1992, the mosque was demolished by members of the VHP, the Bajrang Dal, and RSS-trained cadres. The police did not intervene. The incident sparked violence around the country in which thousands were killed. Since then, the VHP has also organized a program to reconvert those who had been converted from Hinduism to other faiths.

The Bajrang Dal is the militant youth wing of the VHP. It was formed in 1984 during the Babri Masjid conflict, in order to mobilize youth for the Ayodhya campaign. A young women's association, the Durga Vahini, was also founded at this time. Unlike other organizations affiliated to the RSS, the Bajrang Dal is not directly controlled by the sangh parivar. With its loose organizational structure, it initially operated under different names in different states. Its activists are believed to be involved in many acts of violence carried out by Hindutva organizations, including the recent spate of attacks against the Christian community in India.

The Jana Sangh Party was formed in 1951 as the political wing of the RSS. It was later replaced by the Bharatiya Janata Party (BJP) in 1980. The BJP is the largest of the nineteen parties that formed India's coalition government in March 1998. In addition to its important role in national politics, the BJP controls the state legislatures in Maharashtra (in a coalition with the Shiv Sena), Gujarat, and Uttar Pradesh. On April 17, 1999, the BJP-led coalition was voted out of office, losing a motion of confidence by one vote. The government had lost its majority in Parliament when a major coalition partner withdrew its support on April 14. Because the opposition was unable to come up with an alternative government, the BJP-led coalition was to act as the caretaker government until national parliamentary elections in September and October 1999.

Founded by Bal Thackeray on June 19, 1966, the Shiv Sena is a Hindu party based in Maharashtra. Arising out of a campaign against the growing influence of non-Marathi speakers in Bombay, the Shiv Sena became a major force in Indian politics during the 1980s. The Sena is a close ally of the BJP and is part of the ruling central government coalition. An alliance of the Shiv Sena and the BJP, with the Sena as the dominant partner, has also been in power in the state government of Maharashtra since 1995. Leaders of both parties were implicated in the demolition of the Babri Masjid in Ayodhya and the ensuing violence in Bombay, the state capital.

BJP president and Home Minister L. K. Advani and Uttar Pradesh Chief Minister Kalyan Singh were among the forty people accused by the Central Bureau of Investigation (CBI) for the destruction of the mosque. Also on the list were Murli

Manohar Joshi, the former chief minister of Maharashtra, and Bal Thackeray, the leader of the Shiv Sena. The CBI charged all of the accused with "criminal conspiracy, intentional destruction and defiling of a place of worship, criminal trespass and intimidation of public servants on duty." Advani and Joshi were present in Ayodhya when Hindu militants tore down the mosque. The Srikrishna Commission was established in response to the notorious 1992–93 Bombay riots that claimed the lives of 700 people, mostly Muslims, in the aftermath of the mosque's destruction. The report's findings were presented to the government of Maharashtra on February 16, 1998, more than five years after the riots took place. The report determined that the riots were the result of a deliberate and systematic effort to incite violence against Muslims and singled out Shiv Sena leader Bal Thackeray and Chief Minister Manohar Joshi as responsible. The Shiv Sena-BJP government, however, refused to adopt the commission's recommendations and instead labeled the report "anti-Hindu."

RSS Training The structure of the sangh parivar is premised on the notion that a strong and unified Hindu society can only be achieved through discipline and organization. The sangh therefore recruits young boys and men for local cells known as *shakhas* and provides them with extensive physical and ideological training for the purpose of creating a group of volunteers full of "Hindu fervor" with military-like discipline. Organized on the principle that only a militant and powerful Hindu movement can counter threats from outsiders, the sangh has set up approximately 300,000 shakhas all over the country, each with an estimated fifty to one hundred participants. Training typically involves physical-fitness activities as well as the singing of patriotic songs and a discussion of national events and problems. At the end of each session, participants line up in front of the sangh's saffron flag and recite the prayer *Namaste*

Sada Vatsale Matrubhoome (My salutation to you, loving Motherland).

Apart from the shakhas, the sangh also organizes graded-training camps known as *sangha shiksha vargas* at provincial and national levels at regular intervals. These camps attempt to indoctrinate the *swayamsevaks* (RSS volunteers) with the belief that India is a nation for Hindus alone, the nation's original inhabitants who have shaped its culture and society. Participants are also told that Hindus have long suffered at the hands of foreign invaders, namely, Muslim rulers and the Christian British.

Conversions Hindu nationalist leaders continually propagate the notion that Christians, despite their small numbers, could outnumber India's 82 percent Hindu majority early in the next century. Several state governments have threatened to ban Christian conversions altogether, while Hindu nationalists have launched their own "reconversion programs" and have called on the government to expel all missionaries from the country and stop the flow of foreign funding to "proselytizing agencies working under the various humanitarian garbs." B. L. Sharma, central secretary of VHP, has charged: "We were slaves for 1,000 years, and now we have opened our eyes." Sharma demanded that the government "throw out these people who are out to convert Hindus and ruin our culture, language and attire." Onkar Bhave, also a VHP leader, announced: "We want to stop this conversion business . . . They are not propagating religion; it is political slavery . . . They want to turn the poor into Christians so together they can say to Hindus, 'Get out of India.' They want to break India into different pieces."

The RSS sees Christian missionaries as posing a threat to Hinduism, particularly in the northeastern part of the country where three tiny states have Christian majorities. The *sangh* accuses missionaries of being responsible for the insurgencies and separatist movements in the states of this region. It also blames the Indian government's "secular policy" which allowed these missionaries to continue their work even after the British left India in 1947. Of equal concern to the RSS is the work of missionaries in tribal regions. The tribals, they claim, had always been a part of Hindu culture but had been alienated from the national mainstream by the British. Even after independence, they argue, the government followed the steps of the British and allowed missionaries to work in tribal regions. The RSS considers tribals to be particularly vulnerable to exploitation and conversions by Christian missionaries as they are largely illiterate and come from the weaker sections of society.

In January 1999, members of the VHP reportedly drew up an elaborate plan to counter missionary activity by "reconverting" those who had adopted the Christian faith. The plan, conceived of during a nine-day meeting in Jaipur, Rajasthan, reportedly identified 200 "sensitive districts" in the country where missionary conversions had taken place. The "reconversions" were set to take place over a three-year period. A month later, during a three-day plenary session, the VHP demanded that the government ban religious conversions in the country. It claimed, however, that reconverting Christians to Hindus could not be equated with religious conversions as they were mere "home-comings" for those who had be induced out of the Hindu fold. VHP members also pronounced that the burning of churches and prayer halls in Gujarat's Dangs district, further described below, were part of an "international conspiracy" to defame BJP-led governments and to malign the VHP and the Bajrang Dal.

Imposing a "moral code"   The activities of Hindu extremists have touched many aspects of civil society, including sports, arts, economics, and education. On May 2, 1998, as part of an already growing pattern of attacks on art and artists, twenty-six members of the Bajrang Dal allegedly stormed and ransacked the house of M. F.

Husain, a Muslim and one of India's most eminent and revered painters. The attack was meant to protest an "obscene" lithograph of Hindu deities Hanuman and Sita drawn by the painter more than twenty years ago. Several priceless paintings were torn down. Those arrested for the attack were released after providing sureties in the amount of Rs. 1,000 (US$23.81) each. Sena chief Bal Thackeray justified the attack by pronouncing that "[i]f Husain can step into Hindustan, what is wrong if we enter his house?" In a protest letter addressed to the president, several Indian artists warned, "The offense and abuse signals a dangerous move towards an entirely instrumentalised and recognisably fascist use of culture. An attack on creativity, of which this is an instance, is a precursor to an attempt to regiment society . . . " The letter also labeled as "inflammatory" Thackeray's justification of the attack, adding that such justifications "criminally manufacture fear rather as crude bombs are manufactured and placed anywhere to create instant havoc." This and other attempts to impose a "moral code" on Indian society have led to mounting protests against increasing infringements on freedom of expression and the violent tactics used by Hindutva organizations to enforce extra-legal censorship.

The BJP and its allies have also called for the "Hinduization" of education in India. As one of his first acts after taking office, the BJP minister of education, Murli Manohar Joshi, appointed scholars sympathetic to the Hindutva cause to national academic bodies. At a national education conference in October 1998, Joshi introduced a proposal to "Hinduize" the school system. The plan's more controversial points included compulsory courses on "Indian values" from preschool to graduate school, the inclusion of Hindu religious texts into all syllabi, and teacher training in Indian values and culture at all levels. The proposal, drawn up by a group called Vidya Bharati, which functions as the education section of the RSS, was ultimately withdrawn after vociferous objections from several state education ministers. The Minister of Education for West Bengal stated, "The BJP is attempting to destroy the basic secular fabric of [the] country because they don't believe in secularism."

In January 1999, when Pakistan's cricket team was set to travel to India for a series of test matches, members of the Shiv Sena dug up the pitch at the stadium that was to host the first match, while police officers reportedly stood by, and ransacked the headquarters of the Board of Control for Cricket in Bombay. The Shiv Sena also threatened violence against any member of the Indian cricket team who did not boycott the series in fulfillment of his "patriotic duty." Shiv Sena followers reportedly dumped pigs' heads outside Chidambaran stadium in Madras as a deliberate insult to the Muslim players from Pakistan.

Legal Context

Attacks on Christians, the destruction of Christian institutions, forced conversions to Hinduism and numerous other abuses documented in this report constitute violations of domestic and international law. International human rights law, constitutional provisions, and domestic legislation together impose on the government of India a duty to guarantee certain basic rights to minority populations, to prosecute those who participate in communal violence, and to punish complicit state officials who, having the power and duty to stop the violence, do not intervene.

The preamble of the Indian constitution openly declares India as a "sovereign socialist secular democratic republic" which secures to all citizens "liberty of thought, expression, belief, faith and worship." Though many have debated the meaning of the term secular, in the Indian context it has come to imply equality of rights for all regardless of religion, the exercise of religious freedom and tolerance, and the rejection of discrimination based on

religion or belief. Under articles 14, 15, and 16 of the Indian constitution, discrimination on the grounds of religion is prohibited, and all citizens are guaranteed the right to equal treatment before the law and the right to equal protection of the laws. Article 25 guarantees the right to freely practice and propagate religion while articles 26, 28, and 30 ensure the freedom to manage religious affairs, to attend religious instruction or religious worship in certain educational institutions, and the rights of minorities to establish and administer educational institutions, respectively.

Select provisions of the Indian Penal Code make punishable acts of violence or discrimination based on religion. These include:

- Promoting violent attacks against groups on grounds of religion, race, place of birth, or language (sec. 153).
- Injuring or defiling a place of worship with the intention of insulting the religion (sec. 295)
- Committing deliberate and malicious acts intended to outrage religious feelings of any class, by insulting its religion or religious beliefs (sec. 295A).
- Disturbing religious assemblies (sec. 296).
- Trespassing places of worship or places set apart for the performance of funeral rites with the intention of wounding the feelings of any person, or of insulting the religion of any person (sec. 297).
- Promoting enmity between different groups on grounds of religion, race, place of birth, residence, language, caste or community, etc. (sec. 505(2), see also committing such an offense in a place of worship, sec. 505(3))

Three other laws should also provide protection to religious minorities. The Religious Institutions (Prevention of Misuse) Act, 1988, prevents the misuse of religious places for political and criminal activities. It prohibits, among other things, the use of any premises of any religious institution for any act that promotes or attempts to promote disharmony or feelings of enmity or hatred between different religious, racial, language or regional groups. Violations under the act are punishable with imprisonment for up to five years and with a fine of up to Rs. 10,000 (US$238).

The Places of Worship (Special Provisions) Act, 1991, prohibits the conversion of any place of worship of any religious denomination into a place of worship of a different religious institution and for the maintenance of the religious character of places of worship as it existed on 15 August 1947. Violations under the act are punishable with imprisonment for a term of up to three years and also a fine. A person convicted of an offence under the said act shall be disqualified for being chosen as, and for being, a Member of either House of Parliament or of the Legislative Assembly or Legislative Council of a state.

The Representation of the People Act, 1951, prohibits the use of religion or religious symbols to promote one's candidacy or to adversely affect the election of another candidate constitutes a corrupt practice that debases the election and is an offense punishable under the law.

International Law

In addition to its duties under domestic law, India is also party to several international treaties that impose human rights obligations. Article 18 of the International Covenant on Civil and Political Rights establishes the right to freedom of thought, conscience, and religion. It provides that:

> 1 Everyone shall have the right to freedom of thought, conscience and religion. This right shall include freedom to have or to adopt a religion or belief of his choice, and freedom, either individually or in community with others and in public or private, to manifest his religion or belief in worship, observance, practice and teaching.
> 2 No one shall be subject to coercion which would impair his freedom to have or to adopt a religion or belief of his choice.
> 3 Freedom to manifest one's religion or beliefs may be subject only to such limitations as are prescribed by law and are necessary to protect public safety, order, health, or morals or the fundamental rights and freedoms of others.

Articles 2 and 26 bar discrimination on the grounds of religion while Article 27 dictates that "[i]n those States in which ethnic, religious or linguistic minorities exist, persons belonging to such minorities shall not be denied the right, in community with the other members of the their group, to enjoy their own culture, to profess and practice their own religion, or to use their own language."

The right to freedom of religion and prohibitions on discrimination on the grounds of religion are further elaborated upon in the Declaration on the Elimination of All Forms of Intolerance and of Discrimination Based on Religion or Belief. Although not a treaty, this declaration, proclaimed by the General Assembly of the United Nations in 1981, provides authoritative guidelines to UN member states on ways to eliminate religious intolerance and discrimination. Article 4 of the declaration proclaims that, "All States shall take effective measures to prevent and eliminate discrimination on the grounds of religion or belief in the recognition, exercise and enjoyment of human rights and fundamental freedoms in all fields of civil, economic, political, social and cultural life," and that "[a]ll States shall make all efforts to enact or rescind legislation where necessary to prohibit any such discrimination, and to take all appropriate measures to combat intolerance on the grounds of religion or other beliefs in this matter."

Note

Detailed notes and sources related to the above text can be found at _http://www.hrw.org_, following links to Asia and India.

17

"We Have No Orders to Save You": Hindu–Muslim Violence in India

Human Rights Watch

- ◆ Hindu–Muslim violence in Gujarat ◆
- ◆ Conflict over Ayodhya ◆

Thirty-eight-year-old Mehboob Mansoori lost eighteen family members in the massacre of Muslims in the neighborhood of Gulmarg Society, Ahmedabad. He was interviewed by Human Rights Watch three weeks after the attack. His story is representative of many testimonies contained in this report.

They burnt my whole family.

On February 28, we went to Ehsan Jaffrey's home for safety. He is an ex-member of parliament. . . At 10:30 a.m. the stone throwing started. First there were 200 people then 500 from all over, then more. We were 200–250 people. We threw stones in self-defense. They had swords, pipes, soda-lemon bottles, sharp weapons, petrol, kerosene, and gas cylinders. They began shouting, "Maro, kato," ["Kill them, cut them"] and "Mian ko maro." ["Kill the Muslims."] I hid on the third floor.

Early in the day at 10:30 the police commissioner came over and said don't worry. He spoke to Jaffrey and said something would work out, then left. The wall in front of the house was broken at 11:30 a.m. When they entered the hall we had lost our spirit, we had no weapons, we couldn't fight back. Other people also came there for safety. When the gas cylinder exploded I jumped from the third floor. This was around 1:30 p.m.

At 3:30 p.m. they started cutting people up, and by 4:30 p.m. it was game over. Ehsan Jaffrey was also killed. He was holding the door closed. Then the door broke down. They pulled him out and hit him with a sword across the forehead, then across the stomach, then on his legs. . . They then took him on the road, poured kerosene on him and burned him. There was no police at all. If they were there then this wouldn't have happened.

Eighteen people from my family died. All the women died. My brother, my three sons, one girl, my wife's mother, they all died. My boys were aged ten, eight, and six. My girl was twelve years old. The bodies were piled up. I recognized them from parts of their clothes used for identification. They first cut them and then burned them. Other girls were raped, cut, and burned. First they took their jewelry, I was watching from upstairs. I saw it with my own eyes. If I had come outside, I would also have been killed. Four or five girls were treated this way. Two married women also were raped and cut. Some on the hand, some on the neck.

At 5:30 p.m. a car came, it was the assistant commissioner. They brought us out slowly; some were hiding in the water tank underground. Some tried to get out but were attacked. Sixty-five to seventy people were killed inside. After the police came we told them to take us somewhere safe. They brought us to the camp. We didn't go to the police station. Three patients were admitted in the civil hospital. On March 3 and 4 the police came here to file complaints, but only after camp organizers called them.

Indian government officials have acknowledged that since February 27, 2002, more than 850 people have been killed in communal violence in the state of Gujarat, most of them Muslims. Unofficial estimates put the death toll as high as 2,000. At this writing, murders are continuing, with violence spreading to rural areas fanned by ongoing hate campaigns and economic boycotts against Muslims. The attacks against Muslims in Gujarat have been actively supported by state government officials and by the police.

The violence in Gujarat began after a Muslim mob in the town of Godhra attacked and set fire to two carriages of a train carrying Hindu activists. Fifty-eight people were killed, many of them women and children. The activists were returning from Ayodhya, Uttar Pradesh, where they supported a campaign led by the Vishwa Hindu Parishad (World Hindu Council, VHP) to construct a temple to the Hindu god Ram on the site of a sixteenth century mosque destroyed by Hindu militants in 1992. The Ayodhya campaign continues to raise the spectre of further violence in the country – Hindu–Muslim violence following the destruction of the mosque claimed thousands of lives in the city of Bombay and elsewhere in 1992 and 1993. The VHP claims that the mosque was built on a site that was the birthplace of Ram.

Between February 28 and March 2, 2002, a three-day retaliatory killing spree by Hindus left hundreds dead and tens of thousands homeless and dispossessed, marking the country's worst religious bloodletting in a decade. The looting and burning of Muslim homes, shops, restaurants, and places of worship was also widespread. Tragically consistent with the longstanding pattern of attacks on minorities and Dalits (or so-called untouchables) in India, and with previous episodes of large-scale communal violence in India, scores of Muslim girls and women were brutally raped in Gujarat before being mutilated and burnt to death. Attacks on women and girls, including sexual violence, are detailed throughout this report.

The Gujarat government chose to characterize the violence as a "spontaneous reaction" to the incidents in Godhra. Human Rights Watch's findings, and those of numerous Indian human rights and civil liberties organizations, and most of the Indian press indicate that the attacks on Muslims throughout the state were planned, well in advance of the Godhra incident, and organized with extensive police participation and in close cooperation with officials of the Bharatiya Janata Party (Indian People's Party, BJP) state government.

The attacks on Muslims are part of a concerted campaign of Hindu nationalist organizations to promote and exploit communal tensions to further the BJP's political rule – a movement that is supported at the local level by militant groups that operate with impunity and under the patronage of the state. The groups most directly responsible for violence against Muslims in Gujarat include the Vishwa Hindu Parishad, the Bajrang Dal, the ruling BJP, and the umbrella organization Rashtriya Swayamsevak Sangh (National Volunteer Corps, RSS), all of whom collectively form the *sangh parivar* (or "family" of Hindu nationalist groups). These organizations, although different in many respects, have all promoted the argument that because Hindus constitute the majority of Indians, India should be a Hindu state.

Nationwide violence against India's Muslim community in 1992 and 1993 and against India's Christian community since 1998, including in the state of Gujarat, have also stemmed from the violent activities and hate propaganda of these groups. Human Rights Watch and Indian human rights groups have long warned of the potential scale of death and destruction resulting from the sangh parivar's Hindu nationalist agenda. If the activities of these groups remain unchecked, violence may continue to engulf the state, and may spread to other parts of the country.

The state of Gujarat and the central government of India initially blamed Pakistan for the train massacre, which it called a "pre-meditated" "terrorist" attack against Hindus in Godhra. The recent revival of the Ram temple campaign, and heightened fears of terrorism since September 11 were exploited by local Hindu nationalist groups and the local press which printed reports of a "deadly conspiracy" against Hindus by Muslims in the state. On February 28, one local language paper headline read: "Avenge blood for blood." Muslim survivors of the attacks repeatedly told Human Rights Watch that they were told to "go back to Pakistan." Anti-Pakistan and anti-Muslim sentiments had been building up in Gujarat long before the revival of the Ayodhya Ram temple campaign. Human Rights Watch was unable to verify conflicting accounts of what led to the mob attack on the Sabarmati Express in Godhra though local police investigations have ruled out the notion that it was either organized or planned.

The state government initially charged those arrested in relation to the attack on the Godhra train under the controversial and draconian Prevention of Terrorism Ordinance (POTO, now the Prevention of Terrorism Act), but filed ordinary criminal charges against those accused of attacks on Muslims. Bowing to criticism from political leaders and civil society across the country, the chief minister dropped the POTO charges but stated that the terms of POTO may be applied at a later date.

Three weeks after the attacks began, Human Rights Watch visited the city of Ahmedabad, a site of large-scale destruction, murder, and several massacres, and spoke to both Hindu and Muslim survivors of the attacks. The details of the massacres

of Muslims in the neighborhoods of Naroda Patia and Gulmarg Society and of retaliatory attacks against Hindus in Jamalpur are included in this report. Human Rights Watch was able to document patterns in Ahmedabad that echo those of previous episodes of anti-Muslim violence throughout the state and of anti-minority violence over the years in many parts of the country – most notably the Bombay riots in 1992 and 1993, and the anti-Sikh riots in Delhi in 1984. These include the role of *sangh parivar* organizations, political parties, and the local media in promoting anti-minority propaganda, the exploitation of communal differences to mask political and economic motives underlying the attacks, local and state government complicity in the attacks, and the failure of the government to meet its constitutional and international obligations to protect minorities.

Between February 28 and March 2 the attackers descended with militia-like precision on Ahmedabad by the thousands, arriving in trucks and clad in saffron scarves and khaki shorts, the signature uniform of Hindu nationalist – Hindutva – groups. Chanting slogans of incitement to kill, they came armed with swords, *trishuls* (three-pronged spears associated with Hindu mythology), sophisticated explosives, and gas cylinders. They were guided by computer printouts listing the addresses of Muslim families and their properties, information obtained from the Ahmedabad municipal corporation among other sources, and embarked on a murderous rampage confident that the police was with them. In many cases, the police led the charge, using gunfire to kill Muslims who got in the mob's way. A key BJP state minister is reported to have taken over police control rooms in Ahmedabad on the first day of the carnage, issuing orders to disregard pleas for assistance from Muslims. Portions of the Gujarati language press meanwhile printed fabricated stories and statements openly calling on Hindus to avenge the Godhra attacks.

In almost all of the incidents documented by Human Rights Watch the police were directly implicated in the attacks. At best they were passive observers, and at worse they acted in concert with murderous mobs and participated directly in the burning and looting of Muslim shops and homes and the killing and mutilation of Muslims. In many cases, under the guise of offering assistance, the police led the victims directly into the hands of their killers. Many of the attacks on Muslim homes and places of business also took place in close proximity to police posts. Panicked phone calls made to the police, fire brigades, and even ambulance services generally proved futile. Many witnesses testified that their calls either went unanswered or that they were met with responses such as: "We don't have any orders to save you"; "We cannot help you, we have orders from above"; "If you wish to live in Hindustan, learn to protect yourself"; "How come you are alive? You should have died too"; "Whose house is on fire? Hindus' or Muslims'?" In some cases phone lines were eventually cut to make it impossible to call for help.

Surviving family members have faced the added trauma of having to fend for themselves in recovering and identifying the bodies of their loved ones. The bodies have been buried in mass gravesites throughout Ahmedabad. Gravediggers testified that most bodies that had arrived – many were still missing – were burned and butchered beyond recognition. Many were missing body parts – arms, legs, and even heads. The elderly and the handicapped were not spared. In some cases, pregnant women had their bellies cut open and their fetuses pulled out and hacked or burned before the women were killed.

Muslims in Gujarat have been denied equal protection under the law. Even as attacks continue, the Gujarat state administration has been engaged in a massive cover-up of the state's role in the massacres and that of the *sangh parivar*. Eyewitnesses filed numerous police First Information Reports (FIRs), the initial reports of a crime recorded by the police, that named local VHP, BJP, and Bajrang Dal leaders as instigators or participants in the attacks. Few if any of these leaders have been arrested as the police, reportedly under instructions from the state, face continuous pressure not to arrest them or to reduce the severity of the charges filed. In many instances, the police have also refused to include in FIRs the names of perpetrators identified by the victims. Police have, however, filed false charges against Muslim youth arbitrarily detained during combing operations in Muslim neighborhoods that have been largely destroyed. The state government has entrusted a criminal probe into the deadliest of attacks in Ahmedabad, in the Naroda Patia and Gulmarg Society neighborhoods, to an officer handpicked by the VHP, the organization implicated in organizing and perpetrating these massacres.

On April 3, India's National Human Rights Commission (NHRC) released the preliminary findings of its report on the violence, a strong indictment of the failure of the Gujarat government to contain the violence. As the commission awaited a response from the state government before releasing a comprehensive report, its very authority to intervene in the matter was being challenged in the state's High Court based on the fact that a state-appointed judicial commission of inquiry was already in place. Following the trail of other commissions of inquiry appointed by the state in the wake of communal riots in 1969 and 1985 – whose recommendations have yet to be implemented – the current state commission inspires little hope of justice. One lawyer noted, "The state government is involved and is a party to what happened. How can a party appoint a judge? We cannot expect him to give justice." India's National Commission for Minorities (NCM) and National Commission for Women (NCW) have also been severely critical of the Gujarat government's response to the violence and its aftermath.

Government figures indicate that more than 98,000 people are residing in over one hundred newly created relief camps throughout the state, an overwhelming majority of them Muslim. They hold little hope for justice and remain largely unprotected by the police and local authorities. One relief camp resident asked: "The same people who shot at us are now supposed to protect us? There is no faith in the police." A lack of faith has also kept many camp residents from approaching the police to file complaints. Fearing for their lives, or fearing arrest, many have also been unable to leave the camps to return to what is left of their homes.

The state government has failed to provide adequate and timely humanitarian assistance to internally displaced persons in Gujarat. Problems documented in this report include serious delays in government assistance reaching relief camps, inadequate state provision of medical and food supplies and sanitation facilities, and lack of access and protection for non-governmental (NGO) relief workers seeking to assist victims of violence. Muslims have also been denied equal access to relief assistance. Government authorities are also reported to be absent from many Muslim camps. In sharp contrast to the international and Indian community's response following a massive earthquake in the state in January 2001 – when millions of dollars in aid from the international community and civil society poured into the state – the onus for providing food, medical support, and other supplies for victims of violence rests largely on local NGO and Muslim voluntary groups.

The relief camps visited by Human Rights Watch were desperately lacking in government and international assistance. One camp with 6,000 residents was located on the site of a Muslim graveyard. Residents were literally sleeping in the open, between the graves. One resident remarked: "Usually the dead sleep here, now the living are sleeping here."

The disbursement of financial compensation and the process of rehabilitation for victims of the violence has been painstakingly slow and has failed to include all of those affected. Initially compensation was disbursed on a communal basis: the state government announced that the families of Hindus killed in Godhra would receive Rs. 200,000 (US $4,094) while the families of Muslims killed in retaliatory attacks would receive Rs. 100,000 – a statement that was later retracted, in part due to widespread criticism from nongovernmental organizations and Indian officials outside the state of Gujarat.

In the wake of the massive earthquake in January 2001 that, according to government reports, claimed close to 14,000 lives and left over one million homeless, the state of Gujarat also faces economic devastation. The economic impact is felt acutely by both Hindu and Muslim survivors of the attacks whose homes and personal belongings have been destroyed, and whose businesses have been burnt to the ground. Others reside in neighborhoods where curfews have yet to be lifted, limiting their mobility. Thousands are also unable to leave the relief camps to go to work for fear of further attacks. Many Muslims do not have jobs to which to return – their employers have hired Hindus in their place. An economic boycott against Muslims in certain parts of the state has helped to ensure their continued and long-term impoverishment. Acute food shortages resulting in starvation have been reported in areas of Ahmedabad where Muslim communities are forced into isolation, afraid to leave their enclaves to get more supplies. Children's education has also been severely disrupted while the threat of measles and other outbreaks looms large in Ahmedabad camps.

On April 4, Indian Prime Minister Atal Behari Vajpayee visited Gujarat and announced a federal relief package for riot victims. Vajpayee, who earlier described the burning alive of men, women, and children, as a "blot on the country's face," stated that the Godhra attack was "condemnable" but what followed was "madness." His comments stood in deep contrast to those of the state's chief minister, Narendra Modi, formerly a Rashtriya Swayamsevak Sangh volunteer and propagandist, who at the height of the carnage declared that, "The five crore [fifty million] people of Gujarat have shown remarkable restraint under grave provocation," referring to the Godhra attacks.

On April 12, the BJP proposed early elections in Gujarat soon after rejecting Chief Minister Narendra Modi's offer to resign. Early elections in the aftermath of the attacks may favor the Hindu nationalist vote in the state – a primary objective of the sangh parivar nationwide – and Narendra Modi's continued tenure as chief minister. As this report was going to press, national political parties were pressing to remove Modi, leading the BJP to set aside the early election option. The upper and lower houses of the Indian parliament were preparing for parliamentary debates on the violence in Gujarat while opposition parties were pushing for a vote to censure the national government.

This report is by no means a comprehensive account of the violence that began on February 27. Ahmedabad was only one of many cities affected. Reports from other areas indicate that the violence was statewide, affecting at least twenty-one cities and sixty-eight provinces. Information from these areas also suggest a consistent pattern in the methods used, undermining government assertions that these were "spontaneous" "communal riots." As one activist noted, "no riot lasts for three days without the active connivance of the state."

Gujarat is only one of several Indian states to have experienced post-Godhra violence, though elsewhere incidents have been sporadic and were often immediately contained. Events were unfolding every day as this report went to press including developments related to the political future of the Gujarat government.

Both the Godhra incident and the attacks that ensued throughout Gujarat have been documented in meticulous detail by Indian human rights and civil liberties groups and by the Indian press. Their painstaking documentation of the attacks, often under grave security conditions, has been cited throughout this report. In some cases, the names of victims have been changed or withheld for their protection. Names of human rights activists have also been withheld to ensure their ability to continue their important work, an unfortunate indicator of the volatility surrounding the issue of communal violence in Gujarat and beyond.

All of the communities affected continue to live with a deep sense of insecurity, fearing further attacks and a cycle of retaliation. Not included in this report are many heroic accounts of individual police and of Hindu and Muslim civilians who risked their lives and livelihoods to rescue and shelter one another, and the many peace activities that have been organized by citizens amidst the ruins of the state.

The violence in Gujarat has triggered widespread outrage in India. Civil society groups from across the world have also mobilized to condemn the attacks and appeal for justice and intervention. Responding to growing international scrutiny into the violence, however, the Indian government has stated that it "does not appreciate interference in [its] internal affairs." Human Rights Watch calls on the Indian government to prevent further attacks and prosecute those found responsible for the violence in Gujarat, including state government and police officials complicit in the attacks. We call on the international community to put pressure on the Indian government to comply with international human rights and Indian constitutional law and end impunity for current and past campaigns to generate communal violence against Indian minorities.

Assistance from international humanitarian and United Nations agencies is sorely needed for Hindus and Muslims in relief camps. Human Rights Watch urges the Indian government to actively seek the assistance of these groups and to invite United Nations human rights experts to investigate state participation and complicity in the violence in Gujarat.

Note

Detailed notes and sources related to the above text can be found at *http://www.hrw.org*, following links to Asia and India.

Orthodox Christian Intolerance in Georgia

Human Rights Watch

18

- ◆ Orthodox Christianity ◆ "Non-traditional" faiths in Georgia ◆
- ◆ From intolerance to violence ◆ European Convention ◆

Non-Orthodox Christian worshippers throughout Georgia have been the targets of at least eighty violent attacks by civilian groups in the past two years. The government has made no serious efforts to criminally investigate – let alone prosecute – the perpetrators, and in some cases, police themselves violently broke up prayer gatherings. Attacks have grown more frequent with the ensuing atmosphere of impunity. Assailants stalk worshippers on their way to or from prayer meetings, or break up prayer meetings in private homes. They beat congregants, at times inflicting serious injuries, ransack private homes, destroy property, and burn religious literature. The assailants target the victims because of their faith and seek to intimidate congregants into abandoning their religious practices. The victims are primarily Jehovah's Witnesses, Pentacostalists, Baptists, and members of the Assembly of God, also known in Georgia as "non-traditional" worshippers. The evidence indicates that many of the attacks have been led or organized by Vasili Mkalavishvili, a priest from Tbilisi who has been deposed by the Georgian Orthodox Church, and his followers. Religious violence is now also perpetrated by people who have no apparent connection with Mkalavishvili,

including members of nationalist organizations, church clergy, and those who are simply neighbors of so-called non-traditional congregants. Human Rights Watch interviewed twenty-two victims of religious violence in Georgia in 2001. The government's failure to address the attacks, documented in this memorandum, violates its obligations under international law. The International Covenant on Civil and Political Rights (article 18) and the European Convention for the Protection of Human Rights and Fundamental Freedoms (article 9) provide for the right to freedom of religion. The right to religious freedom includes the "freedom to have or to adopt a religion or belief of [one's] choice, and freedom, either individually or in community with others and in public or private, to manifest [one's] religious belief in worship, observance, practice and teaching." Furthermore, "[n]o one should be subject to coercion which would impair [one's] freedom to have or adopt a religion or belief of [one's] choice." As a party to both conventions, the Georgian government has a duty to guarantee basic rights to religious minorities, to prosecute those who participate in religious violence, and to take administrative or legal measures against officials who are complicit in religious violence or who do not exercise their authority to enforce the criminal law. The government's failure to uphold these obligations early on no doubt encouraged further acts of religious violence. In the few instances where the government has acted, the measures adopted were too meager and too late to be effective.

Recommendations for United States Policy

The US government has responded to religious violence in Georgia chiefly through private expressions of concern to the Georgian government at all levels in bilateral relations and in the framework of the Organization for Security and Cooperation in Europe. The US State Department's year 2000 annual *Report on International Religious Freedom: Georgia*, adequately described religious violence, but glossed over the atmosphere of impunity created by the Georgian government's failure to act. The US Embassy in Tbilisi, jointly with the Embassy of the United Kingdom, issued a public statement in response to an incident of police and mob violence in September 2000. While private demarches are welcome, they have been ineffectual in pressing the government of Georgia to take any meaningful action. To address the atmosphere of impunity, the Bush administration should urge the government of Georgia to conduct thorough and impartial investigations of religious violence, and to hold the perpetrators accountable. It should request the government of Georgia to make publicly available a case-by-case description of actions taken to investigate and prosecute cases of religious violence. It should encourage the Georgian government to better publicize its own expressions of concern about religious intolerance. With its mandate under IRFA, the US Commission on International Religious Freedom should make Georgia a priority country and ask the Bush administration for a full accounting of measures

taken to express concern about religious violence in Georgia. It should visit Georgia with a view toward making recommendations to the Bush administration for promoting accountability for religious violence and should include a section on Georgia in its next annual report.

Background

The majority of ethnic Georgians, who make up about 70 percent of Georgia's population, are considered to be associated with the Georgian Orthodox Church. Eastern Georgia adopted Christianity as its state religion in 337 AD, the second state to do so after Armenia. Many Georgians consider affiliation with Orthodoxy an essential feature of Georgian national identity. On March 30, 2001, parliament amended the constitution to establish relations between the Georgian Orthodox Church and the state on the basis of a concordat, which would grant the Church and its clergy a privileged position in Georgian society. Referred to as "nontraditional faiths," Jehovah's Witnesses, Pentacostalists, Baptists, and congregations of other Protestant faiths have been in Georgia for many years. Jehovah's Witnesses, for example, claim to have been present in Georgia since 1953, while Baptist churches there were established in the nineteenth century. The number of adherents is unknown but is believed to be in the tens of thousands. Georgia has no law expressly regulating the activities of religious organizations. Those critical of non-traditional faiths in Georgia argue that the latter are taking advantage of Georgia's economic collapse and political troubles to win converts. They take particular offense at what they perceive as aggressive proselytism by these churches. They claim such faiths eradicate Georgian identity and threaten the Georgian nation, sometimes pointing to refusal by adherents of some faiths to serve in the military. Some claim that the practices of non-traditional faiths "defile" the Orthodox Church. While not all citizens who espouse these views took up the call to violence, perpetrators of violence cited these and other justifications for their actions. Vasili Mkalavishvili, for example, recently stated to the BBC: "It is terrible, terrible that today Georgia is being invaded by dark satanic forces of the outside. Many do not understand that Georgia's salvation is in Orthodoxy, and that those sects, and especially Jehovah's Witnesses, are trying to destroy our centuries'-long tradition. This is why I and my followers have declared a battle against those sects and we are determined to carry on fighting them." In March 2001 he declared that: "We won't allow sectarians to build their Satanic churches", because: "They are against Orthodoxy and insult Jesus Christ. They are selling out Orthodoxy and the Georgian soul." Opponents of non-traditional religions who have not participated in violence against their adherents have a range of views. At a Tbilisi news conference given in July 2000, Guram Sharadze, a member of parliament from the nationalist Georgia First of All Party who filed a lawsuit which resulted in the de-registration of the Jehovah's Witnesses in Georgia, alleged that they were spending hundreds of thousands of dollars to undermine Orthodox Christianity in Georgia and, bizarrely, that they were receiving covert support from the city's American-managed electricity company. Patriarch Ilia II, the head of the Georgian Orthodox Church, has cited the growth of "sects" in Georgia to argue for closer cooperation between the Georgian Orthodox Church and the government. The Georgian Orthodox Church to date has not condemned religious violence against non-traditional faiths. In July 2001, in response to a June attack in Martvili that involved church clergy, Patriarch Ilia II said, "the Georgian Orthodox Church works within the bounds that are acceptable to the Orthodox Church, which is peaceful treatment."

From Intolerance to Violence: 1999–2000

Organized violence against non-Orthodox Christian denominations followed attempts in 1998 and 1999 by the Georgian Orthodox Church to lobby the government to restrict these denominations' activities, as well as several highly publicized actions, some violent, by government agents who sought to break up such activities. The run-up to Georgia's October 1999 parliamentary elections marked a watershed in official intolerance toward non-traditional faiths, and was the context for the first incidents of citizen violence. On May 4, 1999, Guram Sharadze filed suit in Tbilisi's Isani-Samgori district court to annul the Jehovah's Witnesses registration, arguing initially that the organization threatened the Georgian state and national identity. After the court ruled that Jehovah's Witnesses literature constituted no threat to the state, he argued that deregistration was required by Georgia's lack of a law on religion. The court in February 2000 ruled against Sharadze. But on June 27, 2000, an appeals court reversed the district court's decision in a ruling which served to annul the Jehovah's Witnesses' registration. On February 22, 2001, the Supreme Court of Georgia upheld the appeals' court ruling, holding that because the Jehovah's Witnesses is a religious organization it could not, as it had been, be registered as a "legal entity of private law" under the civil code. The Supreme Court ruling stated that deregistration meant neither the banning of the organization and its activities, nor a restriction of its members' "freedom to change their belief, either alone or jointly with others, either publicly or in private" and "freedom to manifest their religion or beliefs, from the viewpoint of religious teachings and having rituals." Some commentators expressed the view that the initial lawsuit and the ensuing violence were intended to exploit voter discontent with the Georgian government's failure to curb rampant corruption and raise living standards. After the lawsuit was filed, law enforcement agencies broke up non-traditional religious gatherings and seized their literature. On May 29, 1999, for example, police in the Gldani district of Tbilisi violently broke up a prayer meeting of the Assembly of God, threatening and beating several participants. In July and August, Georgian customs police impounded six tons of Jehovah's Witnesses' religious literature, claiming that the organization's registration had been revoked. The materials were released in December, after the Jehovah's Witnesses filed suit against the customs service. The first major mob assault took place in on October 17, 1999 in Tbilisi's Gldani district. It was led by Vasili Mkalavishvili, a priest deposed by the Georgian Orthodox Church Patriarchate, who heads what he calls the Gldani Orthodox Eparchy. The attack left at least sixteen people injured, several seriously. Incredibly, the state prosecuted two of the victims, who were convicted on charges of hooliganism, whereas the perpetrators were acquitted of charges of destruction of property. During the trial Mkalavishvili supporters assaulted human rights defenders, a journalist, and Jehovah's Witnesses who were in attendance. Among those beaten were Giga Bokeria and Kote Vardzelashvili, both of the Liberty Institute, a Georgian nongovernmental human rights organization dedicated to defending freedom of expression. The day before, on August 16, 2000, Radio Liberty/ Radio Free Europe correspondent Sozar Subeliani was reportedly assaulted and beaten as he attempted to cover the trial. Canadian human rights lawyer John Burns, who was monitoring the trial as a representative of the Jehovah's Witnesses, also said in a written statement that he was dragged to the ground and struck with a large wooden cross after Mkalavishvili's supporters burst into the court room. They stalked and beat Jehovah's Witnesses in the months that followed, at first chiefly in the Gldani district, and then throughout

Tbilisi. At least two other assaults by Mkalavishvili and his supporters followed in 1999, and violent incidents escalated in 2000: the Jehovah's Witnesses organization claims that thirty-eight incidents took place in 2000. Mkalavishvili's followers were alleged to be involved in the majority of attacks. In several cases, police were involved in violence against non-traditional worshippers. Twice in September 2000, police attempted to prevent Jehovah's Witnesses from mounting large conventions, and stood by idly as organized groups of people attacked those who had tried to gather; some police allegedly beat the congregants. On September 8, police stopped vehicles taking Jehovah's Witnesses to a convention in Zugdidi, and violently dispersed those who had gathered. According to the US State Department, the Zugdidi incident was under investigation, but the results are unknown. On September 16, police turned back nineteen vehicles transporting Jehovah's Witnesses to a convention in Marneuli, about twenty-five kilometers south of Tbilisi. They failed to stop mobs that descended on the convoy at the roadblock, dragged some of the congregants off the buses and beat them; some victims claimed police beat them as well. The mob looted the convention site. Although Mkalavishvili has been indicted for interfering with religious services and violating public order (see below), he and his followers have had little to fear from law enforcement agencies, which have been notoriously unresponsive to episodes of violence and patently unwilling to protect non-traditional religious believers. On some occasions, Mkalavishvili has given public warnings of impending attacks; in September 2000, he boasted on the popular "60 Minutes" weekly investigative reporting program, broadcast on Rustavi-2 TV, that he would break up the Marneuli assembly. In a statement broadcast on Georgian television in May 2001, after he was indicted, Mkalavishvili said that while he would no longer be directly involved in incidents against non-traditional faiths, his followers would continue to do so upon his instructions. During a live television call-in program aired on July 24, Mkalavishvili gave his "blessing to stop Jehovah's Witnesses in the street or wherever they see them, confiscate their literature and burn it in front to them," using violence if necessary. An August 2001 BBC program cited Mkalavishvili's boasting of support from Georgia's law enforcement agencies. He said, " Thank God that among our security services and policemen there are people who are willing to help me: they realize how dangerous it is to have these sects in Georgia."

Human Rights Watch has a leaflet believed to originate with Mkalavishvili's group, found in Tbilisi in March 2001, that warns Jehovah's Witnesses not to gather. Such leaflets are distributed in areas where Jehovah's Witnesses plan to assemble. The leaflet reads:

> A Fatal Warning to All Sects that Defy the Holy Spirit: Temporary leader of Gldani Orthodox Eparchy Father Basili Mkalavishvili with his large number of followers strictly warns various sects like Jehovah's Witnesses, Evangelists, Baptists, Adventists, and Krishnaite... to stop anti-Orthodox activities in Georgia, stop satanic mass meetings against the true Orthodox faith. We call for the Georgian Orthodox nation not to let sectarian meetings take place and to actively defend our ancestors' Christian belief. Gldani Orthodox press service. This is the last warning.

Escalation of Religious Violence in 2001

Given the government's poor record on prosecuting perpetrators of religious violence in 2000, and the police action taken to disrupt non-traditional activities, the rapid escalation of attacks in 2001 is unsurprising. A notable spike in the violence occurred after the Supreme Court's February 22, 2001 decision on the de-registration of Jehovah's Witnesses. According to the Jehovah's Witnesses, forty attacks took place in the first seven months of 2001, more than had occurred throughout 2000; most happened after February 22. Whereas attacks in 1999 and early 2000 were concentrated primarily in Tbilisi and its Gldani district, they later spread to other towns and rural areas of Georgia. Police were involved in some of the incidents. Human Rights Watch interviewed twenty-two victims of eight different acts of religious violence. Mkalavishvili and his followers have been implicated in most of the attacks, but increasingly they are perpetrated by other nationalist organizations, church clergy, and simply neighbors of non-traditional congregants. In seven cases documented by Human Rights Watch, Jehovah's Witnesses had attempted to hold small prayer meetings in private homes; in one incident they were holding a modified congress. In one attack, the assailants beat congregants with wooden clubs spiked with nails. Police in one case cleared the way for mobs to attack worshipers. In no case did police take effective action to prevent or stop the violence, or diligently to investigate it.

Attacks in Tbilisi

On February 27, five days after the Supreme Court decision upholding the de-registration of the Jehovah's Witnesses, about 300 Jehovah's Witnesses gathered at 10:00 a.m. in the courtyard of a private home in the Isani district of Tbilisi for a prayer meeting. At about 3:00 p.m., a group of about fifteen to twenty people led by Basili Mkalavishvili broke up the assembly, breaking into the courtyard and beating those inside. According to Rudolph Mikirtumov, a Jehovah's Witness who was at the gathering, between twenty and thirty policemen were at the scene, but instead of deterring or stopping the attack, they forced open the courtyard gates, allowing the assailants to enter the courtyard. Mikirtumov, an unemployed tailor, told Human Rights Watch that police had told him that they came to the gathering "to protect [the Jehovah's Witnesses] from any possible incidents. At noon Rustavi2 TV showed the assembly on the news, and a bit later the police came." At 3:00 p.m. the Jehovah's Witnesses group received a phone call from other Jehovah's Witnesses who had just left the assembly, warning the group that Mkalavishvili and his supporters were on their way to the gathering. Mikirtumov immediately warned the police and asked for help, to which one policeman reportedly replied, "We can't get beaten up instead of you." Mikirtumov then went inside the courtyard to secure the wires that held the gate closed. Several minutes later, Mkalavishvili's group arrived, but had trouble opening the gate. Three men in plainclothes then jumped over the gate, two showing police badges and saying they were officers, and the third identifying himself as an officer. One of the men bearing a badge forced the gate open, saying he needed to let other police officers in. The attackers rushed through the gate and beat those gathered, using clubs, large crosses, and Bibles. Within thirty minutes, the house was ransacked. Mikirtumov sustained multiple injuries to his face, which required his brief hospitalization. Mikirtumov told Human Rights Watch that instead of questioning him about the details of the attack, procuracy investigators said that local residents had been complaining about the noise level at the gathering, an allegation Mikirtumov believes was fabricated in order to intimidate and dissuade him from pursuing any complaint. They also reportedly stated that information he provided about police having forced open the gate for the attackers was "unnecessary." One of the most vicious incidents in Tbilisi took place on April 30, 2001, when a group wielding sticks spiked with nails broke up a prayer meeting in the Svanetisubani district of Tbilisi. The attackers broke windows, furniture and electrical equipment, beat worshippers with the spiked sticks, and burned religious literature in a large bonfire on the street. As a result, three victims were hospitalized. Among them was Tamaz Nachkebia, who sustained multiple contusions and whose head injuries required five stitches. A Human Rights Watch representative saw the open wounds to Nachkebia's left hand, right arm, left foot, as well as the bruises to his right ribcage and left cheek. Nachkebia told Human Rights Watch what happened to him: "About ten people were beating me, I was lying on the floor and could not move." He also said that the attackers were shouting, "Hit everybody, these little snakes are sons of the devil!" Some of the attackers wore masks that slipped off. Two eyewitnesses identified the attackers as well-known followers of Mkalavishvili. According to an eyewitness, Zviad Dzadzamia, when the attack started one of the congregants phoned the police, who allegedly retorted, "Serves you right, why were you meeting?" According to both Dzadzamia and Nachkebia, a police squad arrived while the attack was in progress, but left without explanation. About a half hour later, another police squad arrived – by this time the assailants had fled – and asked witnesses to write statements. To our knowledge no witnesses were called for questioning, and no one has been arrested in relation to the assault. According to Dzadzamia and Nachkebia, Jemal Gamakharia, a member of parliament from the national opposition Georgian Revival Party, witnessed the attack. When Dzadzamia asked him what he thought of what was going on, Gamakharia allegedly responded, "You deserve it; the worst is yet to come." On May 20, about thirty people believed by eyewitnesses to be followers of Mkalavishvili attacked about sixty people gathered to pray in an apartment in the Mukhiani district of Tbilisi. According to an eyewitness, Zaur Malania, one of the victims was a pregnant woman; another was a seventeen-year-old boy who suffered a concussion and required hospitalization. Another eyewitness, Bakuri Biuglishvili, told Human Rights Watch that he phoned the police, saying that a robbery was in progress. Police arrived within minutes, which is highly unusual in Georgia, caught five of the assailants, took them into custody, released them from custody within a half hour, and asked nine witnesses to write statements. To our knowledge, no questioning took place. Malania told Human Rights Watch that he periodically inquires about the case, but that no criminal charges had been filed. On June 17, a group of fifty or sixty men and women attacked a prayer meeting of eighty-six people in the Ortachala district of Tbilisi. The attackers beat the congregants, several of whom required medical treatment, and burned furniture, personal property, and religious literature on the street. Giorgi Kiknavelidze, a twenty-six-year-old economist, sustained multiple bruises and contusions, mostly to the shoulders and legs. He told Human Rights Watch that the attack seemed very well planned: "They all knew what to do; some of them searched for literature, others beat people, while others made a human gauntlet to the door and assaulted everybody who tried to escape. . . The whole attack lasted about ten to fifteen minutes. . . An Ikarus model bus and one mini-bus were waiting outside and that's how they [the assailants] fled." An eyewitness, Nana Robakidze, an unemployed veterinarian, was able to flee the violence. Her husband, who sustained several bruises to his back, went to the Ponichala police station and returned to the scene with two police officers. "The attackers were still there, getting ready to leave, but police would not act. And only when the mob left, they started asking questions, like why we were gathered, what we wanted." Robakidze, who is thirty-one, said she was not questioned by police about the incident. Kiknavelidze named five of the attackers, all Mkalavishvili followers, but noted that Mkalavishvili himself was not present. That evening he reported the incident to

the Mtatsmindia-Krtsanisi district police. To our knowledge, no investigation is under way.

Attacks outside Tbilisi
Martvili (Western Georgia)

Two priests and their parishioners assaulted a group of Jehovah's Witnesses on their way to a prayer meeting on the morning of June 8, 2001. Kakha Vashakidze, an unemployed economist who serves as the prayer group leader, had arrived early at the home where the prayer meeting was to take place. At about noon, four female congregants arrived, telling Vashakidze that two priests, whom Vashakidze identified by name, and their parishioners had been blocking the road leading to the prayer gathering; the crowd, according to the women, shouted insults and struck the Jehovah's Witnesses who were attempting to pass. The hostess for the prayer meeting complained immediately to the local police chief, who reportedly said that the group had no legal right to gather since they were banned, an oblique reference to the February Supreme Court ruling. Four policemen accompanied her home, to ensure that Vashakidze would leave and that the prayer meeting therefore would not take place. Police formed a cordon through which they instructed Vashakidze to leave the house. As he left, one of the priests implicated in the attack warned Vashakidze not to hold any more meetings on that street because it led to a church, which he said made it holy. "He said if we held any more meetings there he would not be responsible for the consequences," Vashakidze told Human Rights Watch. One week later Vashakidze returned to the police station with copies of the constitution and the Supreme Court decision, which states that deregistration of the Jehovah's Witnesses does not mean denial of their right to gather for prayer. The police officer in charge of the case told Vashakidze to take the documents to the priest and discuss it with him. The following week, Vashakidze returned to the station for further discussions. On that occasion, the priest reportedly threatened, in the presence of the police chief, to use "Basili's methods" (a reference to Mkalavishvili) if the Jehovah's Witnesses attempted to hold another prayer meeting in that area on that street.

Sachkhere

In another incident involving clergy, on March 6, 2001, a group of about 150 people, which included four priests from a local parish, attacked a prayer meeting in the town of Sachkhere, about 270 kilometers northwest of Tbilisi. Savle Gotsadze told Human Rights Watch that on March 5 he was on his way to the home of the B. family, when he saw a mob of people and the four priests, whom he recognized as being from the local parish, in their clerical garb, outside B's building. The priests and several members of the crowd went to B's apartment, where they warned the family not to hold prayer meetings there, and claimed that the patriarchate had authorized them to break up any such gatherings. Gotsadze said that the laymen also struck B. The next day, March 6, the crowd attacked the prayer gathering at B's home, breaking household items and burning religious literature. The crowd broke into another building on B's property, which had been used as the meeting room, looting the premises and burning religious literature. Gotsadze said: "There were about 150 people led by a priest on horseback. . . They started to break the doors. . . For a moment people stopped, but then one priest cried, "What are you doing?! Why did you stop?" That's when the mob got violent. I asked them not to touch the hostess . . . and then I was caught and they started beating me, saying that I talk too much. I fell down and they punched and kicked me . . . " The hostess, Nana, also got severely beaten. Gotsadze told Human Rights Watch that a forensic doctor examined him for injuries he

sustained during the attack. While the chief of police expressed regret to Gotsadze and B. about the incident, to our knowledge, no investigation is under way.

Borjomi District

On April 1, 2001 a crowd of fifteen accosted Jehovah's Witnesses as they were returning from a prayer meeting in the village of Dviri, about 150 kilometers west of Tbilisi. Present during the assault was the village administrator, who upbraided the Jehovah's Witnesses for holding the meeting. Boris Gogoladze told Human Rights Watch that just after the prayer meeting dispersed, as he was on his way home, a group of people drove up in separate cars. Someone called out to him, and when Gogoladze approached, a man whom he identified by name grabbed his bookbag, hit him in the face, ripped off the strap, and began to hit other Jehovah's Witnesses who were waiting at a nearby bus stop. The other members of the crowd observed and allegedly swore at the Jehovah's Witnesses.

The attacker then turned again on Gogoladze, striking him and seizing his religious literature. "The chief administrator of the village shouted at me, 'why are you still gathering, don't you see what happens to you?'" The incident ended when the deputy administrator of the city of Borjomi told the attacker to stop.

Rustavi

On April 7, 2001 a group of about twenty people – led by Paata Bluashvili, a member of "Cross," an ultra-orthodox organization whose explicit aim is to prevent the spread of non-traditional confessions in Georgia – broke up a prayer gathering in Rustavi, ransacking the apartment where the gathering was held, and beating those gathered and neighbors who came to their defense. The mob also seized and burned religious literature in a bonfire. About sixty people had gathered in a private apartment in Rustavi for the prayer meeting; about ten minutes after the meeting started, the mob burst into the apartment, according to Ardoteli Kviria, an eyewitness. Kviria then went with five other congregants to file a complaint with the Rustavi police (first precinct), who, according to Kviria, accused the Jehovah's Witnesses of violating public order by meeting in a private home. The victims were asked to write explanatory statements; to our knowledge no investigation into the attack is under way. Another attack on a prayer meeting, held April 29, was led by the congregants' neighbors. The congregants had begun to disperse after hearing threats shouted through the door. Ilia Eterishvili said he and others had tried to escape through the windows, but that the neighbors beat them as they got outside. "They verbally and physically assaulted me for about ten minutes . . . they took all our bags, books, and personal belongings and made a fire right in the yard and burned everything." Eterishvili said he reported the incident the next day to the police, who instructed him to write an explanatory statement; no investigation followed.

The response by Georgian authorities

In 2001 Georgian officials at the highest level have condemned violence against non-traditional faiths, but throughout the past two years have failed to take action to stop the attacks, to discipline police and local authorities complicit in the attacks, or to protect congregants from further attacks and protect their right to freedom of religion. A March 22, 2001 presidential decree, intended to stem a new crime wave of kidnappings, attacks on foreigners, and trafficking of contraband, also addressed religious violence. Among other things, it ordered the Ministry of Internal Affairs, the General Procuracy, and the Ministry of State Security to stop crimes motivated by religion and "to take extraordinary measures to identify and punish those guilty." Notably, the decree's preamble

cited the damage inflicted on Georgia's international reputation by the deteriorating crime situation. President Eduard Shevardnadze hosted a meeting of seven religious leaders on July 10, 2001 that aimed to find a common strategy for combating religious violence, and reportedly attributed the wave of violence to people's susceptibility to extremism, brought on by their poverty. Reacting to the spike in violent incidents following its ruling upholding the deregistration of the Jehovah's Witnesses, the Georgian Supreme Court condemned the "acts of vandalism" perpetrated by Mkalavishvili "and other expressions of religious extremism and intolerance . . . " The Supreme Court also called on "all law enforcement structures to take appropriate measures against those persons who place themselves above the law and because of religious motives take it upon themselves [to] execute 'justice.' Such acts are not only illegal, but they also create a serious danger for the public and the State." The statement denied any causal link between its February 27, 2001 decision and the escalation in religious intolerance, noting that while its ruling deregistered the Jehovah's Witnesses, it did not restrict their right to practice their faith. However, this aspect of the February ruling received relatively little coverage in the official or independent media, and there are many instances, including those documented by Human Rights Watch, in which local officials have cited the Supreme Court decision as justification for barring prayer gatherings and the like.

On March 30, the same day it adopted a constitutional amendment establishing a concordat between the Georgian Orthodox Church and the state, parliament adopted a resolution condemning religious violence. Also, Human Rights Ombudswoman Nana Devdariani has repeatedly condemned the violence.

While welcome, these statements came far too late and have had little impact. As of this writing, not a single perpetrator of religious violence has been successfully prosecuted. While the victims of religious violence can often identify their attackers, when police react at all to such incidents, most often they do little more than take statements from victims. As noted above, two Mkalavishvili supporters were acquitted on charges of property damage in relation to the October 17, 1999 attack. Under pressure from the international community, Georgian authorities on March 30 charged Mkalavishvili with interfering with religious services and violating public order. The General Procuracy transferred to the Tbilisi City Procuracy ten criminal cases – encompassing seventeen violent incidents – that involve Mkalavishvili. It is unclear which incidents are at issue; the Tbilisi City Procuracy declined a request by the Liberty Institute for information on the subject, citing, inexplicably, the presumption of innocence. Mkalavishvili is currently under a restrain-

ing order not to leave the Tbilisi city limits prior to trial. He has not abided by the order, continues publicly to direct his supporters to break up religious gatherings, and continues to make public announcements to this effect. No trial date has been scheduled in any of the cases involving Mkalavishvili. Human Rights Watch has on several occasions requested information from the Georgian government about steps taken to bring to justice those responsible for the attacks and foster a climate of religious tolerance. To date, we have received no response.

Note

Detailed notes and sources related to the above text can be found at _http_://www.hrw.org; Original title of article:

Memorandum to the US Government on Religious Violence in the Republic of Georgia August 29, 2001

Israel and the Palestinian Authority Territories

Human Rights Watch

19

◆ Israel and the Occupied West Bank and Gaza Strip ◆

◆ Palestinian Authority ◆ Role of the international community ◆

Human Rights Developments

Many civilians were among the over seven hundred Palestinians and over two hundred Israelis who, by November 2001, had been killed in the violence that followed the eruption of clashes between Israelis and Palestinians in September 2000. In addition, some 16,000 Palestinians and some 1,700 Israelis were injured in the violence. The conflict was marked by attacks on civilians and civilian objects by both Israeli security forces and Palestinian armed groups. Both Israeli and Palestinian authorities failed to take the necessary steps to stop the security forces under their control from committing abuses, and failed to adequately investigate and punish the perpetrators.

Israeli security forces were responsible for extensive abuses, including indiscriminate and excessive use of lethal force against unarmed Palestinian demonstrators; unlawful or suspicious killings by Israel Defense Forces (IDF) soldiers; disproportionate IDF gunfire in response to Palestinian attacks; inadequate IDF response to abuses by Israeli settlers against Palestinian civilians; and "closure" measures on Palestinian communities that amounted to collective punishment. They

also mounted a series of killings of suspected Palestinian militants under a controversial "liquidations" policy directed against those they claimed to be responsible for orchestrating attacks against Israelis.

For its part, the Palestinian Authority (PA) did little to exercise its responsibility to take all possible measures to prevent and punish armed attacks by Palestinians against Israeli civilians, including suicide bombings. In addition, the various security forces of the PA carried out arbitrary arrests of alleged Palestinian "collaborators" with Israel. Many were held in prolonged detention without trial and tortured; others were sentenced to death after unfair trials and two were executed. The PA also arrested some Islamist and other militants suspected of responsibility for attacks against Israelis and held them in untried detention.

Israel and the Occupied West Bank and Gaza Strip

The Israeli–Palestinian clashes continued throughout the first ten months of 2001. In December 2000, Israeli Prime Minister Ehud Barak and his Labor Party-led coalition lost office following an early election for prime minister called by Barak. Ariel Sharon, leader of the Likud party, won a decisive victory, replacing Barak as prime minister, and fashioned a governing majority in alliance with Labor and other, mainly right-wing, parties.

The IDF resorted to excessive and indiscriminate use of lethal force, causing civilian deaths and serious injuries and damaging or destroying homes and other property. In one case directly investigated by Human Rights Watch, on December 22, 2000, IDF soldiers used live ammunition against a stone-throwing crowd of Palestinian youth in Hebron district, killing 15-year-old Arafat al-Jabarin with several shots. The soldiers, equipped with several armored cars and a tank, were located in a defensible position above and nearly 150 meters from the youths. Given the distance and the elevation, the stone throwers did not pose the "grave threat to life" that both the United Nations (UN) Basic Principles on the Use of Force and Firearms by Law Enforcement Officials and the IDF's own open fire regulations require before allowing the use of lethal fire. The subsequent IDF account of the incident did not allege any use of firearms by Palestinians, and said that the IDF had responded "with riot dispersal equipment." In another incident, on June 9, an IDF tank fired flechette shells in a populated area between Gaza City and the settlement of Netzarim. The shells, which spread razor-sharp darts over a wide area, killed three Palestinian women and injured three others. IDF officials initially said they fired in response to Palestinian gunfire from the area, but Prime Minister Sharon acknowledged on June 11 that the killing of the three women "should not have happened." IDF officials said that they opened an internal inquiry, but the results had not been made public as of this writing.

As the clashes continued, Palestinians fired at Israeli settlers and carried out suicide bombings against Israeli civilians while the IDF made increasing use of heavy weaponry, including F-16 fighter jets, combat helicopters, tanks, and light rockets against Palestinian targets, including PA police stations, security offices, prisons, and other installations.

Under Prime Minister Sharon, Israel maintained the "liquidations" policy initiated by the previous Barak administration, targeting individuals whom it accused of planning or carrying out attacks on Israeli security forces or civilians. The IDF used snipers, helicopter-fired missiles, tanks, and explosive devices to carry out the assassinations. When first introduced, Israeli authorities justified the policy as necessary to prevent a "clear, specific and imminent terrorist threat," but then expanded it to include those considered responsible for planning or carrying out atttacks on Israelis. In some cases, however, it appeared that those targeted were killed in circumstances where Israeli forces could have arrested them. According to Israeli and Palestinian human rights groups, at least thirty-five Palestinians were targeted under the "liquidations" policy between November 2000 and October 2001. In one case under the Barak government, on December 31, 2000, IDF snipers killed Thabet Thabet, the secretary general of Tulkarem's Fatah branch and director general of the PA's Health Ministry. Israel subsequently accused him of being the regional head of a Palestinian squad responsible for shooting at Israelis. On January 9, Thabet's widow petitioned the Israeli Supreme Court to order Prime Minister Ehud Barak to refrain from "executing people without trial." The court first accepted to hear the petition but then changed its decision when the government contended that the court had no jurisdiction in the matter.

Israeli security forces were responsible for a number of killings and shootings of Palestinian civilians under circumstances that warranted investigation and possible criminal prosecution. In January, the Israeli government publicly categorized the clashes as constituting "armed conflict" and insisted that it was therefore under no obligation to carry out investigations of wrongful deaths at the hands of its security forces. There was no investigation, for instance, of a February incident where soldiers opened fire on a minibus carrying sixteen Palestinian workers to their jobs, killing twenty-year-old Ziad Abu Swayyeh and injuring several others, one seriously. The shootings took place when the minibus, after driving around an army roadblock, followed the soldiers' orders and turned around to go back to al-Khadr, near Bethlehem.

The IDF opened investigations in only a few cases that it characterized as "criminal" and "extreme," but did not contact or interview crucial witnesses to the shootings or inform the relatives of the victims. One case the IDF military police did investigate was the wounding of Jad Allah al-Ja'bari, an elderly Palestinian municipal cleaner, after a journalist filmed most of the incident in which he was shot by an Israeli soldier near a checkpoint. The IDF said that the soldiers responsible had received a "severe reprobation" for violating open-fire instructions and that a military police investigation found that, in addition, the soldiers had failed to follow normal arrest procedures and to provide immediate medical care, interfered with the work of an accredited journalist, and provided inaccurate accounts to their superiors about the incident.

According to B'Tselem (the Israeli Information Center for Human Rights in the Occupied Territories), Israeli settlers killed at least eleven Palestinians between September 2000 and September 2001 and injured dozens more. Settlers attacked Palestinian homes, destroyed stores, automobiles and other property, uprooted trees, prevented farmers from reaching their fields, blocked major roads, stoned Palestinian cars, including ambulances, and targeted humanitarian workers, diplomats, and journalists. Following the killing by a Palestinian gunman of an Israeli settler child, one-year-old Shalhevet Pass, in

Hebron on March 26, some fifty armed settlers fired on the Palestinian Abu Sneineh neighborhood, burned cars and shops, caused other damage to Palestinian property, and wounded six Israeli border police. The Israeli authorities rarely intervened to stop or prevent settler attacks against Palestinians or to investigate them. When they did, perpetrators received disproportionately light sentences if they were punished at all.

Citing security reasons, Israel imposed the most severe restrictions on West Bank and Gaza Strip Palestinians' freedom of movement since it first adopted its "closure" policy in 1993. Israeli authorities sealed off the West Bank and Gaza Strip, restricting movement of Palestinians between and within those areas as well as into Israel, effectively confining them to their towns and villages for extended periods. The IDF blocked or controlled access to towns and villages by placing cement blocks, boulders, earthen dams, and army checkpoints on roads. The IDF also imposed curfews on certain Palestinian areas in response to stone throwing or shootings to protect settlers' movement along "bypass" roads. The 30,000 Palestinian residents of the Israeli-controlled area of Hebron known as H2 were kept under a nearly continuous round-the-clock curfew, but no restrictions were placed on the five hundred Israeli settlers living in the H2 area. Palestinian drivers complained that soldiers enforcing Israel's closure policy often beat and humiliated them and their passengers, slashed tires, shot at vehicles, and confiscated keys for lengthy periods.

Curfews, closures, and blockades had a devastating impact on Palestinians' lives, obstructing access to health care, schools and universities, businesses, and places of worship. According to the World Health Organization (WHO), the closures damaged water, electricity, and sanitation services. The Palestine Red Crescent Society (PRCS) said that delays at Israeli roadblocks and checkpoints contributed to a number of deaths of Palestinians in need of medical treatment. In February, the International Committee of the Red Cross (ICRC) initiated a "Closure Relief Program" and said the policy of isolating whole villages for an extended period was "contrary to International Humanitarian Law."

The UN special rapporteur on the situation of human rights in the occupied Palestinian territories reported that between September 2000 and October 2001 the IDF demolished more than three hundred Palestinian homes throughout the West Bank and Gaza, for alleged security or for punitive reasons, and uprooted 385,000 fruit and olive trees. Israeli authorities also confiscated Palestinian lands in order to expand Israeli settlements and for the construction of bypass roads, as at Deir Qiddis village near Beit Sefer settlement in June. Prime Minister Sharon authorized the construction of additional settlements and settler housing units in the West Bank, in violation of international humanitarian law.

The clashes involved Palestinian Arab citizens of Israel to an extent unprecedented in earlier periods of unrest affecting the Occupied Territories. In early October 2000, Israeli police gunfire killed thirteen Arab citizens and injured hundreds during demonstrations in Arab towns and villages in northern Israel protesting Israeli policies in the West Bank and Gaza Strip. In response, the Barak government set up a Public Commission of Inquiry headed by Supreme Court Justice Theodore Or. Four special anti-terrorist police snipers later testified that they were ordered to fire at unarmed demonstrators and those wielding slingshots in Nazareth and Um al Fahm, and northern district police commander Alik Ron stated that police had not been provided with sufficient non-lethal equipment and that police snipers used live bullets.

There were new reports of torture of detainees by Israeli security forces after October 2000. The Public Committee Against Torture in Israel (PCATI), an Israeli nongovernmental organization (NGO), reported that Israeli security forces kicked detainees and beat them with rifle butts and other implements, deprived them of food and drink for long periods, exposed them to extreme heat and cold, and used other methods that Israel's High Court of Justice explicitly prohibited in a 1999 ruling, including sleep deprivation and prolonged shackling in contorted positions. In March, according to PCATI, General Security Services (GSS) interrogators forced Iyad Nasser to squat in a painful position for an extended period of time and deprived him of sleep for seven consecutive days. At the end of May, PCATI called for Attorney General Elyakim Rubinstein to intervene on behalf of over three hundred Palestinian minors arrested since October 2000 who were reported to have been doused with freezing water, beaten, deprived of sleep, and had their heads covered with sacks during interrogation. On November 23, the UN Committee against Torture expressed its concern that the 1999 Supreme Court decision banning certain interrogation practices did not definitely prohibit torture, and that Israel's policies of closure and house demolitions might, in some cases, constitute cruel, inhuman, or degrading treatment or punishment.

Israel continued to detain Palestinians for extended periods without charge or trial. According to statistics published by B'Tselem in October, Israel held twenty-seven Palestinians under administrative detention, including Hassan Khader Shtiyeh, held since December 1, 2000. For the first time in four years, two Palestinian Arab citizens of Israel – Ghassan Athamneh and Kamal Obeid – were detained under administrative orders. According to B'Tselem, Israeli authorities held more than 1,700 Palestinians in Israeli prisons as of October 2001. Prisoners complained of food shortages and denial of medical treatment. The ICRC reported that its family visits program to prisoners was severely hampered by Israeli closures and administrative requirements.

Discrimination in law and practice against ethnic and religious minorities and other societal groups, especially on issues of employment and social benefits remained major problems. In July, the High Court ruled unanimously when considering a petition by the Association for Civil Rights in Israel (ACRI) that Palestinian Arab citizens were entitled to fair and proportionate representation on governmental bodies. The court ruled that the principle of affirmative action should apply to the Lands Council, responsible for supervising the Israel Lands Administration (ILA) whose twenty-four members included only one Arab, first appointed in May 2000.

On April 2, 2001, the High Court rejected another petition filed by ACRI against the ILA, the Jewish Agency, and the settlement of Katzir for contempt of court. ACRI claimed these bodies had not carried out the High Court's precedent-setting Ka'adan ruling of March 2000 banning discrimination between Jews and Arabs in land allocation. The respondents argued that they retained the right to interview the Ka'adan family before reaching a decision. They were instructed to do so by the court within sixty days. In November 2001, the Katzir admissions board rejected the Arab couple's application.

Israel continued to detain Sheikh 'Abd al-Karim 'Ubayd and Hajj Mustafa al-Dirani, who were abducted by Israeli forces from Lebanon in 1989 and 1994 respectively. Israel said it was holding them as "bargaining chips" for the release of an Israeli pilot, Ron Arad, missing in Lebanon since 1986. On July 4, the Tel Aviv District Court renewed both men's detention orders until December 17, 2001, after the state contended that their release endangered national security. On August 23, a five-judge panel headed by Supreme Court Justice Aharon Barak ruled that the two detainees should be permitted visits by the ICRC; four days later, however, the court delayed implementation of this decision at the request of Arad's family and those of three soldiers abducted by Hizbullah in

October 2000 pending further consideration of the case by a full bench of eleven judges. On October 31, 2001, the government stated officially that the three soldiers captured in October 2000 were dead.

In July 2001, the Israeli ministerial committee for legislation approved an application for continuity of an "Intifada Law" that would end compensation payments to Palestinians whose persons or property were harmed during the 1987-1993 intifada and preclude compensation suits by Palestinians injured during the current clashes.

Palestinian Authority

Security and military courts established by the PA continued to issue death sentences after grossly unfair trials, and the PA carried out two executions, both in January. Palestinians alleged to have collaborated with Israel faced arbitrary arrest and detention, torture and ill-treatment under interrogation, unfair trials, and the death penalty. At least five detainees died in custody; in some cases, there was evidence of torture. Some thirty Palestinians, including suspected collaborators, were victims of vigilante killings by other Palestinians; although no one was held to account for these murders. The PA also arrested and held without trial members of Islamist and other groups that claimed responsibility for attacks on Israelis. The PA released most of these detainees in October 2000, soon after the outbreak of the current intifada, despite concerns that some may have been responsible for attacks on Israeli civilians. Some of those released as well as other suspected militants were briefly detained and released periodically during the year. At the end of October 2001, following a series of attacks on Israeli civilians by Palestinian armed groups, the PA began employing administrative detention orders and detaining larger numbers of suspected militants.

In other incidents, Palestinians shot and killed Israeli drivers and passengers and fired at Israeli settlements. Israel cited the PA's failure to prevent such attacks to justify its "liquidations" policy as well as IDF attacks on PA offices and security installations .

Various PA security forces detained and tortured suspected collaborators. Khaled al-Akra, arrested in February, said that interrogators in Nablus Central Prison handcuffed him to a window and punched and beat him with sticks for six days before releasing him. In March, the British Broadcasting Corporation (BBC) reported that a letter smuggled out by inmates of a West Bank Palestinian prison warned that one of their number had been tortured for weeks to the point where his life was at risk.

Vigilante killings by Palestinians resulted in the deaths of some thirty alleged collaborators. In November 2000, Palestinian gunmen shot dead thirty-seven-year-old Kasem Khlef, suspected of collaborating with Israel in its killing of Fatah leader Hussein Abeyat. In reporting his death, Palestinian TV showed a caption that read, "He lived as a beaver and died as a dog." In February, the PA issued a statement urging Palestinians not to take the law into their own hands. Later that month, however, forty-year-old bus driver, Muhammad Musa Abd al-Rahman, was shot to death when he answered his door. The Palestinian media, citing unnamed Palestinian security officials, reported that he had collaborated with Israeli security services. The PA failed to bring to justice those responsible for those killings.

State security and military courts continued to operate despite the fact that they did not meet minimum international fair trial standards. At least thirteen persons were sentenced to death, most of them on charges of collaboration after summary trials.

The PA briefly reverted to a pattern of executions without due process. On January 13, the PA executed Allam Bani Odeh and Majdi Mikkawi after President Arafat ratified their death sentences. Both men were accused of collaboration with

Israeli security services. Police firing squads carried out the executions after summary trials before Palestinian Authority security courts without access to lawyers and without the right to appeal. Bani Odeh was shot in front of a crowd of thousands in Nablus. Speaking on Israel's Channel 2 television station, Deputy Qadura Fares, chair of the Human Rights Committee at the Palestinian Legislative Council said: "In different circumstances, in the future when we have a democratic country, the defendants will receive all their rights in court, which will assure them a just trial."

As of this writing, President Arafat had not ratified eleven other death sentences, and they had not been carried out.

At least five Palestinians died in custody in 2001, bringing to twenty-eight the number of detainees known to have died in custody since the establishment of the PA in 1994. Thirty-six year-old Salem al-Akra, arrested by Palestinian intelligence officers on February 6 on suspicion of collaborating with Israel, died in a hospital on February 27 after being transferred from Nablus central prison. A witness in Nablus who saw al-Akra's body in the hospital morgue told Human Rights Watch that it bore marks of torture: bruising on the wrists and ankles and head. An autopsy was performed but the results were not made public.

The PA failed to take adequate action against those responsible for killings of Israeli civilians. In January, three members of the Fatah organization's Tanzim militia shot dead sixteen-year-old Israeli Ofir Rahum after he was lured to Ramallah by a Palestinian woman. Six days later, masked Palestinian gunmen apparently belonging to Hamas abducted and killed two other Israelis, restauranteurs Motti Dayan and Etgar Zeitouny, as they dined in Tulkarem. The PA condemned these killings and said it would inquire into them, but no findings of any investigation had been made public by November.

Palestinian militants used firearms and bombings against Israeli settlers traveling on bypass roads and elsewhere. Children were often among the victims, as in an attack in November 2000 near the Kfar Darom settlement in Gaza which killed two adults and injured others, including five children, on a bus. On February 11, Fatah gunmen in Beit Jala shot dead Israeli settler Tsahi Sasson as he drove across a bridge near the Gush Etzion settlement, and continued firing when an ambulance arrived.

At least seventy Israelis were killed and over eight hundred injured in attacks by Palestinian suicide bombers and other militants apparently belonging to groups such as Hamas and Islamic Jihad. On June 1, a suicide bomber killed twenty-one mostly young people and injured over one hundred others outside a Tel Aviv discotheque; on August 9, another suicide bomber, apparently acting on behalf of Hamas, caused an explosion in a Jerusalem restaurant leaving eighteen, including six children, dead and many others wounded. These and other bombings and attacks that targeted or disproportionately affected civilians constituted gross violations of international humanitarian law.

The PA came under severe and repeated pressure from Israel, reinforced by military attacks on PA installations, to arrest those responsible for planning or carrying out suicide bombings and other attacks against Israelis. Under its "liquidations" policy, Israel also directly attacked and killed some of those it said were responsible. The PA took inadequate steps to identify and bring to justice those responsible for attacks on Israeli civilians but it did make some arrests. For example, in October, the PA arrested forty-five people associated with the Popular Front for the Liberation of Palestine (PFLP) after the PFLP claimed responsibility for the October 17 assassination of Israeli Tourism Minister Rehav'am Ze'evi, in retaliation for Israel's "liquidation" of PFLP Secretary General Abu Ali Mustafa a short time earlier. On November 14, the PA released two PFLP leaders after the High Court ruled that there was no

basis in law for the charge brought against them, harming the national interests of the Palestinian people. Also in October 2001, the general director of the Palestinian police issued six-month to one-year detention orders against one Hamas and six Islamic Jihad members; this was the first use of administrative detention by the PA since 1994.

PA police also clashed with Palestinian demonstrators and used excessive force. For example, on October 8, 2001, Palestinian police fired on Islamist students and other stone-throwing demonstrators in Gaza City, reportedly killing a thirteen-year-old boy and a nineteen-year-old student and injuring others.

Defending Human Rights

Israel for the most part permitted human rights organizations to collect and disseminate information in areas under its control, but the policy of closures, blockades, and curfews restricted their freedom of movement within the West Bank and Gaza Strip areas. Palestinian lawyers were unable to visit clients held in prisons in Israel.

Israeli security forces detained several Palestinian and also Israeli human rights activists. The former included Hashem Abu Hassan, a B'Tselem field researcher, as well as Adnan al-Hajjar of the Al-Mezan Center for Human Rights, and Daoud al-Dirawi, a lawyer with the Palestinian Independent Commission for Citizens' Rights (PICCR).

Israeli authorities arrested Abed Rahman al-Ahmar, a Palestinian Human Rights Monitoring Group (PHRMG) researcher, on May 24, and detained him without trial on the basis of secret GSS evidence. His lawyers said he was beaten and shackled in custody. On November 14, a military judge extended al-Ahmar's detention for a further six months.

On June 15, Israeli security forces arrested Sergio Yahni, director of the Alternative Information Center (AIC), during a demonstration organized by

Rabbis for Human Rights and the AIC against the confiscation of Palestinian land in the Bethlehem District.

The PA continued to allow human rights organizations to operate in the territory under its jurisdiction, but continued to deny human rights workers access to prisons. On March 24, Palestinian security forces arrested lawyer Nasir al-Rifa'i at a court in Ramallah: he was reportedly held incommunicado at the Ramallah military intelligence headquarters and lawyers were denied access to him.

The Role of the International Community

United Nations

After visiting Israel and the Occupied Territories at the request of the October 2000 special session of the UN Commission on Human Rights (CHR), UN High Commissioner for Human Rights Mary Robinson issued her report on November 27. She pointed to a range of abuses, including excessive use of force, restrictions on freedom of movement, and the impact of the conflict on children, and said "the bleak human rights situation in the occupied territories" warranted urgent international attention. She called too for an international monitoring presence to be deployed in the territories and for the states that are high contracting parties to the Geneva Conventions to take action "to reduce the terrible violence."

At the behest of the October 2000 special session, the UN established a commission of inquiry composed of three independent experts to investigate human rights and humanitarian law violations in the territories; this reported to the CHR in March. It said the "IDF, assisted by settlers on occasion" was responsible for most violations but noted that Palestinians had also committed violations, either under the authority of the PA or acting in their individual capacity. It too called for an "adequate and effective international pres-

ence" to be established "to monitor and regularly report on" continuing violations. Prior to the CHR, European Union (EU) ambassadors in Israel jointly confirmed that "the issues and findings" in the report "truly reflected facts on the ground" and said all its recommendations could be fully endorsed by the EU. However, the subsequent CHR resolution 2001/7, while condemning and deploring Israeli human rights violations identified in the inquiry's report, omitted any reference to Palestinian violations; although the resolution was adopted by the CHR in April, the United States and Guatemala voted against, and twenty-two states, including the EU countries, abstained.

Earlier, in late 2000, the Security Council informally considered draft proposals to establish a UN military and police observer force in the Occupied Territories but did not proceed to a vote when the US indicated that it would exercise its veto. In March 2001, the US did veto a draft Security Council resolution calling for the secretary-general to consult with the parties to the conflict and recommend "an appropriate mechanism to protect Palestinian civilians, including through the establishment of a UN observer force." Explaining the veto, chief US delegate James Cunningham said the resolution prescribed a role for the secretary-general that was not realistic, given Israel's staunch opposition to a UN observer role, and criticized its failure to call for the protection of all civilians.

In his October 4, 2001 report to the General Assembly, the UN special rapporteur on the situation of human rights in the occupied Palestinian territories also raised the issue of an international monitoring presence. Noting that "International monitors or peacekeepers have been employed in many less threatening situations in the world," he questioned the failure of "the international community to persuade Israel to accept such a presence."

In November, after reviewing Israel's report on compliance with the Convention against Torture and Other Cruel, Inhuman or Degrading Treatment or Punishment, the UN Committee against Torture welcomed the Israeli Supreme Court's 1999 decision banning the application by interrogators of "moderate physical pressure" against persons in custody but expressed concern that the court had not expressly prohibited torture, that Israeli interrogators reportedly continued to use banned methods, and that the authorities had mounted few prosecutions of alleged perpetrators of torture or ill-treatment.

In its annual report to the General Assembly in September 2001, the UN Relief and Works Agency for Palestinian Refugees in the Near East (UNRWA) complained that it had encountered serious problems in providing humanitarian assistance in the July 2000 to June 2001 period due to Israeli restrictions on the freedom of movement of its staff, denial of access to UNWRA staff members who Israel detained, and threats by IDF personnel against UNRWA staff members, including Commissioner General Peter Hansen.

On October 25, 2001, the Security Council issued a Presidential Statement that reproduced and "supported all elements" of a statement that representatives of the US, EU, Russia, and the UN issued earlier in the day in Gaza. This urged the PA to ensure "strict implementation of the ceasefire" and called on Israel to halt extrajudicial killings, ensure greater restraint by the IDF, fully respect the ceasefire, and "move swiftly to ease the closures."

European Union

The EU continued to be the major donor to the Palestinian Authority. Total project support by the European Commission for the year 2000 amounted to US $119 million; $80 million represented a "special cash facility" for the PA's Ministry of Finance. The EU increased its support to compensate in part for the PA's loss of $226 million – approximately 60 percent of its public

revenue – in customs and tax revenues withheld by Israel following the outbreak of the intifada. European Commission funding to the PA amounted to US $106 million from January to October 2001, but this was conditioned on the PA's adoption of an austerity budget, a freeze in public sector employment, and consolidation of all PA public revenues into a single Ministry of Finance account. The EU also conditioned its assistance for the judiciary on the PA's implementation of a judicial reform draft law enacted by the Palestine Legislative Council but still awaiting President Arafat's approval. Other large donors to the PA judiciary, notably Japan via the UN Development Program and Saudi Arabia via the World Bank, did not insist on similar conditions.

Israel was not eligible for direct EU financial aid. According to press reports in December, France declined to sell Israel tear-gas launchers and grenades that it had requested.

The EU strongly criticized the PA's execution of two alleged collaborators with Israel in early 2001 and called for an end to such executions. Subsequently, the State Security Court imposed further death sentences but they were not ratified by President Arafat and the PA had carried out no further executions as of November.

The Swedish government, then holding the presidency, delivered the EU's most comprehensive statement on human rights violations by Israel and the PA at the CHR in April. In this, the EU reaffirmed the applicability of the Fourth Geneva Convention to the Occupied Territories as "binding international humanitarian law," praised the balanced nature of the high commissioner's November 2000 report, and regretted Israel's refusal to cooperate with the special rapporteur. The statement criticized and called for an end to abuses by both sides. With regard to Israel, the EU specifically criticized disproportionate and indiscriminate use of force, extrajudicial executions, closures as a form of collective punishment, and the retention of laws that discriminate against Palestinian Arab citizens of Israel. With regard to the PA, the EU criticized torture, deaths in detention, use of the death penalty, and restrictions on freedom of expression. During the CHR session, the EU abstained on a resolution that condemned Israeli human rights and humanitarian law violations in the Occupied Territories but sponsored another that expressed "grave concern" at continuing Israeli settlement activities "since all these actions are illegal, constitute a violation of the Geneva Convention relative to the Protection of Civilian Persons in Time of War, and are a major obstacle to peace."

In a May 17 resolution, the European Parliament expressed its "deep consternation" at the number of civilian victims of the clashes, condemned excessive use of force by Israel, Palestinian attacks against Israeli civilians, called for the UN Security Council to authorize the dispatch of an observer mission, and regretted the decision of some states not to support the CHR resolution condemning human rights violations in the Occupied Territories. The parliamentary resolution also urged the European Commission and EU member states to "avoid any indirect complicity in illegal settlements" by strictly applying rules-of-origin regulations to EU duty-free imports from Israel.

On November 24, a spokesman for the European Commission stated that the EU's executive arm had decided to advise the customs authorities of member states to require Israeli exporters to deposit funds to cover duties that might be imposed retroactively on imports that are determined to originate from illegal settlements. Some member states, however, reportedly remained reluctant to implement this decision on the grounds that it would impede EU efforts to persuade Israel to resume peace negotiations with the PA.

On June 18, lawyers representing twenty-eight survivors of the 1982 Sabra and Shatila massacres in Lebanon in 1982 filed a complaint against Prime Minister Sharon, who was Israel's defense minister at the time, accusing him of war crimes, crimes against humanity, and genocide. The suit was filed in Belgium under legislation allowing prosecution of such crimes in Belgian courts even if they were committed elsewhere and neither the perpetrators nor the victims were Belgian nationals. A court heard opening arguments from the Belgian prosecutor and Sharon's attorney on November 27 on the issue of whether a Belgian magistrate could continue his investigation into the charges and start legal proceedings in Belgium. Belgian officials expected a decision in late January.

On the day before the November 27 hearing, lawyers representing some thirty Israelis filed a complaint in a Brussels court accusing President Arafat and other Palestinian officials and leaders of "murder, crimes against humanity, and genocide." The complaint named Arafat as the "principal conspirator" in a number of attacks on civilians carried out by Palestinians since 1966 in both Israel and other countries.

In Denmark, there were protests after Israel named Carmi Gillon, former head of the General Security Services, or Shabak, as its ambassador beginning in August. On July 9, Gillon was reported in Denmark's *Jyllands Posten* newspaper to have acknowledged his direct involvement in a hundred interrogations of Palestinian security detainees using techniques widely held to amounting to torture or ill-treatment. In a statement, the Danish Foreign Ministry, which had recently accepted Gillon's accreditation, said the government "strongly oppos[ed] all forms and acts of torture" but that it was a foreign government's "own responsibility" to decide who represented it in Denmark.

United States

Israel, the largest recipient of US military and economic assistance, received an estimated $1,980 million in military assistance and $840 million in Economic Support Funds for fiscal year (FY) 2001, ending in

September. The administration requested $2,040 million in military aid and $720 million in support funds for FY 2002, beginning in October. According to the State Department, these funds "will enable the Israeli government to meet cash flow requirements associated with the procurement of US origin systems such as F-16 fighter aircraft, the Apache Longbow attack helicopter, field vehicles, and advanced armaments."

The US provided an estimated $85 million to the West Bank and Gaza in FY 2001; $75 million was budgeted for FY 2002. This assistance was channeled through US private voluntary organizations and Palestinian NGOs, and was not provided directly to the Palestinian Authority.

The Clinton administration continued its efforts to broker peace talks between Israel and the PA even in its final weeks. On December 23, 2000, President Clinton orally presented "a series of options" to Palestinian and Israeli negotiators in Washington, D.C. These proposals reportedly called for Palestinian refugees to be able to return to their homeland, defined as a "viable and contiguous" Palestinian state comprising approximately 95 percent of the West Bank and Gaza, while land annexed by Israel would include 80 percent of the settler population. Further Israeli-Palestinian talks in Taba, however, failed to reach agreement before President Clinton (and Prime Minister Barak) left office.

The Bush administration conspicuously declined to replicate the same level of involvement in trying to bring the two sides together and confined itself to promoting the recommendations of the Sharm al-Sheikh Fact-Finding Committee, whose report was issued on April 30. The committee, a five-member international body set up at the Sharm al-Sheikh summit in October 2000 and headed by former US senator George Mitchell, proposed sequential steps towards a resumption of peace talks, starting with a ceasefire and "cooling-off" period. The committee, in its introduction to the report, wrote that a resolution to the conflict required that "agreed commitments be implemented, international law respected, and human rights protected." Although its recommendations were not framed in terms of human rights and humanitarian law, many were broadly consistent with those principles, such as adopting non-lethal IDF responses to unarmed demonstrators, conducting impartial investigations into alleged unlawful deaths, and effective PA steps to halt armed attacks against Israeli civilians.

Following the attacks of September 11, the Bush administration intensified its efforts to secure a ceasefire and to restart political negotiations. On November 19, in a major foreign policy speech, Secretary of State Colin Powell called on the PA to "arrest, prosecute and punish the perpetrators of terrorist acts," criticized Israeli settlements, and said that "the occupation must end." He announced that retired Marine Corps Gen. Anthony Zinni would travel to the region as his special advisor to "get that ceasefire in place." Powell later said that Zinni would remain in the region "as long as it takes." As of late November, however, the first steps toward a ceasefire remained elusive.

The State Department's *Country Reports on Human Rights Practices for 2000* was comprehensive in its treatment of Israeli and PA human rights violations. However, generally, the State Department's criticism in response to specific violations was couched in language that labeled them "provocative" or "unhelpful," rather than as violations of international human rights or humanitarian law. Former assistant secretary of state Edward Walker, speaking about Israeli use of US helicopter gunships in residential areas, told the *Baltimore Sun* on May 27, shortly after he left office, "It was a clear administration position that this was an excessive use of force." The public comments of the press spokesperson, however, were typically limited to expressions of "concern," although a press briefing given by State

Department spokesman Philip Reeker on October 23, 2001, was a notable exception, Reeker stating: "We deeply regret and deplore Israeli Defense Force actions that have killed numerous Palestinian civilians over the weekend. The deaths of these innocent civilians under the circumstances reported in recent days are unacceptable, and we call upon Israel to ensure that its armed forces exercise greater discipline and restraint."

Israeli use of US-supplied weapons in the clashes, and in particular the use of helicopter gunships in targeted killings of individual Palestinian militants, raised questions among several members of Congress and in the public as to whether such use violated the Arms Export Control Act (AECA). In a September press briefing, State Department spokesman Richard Boucher said, "We've made it quite clear that we are opposed to the use of heavy weaponry and in these circumstances, particularly in populated areas where the risk of innocent casualties is very high," but he did not comment on this as a possible violation of the AECA on the grounds that he wished to avoid "pushing this into a legalistic discussion."

On September 9, the State Department released an August 17 response of Secretary of State Colin Powell to US Representative John Conyers, who had raised the question of possible AECA violations in a public letter to Powell. "Based on our assessment of the totality of the underlying facts and circumstances," Powell wrote, "we believe that a report [to Congress] under section 3c of the AECA is not required." The administration "has been monitoring Israeli actions carefully and will continue to do so," Powell added.

Note

Detailed notes and sources related to the above text can be found at:
http://www.hrw.org/wr2k2/mena5.html

Further Reading

Ghanem, As'ad, The Palestinian Regime: A "Partial Democracy" (Brighton and Portland: Sussex Academic Press, 2001).

Relevant Human Rights Watch Reports:

Israel: Second Class: Discrimination Against Palestinian Arab Children in Israel's Schools, 12/01

Israel, the Occupied West Bank and Gaza Strip, and Palestinian Authority Territories: Justice Undermined: Balancing Security and Human Rights in the Palestinian Justice System, 11/01

Israel, the Occupied West Bank and Gaza Strip, and Palestinian Authority Territories: Center of the Storm: A Case Study of Human Rights Abuses in Hebron District, 4/01

Indigenous and Minority Traditions:
Case Studies from *Survival*

- ◆ Indigenous and minority rights ◆ Work of Survival ◆
- ◆ Indigenous rights in Africa ◆ Indigenous rights in Australia ◆
- ◆ Indigenous rights in the Americas ◆

Africa

Twa in Rwanda – Rwanda's Hidden Tribe

We used to meet and dance. But now everything has changed. It is very difficult for people to meet and dance, especially because most of them have died. *Twa man, 1995*

Reports of the 1994 bloodbath in Rwanda, and the subsequent exodus of refugees, have highlighted the differences between the Tutsi and the majority Hutu. Concern has rightly focused on the genocide inflicted by Hutu extremists on the Tutsi and moderate Hutu; however, little attention has been paid to the Twa, or Batwa, Rwanda's third "tribe" or (more accurately) caste. (There are also Twa in Burundi, Uganda and Zaire.)

They are among the "Pygmy" peoples of central Africa; but most of them, though short, are not so small as to distinguish them easily from other Rwandans. According to the census of 1991 there were 29,000 of them in Rwanda, though this may have been an underestimate. There are now estimated to be about 11,000 left in the country.

The Twa were already living on the margins of Rwandan society before the 1994 violence erupted. They are divided into two groups.

The majority have lived for generations as the lowest caste in Rwandanese society, dominated by both the Tutsi aristocracy and the Hutu peasants. They rarely possessed land to farm. Their main livelihood came from making pottery; however, the introduction of plastic and metal containers ruined their market. They also worked on Hutu farms as day labourers. The Twa are famous as musicians and dancers, and used to form the majority of the Rwandan national dance troupe.

The second group, also known as Impunyu, have until recently lived in the forests as hunter-gatherers. Some lived in the forest of Gishwati, until most of it was cut down for tea plantations and pasture, in a World Bank-backed development project in the early 1980s. There was no resettlement plan for the Twa, who were left to beg by the roadside. Later charitable projects gave them some land to farm, although this was only partly effective.

The Twa were looked down on by both Tutsi and Hutu. The discrimination took many forms; access to public wells was forbidden, and a cup from which a Twa had drunk might be broken to avoid reusing it. There have been numerous reports of Batwa being wounded or even killed because they had managed to buy some land or accumulate valuables.

In 1991–2 a group of educated Twa set up two organisations to try to improve their economic and social situation. Their projects were wrecked, however, by the violence of 1994.

In the genocide, the Twa community has suffered terribly. Often they were targeted as supposed supporters of the invading Rwandanese Patriotic Front, or more generally as "friends of the Tutsi". Tragically, some Twa are also accused of taking part in the massacres. As a particularly vulnerable group, they could be forced to kill or commit atrocities out of fear for their own lives. About 10,000 Twa joined the flood of refugees that fled to Zaire and Tanzania. In the refugee camps they had even less access to scarce necessities than the other Rwandans.

In the desperation and bitterness following the genocide, many Twa as well as others have been imprisoned or killed without evidence of guilt. It is particularly the Twa men who have been victimised, leaving the women and children to fend for themselves. In 1995 it was estimated that about 30% of the Twa had been killed either in the original massacres or in revenge, or died of hunger or disease; children suffered particularly heavily. By comparison, it is reckoned that 14% of the Rwandan population as a whole (mostly Tutsi) were massacred. A probable further 30% of the Twa (8,000–9,000) are still living outside Rwanda, leaving only 40% of the pre-war population in the country.

As violence escalates once again in Rwanda, the Twa are still among the victims. However, one cause for optimism is that they have re-established their organisations under the umbrella group "Communauté des Authochthones Rwandais" (CAURWA). It is difficult for them to assert a common identity, since the policy of the present Rwandan government is to give no official recognition to ethnic differences. Yet in spite of this and other obstacles, they are working hard to heal the wounds of their people.

Background Reading

Lewis, Jerome & Knight, Judy, *The Twa of Rwanda*, World Rainforest Movement and International Work Group for Indigenous Affairs, 1995 (available from Survival).

"Pygmies" in Central Africa: Peoples of the forest

Today, we don't recognise the forest any more, we don't understand it. The logging companies destroy the forest . . . Our children have no future. Where will they find the animals to hunt? The bark, the leaves and the fruits for food and medicine? We ask the Government not to forget us, to do something so that our life today and tomorrow will not be as black as a night without stars. Protect us, protect the forest. *Jeane Silpen, of the Bakola people, Cameroun*

In the forests of central Africa live the peoples who together are generally known as "Pygmies" (though many of them dislike the name since it is often used as a term of contempt). The different "Pygmy" peoples are widely separated and speak different languages. All, however, share the same deep relationship with the forest which is their home – except in those places, like Rwanda, where the forest no longer exists.

They number perhaps 250,000 altogether, and live in all the central African countries: the Democratic Republic of Congo (DRC, formerly Zaire), Congo, Cameroun, Gabon, the Central African Republic, Rwanda, Burundi and Uganda. Their average height is about 1.5 m (4'8"), though some groups are taller. The languages they use are derived from those of neigbouring peoples; however, certain shared words which are not borrowed suggest that they once had a common language. It is not certain whether they were the original inhabitants of the forest, or whether they moved their alongside the farmers and fishers who expanded from what is now central Cameroun after about 3,000 BC. At all events, the ancestors of the present day "Pygmies" exchanged forest produce with these farmers for foodcrops, iron and pottery, setting up a relationship which continues to this day.

From West to East the main "Pygmy" peoples are: the Bakola and Bagyeli of the Cameroun coast (4,000); the Baka of southeastern Cameroun, Congo and Gabon (40,000–50,000); the Babongo of Gabon and Congo (2,000); the Ba-aka or Babenjele of CAR and northern Congo (8,000–10,000); the various Batwa or Basua groups of DRC; the Bambuti and Efe of the Itrui forest in the northeast of the DRC (30,000–40,000); and the Batwa of Rwanda and Burundi (perhaps 20,000). (The figures are rough estimates.) There are also a number of other smaller groups.

To varying degrees groups such as the Baka, the Ba-aka and the Bambuti still spend long periods of time in the forest, gathering its plants and hunting its animals. Everything the own has to be carried when they move to a new hunting camp, so it is useful to have few possessions. What they do have in abundance is an intimate knowledge of the forest: the ability to read animal tracks, to know the flowering and fruiting cycles of plants, to locate a bees' nest from the flight of a bee. They know the individual properties of thousands of plants for food or medicine. Indeed, scientific studies have shown them to be nutritionally better off than most other peoples of sub-Saharan Africa. They see the forest as a personal god, fruitful and kind, and enact their relationship with it and with the spirits of the forest in ritual and song.

All of them spend part of the year settled near farming villages. They work in the villagers' gardens and provide them with forest produce such as meat and honey in return for food, alcohol, and sometimes small cash payments. Nowadays this period of settlement is tending to get longer. Relations between hunter-gatherers and farmers today range from free exchange to virtual serfdom. Farmers have an ambivalent attitude towards the hunter-gatherers: seeing them on the one hand as slaves and barely human and on the other as having occult wisdom and powers; they are widely consulted as magicians and healers.

None of the "Pygmy" peoples have any "chiefs" or formal system of government. They have, however, a clear system of traditional rights to the forest territories where they live and hunt. They live in bands of between 15 and 60 peoples; within the band, each individual, man or woman, is responsible for his or her own action; but there is also much cooperation in hunting, in music and dance and child care. Quarrels and disputes are worked out by humour and ritual – or by simply separating.

Today the independence and culture of all the "Pygmy" peoples are in danger, above all because of the threat to the forests. The main threats are:

Political Violence Often "Pygmy" peoples are caught up in violence not of their own making. The Batwa of Rwanda and Burundi are suffering appallingly in the ethnic conflicts and genocide, and it remains to be seen how those of the DRC have been affected by the upheavals there.

Logging With West Africa's forests all but finished, exploitation has moved into the vast Central African region; Cameroun is particularly affected. Most logging firms are European, but now companies from Malaysia also moving in. Logging degrades the forest, depriving people of the plants on which they rely and by opening up new roads, lets in commercial hunters, who kill off the animals to supply the demand for "bushmeat" in urban areas.

Landless farmers These move into the forest, often in the wake of logging developments. Generally they are driven by poverty and dispossession, like those made landless in the Kivu region of the DRC, who moved into the Ituri forest. They take up land (eventually causing deforestation) and bring a more commercial way of life. The "Pygmies" are increasingly drawn into the new world of the immigrants, at first as hunters selling their meat, but before long reduced to working as labourers.

National parks and wildlife reserves Generally all inhabitants have been removed from within park boundaries. However, this policy is beginning to change and in some parks, such as the Dzanga-Ndoki in CAR, efforts are made to employ local people, including the Ba-aka "Pygmies", for instance as guides.

Government policies The nation states in which the "Pygmies" live do not recognise that they have any legal right to the forest lands that are their home, although international law recognises such claims.

All the "Pygmy" peoples have suffered intense pressures, first from colonial governments and then from the independent African states, to abandon their forest life and become farmers. This is supposed to "integrate" them into the life of the nation. But as hunter-gatherers they are already part of the economic life of the nation via their economic and exchange relationships. Governments and others need to be convinced that there is room for them to continue their role of "forest specialists" if they wish to do so. There is also a role for training in farming and other occupations, for those who wish to combine them with hunting and gathering, or for those who have already lost their forest way of life, so that they can continue to live independently.

Today the "Pygmy" peoples are increasingly drawn into the mainstream of national life, though generally at the lowest level, as underpaid labourers. However, they are also becoming increasingly conscious of the exploitation. To date there has been almost no political organisation

among them; but the Batwa of Rwanda, who set up their own association in the early 1990s, and the small self-help organisation CODEBABIK started by the Bagyeli of Cameroun in 1996, may point the way to the future.

For the "Pygmy" people today, Survival advocates, firstly, a halt to the destruction of their forest environment, secondly, legal acceptance of their rights to it and thirdly, recognition of their rights as equal citizens in their various states.

Background Reading

Serge Bahuchet, *Les Pygmees Aka et la Forêt Centrafricaine* (SELAF, 1985).

Barry Hewlett, *Intimate Fathers* (Manchester Univesrity Press, 1991).

Justin Kenrick, "People of the African Forests" in *Jungles and Rainforests*, ed. Norman Myers (Weldon Owen, 1992).

Colin Turnbull, *The Forest People* (Chatto and Windus, 1961).

Colin Turnbull, *The Mbuti Pygmies: Change and Adaptation* (Holt, Rinehart and Wilson, 1983).

Niger Delta Peoples: Oil, land and water

For forty years we have borne the pains of pollution, the brutality of the unjust system. We shall unite to fight for equality, fairness and justice. The time is now. *Chief Augustine Anthony, Aleibiri village*

When the writer Ken Saro-Wiwa was executed on 10 November 1995, many people in the West heard for the first time of the Ogoni people, and their homeland in the delta of the river Niger in southern Nigeria. Yet for decades oil from beneath the land and waters of the delta peoples has helped to drive our cars and run our economy.

The peoples The delta region is now divided between eight Nigerian states:

Abia, Akwa Ibom, Delta, Edo, Ondo, Rivers, Bayelsa and Cross River; and contains nearly 20 million of Nigeria's 91 million population. It is a land of rich soil, lagoons, mangrove swamps, rivers and forest. The people are farmers and fishers, in the rivers and the sea.

The roots of these communities go back for thousands of years. Each local clan has its own identity, and often its own language – there are over twenty languages in the region. Yet they are connected by long-established links of trade and migration, and marked by their shared history. They are divided into larger ethnic groupings of which the major one is the Ijaw (Izon) (8,000,000). The Ogoni (est. 500,000) are one of the smaller ones; among the others are the Ikwerre, Etche, Urhobo, Efik, Ibibio, Kale, Isoko, Isekiri and Akwa-Ibom. This is a society of villages and towns, some of which were once powerful city states. Formerly people honoured many deities of earth, sky and water, under a supreme God. Today nearly all are Christians, though the old beliefs are by no means dead. The region's rich tradition of art and folklore includes festivals where masks, costume, song and dance make a total spectacle. From this background spring many modern artists, musicians and writers, of whom Ken Saro-Wiwa was one.

The region was the first in Nigeria to come under British control. Today some Ijaw leaders argue that the agreements that their ancestors made with the then-British government have never been abrogated, so that their status within the Nigerians state is not legitimate.

After Nigeria became independent in 1960, the minority peoples of the delta were shouldered aside in the struggle for power between Nigeria's three main ethnic blocks; the Yoruba in the West, the Hausa-Fulani in the North, and the Ibo in the East. During the Biafran War (1967–70) when the Ibo attempted to secede from Nigeria, the delta peoples were caught between the opposing sides.

The oil companies Oil exports from Nigeria began in the 1950s, and now account for about 90% of foreign exchange earnings, and 80% of the Federal Government's revenue. Over 90% of this comes from the delta area. The principal company involved is the Anglo-Dutch multinational Shell, in the form of its local subsidiary Shell Petroleum Development Company (SPDC). Others are the French company Elf, the Italian Agip, and the Nigerian state company NNPC. Mobile and Chevron are the main offshore producers.

The oil industry has had devastating effects on the Niger Delta peoples and their environment. A report in 1993 found *"badly maintained and leaking pipe lines, polluted water, fountains of emulsified oil pouring into villagers' fields, blow outs, air pollution . . ."* Farms and fisheries are spoiled, and the mangrove swamps, which provide people with building and other materials and are a vital part of the ecosystem, are disappearing. At the same time the people get little benefit from the immense wealth being generated. While the Federal Government gets 80% of the royalties and mining rents, 20% goes to each State government, but the local people see little even of that.

Local political movements Political protest in the delta goes back to the 1960s when Major Boro's "12 day revolution" called for a Niger Delta Republic. The Movement for the Survival of the Ogoni People (MOSOP) started in the 1980s, and in 1990 issued the Ogoni Bill of Rights. This calls for political autonomy within the Nigerian Federation, and the right to control a fair proportion of the resources produced on their land for their own development. MOSOP soon became a powerful mass movement, with such effect that in 1993 Shell halted its operations in Ogoniland. (An attempt to resume them in 1997 is being strongly resisted by MOSOP). However, a split within the movement led in 1994 to the killings for which Saro-Wiwa and his associates were later condemned (on the shakiest of evidence), although Saro-Wiwa himself had denounced violence.

MOSOP was followed in 1992 by the Ijaw (Izon) National Congress. They have produced the Izon Peoples' Charter, which makes similar demands to those of MOSOP. Other organisations with kindred aims are the Movement for the Survival of the Izon (Ijaw) Ethnic Nationality in the Niger Delta (MOSIEND); the Movement for Repar- ation to Ogbia, set up by the Ogbia (Ijaw) Community; the Council for Ikwerre Nationality; and the Southern Minorities Movement, which includes twenty-eight ethnic groups.

Protest and repression The military government of General Sani Abacha, which seized power in November 1993, is guilty of repression, and violations of human rights throughout Nigeria, but particularly in the oil-bearing areas. The oil companies, while denying that they can influence Nigerian politics, have shown themselves ready to call in the security forces when faced with local protests. The first major demonstration against SPDC was that of the Etche people at Umuecchem village, Rivers State, in October 1990. The local Shell manager called in the notorious Mobile Police (known as "Kill and Go"), who attacked peaceful demonstrators with guns and tear gas. About eighty people were killed and the village destroyed.

The Ogoni staged their first mass demonstrations in 1993. A military crack-down followed which amounted to a war against the Ogoni over the next two years. They have suffered shootings, arbitrary arrests, rapes and massive looting. People are tortured and imprisoned in degrading conditions; in 1997, 17 of Ken Saro-Wiwa's associates were still among them. The extreme violence employed by the Abacha regime against Ogoni, and the execution of their leaders, is clearly intended to terrorise other peoples out of any attempt at protest or self determination.

Nevertheless, militancy is increasing among the Ijaw and other delta peoples. This can take the form of violence, which is generally attributed by the Nigerian authorities to "ethnic" or "tribal" rivalries. But there is evidence that these rivalries have been fomented from outside. The fighting between Ijaws, Urhobo and Itshikiris in 1997 is an example. On the other hand, the pressure group "Chicoco" (named after the rich delta soil) was formed in 1997 to unite all the communities in peaceful resistance to the oil companies.

Survival is campaigning for an end to military repression in the Niger delta, and for oil multinationals to cease collusion in repressive measures and hasten cleanup operations. We also call for the rights of the delta's peoples to be fully recognised, within a framework of democracy and social justice.

Background Reading

Human Rights Watch, *Nigeria, the Ogoni Crisis – a case study of military repression* (from Human Rights Watch, 33 Islington High Street, London, N1 9LH, UK).

Jones, G. I., *The Trading States of the Oil Rivers* (Oxford University Press, 1963).

Oshomha, Imoagene, *Peoples of the Cross River Valley and the Eastern Delta*, New Era, Ibadan.

World Council of Churches, *Ogoni: the struggle continues*, World Council of Churches, Geneva, Switzerland.

Bushmen in Southern Africa: Hunters facing change

When someone says, "You Bushmen have no government," we'll say that our old, old people, long ago had a government, and it was a glowing coal from the fire where we last lived, which we used to light the fire at the new place where we were going. So I say, "Don't hold us back, we want to move forward, we have our own talk.'" Di//cao ≠Oma, Bushman woman from Nyae Nyae, Namibia

Many people today still imagine "Bushmen" as untouched "stone age" hunters, roaming freely in the wilderness. In fact this is far from the contemporary reality. Almost no Bushmen still live by hunting and gathering alone, though many do it as a supplementary source of food, and the majority live as herders working for little or no wages, as migrant labourers, as servants, or on government settlements.

Most of the cluster of peoples known as the Bushmen now live scattered in the Kalahari desert of Southern Africa, an area of over 500,000 square km (200,000 square miles), about the size of Kenya or France. However, their ancestors once occupied almost the whole of Southern Africa, and probably parts of East Africa. Outside the Kalahari, some Bushman groups survive in the south of Angola, the Okavango swamps in the north of Botswana, and in western and eastern Botswana. At the latest estimates, there are about 90,500 of them: 8,000 in Angola, 45,000 in Botswana, 33,000 in Namibia, 2,500 in the South African Republican, 1,500 in Zambia, and 500 in Zimbabwe.

The Bushmen are not one but several groups. They speak a number of different languages, nearly all of them "click languages". (These make use of various click and pop sounds made with the tongue – represented in writing by marks such as ! or /.) They do not have a word for themselves as a larger grouping. Other peoples call them by various names; in Namibia they are generally referred to as San, and in Botswana as Basarwa, but both of these are really terms of contempt. Some of them now accept the name "Bushmen", taking it as meaning "people of the land".

We know a lot about the traditional life of the Bushmen because they are one of the most heavily studied peoples in the history of science. An important stimulus to this research was the idea that they were some of the last of the world's original hunting and gathering peoples. Scholars treated them as if they had lived in complete isolation, and this belief soon took hold among the general public. Yet in fact they have interacted and traded with other peoples for centuries.

Bushmen have generally lived as hunter-gatherers or "foragers". The women had great skill in finding the fruits, nuts and roots which provided most of the daily diet. The meat hunted by the men – mainly various kinds of antelope – was a treat, and the most valued food. Some researchers believe that the Bushmen had to work only a short time each day in order to satisfy all their basic needs. At certain times and in certain places this could be true, but at other times life could be harsh, for their desert environment was above all very unpredictable. Mostly they lived in nomadic bands of 25–35 people, made up of several families. They had their own system of land holding: bands had well-defined territories which could measure up to 1,000 square km. During part of the year the whole band would be camped together near a water hole; then in the wet season they would scatter over the country. They had no political hierarchy or chiefs, and decisions were reached by the consensus of the group, women as well as men. Not all of them lived by hunting and gathering alone. In the early 19th century, the Bushmen were responsible for one of the most extensive of the pre-colonial trade networks which extended across the Kalahari. At Tsumeb, in what is now Namibia, they controlled one of the richest copper diggings in Africa.

Of all the peoples in the bloody history of Southern Africa, the Bushmen have been the most brutalised and victimised. In the past, they were hunted down like animals. For instance, in South Africa in the 18th century, special Bushmen commandos were organised by the settlers to hunt down other Bushmen. Large numbers were killed, and women and children were carried off to work for white farmers. Their descendants are today found among the so-called "coloured" population.

In Angola, the Portuguese used the Bushmen as trackers in their fight against independence movements. With the collapse of the Portuguese empire, these soldiers fled to Namibia, where they were incorporated into the South African Army so successfully that the South Africans started recruiting landless and unemployed local Bushmen. Since Namibian independence in 1990, 4,000 of them have been moved to South Africa. In 1993 the South African Defence Force handed over responsibility for them to a Trust largely controlled by the Bushman people themselves.

As recently as the 1950s several Bushman groups in Namibia and Botswana were still living by hunting and gathering. But since then almost all the land on which they depended for hunting has been taken away for farms, ranches or nature reserves. In Botswana, government settlements have been set up for them; in spite of such facilities as clinics and schools, life in the settlements is generally bleak.

The Bushmen people of today are landless and impoverished. However, some are finding new ways of living, such as learning to farm and keeping small numbers of cattle and goats on the land remaining to them, as well as hunting when they still get the chance. A group of such farmers in Namibia have joined together to form the Nyae Nyae Farmers Cooperative (NNFC); this is supported by the Ju/Hoansi Bushmen Development foundation in Namibia.

In the past, the great flexibility of their society helped the Bushmen to evade conquest and control. But at the same time it has made it exceedingly difficult for them to organise themselves so that they can put pressure on others and claim their rights. But now they are beginning to do this, through organisations like the NNFC, or the First People of the Kalahari in Botswana. The first two regional conferences on "Development for Africa's San Peoples" in 1992 and 1993, where Bushman delegations from both Namibia and Botswana made their demands known, seemed like sign of hope.

Since then however the situation of the Bushman peoples has only become harder. For instance, since the 1980s the Botswana Government has tried every means to remove the 1,500 or so Bushman people who live in the Central Kalahari Game Reserve, to make way for conservation, tourism and diamond mining. In 1996 the pressure was increased and by 1998 about a third of the people had been induced by the authorities to move out of the Reserve to a new settlement. However, a vigorous resistance is being led by First People of the Kalahari, who hope to establish their rights in their ancestral land.

Background Reading

Biesele, Megan, *Shaken roots: the Bushmen of Namibia*, EDA Publications (PO Box 62054, Marshalltown, South Africa), 1991.

Katz, Richard, Biesele, Megan, & St Denis, Verna, *Healing makes our hearts happy*, Inner Traditions International (PO Box 388, Rochester, VT 05767, USA), 1997.

Thomas, E. M., *The harmless people* (Penguin, 1959).

van der Post, Laurens, & June Taylor, *Testament to the Bushmen* (Viking/Penguin, 1984).

Australia

Aborigines in Australia: People of the Dreaming

Archaeologists believe that the Aborigines first came to the Australian continent 40,000–60,000 years ago. In time there came to be about 500 different peoples each with their own language and territory, and each made up of several clans. Today many people think of the Aborigines as nomads living in the desert. In fact most of them lived in semi-permanent communities along the coast, where food was more plentiful. They farmed and irrigated the land, and developed sophisticated husbandry techniques such as extending rivers to improve breeding grounds for eels.

In the inhospitable deserts of the bush interior the Aborigines adapted the harsh environment to their needs. They burned the undergrowth the encourage the growth of green shoots, the favourite food of the game they hunted. And they were experts in finding permanent sources of that most valuable of all commodites – water.

Significance of the land To have any understanding of Aborigines it is essential to appreciate what land means to them. Land is crucial to the very core of both their spiritual life and their physical survival. Without land they cannot eat; without land their spiritual being has no meaning. Their concept of land is rooted in the Dreamtime, a time long past when the earth was first created. One Aboriginal man explained it thus:

> By Dreaming we mean that long ago these creatures started human society, they made all natural things and put them in a special place. These Dreaming creatures were connected to special places and special roads or tracks or paths. In many places the great creatures changed themselves into sites where their spirits stayed. Aboriginals have a special connection with everything that is natural. Aboriginals see themselves as part of nature . . . All things on earth we see as part human. It is true that people who belong to a particular area are really part of that area and if that area is destroyed they are also destroyed.

Like so many other indigenous peoples around the world, the Aborigines were devastated by invasion and colonialism. Since the end of the 18th century their land has been taken from them, first for settlement, later for vast cattles ranches and most recently for mining. When Captain Cook landed in 1770 there are thought to have been 300,000–1,000,000 people living in the country. Thousands of Aborigines were wiped out by new diseases brought in by the British colonists. The settlers saw the Aborigines as primitive and massacred

thousands more. *"The government must remove the natives: if not they will be hunted down like wild beasts and destroyed,"* said the *Colonial Times* in 1816. As recently as 1926, Aborigines in the Kimberley region were massacred for killing cattle. Killings, along with the casualties in the Aboriginal wars of resistance, meant that their population plummeted to a low of 60,000 by the year 1990.

The statistics today

- The infant mortality rate for Aborigines is more than three times the national average
- The suicide rate is six times higher for Aborigines than for other Australians
- The proportion of Aborigines imprisoned is 14 times the national average
- Since January 1980 over 130 Aborigines have died in police custody

Since 1900, the population has increased to at least 250,000 (including the Torres Strait Islanders, indigenous people who are ethnically and culturally distinct from Aborigines).

For much of the 20th century, the government pursued a policy of taking small children from their parents and giving them to white families – so that all knowledge of Aboriginal ways would be erased, and their languages would die out.

Fighting back Aborigines have always resisted the theft of their land, but the modern land rights movement really started in 1996, when the Gurindji people walked off the Wave Hill cattle station in the Northern Territory in protest at their appalling work conditions. This inspired Aborigines around the country, as well as focusing attention on the dismal social conditions of many Aboriginal communities. With a sense of their own identity and self-respect assaulted by two centuries of racism and violence, the Aborigines have suffered from high levels of despair, ill-health and alcoholism. They were not even granted Australian citizenship until 1967. Since then, they have organised themselves into Land Councils to fight for recognition of their rights to their lands. They continue to suffer discrimination and persecution.

Today Today roughly half of all Aborigines live in towns, often in "fringe dweller" camps where housing and health conditions are very poor. In an effort to reverse this, the "outstation" movement has recently encouraged many Aboriginal groups to return to their lands. (Survival has helped fund such projects.) This may involve "squatting" on land that officially "belongs" to cattle stations.

In June 1992, the High Court made a historic ruling known as the Mabo case: essentially it recognised "native title" to land in common law. This meant that large areas of Aboriginal land officially held by the Crown can now, at least in theory, be reclaimed by their Aboriginal owners. (Before the ruling, the principle underlying Australian land rights law was known as "terra nullius". This stated that Australia was uninhabited before the British arrived; a devise used to dispossess Aboriginal peoples of their land for the last 200 years.) As a result of the case, in January 1994 Parliament passed the Native Title Act. Under this Act, all freehold and residential leases threatened by the the Mabo decision were validated and any native title over such lands was extinguished. Vacant land site, however, could be claimed by Aborigines showing a *"close and continuing association"* with a particular area. Mining leases did not extinguish native title, which runs alongside the leases until they are renewed or expire. The issue of whether native title could still be claimed on land covered by pastoral leases – the huge cattle ranches which cover much of the Australian outback, and where many Aborigines continue to live – was not resolved. A fund was set up to compensate Aborigines for the loss of native title and to acquire land. Aborigines would have a right to negotiate, but no veto, over devel-

opment on Native title land. Tribunals would arbitrate in cases of dispute. State governments can overrride tribunal decisions *"in the state or national interest"*.

The Native Title Act did not, unfortunately, resolve what became a bitter public debate between politicians, farmers, miners and Aborigines. The issue became even more controversial when a 1996 legal decision known as "Wik" clarified what "native title" meant. In particular, it was clear that native title could still exist on land that was covered by "pastoral leases" – the huge sheep and cattle ranches which cover much of outback Australia, where many Aborigines continue to live.

These two legal decisions, while still leaving Australia far behind many "Third World" countries in its recognition of indigenous rights, have been fiercely opposed by the powerful farming and mining industries. As a result, the government is trying to undermine the Aborigines' legal victories to such an extent as to render them almost meaningless.

The Prime Minister, John Howard, has proposed a new piece of legislation called the Native Title Amendment Bill. Crucially, this will make native title on pastoral leases worthless, and would leave many Aborigines unable to claim native title in the first place. Together, these measures would leave the huge majority of Aborigines with no rights over their land. Sadly, it seems that justice for Australian Aborigines is as far off as ever.

Background Reading

Reynolds, Henry, *Dispossession* (Allen & Unwin, Australia, 1989).

Roberts, Jan, *From Massacres to Mining* (War on Want, London, 1978; out of print but available in libraries).

Layton, Robert, *Australian Rock Art* (Cambridge: Cambridge University Press, 1992).

The Americas

Indians in Amazonia: Land is life

"Our grandparents left this land for our grandchildren. We won't sell the land, and we aren't going anywhere. We used to be able to cut down a tree to make a canoe. Today the colonists are living where we used to walk. We used to live without any problems." *Amazon Quichua Indian, 1992*

Amazonia is a vast region of South America formed by the Amazon and Orinoco rivers and their tributaries. It covers an area of 7.8 million square kilometres, most of which is dense rainforest. The climate is generally hot and humid – the average temperature in Amazonia is 25°C. It can, however, get surprisingly cold at night. There are only two season – the wet and the dry. The average height of the tallest tree is about 40 metres. They act as a kind of umbrella for the human, plant and animal life below.

The Amazon carries more water than any river on earth and is no longer than all others except the Nile in Africa. Its source lies high up in the Peruvian Andes, close to the Pacific Ocean. Two thirds of Amazonia is in Brazilian territory, but the combined Amazon and Orinoco basin spreads over a total of nine countries: Bolivia, Brazil, Colombia, French Guiana, Ecuador, Guyana, Peru, Suriname and Venezuela. The Amazon flows from the Andes in Peru across South America to the Atlantic Ocean 6,500 kilometres away. It is joined by thousands of tributaries in the course of its journey. Not surprisingly, life in Amazonia revolves around the rivers and the forest. There is so much water in Amazonia that the most favoured means of transport is the canoe.

Today there are more than 370 different tribal peoples living the Amazon region. In 1492, when Christopher Columbus first landed in the Americas, there were 1.5–2 million Indians in Amazonia. Today there are approximately 940,000. Western scientists believe that the Indians have been there for at least 15,000 years and that their ancestors were part of a mass migration from central Asia and through the Americas during the last great Ice Age. The Indians adapted to their new environments and developed social systems and ways of life that have been successful for thousands of years.

In Amazonia, most Indians are settled agriculturalists. They clear small areas of forest and plant manioc, plantains, beans, rice and many types of fruit amongst the felled trees. They generally clear a new area every two or three years, once the soil is exhausted. Virtually all Amazonian Indians also hunt animals such as wild pigs and tapir for meat, and fish in the rivers and lakes.

A small minority of Amazonian tribes are more nomadic – they do not live in fixed villages, and rely on hunting, fishing and gathering much more than growing crops. Most surviving Amazonian Indians have had contact with non-Indians for generations, and some for hundreds of years, but have still managed to retain their cultural identities. However, there are also many tribal peoples who have no contact with non-Indians – there are over 40 such "uncontacted" groups in Brazilian Amazonia alone.

The Indians not only use the forest's products for food but to enrich their daily lives. Flutes are fashioned from bamboo or from the hollow leg bones of animals. The maraca, a percussion instrument usually played by men, is made from a small gourd and filled with seeds or pebbles. Houses are built from timber and lianas – the roofs are usually made from palm leaves. Indians hunt with bows and arrows or spears and blowguns, although many today use shotguns. Dyes are used in making clothes and baskets, as well as body decoration. Juice pressed from the fruit of the genipapo tree makes a deep blue-black colour, while the outer coating of seeds from the annatto tree produces a striking orange-red.

Many Indians believe that there are spirits inside animals and plants as well as each human being. Spirits sometimes leave the bodies of their host even while they are alive. They can act as benign protectors, but they can also cause disease and death by blowing invisible darts. Shamans are Indians who can communicate with the spirit world. They do this by dreaming or by using hallucinogenic drugs. Shamans can find out what has angered the spirits and are believed to be able to cure disease. Greed or lack of respect for nature can arouse the wrath of spirits in the forest and bring disaster on families or even whole peoples. The Indians have a wide range of myths and legends to explain their place in the universe; many today have incorporated aspects of Christianity in their beliefs.

There are such a wide variety of Indian societies that it is hard to generalise about them. They range from settled villages with large numbers of people and elaborate dwellings to nomads living in bands of 30–40 moving every few days without need of permanent houses or canoes. Cooperation is central to Indian societies. Many people live in villages and each individual contributes to daily activities by hunting, gathering, looking after the gardens or preparing food. Hunting, warfare and work in the gardens are usually the men's responsibility. Cooking, gathering food in the forest and childcare are usually women's roles. Festivals are almost universal, and are a very important way of expressing a sense of community.

When Europeans arrived 500 years ago it was disastrous for the Indians. Since then, there has been genocide, land theft and the destruction of large areas of forest in the name of profit and greed. After the "discovery" of Columbus, many European settlers moved in and forced the Indians deeper into the forests, destroying the large communities on the banks of the main rivers, Indians were murdered and enslaved in vast numbers; many more died from introduced diseases like measles, smallpox and the common cold to which they had no resistance. (This is, tragically, still a problem today for many isolated tribal peoples.) Their beliefs were considered inferior to Christianity and western notions of "economic growth" have forced aside sustainable agricultural systems. The result of all this has been ecological crisis and human tragedy.

The oppression of Amazonian peoples continues today, largely in the form of racism, destructive "development" projects, illegal settlement on stolen land and the roads, disease and exploitation that the settlers bring. The World Bank, European Union and many multinational "development" agencies underwrite roads, mining, dams and agro-industrial projects that ruin Indian lives. But now, throughout Amazonia, indigenous peoples are fighting back. An increasingly effective combination of Indian rights movements and campaigning organisations like Survival is forcing governments and companies to listen.

Survival is campaigning for recognition that the Indians own their land and are free to decide how it should be used. Land ownership rights are the key to the survival of the Amazonian Indians.

Background Reading

Cunningham, Antonia, *Rainforest Wildlife* (Usborne World Wildlife, London, 1993).

Lewington, Anna, *Rainforest Amerindians* (Wayland, London, 1992).

Survival, *Indians of the Americas* (Survival, 1992).

Survival, *Yanomami Survival Campaign* (Survival, 1990).

WWF/ Survival, *Rainforests: land use options for Amazonia* (Oxford University Press and WWF UK in association with Survival, 1989).

Indians in North America: From the Arctic to the desert

Before Columbus arrived, there were between 5 and 10 million people, speaking over 500 languages, living in North America. These peoples are usually grouped together into nine "culture areas":

The Arctic This huge treeless expanse of

tundra, ice and sea was home to the Inuit (Eskimos) and Aleuts. With no wood for fuel or to use as building material, they made their homes out of animal bones, stones and earth or occasionally from blocks of packed snow (the famous "igloos"). As agriculture was impossible, they lived by hunting mammals such as whales, seals and walruses, and used every part of the animal – for food, clothes, boats, tools and fuel.

The sub-Arctic   The vast pine forests and endless lakes of the sub-Arctic span the continent. The Indian peoples who lived here depended above all on the migrating herds of caribou (reindeer), but they also hunted moose, deer and other small animals, as well as fishing and gathering nuts and berries. They made boats out of birch bark, and clothes out of furs. There were two broad groups: the Cree and other members of the Algonquian language family to the east, and the Athapaskan-speakers to the west.

Northwest Coast   This was a thin strip of land stretching 2,000 miles, squeezed between the Rocky Mountains and the sea. It was home to over 50 different Indian tribes, from the Coos and Umpqua in what is now Oregon, to the Tlingit in modern-day Alaska. Common to all was an abundance of fish and wild animals, nurtured by the warm climate, plentiful rain and lush forests. In this bounteous environment, complex hierarchical societies arose, with permanent villages, totem poles and, above all, the "potlatch" – the ritual of giving away of goods for prestige.

Plateau   Between the Cascade Mountains to the west and the Rockies to the east lies the Columbia Plateau. Over 20 peoples such as the Flathead, Shuswap and Klickitat lived here, fishing the many rivers for trout and salmon, and gathering berries and wild roots.

Great Plains   The grasslands of the Great Plains were bordered by the Rockies in the west and the Mississippi river in the east. What is now thought of as the "classic" Indian lifestyle – tipi-dwelling peoples who used horses to hunt buffalo – actually only evolved after the introduction of the horse by the Spaniards. The arrival of the horse led to a great migration of farming peoples (the Sioux, Crow and Pawnee, for example) onto the previously inhospitable plains, and made this new way of life possible.

Eastern Woodlands   The defining characteristic of the Indians of this region was their settled lifestyle. They tended to live in permanent villages, often with defensive fortifications. They grew corn, beans and pumpkins, and hunted the many animals of the forest. Sometimes different villages would come together in formal alliances, such as the Iroquois League of Five Nations and the Abnaki Confederacy.

California   Over 100 languages such as Yokut, Chumash, and Tolowa were spoken in the mountain ranges between the Sierra Nevada and the Pacific, where animals and edible plants were so plentiful that no agriculture was necessary to support a relatively high population. Acorns were a staple food, along with other nuts and berries, shellfish, and small game. Small numbers of related families lived together in villages, and usually had little contact with their neighbours in nearby valleys.

Great Basin   Baked by the sun, with very little rainfall, life in this desert basin was extremely harsh. The only people who could live here were small groups of Paiute, Ute and Shoshone families, permanently searching for water and food. Agriculture or a settled life was impossible – their food consisted of roots, nuts, snakes and anything else edible that could be hunted or dug out of the ground.

Southwest   There were two distinct lifestyles in the southwestern desert – farmer and nomad. The farming peoples, such as the Pueblos (Hopi, Zuni and others), Tohono O'Odham and Havasupai, were strongly influenced by Mexican Indians, and were masters at coaxing corn, squashes and beans from the desert sand. The nomads, like the Apaches and Navajos, were more recent arrivals in the area, having journeyed from the cold forests of western Canada.

The arrival of Europeans The earliest European arrival on the continent was not British or French, but Viking – Leif the Lucky landed in Newfoundland in about 1000 AD, and the remains of his settlement can still be seen. However, the disturbance the Vikings caused to the Indians (eight were killed and two children kidnapped and taken back to Greenland) was nothing compared with what was to come.

The Spanish, French and English spear-headed the subsequent invasion, although the Russians and Dutch were also active. Their primary motive was greed: they were after gold, and later slaves, fur and land. The Indians died in their millions; most not from war or massacre (though these were frequent) but from the spread of European diseases (such as influenza and measles) which they had never encountered before. Typically, 90% of the Indian population died following the shock of first contact. As Massasoit, chief of the Wampanoags said in 1621 when signing a treaty, *"Englishmen, take that land, for none are left to occupy it. The Great Spirit . . . has swept its people from the face of the earth."* An English settler had a different view, *"The woods were almost cleared of these pernicious creatures [the Indians] to make room for a better growth."*

There were some early attempts to protect the Indians from this devastation – the work of the Spanish priest Bartolome de las Casas, for example, or the 1512 declaration by Pope Julius II that Indians were after all descended from Adam and Eve – but their overall effect was negligible.

Trade with the white settlers had profound effects on the Indians. It not only led to dramatic shifts in lifestyle (for instance, the fur trade transformed the lives of the Algonquian and Iroquoian Indians), but caused sharp changes in the balance of power; the arrival of such things are firearms or horses could confer a sudden, devastating advantage to one tribe over its neighbours. Together with the soldiers and settlers came missionaries, who attempted to suppress the Indians' culture, languages and beliefs, and impose their own religion and moral code.

Besides death through disease and geno-cide, the single most devastating effect of this invasion was the Indians' loss of their land. Although the British Royal Proclamation of 1763 stated that the Indians had legal title to their land which could only be "extinguished" through treaty, the westward expansion of the white frontier was so remorseless that this was frequently ignored. A typical example was the 1868 Treaty of Fort Laramie between the Sioux and the United States govern-ment, which left the Sioux with about half of South Dakota. It was only respected for six years, when gold was discovered in the Sioux's sacred Black Hills, and the reserva-tion was invaded.

Throughout North America, the Indians fought against this takeover of their land. From Arizona, where Cochise and Geronimo led the apaches in raids against the Mexicans and Americans, to Alaska, where the Aleuts attacked their Russian oppressors, this was no passive acceptance of invasion. Ultimately how-ever their resistance was useless, as these examples illustrate: Geronimo spent the last 23 years of his life as a prisoner; Russian ships bombarded Aleut villages, killed most of the people, and enslaved the survivors.

The Indians were confined to reserva-tions in the USA (though most of that land was later stolen from them) and reserves (small parcels of government land) in Canada. They were also forced to organise themselves along western lines: in both Canada and the USA, tribes were made to form councils which governed them in a totally alien manner.

The situation today Today, there are about 1 million Canadian Indians and 2 million Native Americans. In spite of their terrible suffering, they have managed to retain much of their culture, particularly where they still have access to their land. There are Indians in every state of the USA and every Canadian province; in the USA, about half of the Native Americans live in towns rather than on the reservations. The remarkable persistence of Indian identity can be seen in the example of the Mashantucket Pequots of Connecticut, who were almost wiped out in the Pequot Wars of 1636–7, but survived virtually hidden and are now thriving once more.

The Indians continue to suffer persistent racism and persecution. Conditions on most reservations and reserves are appalling. In the USA, American Indians are eight times more likely to contract tuberculosis than other US citizens, and 37% of all Indians die before the age of 45. In Canada, the Indian suicide rate is three times the national average, while Indian infant mortality is 60% higher than for the population as a whole.

The theft of Indians' resources is not confined to the past. Throughout the continent, their lands, forests, minerals, even their water, are taken from them. Indian resistance goes on, and Survival continues to campaign alongside them.

Background Reading

Survival, *Indians of the Americas*, Survival, London, 1992.

Survival, *Guardians of the Sacred Land*, Survival, London, 1994.

Wilson, James, *Canada's Indians*, Minority Rights Group Report, London, 1982.

Wilson, James, *The Original Americans: US Indians*, Minority Rights Group Report, London, 1986.

Wilson, James, *The Earth shall weep*, Picador, London, 1998.

Innu in Canada: Hunters and bombers

The Innue, who number approximately 16,000 are the indigenous people of Labrador and eastern Quebec. They are unrelated to the Inuit (or Eskimo) who live further north.

The Innu are a hunting people who have lived for millennia in the sub-arctic pine forests of eastern Canada. They are heavily dependent on the migratory herds of caribou (reindeer) in the region, and they also hunt many other animals, as well as fish, and gather fruits and berries. Today, many have paid jobs as well.

In the 1950s and 60s, under the combined pressure of the government and the Catholic Church, the formerly nomadic Innu were settled in fixed communities. They were particularly attracted by the promise of western education for their children. As an Innu man says, *"People thought it would be good. They saw white people were successful with their education. But white people have different aims, a different way of life."*

The transition from a mobile to a fixed lifestyle has been an extremely difficult one. Innu life in the communities is marked by extremely high levels of alcoholism, violence and despair. Elizabeth Penashue, an Innu woman, says,

> It was a mistake. Education is somehow connected with the problems we see today with children: a sense of rage, they break things, they end up in jail . . . They are made to feel inferior at school, they are depressed and unhappy . . . They are unsure of their direction. Before, they were proud to hunt with their fathers. Things fitted together and made sense.

However, it would be wrong to think that the Innu are now a settled people in the process of becoming "white". They have fought to retain much of their culture, and many continue to leave the communities for six months of the year to live in small camps in the country, where they can hunt, fish and bring up their children as Innu.

Adapting to this sudden, forced change in lifestyle has been extremely traumatic for the Innu, as for so many other indigenous peoples. Working out how to combine Innu culture with the Canadian culture that surrounds and invades them requires both time and space. This is why being able to live on their own land in peace is so important. But the Canadian government denies them this internationally-recognised right, and persecutes them relentlessly.

Low-level flying   The Canadian Air Force base at Goose Bay (formerly an area where Innu women used to gather berries) is used by the British, Dutch and German Air Forces for low-level flying practice. They currently fly up to 8,000 sorties per year. All this takes place directly over the heads of the Innu. The areas most over-flown, the lakes and river valleys, are precisely those areas most used by the Innu. The peace of the countryside is therefore constantly being shattered, making it very difficult for the Innu to continue to hunt. A Federal Environmental Assessment recently recommended that the number of flights per year be increased to 18,000, even though they admitted they did not know what the impact of this would be. They also backed the expansion of the low-level flying are from 100,000 km² to 130,000 km², and the construction of a new bombing range – all on Innu hunting territory. Furthermore, the Canadian government has now invited the Belgian, Italian and French Air Forces to use Goose Bay.

In 1996 Canada, the United Kingdom, Germany and the Netherlands signed a new Multinational Memorandum of Understanding for low-level flight training over Innu territory in eastern Quebec and Labrador, which made it clear they intend to continue the low-level flying despite the Innu's vigorous opposition.

Mining   The Newfoundland government

is handing out mining concessions to scores of companies on land which the Innu have never signed away. Not only is this ignoring the wishes of the Innu, but it is leading to a steep increase in the degree of industrial activity on Innu land. For example, in Eimish (Voisey Bay), two companies – Diamond Fields Resources and Archean Resources – announced a massive find of nickel, cobalt and copper in November 1994. The Innu were not consulted over this development despite the fact that they have burial sites in the area. Simeon Tshakapesh, ex-Chief of the Mushuau Innu has said, *"If exploration and development of our land continues, we will lose everything. The company is talking about jobs and opportunities, but we are talking about our land, our rights and our way of life."*

The discovery of this deposit has resulted in an intense level of mineral exploration and development activity on Innu and Inuit land in Labrador. On one hand, the Voisey Bay Nickel Company (the company formed to exploit the mine) is attempting to transform their discovery into a working open-pit nickel mine and mill facility as quickly as possible. On the other, several dozen companies have initiated active exploration programmes over the more than 250,000 mineral claims that now cover roughly 60,000 km² of Labrador.

The goal of the Innu Nation, the political organisation of the Labrador Innu, is for the land rights issue to be settled before the mine goes ahead. Survival is campaigning for this to be achieved.

The Newfoundland government is vigorously promoting other industrial developments on the Innu's land without their consent, such as roads, hydroelectric dams and snowmobile trails.

Survival has taken the following action in support of the Innu:

- organised letter writing campaigns;
- published numerous articles in our newsletters;

- coordinated five visits by Innu leaders;
- made many formal protests and organised several demonstrations, including an ascent of Nelson's Column in London;
- publicised their plight in the media;
- repeatedly lobbied the governments concerned;
- financially supported an Innu Newsletter;
- presented a report to the United Nations on the legal basis for the Innu land claim in 1987;
- made a submission to the United Nations Human Rights Commission in February 1995;
- arranged for questions to be asked in the French and Italian Parliaments.

Background Reading

Henriksen, Georg, *Hunters in the Barrens – the Naskapi on the edge of the white man's world* (Institute of Social and Economic Research, Memorial University of Newfoundland, St. John's, 1993).

Wadden, Marie, *Nitassinan – the Innu struggle to reclaim their homeland* (Douglas and McIntyre, Vancouver and Toronto, 1991).

Global Prospects

PART

IV

Introduction to Part IV

Human Rights & Religion: A Reader ends with reflections on the global prospects for human rights and religion.

Paul Marshall's chapter opens **Part IV** and draws from extensive international research on religious freedom throughout the world compiled by the US-based human rights organisation, Freedom House. The work is controversial in the sense that its approach provides a grading system based on set criteria for the assessment of religious freedom within a particular country. Such measured approach runs a number of risks. The notion of a league table of religious freedom is something that might run counter to the notion of freedom in religions itself. It is inherently judgmental, and could be put to cruder judgmental purposes in the wrong political hands. Most fundamentally, the notion of a grading system and the league table that could be assembled from the results – running from the high of 1 to the low of 7 – presents a hierarchical model which encourages an unhelpful trend towards national superiority. Indeed, the United States, from where the research was compiled, receives the highest grade for religious freedom of 1. Yet the work highlights some very important trends within nations and provides and accessible guide to major fault lines in human rights and religion globally. "It is clear from the Freedom House Report, as well as State Department reports and other surveys, that violations of religious freedom worldwide are massive, widespread, and, in the last five years, growing. This leads to three other conclusions. First, that attention to and action on religious freedom have been comparatively weak. Second, that the important role of religion in conflicts and in political orders has been comparatively neglected. Third, that both of these situations are now beginning to change, a change that we hope this present survey will accelerate."

Tony Coates's chapter on "International Justice and Just War Theory" presents an analysis of when war is justified and when it is not. Not only is this pertinent to the present-day crusade – the "War on Terrorism" – but the "just war" frame of reference had in part a theological origin. Coates examines the question of justification for war in international relations and his discussion of the universal versus the particular – an opposition which has permeated this book – is seen to be a false opposition, or one which has been drawn too sharply. Post September 11 it is a division that has been drawn more sharply still: "As often happens in a fiercely contested debate, where each side develops its own self-image largely in opposition to the other, the tendency is to concentrate on the points of difference rather than the points of contact or affinity. The result is a polarization of the argument in which universalism comes to be understood as the very antithesis of particularism (and vice versa), and in which the claims of the world community are seen to vie with the claims of particular states. Polarization, therefore, has a thoroughly distorting effect leading, inevitably, to one-sided and incomplete conceptions of international relations and, by extension, of international justice." Coates's discussion of the just war presents a context for considerations of human rights and religious/ cultural difference. We live in a world that has gone to war on these issues, even if the aims of the war and the issues that are contested are not always so clearly formulated. In many respects, however, whether or not Wellman's "proliferation of rights" is "moral progress" the consequences of dispute are far from "rhetoric."

Carl Wellman's "The Proliferation of Rights: Moral Progress or Empty Rhetoric?" concludess **Part IV**. Wellman begins with philosophical and political reflections on the origins of contemporary human rights discourse in the twentieth century, a revival that "reflected two world wars that not only caused the death of vast numbers of individuals and the destruction of immense amounts of property but also exposed the world to the dreadful experience of totalitarian regimes, especially in Nazi Germany, that grossly violated the basic rights of so many human beings." Here Wellman notes, "These fundamental moral 'rights of man' were renamed 'human rights' to avoid any insinuation that only males are qualified to possess them and to eliminate the dubious presuppositions of traditional theories of natural rights. Hence, a new era of human rights began in 1945 when the United Nations Charter reaffirmed faith in fundamental human rights and announced that one of its primary purposes was "to achieve international co-operation . . . promoting and encouraging respect for human rights and for fundamental freedoms for all without distinction as to race, sex, language, or religion." But Wellman goes on to provide a detailed analysis of the development of

three subsequent "generations of rights": the first, civil and political rights; the second, economic, social and cultural rights; the third, rights pertaining to "human solidarity." Wellman's critique is highly useful because he provides a summary of major trends in human rights discourse since the founding Universal Declaration of Human Rights in 1948 and because he rightly points out that rights themselves are highly contested. Human rights are, as we have seen, nowhere more contested than in the field of religion and cultural difference.

Human Rights & Religion: A Reader presents a wide-ranging set of analyses and case studies with a view to making a continued constructive contribution to debate on human rights and religion in global politics.

Further Reading

Arts, Karin *Integrating Human Rights into Development Cooperation: The Case of the Lome Convention* (The Hague: Kluwer Law International, 2000).

Coates, Tony (ed.) *International Justice* (Aldershot, Hampshire: Ashgate Publishing, 2000).

Küng, Hans 'The History, Significance and Method of the Declaration Toward a Global Ethic' in Küng, Hans and Schmidt, Helmut (eds), *A Global Ethic and Global Responsibilities: Two Declarations* (London: SCM, 1998).

Marshall, Paul (ed.) *Religious Freedom in the World: A Global Report on Freedom and Persecution* (London: Broadman and Holman, 2000).

Midgley, Mary 'Toward an Ethic of Global Responsibility' in *Human Rights in Global Politics* (Cambridge: Cambridge University Press, 1999).

Wellman, Carl *The Proliferation of Rights: Moral Progress or Empty Rhetoric?* (Oxford: Westview, 1999).

Religious Freedom

Paul Marshall

21

◆ Defining religious freedom ◆ Distribution of religious freedom ◆

◆ Religious freedom and other human rights ◆

◆ US State Department on religious freedom ◆

One goal of this survey is to rank countries on a standard scale of religious freedom so that we can compare them with one another, see whether any patterns occur, and eventually discern whether any systematic change occurs over time. Some people have objected to the very idea of rating and ranking countries as necessarily an invidious, even imperialistic, exercise. However, it is a fact that some countries, such as Norway, have more religious freedom than others, such as Sudan. If we cannot say that, then there is little point in any general survey.

What critics may mean is that any attempt to rate countries is very difficult, liable to error, and in need of copious self-criticism. This is certainly correct. In particular, there are two major methodological problems: the use of standardized criteria, and what those criteria should be.

Clearly, since countries are different, then the facets and problems of religious freedom will be different in each country: Hence, any standard set of criteria will be disproportionate. It will highlight things in some countries that may, in practice, be of little relevance. In other countries it may not give adequate place to idiosyncratic features that are of great relevance. There is

no "solution" to this problem: it is an inbuilt and inescapable feature of using any universal criteria for any particular situations. All we can do is the best we can and be open to refining the criteria as the results come in.

The survey criteria are developed from the International Covenant on Civil and Political Rights, the United Nations Declaration on the Elimination of All Forms of Intolerance and of Discrimination Based on Religion or Belief, the European Convention on Human Rights, and from a list of criteria developed by Willy Fautre. They are based on the fact that surveying religious freedom is more limited than surveying human rights in general, but also it is different from surveying particular human rights, such as press freedom, which focus only on particular organizations or practices. With freedom of the press, one can look at the intensity of controls on particular media and the weight of penalties applied with those controls. But, unlike press freedom, religious freedom cannot be focused on the freedoms of certain organizations and individuals. Religious freedom cuts across a wide range of human rights.

First, it refers to the freedoms of

particular bodies, houses of worship, humanitarian organizations, educational institutions, and so forth. Second, it refers to freedom for particular individual religious practices – prayer, worship, dress, proclamation, diet, and so forth. Third, it refers to human rights in general in so far as they involve particular religious bodies, individuals, and activities. For example, the freedom to proclaim one's religion or belief is an issue of freedom of speech generally and is parallel to freedom of speech in other areas of life. Similarly, for freedom of the press or freedom of association. This means that we are looking not only at particular "religious rights" but also at any human right, insofar as it impacts on freedom of religion or belief. In particular, we need to be aware of any different and unequal treatment of particular religions. This means that the question of adverse discrimination needs specific attention.

There are, of course, many situations where it is not immediately clear whether there is a violation of religious freedom. Some examples, with my own analysis:

- A priest acting alone in Central America is killed because of his human-rights work, and he regards such human-rights work as a necessary consequence of his faith. This is not an instance of religious persecution because any other person of a different faith, or no faith, in the same situation would face the same attack. (Note that this is certainly a human rights violation but not a violation of religious freedom per se.) However, if a church has a pastoral policy that includes such human rights work, then any limits on this are limits on the believing practice of the church and of its clergy, and so are a violation of religious freedom.
- A European country bans Islamic dress in schools. This is a violation of religious freedom since, while the school may legitimately want to enforce a dress code, that should be outweighed by a right to live according to one's religion.

If it were a case of a full covering and veil and the school were worried about checking someone's identity, say at exam time, then there might be additional legitimate concerns, but a way could be found around them.

- A country bans polygamy or polyandry whereas some religions allow it. This is not a violation of religious freedom since, as far as I know, no religion requires polygamy or polyandry.
- A country has a state church or its equivalent but otherwise allows freedom of religion. This is always an instance of religious discrimination and, therefore, a limit on religious freedom; however, its importance may vary greatly. Does the state fund the church in a way that it does not fund other religious bodies? Does the church have political privileges or privileges in areas such as education? (International human-rights documents do not reject a state church per se.)
- A religious group is also a politically separatist group. This can be a very difficult area as states have a legitimate interest in avoiding fragmentation. However, international law also recognizes a "people's right to self-determination." The question of whether the repression of such a group is a violation of religious freedom would depend on whether the group had a religious identity and on the justice of their cause. (Have they been previously repressed, discriminated against, or had their religion violated?) If there has been such a previous threat to the religious identity of the group, then the repression even of a separatist group would be a violation of religious freedom, and any human rights violations in the area are also violations of religious freedom. Consequently, even if religiously identified groups in Tibet and southern Sudan were separatist, which both sets of groups deny, their repression would still be a violation of religious freedom.
- If a religiously identified separatist or

other group is violent, the answer would depend on whether their violence is a legitimate form of self-defense or whether the group is inherently violent or terrorist. In the former case any human rights violations against them would also be violations of religious freedom.

- A family disinherits or ostracizes an (adult) child because the child converts to another religion. This is not a violation of religious freedom since under international standards families can legitimately make such decisions. However, any physical attack on the child would be a violation of religious freedom.
- A family forbids an underage child to convert or marry someone of different religion. International standards allow families to make such decisions.
- In many countries, much law (especially on family and marriage) is divided along confessional lines, with different marriage and divorce rules for different groups. This is not a violation of religious freedom as long as: the groups are treated equally, people can voluntarily change their group, and there are avenues for marriage, and so forth, for those who may not fit in any particular group.
- Are restrictions on the entrance of missionaries or other religious workers a violation of religious freedom? Not necessarily, as there is no universal right to be able to work in a country other than one's own. It would depend on whether such restrictions discriminated between (and within) religions and whether they had an adverse effect on domestic groups that are denied adequate, trained leadership.
- A decision by a country either to fund or not to fund education by religious groups can be consistent with religious freedom. The question is one of discrimination, that is, whether some groups are denied funds because of their beliefs while others are given funds.

Many more examples clearly could be given of situations where answers to questions of religious freedom are by no means obvious. Nevertheless, from the above, we can suggest some guidelines:

- Are restrictions on religious groups "reasonable"? In the words of many international human-rights documents, are they "subject only to such limitations as are prescribed by law and are necessary to protect public safety, order, health, or morals or the fundamental rights and freedom of others"?
- The question of whether something is a violation of religious freedom (as distinct from a violation of some other human right) depends on whether someone's religion is a factor (usually not the only one) in the treatment they give or receive. To put this another way, would someone of different religious beliefs or no religious beliefs in the same situation mete out or suffer the same treatment? (Of course, groups with different beliefs may, by that fact, also not fall into the same situation.)
- Is there discrimination; is different treatment given to different religious groups?
- Religious freedom can be violated by a government or another religious group even if the violation is not itself for religious motives. The motive is not, *per se*, the issue; the key question is, what is the result? If a government represses churches, mosques, and temples in the same way it represses political parties, newspapers, and other groups, simply because the government wants no other centers of loyalty or authority in the society, then this is still a violation of religious freedom.

Particularly with respect to this latter point, it is vitally important to realize that the fact that something is "political," "economic," or "cultural" does *not* mean that it is not religious (and vice versa). Many things are both "political" *and* "religious":

Europe and Latin America have many Christian Democratic parties. China is officially atheist, and Iran is officially Islamic. Or "cultural" and "religious": Tibetan culture and religion are interwoven, as are Mexican or Indian culture and religion. Or "economic" *and* "religious": the Sudanese government's self-proclaimed *jihad* strives for control over oil fields and hydroelectric power stations. In Chiapas, Mexico, Protestants are persecuted by local *caciques* because they refuse to pay extortionate prices for goods to be used in religious ceremonies that they reject. In fact, outside of communist and radical Islamicist settings, it is comparatively rare for someone to be repressed merely for their individual confessional beliefs if these beliefs do not affect some other facet of life. It is usually the very interrelation that leads to persecution. Furthermore, religion is usually not merely an additional factor but is also intimately interwoven with other factors. Since religion refers to our ultimate beliefs, it is only to be expected that it is deeply connected to every other area of human life, a fact emphasized by nearly every religion in the world.

We need to take account not only of individual acts but also the religious context in which they occur. This may be illustrated by a comparison with the role of race in South Africa in the period of apartheid. Some blacks were allied with the government, and some whites were fighting for the African National Congress. Nelson Mandela was not imprisoned for his race but because he was accused of terrorism. The government would have imprisoned anyone, of any race, whom it believed to be a terrorist, and it would have imprisoned anyone for terrorism even for a reason unconnected to *apartheid*. The South African troops in Namibia and Angola were not fighting on direct racial grounds but to prevent infiltration. Would we say then that the South African conflict was political not racial, economic not racial, and cultural not racial? Of course not, because we are well aware that it was the policy of *apartheid* and the exclusion of nonwhites from the political process that drove the government's opponents, black and white, to take the steps they did. Racial division lay behind nearly all government policies, hence acts that were not themselves *individually* racially motivated were undertaken to defend a system that was. Similarly, people, regardless of their religion, may be repressed in order to maintain a religious hegemony.

The Current State of Religious Freedom

The survey does not compare the current situation with the patterns of earlier years. However, each country profile includes, where relevant, a brief history of religious freedom. These histories indicate that, during the mid- to late-1990s, the overall situation of religious freedom in the world has deteriorated. This is particularly so in the larger Asian countries, such as China, India, Pakistan, and Indonesia. Western Europe has also become less religiously free due to widespread hysteria over "cults." Some areas, such as Latin America, have improved, while others such as Africa, the former Soviet Union and the Middle East have remained fairly stable, the latter two at a low level of religious freedom and the last being one of the worst in the world.

The Spread of Religious Freedom

Religious freedom and religious persecution affect all religious groups. A variety of groups – Christians and animists in Sudan, Baha'is in Iran, Ahmadiyas in Pakistan, Buddhists in Tibet, and Falun Gong in China – are now perhaps the most intensely persecuted, while Christians are the most widely persecuted group. But there is no religious group in the world that does not suffer to some degree because of its beliefs. Religions, whether large, such as

Christianity, Islam, Hinduism, or Buddhism, or small, such as Baha'i, Jehovah's Witnesses, or Judaism, all suffer to some degree. In many cases these restrictions come from people who are members of the same general religious group but who are part of a different subgroup. Thus non-Orthodox Christians in Russia, Greece, and Armenia suffer discrimination from the Orthodox, while Shi'ite Muslims in Pakistan and Afghanistan suffer persecu-

tion and even death from some of the dominant Sunni groups.

Religious freedom is also not confined to any one area or continent (see **figure 21.1**). There are relatively free countries in every continent. South Korea, Taiwan, Japan, Brazil, South Africa, Botswana, and Namibia score higher in this survey than do France and Belgium. Latin America also has relatively high scores. There are absolutely no grounds for thinking that religious

Figure 21.1 Religious freedom by area

Religious Freedom Rating	Former Soviet Union and Eastern Europe	North Africa and West Asia	Western Europe and North Atlantic	Asia	Africa	Latin America
1	Estonia		Finland Ireland Netherlands Norway United States			
2	Lithuania Poland		Austria Sweden United Kingdom	Japan South Korea Taiwan	Botswana Namibia South Africa	Brazil
3	Hungary Latvia Romania Ukraine	Israel	Belgium France Germany Spain	Mongolia Philippines	Zimbabwe	Argentina Chile El Salvador Guatemala
4	Armenia Bulgaria Georgia Kazakhstan Macedonia Moldova Russia	Greece Lebanon Morocco		Malaysia Singapore Sri Lanka	Tanzania	Colombia Mexico
5	Azerbaijan Belarus	Egypt Turkey		East Timor India Indonesia Nepal	Nigeria	
6	Uzbekistan	Mauritania Pakistan		Bangladesh Bhutan China Vietnam		Cuba
7	Turkmenistan	Iran Saudi Arabia Sudan		Burma North Korea Tibet (China)		

    "free"   "partly free"   "unfree" freedom is an exclusively Western concern or achievement.

Some Westerners and Third World tyrants in China and Vietnam elevate "economic rights," "Asian values," and "cultural relativism" and denigrate civil rights, such as religious freedom, as quasi-luxuries that need be advanced, if at all, only when more basic needs such as food and shelter have been achieved. Proponents of these views should be asked why several Asian countries, such as South Korea and Taiwan, which have a background of poverty and exploitation, and with Confucian traditions as strong as China and Vietnam, both value and successfully defend religious freedom, and why desperately poor African countries can do the same. Religious freedom is desired throughout the world and has been achieved throughout the world. It is a moral travesty of the highest order to pretend that because people are hungry and cold it is legitimate to repress and persecute them as well.

While high levels of religious freedom occur in every area, there are still large regional variations. The Western European and North Atlantic area countries covered in this survey all score from one to three, and thus all show a high level of religious freedom (following Freedom House practice, this survey calls countries with a score of one to three "free," four to five "partly free," and six to seven "not free"). The countries of Latin America also score highly, with only Colombia, Mexico, and Cuba scoring less than three (Sigmund, 2000). A similar pattern occurs in sub-Saharan Africa where Nigeria scores a five and Tanzania scores a four and the other countries surveyed scored higher. However, in the African case, the survey covers relatively few countries, and there are signs that other countries (such as war-torn Angola, Congo, Liberia, or Sierra Leone) would score much less. However, the completed profiles show that several African countries score highly.

The countries of Eastern Europe and the former Soviet Union cover a wide spread, from Estonia, rated a one, to Turkmenistan, rated a seven. There are countries at each level, with those bordering the Baltic (Estonia, Latvia, Lithuania, and Poland) as well as Hungary, Romania, and Ukraine scoring higher. Most countries (ten out of nineteen) are at the intermediate levels of four and five (Bourdeaux, 2000). Other Freedom House surveys indicate that these countries are in transition and are likely to move to higher or lower levels.

Asian countries also show a wide spread, though with more countries at the intermediate and lower levels. East Asian countries (Taiwan, South Korea, Japan, and the Philippines, as well as Mongolia) score higher. The low scores are dominated by communist powers (China, Tibet, North Korea, and Vietnam) and the chaos in East Timor. Apart from these, the only "unfree" countries surveyed are Burma and Bhutan.

The area from northern Africa through the eastern Mediterranean to West Asia tends to have low scores. Israel (excluding the occupied territories) scores a three, and Lebanon, Malaysia, Morocco, and Greece a four, with Egypt and Turkey a five. The others are sixes (Mauritania, Pakistan) and sevens (Saudi Arabia, Sudan, Iran). These findings (as well as those for other areas) are consistent with the general area findings for all political rights and civil liberties contained in *Freedom in the World*.

There is similar variation in the religious background of religious freedom. This is obviously a complex matter, since current regimes may reflect comparatively little of a country's religious background. China, Tibet, and Vietnam all have a largely Buddhist background, but current religious repression comes at the hand of communist regimes who profess to be atheistic materialists. Similarly Catholic East Timor had, until the fall of 1999, been under Indonesian occupation, and its lack of religious freedom reflected the damage and chaos left in the aftermath of Indonesian military withdrawal. Nevertheless, since the survey usually covers several countries of each religious background, the overall patterns can be revealing (see **figure 21.2**).

Historically Christian countries tend to score the highest in religious freedom, with an average rating of three. This parallels other Freedom House findings, which have found that traditionally Christian countries have tended to score higher on political

Figure 21.2 Religious freedom by religious background

Religious Freedom Rating	Catholic	Protestant	Orthodox	Mixed Christian	Hindu	Buddhism and related religions	Islam	Other	Mixed Muslim/Christian
1	Ireland	Estonia Finland Netherlands Norway United States							
2	Austria Brazil Lithuania Poland	Botswana Namibia South Africa Sweden United Kingdom				Japan South Korea Taiwan			
3	Argentina Belgium Chile El Salvador France Guatemala Hungary Philippines Spain	Zimbabwe	Romania Ukraine	Germany Latvia		Mongolia		Israel	
4	Colombia Mexico	Tanzania	Armenia Bulgaria Georgia Greece Macedonia Moldova Russia			Singapore Sri Lanka	Kazakhstan Kyrgystan Malaysia Morocco		Lebanon
5	East Timor		Belarus		India Nepal		Azerbaijan Egypt Indonesia Turkey		Nigeria
6	Cuba					Bhutan China Vietnam	Bangladesh Mauritania Pakistan Uzbekistan		
7						Burma North Korea Tibet (China)	Iran Saudi Arabia Sudan Turkmenistan		

▢ "free"   ▢ "partly free"   ▢ "unfree"

rights and civil liberties. Of the thirty four countries that can be rated as religiously "free" (i.e., scoring three or above), twenty-nine of them are traditionally Christian. Conversely, only one of the forty-two traditionally Christian countries surveyed (Cuba) is "not free" (i.e., scoring six or seven). Within Christianity, Protestantism tends to score higher than Catholicism, and both higher than Orthodoxy.

The other religiously "free" countries are Israel and then four countries of largely Buddhist background Japan, Mongolia, South Korea, and Taiwan. This suggests that a Buddhist tradition also has had a tendency to produce relatively high religious freedom. The Buddhist countries with markedly low scores reflect the communist regimes in China, Tibet, North Korea, and Vietnam. If these are excluded, the remaining countries, except Bhutan and Burma, score relatively high. These patterns are also congruent with the findings of *Freedom in the World.* There is, however, some difference with respect to Hindu countries. Whereas both India and Nepal have relatively free elections, they have tended to score low on civil liberties generally and, in this survey, score even lower on religious freedom. In Nepal the difference is not great, but in India the difference reflects the upsurge in India within recent years of a militant Hinduism coupled with attacks on religious minorities, especially Christians.

The religious areas with the largest current restrictions on religious freedom are the Islamic countries. This parallels problems with democracy and civil liberties, but the negative trend with respect to religion is even stronger. No traditionally Islamic country surveyed is religiously "free" while almost half of those surveyed are "not free." Four countries (Iran, Saudi Arabia, Sudan, and Turkmenistan) score a seven, the lowest category. This situation may soon show some improvement since Indonesia, the country with by far the world's largest Muslim population, is rapidly becoming freer following its 1999 election, and Nigeria, which is about half Muslim, may also be establishing itself as a democracy.

Religious Freedom and Other Human Rights

A comparison of ratings for religious freedom with ratings for political rights and civil liberties allows us to see how the degree of religious freedom in a country compares to its record of human rights in general, and vice versa. In thirty-seven out of the seventy-five countries covered, the score for religious freedom is identical to the score for civil liberties in general. For the rest, except for three countries, the religious freedom score is within one point of the score for civil liberties in general. These other three are within two points. Consequently, freedom of religion correlates very closely with civil liberties in general.

A skeptic may suggest that this might merely reflect methodology – a result of the fact that the criteria for religious freedom in this survey and the criteria for civil liberties in *Religious Freedom in the World* actually overlap considerably. This overlap is real, but it is not merely a methodological accident, but a reflection of the simple reality that religious freedom is necessarily a part of civil rights in general. In practical terms this means that restrictions on the press necessarily involve restrictions on the religious press, that restrictions on freedom of association necessarily imply restrictions on religious association, that restrictions on speech necessarily imply restriction on religious speech. Consequently, it is only to be expected that freedom of religion and other freedoms will usually go together. Religion exists not (only) in a transcendent realm but is a fundamental and integral part of all human freedom.

Given the fact that these various dimensions of human freedom usually go together, it is also useful to consider situations where differences for religious freedom and for human rights in general are systematic, though small.

Those countries in which the score for religious freedom is less than for civil liberties in general are Austria, Azerbaijan, Bangladesh, Belgium, Bulgaria, Chile, France, Germany Greece, Hungary, Indonesia, Iran, Latvia, Macedonia, Mauritania, Nigeria, Pakistan, Romania, Sweden, and Spain. While these, along with all the countries surveyed, obviously have idiosyncrasies, nevertheless they also reflect some systematic variations. Many of these countries are Western European ones (Austria, Belgium, France, Germany, Spain, and Sweden) that have both a history and a current practice wherein their reaction to religious nonconformity is more repressive than their response to nonconformity in general. They reflect an attachment to a traditional dominant religions (Austria, Belgium, France, Germany Spain, Sweden, Bulgaria, Romania, Latvia, Hungary, and Macedonia) and an antipathy to new, unorthodox religions (Austria, Belgium, France, and Germany). This illustrates two real trends in the world: the increasing Western European phobia of "sects" (Fautre, 2000) and an Eastern European fear of anything that challenges the hegemony of the dominant religious group.

Another group that has a comparatively lower rating for religious freedom consists of Azerbaijan, Bangladesh, Iran, Mauritania, and Pakistan. All of these countries have governments or opposition groups committed to radical forms of Islam that would relegate other religions to second-class status, or who think that they must accommodate or defer to such militant forms of Islam. Because of this, in many Islamic countries religious freedom lags behind even other freedoms.

Apart from the above two trends, there are the examples of Chile, Nepal, and India (which is two points below). Like the example of the Islamic countries cited, these reflect the influence of a dominant religion (Catholicism or Hinduism) that is currently more wary of the possible consequences of religious competition than it is of human freedom in general. In the case of India, there has recently been a rapid increase in religiously motivated assaults on minority religions.

Finally there are the examples of Indonesia and Nigeria. Their differential scores do not indicate any systematic variance of religious freedom but merely (like India) a process of rapid change. Both have experienced recent major changes, and their scores simply reflect this.

The countries that score higher on religious freedom than they do for civil rights in general are equally varied. However, here too some general patterns emerge. Several of these countries (Belarus, Estonia, Kazakhstan, Kyrgyzstan, and Ukraine) are remnants of the former Soviet Union. While they vary from comparatively free (Estonia) to comparatively repressive (Belarus), each has found the freedom of its religious institutions easier to achieve, and perhaps less of a threat to power holders, than the freedom of other groups. The rest of this group – Cuba, Egypt, Malaysia, East Timor, Guatemala, Lebanon, Namibia, Vietnam, Singapore, Brazil, and Zimbabwe (the latter two are two points above) – are more idiosyncratic. However, in each case, their religious institutions are comparatively large and are, in fact, the major portion of civil society Consequently, they may be harder to repress than other bodies. In addition, in most of these instances, the religious bodies have been relatively apolitical and, thus, have not provoked much opposition. The case of Cuba also reflects a slight slackening of religious control, while East Timor has eased due to the United Nations takeover in the fall of 1999.

State Department Reports on Religious Freedom

In September 1999, as required by law under the 1998 *International Religious Freedom Act,* the US State Department released its first annual *Report* on religious freedom worldwide. The *Report* is an impressive piece of work and, by and large, gives a detailed and comprehensive overview of the state of religious freedom in each country in the world. However, the compilation of Freedom House's own survey gives us a basis to evaluate and to point out some weaknesses in the State Departments work.

First, because its material is not standardized and, hence, gives simply an ordered compilation of information about each country, the *Report* makes it difficult to compare one country to another. This has the effect of blurring distinctions so that many countries appear to be equally repressive. The very breadth of the material tends to repress important differences. Indeed, the largest single section on the problems of any individual religious group concerns the situation of Scientologists in Germany. No doubt this is a topic worthy of attention, but does it deserve more attention than the situation of any other group in the world, including Tibetan Buddhists, Iranian Baha'i, and Sudanese Christians?

In other instances the *Report* downplays the severity or significance of restrictions on religious freedom, perhaps in deference to the governments concerned. This appears in reports on Egypt, China, and Saudi Arabia.

- The *Report* says that the Egyptian Coptic Orthodox Church was established in the fifth century, but Egypt has been a major center of Christianity since the first century. It is noteworthy that Egyptian textbooks also omit the first five centuries of Coptic history. The *Report* also merely notes "discrepancies in official and unofficial accounts" of the torture and abuse of more than one thousand Copts in El-Khosheh in 1998, when there is copious detail of these abuses. Finally, it credits Egypt for improvements in permits for church construction and repair. But some of the construction permits were

given for churches that had already been built – some in the fourth century.
- While the China section contains numerous details of persecution, it eschews the conclusion that China persecutes believers, stating the weaker conclusion that it "restricts" some religious believers (although the *Report's* executive summary does use the term *persecution*). It even avoids making conclusions as to the situation of the highest ranking member of the Roman Catholic Church in China, Bishop James Su Zhimin, stating only that his whereabouts "remain unclear," though Catholics from his diocese state he was arrested two years ago. The report flags the early release from reeducation camp of seventy-eight year-old Bishop Zeng Jingmu when, in fact, as the report itself states, he was simply transferred to house arrest and is thus still prevented from carrying out his episcopal duties.

Perhaps most importantly, the *Report* sometimes gives a truncated view of religion. This is not a mere definitional quibble of interest only to academics: it is central to the proper implementation of the entire 1998 *International Religious Freedom Act*. The focus of the act is not human rights violations against "religious" people. After all, as noted above, since most people in the world claim some form of religious identity, the most human rights violations of *any* kind are against religious believers. The act is concerned not with all forms of restrictions or persecution of religious people, *but with persecution where the focus or the grounds are themselves in part religious* where a person's or community's religion is a component of the persecution or discrimination they suffer. (Therefore it would not address genocide in Rwanda – even though most of those killed had a religious identity – since their death was related to their being Tutsis.) Hence a truncated view of religion would lead inevitably to a truncated implementation of the act. The *Report is* aware of the difficulties of defining the role of religion and very carefully and lucidly uses the example of Kosovo to illustrate it ("Introduction," 3–4):

> In Kosovo, for example, Serb atrocities were visited predominantly on Kosovar Albanian Muslims. The key question for this report is the extent to which the religion of the victims played a part in Serb behavior. If religion were a significant factor, then the Milosevic regime is responsible for a partic- ular virulent form of religious persec- ution – alongside its other crimes against humanity – involving prolonged arbitrary detention, torture, mass executions, mass deportations, and rape. By the same token, if religion were not a factor, or constituted an insignificant factor, then religious perse- cution should not be added to the bill of particulars against the regime.
>
> This is an issue on which people of good will hold strongly differing views. In the Kosovo case, many would argue that the predominant causes of the Serb campaign were political (Milosevic's usual tactic of initiating conflict as a means of retaining power), nationalist (the drive to retain a province central to Serbian identity and power), and ethnic (a determination to cleanse the nation of a non-Serb, unassimi- lated ethnic minority, the Kosovar Albanians). This view would hold that religion played an insignificant role in the conflict.
>
> . . . By contrast, others argue that the ethnicity of the Kosovar Albanians is inex- tricably bound to their Muslim heritage, both in their own minds, and more im- portantly, in the minds of their Serb tormentors .
>
> . . . Serbia is not the only case. In many countries where there is violent persecu- tion against a religious minority, there are also nonreligious factors at work – the ethnicity and separatist policies of the minority, for example. In Sudan, Christians are being persecuted by an Arab regime that is Muslim. In China Tibetan Buddhists who are associated with separatism are being persecuted by an atheist government.

Clearly, as the *Report* says, people of goodwill can have differences about such things. However, it is troubling that at times it contrasts politics, nationalism, and ethnicity to religion, as though concrete acts, events, and movements were neces- sarily only one or another. In fact, most things human are several of these things at once. A war can be both economic and reli- gious just as a wall can be both thick and tall. Cultures are usually religious, and reli- gions are usually cultural. While the *Report* is often sensitive to these points, at times the tendency to separate religion from other factors leads it astray.

This tendency to minimize religion creates problems with coverage of Sudan. The Sudan section does a very good job of detailing religious persecution in areas under the direct control of the Khartoum regime, and it describes the practice of slavery. However, the conduct of the war itself – with a death toll higher than that of Rwanda, Bosnia, Kosovo, Chechnya, Algeria, and all the Arab–Israeli wars combined, with up to five million displaced people, and widespread massacre, rape, torture, and forced starvation – is absent. The reason, we must assume, is that the war itself is not understood as "religious." Consequently, the *Report* neglects what may be, in terms of size and intensity, the world's worst situation of religious oppres- sion. This is akin to disregarding race in describing South Africa's military actions and repression of the opponents of apartheid.

In contrast to its treatment of Sudan, the *Report* correctly and fully outlines Saddam Hussein's vicious persecution of Shi'ite Muslims and of Assyrian and Chaldean Christians. However, the grounds for calling these depredations matters of reli- gious freedom or religious persecution are less than they are in the Sudanese war. Clearly Saddam will, without discrimina- tion, kill anyone of any or no religion whom he perceives as a political threat. Religion *per se is* not, apparently, a motive or independent factor for him. Yet the *Report is* correct to detail his depravities, since their result, regardless of motive, is a monumental denial of religious freedom. However, the State Department should have addressed Saddam's ally, Sudan, with the same insight.

Some other examples:

- In Indonesia, conflict in Ambon between Christians and Muslims, claiming hundreds, perhaps thousands of lives, is related to immigration that has disturbed the "ethnic balance" of the area. But the crucial change has been in the *religious* balance, which is what has precipitated the conflict.
- In Nigeria, the report describes thirty-one followers of Shi'ite leader Ibrahim El-Zakzaky as having been detained for "political" not "religious beliefs." But, since for El-Zakzaky there "is no government but Islam," here the distinction of "political" and "religious" does not make much sense.
- In Taiwan, in reference to Jehovah's Witness conscientious objectors who have been imprisoned for refusing military service, the *Report* says there "is no indication [they] have been singled out for their beliefs." But their *religious* beliefs in this instance are *precisely* that they must not do military service.
- In Bhutan, the expulsion of Nepalese is described as "political," "economic," and "cultural" rather than "religious." However, it is also noted that the Hinduism of the ethnic Nepalese is one way of identifying them. Surely it is clear that here "religion" permeates "politics," "economics," and "culture."
- In India the caste system is described

"as much a cultural and social phenomenon as a religious one" – but all religious phenomena are also always cultural and nearly always social.

Despite these critical comments, it must be reemphasized that the State Department *Report* is an exemplary piece of work and marks a milestone in reporting on religious freedom. It does highlight, however, the need for standardized criteria.

Conclusions

It is clear from the Freedom House Report, as well as State Department reports and other surveys, that violations of religious freedom worldwide are massive, widespread, and, in the last five years, growing. This leads to three other conclusions. First, that attention to and action on religious freedom have been comparatively weak. Second, that the important role of religion in conflicts and in political orders has been comparatively neglected. Third, that both of these situations are now beginning to change, a change that we hope this present survey will accelerate.

References

Fautre, Willy (2000) "Western Europe: Trends in Religious Liberty," in Paul Marshall *Religious Freedom in the World*. Nashville: Broadman and Holman.

Sigmund, Paul (2000) "Religious Freedom in Latin America," in Marshall *Religious Freedom in the World*. Nashville: Broadman and Holman.

International Justice and Just War Theory

Tony Coates

22

◆ Cosmopolitanism, realism and the morality of states ◆

◆ Realism, morality of states and Just War theory ◆

◆ Cosmopolitanism and Just War theory ◆

Deep divisions mark the contemporary debate about international justice. Realists are ranged against idealists, communitarians against cosmopolitans, particularists against universalists. The differences relate to methods or approaches as well as matters of substance. Realists and communitarians criticize idealists and cosmopolitans for their prescriptivism or utopianism; for their atomistic understanding of international relations with its exclusive and artificial focus on rational individuals abstracted from their social and historical situation; and for their ensuing neglect of real, particular and communal, identities and values. Conversely, cosmopolitans criticize realists and communitarians for their positivism and uncritical acceptance of the status quo; for their preoccupation with the state and the claims of particular moral and political communities; and for their consequent denial or neglect of universal or global values and needs.

Within the terms of the debate thus conceived international justice, in its fullest sense, comes to be regarded as the preserve of cosmopolitanism. In its pure or classical form realism is seen to dispense entirely with considerations of justice, regarding ethical concerns in general as essentially alien, even hostile, to the proper conduct of international relations. In a more moderate, or "liberal," guise realism is able to admit justice but only in a narrow legalistic or corrective sense and mainly as a way of preserving state autonomy; the domain of distributive or substantive justice remains a purely domestic one.

By contrast, cosmopolitanism's uncompromising universalism makes imperative the application to international relations of substantive and distributive as well as formal and legal justice. From this cosmopolitan perspective the boundaries of particular states and societies, or the political and social identities of individual human beings, appear largely irrelevant to questions of justice comprehensively understood. What matters is whether or not the needs of individual human beings are being met and their rights upheld. For citizens of the cosmopolis rights and duties cannot be confined within state boundaries or restricted to formal principles that maintain the security and integrity of states without reference to their internal constitution or their impact on individuals. To suggest otherwise is to renounce any real notion of the universal community of humankind in favour of some form (more or less extreme) of moral particularism.

As often happens in a fiercely contested debate, where each side develops its own self-image largely in opposition to the other, the tendency is to concentrate on the points of difference rather than the points of contact or affinity. The result is a polarization of the argument in which universalism comes to be understood as the very antithesis of particularism (and vice versa), and in which the claims of the world community are seen to vie with the claims of particular states. Polarization, therefore, has a thoroughly distorting effect leading, inevitably, to one-sided and incomplete conceptions of international relations and, by extension, of international justice.[1]

By drawing on a just war tradition that is neither realist nor cosmopolitan the argument of this chapter attempts to construct more rounded concepts of international relations and international justice. In Section 1 the current polarity between realism and cosmopolitanism is examined in the light of the morality of states. The assimilation of the just war tradition to realism (in the guise of the morality of states) is noted in section 1 and criticized in Section 2. While the universalist principles of just war theory are seen to belie its realist image (Section 2), in Section 3 the concrete or rooted universalism of just war theory is contrasted with the abstract universalism of cosmopolitanism. The conclusion reached is that the merit of the just war approach lies in its transcendence of the realist–cosmopolitan divide through its upholding of the claims of *both* particularity and universality.

I The Current Polarity: Cosmopolitanism, Realism and the Morality of States

The polarized or dualistic way of thinking is evident in the accounts given of the range of conceptions (past and present) of international relations and, by implication, international justice. In his *Political Theory* *and International Relations* (a book that has exercised a considerable influence on contemporary cosmopolitan thought) Charles Beitz (1979: vii) positions cosmopolitanism in relation to what he considers to be the traditional and main alternatives:

> To assert the possibility of international political theory, one must first reexamine the traditional image of international relations as a state of nature and purge it of its skeptical elements. The traditional alternative to this view, which I call the morality of states, must be reconstructed to correct for the persistent misunderstanding of the notion of state autonomy. The result is a third view of international morality, which might be described as cosmopolitan.

This tripartite characterization of past and present thinking about international relations ("realism," "morality of states," "cosmopolitanism") is a commonly accepted one (see, for example, Vincent, 1986; Nye, 1997: 19–24; Dower, 1998: 17–20; Barry, 1999). Despite its more complex appearance it does little to undermine the dualistic opposition of realism and idealism, or of communitarianism (or statism) and cosmopolitanism. In fact it reinforces it since, from a cosmopolitan standpoint at least, the distinction between realism and the morality of states is of minor significance.

The morality of states is not seen to constitute a decisive enough break with realism. In fact it is thought to amount to a distinction within realism, being seen (perhaps correctly) as no more than a moderate or liberal form of realism that leaves the fundamentals of realism intact. Though, unlike pure or classical realism, it accepts the moral or ethical determination of international relations, the form of international ethics it upholds is limited in nature and scope. It is an ethic with a negative rather than a positive emphasis, in which order may be seen to dominate justice. Its object is to regulate the external relations of states with a view to curtailing (rather than resolving) conflict by safeguarding the integrity and autonomy of each state. Insofar as justice is seen to apply at all to the domain of international relations it applies in the restricted sense of corrective justice. The idea of distributive justice, with its universalist assumptions and intrusive implications, is seen to conflict with those key principles of the system of states, state sovereignty and nonintervention, that the morality of states is meant to uphold.

Understandably, cosmopolitans find the morality of states wholly inadequate. Like realism, it fails to articulate a community of interest or need, grounded in a common humanity and transcending particular states. It seems designed rather to allow states to go their own ways, in a state of mutual indifference, than to realize a common identity or to work out a common fate. This is not an alternative to realism but simply a more presentable form of realism, realism with a moral face. Some cosmopolitans are even inclined to doubt that: "Is the morality of states a morality at all?," asks Brian Barry (1999: 16) – "if universal egoism counts as a morality, then so does its statist analogue."

The morality of states, therefore, does little to shake the duopoly of statism and cosmopolitanism or to produce a more balanced understanding of international relations. It is far too closely identified with one side of the argument for that. Inevitably, its defence of the state and the states-system is at the expense of those global and universalist considerations that are central to international justice. The morality of states is too narrow in its scope to embrace the agenda of international justice, of which regulative or corrective justice forms only a part (and a part that depends for its validity on its connection with the whole).

But does this trinity of realism, morality of states, and cosmopolitanism exhaust the possibilities so far as conceptions of international relations and international justice are concerned? It seems an unduly economical or abbreviated account of the potential, or actual, spectrum of thought. Even recent thinking about international relations is more varied and complex than that. Recognition of that variety and complexity seems a matter of some urgency given the polarized or dualistic state of the argument. The variety and complexity of thought suggest that the choice is not simply between realism and cosmopolitanism, or between title claims of particular polities and those of the universal or global community. The polarized nature of the debate has obscured those concepts of international relations that are not classifiable as either realist or cosmopolitan.

Chris Brown alludes to this variety in his review of postwar international theory. Even though international relations theory has been dominated throughout most of the twentieth century by the struggle for mastery between realists and idealists, statists and cosmopolitans, dissenting voices have been heard from time to time. One such voice (Brown suggests) is that of the just war tradition with its roots in natural law theory. In the context of the debate about international justice what is interesting about this tradition is its claim to transcend the conventional division between realism and cosmopolitanism through its reconciliation of particular and universal values.

It is a claim that is frequently denied or overlooked. The reason for this oversight is significant and points to the internal variety and ambiguity of the just war tradition itself as well as to partial and incomplete readings of that tradition. In its contemporary form just war theory is commonly regarded (especially, perhaps, by cosmopolitans) as a version of the morality of states, that is, not as a theory spanning the realist–cosmopolitan divide, but as a theory firmly planted on the realist side of that divide, a form of moral particularism. As such it appears incapable of grounding any concept of international distributive justice. Is this view of just war theory warranted?

2 Realism, Morality of States and Just War Theory

The view of just war theory as a form of realism owes much to the identification of contemporary just war theory with the work of Michael Walzer. More often than not the critique of just war theory amounts to little more than a critique of Walzer (see Holmes, 1989; Thompson, 1992; Campbell, 1993; Norman, 1995; Zolo, 1997). It is the assimilation of the tradition as a whole with the specific form or shape that Walzer has given it that largely accounts for its "realist" or "statist" reputation. Here, according to one critic, is "a theory of justice based on the entitlements of sovereign states," an "inherently conservative" theory that "takes the entitlements of sovereignty for granted and [that] closes off attempts to criticise these entitlements" (Thompson, 1992: 13 and 17). Another claims that "in Michael Walzer's extended discussion of just-war theory, territorial integrity and political sovereignty are the absolute rights of nations in a world comprised of sover-eign states." As a result "just-war theory is woefully inadequate as a concept for anything other than the rationalization of war" (Campbell, 1993: 23 and 80). Yet another suggests that "national survival, or more basically, national egoism is the governing norm" of Walzer's theory with the result that "reason of state begins to show itself in the guise of the just war theory" (Holmes, 1989: 170).

The concept of international justice asso-ciated with such a statist version of just war theory cannot be other than minimal. "It is an immediate implication of Walzer's particularism," writes Brian Barry (1995: 79), "that there can be no such thing as international distributive justice." At best, it yields a legalistic notion of international justice that "consists in people recognising and respecting the sovereignty exercised by others unless there are very good reasons for intervention" (Thompson, 1992: 12). As a response to the pressing problems and urgent needs of the global community it appears wholly inadequate

The attention paid to Walzer's work is neither surprising nor unjustified. He has done, perhaps, more than any other contemporary writer to breathe life into a tradition that, for a variety of reasons, had become somewhat moribund. That said it would be a mistake to regard Walzer's version of just war theory as definitive or exhaustive. In many fundamental respects Walzer's interpretation may be at odds with the classical tradition of just war thought (and with the pre-modern or pre-enlightenment tradition of natural law on which the classical version – but not, it seems, Walzer's – rests). Significantly, conflict-orxensionoften coincide with the points of criticism raised by those of a more universalist persuasion and critical disposition.

The charge levelled at just war theory – that by giving normative primacy to state sovereignty it lapses into moral particu-larism – may have some foundation in Walzer's work[2] but as a statement about the tradition as a whole it appears wide of the mark. It is true that within the tradition the 'state,' or (more neutrally) the political community, is seen to play a key, even constitutive, role and to enjoy a certain moral entitlement (a role and an entitlement denied, or at any rate obscured, by the cosmopolitan tradition). To claim, however, that this theory of justice is *based* on the entitlement of sovereign states is a gross distortion of a tradition that, in its classical (and pre-Westphalian) form at least, grounds the rights of states or polities (including the right to war) in a conception of natural law and the moral community of mankind. It is this grounding that gives just war theory a critical edge and universalist orientation that are missing from realism and the morality of states. The fact is that in just war theory, at least in its classical version, the idea of the universal com-munity of mankind is the basic norm that structures the entire theory. It is this universalist principle that underpins those concepts that make the tradition's understanding of war and peace.[3]

The concept of legitimate authority, for example, that establishes the right to war or to the use of coercive force, is not to be confused with the "weak" or realist version of conventional usage From the realist – even the moderate realist – standpoint this is a criterion that any state would find it easy to satisfy. The *competence de guerre* is, in realist terms, simply a formal accompaniment of state sovereignty that all states enjoy merely by being in effective control of their territory. Conversely, the resort to force by non-state or sub-state agents is automatically ruled out.[4]

This "realist" understanding of legitimate authority or the right to war is frequently assumed in criticisms of just war theory. One criticism, for example, makes much of the fact that "[governments] tend to assume that they have an automatic right of military resistance to any violation of national sovereignty [yet] tend to regard armed resistance to internal oppression as much less justifiable" (Norman, 1995: 156). No doubt this is the case but it hardly seems relevant to the criticism of a tradition that accepts, in principle, the right of revolution (or at any rate of resistance), and that derives the state's right to war not from its de facto sovereignty but, proximately, from the political community on whose behalf power is exercised and force employed and, ultimately, from its membership of an international community to the law and common good of which it is seen to be subject. In the light of that framework of moral universalism the sovereignty of the state must be seen as relative and conditional, not as an absolute sovereignty. The view that Thompson attributes to cosmopolitanism, allegedly in contradistinction to just war theory, that "the entitlement of states to exist and exercise sovereignty is a derivative and conditional right" (Thompson, 1992: 76), is as much a principle of just war reasoning as it is of cosmopolitan thinking (even though the

specific grounding of the right may be understood differently).

A similar logic is discernible in reasoning about just cause. Conventional thinking about just cause is often dominated by the aggressor–defender distinction, a just war being equated simply and uncritically with a war of self-defence and an unjust war with a war of aggression. This way of thinking reflects the prevalent states system with its established principles of sovereignty and nonintervention. It fits much less comfortably with a tradition, like the just war tradition, that rests the assessment of war on the premise of the universal community of mankind.

The right of self-defence is an important part of just war reasoning but it does not monopolize that reasoning in the way that it has monopolized recent thinking about war. What is really at issue is the grounding or derivation of the right. Whereas in realist thought the state's right of self-defence is seen to follow automatically from its independent sovereignty, in the just war tradition. it is seen as a vindication of the legal and moral community or whole of which states form a subordinate part. In upholding its own right the state is at the same time upholding the legal and moral system from which its right is derived. This different grounding gives just war reasoning a critical force that is missing in the case of realism. The right of self-defence can no longer be taken for granted. A state that habitually contravened the moral law could not plausibly be construed as upholding that law by exercising its "right" of self defence. Some states may, by virtue of their disordered internal constitution, lack the right of self-defence.

The universalist assumptions of just war theory cast further doubt on the moral adequacy of the aggressor–defender distinction. Not only is the justice of a defensive war questionable so too is the presumed injustice of offensive recourse. Traditionally, the vindication of the universal community included the use of war in an offensive role, the protection of the innocent being considered a duty that befell rulers even when the innocent in question were citizens of another state or political community. This duty of humanitarian intervention sprang from the notion of a universal moral community whose members enjoyed reciprocal rights and duties, precisely as members of that community and not just as citizens of particular states.

The moral primacy of the community of mankind is evident in the other criteria of just war theory. Proportionality, for example, is a central criterion of just recourse: do the potential benefits of war outweigh the potential costs? Just war theory in its traditional form brings to this principle too a universalist perspective. "since one nation is a part of the whole world," wrote Vitoria, "if any war should be advantageous to one . . . nation but injurious to the whole . . . that war is unjust" (quoted in Fernandez-Santamaria, 1977: 141). The proportionate worth of a war must be assessed in the light of the state's membership of a global community and of a global common good to which the good of the state is seen to be essentially related.

The same approach is evident in the moral treatment of the *conduct of* war. The just war category of *ius in bello* is informed by a sense of moral community. It is the recognition of an adversary's common humanity that dictates his just treatment (just as its suppression by some process of dehumanization leads in a contrary direction). The proportionate and discriminate conduct of war that just war theory stipulates assumes membership of a community transcending the warring states. As members of that universal moral community belligerents enjoy reciprocal rights and duties that are rooted in their common humanity and that remain in force even in the midst of war. The moral claims that belligerents rightly make upon each other are grounded in their membership of the universal community of mankind.

But what moral force or impact does the theory have as a whole? Critics of just war theory have argued that, whatever the specific merits or demerits of this theory of war, that is what it remains – a theory of *war* – and, therefore, a system of thought that is quite incapable of generating a comprehensive and at all adequate account of international justice. Geyer and Green, for example, voice a common criticism when they write of the just war tradition's "essentially negative preoccupation with questions as to whether, or when, or how to resort to war." As such this is "an ethic of war" only – not "a complete ethic of war and peace" that includes "the positive imperatives and strategies of peacemaking" (Geyer and Green, 1992: 24).

This alleged preoccupation with war is seen as confirmation of the realist nature of just war theory. Like realism, it is argued, just war theory sees war as paradigmatic. The realm of international relations is understood as a natural state of war with the moderation of conflict defining the limit of moral ambition or aspiration. Both realism and just war theory are understood to be theories that regard international relations as intrinsically conflictual and that, therefore, put a premium on order rather than on justice. The "peace" that both uphold is really a covert form of war, an interlude between hostilities, a cessation of conflict that does little to remove the causes of war or to secure a lasting peace. Both take war for granted and regard its abolition or supersession as a utopian and moralistic fancy that, if acted upon, seems likely to worsen the state of international relations.

It is true that for many realists the balance of power has often exhausted the concept and the strategy of peace – "this approximate, tenuous equilibrium that provides whatever peace and order exists in the world of nation states" (Morgenthau and Thompson, 1985: 388) – but can the same be said of just war theorists? A partial recognition and acceptance of the utility of balance of power politics is not inconsistent with just war thinking. The tradition is worldly enough – realistic enough perhaps – to acknowledge the limits as well as the possibilities of a peaceful ordering of international relations, and modest enough to accept the instrumentality, if not of evil, then of impure or tainted means. Yet the balance of power remains something about which just war theory seems bound to harbour grave reservations.

In the first place the policy is open to abuse. Though it can be understood as a strategy consistent with a global concern and pacific purpose, the likelihood is that considerations of global peace and security will be sacrificed to the advancement of a national or imperial interest. Secondly, the policy itself seems intrinsically disordered or unethical, the logic of the balance of power appearing to dictate policies of dubious moral worth, more in tune with *raison d'état* than with a strategy that serves a moral or ethical purpose. Operationally, the balance of power may dictate not merely the toleration of injustice but the collusion with, and even perpetration of, injustice. Thirdly, its pacific consequences, by which so much store is set, are themselves questionable. Far from preventing war the pursuit of this policy can become one of the principal causes of war.

For reasons such as these just war theory's acceptance of balance of power politics must remain strictly guarded or inhibited, even though the complexities and difficulties that beset the international realm in its present condition are seen to give those politics some limited and contingent justification. Fundamentally, the realist concept of peace is too conservative to comply with just war criteria. What realism lacks is that idea of peace that just war theory shares with more critical and more utopian ways of thinking and that springs from a deep dissatisfaction with the present state of international relations – the idea of the qualitative improvement of the international order, its radical transformation from something akin to a state of war to something akin to a state of genuine peace.

It is peace in this dynamic sense that structures just war theory, a theory that is not, despite what critics might say, a theory of war, primarily, but a theory of peace. The *ius ad bellum* is subordinate throughout to the *ius ad pacem.* What just war theory affirms, quite unequivocally, is the moral primacy of peace over war. This search for a more authentic peace corrects the realist imbalance between the values of order and justice. The idea of peace without justice is in just war terms a self-contradictory notion. That is why the work of peace-making does not end with the cessation of war. The agenda of peace is not limited to the control of conflict but includes the positive and progressive removal of the causes of conflict.

The reason for realism's lack of ambition is that it is without a sense of international community. Being founded precisely on the reverse assumption of a natural or essential *dis*unity, it cannot see beyond the requirements of order, an order that is thought too fragile a construct to bear the weight of justice. By contrast, in just war theory, the paradigm of international relations is a state of peace not a state of war, a harmony or unity of parts not a conflict between sovereign and independent entities. Peace in this positive and radical sense *is* a kind of community and to be just war itself must constitute a vindication of that community, both actual and potential.

3 Cosmopolitanism and Just War Theory

What kind of international community does just war theory uphold? The question is a decisive one so far as peacemaking is concerned for not all concepts of unity (or community) promote peace. Some have quite the reverse effect, deepening divisions, multiplying grievances, exacerbating the state of war. Such is the case with an imperial unity where the claims of a particular polity, culture, religion or ideology are imposed upon the rest. By contrast the natural law tradition on which just war theory draws (an earlier Thomist and Aristotelian tradition very different from the modern natural law tradition out of which the morality of states and cosmopolitanism have developed[5]) conceives of the community of mankind as a plurality, a differentiated whole made up of parts that, in the interests of unity itself, are themselves to be considered wholes.

It is here, perhaps, that the essential difference between the just war approach and that of cosmopolitanism is to be located. Unlike realism, both just war theory and cosmopolitanism are forms of universalism but the concepts of universalism that they uphold seem worlds apart. Unlike cosmopolitan universalism, the universalism of just war theory remains open to the realm of the particular. There is here none of that hostility to particular societies commonly, and rightly, associated with cosmopolitanism. The universal is not regarded as the particular's polar opposite precisely because it is understood to be the particular's own internal principle (and *vice versa*). The relation between particular and universal in just war thought is understood to be one of mutual reciprocity not, as in the cosmopolitan conception, one of mutual antagonism. As a result, while both just war theory and cosmopolitanism employ the idea of the universal community of mankind as a normative principle, they conceive of that community in radically different ways and to radically different effect.

The source of the difference lies, perhaps, in their contrasting conceptions of human nature. Unlike cosmopolitanism (and, in this respect at least, like communitarian thought), the just war tradition conceives of human nature in social and political terms. The atomistic conception of the rational, autonomous and self-constituted individual that structures the liberal cosmopolitan tradition vies with the Thomist–Aristotelian concept of "man as social and political animal." According to the latter, the social and political community with its complex of institutions is to be understood not contractually and instrumentally (and, therefore, purely deriv-

atively), as a means to the advancement of autonomously chosen ends, but constitutively, as the real foundation and essential context of human growth and fulfilment. Viewed from within this tradition, the achievement of human well-being is as much a communal achievement as it is an individual one, an achievement crucially dependent upon the moral and not just the material resources of a society. Here is a way of thinking that is deeply sympathetic to social and political institutions by virtue of its understanding of human nature itself.

By contrast, the rational–individualist premise of liberal cosmopolitan thought (according to which "human beings [are] . . . only incidentally members of polities" (Barry, 1999, 35)) creates a natural antagonism to all inherited social institutions and historic communities. Those institutions (and communities) are seen to confront rational and autonomous individuals with the threat of heteronomy. The only form in which institutions appear at all acceptable is when they are seen to result from rational planning or construction and, in that way, are able to be construed entirely as the work of autonomous individuals.

The idea of the moral as well as material dependence of individuals on society that is so central to just war theory is here denied or suppressed. The contrary view that "membership of a society does not have deep ethical significance" (Barry, 1998, 145) seems representative of the tradition as a whole. As a result "cosmopolitan liberalism [unlike just war theory] accords no ethical privilege to state-level societies" (Beitz, 1999a; 519). "There would have to be something crazy," Barry writes (1999: 38), "about giving value to states as such."

The anti-communal and anti-statist sympathies of liberal cosmopolitanism are reinforced by the common cosmopolitan assumption that the advocacy of the particular community will invariably take a "closed" form, one that is fundamentally hostile to universalist values. Cosmopolitan criticisms of "statist" or "communitarian" thought often assume a nationalist, even xenophobic and militarist, concept of the state or community (see Barry, 1999). There are good grounds for criticizing the nationalist concept of the state (not just in its extreme form) but that criticism is not the monopoly of cosmopolitans. As the case of just war theory exemplifies, acceptance of the claims of particular states or political communities does not entail support for nationalist politics (whether moderate or extreme), much less the denial of universalist values. In that theory the claims of particular communities are upheld but only in a form that is reconcilable with the moral community of mankind.

Cosmopolitans may argue, however, that although the *concept* of the state articulated by "statist" theorists need not (and in some cases does not) take a "closed" form, that is where, in practice, such advocacy leads. Brian Barry, for example, appears to argue along such consequential lines when he writes about "the disjunction between what nationalists do and what their apologists among the political theorists defend";[6] or, when he suggests "that those sympathetic to nationalism, while talking a different language, are in fact acting as a front for blood and soil nationalism" (Barry, 199: 25 and 41). Though a liberal form of nationalism (or statism) is conceivable, it is not the form that tends to prevail in the real world (or the form to which, for all its good intentions, liberal statism tends to give rise).

This practical or consequential criticism may be a double-edged sword as far as cosmopolitanism is concerned. The tendency of cosmopolitanism (and cosmopolitan politics) to devalue particular and historic social and political attachments in favour of a more abstract and rational–legal order might be expected to encourage those attachments, real as they are, to reassert themselves in a more virulent and aggressive form. Arguably, this is at least as likely a consequence of cosmopolitanism as it is of "statism." Cosmopolitanism's assumption of a "closed" and particularist form of "statism" simply makes things worse, reinforcing the opposition between particularist and universalist values and encouraging states to disown universalism in favour of a narrow and parochial particularism.

In contrast to its cosmopolitan counterpart, the just war concept of the community of mankind is built on the ethical recognition of particular communities. Like cosmopolitanism just war theory conceives that universal community in progressive terms. On this view, however, its development is seen as a social and historical process that is not impeded but strengthened and enriched by a plurality of cultures. It is not the work of individual human beings but of culturally situated and culturally endowed individuals. It is the work, moreover, not of any one culture but of the many. Recognition of the integrity and the worth of those cultures is an essential requirement. The community of mankind is conceived as a unity but as a unity of particulars, a unity in which no one culture is allowed to lord it over the rest.

It is important not to conceive of international justice in material terms alone. The extreme poverty and physical degradation of life in the Third World encourages us to do so but this is a form of reductionism which perhaps says more about the values of the First World than it does about the values and consequent needs of the Third. International justice consists in more than dealing with the problems of material deprivation. It involves doing justice to the social, cultural and moral complexity of the particular communities that make up the community of mankind. It would be an injustice if the price that poor nations were forced to pay for the satisfaction of their material needs was the loss of cultural autonomy through their subjection to Western values and institutions. That loss would be of as much consequence to the universal community as it would to the particular communities themselves.

Does cosmopolitanism promote international justice in this inclusive sense? It seems not. Its rational–individualism precludes the kind of distributive recognition that international justice demands. The community, the social identity of individuals, is its traditional blind spot and one that leads to a distorted concept of what international justice entails. As one of its foremost contemporary advocates argues: "cosmopolitan liberalism" consists in "the application to the global level of the individualist moral egalitarianism of the Enlightenment" (Beitz, 1999a: 518).[7] In other words, a creed that is contentious even within its own Western cultural confines (partly because of its perceived corrosive effect on society) is to be used to determine the fate of the global community.[8]

The temptation to conceive the unity of mankind as an imperial unity is a long-standing one. Arguably, cosmopolitanism in its ancient and Stoic form succumbed to it (see Germino, 1982: ch. IV). It is to be hoped that cosmopolitanism in its modern form does not suffer the same fate.

"It is often," wrote Eliot (1962: 91–2),

> the anti-imperialists who, being liberals, are the most complacent believers in the superiority of Western civilisation . . . According to such enthusiasts, we do well to intrude ourselves upon another civilisation, equip the members of it with our mechanical contrivances, our systems of government, education, law, medicine and finance, inspire them with a contempt for their own customs and with an enlightened attitude towards religious superstition – and then leave them to stew in the broth which we have brewed for them.

Conclusion

Universalism in its abstract cosmopolitan form appears indifferent, or even hostile, to the particular, while a reverse preference is evident in realist particularism. What is precisely required is the avoidance of this polarization of the debate. Universalism need not take a cosmopolitan form, particularism need not take a realist form as the just war idea of a global or world community that recognizes the value and respects the integrity of particular states or polities suggests. Global unity is best conceived not as an imperial and uniform unity but as an ecumenical unity, one that not only tolerates cultural differences, grudgingly and patronizingly, but that recognizes the superiority and added strength of a unity based on diversity. What is needed (and what just war theory has traditionally upheld) is a unity conceived as a plurality.[9]

Notes

1   The phenomenon is not new. Rousseau provides a good example of such thinking when he writes: "The patriotic spirit is an exclusive spirit which makes *us* look on everyone but our fellow citizens as strangers, and almost as enemies . . . The spirit of Christianity on the contrary makes *us* look on all men as brothers, as the children of God . . . its ardent zeal embraces indifferently the whole human race. Thus it is true that Christianity is in its very sanctity contrary to the particular social spirit" (quoted in Colletti, 1974: 177).

2   The criticism even of Walzer's work often seems selective and tendentious, exaggerating its realist and positivist aspects and suppressing its moral or critical force. It is difficult, for example, to reconcile the charge that Walzer regards state entitlements uncritically with the claim advanced in *Just and Unjust Wars* that "[t]he moral standing of any particular state depends on the reality of the common life it protects and the extent to which the sacrifices required by that protection are willingly accepted and thought worthwhile," or with the view that "[i]f no common life exists, or if the state doesn't defend the common life that does exist, its own defense may have no moral justification" (Walzer, 1992: 54).

3   For a fuller discussion see Coates, (1997).

4   It is this positivist conception of legitimate authority that Brian Barry seems to have in mind when, in his criticism of statism, he contrasts the universal condemnation of insurgent terrorism by the "trade union of states" with the self-indulgent condoning of much more destructive acts of violence by the states themselves (Barry, 1999: 37).

5   "The new natural law," wrote Rommen

(1947: 75), "differed in many respects from the traditional one. It represented a peculiar hypertrophy of the older conception." A key feature of the modern version is "the individualistic trait manifesting itself in the predominance of the doctrine of the state of nature [or "original position"] (*ibid.*, 93). In Rommen's view, "Kant exhibits . . . the individualistic natural law in its final, highest form" (*ibid.*, 100). In similar vein, Midgley writes of Grotius's "individual-istic formulations [that] represent a grave emasculation of the traditional doctrine [of natural law]" (Midgley, 1975: 159). For a fuller discussion of the distinction's impact on the realist-cosmopolitan debate see Coates, 1999; see also Hayek, 1973: 21).

6   Among the apologists Barry identifies are Walzer, Taylor, Kymlicka, Miller and Elshtain.

7   Elsewhere Beitz (1999b: 296) writes:

[C]osmopolitan liberalism takes the inter-ests of individuals as fundamental and as entitled to equal concern on a global scale, and it holds that the basic institutions of society, at both the global and sectional levels, should be justified in ways consistent with this fundamental commitment.

8   According to Barry (1999: 32–3 and 57) "the fundamental human right [is] to live in a liberal society." "There is," he writes, "a straightforward conflict between the values of group autonomy and liberalism here, and a cosmopolitan is bound to say that the latter should take precedence" . . . "Liberals are first and foremost people who want to see liberal institutions thrive."

9   The argument is considered further in Coates (1999).

References

Barry, B. (1995) 'Spherical Justice and Global Justice" in D. Miller and M. Walzer (eds.), *Pluralism, Justice and Equality*. Oxford: Oxford University Press.

Barry, B. (1998) "International Society from a Cosmopolitan Perspective" in D. Mapel and T. Nardin (eds.) *International Society: Diverse Ethical Perspectives*. Princeton: Princeton University Press.

Barry, B. (1999) 'Statism and Nationalism: A Cosmopolitan Critique" in I. Shapiro and L. Brilmayer (eds.) *Global Justice. NOMOS*

XLI. New York: New York University Press.

Benz, C. R. (1979) *Political Theory and International Relations*. Princeton: Princeton University Press.

Benz, C. R. (1999a) "Social and Cosmopolitan Liberalism," *International Affairs*, 75, 3.

Benz, C. R. (1999b) "International Liberalism and Distributive Justice," *World Politics*, 51, 1, 269–96.

Campbell, D. (1993) *Politics Without Principle*, Boulder, CO and London, Lynne Rienner.

Coates, A. J. (1997) *Ethics of War*. Manchester: Manchester University Press.

Coates, A. J. (1999) "Neither Realism Nor Cosmopolitanism: A Response to Danilo Zolo" in B. Holden (ed.) *Global Democracy*. London: Routledge.

Colletti, L. (1974) *From Rousseau to Lenin*. New York: Monthly Review Press.

Dower, N. (1998) *World Ethics*. Edinburgh: Edinburgh University Press.

Eliot, T. S. (1962) *Notes Towards the Definition of Culture*. London: Faber & Faber.

Fernandez-Santamaria, J. A. (1977) *The State, War and Peace*. Cambridge: Cambridge University Press.

Germino, D. (1982) *Political Philosophy and the Open Society*. Baton Rouge: Louisiana State University Press.

Geyer, A. R and Green, B. G. (1992) *Lines in the Sand*. Westminster/John Knox Press.

Hayek, R. A. (1973) *Law, Legislation and Liberty*, Vol. I. Routledge & Kegan Paul.

Holmes, R. L. (1989) *On War and Morality*. Princeton: Princeton University Press.

Midgely, E. B. (1975) *The Natural Law Tradition and the Theory of International Relation*. London: Paul Elek.

Morgenthau, H. J. and Thompson, K. W. (1985) *Politics Among Nations*. 6th edn. New York.

Norman, R. (1995) *Ethics, Killing and War*. Cambridge: Cambridge University Press.

Nye, J. S. (1998) *Understanding International Conflicts*. New York: Longman.

Rommen, H. A. (1947) *The Natural Law*. London: Herder.

Thompson, J. (1992) *Justice and World Order*. London: Routledge.

Vincent, R. J. (1986) *Human Rights and Inter-national Relations*, Cambridge University Press.

Walzer, M. (1992) *Just and Unjust Wars*. New York: Basic Books.

Zolo, D. (1997) *Cosmopolis*. Polity Press.

23

The Proliferation of Rights: Moral Progress or Empty Rhetoric?

Carl Wellman

◆ Development of human rights ◆ Legal critiques and moral criticisms ◆

◆ First generation rights ◆ Second generation rights ◆

◆ Third generation rights ◆

The rights to seek and enjoy asylum are similar to the civil and political rights traditionally recognized in political theory and democratic constitutions. The right to work has been widely asserted to be a moral right and has become a legal right only in the twentieth century. The right to existence of any people has been alleged to be a moral right most recently and has yet to become established in international or national law. One goal of this chapter will be to understand the nature of these quite different kinds of human rights, both as alleged moral rights and as rights in international law.

The Development of Human Rights

Each of these human rights has occasioned vigorous debates. Considered in their legal guise, these rights raise questions concerning whether they can be effectively protected by international courts and political action and, if so, whether this protection would be desirable. Debates concerning declarations of these rights as fundamental moral rights focus on both whether one should take them to be mere ideals or aspirations rather than rights in any strict sense and, however they are interpreted, whether there are reasons to justify their assertion. Hence, a second goal of this chapter will be to understand the arguments advanced in these debates.

Although the term "human rights" did not gain currency until after the Second World War, the idea it expresses is an ancient one, for what we call human rights today are the descendants of the traditional natural rights of man. These are the fundamental moral rights each and every individual possesses simply as a human being. They are natural both because they are grounded on human nature and because their existence is independent of any artificial social institutions, such as the positive law created by human legislation and enforced in the courts. At the same time, these fundamental moral rights were originally thought to be analogous to legal rights in the sense that they are conferred upon the right-holder by law – not the law posited in any society but the natural law conceived of either as the commands of God or the moral rules self-evident to the natural light of reason. These natural rights, especially the inalienable rights to life, liberty, and property, are central to the political theory used to justify the American and French Revolutions. Because the primary purpose of the state is to protect the natural rights of the individual, any government that violates these rights may legitimately be resisted and replaced by one that will respect these fundamental moral rights of its citizens.

Thus natural rights were traditionally thought to be independent of human legislation and a moral standard to which one could appeal in the criticism or reform of any legal system. Nevertheless, the history of natural rights in theory and practice reveals a continuous interaction between moral philosophy and the law. The concept of a natural right was first defined by William of Ockham, the fourteenth-century philosopher who united the Stoics' conception of a natural law of the divine reason immanent in nature with the conception of a legal right found in Roman jurisprudence. Hugo Grotius, the seventeenth-century founder of the modern philosophical theory of natural rights, also contributed mightily to the development of the modern international law governing the relations between nation states. John Locke, the seventeenth-century moral and political philosopher who was highly influential in the framing of the constitutions adopted in America and France after their respective revolutions, was himself deeply influenced by the development of English constitutional law from the Magna Carta to the Bill of Rights of 1689. William Blackstone, the great eighteenth-century commentator upon the common law, even believed that the traditional rights of Englishmen coincided almost perfectly with the natural rights of all mankind. It is no wonder, then, that the recent development of human rights reflects both philosophical theory and legal practice.

During the nineteenth century, natural rights theories were increasingly ignored or even rejected. Probably this was due in large part to the influence of Jeremy Bentham, an exponent of classical utilitarianism, which maintained that the moral standard of individual actions and social institutions is whether they promote or prevent human happiness. Alarmed by the violence of the French Revolution, he argued that declarations of natural rights are groundless, dogmatic assertions leading to anarchy and that the only real rights are legal rights. Later moral philosophers were by and large skeptical of the existence of any personal God to legislate the law of nature and of any self-evident truths to enunciate it. Political philosophers looked to utilitarianism rather than natural rights theory as the basis for social criticism and legal reform. Most jurists adopted legal positivism, the view that whatever rules are posited or willed by legislative or judicial action are valid law. According to legal positivism, law and morals, including legal and moral rights, are logically distinct and radically separate. Lawyers became almost completely absorbed in the empirical facts of legislation and adjudication and uninterested in the moral standards they thought irrelevant to their legal practice.

In the twentieth century, however, there was a marked revival of interest in the natural rights of man. This revival reflected two world wars that not only caused the death of vast numbers of individuals and the destruction of immense amounts of property but also exposed the world to the dreadful experience of totalitarian regimes, especially in Nazi Germany, that grossly violated the basic rights of so many human beings. These fundamental moral "rights of man" were renamed "human rights" to avoid any insinuation that only males are qualified to possess them and to eliminate the dubious presuppositions of traditional theories of natural rights.

Hence, the development of human rights as such began in 1945 when the *United Nations Charter* reaffirmed faith in fundamental human rights and announced that one of its primary purposes was "to achieve international co-operation . . . promoting and encouraging respect for human rights and for fundamental freedoms for all without distinction as to race, sex, language, or religion."[1] It will be useful to adopt the usual genealogy in which the first generation of human rights are civil and political rights; the second generation are the economic, social, and cultural rights; and the third generation are the human rights of solidarity. As one would expect from the biological metaphor, these successive generations overlap somewhat in their temporal development.

First Generation Rights

The first generation of human rights consists of civil and political rights. Civil rights are rights possessed by every citizen, or in a wider and more relevant sense, by every inhabitant of some state or society. These are basic rights, such as the right to own property or to a fair trial, belonging to every individual person. Political rights, such as the right to vote or to stand for public office, are those that enable the individual to participate either directly or indirectly in the establishment or administration of the government. These categories are not mutually exclusive; for example, the right to free speech is a civil right that also enables the citizen to take part in political campaigns and to criticize public officials or policies.

Historical origins

These civil and political rights are known as the first generation of human rights because they are, for the most part, of ancient lineage. Their philosophical foundations were laid in the seventeenth and eighteenth centuries. John Locke argued that the law of nature confers on each human being the inalienable moral rights to life, liberty, and property. Although all persons would possess these rights in a state of nature, a condition in which they live without any legally organized society, their natural rights would be frequently violated. Hence, individuals enter into a social contract by which they agree to limit their natural

liberty by forming a commonwealth and subsequently a government in order to secure these fundamental moral rights. However, if the state neglects the common good or violates individual rights, then the citizens have a right to revolt and to form a new state.

This and similar political theories underlie the classic natural rights documents. The American *Declaration of Independence* of 1776 asserts "that all men are created equal; that they are endowed, by their Creator, with certain unalienable rights; that among these are life, liberty, and the pursuit of happiness." The French *Declaration of the Rights of Man and of the Citizen* of 1789 proclaims "The purpose of all civil association is the preservation of the natural and imprescriptible rights of man. These rights are liberty, property and resistance to oppression."

The process of establishing these fundamental moral rights of man in the constitutional law of the modern nation-states began at least with the Magna Carta of 1215 and the English Bill of Rights of 1689. It continued with the inclusion of bills of rights in the constitutions ratified in France and the United States after their revolutions, an example that was later imitated by many other nations. The inclusion of human rights in international law began even earlier under the influence of Hugo Grotius and other natural law philosophers. More recently, natural rights have been protected by international treaties and recognized by the international *Cour Permanente de Justice*. Thus the United Nations could very reasonably have taken itself to be *reaffirming* traditional moral and legal principles when it announced in the preamble to its charter that "We the peoples of the United Nations determine . . . to reaffirm faith in fundamental human rights in the dignity and worth of the human person, in the equal rights of men and women and of nations large and small . . . do hereby establish an international organization to be known as the United Nations." Three years later in its *Universal*

Declaration of Human Rights it first defined these rights in general terms.

When one compares the more than twenty-six civil and political rights listed in Articles 3–21 of the *Universal Declaration of Human Rights* with the rights to life, liberty, and the pursuit of happiness in the *Declaration of Independence,* it might appear that the first generation of human rights vastly outnumbers the previously accepted natural rights. This would be to misunderstand the logical structure of traditional theories of fundamental civil and political rights. These theories distinguish between primary rights that are not grounded on some logically prior right and the other rights derived from them. Derived rights may be either more specific forms of some generic right, as the right to freedom of the press is a special case of the right to free speech, or auxiliary rights that serve to protect some primary right, as the right to *habeas corpus* (by which a person can demand to be brought before a judge to obtain release from unlawful confinement) serves to prevent the violation of the individual's right to liberty. The same sort of logical structure is presupposed by the *Universal Declaration.* Article 3 affirms the human rights to life, liberty, and security of person; most of the following rights are assumed to be derived from these primary rights. Also, one must not overlook the manner in which national and international law had previously defined a wide variety of civil and political rights in order to recognize and protect the fundamental natural rights of all persons.

The rights to asylum

Nevertheless, the United Nations has introduced a few new civil and political rights. One new right declared by the United Nations is the human right to asylum. As early as 1625 Grotius had asserted the natural right of a state to grant asylum on the ground that this humane act is not contrary to friendship between states. This right to grant asylum gradually became established in international law. But this right of a state was not a human right, not a right of the individual human being. What was new about the UN declaration was that every human being has the right to asylum. No such right then existed in international law; nor was this right generally accepted in moral theory. Although some moral philosophers held that the state has a humanitarian duty to grant asylum to a refugee fleeing from persecution, they did not assert that this is because the refugee has any correlative right to asylum.

Article 14 of the *Universal Declaration of Human Rights* reads in part, "Everyone has the right to seek and to enjoy in other countries asylum from persecution." Although this is frequently called "the right of asylum," it is really a pair of rights. One is the liberty-right to seek asylum from persecution, for example, by asking to be granted asylum or simply by fleeing to another country; the other is the liberty-right to enjoy asylum from persecution, that is, of remaining within the territory of another country and refusing to return to the pursuing state. Asylum is a sanctuary, a place of refuge and safety. The individual is at liberty to seek and enjoy asylum, but only when he or she is a refugee in the restricted sense of someone subjected to or threatened with persecution. The United Nations seems to have adopted a broad conception of persecution, which includes ill treatment for reasons of race, color, national or ethnic origin, religion, nationality, kinship, membership of a particular social group, or the holding of a particular political opinion – including the struggle against colonialism and apartheid, foreign occupation, alien domination, and all forms of racism. What unifies this list of diverse reasons for asylum is that ill treatment on any of these grounds violates one or more human rights. Although some nations argued that the liberty-rights to seek and enjoy asylum would be of very little value unless the individual also possessed a claim-right to be granted asylum, a right implying a duty of other countries to grant asylum to any genuine refugee, the United Nations has refused to recognize this additional right because it would conflict with the unquestioned right of the sovereign state to refuse to grant asylum at its discretion.

Since 1948, the human rights to seek and to enjoy asylum from persecution have become firmly established in international law. In addition to defining the core liberties of the individual to seek and to enjoy asylum in another country, these rights include several associated elements – legal positions of other parties that tend to confer freedom or control over the exercise of these liberties upon the right-holder. For example, although no state has a legal duty to admit a refugee at its frontier, it does have a legal duty not to forcibly return any refugee, even one who has entered the country illegally, to the pursuing state. This duty not to return an alien is limited by any extradition treaty binding upon the state; however, most such treaties require the extradition of common criminals but not of refugees from persecution. Any state has the traditional liberty-right to grant asylum at its discretion, and the pursuing state has a duty under international law to respect any asylum granted by another state.

The alleged moral rights to seek and enjoy asylum as defined by the United Nations and other international bodies have the same complexity. There are associated moral duties and liberties corresponding to the duties and liberties under international law. In 1967, Article 3 of the *Declaration on Territorial Asylum* added the moral duty, not yet recognized as a legal duty, of any state not to reject a refugee at the frontier. Although this does require the state to admit the refugee to its territory, this may be only for temporary asylum. Thus each state is declared to have a moral duty to admit refugees only as long as this does not require any excessive sacrifice by that state.

Critique

Considered as legal rights, there can be no doubt that the human rights to seek and to enjoy asylum are real. They have been increasingly recognized in the authoritative sources of international law. But international lawyers and political scientists insist that what can and should be doubted is their effectiveness. Because there is no human right to be granted asylum in any other country, the individual who seeks asylum has no assurance of finding and enjoying it. Moreover, the legal rights to asylum have clearly failed to provide adequate refuge for the vast numbers of human beings fleeing from persecution. This is illustrated dramatically by the case of Rwanda, where about 500,000 Tutsi fled to avoid annihilation by the Hutu and then, after the Tutsi regained power, over 2 million Hutu fled to escape retaliation. The refugee problem became most obvious and urgent in the United States recently with the flood of Cuban refugees seeking to escape persecution. Nevertheless, inadequacy is not the same as complete ineffectiveness. Most states have fulfilled their duty not to forcibly return refugees to the state where they face persecution and have refused to extradite individuals who may be political offenders but not common criminals. What is needed is probably not so much a stronger human right to asylum in international law as a more effective international action to reduce persecution.

Human rights organizations report that the rights to seek and to enjoy asylum, when considered as moral rights, also have a genuine but very limited effectiveness. Although states have no legal duty to admit refugees, most of them try to fulfill their moral duty not to reject at the frontier anyone fleeing from persecution, even if only to offer temporary asylum. Also the duty of other states merely "to consider . . . appropriate measures to lighten the burden" on any state flooded with refugees has been more effective than one might have predicted. On a variety of occasions, several states have combined under the auspices of the United Nations to provide relief to large numbers of refugees and to enable them either to return to their original countries safely or to be admitted to some other country for protection.

Are the human rights to seek and enjoy asylum as declared and defined in various documents of the United Nations real moral rights? That is, are those pronouncements that affirm them rationally justified or merely dogmatic assertions? This depends not upon whether they are asserted or even widely accepted as such but on whether they have adequate moral grounds. Unfortunately, no UN document contains moral reasoning to justify its assertions that there are rights to seek and to enjoy asylum, and moral philosophers have neglected to inquire into the grounds of these rights. My guess is that they should be regarded as auxiliary rights, rights grounded upon their necessity for the protection of other prior human rights. This is suggested by the facts that they are rights to asylum from persecution and that persecution consists in the violation of certain human rights. To be sure, the rights to seek and enjoy asylum do not protect the individual from having his or her human rights violated, but to the degree that they are effective they do lessen the danger of exercising or insisting upon these other human rights by providing for some escape from retaliation, should it occur.

Second Generation Rights

In addition to civil and political rights, the UN *Declaration* of 1948 includes a number of economic, social, and cultural rights. These have come to be known as second generation rights because no rights of this kind were affirmed in either the American *Declaration of Independence* of 1776 or the French *Declaration of the Rights of Man and the Citizen* of 1789. To be sure, Thomas Paine, an eighteenth-century radical advocate of natural rights, did include social provisions regarding education, welfare, and work in *The Rights of Man,* published in 1792; and then the French *Declaration* of 1793 did affirm the right to education. But these rights did not fit easily into the traditional natural rights theories and were not very widely recognized as fundamental moral or constitutional rights until this century. Although the right to education was introduced into many legal systems long ago, this was done by simple legislation rather than constitutional amendment, and the same is true of the various welfare rights more recently enacted. Only in 1936 did the USSR Constitution give fundamental status to the rights to work, to rest and leisure, to maintenance in old age and in case of sickness or disability, and to education.

How should one define these second generation human rights? The usual label "economic, social, and cultural rights" is not very illuminating, for it tells us neither what distinguishes these rights from the more traditional civil and political rights nor what these kinds of economic, social, and cultural rights have in common. We can learn something of what distinguishes these rights from more traditional rights by consulting the early history of human rights.

When it adopted its *Universal Declaration of Human Rights,* the United Nations understood that these declared rights could not be secured in practice until they were spelled out in terms that could be embodied in international law and in national constitutions. But as it drafted a more detailed covenant, it came to recognize that economic, social, and cultural rights must be institutionalized very differently from more traditional civil and political rights. For one thing, although rights such as the rights to life or liberty or due process could be enforced in the courts, this enforcement would require the construction of schools and hospitals, the improvement of irrigation and agriculture, the industrialization of production, and the creation of an elaborate system of welfare agencies to ensure the rights to education, to an adequate standard of living, and to social security. For another thing, and as a consequence, although the civil and political rights could be introduced almost immediately into every legal system, the economic, social, and cultural rights could be achieved only gradually and over a considerable period of time in the less affluent nations. Because of these differences, first and second generation human rights were articulated in two separate UN covenants.

What, then, do the various rights included in the *International Covenant on Economic, Social and Cultural Rights* have in common? They all presuppose the recognition that the welfare of the individual human being depends upon certain social conditions, such as an opportunity to earn one's living by productive labor, the availability of physicians with access to hospitals, and public or private agencies to provide subsistence in the event of unemployment or disability. These rights also presuppose the conviction that because these conditions cannot be effectively achieved by individual effort, one's society has a moral obligation, and ought to have a legal duty, to provide them. Hence, second generation human rights might best be thought of as social welfare rights.

The right to work

A good example of a social welfare right is the human right to work. It is not at all clear whether Article 23 of the *Universal Declaration of Human Rights* affirms a single but complex right to work or a number of distinct rights concerning work. Later human rights documents, beginning in 1961 with the *European Social Charter,* distinguish between the right to work itself and the right to just or fair working conditions. Probably the most authoritative definition is contained in Article 6 of the UN *International Covenant on Economic, Social, and Cultural Rights* of 1966: "The

States Parties to the present Covenant recognize the right to work, which includes the right of everyone to the opportunity to gain his living by work which he freely chooses or accepts, and will take appropriate steps to safeguard this right." Thus the core of this human right is the claim of every individual human being against his or her state to be provided with the opportunity to gain a living by work and to freely choose between working positions. This right implies the correlative duty of one's government to take the appropriate steps to provide this opportunity. The underlying assumption is clearly that the welfare of the individual human being requires this opportunity and that only the state has the ability to fulfill this fundamental human need.

Because each of the key concepts in this definition of the right to work is vague, some explanation is required. Work is a purposive, presumably useful, activity involving effort or exertion. This distinguishes the right to work from other rights such as the right to rest and leisure or the right to take part in the cultural life of one's society. Finally, the conditions should allow the individual a reasonable choice between working positions in society. This does not mean that the individual should be able to work when and where and how he or she most desires, but at the very least it does exclude forced labor, except perhaps as punishment of a convicted criminal.

Legal doubts

Human rights frequently exist both as fundamental moral rights and as rights in force under international law. However, jurists have questioned the reality of social welfare rights considered as legal rights. Are economic, social, or cultural rights genuine legal rights today? If not, could they become so as the international law of human rights continues to develop?

One challenge to the reality of social welfare rights under international law arises from what David Trubek, a jurist who has published extensively on international law, has called the principle of progressive realization. Article 2 of the *International Covenant on Economic, Social, and Cultural Rights* reads in part: "Each State Party to the present Covenant undertakes to take steps . . . with a view to achieving progressively the full realization of the rights recognized in the present Covenant by all appropriate means." For example, the steps to be taken to achieve the full realization of the right to work include the creation of vocational guidance and training programs as well as of policies to achieve full and productive employment. But steps like these would not ensure the enjoyment of the right to work for each and every individual human being in a society. A genuine right, such as the creditor's right to be paid, imposes a present duty upon some second party, in this case the debtor. The debtor's duty is not merely to take steps to earn the money to repay the loan or to do his best to repay the loan in the future; it is to pay in full on the due date. And if payment is not forthcoming, the right-holder can take legal action to claim performance of the duty correlative to her right. Hence, some jurists argue that the principle of progressive realization defines a social ideal but does not recognize any legal right.

Other jurists reply that the *Covenant* does more than define an ideal to be achieved in the indefinite future; it imposes definite obligations upon the states parties today. Those states that have ratified this international treaty have bound themselves to legislate specific economic, social, and cultural programs to satisfy certain fundamental human needs. Thus each human being does have a right that demands of his or her government that it actually adopt the appropriate policies and effectively administer the agencies necessary to ensure the enjoyment of each social welfare right.

Even granted that the *Covenant* does impose programmatic obligations – such as the obligations to provide institutions for vocational training and to take steps to

achieve full employment – these would fall short of ensuring for every individual his or her right to work. Some job-seekers will still lack the opportunity to gain their living by work they have chosen or accepted freely. There is and always must remain a gap between any obligation to undertake programs to achieve social goals and any corresponding duty to each and every individual that would enable him or her to enjoy a human right. Thus what international law calls economic, social, and cultural rights are really social ideas rather than individual rights.

Another challenge to the reality of social welfare rights as legal rights is that they permit such extensive derogations and limitations that they do not impose any binding obligation upon the states parties that have ratified treaties such as the *International Covenant*. Any real right implies one or more correlative obligations, and to be bound by an obligation is to have one's freedom of action constrained in some manner. But any state can always evade any burdensome obligation by taking advantage of one of the provisions in the human rights treaties. Under the *Covenant* each state undertakes only to take steps "to the maximum of its available resources" (Article 2.1), and developing countries "may determine to what extent they would guarantee the economic rights recognized in the present Covenant to non-nationals" (Article 2.3). Moreover, Article 4 permits each state to abridge the recognized rights by "such limitations as are determined by law . . . and solely for the purpose of promoting the general welfare in a democratic society." Because each state can interpret the meaning and force of these derogations for itself, it can always decide that it lacks the resources to realize these social welfare rights or that the attempt to guarantee them to needy individuals would conflict with policies required to maximize the general welfare.

However Louis Henkin, a specialist on international law and a recognized authority on human rights, believes that these derogations and limitations do not render the undertakings of the states parties illusory, provided that international bodies and other states scrutinize the interpretation and application of the relevant provisions in international human rights treaties. The question remains, of course, as to how effectively international supervision would enforce social welfare rights.

Accordingly, a third challenge to the reality of social welfare rights is that they are not enforceable. Any real legal right must be enforceable in the courts. If a debtor fails or refuses to repay a loan, for example, the creditor has the power to take legal action to force the debtor to pay the amount owed or to pay compensation for any damages suffered as a consequence of the violation of his or her right. Without some such power to sue, the alleged right would be a merely paper right rather than a real right because the document in which it is said to exist makes no difference in the way the legal system really functions.

The *International Covenant on Economic, Social, and Cultural Rights* provides for what Trubek has aptly called a system of generic implementation. Articles 16 and 21–3 require the states parties to submit reports on both the measures they have adopted and the progress they have made in achieving the recognized rights. These reports shall be transmitted by the secretary-general of the United Nations to the Economic and Social Council. This council may submit recommendations of a general nature (not mentioning any particular state) to the General Assembly and to the specialized agencies of the United Nations and may assist such bodies in deciding on the advisability of international measures likely to contribute to the progressive implementation of the social welfare rights. This method is clearly designed to assist the states parties and not to embarrass or censure any that fail to ensure the recognized rights. It is not, and is not intended to be, a system of legal enforcement. Many jurists conclude that there are no real social welfare rights under existing international law. Others point to the fact that many such rights are already enforced in the domestic law of several welfare states to show that social welfare rights could, given the necessary modifications in the system for their implementation, become real rights under international law also.

What should a jurist or philosopher of law conclude from these debates? Probably that there are no economic, social, or cultural human rights under existing international law. It may well be that no international social welfare rights are real legal rights because none of them imposes any definite obligation upon any state party and none can be enforced through the courts of human rights. Even if a few such rights are currently enforceable, they are not human rights in the strict sense because individual human beings lack access to these courts. However, it seems that at least some social welfare rights could become real rights if the human rights documents were amended in a way that would impose more definite duties upon the states and would give the individual right holders the power to go to court to enforce their rights.

Moral arguments

Rights are negative   Jurists and international lawyers tend to be concerned with institutional issues: whether social welfare rights could be enforced in the courts and what role individual right-holders might have in any judicial processes. Moral philosophers, on the other hand, focus more on conceptual and moral issues: what the expression "a human right" does or should mean and what moral implications would follow from the recognition of any alleged right.

Thus some moral philosophers argue that so-called social welfare rights cannot be human rights in the strict sense because human rights are essentially negative. They distinguish between negative rights – such as one's right not to be killed, which imposes a duty upon others not to kill one and positive rights – such as the creditor's right to be repaid, which imposes upon the debtor the correlative duty to pay the amount borrowed by the due date. Moral philosophers maintain that human rights are essentially negative rights, rights correlative to the duties of others, primarily governments, *not* to mistreat individuals in fundamentally immoral ways. Hence, genuine human rights could not impose any positive social obligations to promote individual welfare. Robert Nozick, a libertarian philosopher who holds that government welfare programs violate the basic rights of those taxed to support them, expresses this conception of a right succinctly when he addresses the question of whether every right necessarily confers upon its holder a right to enforce that right: "Yet rights of enforcement are themselves merely rights; that is, permissions to do something and obligations on others not to interfere."[2]

Why should one accept this purely negative conception of rights? Nozick himself grounds his theory of rights upon a Kantian moral theory. Along with many others, he believes that the import of moral rights cannot be explained by a utilitarian theory. If rights were justified by their utility, their contribution to human welfare, then it would be permissible or even required to violate someone's rights whenever it would be useful to do so. This implies that one might, for example, have an obligation to punish an innocent person in order to prevent a riot in which large numbers of persons might be seriously harmed. Such an act would clearly be morally wrong because it would be using an innocent person merely as a means to benefit others. To avoid this immoral conclusion, Nozick contrasts rights with goals. Rights are not goods or benefits to be pursued by human action; they are side constraints that limit what one may do to right-holders in promoting one's own welfare or even the general welfare. Rights must be purely negative because their moral function is to constrain or limit permissible kinds of action; they tell one only what one must not

do in the pursuit of one's goals. The import of moral rights can be explained best with recourse to Kantian theory, in which the most basic moral principle is the respect for persons. What commands our respect in each individual person is his or her practical rationality, the ability to choose and act on moral reasons. Therefore, one ought always to treat others as ends-in-themselves, as individuals capable of choosing for themselves how to live their own lives. This is why moral rights are essentially both freedoms to act as one chooses and obligations on the part of others not to interfere with one's liberty of action.

There are at least two ways in which moral philosophers have tried to avoid this Nozickian challenge to social welfare rights. One is to rebut his rejection of all utilitarian theories of moral rights. David Lyons, a contemporary moral philosopher and interpreter of utilitarianism, has advanced an interpretation of John Stuart Mill that would enable us to integrate human rights into his utilitarian moral philosophy. Another way to avoid the Nozickian challenge is to explain how a moral right could impose some positive obligation even according to Kantian theory. Immanuel Kant, an eighteenth-century German philosopher, argued that one has a moral duty to rescue someone in dire need of help, and this might well imply that the individual in distress has the right to be rescued. Kant could argue that although a right is a purely negative side constraint, a drowning person's right to life implies an obligation that one who could save her life *not* refrain from doing so.

Nozick is not the only one to deny the existence of positive human rights. There is another sort of reasoning advanced to defend a purely negative conception of human rights. It is not based upon any Kantian theory of the grounds of moral rights or any general conception of the nature of rights; it is based upon our paradigms of human rights, those traditional natural rights that were the first generation of civil and political rights. An examination of the great natural rights documents, such as the American *Declaration of Independence* and the French *Declaration of the Rights of Man and of the Citizen,* shows clearly that their essential purpose is to protect individuals from state action. Hence, the function of human rights is purely negative; it is to limit state interference with individual liberty.

This reasoning is not, however, conclusive. Some moral philosophers accept this characterization of the traditional natural rights documents but suggest that they reflect the political issues of their times rather than the nature of human rights. When the main threat to individual welfare was governmental oppression, it was only natural that moral and political philosophers would assert negative rights. But when new social and economic institutions result in vast unemployment, the poverty of many dependent children, and great financial insecurity of elderly individuals, then it is time to recognize a second generation of social welfare rights. Others reject the view that our paradigms of natural rights are purely negative. The rights to life and liberty impose upon the state not merely the negative duties to refrain from the arbitrary killing or imprisonment of individuals but also the positive duties to provide police protection so that other individuals will not kill or kidnap one. Similarly, the right to due process requires the state to create and maintain an expensive system of courts before which its citizens can obtain fair trials in criminal and civil cases.

Scarce resources Even granted that moral rights often imply positive duties, there remains the problem of scarce resources. Most moral philosophers accept the Kantian principle that there can be no moral obligation to do the impossible. Maurice Cranston asserts the corollary: No right can imply a duty to do the impossible. Hence, the primary test for the reality of any moral right is practicability. He argues that the alleged social welfare rights fail this test.

If social welfare rights were a second generation of human rights, they would be universal rights – rights of *all* human beings to certain benefits, such as work or social security, essential for their welfare. But many societies lack the resources to fulfill the duties that would be implied by such rights. Periodic famines make it impossible for some African countries to protect all their citizens at all times from malnutrition, even from starvation. Many countries lack the physicians, hospitals, and medicines that would be required to provide everyone with necessary medical care in the event of sickness. Even affluent societies are finding themselves unable to contain the costs of medical care sufficiently to ensure high quality care to all their citizens. And we in the United States are discovering how frightfully expensive it is to provide the disabled and the handicapped with an opportunity to work. Cranston and others conclude that social welfare rights cannot be real human rights because many societies lack the resources to make them practicable.

There are at least three ways to rebut this argument against second generation human rights. One is to limit the content of social welfare rights in a way that reduces the implied duties sufficiently to render them practicable. The *International Covenant on Economic, Social, and Cultural Rights* does this when it requires only that "Each State Party to the present Covenant undertakes to take steps . . . to the maximum of its available resources." Similarly, D. D. Raphael, a British moral and political philosopher, argues that it is always possible for a society to do something to control unemployment or to provide security against hunger. After all, we do not conclude that there is no human right to life simply because no amount of police protection will prevent all homicides. Thus any social welfare right implies the correlative duty of one's state to do as much as it can to fulfill the demands of the right.

Paradoxically, a second way to respond to the problem of scarce resources is to multiply the number of correlative duties implied by any human right. Henry Shue, a moral philosopher who has argued that American foreign policy ought to take human rights more seriously, suggests that the basic right to subsistence implies three types of correlative duties – duties to avoid depriving anyone of subsistence, duties to protect everyone from such deprivation, and duties to aid the deprived. He points out that the first sort of duty is purely negative and that the second type is no more demanding than the duties implied by such first generation human rights as the rights to life or liberty. He then argues that by fulfilling these two types of duties, any society can greatly reduce the amount of resources needed to aid those who find themselves deprived of the means of subsistence. Presumably an analogous argument could be advanced to defend other social welfare rights.

Finally, H. J. McCloskey, an Australian philosopher who has articulated one of the more important theories of rights, rejects the correlativity of rights and duties. He holds that a right is an entitlement to do, have, enjoy, or have done. Although any right will imply one or more claims against others, it is a mistake to identify a right to something with a claim against some duty-bearer. According to McCloskey's theory, a social welfare right is an entitlement to the efforts of others to aid and promote one's seeking after or enjoying some good. But the duties implied by such a right will depend upon the circumstances and never demand more than is practicable.

The violation of fundamental rights   A third argument against the existence of social welfare rights is that they would require the state to violate fundamental moral rights of its citizens. As all the international documents defining these rights show, each economic, social, or cultural right imposes upon the state the appropriate programmatic obligations. Any governmental program, such as one to provide unemployment benefits or medical care to those in poverty, would have to be funded through taxation of the incomes or real estate of the more fortunate members of society. Robert Nozick argues that such taxation would violate their human right to property. The central core of a property right is the right to determine what shall be done with one's property. But the state violates this right when it takes a portion of one's property and thereby deprives one of the choice of whether to give this amount to charity or to spend it oneself. The taxation of one's income also violates the individual's human right to liberty. To take away part of one's income is, in effect, to force one to work part of the time for the state. This constitutes forced labor and amounts to a partial ownership in one's person. In this respect it violates the human right to liberty much as the institution of slavery does.

One criticism of this argument, a criticism advanced by Tony Honore, a contemporary British jurist, is that human rights are more limited than Nozick recognizes. Nozick does admit that one's right to property is limited by the Lockean rights of others. Regarding the core right to decide what shall be done with one's property, he says, "My property rights in my knife allow me to leave it where I will, but not in your chest."[3] Thus the scope of the human right to property is limited by the human right to life. But why assume that the only limits to one's property rights are the three natural rights asserted by Locke – the rights to life, liberty, and property? If there is a second generation of human rights, these will also limit the individual's human rights to property and liberty. And if these Lockean rights are thus limited, then taxation need not infringe them. To assume that the fundamental rights of the individual are not limited by social welfare rights is to beg the question.

Another criticism of Nozick's reasoning is that he mistakenly presupposes that the rights to property and liberty are absolute, that they are never overridden by other rights. In a footnote, Nozick writes, "The question of whether these side constraints are absolute . . . is one I hope largely to avoid."[4] However, he cannot evade this issue. Samuel Scheffler, a contemporary moral philosopher, proposes a wider range of human rights, including social welfare rights. He admits that these may conflict under some circumstances, but explains that this does not show that any of them are unreal. This is because our fundamental moral rights are prima facie rather than absolute. A *prima facie* right is a right that imposes a duty upon some second party *unless* it is outweighed by some more important moral factor; an absolute right is one that always imposes a correlative duty whatever the circumstances. Thus taxation to fund social welfare programs will be morally justified when, but perhaps only when, the social welfare rights of the deprived override the property rights of the more fortunate members of society.

The debate about whether second generation human rights are real moral rights continues. Although it would be premature to predict its outcome, perhaps one can draw some tentative conclusions. The repeated attempts to introduce such rights into international law have been only partially successful because it has proven difficult to define with precision the obligations they are supposed to impose, and no effective procedures for enforcing them have been firmly established. There are very plausible arguments against the moral credentials of social welfare rights, but by far the most serious of these is posed by the problem of scarce resources. Still, there are equally plausible replies to each of these moral arguments. Thus both the legal and moral status of second generation human rights remain to be decided.

Third Generation Rights

Today a third generation of human rights is emerging in international law and moral theory. Although there is almost no doubt about the birth of several new rights, there is very considerable uncertainty about what, if anything, they have in common and how, if at all, they differ from human rights of the first and second generations.

These new human rights are most often labeled rights of solidarity. Solidarity is the mutual support or cohesiveness within a group, especially among individuals with strong common interests, sympathies, or aspirations. Solidarity enters into the definition of this third generation of human rights in two ways. First, they are rights of social groups rather than of individual human beings. They include the rights of all humanity to peace and to a healthy environment and the rights of any people to self-determination and to its own culture. Second, they hold against all humanity. Because they demand worldwide action, the duties they impose fall primarily upon international institutions – including the United Nations, regional organizations such as the Council of Europe and the Organization of American States, and a variety of more specialized associations of nation states, such as the Organization for Economic Cooperation and Development and the North Atlantic Treaty Organization.

The difference between third generation human rights and those of the first two generations is one of degree. Civil and political rights, especially the economic, social, and cultural rights, impose duties upon states and international organizations as well as upon individual persons; conversely, third generation rights impose duties upon individuals as well as upon social groups. What is new, or at least relatively new, is the assertion of human rights of groups with correlative obligations falling collectively upon all humanity. What is distinctive about each generation of human rights is probably the emphasis it places upon the aspirations of the French Revolution – Liberty, Equality, Fraternity. The civil and political human rights serve primarily to protect the liberty of the individual against the oppression of the nation state. The social welfare rights function mainly to reduce social inequalities and to assist the most deprived members of a society to live a more nearly normal human life. The solidarity rights are needed to protect vulnerable groups of people and to advance the unity and well-being of humanity in general.

It will be useful to have an example of this third generation of human rights in mind in order to enable us to discover what they have in common and to illustrate their problematic aspects. The rights of peoples are the best paradigms both because they are more firmly established in international law and because they are discussed more fully in the legal and philosophical literature.

The right to existence

Article 1 of the *Universal Declaration of the Rights of Peoples* asserts, "Every people has the right to existence." This is also the first peoples' right explicitly affirmed in the *African Charter on Human and Peoples' Rights*.[5] Although neither of these is a document issued by the United Nations, they can be taken to reaffirm its previous conventions on genocide. This may be why they do not spell out the specific content of this peoples' right.

In the *Convention on the Prevention and Punishment of the Crime of Genocide, 1948*, the General Assembly defined genocide in some detail:

> In the present Convention, genocide means any of the following acts committed with intent to destroy, in whole or in part, a national, ethnical, racial or religious group, as such: (a) Killing members of the group; (b) Causing serious bodily or mental harm to members of the group; (c) Deliberately inflicting on the group conditions of life calculated to bring about its physical destruction in whole or in part; (d) Imposing measures intended to prevent births within the group; (e) Forcibly transferring children of the group to another group.

When this *Convention* was adopted, the United Nations was no doubt motivated primarily by the Holocaust, the wholesale killing of Jews by the Nazi regime; but today we might think first of the recent ethnic cleansings in what used to be Yugoslavia.

Presumably, then, the peoples' right to existence concerns its physical existence rather than its cultural identity; it is the right that others not act with intent to annihilate the group. Although genocide is most frequently committed by acts of killing a number of individual human beings, what makes it a violation of the peoples' right to existence is that these individual murders are done with intent to destroy the group as such. And the kinds of groups protected by this right are or include national, ethnical, racial, or religious groups.

The peoples' right to existence is a solidarity right not only because it is the right of a people rather than an individual person, but also because it holds primarily upon the international community. Because genocide is typically committed by military personnel on the command of, or at least with the acquiescence of, the political authorities, it is unrealistic to rely upon the individual nation-states to prevent or punish it. Hence, the *Convention on Genocide* declares that "to liberate mankind from such an odious scourge, international co-operation is required." To this end, it recognizes the jurisdiction of international penal tribunals to adjudicate cases involving persons charged with genocide. The *Convention* asserts that genocide is a crime even when committed by constitutionally responsible rulers or public officials, and it imposes an obligation upon each state party to extradite such persons and not to refuse to do so – on the grounds that genocide is a political crime analogous to resistance to colonial rule. Finally, it obliges the competent organs of the United Nations to take such actions as they consider appropriate for the prevention and suppression of acts of genocide.

Legal critique

Although there is often debate about the legal status of this or that particular third-generation human right, most jurists do not doubt that solidarity rights can be real human rights, for both advocates and opponents agree that they are emerging rights in international law. Disagreements between jurists concern primarily questions of whether to encourage or discourage this development and of how such rights could be institutionalized.

First, many jurists maintain that it is unnecessary to add a third category of solidarity rights to the first and second generations of human rights. To be sure, individual persons cannot enjoy their human rights in isolation from the groups of which they are members. But there is obviously a social dimension to most civil and political rights and to all economic, social, and cultural rights. These rights hold against one's state and impose obligations upon the United Nations and other international organizations. The civil right to life, for example, requires that one's state take measure to protect one's life, and the economic right to an adequate standard of living imposes a duty upon the United Nations and various international bodies to assist the developing countries to progress economically. Rather than introduce a third generation of human rights, it would be better to develop more fully the solidarity aspects implicit in the human rights of individuals.

Thus Article 22 of the *Universal Declaration of Human Rights* asserts, "Everyone, as a member of society, has the right to social security." And Article 27 of the *International Covenant on Civil and Political Rights* reads: "In those States in which ethnic, religious or linguistic minorities exist, persons belonging to such minorities shall not be denied the right, in community with other members of their group, to enjoy their own culture, to profess and practice their own religion, or to use their own language." There is no need to introduce rights of peoples as such because international law already recognizes that many of the human rights of individuals belong to them as members of social groups.

Other jurists reply that this individualistic approach to group rights does not go far enough. To be sure, it is individual persons who speak their own language to one another or participate in the culture of their community. But some rights essential to human flourishing cannot be exercised by individual persons, even as members of some social group. The right to self determination can be exercised only by a people collectively. Although this right can be, and has been, exercised by means of a plebiscite, in which each member of the group votes, it is the aggregate outcome that determines the people's choice of its political status. No individual member of the minority has the right to a form of government different from that chosen by the majority. Similarly, the peoples' right to not be reduced physical existence canto the individual rights to life of the members of the group. Why is genocide such a monstrous crime against humanity? It is not merely that so many individuals are destroyed; many lives are lost in any major war. The essence of genocide lies in the intention to destroy a racial, religious, or national group as a whole.

A second legal issue concerns this proliferation as such. Many jurists believe that it is undesirable to add an entire third generation of human rights to those previously established in international law. Any such inflation will devalue the currency of human rights. The more human rights there are the less weight each will carry, for the resources of the international community are very limited. It is especially unfortunate to introduce a new category of less urgent rights while such fundamental human rights as the rights to life, liberty, social security, and political participation are so widely violated. It would be better to concentrate on the more effective realization of the most necessary human rights rather than to burden our legal system with an additional set of rights that do not yet command widespread respect among the nation-states, which must cooperate to secure any human right in international law.

Other jurists concede that it is a mistake to attempt to introduce impractical aspirations into human rights law; to do so would merely create unrealistic expectations and, when these expectations fail, lead to a general disillusionment with human rights. Nevertheless, they argue that it is not always possible to enforce the human rights of individuals without the legal recognition of peoples' rights. As long as the Jews remain a despised people in some states, it will not be possible to protect the right to life of Jewish individuals without international action to outlaw the genocide of the Jewish people. And the human right to enjoy one's own culture, in community with others, of individual American Indians or Australian Aborigines becomes empty unless the human right of indigenous peoples to preserve and develop their shared cultures is respected. Therefore, the introduction of a very few solidarity rights is desirable and can be accomplished without any devaluation of the entire currency of human rights.

A third objection of some international lawyers to the introduction of solidarity rights is the fear that they pose a threat to the human rights of individuals. Group rights will often conflict with individual rights, so that the protection of peoples' rights will sometimes require the violation of fundamental human rights of persons. The right of a people to preserve its own culture may well conflict with the right of parents to choose how their child shall be educated; for example, the right of the Amish people to preserve their religious tradition might conflict with the right of Amish parents to decide that their children would be better prepared for life in the United States by public schools than by schools in which the values of the Amish religious community are taught. Again, the right of an Indian tribe to preserve its own

culture implies a claim over its traditional lands, for the two are inseparably connected; but this conflicts with the human right to property of those members of the Indian tribe that might purchase portions of that land and subsequently wish to sell it to someone other than another member of the tribe.

Other jurists reply that there will inevitably be conflicts between rights within any system of specific rights. Conflicts between civil rights or between civil rights and social welfare rights have been resolved by the gradual redefinition of each specific right to avoid future conflicts and, where this is impossible, by balancing one right against another in each particular case. Because no legal right is immutable or absolute, the conflict between group rights and individual rights is no more serious than the many conflicts between the human rights of individual persons. Moreover, the debate about individual rights versus collective rights becomes much less crucial once it is accepted that certain individual rights cannot be exercised in isolation from the community.

Moral Criticisms

In addition to the debates among jurists as to whether solidarity rights can and should become real human rights under international law, there are philosophical criticisms of the recent assertions of these rights considered as a new category of moral rights. For one thing, these group rights seem to be incompatible with the nature of human rights. Because human rights are rights one possesses merely as a human being – not by virtue of some special status, such as one's citizenship or moral virtue – they must be possessed equally by all human beings. Article 1 of the *Universal Declaration of Human Rights* asserts, "All human beings are born free and equal in dignity and rights." Then Article 2 asserts as a corollary: "Everyone is entitled to all the rights and freedoms set forth in this Declaration, without distinction of any kind, such as race, colour, sex, language, religion, political or other opinion, national or social origin, property, birth or other status." Thus the fundamental principle that human rights are universal and equal implies that any racial, religious, sexual, or similar discrimination is morally wrong.

This seems to exclude recognizing any basic moral rights of peoples. What defines any people is its culture, consisting in its distinctive language, religion, traditions, and such characteristics. Therefore, to admit special rights for a people would be to give the members of this limited community special privileges denied to other human beings. For example, to establish Spanish as a second language in the public schools in states such as California and Texas in order that Hispanics could preserve their traditional culture would be to discriminate against those Italian, Polish, and Russian immigrants, among others, who are denied equal treatment in this respect. This policy would seem to be discrimination on the basis of language or national origin, thereby a violation of human rights, and not a new sort of protection for human rights. Therefore, some argue that there cannot be a third generation of human rights because they would be inconsistent with the principle of the universality and equality of human rights.

In reply, others argue that solidarity rights need not confer special privileges upon any human being. Although it might be discriminatory to establish the Spanish language in our public schools, while excluding Italian, Polish and Russian, it does not necessarily follow that group rights are discriminatory. Genuine solidarity rights are universal; they are rights of *all* peoples and thereby beneficial for every member of every people. If any people has a right to preserve its language, so does every group; and if a state assists one ethnic community in this endeavor, it ought to give equal assistance to all the other ethnic communities within its territory. Also, far from inevitably perpetuating inequality, solidarity rights are sometimes necessary to

preserve or promote equality. In a pluralistic society, some ethnic minorities may be so small that without special rights they would be swallowed up by the majority culture. Even in a democratic society, the equal universal rights of the members of a minority will often count for nothing against an overwhelming majority of voters indifferent or even antagonistic to the minority's special interests. Full equality for these human beings requires more than that they have human rights as individual members of some minority; the minorities to which they belong must have fundamental moral and legal rights as peoples.

The most fundamental criticism of recent declarations of peoples' rights is that a people is not the kind of being that could possibly possess any moral rights. When someone picks a flower, does she violate its moral right to life? Presumably not. This is not because the flower is not killed by her action; plants are simply not the kind of beings that could possess any moral rights at all. Why not? Why is it that normal adult human beings can and do possess moral rights but sticks, stones, and plants cannot? What qualifies some entities to be possible moral right-holders?

I have argued in *Real Rights* that only moral agents can possess moral rights. This is because according to my conception of a right, every right includes liberties and powers, and one exercises a liberty or power by acting in the appropriate manner. For example, one exercises one's liberty of free speech by public speaking or one exercises one's power of disposing of one's property by handing one's book to another while saying, "here, this is yours." Because it would be pointless and misleading to ascribe a liberty or a power to any being incapable of exercising either, moral theory should ascribe rights only to moral agents. Because I believe that groups, including peoples, are incapable of acting collectively, I deny that a people as such could have any moral rights.

Other moral philosophers disagree and try to explain how group action is possible.

Thus Peter French, an important contributor to business ethics, has argued that corporations have an internal organizational decision procedure by virtue of which they can and do act. Even if this is true, it seems irrelevant to third generation human rights. A people is not a corporate body, not an organized group like a nation-state or a private corporation. Vernon Van Dyke, a political scientist especially interested in the status of minorities, offers one of the most clear and accurate definitions of a people:

> Two definitions of a people show up in UNESCO's deliberations. According to one, a people is identified with a distinctive culture: those who share a given culture are a people. I will assume that a culture is distinguished by such characteristics as language, religion, and race, and more broadly by shared attitudes, customs and traditions. To qualify as a people, those sharing a culture should think of themselves as collectively possessing an enduring, separate identity, and they are likely to be predominantly of common descent.[6]

Those who assert solidarity rights typically believe that such a people has a human right to self-determination whether or not they are organized into a nation-state or any other sort of corporate body.

The question then becomes whether only organized groups are capable of acting. Larry May, a moral philosopher who has defended the existence of group rights, argues that this is not so. He holds that the storming of the Bastille cannot be reduced to the individual actions of the members of the Paris mob of 1789. To be sure, this mob action consisted of the actions of the individual members of the group, but it also consisted of the concerted actions of these persons as a group. What enabled them to act collectively or "as one person" was their solidarity: their common reaction to the injustices that had been perpetrated upon the lower classes and their implicit agreement to take action against the perpetrators. Quite possibly this

sort of explanation can be extended to apply to a people. They are capable of genuine group action by virtue of their solidarity, their thinking of themselves as collectively possessing an enduring, separate identity. Still, whether the actions of a mob can be reduced to the actions of its members and whether a people can really possess any solidarity like that of the Paris mob remain controversial questions.

Equally controversial is the question of what does qualify an entity to possess moral rights. One would expect Joel Feinberg, perhaps the most influential contemporary American moral and legal philosopher, to agree with me that only beings capable of action are possible right-holders. This is because Feinberg maintains both that to have a right is to be in a position to claim the performance of the correlative duty and that this claiming should be understood as the process or action of demanding something as one's due. But this seems to imply that tiny babies could not have any right to life or to be cared for by their parents, for they have not yet learned the language of claiming and have no conception of what might be due to them. Feinberg points out, however, that parents or guardians can claim the legal, and presumably the moral, rights of young children. Hence, a right-holder can be either someone capable of claiming or someone on behalf of whom a representative can make claims. Because claiming would be pointless were one not claiming something in one's interest, and because to act on behalf of someone is to act in the interests of that person, Feinberg concludes that it is having interests that qualifies an entity to be a genuine right-holder.

Jeremy Waldron, a philosopher on the law faculty of Columbia University, arrives at the same conclusion by a more direct route. Instead of accepting Feinberg's claim theory of rights, he adopts the interest theory of Joseph Raz, an Oxford jurist and philosopher. Raz defines a right as an interest-based reason sufficiently important to impose one or more duties upon others to promote, or at least not damage, that interest. For example, there is a human right to life because the interest one has in his or her own life is important enough to impose a duty both upon others not to kill one and upon one's state to protect one's life. On this basis, Waldron defends the reality of third generation human rights. An interest is something that is in the interest of someone, some component of that being's good. Now some public goods cannot be properly valued as merely goods for the individual members of the public. For example, when one enjoys the conviviality of a party, one is not merely enjoying oneself but is aware that others are enjoying similar pleasures. One's enjoyment is partly constituted by the enjoyment of others; indeed, one person's enjoyment of conviviality is unintelligible apart from the enjoyments of others. Therefore, conviviality is necessarily an essentially communal good. Examples of communal goods more relevant to a people include the value of a cultured or tolerant society or the value of a general respect for persons. Because values such as these can be interests of a people collectively, a people could have a moral or legal right to these sorts of collective goods.

Those who advocate third generation human rights frequently speak on the side of the angels: They champion morally worthy causes and seek to advance the freedom and welfare of human beings around the world. The question remains, however, whether these worthy aspirations can best be achieved by the appeal to a new generation of solidarity rights. Here the lawyer's doubt that there is any way to identify the person or persons legally empowered to claim or waive a people's right before an international court merges with the philosopher's doubt about whether a people as such is capable of exercising the power of claiming or waiving any right. Perhaps the proliferation of alleged moral rights has gone too far.

Even if peoples do have moral rights that can and should be recognized in interna-

tional law, these probably should not be thought of as a third generation of human rights. A human right is by definition a right one possesses as a human being. Although a people is a cultural community of human beings, it is not itself a human being. At the very least, this distinction between individual and group rights should not be obscured in moral and political discourse.

Fragmentary Conclusions

The debates concerning the development of human rights continue undiminished. Nevertheless, it may be possible to draw a few relatively noncontroversial conclusions. Clearly there has been a proliferation of human rights in the five decades following the formation of the United Nations. This proliferation has taken two very different forms. There have been a number of attempts to introduce new human rights into international law. Where these have been successful, new human rights have actually been created. There have also been numerous assertions by moral reformers and moral philosophers of new human rights. But success in convincing others to agree with such an assertion does nothing to bring a new moral right into existence. This is because genuine moral rights, if they exist, are different from the conventional rights created by the moral code of a society. An alleged moral right is real only if there exist moral reasons sufficient to justify its assertion. Thus there have been both a proliferation of legal human rights and a proliferation of assertions of moral human rights.

Rather different considerations are relevant to these two strands in the proliferation of rights. Any attempt to introduce a new legal right should be evaluated on institutional and pragmatic grounds. Such an introduction will be successful only if the legally authoritative documents can be effectively applied by the relevant states parties and international bodies, especially in some court of human rights. The introduction of a new legal right is wise only if creating an additional human right is a useful method of advancing the cause of human freedom and welfare in some important way. Any assertion of a new moral right should be assessed more in terms of theory than of utility. Is the newly asserted human right a right in the sense defined by the most adequate theory of the nature of rights? And is the alleged possessor of the right a possible moral right-holder? As we have seen, these considerations are very complicated. It is no wonder that there is little agreement about whether these parallel strands in the proliferation of human rights are desirable or undesirable.

Notes

1   The most convenient place to find this and many other human rights texts is Ian Brownlie (ed.), *Basic Documents on Human Rights,* 3rd edn. (Oxford: Clarendon, 1992).
2   Robert Nozick, *Anarchy, State and Utopia* (New York: Basic Books, 1974), 92.
3   Nozick, *Anarchy,* 171.
4   Nozick, *Anarchy,* 30.
5   These and other related documents are reprinted in James Crawford (ed.), *The Rights of Peoples* (Oxford: Clarendon Press, 1988).
6   Vernon Van Dyke, "The Cultural Rights of Peoples," *Universal Human Rights* 2 (1980): 2–3.

Further Reading

Brownlie, Ian, 1992. *Basic Documents on Human Rights*, 3rd edn. Oxford: Clarendon Press. — A convenient source for the most important texts.

Cranston, Maurice. 1967. "Human Rights, Real and Supposed." In *Political Theory and the Rights of Man*, D. D. Raphael (ed.) Bloomington, IN: Indiana University Press. — This essay is a clear and powerful criticism of the alleged economic, social, and cultural human rights.

Crawford, James (ed.) 1992. *The Rights of*

Peoples. Oxford: Clarendon Press. — An excellent collection of papers on the rights of peoples with selected relevant documents.

Feinberg, Joel. 1980. *Rights, Justice, and the Bounds of Liberty*. Princeton: Princeton University Press, esp. 143–58. The best explanation of the view that rights are claims.

French, Peter A. 1979. "The Corporation as a Moral Person." *American Philosophical Quarterly* 16, 133–49. — An influential argument to show that corporate bodies are capable of moral action.

Goodwin-Gill, Guy S. 1983. *The Refugee in International Law*. Oxford: Clarendon Press. — 101–23 give a clear and accurate description of the human right to asylum.

Hartney, Michael. 1991. "Some Confusions Concerning Collective Rights." *Canadian Journal of Law and Jurisprudence* 4, 293–314. — This article provides an illuminating discussion of theories of group rights.

Henkin, Louis. 1981. "International Human Rights as 'Rights.'" In *Human Rights*, J. Roland Pennock and John Chapman (eds.). New York: New York University Press. — Henkin responds to those who argue that human rights are not real human rights under international law.

Honoré, Tony. 1977. "Property, Title and Redistribution." In *Equality and Freedom: Past, Present and Future*, Carl Wellman (ed.). Wiesbaden: Franz Steiner Verlag. — A critique of Nozick's view that welfare rights would be inconsistent with the natural right to property.

Kymlicka, Will. 1989. *Liberalism, Community, and Culture*. Oxford: Clarendon Press. — 135–61 argue for the recognition of group rights of minorities.

Lyons, David. 1977. "Human Rights and the General Welfare." *Philosophy & Public Affairs* 6, 113–29. — Argues against the view that utilitarianism could not explain our fundamental moral rights.

Marks, Stephen P. 1981. "Emerging Human Rights: A New Generation for the 1980s?" *Rutgers Law Review* 33, 435–52. — An informative article on the new third generation human rights.

May, Larry. 1987. *The Morality of Groups*. Notre Dame, IN: University of Notre Dame Press. See especially 31–57. — An explanation of how unorganized groups can and do act collectively.

McCloskey, H. J. 1965. "Rights." *Philosophical*

Quarterly 15, 115–27. — McCloskey explains and defends the view that rights are entitlements rather than claims.

Nozick, Robert. 1974. *Anarchy, State, and Utopia.* New York: Basic Books. — 26–53 reject the conceptual possibility and moral legitimacy of human rights to welfare benefits.

Raphael, D. D. 1967. "Human Rights, Old and New." In *Political Theory and the Rights of Man*, ed. D. D. Raphael. Bloomington, IN: Indiana University Press. — Raphael defends economic, social, and cultural human rights against the attack by Cranston.

Raz, Joseph. 1986. *The Morality of Freedom.* Oxford: Clarendon Press. See esp. 165–92. — A sophisticated explanation of the theory that rights are interest-based reasons sufficient to impose one or more duties.

Scheffler, Samuel. 1976. "Natural Rights, Equality, and the Minimal State." *Canadian Journal of Philosophy* 6, 59–76. — Rebuts Nozick's arguments against moral rights to welfare benefits.

Shue, Henry. 1980. *Basic Rights.* Princeton: Princeton University Press. See esp. 35–64. — Shue argues that any basic right implies three kinds of correlative duties.

Trubek, David M. 1984. "Economic, Social and Cultural Rights in the Third World: Human Rights Law and Human Needs Programs." In *Human Rights in International Law*, Theodore Meron (ed.). Oxford: Clarendon Press. — A clear informative account of second generation human rights.

Tuck, Richard. 1979. *Natural Rights Theories.* Cambridge: Cambridge University Press. — Probably the best account of the historically important theories of natural rights.

Van Dyke, Vernon. 1980. "The Cultural Rights of Peoples." *Universal Human Rights* 2, 1–21. — A strong defense of the human rights of peoples.

Waldron, Jeremy. 1993. *Liberal Rights.* Cambridge: Cambridge University Press. — 339–69 argue that groups can possess some collective rights.

Wellman, Carl. 1995. *Real Rights.* New York: Oxford University Press. — See esp. 105–36. A controversial argument for the conclusion that only moral agents could possess either moral or legal rights.

Appendix: International Documents and Further Reading/Research

The Appendix contains extracts of two documents relating to human rights and religion. It is worthwhile bearing in mind that the issues discussed in *Human Rights & Religion: A Reader* demonstrate that the influence of religion in global politics extends beyond matters that might be directly affected by statutes explicitly referring to religion. On generic guidance to human rights and religion in world politics, the reader is referred to the first three chapters in this volume. The following are key international documents on human rights in which religion is featured:

- United Nations Declaration of Human Rights (1948)
  [Article 16 being of explicit reference to religion]
- Convention on the Prevention of Genocide and Punishment of the Crime of Genocide (1948)
  [Article II being of explicit reference to religion]
- International Covenant on Civil and Political Rights (1996)
  [Article 18 being of explicit reference to religion]
- United Nations Declaration on the Elimination of All Forms of Intolerance and Discrimination Based on Religion or Belief (1981)
- United Nations Declaration on the Rights of Persons Belonging to National or Ethnic, Religious, and Linguistic Minorities (Adopted 1992)
- The Cairo Declaration on Human Rights in Islam (1990)

- Fundamental Agreement between the Holy See and the State of Israel (1993)
- Vienna Declaration and Plan of Action (1993)
  [From the World Conference on Human Rights; Article 16 being of explicit reference to religion]
- Follow-up to the World Conference on Human Rights (held in Vienna, 1993). United Nations High Commissioner on Human Rights (1998)
  [Paragraph 34–39 being of explicit reference to religion]
- Oslo Declaration on Freedom of Religion and Belief (1998)
- Declaration of World Conference Against Racism, Racial Discrimination, Xenophobia and Related Intolerance (2002)

Declaration on the Elimination of All Forms of Intolerance and of Discrimination Based on Religion or Belief (Proclaimed by General Assembly resolution 36/55 of 25 November 1981)

Article 1
1. Everyone shall have the right to freedom of thought, conscience and religion. This right shall include freedom to have a religion or whatever belief of his choice, and freedom, either individually or in community with others and in public or private, to manifest his religion or belief in worship, observance, practice and teaching.

2. No one shall be subject to coercion which would impair his freedom to have a religion or belief of his choice.

3. Freedom to manifest one's religion or belief may be subject only to such limitations as are prescribed by law and are necessary to protect public safety, order, health or morals or the fundamental rights and freedoms of others.

Article 2

1. No one shall be subject to discrimination by any State, institution, group of persons, or person on the grounds of religion or other belief.

2. For the purposes of the present Declaration, the expression "intolerance and discrimination based on religion or belief" means any distinction, exclusion, restriction or preference based on religion or belief and having as its purpose or as its effect nullification or impairment of the recognition, enjoyment or exercise of human rights and fundamental freedoms on an equal basis.

Article 3

Discrimination between human beings on the grounds of religion or belief constitutes an affront to human dignity and a disavowal of the principles of the Charter of the United Nations, and shall be condemned as a violation of the human rights and fundamental freedoms proclaimed in the Universal Declaration of Human Rights and enunciated in detail in the International Covenants on Human Rights, and as an obstacle to friendly and peaceful relations between nations.

Article 4

1. All States shall take effective measures to prevent and eliminate discrimination on the grounds of religion or belief in the recognition, exercise and enjoyment of human rights and fundamental freedoms in all fields of civil, economic, political, social and cultural life.

2. All States shall make all efforts to enact or rescind legislation where necessary to prohibit any such discrimination, and to take all appropriate measures to combat intolerance on the grounds of religion or other beliefs in this matter.

Article 5

1. The parents or, as the case may be, the legal guardians of the child have the right to organize the life within the family in accordance with their religion or belief and bearing in mind the moral education in which they believe the child should be brought up.

2. Every child shall enjoy the right to have access to education in the matter of religion or belief in accordance with the wishes of his parents or, as the case may be, legal guardians, and shall not be compelled to receive teaching on religion or belief against the wishes of his parents or legal guardians, the best interests of the child being the guiding principle.

3. The child shall be protected from any form of discrimination on the ground of religion or belief. He shall be brought up in a spirit of understanding, tolerance, friendship among peoples, peace and universal brotherhood, respect for freedom of religion or belief of others, and in full consciousness that his energy and talents should be devoted to the service of his fellow men.

4. In the case of a child who is not under the care either of his parents or of legal guardians, due account shall be taken of their expressed wishes or of any other proof of their wishes in the matter of religion or belief, the best interests of the child being the guiding principle.

5. Practices of a religion or belief in which a child is brought up must not be injurious to his physical or mental health or to his full development, taking into account article 1, paragraph 3, of the present Declaration.

Article 6

In accordance with article I of the present Declaration, and subject to the provisions of article 1, paragraph 3, the right to freedom of thought, conscience, religion or belief shall include, inter alia, the following freedoms:

(a) To worship or assemble in connection with a religion or belief, and to establish and maintain places for these purposes;

(b) To establish and maintain appropriate charitable or humanitarian institutions;

(c) To make, acquire and use to an adequate extent the necessary articles and materials related to the rites or customs of a religion or belief;

(d) To write, issue and disseminate relevant publications in these areas;

(e) To teach a religion or belief in places suitable for these purposes;

(f) To solicit and receive voluntary finan-cial and other contributions from individuals and institutions;

(g) To train, appoint, elect or designate by succession appropriate leaders called for by the requirements and standards of any religion or belief;

(h) To observe days of rest and to celebrate holidays and ceremonies in accordance with the precepts of one's religion or belief;

(i) To establish and maintain communica-tions with individuals and communities in matters of religion and belief at the national and international levels.

Article 7

The rights and freedoms set forth in the present Declaration shall be accorded in national legislation in such a manner that everyone shall be able to avail himself of such rights and freedoms in practice.

Article 8

Nothing in the present Declaration shall be construed as restricting or derogating from any right defined in the Universal Declaration of Human Rights and the International Covenants on Human Rights.

© Copyright 1997–2000 Office of the United Nations High Commissioner for Human Rights, Geneva, Switzerland

Appendix II   United Nations Declaration on the Rights of Persons Belonging to National or Ethnic, Religious and Linguistic Minorities (Adopted by the General Assembly in its resolution 47/135 of 18 December 1992)

Article 1

1. States shall protect the existence and the national or ethnic, cultural, religious and linguistic identity of minorities within their respective territories and shall encourage conditions for the promotion of that identity.

2. States shall adopt appropriate legislative and other measures to achieve those ends.

Article 2

1. Persons belonging to national or ethnic, religious and linguistic minorities (here-inafter referred to as persons belonging to minorities) have the right to enjoy their own culture, to profess and practise their own religion, and to use their own language, in private and in public, freely and without interference or any form of discrimination.

2. Persons belonging to minorities have the right to participate effectively in cultural, religious, social, economic and public life.

3. Persons belonging to minorities have the right to participate effectively in decisions on the national and, where appropriate, regional level concerning the minority to which they belong or the regions in which they live, in a manner not incompatible with national legislation.

4. Persons belonging to minorities have the right to establish and maintain their own associations.

5. Persons belonging to minorities have the right to establish and maintain, without any discrimination, free and peaceful contacts with other members of their group and with persons belonging to other minorities, as well as contacts across frontiers with citizens of other States to whom they are related by national or ethnic, religious or linguistic ties.

Article 3

1. Persons belonging to minorities may exercise their rights, including those set forth in the present Declaration, individually as well as in community with other members of their group, without any discrimination.

2. No disadvantage shall result for any person belonging to a minority as the conse-quence of the exercise or non-exercise of the rights set forth in the present Declaration.

Article 4

1. States shall take measures where required to ensure that persons belonging to minorities may exercise fully and effectively all their human rights and fundamental free-doms without any discrimination and in full equality before the law.

2. States shall take measures to create favourable conditions to enable persons belonging to minorities to express their char-acteristics and to develop their culture,

language, religion, traditions and customs, except where specific practices are in violation of national law and contrary to international standards.

3. States should take appropriate measures so that, wherever possible, persons belonging to minorities may have adequate opportunities to learn their mother tongue or to have instruction in their mother tongue.

4. States should, where appropriate, take measures in the field of education, in order to encourage knowledge of the history, traditions, language and culture of the minorities existing within their territory. Persons belonging to minorities should have adequate opportunities to gain knowledge of the society as a whole.

5. States should consider appropriate measures so that persons belonging to minorities may participate fully in the economic progress and development in their country.

Article 5

1. National policies and programmes shall be planned and implemented with due regard for the legitimate interests of persons belonging to minorities.

2. Programmes of cooperation and assistance among States should be planned and implemented with due regard for the legitimate interests of persons belonging to minorities.

Article 6

States should cooperate on questions relating to persons belonging to minorities, inter alia, exchanging information and experiences, in order to promote mutual understanding and confidence.

Article 7

States should cooperate in order to promote respect for the rights set forth in the present Declaration.

Article 8

1. Nothing in the present Declaration shall prevent the fulfilment of international obligations of States in relation to persons belonging to minorities. In particular, States shall fulfil in good faith the obligations and commitments they have assumed under inter-national treaties and agreements to which they are parties.

2. The exercise of the rights set forth in the present Declaration shall not prejudice the enjoyment by all persons of universally recognized human rights and fundamental freedoms.

3. Measures taken by States to ensure the effective enjoyment of the rights set forth in the present Declaration shall not prima facie be considered contrary to the principle of equality contained in the Universal Declaration of Human Rights.

4. Nothing in the present Declaration may be construed as permitting any activity contrary to the purposes and principles of the United Nations, including sovereign equality, territorial integrity and political independence of States.

Article 9

The specialized agencies and other organizations of the United Nations system shall contribute to the full realization of the rights and principles set forth in the present Declaration, within their respective fields of competence.

Further Reading/Research

Paul Marshall (ed.), *Religious Freedom in the World: A Global Report on Freedom and Persecution* (Nashville: Broadman and Holman, 2000) contains about the most easily accessible, comprehensive single volume guide to the appearance of religion within human rights legislation in countries around the world.

The United Nations Dag Hammarskjöld Library (http://www.un.org/ Depts/ dhl/resguide/basic.htm) has links to "Special Subject" including the heading "Human Rights."

General Index

Index of Articles, Charters and Conventions